Realism, Naturalism, and Local Color, 1865-1917

Concise Dictionary of American Literary Biography

Realism, Naturalism, and Local Color, 1865-1917

A Bruccoli Clark Layman Book
Gale Research Inc. • Book Tower • Detroit, Michigan 48226

Matthew J. Bruccoli and Richard Layman, *Editorial Directors*
C. E. Frazer Clark, Jr., *Managing Editor*

Manufactured by Edwards Brothers, Inc.
Ann Arbor, Michigan
Printed in the United States of America

Library of Congress Cataloging-in-Publication Data

Realism, naturalism, and local color, 1865-1917.
   (Concise dictionary of literary biography; v. 2)
   "A Bruccoli Clark Layman book."
   Includes index.
   1. American literature—19th century—History and criticism. 2. American literature—19th century—Bio-bibliography. 3. Realism in literature. 4. Naturalism in literature. 5. Local color in literature. 6. American literature—20th century—History and criticism. 7. American literature—20th century—Bio-bibliography. 8. Authors, American—Biography—Dictionaries. I. Gale Research Inc. II. Series
PS217.R4R43   1988   810'.9'004   [B]   88-6016
ISBN 0-8103-1821-0

Contents

Plan of the Work

The six-volume *Concise Dictionary of American Literary Biography* was developed in response to requests from high school and junior college teachers and librarians, and from small- to medium-sized public libraries, for a compilation of entries from the standard *Dictionary of Literary Biography* chosen to meet their needs and their budgets. The *DLB*, which comprises over ninety volumes as of the end of 1987, is moving steadily toward its goal of providing a history of literature in all languages developed through the biographies of writers. Basic as the *DLB* is, many librarians have expressed the need for a less comprehensive reference work which in other respects retains the merits of *DLB*. The *Concise DALB* provides this resource.

This series was planned by a seven-member advisory board, consisting primarily of secondary school educators, who developed a method of organization and presentation for selected *DLB* entries suitable for high school and beginning college students. Their preliminary plan was circulated to some five thousand school librarians and English teachers, who were asked to respond to the organization of the series and the table of contents. Those responses were incorporated into the plan described here.

Uses for the Concise DALB

Students are the primary audience for the *Concise DALB*. The stated purpose of the standard *DLB* is to make our literary heritage more accessible. *Concise DALB* has the same goal and seeks a wider audience. What the author wrote; what the facts of his life are; a description of his literary works; a discussion of the critical response to his works; and a bibliography of critical works to be consulted for further information: These are the elements of a *Concise DALB* entry.

The first step in the planning process for this series, after identifying the audience, was to contemplate its uses. The advisory board acknowledged that the integrity of *Concise DALB* as a reference book is crucial to its utility. The *Concise DALB* adheres to the scholarly standards established by the parent series. Thus, within the scope of major American literary figures, the *Concise DALB* is a ready reference source of established

value, providing reliable biographical and bibliographical information.

It is anticipated that this series will not be confined to uses within the library. Just as *DLB* has been a tool for stimulating students' literary interests in the college classroom—for comparative studies of authors, for example, and, through its ample illustrations, as a means of invigorating literary study—the *Concise DALB* is a primary resource for high school and junior college educators. The series is organized to facilitate lesson planning, and the contextual diagrams (explained below) that introduce each entry are a source of topics for classroom discussion and writing assignments.

Organization

The advisory board further determined that entries from the standard *DLB* should be presented complete—without abridgment. Their feeling was that the utility of the *DLB* format has been proven, and that only minimal changes should be made.

The advisory board further decided that the organization of the *Concise DALB* should be chronological to emphasize the historical development of American literature. Each volume is devoted to a single historical period and includes the most significant literary figures from all genres who were active during that time. Thus, the volume that includes modern mainstream novelists Saul Bellow, Bernard Malamud, and John Cheever will also include poets who were active at the same time—such as Allen Ginsberg, Lawrence Ferlinghetti, and John Berryman—and dramatists who were their contemporaries—such as Tennessee Williams, Arthur Miller, and William Inge. It should be noted that the volume of the *Concise DALB* that includes these authors comprises thirty-six entries, while the volumes in the standard *DLB* covering the same period include some four hundred author biographies. The *Concise DALB* limits itself to major figures, but it provides the same coverage of those figures as the *DLB* does.

The six period volumes of the *Concise DALB* are *Colonization to the American Renaissance, 1640-1865; Realism, Naturalism, and Local Color, 1865-1917; Literary Responses to the Jazz Age, 1917-1929; The Age of Maturity, 1929-1941; The New Conscious-*

ness, 1941-1968; Broadening Views, 1968-1987. The sixth volume will also contain a comprehensive index by subjects and proper names to the entire *Concise DALB*. (As in the standard *DLB* series, there is a cumulative index to author entries in each *Concise DALB* volume.)

Form of Entry

The form of entry in the *Concise DALB* is substantially the same as in the standard series, with the following alterations:

1)   Each entry has been updated to include a discussion of works published since the standard entry appeared and to reflect recent criticism and research of interest to the high school audience.

2)   The secondary bibliography for each entry has been selected to include those books and articles of particular interest and usefulness to high school and junior college students. In addition, the secondary bibliography has been annotated to assist

students in assessing whether a reference will meet their needs.

3)   Each entry is preceded by a "contextual diagram"—a graphic presentation of the places, literary influences, personal relationships, literary movements, major themes, cultural and artistic influences, and social and economic forces associated with the author. This chart allows students—and teachers—to place the author in his literary and social context at a glance.

It bears repeating that the *Concise DALB* is restricted to major American literary figures. It is anticipated that users of this series will find it advantageous to consult the standard *DLB* for information about those writers omitted from the *Concise DALB* whose significance to contemporary readers may have faded but whose contribution to our cultural heritage remains meaningful.

Comments about the series and suggestions for improvement are earnestly invited.

A Note to Students

The purpose of the *Concise DALB* is to enrich the study of literature. In their various ways, writers react in their works to the circumstances of their lives, the events of their time, and the culture that envelops them (which are represented on the contextual diagrams that precede each *Concise DALB* entry). Writers provide a way to see and understand what they have observed and experienced. Besides being inherently interesting, biographies of writers provide a basic perspective on literature.

Concise DALB entries start with the most important facts about writers: What they wrote. We strongly recommend that you also start there. The chronological listing of an author's works is an outline for the examination of his or her career achievement. The biographies that follow set the stage for the presentation of the works. Each of the author's important works and the most respected critical evaluations of them are discussed in *Concise DALB*. If you require more information about the author or fuller critical studies of the author's works, the annotated references section at the end of the entry will guide you.

Illustrations are an integral element of *Concise DALB* entries. Photographs of the author are reminders that literature is the product of a writer's imagination; facsimiles of the author's working drafts are the best evidence available for understanding the act of composition—the author in the process of refining his work and acting as self-editor; dust jacket and advertisements demonstrate how literature comes to us through the marketplace, which sometimes serves to alter our perceptions of the works.

Literary study is a complex and immensely rewarding endeavor. Our goal is to provide you with the information you need to make that experience as rich as possible.

Acknowledgments

This book was produced by Bruccoli Clark Layman, Inc. Karen L. Rood is senior editor for the *Dictionary of Literary Biography* series. Laura Ingram was the in-house editor.

Production coordinator is Kimberly Casey. Art supervisor is Cheryl Crombie. Copyediting supervisor is Joan M. Prince. Typesetting supervisor is Kathleen M. Flanagan. Michael D. Senecal is the editorial associate. The production staff includes Rowena Betts, Charles D. Brower, Joseph Matthew Bruccoli, Patricia Coate, Mary Colborn, Mary S. Dye, Sarah A. Estes, Cynthia Hallman, Judith K. Ingle, Maria Ling, Warren McInnis, Kathy S. Merlette, Sheri Neal, Joycelyn R. Smith, and Virginia Smith. Jean W. Ross is permissions editor. Joseph Caldwell, photography editor, and Penney Haughton did photographic copy work for the volume.

Walter W. Ross and Rhonda Marshall did the library research with the assistance of the staff at the Thomas Cooper Library of the University of South Carolina: Daniel Boice, Cathy Eckman, Gary Geer, Cathie Gottlieb, David L. Haggard, Jens Holley, Dennis Isbell, Jackie Kinder, Marcia Martin, Jean Rhyne, Beverly Steele, Ellen Tillett, Carol Tobin, and Virginia Weathers.

Realism, Naturalism, and Local Color, 1865-1917

Concise Dictionary of American Literary Biography

Louisa May Alcott

This entry was updated by Daniel Shealy (Clemson University) from the entry by Ruth K. MacDonald (New Mexico State University) in DLB 42, American Writers for Children Before 1900.

Places	New England	Concord, Mass.	Boston
Influences and Relationships	Amos Bronson Alcott Theodore Parker Mary Mapes Dodge	Ralph Waldo Emerson Thomas Niles	Henry David Thoreau Margaret Fuller
Literary Movements and Forms	Children's Literature Local Color	Transcendentalism Didacticism	Realism
Major Themes	Woman's Role in Society Domestic Life	Abolitionism	Educational Reform
Cultural and Artistic Influences	Religion as Emotional Support	Utopian Communities	German Philosophy
Social and Economic Influences	Health Reform–Temperance and Vegetarianism	Woman's Rights Education	Slavery Civil War

See also the Alcott entry in DLB 1, The American Renaissance in New England.

BIRTH: Germantown, Pennsylvania, 29 November 1832, to Amos Bronson and Abigail May Alcott.

DEATH: Roxbury, Massachusetts, 6 March 1888.

BOOKS: *Flower Fables* (Boston: George W. Briggs, 1855);
Hospital Sketches (Boston: James Redpath, 1863); republished in part in *Something to Do* (1873);
The Rose Family. A Fairy Tale (Boston: James Redpath, 1864);
On Picket Duty, and Other Tales (Boston: James Redpath, 1864);
Moods (Boston: A. K. Loring, 1865; revised edition, Boston: Roberts Brothers, 1882);
Nelly's Hospital (Boston, 1865);
The Mysterious Key, and What It Opened (Boston: Elliott, Thomes & Talbot, 1867);
Morning-Glories, and Other Stories (Boston: Horace B. Fuller, 1868);
Louisa M. Alcott's Proverb Stories (Boston: Loring, 1868); republished in *Something to Do* (1873);
Little Women or, Meg, Jo, Beth and Amy, 2 volumes (Boston: Roberts Brothers, 1868-1869; London: Low, 1868-1869); volume 2 republished as *Little Women Wedded* (London: Low, 1872), *Little Women Married* (London: Routledge, 1873), and *Nice Wives* (London: Weldon, 1875); both volumes republished in one as *Little Women and Good Wives* (London: Nisbet, 1895);
Hospital Sketches and Camp and Fireside Stories (Boston: Roberts Brothers, 1869);
An Old-Fashioned Girl (Boston: Roberts Brothers, 1870; London: Low, 1870);
Will's Wonder Book (Boston: Fuller, 1870);
V.V.: or, Plots and Counterplots, as A. M. Barnard (Boston: Thomes & Talbot, circa 1870);
Little Men: Life at Plumfield with Jo's Boys (London: Low, Son & Marston, 1871; Boston: Roberts Brothers, 1871);
Aunt Jo's Scrap-Bag. My Boys, Etc. (Boston: Roberts Brothers, 1872; London: Low, 1872);
Aunt Jo's Scrap-Bag. Shawl-Straps, Etc. (Boston: Roberts Brothers, 1872; London: Low, 1872);
Something to Do (London: Ward, Lock & Tyler, 1873);

Work: A Story of Experience (1 volume, Boston: Roberts Brothers, 1873; 2 volumes, London: Low, 1873);
Aunt Jo's Scrap-Bag. Cupid and Chow Chow, Etc. (Boston: Roberts Brothers, 1874; London: Low, 1874);
Eight Cousins; or The Aunt-Hill (Boston: Roberts Brothers, 1875; London: Low, 1875);
Silver Pitchers: And Independence, A Centennial Love Story (Boston: Roberts Brothers, 1876; London: Low, 1876);
Rose in Bloom. A Sequel to "Eight Cousins" (Boston: Roberts Brothers, 1876; London: Low, 1876);
A Modern Mephistopheles, anonymous (Boston: Roberts Brothers, 1877; London: Low, 1877);
Aunt Jo's Scrap-Bag. My Girls, Etc. (Boston: Roberts Brothers, 1878);
Under the Lilacs (11 parts, London: Low, Marston, Searle & Rivington, 1878; 1 volume, Boston: Roberts Brothers, 1878);

Aunt Jo's Scrap-Bag. Jimmy's Cruise in the Pinafore, Etc. (Boston: Roberts Brothers, 1879; London: Low, 1879);

Jack and Jill: A Village Story (Boston: Roberts Brothers, 1880; London: Low, 1880);

Aunt Jo's Scrap-Bag. An Old-Fashioned Thanksgiving, Etc. (Boston: Roberts Brothers, 1882; London: Low, 1882);

Spinning-Wheel Stories (Boston: Roberts Brothers, 1884; London: Low, 1884);

Lulu's Library. Vol. I. A Christmas Dream (Boston: Roberts Brothers, 1886; London: Low, 1886);

Jo's Boys, and How They Turned Out. A Sequel to "Little Men" (Boston: Roberts Brothers, 1886; London: Low, 1886);

Lulu's Library. Vol. II. The Frost King (Boston: Roberts Brothers, 1887);

A Garland for Girls (Boston: Roberts Brothers, 1887; London: Blackie, 1887);

A Modern Mephistopheles and A Whisper in the Dark (Boston: Roberts Brothers, 1889; London: Low, 1889);

Lulu's Library. Vol. III. Recollections (Boston: Roberts Brothers, 1889); republished as *Recollections of My Childhood Days* (London: Low, 1890);

Comic Tragedies Written by "Jo" and "Meg" and Acted by the Little Women (Boston: Roberts Brothers, 1893; London: Low, 1893);

Behind a Mask; The Unknown Thrillers of Louisa May Alcott, edited by Madeleine B. Stern (New York: Morrow, 1975);

Louisa's Wonder Book: An Unknown Alcott Juvenile, edited by Stern (Mount Pleasant: Central Michigan University & Clark Historical Library, 1975);

Plots and Counterplots; More Unknown Thrillers of Louisa May Alcott, edited by Stern (New York: Morrow, 1976).

Though she also wrote adult novels, Louisa May Alcott is known primarily for her eight novels for children in the *Little Women* series. Her children's novels are characterized by their glorification of family life, by their wholesomeness and high spirits, and by their lack of preachiness, which was evident in most other children's novels of her time. Though she did not set out to be a children's writer, it is in this field that her greatest achievement was made. Her most popular characters are more than mouthpieces and moral exemplars for the author; they are well-rounded individuals and independent thinkers. In her novels Alcott criticized many of the current philosophies of education and notions of fashionable behavior. Throughout her works the ideas of religious faith, sensible eating, learning, and play are dominant themes investigated in a variety of real-life situations. Though her works for children have recently received adverse criticism as compared to her more complex and sometimes sensational adult works, for their time they set a new high standard for excellence in full characterization, both of the attractive and unattractive qualities of children, for the warmth with which she portrayed American family life, for her simple but precise style, and for her New England local color.

Her early life was dominated by the high-minded idealism characteristic of the American transcendentalist movement and by the poverty which necessitated the upheaval of her family as they moved frequently to meet financial exigencies. Born in Germantown, Pennsylvania, on 29 November 1832, Louisa May Alcott was the second of the four daughters of Amos Bronson Alcott, transcendentalist philosopher and educational theorist, and Abigail May Alcott, a descendant of one of the leading families of Boston. Bronson Alcott's philosophical flights were outlandish and his educational ideas eccentric. He frequently found himself with no pupils as he tried to establish several different schools, and for most of Louisa's life he failed to support his family by holding a steady job. The most formative event in Alcott's life was her father's attempt to establish a utopian community called Fruitlands in Harvard, Massachusetts, in 1843. After the failure of this endeavor it became apparent that the family could rely no longer on the father and husband for its direction and financial stability; it was at this point, when Louisa Alcott was a mere twelve years old, that she decided to take on the burden of providing for the family. This resolve lasted her whole life.

Though Bronson Alcott was a financial failure, he did provide his daughters with an exceptional, although somewhat erratic, education. When the family lived in Concord, as it did sporadically throughout Louisa Alcott's life, Bronson as well as his daughters were in frequent contact with the leading intellectuals of Boston at the time. Ralph Waldo Emerson was a great friend and near neighbor; the young Louisa May Alcott had free access to his library and read widely there both in the classics and in the masters of English and German philosophy and literature. She later became a tutor to Emerson's daughter Ellen. Though Nathaniel Hawthorne remained aloof from his neighbors in Concord, the Alcott children often met socially with the Hawthorne children, and Alcott knew and read his works. Henry David Thoreau was her botany teacher. The family also had as acquaintances at different times during Alcott's childhood Margaret Fuller, Elizabeth Peabody, William Lloyd Garrison, Theodore Parker, William Ellery Channing, Lydia Maria Child, James Russell Lowell, and Julia Ward and Samuel Gridley Howe. Though she had almost no formal schooling, Alcott was widely read and was familiar with many of the social reform movements of the time. She and her family were avid supporters of woman's rights and woman suffrage, abolitionism, temperance, vegetarianism, and dress and educational reform. Many of these causes appear as themes in her novels.

Though her novels are didactic, the most successful of them endure because of the realism with which she portrayed childhood and adolescence. The reputation Alcott garnered as the "Children's Friend" because of the overwhelming popular reception of *Little Women* (published in two volumes in 1868 and 1869) is justly deserved. In this autobiographical novel Alcott captures the speech patterns and behavior of children, in this case teenagers, with a reporter's eye for detail. And in Jo March, Alcott's literary re-creation of herself, she portrays one of the most enduring and endearing characters in all of children's literature. Jo is ambitious and energetic, loving and charming, awkward and temperamental. Her character is so universally appealing that even boy readers identify with her, though Alcott's expressed intent was to write the novel for girls. The March family is portrayed as a close and loving one and their home a warm nest in which children are nurtured gently before they take flight into the outside world; it is the kind of family that every reader would like for his own. Though as the years progressed Alcott's imitation of her earlier success with Jo and the Marches sometimes became mechanical, there is always the spark of the joy of childhood and the satisfactions of family living that rescue the more dismal examples. Alcott was also adept as a local colorist; her children's novels are all set in New England, and she captures the pleasures of New England weather and the childhood activities and celebrations that go with the passing seasons with a particularly fine eye. But the local color does not dominate so much that the novels lose their universal appeal.

Alcott's early career as a writer began with her frequent contributions of sentimental short stories and Gothic thrillers to such diverse magazines as the *Saturday Evening Gazette, Atlantic Monthly, Frank Leslie's Illustrated Newspaper,* and the *Flag of Our Union.* Though these stories were for adults, Alcott also showed an early predilection to write for children when George Briggs of Boston published her *Flower Fables* (1855), a collection of fairy tales which Alcott had written for Ellen Emerson when Alcott was her tutor. These fairy tales are all heavily didactic. They are concerned with various flowers, animals, fairies of nature, and occasional children, who, through the progress of the short stories, are taught lessons about selflessness, control of temper, gratitude, and the power of love to overcome obstacles and reform the most obdurate sinners. The themes are all ordinary, commonplaces of literature for children at the time, and the collection is altogether undistinguished. Alcott earned thirty-two dollars for the limited edition; it is rarely read now except by Alcott scholars.

Though such writing for children brought in money, it was obvious to Alcott that much more was to be made from the short stories which she could turn out quickly for a profit with which to support her family. Before the Civil War started Alcott's younger sister Elizabeth died, and her older sister Anna married and moved away from the family. At the beginning of the war Alcott found herself lonely and without purpose; she felt keenly the loss of both sisters and realized that it was unlikely that she would marry and find fulfillment in a family of her own, especially given her commitment to the care and financial support of her parents and remaining sister May. But her high ambition was not satisfied with the hack writing she had been doing for profit, and her two adult novels were progressing slowly. The war provided Alcott with the idea of army nursing. Always eager to support a worthy humanitarian cause and never content to stay at home on the sidelines of the action as women were supposed to, Alcott had had much experience in nursing her sister through her terminal illness. In December 1862 she left home to become one of Dorothea Dix's nurses in the U.S. Sanitary Commission at the Union Hotel Hospital in Washington, D.C.

Her nursing experience was a crucial part of her life in two ways, though she remained in

Washington for only about six weeks. First, she contracted typhoid fever, which was the cause of her early departure from the city, and was never well again, due to the effects of mercury poisoning from the treatment prescribed for the fever. For the rest of her life she suffered from spells of nervousness and a variety of aches and pains which plagued her and hampered her writing. For a woman as active as Alcott was, the extended periods of bed rest were a particular trial. Second, she edited and published the letters she had written to her family about the men whom she had nursed. *Hospital Sketches* (1863) was a commercial and popular success, not only because it had an obvious appeal for the readers of the North but also because of the wry humor and plain, reportorial style in which the book was written. The story collection brought Alcott a modicum of literary fame, enough for her to attempt a serious adult novel, *Moods* (1865), which was not so warmly received. As she left for a European tour, she was disappointed about her writing career.

In 1867 Alcott's career had not progressed much beyond the initial popular and critical success of *Hospital Sketches*. She was still writing her anonymous and pseudonymous Gothic thrillers to make money. When Thomas Niles of Roberts Brothers approached her about writing a novel for girls, she was not enthused with the suggestion. She had just accepted the editor's position at *Merry's Museum*, a children's monthly magazine. For the January 1868 issue she wrote a short story about a family of four girls who give their Christmas breakfast to a poor German immigrant family. That story later became one of the opening scenes in *Little Women*. Though the novel project did not interest her, she found that the book was easy enough to write. In six weeks' time, from May to July 1868, she completed the first volume. Though the finished manuscript excited neither Alcott nor her editor, when it finally appeared in print in September 1868 it was an overnight success. Prompted by the success of volume one, she began a sequel. It took her another two months to write the second volume, which had the working title "Good Wives"; when it was published as *Little Women or, Meg, Jo, Beth and Amy, Part Second* in January 1869, it too was a commercial and critical success.

The story of the four teenaged sisters, Meg, Jo, Beth, and Amy, and their growing up into young women succeeded partly because the material was autobiographical and Alcott knew it so

well. Though each of the sisters receives equal attention in the novel, it is clear that Jo is the most interesting and best-drawn character, probably because she was Alcott's re-creation of herself. Jo's struggles with her temper, her ambition, and her fervent desire to be a boy are well realized in the novel because they are so heartfelt. One identifies with the girl who wishes that she could enjoy the freedom of boys in clothing, manners, and career. One also sympathizes with Jo's attempts to curb her temper and her boyish enthusiasm and with her occasional relapses. Though all four girls have faults which they resolve to conquer at the novel's opening, Jo's are the most difficult and therefore her victory over them the most hard-won.

The faults or "burdens" of the four girls take on a religious cast since they are likened to the symbolic burdens of Christian, the hero of John Bunyan's *Pilgrim's Progress*. As Christian in Bunyan's allegory must deal with his burden of sin on his journey to heaven, so the girls seek to cast off their burdens in their quest to become "little women." Alcott uses *Pilgrim's Progress* as a patterning device in the novel. The book begins at Christmastime with each of the girls deciding what her main fault is. In the following year each goes through major changes so that by the next Christmas at the close of the book's first part they are all much improved. Each girl has a chapter devoted to her and her struggles, with the title of the chapter taken from an incident in *Pilgrim's Progress*–"Meg goes to Vanity Fair," "Amy's Valley of Humiliation," "Beth Finds the Palace Beautiful," and "Jo Meets Appolyon." The girls are assured that God will help them on their journey if they will only appeal to Him. Though Alcott was never a member of a particular religious faith, it is clear that for her, religion was an important part of being a complete woman, and that trust in God was the major emotional support in a woman's life.

It is also important in *Little Women* that a girl learn housewifely accomplishments, such as sewing, cooking, and good manners in society. Though the March sisters show talents which might lead them to careers–Jo as a writer, Meg as an actress, Beth as a pianist, and Amy as an artist–career aspirations by themselves are shown to be inadequate as a complete definition of womanhood. In the novel each girl must learn to keep house and to master the feminine accomplishments of conversation, entertaining, and being pleasant and cheerful even under the most

Frontispiece illustration by May Alcott for the first part of her sister Louisa's book Little Women or, Meg, Jo, Beth and Amy

trying circumstances. Mrs. March, known as Marmee, is the model for all the girls to follow. She is a strong woman, the head of a household while her husband is away as a Union Army chaplain during the Civil War. She guides her daughters through their troubles with their faults. Throughout the novel she is a reliable source of loving wisdom, strong as a rock and as imperturbable as one. She is the mother that all readers would like to have–always available, always loving, always compassionate. Indeed, she was the model woman for the Victorian period and stands as the emotional center of the book.

The second volume of the book was written at least partly in response to Alcott's readers' demands to see how and whom the March sisters marry. Though it is difficult to ascertain whether Alcott had the sequel to volume one clearly designed when she wrote the first volume, it is clear

that her readers' demands changed markedly the direction that the second volume took. Though in real life Alcott's older sister Anna, the model for Meg, had married, neither Alcott nor her younger sister May, the models for Jo and Amy, had marital prospects. Her sister Elizabeth, Beth in the novel, was dead, so finding a partner for Beth to marry was unthinkable. If Alcott were to continue in her autobiographical vein, it was clear that she would frustrate her readers by not marrying off Jo and Amy, which might hinder the sales of the novel and might endanger future books that she might write. On the other hand, were she to proceed to marry off the March sisters, she would have some strenuous fictionalizing to do.

Alcott would also have to manage her own feelings about marriage. She herself never married; she knew that to marry might not be as desirable as was popularly thought in Victorian America and that there were other ways of leading a satisfying life if a woman were bold enough to try them. She could not consent to marry her own character Jo to the obvious choice in the novel, Laurie, the high-spirited and adventuresome boy next door. Throughout the first half of the novel the two had been fast friends and constant companions; there are even hints that Laurie is interested in Jo romantically. But in the second half of the novel Jo flatly turns him down. Though some readers may be disappointed that Jo does not choose the most handsome and most eligible bachelor in the novel and may not accept Jo's explanation that she and Laurie "don't agree and we never shall," that "our quick tempers and strong wills would make us very miserable," others may laud Jo's resolution to remain single: "I don't believe I shall ever marry. I'm happy as I am, and love my liberty too well to be in any hurry to give it up for any mortal man." Laurie, the handsome prince of the story, finally marries Amy, the golden-haired princess; this was Alcott's conciliatory gesture to those readers who wanted a typical fairy-tale, happy-ever-after ending.

Writing of her sister Elizabeth's death was particularly painful for Alcott, but at least it gave her an excuse for not marrying Beth to some invented character. And her sister Anna's marriage could simply be transported whole into the fictional world of the novel. But Alcott's sense of her audience's limits told her that her readers would not be willing to accept an unmarried spinster who wrote books for a living as an acceptable ending for Jo. Though Alcott herself had a fulfilling life in just such a role, she was convinced that her public would accept nothing less than marriage as a satisfying happy ending; they were not open-minded enough to accept less traditional possibilities.

What the readers probably did not expect was the kind of character that Alcott finally chose for Jo to marry–Professor Bhaer, the poor German intellectual who is not handsome, young, dashing, or anything else that might have qualified him as a proper romantic hero in a sentimental novel. But Professor Bhaer provides Jo with a married life that suits her. He does not approve of her sensational writing, but he does encourage her intellectually. He also does not expect that she will stay home and take care of him and their children. At the end of the novel the two have established a school, so that both continue to work.

They also have two sons, both reincarnations of Jo's energy and high spirits. Though Jo's future does not seem to be the "something splendid" that she aspires to in the first part of the novel, it is more satisfying than the more traditional wifely roles that Amy and Meg take on in their respective marriages.

There are other ways in which Alcott's novel was unconventional for its time. The girls are not perfect models of behavior or of speech. They sometimes utter mild curses and speak in slang. Even though some of her critics attacked *Little Women* and other Alcott novels on this score, Alcott was quick to point out that there was nothing immoral about such language, and that it was more realistic than the pious, perfect little mouthpieces that passed for characters in other children's novels of the time. She avoided the extreme sentimentalism that was characteristic of many deathbed scenes in children's literature when she described Beth March's final moments. Beth utters no parting words, and there is no profusion of tears from those she leaves behind. There is only a simple, heartfelt paragraph which is moving and understated while not resorting to bathos to influence the reader: "As Beth had hoped, the 'tide went out easily,' and in the dark hour before the dawn, on the bosom where she had drawn her first breath, she quietly drew her last, with no farewell but one loving look, one little sigh."

Alcott presents the first of a long line of imperfect and sometimes outright naughty children in American children's literature. The March sisters are the first in a line of such children which would later include Tom Bailey in *The Story of a Bad Boy* (1870) by Thomas Bailey Aldrich; Katy Carr in *What Katy Did* (1872) by Susan Coolidge; Tom Sawyer (1876) and Huckleberry Finn (1884) in the novels of Mark Twain; and Rebecca Rowena Randall in *Rebecca of Sunnybrook Farm* (1903) by Kate Douglas Wiggin.

Finally, though she may not have been interested in writing the novel to begin with, Alcott was one of the first writers in American children's literature to take seriously the critical questions involved in writing for children. She may seem today to be preaching in *Little Women*, but given the didactic intent of most literature at the time, she showed remarkable restraint. She did not tell but rather showed, by putting her characters in real-life situations, the dilemmas of deciding what is right action and the thoughts and feelings involved in arriving at a difficult moral

Proof of a wood engraving by Hammatt Billings for the frontispiece of Little Women, *part two. Alcott returned the proof, with her annotations in the margins, to Roberts Brothers, who had Billings redo the illustration.*

choice. Her work was influential in encouraging other writers for children to create real situations and real characters, having them act and speak as real children would.

Though *Little Women* was warmly received by its original readers, the book has not fared so well at the hands of modern critics, who see it as too sweet and sentimental for modern tastes. Martha Saxton, in the 1977 biography *Louisa May*, sees *Little Women* as an artistic compromise for Alcott, a retreat into easy moralizing and simplistic characterization after the complexity of her adult novel *Moods* and its lukewarm critical reception. In a 1965 essay entitled "A Masterpiece, and Dreadful" Brigid Brophy criticizes Alcott for being unwilling to analyze characters or to devise situations which might test them and their virtues. In *Women's Fiction* (1978) Nina Baym, while

praising Alcott for her artistic accomplishment and her ability to create authentic characters, notes that Alcott took over the themes of adult women's fiction of the time and turned them into a didactic device for girls, simplifying the themes rather than preserving the complexity with which they were illustrated in adult works. David E. Smith, studying the uses of *Pilgrim's Progress* in *John Bunyan in America* (1966), levels the same kind of criticism, that Alcott oversimplifies Christian's struggles so that they will fit into the uncomplicated structure and symbol pattern in *Little Women*.

In spite of such criticism the book endures and continues to be read with pleasure by children and by adults who return to the novel. The reason for the novel's popularity has been identified by Nina Auerbach, whose 1976 article "Austen and Alcott on Matriarchy" points to the warmth and solidarity of the circle of women in the novel and to the nostalgic appeal which makes readers wish for a time when domestic harmony of this order really existed. Though Alcott's own home life was never as placid or as warm as she presents it in the novel, she does create and sustain the atmosphere of emotional and physical sufficiency in the home, where Marmee allows the girls to remain always young and cared for. Readers continue to be enchanted by this never-never land set in New England and to be lulled and comforted by its emotional richness.

Alcott capitalized on her success in *Little Women* by writing another girls' novel almost immediately. In 1869 *An Old-Fashioned Girl* was published in *Merry's Museum* in two separate parts, the second part again demanded by readers who wanted to know what happened to the characters as they grew up. Book publication followed in 1870. The novel is the story of a poor girl, fourteen-year-old Polly Milton, the old-fashioned girl of the title, who is visiting the rich Shaw family and their three children: six-year-old Maud, fourteen-year-old Fanny, and sixteen-year-old Tom. Though the Shaw family is wealthy and seems to have everything to make them happy, they are not. All the family members are materialistic and self-absorbed; they care little for each other and do nothing to make home life harmonious or comfortable. Mrs. Shaw is a neurasthenic invalid. Mr. Shaw is completely preoccupied by his business dealings. The children are left to their own devices, and their grandmother is ignored by all. Though Polly's own home is never shown in detail, the reader is assured that, in spite of the family's poverty and many children, they are happy, the children well cared for and well behaved.

In the book Alcott demonstrates the carelessness with which rich people treat other people as well as material goods. She points out how snobby rich people are and how little they realize their complicity in the poverty and social isolation of working women: Fanny's rich friends snub Polly when she decides to make her own living as a music teacher, and women who work, such as seamstresses and servants, are not paid enough money to keep themselves. Alcott points to the silliness of fashionable girls' finishing schools where the girls go, not to learn useful accomplishments but rather to show off their clothes, to flirt, and to gossip. Alcott sets Polly as

a positive example to the rich people. She is friendly even when the rich girls snub her; she is helpful around the Shaw house and shows the Shaws how happy home life can be if they make the effort to care for each other. She dresses simply and in the style of the young girl she is, instead of as the fashionable young woman Fanny Shaw prinks herself up to be.

In fact, Polly is too good to be true. Alcott does give her one fault, vanity, which makes her envy her rich friends for their finery and many changes of clothes and hats and gloves, but this one fault does not rescue Polly from seeming the perfect domestic little woman. In the book she is called "sweet P" and "Polly peacemaker." She comes from the same social background as does Jo March but has none of Jo's spirit and ambition; her value in the novel is primarily symbolic. When Polly decides to become an independent working woman and support herself, she does have the urge to break loose from the severe domestic economy she practices and to spend money extravagantly though she cannot afford it. But it is only here that Polly's character becomes more than just a symbol of "old-fashioned" girlhood based on domestic virtues.

As she shows the joys of poverty in *Little Women,* so in *An Old-Fashioned Girl* Alcott shows the misery of wealth. Though the Shaws try to learn from Polly how to make their house a home, it is not until they lose their fortune that they are properly reformed and learn to be a happy family. The book ends with the traditional marriages, of Fanny to an ardent admirer who loves her even though she is now poor because she has learned to make a proper home for him, and of Polly to Tom Shaw, who has been sobered by the realization that he must work diligently for a living rather than rely on his father's wealth. Alcott uses many of the same formulas she did in *Little Women* but this time without the vibrancy or vigor that makes *Little Women* distinctive. The book did not sell as well as *Little Women* did, although it did well enough: 12,000 copies were sold by the initial publication date, and Alcott's first royalty check arrived for over $6,000.

Having established herself as a wealthy and successful author, Alcott took a prolonged European holiday with her sister May and a mutual friend. While they were in Italy they heard of the death of Alcott's sister Anna's husband, John Pratt. Though Pratt had arranged his affairs so that his widow and sons would be provided for, Alcott decided to write a book and give the proceeds to them. It was as though providing for her family had become a habit which she practiced even when the situation did not call for it. The result was *Little Men* (1871), a sequel to *Little Women*, the story of the Plumfield School which Professor Bhaer and Mrs. Jo had established at the end of *Little Women*. Alcott wrote the novel while she was in Europe and sent the manuscript to her publishers, Roberts Brothers, in Boston. It was published the day she arrived home and has continued to sell as well as *Little Women*.

Little Men is an educational novel in the manner of *Tom Brown's Schooldays* (1857) and *Tom Brown at Oxford* (1861) by Thomas Hughes. But Alcott's purpose is more than simply to celebrate the joys of school and the high spirits of schoolchildren. She wrote the novel to justify her father's educational methods and ideas. Many of the characters from *Little Women* reappear in *Little Men*—the March sisters and their husbands and offspring, Mr. and Mrs. March—and several children are introduced to demonstrate the effectiveness of Bronson Alcott's theories. The children spend little time in the classroom, though it can be assumed that they do have lessons in traditional subjects such as mathematics, composition, and geography, since the children discourse about these subjects at various points in the novel. Although Bronson Alcott did see that his daughters and the other pupils he taught were grounded in standard academic fare, he felt that other parts of their education were more important. As a consequence, even the most bookish of the children is never allowed to overindulge for fear he may neglect the other aspects of the educational regime at Plumfield.

Even more important to Bronson Alcott was the education of the child's body and spirit. Louisa May Alcott sees to both of these matters at the fictional Plumfield. The children each receive a garden plot in which they must work; they are encouraged to play cricket, fly kites, go berry-picking, and participate in the household chores, not only to develop their bodies but also to cultivate their senses of responsibility and good sportsmanship. Much of the time is spent romping about Plumfield, since neither Bronson nor Louisa Alcott thought that youthful high spirits should be suppressed; rather they needed to be channeled into healthful, harmless fun. The book opens with a pillow fight at the school. Mrs. Jo has realized early in her career as a teacher that though she might prefer that the boys not

sport about this way, such fighting is inevitable; she permits one fifteen-minute pillow fight a week, since everyone is the better for it–the boys for the fun and the release of energy and Mrs. Jo for not having to enforce an unenforceable and unnecessary rule.

But education at Plumfield has a more reflective and meditative side to it. Each Sunday the children attend church, and in the afternoon the professor takes them for a nature walk, not only so that they may learn botany but also so that they may observe and appreciate God's handiwork in nature. They say grace at meals and sing hymns in the evenings while the school orchestra plays. Though Alcott does not press any sectarian belief in the book, she does make clear, as she does in *Little Women*, that the proper education of children requires that they understand religious matters.

Bronson and Louisa May Alcott both believed in coeducation, though Bronson was not as ardent a supporter of the cause of educational opportunity for women as was his daughter. In any case there are girls at the school, both the traditional feminine domestic kind and the more independent, physically and mentally ambitious kind. Alcott claims in the book that exposing the boys to the girls makes the boys improve their manners, social graces, and standards of cleanliness. They also come to realize that girls can be their physical and educational equals when Nan Harding, one of the girls at the school, competes with them in the classroom and on the playing field, frequently besting them both at games and in schoolwork.

The children are for the most part well behaved and well motivated, but there are times when their desire to please Professor and Mrs. Bhaer is simply not enough to keep them good. Bronson Alcott did not believe in corporal punishment, a revolutionary idea for the time, so he had to devise a number of other ways to chastise his pupils. One, which shows up in *Little Men*, was to have the student strike the teacher as punishment when the student had committed an error. Another was to keep a ledger or an account of each pupil's behavior and to discuss it once a week with the student, rewarding good behavior with praise and a check mark, but punishing misbehavior with a black mark and an expression of the teacher's disappointment. In the case of both punishments the primary result is guilt on the student's part, which the modern reader may find distasteful. However, guilt can be quite motivating, as Louisa May Alcott knew, and both punishments are shown to work effectively in the novel.

That such mild punishments should succeed so splendidly indicates the major problem in the novel. The children are not well individualized; they are one-dimensional, each having one prevailing fault which they improve upon in the course of the novel. The metaphor which dominates the book is agricultural; the novel begins in the spring with Professor and Mrs. Bhaer planting the seeds of improvement; by the Thanksgiving celebration which closes the book, they reap a bountiful harvest of good deeds from each of the students. There is no really bad child who challenges the educational method, not even Dan Kean, the firebrand "berserker" who smokes, drinks, gambles, and swears. Even he is brought around by being thrown out of the school, the worst punishment available. His longing to return is so great that he promises and delivers reform in order to obtain a second chance at Plumfield.

The atmosphere of the book is tender and sweet; it has long been a favorite both of children and of educational theorists. But the sunny, cheerful surface of the book is not as simple and as harmonious as it seems at first glance. Dan Kean may be reformed, but the bond that results between him and Mrs. Jo is one that Alcott describes in peculiarly sexual terms. Once when she is particularly grateful, Mrs. Jo gives him "a kiss that made Dan entirely hers." When he feels the urge to run away again, Mrs. Jo says, "don't run far, and come back to me soon, for I want you very much." The happiness of the extended family is further called into doubt when Nan Harding tomahawks her dolls and abandons them in a particularly unmotherly way. Mrs. Jo's own five-year-old son Robby makes up a story about "a lady who had a million children, and one nice little boy" who subsequently drowns. It seems that Alcott is indicating here that in spite of her obvious purpose to show that family life and youth in general are happy, there is a darker side to human emotion and the intimacy of families which would destroy such happiness and which will intrude, even when perfect harmony seems to be prevailing. A careful reading of the novel rescues it from the charges of modern critics that the children are too good and the book too simple-minded in its belief that proper education can reform mankind.

After *Little Men* Alcott did not write another children's novel for four years. In the interim she rewrote one of the adult novels she had started during the Civil War, a largely autobiographical book entitled *Work: A Story of Experience,* and had it published serially in Henry Ward Beecher's weekly magazine the *Christian Union* and as a single volume with Roberts Brothers in 1873. She also wrote several short stories for children which appeared in magazines such as the *Youth's Companion,* the *Independent,* the *Christian Register,* and *St. Nicholas.* Many of these short stories were collected and republished in the six books of the *Aunt Jo's Scrap-Bag* series (1872-1882) and in other volumes as her career continued. Always one to turn a profit, Alcott realized that she could be paid twice for novels and stories if she sold them to magazines and then had them republished. Her reputation as a writer was well established, and her public was eager to read whatever she wrote, even if it had already appeared elsewhere.

In 1874 Alcott wrote *Eight Cousins* with its sequel, *Rose in Bloom,* clearly in mind. She wrote the former in serial form, to be published in installments in two children's magazines, *Good Things: A Picturesque Magazine for the Young of All Ages* (December 1874-November 1875) and *St. Nicholas* (January-October 1875). Roberts Brothers published the book as *Eight Cousins; or The Aunt-Hill* in 1875, with a promise in the preface of a sequel, which appeared the next year, although it was not serialized. Both novels show a technical accomplishment in plotting and characterization which Alcott had not formerly achieved. *Little Men* and *Little Women* are both episodic, devoting individual chapters to single characters. Though *An Old-Fashioned Girl* is concerned with one main character, Polly Milton, Polly's relations with individual members of the Shaw family tend to occupy individual chapters. But Alcott's treatment of Rose Campbell, the central character in *Eight Cousins* and *Rose in Bloom,* shows that she was capable of writing one continuous novel about a single character. Though the story line sometimes becomes episodic when dealing with Rose's seven male cousins, Rose is still the central focus, and it is her progress that dominates the novel.

The two novels taken together comprise a treatise on female education. Rose Campbell is a thirteen-year-old orphaned heiress who comes under the guardianship of her Uncle Alec, a young physician. He takes care of her at their ancestral home, a large house on a hill, near which and in which his many aunts, sisters, and sisters-in-law live; hence the subtitle of *Eight Cousins, The Aunt-Hill*. Rose is surrounded by her many female relatives, each of whom has a different idea about how the young heiress should be brought up. To relieve this female tyranny, Alcott provides Rose with seven male cousins of different ages, all of whom wish to make her one of their set. Uncle Alec is most willing that she should join with them in their games and sports, for Rose has led a rather sheltered life and feels awkward around company, especially boys; she also needs the physical exercise that playing with the boys will provide in order to perk up her spirits and to help her sleep more soundly. In this case Alcott reverses the rationale for coeducation as she presented it in *Little Men;* whereas in the earlier novel it was for the improvement of the boys that girls were introduced, in *Eight Cousins* it is decidedly for Rose's benefit that boys should be her companions.

Though it is clear that vigorous physical education is one reason for the presence of the seven male cousins, it is apparent later in the novel that Rose is present to exert her influence on her cousins so that they will refrain from the temptations that beset growing boys–smoking, drinking, and reading unhealthy novels. Though Alcott uses Rose as a vehicle to rail against these errors, it is also clear that these issues point to one of the aspects of female education important to Alcott. Rose's education takes place not only so that she can improve herself but also so that she may learn to improve her cousins. At one point in *Eight Cousins* Rose says, "I have discovered what girls are made for. . . . To take care of boys." As independent and strong-minded as Alcott would have her heroines be, she clearly does not have them achieve independence only for their own sakes.

But Alcott does advocate that Rose learn a "trade" so that she can take care of herself should she ever have to and so that her life will not be an idle one. Part of Alcott's educational regime for Rose is that she learns as her trade housekeeping from her aunts. Her accomplishments in this field are symbolized by her ability to make a wholesome loaf of bread and to sew a shirt with neat buttonholes for her Uncle Alec, both without assistance. These two tasks symbolize in the novel competence in a variety of other household tasks which may be performed easily once these two basic skills are mastered. Alcott's points are

two: first, that all women, no matter how wealthy, should be able to earn their own livings; and second, that all women should master the traditional female chores of cooking and sewing, even if they are likely to have servants. Though the first message is decidedly untypical and rather feminist for its time, the second is not. Alcott is again careful not to offend her audience by not being too strident in her ideology about women's work and educational reform.

Alcott also takes up the issue of female dress reform, which was suggested but not examined in depth in *An Old-Fashioned Girl*. Though she does not go as far as to have Rose wear bloomers, assuaging the more fashionable aunts and less daring readers, Alcott does criticize a stylish walking suit as unbecoming, unhealthful with its high boots and open neckline which do not protect the body against inclement weather, and unmanageable and confining because of the tightness of the skirt and the restrictions of the corset. What the aunts propose is that Rose wear a walking suit in which she cannot walk. The suit that Uncle Alec proposes for her is comfortable, warm, attractive in color and design, and decidedly made for moving and playing in. It is eminently sensible and makes Rose look like the schoolgirl she is rather than a young lady, which as yet she is not. Alcott is not saying that women should look unattractive or that they should wear no ornaments; she does allow Rose to pierce her ears and to enjoy the earrings, although Uncle Alec is disappointed in the girl's vanity about them. But Alcott does indicate that the Victorian way of dressing young girls, and even stylish older women, is unflattering and not conducive to good health.

Rose does study traditional school subjects, but in nontraditional ways. The geography and economy of China are taught by visiting a merchant ship newly arrived from the Orient. Rose learns mathematics by keeping records of the expenditures from her allowance. Uncle Alec points out that this will be particularly important for Rose if she is to manage her own estate when she comes of age. She does study books, but not by doing assigned reading in them; instead she learns while she is reading aloud to one of her cousins who is ill and while she is teaching one of the household servants to read and write. And finally, she learns anatomy and physiology when her physician uncle brings home a real skeleton for her to study. Alcott is posing this curriculum as a much more useful and enjoyable course of study, different from that which girls, or even boys, usually pursued at schools of the time. There is no grinding away at learning useless facts, to the detriment of both health and intellectual progress; nor is there the trivial study typical of finishing schools which might teach a little music and painting and dancing, but nothing of real use in the adult world.

In *Rose in Bloom* Alcott returns to the Campbell clan of cousins. Her activities in the interim between the composition of *Eight Cousins* and that of *Rose in Bloom* are embodied in the latter book in several ways. Alcott had spent a year attending meetings of women's reform movements, including the Women's Congress in Syracuse in 1875, and had spent the winter holidays in New York, visiting philanthropic institutions, including orphanages and prisons. The novel opens seven years after the close of *Eight Cousins*. Rose and her cousins are now young people considering marriage and a choice of vocation. Rose has just returned from Europe, where her Uncle Alec has taken her to visit philanthropic institutions like those Alcott had observed. Rose has decided to become a professional philanthropist. She converts one of her properties into a lodging house for poor working women. She also adopts an orphan from a workhouse and sponsors outings and picnics for children from a nearby orphanage. Her male cousins find her decidedly strong-minded in her pursuit of these causes, but Rose attributes her resolution to her desire to have a career and be more than a social ornament of a wife and mother: "I believe that it is as much a right and a duty for women to do something with their lives as for men; and we are not going to be satisfied. . . . Would *you* be contented to be told to enjoy yourself for a little while, then marry and do nothing more till you die?" The sermon continues: "We've got minds and souls as well as hearts; ambition and talents, as well as beauty and accomplishments; and we want to live and learn as well as love and be loved. I'm sick of being told that is all a woman is fit for! I won't have any thing to do with love till I prove that I am something besides a housekeeper and baby-tender!" Here is the feminism that Alcott had been experimenting with in her leisure time between books.

In spite of Rose's high-mindedness about a career and philanthropy, in the course of the novel she does marry. Much of the book is devoted to her decision about which of her cousins to choose. At first it seems that she will marry Charlie, but he proves unsuitable. As an only

child, he has been spoiled by his mother, and he is now unable to concentrate on either studies or a vocation long enough to make a success of himself. He also runs with a bad crowd of other boys and drinks. Though he promises Rose to abstain, one night he breaks his promise. One glass of champagne makes him unable to control his horse; he is thrown and dies of his injuries. Though this may seem like rather drastic punishment for one indulgence in champagne, it is clear that Charlie is unsuitable for Rose because of his irresolution.

After a suitable period of mourning Rose turns her interest to her bookish cousin Mac. He is the cousin who most resembles her admirable Uncle Alec, for Mac is studying to be a doctor. But even Mac needs improvement, for his manners in social settings are abominable. He does not dress himself neatly, and when he escorts Rose to a ball he leaves her to her own devices, going off in a corner to talk science with another man rather than dancing with Rose and seeing her home. Rose sends him off to make a success of himself. He does so not only by becoming a worthy physician but also by writing a volume of poetry which makes him sought after by fashionable society, where he shows off his newly acquired social graces. When he arrives home, he has thoroughly demonstrated his fitness to be Rose's husband.

At the end of the novel several other cousins marry, too, but one of the marriages is noteworthy for the social snobbery which is clear in the conduct of the courtship. In *Eight Cousins* Rose "adopts" as a sister an orphaned servant girl her own age. She sees to it that Phebe has all the educational advantages that she has, especially voice lessons, for Phebe is a natural singer. When Alec, Rose, and Phebe return from Europe one of Rose's cousins falls in love with Phebe, and she with him, but the family opposes the match because of Phebe's social inferiority. Phebe goes away to a big city where she earns a reputation for herself as a singer in one of the prestigious churches. Both she and cousin Archie prove their love by remaining true to each other during their separation. When Phebe arrives home with sufficient public acclaim to prove her worthiness, then the family consents to the match, but not until then. Though Alcott in other places supports the lot of decent and respectable working women, she will only allow them into the upper class when they prove extraordinarily meritorious, as Phebe does.

Alcott in 1887

Eight Cousins and *Rose in Bloom* are more issue oriented than any of Alcott's earlier books. She does not hesitate to have her characters preach when she feels strongly about an issue. And though Rose is characterized by many of the high-spirited qualities of children that the girls in *Little Women* have, she too can be preachy and straitlaced, especially when it comes to drinking, smoking, and application to a vocation. The feminism she expresses at the beginning of *Rose in Bloom* seems too bitter for a young girl who has led a privileged and sheltered life; the acerbity is Alcott's, and the didacticism in both novels sometimes overshadows the technical achievements of plot and characterization.

Both Alcott and her mother were ill during the time that the two books were written. By 1877 it became apparent that Abigail Alcott was dying. While Alcott attended her mother's sickbed, Mary Mapes Dodge, the editor of *St. Nicholas*, appealed to her for another children's novel to be serialized in her magazine. *Under the Lilacs* was written in snatches while Alcott nursed her mother. It is the least successful of her juvenile

novels. It was published serially from December 1877 to October 1878 in *St. Nicholas*. Her publisher, Roberts Brothers, gave her a $3,000 advance on the book's publication in 1878 which Alcott felt she would need for the extra expenses in nursing her mother.

Under the Lilacs is the story of a circus boy and his trained poodle who run away from the circus to find the boy's father. His father had left to find his fortune in the West, promising to return. When he does not and when the boy and the dog are abused by the circus master, they leave. On their way they encounter two young girls and their mother, who take over the care of both boy and dog, giving them a home and the boy schooling to make him respectable. In the process they stifle the boy's fun-loving nature. The best scenes in the book are Alcott's descriptions of the children at their games and the dog doing his tricks. Otherwise Alcott turns the circus boy into a respectable but boring middle-class schoolboy entirely too quickly. The girls' characters are flatly drawn, and the plot shows little inventiveness. Perhaps Alcott was too involved in caring for her mother to give the novel the attention needed for it to succeed.

At this time Alcott rewrote one of her Gothic thrillers to be published in the No-Name series of books published anonymously by famous American authors. Her own publisher, Roberts Brothers, produced the series and wanted a book by their best-known author in disguise. *A Modern Mephistopheles* (1877) is full of Gothic horror and evil and might have shocked Alcott's reading public, who expected wholesome juvenile writing. But nothing in the book is really so horrible, and Alcott later consented to have the book republished under her own name.

Just before her mother's death Alcott and her family moved from their home at Orchard House on the outskirts of Concord to the Thoreau house in Concord village. After her mother's death Alcott was drawn into the activities of the village children—their sports, dramatic productions, and holiday celebrations. When one of the children died she was moved to write *Jack and Jill: A Village Story*, which was serialized in *St. Nicholas* from December 1879 to October 1880 and also published by Roberts Brothers in 1880. It is the story of a group of children and uses Alcott's earlier episodic technique of devoting individual chapters to individual children. The book takes place in Harmony Village, the fictional equivalent of Concord, over the course of about a year. Alcott chronicles a Christmas party, the children's dramatic presentation in honor of George Washington's birthday, a May Day celebration, a weekend at a shore resort, and a school exhibition. Her eye for journalistic detail did not fail her, for these are the most interesting incidents in the book. *Jack and Jill* is also the work that succeeds best in capturing the New England setting, which dominates the action and dictates much of the ordering of the celebrations.

Jack and Jill also tells the story of the death of Ed Devlin, the fictional equivalent of a neighboring Concord schoolboy, Ellsworth Devens, to whose memory the book is dedicated. Ed is a good boy, perhaps too angelic in his protection of the younger children from the bullying of the older ones and in his willingness to leave school and go into business in order to support his mother. But Alcott does relieve this portrait of overwhelming goodness by pointing out that Ed is something of a flirt, for he is particularly gallant around girls. In any case Ed dies of a mysterious fever, and all the children attend his funeral. They realize that Ed is sincerely mourned in

death because of his goodness in life, and they all resolve to follow his good example in their own lives. Although Ed's death is not described by Alcott, the scene of the funeral is overdone, partly because Alcott does not resist the urge to intrude and preach on the appropriateness of the subject of death in children's books, and partly because Ed was so good. If she had resisted both impulses, she might have written about death with the same sensitivity with which she portrayed Beth's demise in *Little Women.* As it stands in the novel, Ed's death is too sweet and precious to be believed.

Some episodes in *Jack and Jill* are devoted to showing the efficacy of Bronson Alcott's childrearing principles of "good health, good principles, and a good education." The girls of the village take it upon themselves to reform their male siblings and friends, again by influencing them to be gentlemen in their ladylike presences. The boys, of course, are duly reformed. The boys have a debating team which discusses the idea of coeducation and decides in its favor. They also form an antismoking league to help one another resist the boyish temptation to indulge. What saves *Jack and Jill* from being a slavish imitation of Alcott's earlier books is the portrayal of the children's celebrations. Otherwise Alcott takes no chances in this novel with inventing new or daring characters and situations or trying out new social ideas.

Alcott continued to be a popular author with children and to write short stories for them; she also kept on with her practice of collecting those short stories for republication in book form. When her younger sister May died from the complications of childbirth and left the guardianship of her baby daughter, Louisa ("Lulu") May Nieriker, to the baby's Aunt Louisa, Alcott started writing stories for the little girl's amusement. The three-volume *Lulu's Library* series (1886-1889) collected these stories and republished some of Alcott's older stories from *Flower Fables.* Alcott also found time to revise her favorite novel, *Moods,* for republication in 1882. Its commercial success no doubt rested on Alcott's fame as a juvenile writer.

Alcott became increasingly ill toward the end of her life. Nannies took over the care of her niece, and Alcott began to settle her financial affairs by adopting her nephew John Sewell Pratt (who took the name John S. P. Alcott) so that there would be no legal problems about the proceeds from her books staying in the family. As early as 1880 Mary Mapes Dodge and Alcott's editor had asked for a sequel to *Little Men.* Alcott began to write one, but due to ill health, the death of her sister, her grief over the death of her mother, and her father's stroke and deteriorating health, all progress halted. The family moved from Concord to Boston to be nearer to Alcott's doctors. The sequel, *Jo's Boys, and How They Turned Out,* was finally finished and published in 1886 by Roberts Brothers. The pain in which the book was composed is evident from the first chapter, in which the remaining March sisters, Mrs. Jo and Mrs. Meg, mourn the deaths of Beth, Marmee, Meg's husband, and others; it was difficult for Alcott to think about, much less write about, those deaths, and the mental anguish slowed down her progress on the book.

Jo's Boys is set at the Plumfield School, which has been expanded to include Laurence College for both young men and women. The role of the college in the book is to show the success of Bronson Alcott's educational methods as children grow into young adulthood. The many successful careers and marriages pursued and achieved in the novel are indications of the soundness of Bronson Alcott's principles, though it is not always clear from the characterizations that the successes are due solely to the children's educations.

In spite of the educational theme, the novel's main emphasis is on woman's rights. Though in other novels Alcott refrained from preaching the feminist gospel and from having her female characters follow it too closely, in *Jo's Boys* she shows no such restraint. She has Mrs. Jo reproach the male students for their condescending attitudes toward their fellow female students; when the women students meet together for a sewing circle, Mrs. Jo reads to them from feminist tracts while they attend to their needlework. Finally, the girls in the novel have successful careers, whereas in *Little Women* they do not. One of the girls in *Jo's Boys,* Nan Harding, becomes a doctor and remains a happy and satisfied spinster. Though there are more conventional "little women" in the book who become happy housewives, they are not as convincingly or as sympathetically drawn as are the career women. The little women seem to be a sop that Alcott throws to readers who might find such strident feminist talk and action distasteful.

At the end of the novel Alcott ties up the loose ends of the plot, disposing of all the characters so thoroughly that no sequel would be possible. The exhaustion and relief she felt at finally

finishing with the March family are evident at the end when she threatens to destroy Plumfield with an earthquake to prevent clamor from her readers for yet another sequel. The episodic quality of the book, no doubt resulting at least partly from Alcott's sporadic attempts at writing it over a period of six years, is particularly noticeable. The sharpness of the woman's-rights diatribes and the speedy dispatch with which the characters are disposed of and the novel ended underscore Alcott's physical and creative exhaustion. Though it is pleasing to meet the same familiar characters again, *Jo's Boys* is the least satisfactory of the March family stories. No doubt its commercial success and acceptance by the critics owed much to the quality and reputation of its two predecessors.

Alcott's health deteriorated rapidly in early 1888. When on 4 March she was allowed to leave the rest home where she was staying to visit her father on his deathbed, the outing was too much for her both physically and emotionally. Bronson Alcott died that day; early on the morning of 6 March Louisa May Alcott died in her sleep at the rest home in Roxbury, Massachusetts. The two were eulogized at a joint funeral, and both were buried in the family plot in Sleepy Hollow Cemetery, Concord.

Alcott's reputation as a children's writer was and still is based primarily on her accomplishment in *Little Women.* None of the books that followed reach the same level of technical accomplishment in characterization and structure, and it is this book to which most modern criticism has been directed. The rediscovery of Alcott's adult works inspired by the new interest in nineteenth-century women's fiction has undercut favorable evaluation of the juvenile novels. It is necessary to remember that for her time Alcott showed surprising honesty in her portrayal of authentic human characters with recognizable human feelings. She institutionalized the family story as a staple of American children's fare; she maintained a plain, honest, and yet pleasing style; and even if she did descend into preachiness at times, she did it with a restraint lacking in her contemporaries. Her novels are particularly adept at capturing the high spirits of children at play, and if those children today seem too good to be true, they were much truer to life than other fictional children of the time. Finally, Alcott filled a void in children's literature, for there were no good books for adolescents, especially not for girls. The March sisters, especially Jo, stand as the crowning achievement of Alcott's literary career and as a model for writers of domestic fiction who followed.

Letters:

The Selected Letters of Louisa May Alcott, edited by Joel Myerson and Daniel Shealy; associate editor, Madeleine B. Stern (Boston: Little, Brown, 1987).
> A collection of over 260 letters by Alcott, all fully annotated, with an introduction by Madeleine B. Stern.

Bibliography:

Alma J. Payne, *Louisa May Alcott; A Reference Guide* (Boston: G. K. Hall, 1980).
> Primary and annotated secondary bibliography which contains references to reviews, articles, and books.

Biographies:

Ednah Dow Cheney, *Louisa May Alcott, Her Life, Letters and Journals* (Boston: Roberts Brothers, 1889).
> First book-length biography of Alcott written by one of her contemporaries.

Madeleine B. Stern, *Louisa May Alcott* (Norman: University of Oklahoma Press, 1950; revised, 1971).
> Most definitive biography yet, with excellent bibliography and notes on the sources.

Martha Saxton, *Louisa May: A Modern Biography of Louisa May Alcott* (Boston: Houghton Mifflin, 1977).
> Psychoanalytical biography which interprets various themes in Alcott's life.

Madelon Bedell, *The Alcotts* (New York: Clarkson Potter, 1981).
> Critical biography which focuses on the entire Alcott family, especially Bronson and Abigail Alcott.

References:

Nina Auerbach, "Austen and Alcott on Matriarchy: New Women or New Wives?," *Novel*, 10 (Fall-Winter 1976): 6-26.
> Comparison of *Pride and Prejudice* and *Little Women* as representations of matriarchal families.

Nina Baym, *Women's Fiction; A Guide to Novels by and about Women in America, 1820-1870* (Ithaca & London: Cornell University Press, 1978), pp. 296-298.
> Critical analysis of novels written between 1820 and 1870 by American women authors about women.

Brigid Brophy, "A Masterpiece, and Dreadful," *New York Times Book Review*, 10 January 1965, p. 44.
> Examines the popularity of *Little Women* and focuses on Alcott's technical skills and her use of sentimentality.

Sarah Elbert, *A Hunger for Home: Louisa May Alcott and Little Women* (Philadelphia: Temple University Press, 1984).
> Exploration of Alcott's use of feminist ideas in her fiction.

Elizabeth Janeway, "Meg, Jo, Beth, Amy, and Louisa," *New York Times Book Review*, 29 September 1968, pp. 42-46.
> Discussion of why *Little Women* continues to be popular today.

Ruth K. MacDonald, *Louisa May Alcott* (Boston: Twayne, 1983).
> A broad, general biographical and critical overview of Alcott's life and career.

Joy Marsella, *The Promise of Destiny: Children in the Short Stories of Louisa May Alcott* (Westport, Conn.: Greenwood Press, 1984).
> A critical examination of the sixty stories collected in the six volumes of *Aunt Jo's Scrap-Bag*.

Leona Rostenberg, "Some Anonymous and Pseudonymous Thrillers of Louisa May Alcott," *Papers of the Bibliographical Society of America*, 37, no. 1 (1943): 131-140.
> Recounts how Alcott's anonymous sensational stories were discovered in the twentieth century.

David E. Smith, *John Bunyan in America* (Bloomington & London: Indiana University Press, 1966), pp. 93-102.
> Examines Alcott's use of *Pilgrim's Progress* as a structural device and symbolic pattern in *Little Women*.

Patricia Meyer Spacks, *The Female Imagination* (New York: Knopf, 1975), pp. 95-101.
Discussion of Jo March and the role of women in *Little Women*.

Madeleine B. Stern, *Critical Essays on Louisa May Alcott* (Boston: G. K. Hall, 1984).
Excellent collection of reviews and critical articles covering all aspects of Alcott's career.

Charles Strickland, *Victorian Domesticity: Families in the Life and Art of Louisa May Alcott* (University: University of Alabama Press, 1985).
Critical examination of American family life in relation to Alcott's own family and fiction.

Papers:
The Alcott family papers are in the possession of the Houghton Library at Harvard University.

Ambrose Bierce

*This entry was updated by M. E. Grenander (State University of New York at Albany)
from her entry in* DLB 12, American Realists and Naturalists.

Places	Ohio Civil War Battlefields England Washington, D.C.	Kentucky Alabama Dakota Territory	Indiana San Francisco Bay Area Mexico
Influences and Relationships	Bret Harte George Sterling Herman Scheffauer	William Randolph Hearst Gertrude Atherton	Mark Twain Gustav Adolf Danziger Percival Pollard
Literary Movements and Forms	Impressionism Epigram Satire	Naturalism Fable	Short Story Journalism
Major Themes	Individualism Political Corruption	Mistrust of the Law Determinism	Death
Cultural and Artistic Influences	Rejection of All Theological and Moral Systems	Darwin's Theory of Evolution	Anti-Idealism
Social and Economic Influences	Civil War Revolution in Mexico	Reconstruction Spanish-American War	America's "Age of Plutocracy"

See also the Bierce entries in DLB 11, American Humorists, 1800-1950, *and* DLB 23, American Newspaper Journalists, 1873-1900.

BIRTH: Meigs County, Ohio, 24 June 1842, to Marcus Aurelius and Laura Sherwood Bierce.

EDUCATION: Kentucky Military Institute, 1859-1860.

MARRIAGE: 25 December 1871 to Mary Ellen (Mollie) Day; children: Day, Leigh, and Helen.

DEATH: Disappeared in battle somewhere in Mexico, January 1914.

SELECTED BOOKS: *The Fiend's Delight,* as Dod Grile (London: John Camden Hotten, 1873; New York: A. L. Luyster, 1873);
Nuggets and Dust Panned Out in California, as Dod Grile (London: Chatto & Windus, 1873);
Cobwebs from an Empty Skull, as Dod Grile (London & New York: Routledge, 1874);
The Dance of Death, by Bierce and Thomas A. Harcourt, as William Herman (San Francisco: Privately printed, 1877; corrected and enlarged edition, San Francisco: Henry Keller, 1877);
Tales of Soldiers and Civilians (San Francisco: E. L. G. Steele, 1892; published simultaneously as *In the Midst of Life* (London: Chatto & Windus, 1892; revised and enlarged edition, New York & London: Putnam's, 1898);
Black Beetles in Amber (San Francisco & New York: Western Authors Publishing, 1892);
Can Such Things Be? (New York: Cassell, 1893; London: Cape, 1926);
Fantastic Fables (New York & London: Putnam's, 1899);
Shapes of Clay (San Francisco: W. E. Wood, 1903);
The Cynic's Word Book (New York: Doubleday, Page, 1906); enlarged as *The Devil's Dictionary,* volume 7 of *The Collected Works of Ambrose Bierce* (New York & Washington: Neale, 1911);
A Son of the Gods and A Horseman in the Sky (San Francisco: Elder, 1907);
The Shadow on the Dial and Other Essays, edited by S. O. Howes (San Francisco: A. M. Robertson, 1909); revised and republished as *Antepenultimata,* volume 11 of *The Collected Works of Ambrose Bierce* (New York & Washington: Neale, 1912);

Write It Right (New York & Washington: Neale, 1909);
The Collected Works of Ambrose Bierce, 12 volumes (New York & Washington: Neale, 1909-1912)–1) *Ashes of the Beacon, The Land Beyond the Blow, For the Ahkoond, John Smith, Liberator, Bits of Autobiography;* 2) *In the Midst of Life;* 3) *Can Such Things Be?, The Ways of Ghosts, Soldier-Folk, Some Haunted Houses;* 4) *Shapes of Clay, Some Antemortem Epitaphs, The Scrap Heap;* 5) *Black Beetles in Amber, The Mummery, On Stone;* 6) *The Monk and the Hangman's Daughter, Fantastic Fables, Aesopus Emendatus, Old Saws with New Teeth, Fables in Rhyme;* 7) *The Devil's Dictionary;* 8) *Negligible Tales, The Parenticide Club, The Fourth Estate, The Ocean Wave, "On with the Dance!," Epigrams;* 9) *Tangential Views;* 10) *The Opinionator, The Reviewer, The Controversialist, The Timorous Reporter, The March Hare;* 11) *Antepenultimata;* 12) *In Motley, Kings of Beasts, Two Administrations, Miscellaneous;*
Battlefields and Ghosts, edited by Hartley E. Jack-

21

son and James D. Hart (Palo Alto: Harvest Press, 1931);

Selections from Prattle by Ambrose Bierce, edited by Carroll D. Hall (San Francisco: Book Club of California, 1936);

Enlarged Devil's Dictionary, edited by Ernest J. Hopkins (Garden City: Doubleday, 1967);

The Ambrose Bierce Satanic Reader, edited by Hopkins (Garden City: Doubleday, 1968);

Ambrose Bierce–Skepticism and Dissent: Selected Journalism from 1898-1901, edited by Lawrence I. Berkore (Ann Arbor, Mich.: Delmas, 1980).

OTHER: *Mark Twain's Library of Humor,* contains contributions by Bierce (New York: Webster, 1888);

Richard Voss, *The Monk and the Hangman's Daughter,* Gustav Adolf Danziger's translation, revised by Bierce (Chicago: Schulte, 1892).

The late Carey McWilliams, himself an astute observer of the national scene, has pointed out that every American should have some familiarity with Ambrose Bierce, that aloof and independent iconoclast who was in the thick of some of the most important developments of our history. Like other gallant young men of his generation, he sacrificed his youth to the military holocaust that blazed through and almost destroyed the United States from 1861 to 1865. As he grew older his magnetic personality attracted respect and esteem in England, California, and Washington, D.C. Many of his admirers recorded their impressions of him; and his incisive journalism, witty epigrams, and brilliant stories are now part of the American heritage. Nevertheless, for more than one hundred years his life and his writings have resisted easy generalizations.

The reason lies in the fact that Bierce was the completely self-reliant man, whose nonconformity permeated almost every aspect of his thinking. He set his face not only against literary fashion, but against dominant social and political theories as well. Basic to his position was his dark view of the human soul. Given the nature of man, he felt, programs based on rigid principles of any stripe were doomed to failure. What might be abstractly preferable was irrelevant to the solution of problems whose answers must be devised and implemented by human beings. The starry-eyed idealist who oversimplified issues did more harm than good in the long run; his visionary promises deluded the very people he sought to help, leading them to cynicism and despair.

Not only about theological and scientific matters, but about literary, moral, ethical, social, and political ones as well, men and women should reserve judgment on problems which cannot be solved by reason. They should not leap blindly into an uncritical acceptance of dogma by faith. Anyone holding such views is unlikely to maintain doctrinaire tenets, and here lies the crux of Bierce's nonconformity. He could hardly be expected to follow the majority, but what is perhaps more interesting is that he refused to enlist in any minority-*ism*, either. Such a man is clearly provocative rather than popular, since there is no group for whom he will have mass appeal. Rather, his charm lies in his affinity for the small number of people in any age who are as strongly individualistic as he.

Ambrose Gwinnett Bierce was born on a farm in southeastern Ohio on 24 June 1842, the tenth of thirteen children (all of whose first names began with *A*) born to Marcus Aurelius and Laura Sherwood Bierce and the youngest to survive to adulthood. Although the Ohio of his early childhood furnished the background for two of his short stories, "The Suitable Surroundings" and "The Boarded Window," his family moved to northern Indiana near the village of Warsaw four years after his birth, and he grew up a Hoosier except for a brief period in 1859-1860 when he studied draftsmanship, surveying, and engineering at the Kentucky Military Institute in Franklin Springs, Kentucky. His nonconformity was nurtured when, as a teenager, he worked on an antislavery paper in Warsaw, the *Northern Indianan*. And in April 1861, when the Civil War broke out, he enlisted at the age of eighteen as a private in the Ninth Indiana Infantry.

This decision, at the beginning of four of the most impressionable years of his life, was to have lasting consequences in molding his character. He fought bravely and skillfully throughout the war, rising eventually to the rank of first lieutenant and the staff position of topographical engineer. As a brigade headquarters officer he was in a position not only to engage in firsthand combat but also to understand the larger strategic picture of some of the Civil War's most famous battles: Shiloh, Stones River, Chickamauga, Missionary Ridge, and Kennesaw Mountain, where he was shot in the head in June 1864. After hospitalization and a brief convalescent furlough he returned to service in September, in time to participate in the battles of Franklin and Nashville. During Reconstruction after the war, he worked as a U.S. Treasury agent in Alabama for several months in 1865. The next year, however, he joined his wartime commander, Brig. Gen. William Hazen, as engineering attaché on an army mapping expedition from Omaha to the West Coast. But when he arrived in San Francisco, he resigned his army post, angered at not receiving the captain's commission he had been promised. (He was brevetted to major in 1867 for his distinguished military service.)

In 1867, while holding minor, undemanding jobs at the U.S. Sub-Treasury in San Francisco, he began having his work published in the *Californian,* the *Golden Era,* and the *Alta California,* as well as in the *San Francisco News Letter and California Advertiser,* of which he became editor in December 1868. In 1871 his "Grizzly Papers" began to appear in the *Overland Monthly,* then under Bret Harte's editorship. These essays contain some of Bierce's best and most distinctive early work. For example, in a public statement of the principles that governed his own life, he attacked conformity to fickle public opinion and defended self-reliance, on the ground that "If a man have a broad foot, a stanch leg, a strong spine, and a talent for equilibrium, there is no good reason why he should not stand alone. . . . A mind that is right side up does not need to lean upon others: it is sufficient unto itself. The curse of our civilization is that the 'association' is become the unit, and the individual is merged in the mass." According to Bierce, civilization owed its advances to the courageous minority, not to the powerful but mediocre majority. His first published story, "The Haunted Valley," a tale of murder and mystery which was republished in *Can Such Things Be?* (1893), also appeared in the *Overland Monthly.*

On Christmas Day 1871 Bierce married Mary Ellen (Mollie) Day, the daughter of a well-to-do miner; and in March 1872, financed by his father-in-law, he and Mollie Bierce left for England. They lived there from 1872 to 1875, a period he later characterized as "the happiest and most prosperous period" of his life. Tall, well-dressed, and handsome, with gray eyes and blond hair and mustache, the witty Bierce appealed to the British, and he quickly became active in London journalism and publishing. He wrote for Tom Hood's *Fun,* a humorous weekly; for *Figaro;* and for the San Francisco *Alta California,* to which he sent accounts of English current events. He also wrote in their entirety the two issues of the *Lantern,* a gorgeously polychromatic

publication, which appeared on 18 May and 15 July 1874. A footnote to the French revolution of 1870-1871, which had toppled Napoleon III from his throne and established the short-lived Paris Commune, the *Lantern* was subsidized by the Empress Eugénie, Napoleon's widow and a wealthy exile in England.

Using the pen name Dod Grile, Bierce also had his first three books published in England: *The Fiend's Delight* and *Nuggets and Dust Panned Out in California* in 1873, and *Cobwebs from an Empty Skull* in 1874. Four thousand copies of *Cobwebs from an Empty Skull* were printed, with a second printing of four thousand several years later. All three of these early books were composed of sketches, paragraphs, short narratives, epigrams, and fables collected from Bierce's journalistic writings. *The Fiend's Delight* shows him at his epigrammatic best in selections such as "Those who are horrified at Mr. Darwin's theory, may comfort themselves with the assurance that, if we are descended from the ape, we have not descended so far as to preclude all hope of return." *Nuggets and Dust* included appreciative little essays on aspects of England that had appealed to Bierce: "St. Paul's," "The Size of London," and "Stratford-on-Avon," his homage to Shakespeare. Typical of the short fables in *Cobwebs from an Empty Skull* is one in which an oak agrees to let an ivy vine climb him: "So she started up, and finding she could grow faster than he, she wound round and round him until she had passed up all the line she had. The oak, however, continued to grow, and as she could not disengage her coils, she was just lifted out by the root. So that ends the oak-and-ivy business, and removes a powerful temptation from the path of the young writer." Such fables, with their compression, wit, stylistic elegance, and reversal of conventional opinion, were admired by Mark Twain, and he included seven of them in his *Library of Humor* (1888), their first publication in America. Bierce, however, always expressed contempt for his early London books and refused to have them republished during his lifetime. Nevertheless, they were moderately successful in England, where Prime Minister William Ewart Gladstone, twenty years after their original appearance, started a Bierce boom by praising their wit. And in spite of his announced distaste for them, Bierce culled from all three books for volumes 6, 8, 9, and 12 of his *Collected Works* (1909-1912).

His chronic asthma had prevented the Bierces from settling permanently in London.

They lived in a number of attractive places: Bristol, where their first son, Day, was born in 1872; Bath; and Leamington, birthplace of their second son, Leigh, in 1874. However, Mollie Bierce, burdened with two small children and pregnant with a third, was not as enchanted with England as her husband, and in April 1875 she returned to San Francisco. Bierce joined her in September, and on 30 October their third child–a daughter, Helen–was born there. Bierce had had to leave a promising writing career in England, and it took him more than a decade to establish himself professionally in the United States. Initially he got a job in the assay office of the San Francisco branch of the U.S. Mint and wrote a column, "The Prattler," for a newly founded magazine called the *Argonaut*, beginning the satiric definitions which later became famous in *The Devil's Dictionary* (1911–after an intermediate appearance in *The Cynic's Word Book*, 1906). With Thomas A. Harcourt he concocted an elaborate hoax called *The Dance of Death* (1877), supposedly written by a William Herman. The book purported to be a vicious attack on the waltz, but was so suggestively written as to be a popular success whose appeal Bierce augmented by stern strictures against it in his column.

However, his most serious efforts at establishing himself in a career were devoted to an ill-starred gold-mining venture in the Dakota Territory. Financed by Wall Street capitalists, the Black Hills Placer Mining Company was run by incompetents and headed by a president who later barely escaped being sent to Sing Sing on charges of graft and corruption. In the spring of 1880 Bierce was appointed general agent of the struggling mining company and left for Deadwood, his wife and children remaining in California. For four months he drudged ably and conscientiously for the company, but its affairs were so snarled by foolish and dishonest managers that, despite his skill and hard work and the mine's potential for success, the enterprise collapsed. He wound up with little money for his exhausting labors and the burden of a complicated lawsuit which dragged on for nine years, ending up in the U.S. Supreme Court. As nominal plaintiff Bierce won the suit, but he got nothing out of it and even had to pay the court costs. Although this single episode was not the only basis for his continuing satire against the law and lawyers, it could hardly have failed to add to his disillusionment with them.

In 1881 he returned to San Francisco and

his family and once again had to find a new career. This time, however, he was able to secure the editorship of the weekly *San Francisco Wasp*, with which he was associated from 1881 to 1886. He continued his column in this journal, renaming it "Prattle" and including in it many more of the definitions collected in *The Cynic's Word Book*, and published "What I Saw of Shiloh," an eyewitness account of one of the Civil War's most memorable battles. The *Wasp* also offered Bierce a journalistic outlet for attacking the "Big Four," whose depredations were later to be documented by Gustavus Myers in his *History of the Great American Fortunes* (1910). Primarily through the Central Pacific and Southern Pacific Railroads, they had seized control of California, dominating not only the press but the state's corrupt politicians in Washington as well as in Sacramento. Bierce denounced these malefactors of great wealth–Mark Hopkins, £eland $tanford (as Bierce called him), Collis P. Huntington, and Charles Crocker–while they were at the very height of their power. An honest and courageous man, he was throughout his life filled with disgust at the chicanery and greed that scarred American life after the Civil War. He had seen these traits of the national character while still a young man, in the days of his Alabama service during Reconstruction; and one of the reasons he had been so taken with England in the three and a half years he lived there was that he felt Englishmen were morally superior to Americans. His months in the Black Hills, when he watched what could have been a valuable gold mine destroyed by incompetent and fraudulent management, had reinforced his contempt for deceit and graft. Much of his reputation on the West Coast stemmed from his audacity and skill in attacking the Big Four, whom he called feudal overlords. Bierce accused these men of holding the economic and political life of California in their viselike grip and demonstrating on a grand scale the worst qualities of America's Age of Plutocracy. Unfortunately, however, the owner of the *Wasp* was too vacillating and dependent to succeed in journalism. After an embarrassing series of policy changes, he sold his periodical in 1886, and Bierce was once more out of a job.

But the next twelve years were to be the most significant of his personal and professional life. In 1887 the young William Randolph Hearst hired him, at a generous weekly salary, to write for his newly acquired *San Francisco Examiner*, and Bierce henceforth had a powerful weapon at hand for attacking the objects of his scorn, which

Bierce in his study, 1899

included not only political and economic malfea-
sance but also bad writing. The scourge of poetas-
ters, he became the literary dictator of the West
Coast. His living arrangements, however, were
controlled by the asthma which prevented his settling in any of the Bay Area cities where he
earned his living–San Francisco, Berkeley, and
Oakland. Instead, he retreated to lonely hotels in
out-of-the-way mountain resorts, his solitude miti-
gated by an occasional visitor and by a number
of pets, not only cats, birds, and squirrels but
also those rejected by most people: horned toads,
lizards, and snakes. Troubled by insomnia as well
as bronchial ailments, he spent much time in the
open air, hiking and bicycling along woodland
trails.

Two crises blighted this period. One was his
separation from Mollie Bierce, which occurred
after he discovered some indiscreet letters an ardent admirer had written her. Although nothing
seriously improper had occurred, Bierce refused
to compete for the affection of his own wife; the
rupture was complete and final. Even more shat-
tering was the death of the Bierces' older son,

Day, at the age of sixteen, when he and a young
rival killed each other in a gun duel over a girl.

Although Bierce confronted these tragedies
stoically, it seems inescapable that he sought catharsis in creative work. In a burst of consummate art he wrote in rapid succession, between
1888 and 1891, the series of short stories on
which his reputation today largely rests: "One of
the Missing," "A Son of the Gods," "A Tough Tus-
sle," "Chickamauga," "One Officer, One Man,"
"A Horseman in the Sky," "The Suitable Surroundings," "The Affair at Coulter's Notch," "A
Watcher by the Dead," "The Man and the
Snake," "An Occurrence at Owl Creek Bridge,"
"Parker Adderson, Philosopher," and "The Death
of Halpin Frayser." These tales, published initially in ephemeral periodicals, deal with the psychological traumas of a protagonist suddenly forced
into agonizing and deadly straits. For most of the
settings Bierce returned to the Civil War battles
of his youth. Now, however, he distilled those experiences, catalyzed by a polished craft, through
the alembic of a mature wisdom. The results,
among the English-speaking world's greatest crea-

tions in the demanding art of the short story, were eventually collected in two volumes. The first was published simultaneously in 1892 in San Francisco by E. L. G. Steele as *Tales of Soldiers and Civilians* and in London by Chatto and Windus as *In the Midst of Life*. The London title, derived from the burial service in the Anglican *Book of Common Prayer* ("In the midst of life we are in death"), was a brilliant contribution of Andrew Chatto's. Bierce was slow to appreciate this title, although in 1898 he took it over himself for the new American edition. The book was favorably received on both sides of the Atlantic, with Bierce being ranked alongside Edgar Allan Poe and Nathaniel Hawthorne. It suffered, not from lack of critical appreciation, but from a failure of business acumen. Steele was not a publisher, but a moderately well-to-do friend of Bierce's. Two subsequent publishers of the book went bankrupt, as did the publisher of a second collection of Bierce's stories which appeared as *Can Such Things Be?* (1893), a title derived from Shakespeare's *Macbeth*.

Meanwhile Bierce was becoming involved in one of the most tangled episodes of his career. A young German-Jewish dentist, Gustav Adolf Danziger, had brought him a rough translation of a short novel by Richard Voss, *Der Mönch von Berchtesgaden*, which had appeared in a German monthly. Bierce rewrote the story from Danziger's translation, and the two signed a complicated contract dividing the rewards they expected to get. Their work appeared serially under the title *The Monk and the Hangman's Daughter* in the *Examiner*; then in 1892 it was published by F. J. Schulte of Chicago, who went bankrupt. For years Danziger squabbled with Bierce over *The Monk and the Hangman's Daughter*.

Bierce's next book, a volume of satirical verse entitled *Black Beetles in Amber* (1892), was published by the Western Authors Publishing Company, a shaky vanity enterprise formed by Danziger and William M. Langton. This company also failed. Although Bierce's satire was superb, its targets were so insignificant that a new firm in Cambridge, Stone and Kimball, decided not to go through with their plans for publishing a selection from his book. Bierce defended his concentration on minor insects, however, by referring to the examples of Lord Byron and Alexander Pope and revealing his theory of satire: "I cannot see how the quality or interest of a piece is affected by application to a real, though unknown, person instead of presenting it as a gen-

eral satire, with perhaps a fictitious name. If the verse is good it *makes* the victims known; if not good it is not worth publishing anyhow." But his work was soon taken in hand by a competent firm. In 1898 Putnam's published a revised and enlarged edition of *In the Midst of Life*, which earned favorable reviews and royalties on the sale of over three thousand copies; Chatto and Windus brought out a second printing; and in 1899 Putnam's published *Fantastic Fables*, whose sales approached one thousand.

In journalism, too, this period saw Bierce's greatest triumphs. Hearst had decided to direct his minions to attack a railroad refunding bill introduced in Congress in 1896. The bill would have written off the tremendous sums the federal government had loaned the railroads, gouging the American taxpayers for $130 million. Collis Huntington, the only surviving member of California's Big Four, was leading the Washington lobby favoring the bill; Bierce was sent to the nation's capital to head the opposition deployed by Hearst, who had recently acquired the *New York Journal*. Bierce wrote for both the *Journal* and the *San Francisco Examiner*, traveling frequently from Washington to New York and pointing out in powerful prose in these two widely circulated papers the web of deceit on which the funding bill rested and its cost to the nation. Telegrams and letters streamed from the San Francisco staff of the *Examiner*, furnishing him a constant source of ammunition that he supplemented with what he picked up himself on the East Coast. The bill was eventually defeated, and the railroads paid off their debt in twenty semiannual installments from 1899 to 1909.

Bierce had planned to join his second son, Leigh, in New York, but poor health and changes in the political scene caused his return to California in 1896. Although he had numerous conflicts with the editorial staffs of both the *Examiner* and the *Journal* because they mangled his copy and failed to print some of what he considered his best work, Hearst himself insisted on paying his weekly salary, leaving him free to decide when and what he wanted to write. Bierce then began a journalistic crusade with a column, "War Topics," that, contrary to Hearst's own stand, opposed the Spanish-American War. Bierce considered it unnecessary and imperialistic, describing it as the first step in America's march to world power, global wars, and eventual destruction of the planet by airborne superbombs.

Meanwhile his ties to California were loosening. Most of his early literary friends were his "pupils"—young writers such as George Sterling, Gertrude Atherton, and Danziger—who lived in California and who had come to him with their manuscripts for advice and encouragement. But as his fame spread, his friends who were not necessarily Californians became admirers of his work. Moreover, he wanted to be nearer Leigh Bierce, a reporter for the *New York Journal*. Consequently Bierce left San Francisco in December 1899 to return to Washington, where he lived for most of the remainder of his life.

His last thirteen years were shaken by two further tragedies: the death of his second son, the twenty-six-year-old Leigh Bierce, from pneumonia in 1901; and the death of his former wife, Mollie Bierce, four years later, shortly after their divorce. Yet his daughter, Helen, despite a serious illness and repeated marital difficulties, remained a solace to him. And, most important, Carrie Christiansen, a middle-aged schoolteacher whom the Bierces had befriended when she was a young girl, moved to Washington and lived near him as friend and secretary. Consequently this period was in many ways the most serene and contented of Bierce's life. He joined the Army and Navy Club, where military friends revived his post-Civil War brevet rank of major; his writing enjoyed a growing reputation; and he was earning a steady salary from William Randolph Hearst, contributing to the *San Francisco Examiner*, the *New York Journal*, the *New York American*, and *Cosmopolitan* magazine. Although such former "pupils" as Sterling, Herman Scheffauer, and Danziger (who changed his name to De Castro) created friction in his life, other young men and women made much of his work: Gertrude Atherton, Percival Pollard, H. L. Mencken, and, most important, an aggressive publisher, Walter Neale.

Shapes of Clay, a second volume of satirical verse, came out in 1903. Although in this book Bierce calls the pun the bequest of a "dying idiot," the following stanza from "For Merit" is typical:

> Let meaner men the poet's bays
> Or warrior's medal wear;
> Who cooks potatoes fifty ways
> Shall bear the palm—de terre.

In 1906 Bierce's satirical definitions, which are still current, appeared in book form as *The Cynic's Word Book*, a weak title insisted upon by a timorous publisher afraid of his author's forthright choice, *The Devil's Dictionary*. In 1907 two of his short stories were published in book form as *A Son of the Gods and A Horseman in the Sky*; and Neale brought out *The Monk and the Hangman's Daughter*, Danziger having turned over his rights in it to Bierce in 1902. In 1909 Neale also published a small handbook of grammatical usage, *Write It Right*, which is not included in Bierce's *Collected Works*. *Write It Right* was reprinted many times and remained a newspaperman's bible for decades; much of the advice in it is still valuable. Typical of its strictures is the following: "*Badly* for *Bad*. 'I feel badly.' 'He looks badly.' The former sentence implies defective nerves of sensation, the latter, imperfect vision. Use the adjective." Still another book appeared under the aegis of Silas Orrin Howes, a young Texas newspaperman, who edited a collection of Bierce's essays bearing the title *The Shadow on the Dial and Other Essays* (1909); it reappeared as *Antepenultimata* in volume 11 of *The Collected Works*.

By far the most important publishing project of Bierce's entire life was his *Collected Works*, a twelve-volume set he prepared himself, which Neale published from 1909 to 1912 and marketed through subscription. Bierce was not always discriminating in what he chose to include, and since he was a prolific journalist throughout his life, much is left out. Nevertheless, this collection, which contains much material that had not previously been published in book form, is essential for any serious study of its author. Bierce expended years of devoted labor on its twelve volumes—gathering, revising, editing, and proofreading.

After the monumental task was completed in 1912, Bierce's thoughts began turning to death. He had stated repeatedly that he did not want to die in bed, and after more than a decade of relative quiet he craved action. Consequently he began writing farewell letters to his friends and relatives, telling them that he intended to visit Mexico to observe the revolutionary forces of Pancho Villa, who was leading a popular insurrection against the reactionary government. Early in October 1913 Bierce left Washington and made a leisurely tour of his old Civil War battlefields. Reaching New Orleans, he granted interviews to newspaper reporters, then traveled to Texas. From El Paso he went to Juarez, which Villa had captured on 15 November. Thence he proceeded to Chihuahua, occupied by Villa on 8 December. Bierce's last letter was dated 26 De-

Bierce, age sixty-nine, with two close friends from the latter part of his life: Carrie Christiansen, his secretary and platonic companion, and Walter Neale, his publisher

cember 1913. In it he stated that he intended to go from Chihuahua to Ojinaga the next day. Circumstantial evidence indicates that almost certainly he was killed in the battle of Ojinaga, which took place on 11 January 1914. Although many fanciful theories–the most recent being Carlos Fuentes's novel *The Old Gringo* (1985)–have been advanced outlining his continued activities in Mexico or South America after this date, none of them was convincing, and none stood up to investigation. His disappearance, the most dramatic exit from life in American literary history, caused a flurry of excitement whose fallout still drifts about his name. His mysterious end had an effect that he himself would have deplored: for years interest focused not on his work, but on his colorful life and commanding personality. Even today the student of Bierce is often forced to preface any discussion of his writing by answering the

question: "What happened to him after he went to Mexico?"

However, serious critical examination of his work is now well under way. Since he wrote entirely in short forms–some very short indeed–his writing demands the scrupulous attention to detail at the level of sentences, phrases, and even words that is normally reserved for poetry. In some cases, to be sure, he strikes a false note in these short works that spoils their tone. But many are masterly, ranking at or near the peak of the brief forms in which he chose to write. His ability to create an astounding array of effects within such narrow compass is a magnificent encomium to the versatility on which he prided himself. At his best Bierce makes us think about ourselves, about our relations with others, and about our society.

His short stories fall into four broad categories: didactic tales, mimetic tales of passion, mimetic tales of moral choice, and mimetic tales of action. Didactic tales like "Haita the Shepherd," "Parker Adderson, Philosopher," and "The Famous Gilson Bequest" are fictional arguments persuading the reader to accept particular theses about such questions as the nature of happiness, the meaning and acceptance of death, and the destructive effects of avarice. All the mimetic tales, however, are imitations of human experience so represented as to arouse in the reader a sequence of expectations and emotions. In mimetic tales of passion like "An Occurrence at Owl Creek Bridge," "A Resumed Identity," and "The Death of Halpin Frayser," the protagonists undergo changes in thought and feeling as reactions to the situations in which they find themselves. Mimetic tales of moral choice–like "The Affair at Coulter's Notch," "A Son of the Gods," and "A Horseman in the Sky"–place their protagonists in situations where they must make crucial decisions involving a conflict between two value systems, both of which they adhere to. And finally, the mimetic tales of action present protagonists who act in relation to their situation. Examples of these stories are "Jupiter Doke, Brigadier-General," "A Watcher by the Dead," and "The Suitable Surroundings."

Bierce's narratives are represented in such a way as to create different kinds of emotional effects on the reader: ironic terror, pathos, tragic pity and fear, the moral satisfaction of retributive tragedy, uncanny dread, or moral indignation. The effect may even be one of absurdity in tales like "Jupiter Doke, Brigadier-General," "The Widower Turmore," "My Favorite Murder," and "An Important Conflagration." Such stories force the reader to reexamine accepted values in human ties and social relationships, an aim accomplished by a reversal of genuine standards, hyperbolic exaggeration, and understatement.

But Bierce's fame also rests on forms which are even briefer than the short story: fables, epigrams, verse satires, and sardonic definitions. Although enormous variety exists in these works, four features at which Bierce explicitly aimed can be found in them: clear thinking, wit, precision, and taste. In *Write It Right* he had stated that good writing, "essentially, is clear thinking made visible." Wit, he believed, was different from humor, conveying a sudden, sharp insight that reverses conventional attitudes and overturns stereotyped values; it "stabs, begs pardon–and turns the weapon in the wound." Precision was

achieved through writing so that the "reader not only may, but must, understand." Bierce was a linguistic liberal, not a purist; he believed that dictionaries were poor guides to the precise use of language because they tended to rigidify usage. For taste, since "there are neither standards nor arbiters," what the reader gets, of course, is Bierce's own.

Certain subjects run through his short forms: international relations, politics, religion, medicine, business, the pleasures of good food and drink, science, law, and the war between the sexes. Illustrating the last is his definition of *Marriage* in *The Devil's Dictionary*: "The state or condition of a community consisting of a master, a mistress and two slaves, making in all, two." An epigram also illustrates this theme: "For study of the good and the bad in woman two women are a needless expense." And finally, a fable called "The Inconsolable Widow" represents one pole of his complex attitude:

> A Woman in widow's weeds was weeping upon a grave.
> "Console yourself, madam," said a Sympathetic Stranger. "Heaven's mercies are infinite. There is another man somewhere, besides your husband, with whom you can still be happy."
> "There was," she sobbed,–"there was, but this is his grave."

Thus, Bierce claimed that "A virtuous widow is the most loyal of mortals; she is faithful to that which is neither pleased nor profited by her fidelity." And he also wrote this forthright definition of *Widow*: "A pathetic figure that the Christian world has agreed to take humorously, although Christ's tenderness towards widows was one of the most marked features of his character."

Probably the most coruscating examples of Bierce's wit, many of which are still in circulation, can be found in his *The Devil's Dictionary*. The following selections are representative:

> BRUTE, *n.* See HUSBAND.
> CONSOLATION, *n.* The knowledge that a better man is more unfortunate than yourself.
> CONSULT, *v.t.* To seek another's approval of a course already decided on.
> HERS, *pron.* His.
> INSURRECTION, *n.* An unsuccessful revolution.
> Disaffection's failure to substitute misrule for bad government.

PREJUDICE, *n.* A vagrant opinion without visible means of support.

QUEEN, *n.* A woman by whom the realm is ruled when there is a king, and through whom it is ruled when there is not.

Although it is a scholarly convention to call the period in which Bierce wrote the age of realism and naturalism, he does not fit neatly into either of these categories. Nevertheless, the dominant trends in a period can sometimes be defined by their opponents as well as by their adherents. From this point of view, Bierce helps to explain realism and naturalism by exposing the limitations of the movement. In his critical writings he repeatedly attacked realism and realists, his favorite target being William Dean Howells. One reason he preferred the short story to the realistic novel, with its slow, painstaking accretion of detail, was that his artistic aims were radically different from those of the realists. A third movement–international in scope–dominant during the late nineteenth and early twentieth centuries was literary impressionism. Bierce fits far better under the heading of impressionism than he does under the rubrics of either realism or naturalism.

According to the impressionists, a verifiable description of reality is impossible; rather, the writer must concentrate on the perceptual awareness which links the subjective response of the perceiver to the objective reality he perceives. It is this interaction between perceiver and perceived that constitutes "reality" for the literary impressionist. Moreover, neither space nor time is regarded as a fixed and rigid category. Both are fluid, depending on how the observer apprehends them. Consequently time can be either speeded up tremendously or slowed down to an extraordinary degree. Space, likewise, can be expanded exponentially or contracted to the merest pinpoint. Finally, the protagonist in impressionistic writing experiences a moment of epiphany, a flash of illumination during which he has an immediate and blinding revelation of what constitutes for him the ultimate nature of reality.

These defining characteristics of literary impressionism–which have already been explored in connection with Henry James–fit the work of Ambrose Bierce much better than do those of realism and naturalism. Indeed, the focal point of many of his stories is precisely the relativistic perception of the external world. In "An Occurrence at Owl Creek Bridge" and "Chickamauga,"

Peyton Farquhar and the deaf-mute boy misperceive lethal military situations as ones in which the appropriate responses are happiness and glee. And the sensations of time and space are both radically affected by the protagonists' emotional states. Moreover, Bierce's impressionistic attitude toward time was not limited to his stories. In "The Chair of Little Ease," an essay on the newly introduced electric chair as a device for capital punishment, he questioned the easy assumption that execution by such means would be mercifully quick and painless. He pointed out that it is impossible for any observer to tell whether the dying criminal, his body jolted by electric shocks and his face contorted, perceives his death as quick or not. Indeed, an "unnatural exaltation of the senses" might commute a moment "into unthinkable cycles of time."

The epiphany, too, is of extraordinary importance in Bierce's work. In his short stories he is, above all, interested in the brief but devastating crises most individuals face only once or twice in the course of their lives, when they must confront not only other people or dangerous situations but, at the most fundamental level, themselves. The unwary reader is often lured into believing a tale to be one of the supernatural. The real terror, however, derives from the irrational powers of the human psyche, whose depths Bierce was probing long before Freud. His investigations reveal his great understanding of, and deep compassion for, the soul tortured by circumstances it can face only with the agonized courage of supreme suffering. Given this philosophy, it is not surprising that many of Bierce's stories deal with the Civil War. But in the midst of civilian life, too, his protagonists may find themselves in death.

While Bierce's work is impressionistic rather than realistic, it does express a sense of the determinism that is characteristic of naturalism. Bierce was keenly interested in tracing effects to their ineluctable causes, carrying the process back almost as far as any Calvinist theologian. But he was not a Christian, even in the nominal sense; and his brand of determinism was precisely the secular one held by the naturalists: he believed that all human events were necessarily controlled by ancestry and environment. His interest in the transmission of character traits from one generation to another is discussed theoretically in his essay "The Ancestral Bond." He uses the theory in various ways in such stories as "Beyond the Wall," "John Bartine's Watch," "The Death of Halpin

Bierce in Washington, D.C.

Frayser," and especially "One of Twins." Even the actions of the deaf-mute boy in "Chickamauga" are explained in large part by tracing his genealogy, and "A Watcher by the Dead" concerns the influence of racial memory in antipathy to cadavers. In other stories Bierce traces the interlocking relationships of past events moving onward into the present to determine a given incident which may be the subject of his story. In "One of the Missing," for example, Jerome Searing, a Federal scout, has been sent out on a reconnaissance mission during the Civil War engagement at Kennesaw Mountain, Georgia. Seeing a column of retreating Confederate troops in the distance, he raises his rifle and plans to shoot into their midst: "but it was decreed from the beginning of time that Private Searing was not to murder anybody that bright summer morning, nor was the Confederate retreat to be announced

by him. For countless ages events had been so matching themselves together in that wondrous mosaic to some parts of which, dimly discernible, we give the name of history, that the acts which he had in will would have marred the harmony of the pattern. Some twenty-five years previously the Power charged with the execution of the work according to the design had provided against that mischance by causing the birth of a certain male child in a little village at the foot of the Carpathian Mountains, had carefully reared it, supervised its education, directed its desires into a military channel, and in due time made it an officer of artillery. By the concurrence of an infinite number of favoring influences and their preponderance over an infinite number of opposing ones, this officer of artillery had been made to commit a breach of discipline and flee from his native country to avoid punishment." Arriving in

New Orleans, he has enlisted in the Confederate army and eventually ended up commanding a Confederate battery that at the moment was standing about two miles away from Searing. "Nothing had been neglected—at every step in the progress of both these men's lives, and in the lives of their contemporaries and ancestors, the right thing had been done to bring about the desired result. Had anything in all this vast concatenation been overlooked Private Searing might have fired on the retreating Confederates that morning, and would perhaps have missed. As it fell out, a Confederate captain of artillery, having nothing better to do while awaiting his turn to pull out and be off, amused himself by sighting a field-piece obliquely to his right at what he mistook for some Federal officers on the crest of a hill, and discharged it."

The aspect of naturalism in which Bierce was primarily interested was the moral determinism examined in depth by Jonathan Edwards in *Freedom of the Will.* For him, as for Edwards, it is morally impossible for a man with a certain character to respond to a given situation other than as he does respond. His character determines the way in which he thinks and feels, makes crucial choices, and acts at decisive points in his life. Bierce's interest in determinism and its relation to freedom of the will is apparent in a civilian tale, "The Death of Halpin Frayser." Bierce not only traces Halpin Frayser's ancestry back through several generations; he also peels away layer after layer of Frayser's personality to expose his underlying character structure, determined in large part by what today would be called the Oedipus complex, in order to explain why he must necessarily act as he does act.

Because Bierce does not fit easily into the literary *-isms* of his time, literary historians have had difficulty in placing his work, and a good part of his reputation has always rested on his appeal to readers as independent and iconoclastic as he was. Only in the last three decades have scholars and critics begun to recognize that their theoretical concepts must be expanded if they are to include a writer as nonconformist as Ambrose Bierce.

As more biographers investigate Bierce's life and more critics examine his work, misinterpretations of his personality and his writing are fading. Scholars have begun to dispel the fog of innuendos and falsehoods (which originated with people who had known him and created a smokescreen after his death to conceal the nature of their relations with him) that have marred many biographical studies. It is no longer said that "Bitter" Bierce's output is mediocre and that he is interesting only as a misanthropic cynic incapable of human emotions. But if he is not to remain elusive as a man, future investigations will have to be undertaken on the careful, detailed model of Paul Fatout's *Ambrose Bierce and the Black Hills* (1956), an authoritative and absorbing account of Bierce's abortive mining venture in the Dakota Territory.

Critics, too, are now evaluating his work on its merits. Even as a young man he had a reputation in several English-speaking countries. After his death his work was translated into French, German, Spanish, Italian, and Japanese. His writing has been popular with Russians since czarist times. Much of the best work on Bierce is found in doctoral dissertations which began to appear after World War II, both in the United States and abroad. It is therefore safe to say that his place in American literature is secure. And those who give Bierce's work their careful attention will be able to render him a juster homage than the interest accorded a fascinating newspaperman who disappeared mysteriously in Mexico.

Letters:
The Letters of Ambrose Bierce, edited by Bertha Clark Pope (San Francisco: Book Club of California, 1922);
M. E. Grenander, "H. L. Mencken to Ambrose Bierce," *Book Club of California Quarterly News Letter,* 22 (Winter 1956): 5-10;
Grenander, "Seven Ambrose Bierce Letters," *Yale University Library Gazette,* 32 (July 1957): 12-18;
Grenander, "Ambrose Bierce and Charles Warren Stoddard: Some Unpublished Correspondence," *Huntington Library Quarterly,* 23 (May 1960): 261-292;
J. V. Ridgely, "Ambrose Bierce to H. L. Mencken," *Book Club of California Quarterly News Letter,* 26 (Fall 1961): 27-33;
Grenander, "A London Letter of Joaquin Miller to Ambrose Bierce," *Yale University Library Gazette,* 46 (October 1971): 109-116.

Bibliographies:
Vincent Starrett, *Ambrose Bierce, A Bibliography* (Philadelphia: Centaur Book Shop, 1929);
Joseph Gaer, ed., *Ambrose Gwinett* [sic] *Bierce, Bibliography and Biographical Data* (1935; republished, New York: Burt Franklin, 1968);

Paul Fatout, "Ambrose Bierce (1842-1914)," *American Literary Realism, 1870-1910*, 1 (Fall 1967): 13-19;

John C. Stubbs, "Ambrose Bierce's Contributions to *Cosmopolitan:* An Annotated Bibliography," *American Literary Realism*, 4 (Winter 1971): 57-59;

Philip M. Rubens and Robert Jones, "Ambrose Bierce: A Bibliographic Essay and Bibliography," *American Literary Realism*, 16 (Spring 1983): 73-91.

Biographies:

Carey McWilliams, *Ambrose Bierce, A Biography* (New York: A. & C. Boni, 1929).
One of the earliest full-length studies; still valuable.

Paul Fatout, *Ambrose Bierce, the Devil's Lexicographer* (Norman: University of Oklahoma Press, 1951).
Contains much useful factual information.

Fatout, *Ambrose Bierce and the Black Hills* (Norman: University of Oklahoma Press, 1956).
A penetrating examination, based on primary sources, of a critical period in Bierce's life which had previously not been fully investigated.

Richard O'Connor, *Ambrose Bierce, A Biography* (Boston: Little, Brown, 1967).
A "popular" biography, smoothly written but with little new information and some misinformation.

M. E. Grenander, "California's Albion: Mark Twain, Ambrose Bierce, Tom Hood, John Camden Hotten, and Andrew Chatto," *Papers of the Bibliographical Society of America*, 72 (Fourth Quarter 1978): 455-475.
Biographical information on Bierce's stay in London.

References:

Howard W. Bahr, "Ambrose Bierce and Realism," *Southern Quarterly*, 1 (July 1963): 309-331.
Useful critical interpretation.

Lawrence I. Berkove, "Arms and the Man: Ambrose Bierce's Response to War," *Michigan Academician*, 1 (Winter 1969): 21-30.
Argues that Bierce's response to war was much more complex than is conventionally assumed.

Berkove, "The Man with the Burning Pen: Ambrose Bierce as Journalist," *Journal of Popular Culture*, 15 (Fall 1981): 34-40.
Considers Bierce's journalism "one of the most extensive and able critiques of America in print," much of it still vital.

Berkove, " 'A Strange Adventure': The Story Behind a Bierce Tale," *American Literary Realism*, 14 (Spring 1981): 70-76.
A biographical anecdote by W. C. Morrow which casts light on Bierce's story "The Lady from Redhorse."

Berkove, "Two Impossible Dreams: Ambrose Bierce on Utopia and America," *Huntington Library Quarterly*, 54 (Autumn 1981): 283-292.
Asserts that Bierce considered utopian communities "foolish" and republican democracy "insidiously dangerous."

E. F. Bleiler, "Who Was Moxon's Master?," *Extrapolation*, 26 (Fall 1985): 181-189.
Argues that "Moxon's Master" is not science fiction, but a murder mystery.

Cathy N. Davidson, *The Experimental Fictions of Ambrose Bierce: Structuring the Ineffable* (Lincoln: University of Nebraska Press, 1984).
Applies postmodern literary theory to an analysis of a number of Bierce's stories.

Davidson, "Re-Structuring the Ineffable and Ambrose Bierce's 'The Secret of Macarger's Gulch,' " *Markham Review*, 12 (Fall 1982): 14-19.
This story is superficially a traditional ghost story, but the protagonist tries to explain it in terms of his own perceptual processes.

Davidson, ed., *Critical Essays on Ambrose Bierce* (Boston: G. K. Hall, 1982).
Useful anthology of secondary references.

Paul Fatout, "Ambrose Bierce, Civil War Topographer," *American Literature*, 26 (November 1954): 391-400.
Provides useful information about Bierce's technical assignments in the Civil War.

Fatout, "Ambrose Bierce Writes about War," *Book Club of California Quarterly News Letter,* 16 (Fall 1951): 75-79.
Discusses Bierce's attitude toward the Spanish-American War.

Wilson Follett, "Ambrose Bierce—An Analysis of the Perverse Wit that Shaped His Work," *Bookman,* 68 (November 1928): 284-289.
Ingenious dissection of Bierce's short forms.

M. E. Grenander, *Ambrose Bierce* (New York: Twayne, 1971).
Provides biographical information based on primary sources and critical analyses of Bierce's writing.

Grenander, "Ambrose Bierce and *In the Midst of Life,*" *Book Collector,* 20 (Autumn 1971): 321-331.
Examines in detail the problems posed by international copyright in connection with Bierce's most famous book of stories.

Grenander, "Au Coeur de la vie: a French Translation of Ambrose Bierce," *Boston University Studies in English,* 1 (Winter 1955-1956): 237-241.
Discusses French interest in Bierce's work.

Grenander, "Bierce's Turn of the Screw: Tales of Ironical Terror," *Western Humanities Review,* 11 (Summer 1957): 257-263.
Detailed critical analyses of a number of Bierce's stories.

Grenander, " 'Five Blushes, Ten Shudders and a Vomit': Mark Twain on Ambrose Bierce's *Nuggets and Dust,*" *American Literary Realism,* 17 (Autumn 1984): 169-179.
Publishes a letter by Mark Twain, who, failing to understand that *Nuggets and Dust* is not humor but wit, criticizes the book violently.

Carroll D. Hall, *Bierce and the Poe Hoax* (San Francisco: Book Club of California, 1934).
Describes the pretended "discovery" of a purported lost Poe work actually by Herman Scheffauer.

F. J. Logan, "The Wry Seriousness of 'Owl Creek Bridge,' " *American Literary Realism,* 10 (Spring 1977): 101-113.

One of the best analyses of "An Occurrence at Owl Creek Bridge."

Fred H. Marcus, "Film and Fiction: 'An Occurrence at Owl Creek Bridge,' " *California English Journal,* 7 (1971): 14-23.
Describes a cinematic adaptation of Bierce's story.

Jay Martin, "Ambrose Bierce," in *The Comic Imagination in American Literature,* edited by Louis D. Rubin, Jr. (New Brunswick: Rutgers University Press, 1973), pp. 195-205.
Asserts that Bierce's humor is destructive and questions accepted conventions in the classic satiric tradition.

Robert C. McLean, "The Deaths in Ambrose Bierce's 'Halpin Frayser,' " *Papers on Language and Literature,* 10 (Fall 1974): 394-402.
Theorizes that "Jaralson" is actually Halpin Frayser's father, and that he killed his son.

Carey McWilliams, Introduction to Bierce's *The Devil's Dictionary* (New York: Sagamore Press, 1957), pp. v-xii.
Brilliant short essay summarizing years of thoughtful study.

H. L. Mencken, "Ambrose Bierce," in his *Prejudices, Sixth Series* (New York: Knopf, 1927), pp. 259-265.
Valuable for Mencken's judgment of Bierce.

Frank Monaghan, "Ambrose Bierce and the Authorship of *The Monk and the Hangman's Daughter,*" *American Literature,* 2 (January 1931): 337-349.
Compares the Bierce-Danziger version with Richard Voss's German original.

Matthew C. O'Brien, "Ambrose Bierce and the Civil War: 1865," *American Literature,* 48 (November 1976): 377-381.
Examines Bierce's Civil War notebook to determine the date of his discharge.

James W. Palmer, "From Owl Creek to *La Rivière du hibou:* The Film Adaptation of Bierce's 'An Occurrence at Owl Creek Bridge,' " *Southern Humanities Review,* 11 (Fall 1977): 363-371.
Describes a cinematic adaptation of Bierce's story.

Lois Rather, *Bittersweet: Ambrose Bierce & Women* (Oakland, Cal.: Rather Press, 1975).
Discusses Bierce's ambivalence toward women.

William Bysshe Stein, "Bierce's 'The Death of Halpin Frayser': The Poetics of Gothic Consciousness," *ESQ: Emerson Society Quarterly*, 18 (Second Quarter 1972): 115-122.
One of the many analyses of this civilian story now engaging the attention of critics.

Franklin Walker, *San Francisco's Literary Frontier* (New York: Knopf, 1939).
Valuable study of the local milieu in which Bierce operated during much of his career.

David R. Weimer, "Ambrose Bierce and the Art of War," in *Essays in Literary History*, edited by Rudolf Kirk and C. F. Main (New York: Russell & Russell, 1965).
Analyzes seven of the war stories.

Napier Wilt, "Ambrose Bierce and the Civil War," *American Literature*, 1 (November 1929): 260-285.
Study based on government documents of Bierce's Civil War career.

Papers:
The most important holdings of Bierce's papers are in the Bancroft Library of the University of California at Berkeley; the Clifton Waller Barrett Collection at the University of Virginia; the University of Cincinnati; the Huntington Library in San Marino, California; the Berg Collection of the New York Public Library; the Division of Special Collections at Stanford University; the George Arents Research Library at Syracuse University; and the Beinecke Library of Yale University.

Willa Cather

*This entry was updated by James Woodress (University of California, Davis) from his
entry in DLB 9, American Novelists, 1910-1945, Part 1.*

Places	Webster County, Nebr. Pittsburgh Grand Manan Island, New Brunswick	Red Cloud, Nebr. New York Frederick Co., Va.	Lincoln, Nebr. The Southwest Jaffrey, N.H.
Influences and Relationships	Henry James Ralph Waldo Emerson Edgar Allan Poe Gustave Flaubert George Sand	Sarah Orne Jewett Nathaniel Hawthorne Thomas Carlyle Ivan Turgenev William Shakespeare	Walt Whitman John Ruskin Leo Tolstoy George Eliot
Literary Movements and Forms	Romanticism Anti-materialism Epic Tradition	Regionalism Minimalism (The Novel Démeublé)	Modernism Pastoral Tradition

Major Themes	Old World vs. New World
	The Corrupting Effect
	  of Materialism
	The Divided Self
	Faith in the Power of
	  the Imagination to
	  Shape One's Destiny
		East vs. West
		Nostalgia
		Destructiveness of
		  Romantic Love
			Culture vs. Primitivism
			Female Strength
			  of Character

Cultural and Artistic Influences	Opera
	Dutch Genre Painting
	Henri Bergson's
	  Philosophy
		Impressionistic Painting
		Greek and Latin Classics
		The Bible
			Episcopalianism
			  and Catholicism

Social and Economic Influences	The Frontier Loss of Old Values	World War I	Stock Market Immigration

See also the Cather entries in DLB 54, American Poets, 1880-1945, Third Series, Part 1; *and* DLB: Documentary Series 1.

BIRTH: Back Creek Valley, Virginia, 7 December 1873, to Charles F. and Mary Virginia Boak Cather.

EDUCATION: University of Nebraska, A.B., 1895.

AWARDS AND HONORS: Litt.D., University of Nebraska, 1917; Pulitzer Prize for *One of Ours*, 1922; Litt.D., Yale University, 1929; William Dean Howells Medal of the American Academy of Arts and Letters for *Death Comes for the Archbishop*, 1930; Litt.D., Princeton University, 1931; LL.D., University of California, Berkeley, 1931; Prix Femina Américain for *Shadows on the Rock*, 1933; L.H.D., Smith College, 1933; National Institute of Arts and Letters Gold Medal, 1944.

DEATH: New York, New York, 24 April 1947.

BOOKS: *April Twilights* (Boston: Badger, 1903);
The Troll Garden (New York: McClure, Phillips, 1905);
Alexander's Bridge (Boston & New York: Houghton Mifflin, 1912); republished as *Alexander's Bridges* (London: Heinemann, 1912);
O Pioneers! (Boston & New York: Houghton Mifflin, 1913; London: Heinemann, 1913);
The Song of the Lark (Boston & New York: Houghton Mifflin, 1915; London: Murray, 1916); revised edition, volume 2 of *The Novels and Stories of Willa Cather* (Boston: Houghton Mifflin, 1937);
My Ántonia (Boston & New York: Houghton Mifflin, 1918; London: Heinemann, 1919);
Youth and the Bright Medusa (New York: Knopf, 1920; London: Heinemann, 1921);
One of Ours (New York: Knopf, 1922; London: Heinemann, 1923);
April Twilights and Other Poems (New York: Knopf, 1923; London: Heinemann, 1924; enlarged edition, New York: Knopf, 1933; abridged edition, in volume 3 of *The Novels and Stories of Willa Cather* (Boston: Houghton Mifflin, 1937);
A Lost Lady (New York: Knopf, 1923; London: Heinemann, 1924);
The Professor's House (New York: Knopf, 1925; London: Heinemann, 1925);

My Mortal Enemy (New York: Knopf, 1926; London: Heinemann, 1928);
Death Comes for the Archbishop (New York: Knopf, 1927; London: Heinemann, 1927);
Shadows on the Rock (New York: Knopf, 1931; London, Toronto, Melbourne & Sydney: Cassell, 1932);
Obscure Destinies (New York: Knopf, 1932; London, Toronto, Melbourne & Sydney: Cassell, 1935);
Lucy Gayheart (New York: Knopf, 1935; London, Toronto, Melbourne & Sydney: Cassell, 1935);
Not Under Forty (New York: Knopf, 1936; London, Toronto, Melbourne & Sydney: Cassell, 1936);
Sapphira and the Slave Girl (New York: Knopf, 1940; London, Toronto, Melbourne & Sydney: Cassell, 1941);
The Old Beauty and Others (New York: Knopf, 1948; London: Cassell, 1956);
Willa Cather on Writing (New York: Knopf, 1949);
Writings from Willa Cather's Campus Years, edited by James R. Shively (Lincoln: University of Nebraska Press, 1950);
Willa Cather in Europe, edited by George N. Kates (New York: Knopf, 1956);
Early Stories, edited by Mildred R. Bennett (New York: Dodd, Mead, 1957);
Willa Cather's Collected Short Fiction, 1892-1912 (Lincoln: University of Nebraska Press, 1965);
The Kingdom of Art: Willa Cather's First Principles and Critical Statements, 1893-1896, edited by Bernice Slote (Lincoln: University of Nebraska Press, 1966);
The World and the Parish: Willa Cather's Articles and Reviews, 1893-1902, 2 volumes, edited by William M. Curtin (Lincoln: University of Nebraska Press, 1970);
Uncle Valentine and Other Stories, edited by Slote (Lincoln: University of Nebraska Press, 1973).
Collection: *The Novels and Stories of Willa Cather*, Autograph Edition, 13 volumes (Boston: Houghton Mifflin, 1937-1941).

OTHER: Georgine Milmine, *The Life of Mary G. Baker Eddy*, ghostwritten by Cather (New York: Doubleday, Page, 1909);
S. S. McClure, *My Autobiography*, ghostwritten by Cather (New York: Stokes, 1914; London: Murray, 1914);

Willa Cather in Person: Interviews, Speeches, and Letters (Lincoln: University of Nebraska Press, 1986).

Willa Cather is an outstanding example of a writer whose work is deeply rooted in a sense of place and at the same time universal in its treatment of theme and character. The corner of earth that she is best known for depicting is Nebraska, where she lived as an adolescent and young woman and where she was educated. This dominant subject is the setting for all or significant parts of six of her twelve novels and many of her short stories. Her typical preoccupation with her Nebraska material is, as one of her oldest friends, Dorothy Canfield Fisher, put it in a summarizing article, "the effect of a new country . . . on people transplanted to it from the old traditions of a stable, complex civilization." She evokes indelibly the shaggy virgin prairie around Red Cloud, Nebraska, during the late decades of the nineteenth century, the Scandinavian, Bohemian, German, and other immigrant peoples who settled that area, and their problems in populating the new land. In a sense Cather's work is a metaphor for the American westering experience.

Her work is not confined to Nebraska, however, and a second large area of her interest is the Southwest, which she discovered and fell in love with when she was thirty-eight and used as the setting for *Death Comes for the Archbishop* (1927), the novel she thought her best, and significant parts of two other novels. Her interest in the Southwest, which included the people and their culture as well as the land, turned her attention to the history of that region and to history in general. As a result, three of her last four novels are historical reconstructions of the Southwest, Quebec, and Virginia (her natal state), and she was at work on a fourth historical novel to be laid in medieval France when she died in 1947.

Whether she is writing of the Nebraska of her youth or seventeenth-century Quebec, her work is always meticulously crafted. She wrote slowly, averaging no more than one novel every three years, and regarded the writer's art as an activity that required complete dedication. Her fiction is written in language that is disarmingly clear and simple but at the same time richly allusive and subtle. It also obtains its effect by a careful selection of detail, never a heaping up of incident, to achieve verisimilitude. She describes her method as "unfurnished" in an essay she entitled "The Novel Démeublé." She said: "If the

Willa Cather in her early teens (Willa Cather Pioneer Memorial Collection, Nebraska State Historical Society)

novel is a form of imaginative art, it cannot be at the same time a vivid and brilliant form of journalism. Out of the teeming, gleaming stream of the present it must select the eternal material of art." She wants to throw all the furniture out and leave the room as bare as the stage of a Greek theater. "The elder Dumas enunciated a great principle when he said that to make a drama, a man needed one passion, and four walls."

Cather divided her childhood and adolescence between the Shenandoah Valley of Virginia and Webster County, Nebraska. The oldest child in a family that eventually included seven children, she was only nine when her father moved his family west to join his brother and parents, who already had migrated to Nebraska. Cather remembered vividly the trauma of leaving a hill farm that raised sheep for the Baltimore market for a flat, empty land that seemed as bare as a piece of sheet iron. But she also remembered the subsequent excitement of growing up in the new country and the intense pleasure she got from riding her pony to neighboring farms and listening to the stories of the immigrant farm women who had come from various parts of Europe. Charles Cather, however, was not cut out for farming the prairie, and eighteen months later he moved his family into Red Cloud and went into the insurance business.

Cather spent her high-school years in Red Cloud, a farm-to-market town of 2,500 people and a division point on the Burlington Railroad. Although it was a raw, new town, there was a good deal of intellectual nourishment there. The Weiner couple around the corner were educated Europeans who spoke French and German and encouraged Cather to read in their well-stocked library. Cather also studied Latin and Greek with William Drucker, an Englishman who clerked in his brother's store. Another neighbor was Julia Miner, who had been born in Oslo, the daughter of an oboist in the Royal Norwegian Symphony. She played the piano expertly, to her young neighbor's perennial delight. Cather also took part in amateur theatricals and attended performances of road companies that played in the Red Cloud opera house. Then at the age of sixteen and a half she finished high school along with two other students in the second class to graduate. After delivering a commencement oration on "Superstition versus Investigation," a ringing defense of experimental science, she left for Lincoln and the University of Nebraska, but she had to complete an additional year of prep school there before she could become a regularly matriculated freshman in the fall of 1891.

Cather's career as a novelist began with a long foreground of apprenticeship. But she knew that she wanted to be a writer from the moment her freshman English instructor gave an essay she had written on Thomas Carlyle to a Lincoln newspaper, which published it. She had until then planned to study medicine. From that day on, however, until she left her position as managing editor of *McClure's Magazine* in 1912, she wrote an enormous quantity of newspaper copy and published forty-five short stories. Beginning in her junior year at the University of Nebraska, she supported herself as a journalist, first as a reviewer and columnist for the *Nebraska State Journal*, then after graduation as a magazine editor and newspaper writer in Pittsburgh. Then she quit daily journalism and for five years was a high school teacher of Latin and English in Pittsburgh. During these years she published her first book, *April Twilights* (1903), a collection of verse brought out by a vanity press. This period of teaching, however, was most important in giving Cather her summers to concentrate on fiction,

and in 1905 she was able to have published her first collection of stories, *The Troll Garden*.

The seven stories in this volume, which range from good to excellent, all deal with art in one way or another. "Flavia and Her Artists" is about a woman who collects artists, "The Garden Lodge" about a woman who gave up a concert career for marriage, and "The Marriage of Phaedra" about a British painter. These three were written when Cather was in her Henry James period, and she never thought them good enough to reprint. "Death in the Desert" deals with a singer dying on her brother's ranch in Wyoming; "A Wagner Matinee" details the reaction of a Nebraska farm wife to a Boston concert; "The Sculptor's Funeral" describes the return home in death of a midwestern boy who had become a famous sculptor; and "Paul's Case" is the tragedy of a Pittsburgh high-school youth who is seduced by art. These four all were revised and reprinted, and the last is the only story Cather, in her later years, ever would allow to be anthologized.

The year after the publication of *The Troll Garden*, when S. S. McClure hired her to help edit his magazine, she settled down in New York. She lived there for the rest of her life except for trips back to Nebraska to visit and to the Southwest, Canada, and New England in the summers. From 1906 until she left *McClure's* she was deeply immersed in editing one of the leading muckraking magazines. Her interest in muckraking, however, was nil, and she concentrated on buying fiction from the prominent writers of the day—Arnold Bennett, O. Henry, Theodore Dreiser, Jack London, and others. Cather enjoyed this part of her job and particularly liked being sent by McClure to London in search of manuscripts. These activities perhaps kept her in her editorial position long after she should have struck out as a free lance.

She had a difficult time breaking away from the magazine despite the urging of her older literary friend Sarah Orne Jewett, who wrote her in 1908: "you must find your own quiet centre of life, and write from that to the world. . . ." As long as Cather stayed with *McClure's*, Jewett said, she would be caught up in the hectic life of a magazine office and what might be strength in a writer would be only crudeness, what might be insight would be only observation, and what might be sentiment would be only sentimentality. Under such conditions, she added, "you can write about life, but never life itself." Still, Cather did not feel secure enough to cut loose. Perhaps it was hard to give up a position as one of the most successful women editors at a time when journalism was almost wholly dominated by men. At any rate she did not quit for three more years.

When she did make the break, she was ready emotionally to use her youthful memories of Nebraska. She had been living in the East for fifteen years, and the Nebraska experience had by that time penetrated deeply and matured. As Jewett also said in a statement that Cather was fond of repeating: "The thing that teases the mind over and over for years, and at last gets itself put down rightly on paper–whether little or great, it belongs to Literature." Cather found that she had distanced herself enough from Nebraska by 1912 to turn the memories into art. It is this long perspective on her experience that gives Cather's best work about Nebraska a rich aura of nostalgia and converts it into a drama of memory. The slag has burned off, and what remains is the pure ore of enduring literature. Cather is a retrospective writer, a romantic, though she wrote in an age of realism and naturalism.

She had, of course, been using Nebraska material in her short fiction ever since she was an undergraduate at the University of Nebraska. Her first story, "Peter," makes use of the real-life episode of a Bohemian immigrant's suicide that Cather reuses as a central scene in *My Ántonia* (1918). But the early use of Nebraska often has the critical tone of writers such as Hamlin Garland writing bitterly about the hardships of farming on the prairie in the 1870s and 1880s. Among such stories are "Lou the Prophet" and "The Clemency of the Court." Also some of the early stories suggest the "revolt-from-the-village" motif that one associates more with later works like Edgar Lee Masters's *Spoon River Anthology* (1915) or Sinclair Lewis's *Main Street* (1920). Examples of these are "The Wagner Matinee" and "The Sculptor's Funeral." When Cather turned to the Nebraska material after 1911, she affirmed the positive values of the midwestern experience. She had been out in the world, and she now was returning home. Again, Jewett had told her: "One must know the world *so well* before one can know the parish."

Before she could begin a story laid in Nebraska, however, she had to revise for serialization in *McClure's* a short novel that she had managed to write despite the organized chaos of the magazine office. This was *Alexander's Bridge* (1912), the story of Bartley Alexander, a bridge builder from Boston. The novel is very Jamesian in its structure and thematic treatment, and Cather in later years never thought very much of it. She later said that she had written two first novels, *Alexander's Bridge* and *O Pioneers!* (1913), her first major use of the Nebraska material. The story takes place in Boston, London, and Quebec where Bartley Alexander is building a bridge across the Saint Lawrence. Bartley is married to a Boston socialite but in love with a London actress. During the course of the novel he makes the decision to leave his wife for the actress, but before he is able to do so, his lieutenants at the bridge site summon him to troubleshoot structural problems that have developed. He arrives in Quebec too late, and as he inspects the bridge, it collapses and carries him to his death. A flaw in the bridge's design tallies with a flaw in Bartley's character and both go down together.

Cather's low opinion of this novel rested mainly on the subject matter. It derives from her years as a magazine editor and her visits on editorial assignment to Boston and London. She felt that she had been too much the observer of a life that she found exciting but was not really a part of. The beginner, she said, has to "work through his youthful vanities and gaudy extravagances before he comes to deal with the material that is truly his own." Yet this novel is well written, carefully plotted, and, Cather's opinion notwithstanding, a good piece of fiction. Although the world of Bartley Alexander is not the world of Willa Cather's most characteristic fiction, the novel fits in well with her themes and preoccupations. Bartley, like Cather, is a self-made westerner who has made his success in the East. As a middle-aged man who feels that he has not gotten all he wants from life, Bartley anticipates Professor St. Peter in *The Professor's House* (1925) and Jim Burden, the narrator in *My Ántonia*. His desires and yearnings are similar to those that trouble Marian Forrester in *A Lost Lady* (1923) and destroy Myra Henshawe in *My Mortal Enemy* (1926), and Bartley is killed by his inability to reconcile contradictions in his character, a theme frequently found in Cather's fiction.

When Cather left *McClure's* in the fall of 1911, she and her Pittsburgh friend Isabelle McClung rented a house in Cherry Valley, New York. The quiet and seclusion produced a great burst of creative energy, one result of which was a story called "Alexandra," which later became part of *O Pioneers!*, and another story of foreigners on the "Divide," as the area north of Red Cloud, Nebraska, was called, which she entitled

"The Bohemian Girl." This second story is vintage Cather and recounts the story of Nils Ericson's return to his prairie home after he has been off in the world seeking his fortune. His mother and brothers have remained on the farm and grown up with the country. It ends with the elopement of Nils and his former sweetheart, the Bohemian Clara Vavrika, a heroine who anticipates Marie Shabata in *O Pioneers!* Nils's delight in the beauty of the wheat fields as he returns home mirrors Cather's delight, and his disgust at his brothers' smug materialism amid the prosperity of the postpioneer era is Cather's disgust.

The following year after a trip to the Southwest to visit her brother who worked for the Santa Fe Railroad, Cather stopped off in Red Cloud to visit her family. On the edge of a wheat field as she watched her first harvest in years, she had the idea for a story to be called "The White Mulberry Tree." This is the tragic tale of Marie Shabata and Emil Bergson, who are killed under the tree by Marie's enraged Bohemian farmer-husband. When Cather looked this story over and reread the previously completed "Alexandra," there occurred what she later described as an "inner explosion and enlightenment." She had the idea of putting the two together to form a novel. Such was the genesis of *O Pioneers!*, the novel that Cather preferred to think of as her first.

This novel is the story of Alexandra Bergson, the oldest child of a Swedish immigrant who dies in the struggle to tame the wild land. Alexandra holds the family together with her industry and vision, keeps her plodding brothers from giving up the struggle, and plans a brilliant future for her beloved younger brother Emil. Alexandra and her brothers prosper, but the brothers turn out mean-spirited, as do Nils Ericson's brothers, and when Emil falls in love with their neighbor's wife Marie, tragedy ensues. But Alexandra endures, and when her old friend Carl Lindstrom returns from years of wandering, she can look forward to a serene middle and old age with him. The novel ends on a note of transcendental renewal: "Fortunate country, that is one day to receive hearts like Alexandra's into its bosom, to give them out again in the yellow wheat, in the rustling corn, in the shining eyes of youth."

The novel is suffused with nostalgia for the pioneer days, as is much of Cather's best fiction. The poignancy in her best fiction derives from the remembrance of things past, the evocation of a departed grandeur seen in contrast with a

Cather as managing editor of McClure's, *1912 (Willa Cather Pioneer Memorial Collection, Nebraska State Historical Society)*

lesser present. The novel begins in 1883, the year that the Cathers moved from the Shenandoah Valley in Virginia to Nebraska. The pioneer days are sketched briefly but lovingly with the focus on Alexandra, then about twenty years old. She is the great earth mother, the pioneer woman, like Nils Ericson's mother or Ántonia Shimerda, the heroine of Cather's fourth novel. It is her courage and vision that bring civilization to the new land. Cather writes, as Alexandra faces the future after her father's death: "For the first time perhaps, since that land emerged from the waters of geologic ages, a human face was set toward it with love and yearning. . . . The history of every country begins in the heart of a man or a woman."

The critics treated *O Pioneers!* very well, and Ferris Greenslet, Cather's editor at Houghton Mifflin, had been right when he had told his colleagues that the novel "ought to . . . definitely establish the author as a novelist of the first rank." Although the novel is flawed by an uneasy joining of the stories that were put together to create it, it is an impressive performance and still has wide appeal. The rather formless structure Cather defended as having been dictated by the land itself, which had no skeleton, no rocks, no ridges. But she wrote it to please herself and did not try to devise an elaborate plot structure. She wrote in a presentation copy given to a friend: "This was the first time I walked off on my own feet—everything before was half real and half an imitation of writers whom I admired. In this one I hit the home pasture. . . . "

The organic principle that she describes in her next novel, *The Song of the Lark* (1915), applies to all of her fiction after *O Pioneers!* In that novel her heroine, Thea Kronborg, spends her summer in the Southwest, and as she bathes in the stream at the bottom of Panther Canyon after having climbed down from an ancient cliff dwelling below the rim of the mesa, she reflects. Why had the Indian women lavished such loving care on the pottery they had made for the mere purpose of carrying water? The shards of the broken pottery she had been admiring suggested grace and beauty in the work. Then it came to her. The world of the mesa Indians centered on water, the life-giving liquid that she was then pouring over herself. "The stream and the broken pottery: what was any art but an effort to make a sheath, a mould in which to imprison for a moment the shining, elusive element which is life itself."

The Song of the Lark is the story of a Swedish girl from Colorado who becomes a great Wagnerian soprano. After finishing *O Pioneers!*, Cather had turned to fulfilling her promise to *McClure's* to write five articles. One of these articles was a trio of profiles of American opera singers—Louise Homer from Pittsburgh, Geraldine Farrar from Massachusetts, and Olive Fremstad from Minnesota—who had been born in Sweden. Fremstad was the reigning diva of Wagnerian roles at the Metropolitan Opera in New York, and when Cather interviewed her for the article, she realized in a flash that here was Alexandra Bergson with a voice. The story of a gifted western girl of Swedish extraction—the sort of person Cather had known on the Divide—fighting her way to the top in the world of art in the East combined themes that fascinated Cather. She herself was a great devotee of opera and also had made good

in the highly competitive world of journalism and now literature. Fremstad's career provided a perfect vehicle for a fictional portrait, partly autobiographical, of a great artist.

Although this novel is Cather's longest and is definitely not written in her *démeublé* manner, it is an extraordinarily interesting one. The early parts of the story are fashioned from Cather's own memories of childhood in Red Cloud, even though the fictional locale is Moonstone, Colorado. The youthful aspirations of Thea Kronborg are the youthful aspirations of Willa Cather, and the departure from home to study music in Chicago also has the authenticity of the author's memories. A midsection that takes place in Arizona, including Thea Kronborg's visit to the cliff dwellings, derives from Cather's first visit to the Southwest. Just as Cather broke loose from journalism after years on the treadmill, Thea in the novel goes west for rest and reflection after a period of intense study of music in Chicago, and for the first time in years she has time to think about her life.

From this point the novel is built more on observed facts, not Cather's preferred technique, rather than on material assimilated through long immersion. The novel is engrossing as the reader sees Thea Kronborg scoring a great triumph as Sieglinde in *Die Walküre*, but it does not have the authenticity of the earlier sections. Later in her life when, realizing that she had greatly overwritten, Cather made a great many cuts in this novel for a revised edition, most of the excisions came from the later parts of the book. Had she been writing the novel then, she would have left her heroine at the threshold of success. Struggle always interested her more than success, both in her fiction and in her own life.

The greatest of her Nebraska novels, *My Ántonia*, followed *The Song of the Lark*, and with it Cather reached a level of artistic excellence that she perhaps equaled but never surpassed. This novel creates an unforgettable heroine in Ántonia Shimerda, a Bohemian immigrant farm girl, who is one of the great characters in twentieth-century American fiction. The story is told in the loose episodic fashion that Cather had developed in *O Pioneers!*, but it has more focus and better direction. She told her friend Elizabeth Sergeant that when she was planning the novel she wanted her new heroine to be "like a rare object in the middle of a table, which one may examine from all sides . . . because she is the story." While there are small stories within the story and Ántonia is offstage during the third of the five books of the novel, there is never any doubt that this is her story, although some critics have argued that Jim Burden, the narrator, is the chief character.

The narrative point of view, however, is important, for Jim Burden is Cather's persona, and the reader sees Ántonia through his eyes. Jim comes to Nebraska as a boy, about the time the Cathers moved west, and he lives on a farm for a time with his grandparents, as Cather did. Jim's neighbors are the Shimerdas, a Bohemian immigrant family trying to gain a toehold in the new country, as were the Sadileks, who lived near the Cathers. There is no evidence that Cather met Annie Sadilek, Ántonia's prototype, until after the Cathers moved into Red Cloud, but as Cather was growing up in Red Cloud, Annie worked for the nearby Miner family, who become the Harlings of the novel. And when Jim goes to college and Ántonia drops out of the story except as someone to talk about, his experiences parallel Cather's life as a student at the University of Nebraska. The story of Ántonia's seduction and abandonment and the birth of an illegitimate child is told to Jim, as the real-life story probably was related to Cather by letter. The final book of the novel, in which Jim Burden returns to Nebraska after having made his career in the East as a lawyer, derives its emotional impact from Cather's own return to Red Cloud, probably in the summer of 1914. She visited Annie, who then was surrounded by a large brood of children and happily married to a Czech farmer named Pavelka (Cuzak in the novel). Ántonia is the mother of races, the madonna of the wheat fields, a heroic figure in myth and symbol.

My Antonia ends on a happy note, as Jim visits her on her farm. Although her father had committed suicide in her childhood, she has had to work in town as a hired girl, and she has been abandoned at the altar, she endures triumphantly. Cather's earlier heroines, Alexandra Bergson and Thea Kronborg, do not achieve happiness. Alexandra tames the wild land at the expense of personal tragedy, and Thea becomes a great singer at the cost of having no private life. Other Cather heroes and heroines in her later novels also are denied happiness: Marian Forrester, Godfrey St. Peter, Myra Henshawe; and Lucy Gayheart dies before having a chance for a career. Only Archbishop Latour and Ántonia achieve real fulfillment in their fictional lives.

Dust jacket for Cather's fourth novel

This novel is compounded of the things that had "teased" the mind of Willa Cather for many years. To her thorough assimilation of the material may be added her complete and abiding love for the people and the country, what she later called "the gift of sympathy." Perfect knowledge and boundless enthusiasm, however, would count for little if the artist had not mastered her instrument. Willa Cather's technical skill after twenty-five years of steady practice enabled her to create a virtuoso performance. When Thea Kronborg's old music teacher is asked, as he listens to her perform at the Met, what is the secret of her success, he replies: " 'Her secret? It is every artist's secret'—and he waves his hand—'passion. That is all. It is an open secret, and perfectly safe. Like heroism, it is inimitable in cheap materials.' " That also was Cather's secret.

Cather's next book was a collection of stories, *Youth and the Bright Medusa* (1920), her first book published by young Alfred Knopf, who became her friend and remained her publisher for the rest of her life. She continued with the subject of art, which had unified *The Troll Garden* in 1905, and gathered together eight stories, four of which were reprinted from the earlier collection. The new ones were "Coming, Aphrodite!," "The Diamond Mine," "A Golden Slipper," and "Scandal," all of which deal with opera singers. The last two create a star more like a Mary Garden than an Olive Fremstad; "The Diamond Mine" depicts a character who might have been Thea Kronborg ten years later. She goes down on the *Titanic*, worn out by the rapacity of her relatives, her singing coach, and her husbands. The most interesting tale is "Coming, Aphrodite!," which juxtaposes a young artist and a young singer who in their struggling days find themselves living side by side in a Greenwich Village rooming house. They fall in love but ultimately go their own ways–Eden Bower to become a popular opera star, Don Hedger to become an influential though not popular painter. Each achieves the kind of success she or he wants.

Cather's novel about World War I, based on the life of her cousin who was killed in France in 1918 during the Argonne Forest offensive, appeared in 1922 as *One of Ours*. This novel, which was four years in the making, cost Cather more effort than any other work and, as an artistic achievement, is a disappointment. It is a story she wanted very much to do, however, and she was inspired to write it by reading her cousin's letters to his mother, her Aunt Franc. She had not known her cousin very well, but in the letters she found a sensitive, idealistic young man who was dissatisfied with the materialistic prosperity of Nebraska in 1917. He found fulfillment in enlisting in "the war to end all wars" and went off to France like a medieval crusader to the Holy Land.

The early parts of the novel are excellent Cather. Claude Wheeler, the protagonist, is first seen as a farm boy growing up in Nebraska. He is too sensitive and fine-grained to accept the coarse realities of farm life. His father is prosperous, good-natured, materialistic; his older brother is a money-grubbing farm implement dealer. Claude suffers too much over little things and feels that somehow life ought to be splendid. He goes to college, but after two years his father decides that he is needed on the farm and forces him to return to a life he hates. Then he falls in love and marries a frigid woman. So far the material is authentic and is written out of sympathy

and knowledge; the Nebraska farm background is authentic and the characterizations believable.

When Claude goes off to war, however, Cather has to get her material from observation and reading. She used a doctor's diary to work up the troopship crossing and conversations with soldiers to get the feel of military life. She wisely kept the battle scenes to a bare minimum, and she handled the garrison life in France successfully by drawing on her own memories of her reaction to France during her first visit with Dorothy Canfield in 1902. But the final scene, in which Claude is killed in battle, is a stereotype, which Hemingway told Edmund Wilson must have come from D. W. Griffith's film *The Birth of a Nation* (1915): "Poor woman, she had to get her war experience somewhere."

The critical reception of this novel was mixed. H. L. Mencken, who had been a great admirer of Cather's earlier novels, wrote that the appearance of John Dos Passos's *Three Soldiers* the year before had changed forever the war novel and at one blast had "disposed of oceans of romance and blather." Any subsequent war novel would inevitably be compared to it, and in this comparison he found Cather's novel wanting. By the time *One of Ours* came out, the postwar disillusionment already had set in, and any war novel in which the protagonist dies believing he is saving the world for democracy–appearing in the same year as T. S. Eliot's *The Waste Land*–was doomed to critical disapprobation. But there was a supreme irony in the whole venture: the novel was a best-seller, whereas *My Ántonia* had earned very little money, and also *One of Ours* won Cather the Pulitzer Prize.

There were many favorable reviews, however, and modern readers are likely to find much of the criticism wrong-headed. It was as though the male reviewers thought a woman had no business writing a war novel. In charging her with lack of firsthand war experience, they never bothered to reflect that Stephen Crane had not even been born when the action in *The Red Badge of Courage* took place. The novel presents a broad panorama: Nebraska before and during the war, France in the war zone and behind the lines, a well-developed cast of male and female characters. As well, the reviewers missed a great deal of irony and satire. *One of Ours* may outlast many other World War I novels.

Cather bounced back with a great critical success in *A Lost Lady* the following year. In this novel she returns to memories of childhood when ex-governor Silas Garber and his young wife were the leading citizens of Red Cloud. When Cather read about the death of Garber's widow while she was finishing her war novel, the past came flooding back. She remembered in vivid detail Mrs. Garber's voice and eyes, the big house on the hill east of town, and the cottonwood grove nearby where she had gone for picnics. The result was another of Cather's inner explosions that brought the entire story to her mind within an hour, as though she had read it somewhere. Marian Forrester, the lost lady, is one of Cather's most memorable creations.

The story is a good example of the "unfurnished" novel. Told in about fifty thousand words, it begins with a brief stage-setting, then a picnic in the cottonwood grove where Mrs. Forrester is seen through the eyes of twelve-year-old Niel Herbert. Next the novel skips seven years and then a series of sixteen chapters covers four years, ending with Niel's departure from Sweet Water for good. No effort is made to supply a continuous narrative, but each chapter recounts a key episode: a carefree dinner party before Captain Forrester's bank fails; a winter sleigh ride during which Mrs. Forrester and Frank Ellinger are seen coming out of the woods together; Niel's overhearing Frank's voice from outside Mrs. Forrester's bedroom during the captain's absence on business; the bank failure; the captain's stroke; Niel's departure for college. After the captain dies Marian slowly remakes her life under the blight of poverty and accepts the attentions of Ivy Peters, an unscrupulous lawyer who represents the soulless materialism that has replaced the pioneer generation of men like Captain Forrester.

In this novel Cather creates indelible pictures through her remarkable ability to conjure up the past. The figure of Marian Forrester is authentic, three-dimensional. The town of Sweet Water (Red Cloud) is as real as Moonstone in *The Song of the Lark* or Black Hawk in *My Ántonia*, and the character of old Daniel Forrester, ex-governor and railroad builder, is as solid and believable as the stone bank building that still stands in Red Cloud. The creation of Niel Herbert, son of the town lawyer, provides an excellent persona for Cather, from whose perceptions most of the drama is developed. The novel is written in the third person, however, which gives Cather the latitude to show Mrs. Forrester both through the boy's eyes and through the perceptions of other people in the town. For example, it

is another boy, Adolph Blum, the butcher's son, who sees Marian and Frank emerge from the woods. Niel's disillusionment with his idolized Mrs. Forrester comes all at once when he lays a bouquet of roses outside the French doors of her bedroom and hears Frank's voice from inside.

It is only from Niel's point of view, however, that Marian disappoints the novel's romantic image of her. The authorial voice in the novel never passes judgment on Marian's adultery. She has a strong will to live and survives under difficult circumstances. Never does she fail to take care of her husband, and although Niel would have preferred to have her immolate herself on the captain's funeral pyre, it is clear from the text that Cather believes that one must adapt to change. The captain cannot do this and goes down with the pioneers.

The Professor's House, more than any other novel, reflects the malaise that Cather felt in the decade of the 1920s. She wrote in a prefatory note to her essay collection, *Not Under Forty* (1936), that "the world broke in two in 1922 or thereabouts," and this view of the world mirrored her own personal feelings about life. She solved one problem by joining the Episcopal church in 1922, but she felt alienated by the moral climate of the decade, and for a writer who believed that struggle was more important than success, achieving best-sellerdom was a hollow victory. Professor St. Peter in her next novel also suffers from a middle-age weariness and a sense of loss after winning a great literary prize for his history of the Spanish adventurers in North America.

The novel begins at the point where St. Peter's wife is building a pretentious new house with his prize money. The professor is reluctant to leave the modest house where he raised his children and struggled with his history, especially his attic study. He and his wife have grown apart; his daughters are married, the younger to a mediocre journalist and the elder to an aggressive Jewish engineer who has made a fortune promoting an invention of prime importance to the aviation industry. While Kathleen, the younger daughter, remains unchanged, the older Rosamond has been thoroughly corrupted by her husband's money.

The midsection of the novel is a story within the story, the tale of Tom Outland, the professor's best student who has been killed in the war. He had loved Rosamond and had willed her the patent to the invention on which her husband's fortune is based. The story of Tom Outland relates his activities before he turns up as a student at the professor's college. Tom had participated in the discovery of the ancient cliff dwellings in what is now Mesa Verde National Park. The discovery had made an indelible impact on the uneducated boy, who was then working as a cowhand. But when he went to Washington, D.C. to try to interest the government in preserving the cliff dwellings and the artifacts, he encountered only indifference. Then he returned to the Southwest to find that his partner had sold the artifacts to a German collector. Disillusioned, Tom left the Southwest and went to college.

After the Tom Outland story the novel returns to St. Peter, whose family goes off to Europe leaving him alone in the old house. Just before they return, as he wonders how he can go on living with them, he lies down for a nap in his attic study. He is nearly asphyxiated when the gas stove goes out, but while he is unconscious something lets go within him. His family will not know he is not the same man, but he now feels that he can face life, a diminished life to be sure, but he can go on. Cather also picked herself up from her malaise and went on to write five more novels, including *Death Comes for the Archbishop.*

Despite the unusual structure of the novel, containing a seventy-page story within the story, the work is unified by the house symbolism. In the sections dealing with the professor there are the old and new houses, the comfortable old one and the detested new one. Also there is the security of the attic workroom (womb, if one wishes to give the novel a psychoanalytic reading). Contrasted with these houses is the image of the cliff dwellings, which are simple, functional, open to the wind and sky. Tom Outland's love for this ancient civilization is Cather's, and Tom's adventures in Mesa Verde are her own dream adventures. Cather's ability to cast a nostalgic aura over the past makes "Tom Outland's Story" a vivid piece of fiction. Cather defended the structure of this novel by explaining that she was trying to do in fiction what the Dutch genre painters did in painting interior pictures that show open windows from which outdoor scenes may be viewed. She wanted to open a window in the professor's house and let in the fresh air of the Blue Mesa.

The use of the Southwest in *The Professor's House* presages the setting of an entire novel in that area in *Death Comes for the Archbishop* and a turn to historical fiction. But Cather still had one more story to write out of her spiritual malaise of

the mid 1920s, *My Mortal Enemy,* the angriest piece of fiction she ever wrote. It is the story of Myra Henshawe, a woman who feels cheated by life and who dies of cancer, alone, embittered, and impoverished at the age of fifty-five. This time Cather turns to a first-person narrator, a young woman from Myra's midwestern hometown. We see Myra on three different occasions, twice when she is forty-five and a third time just before her death. She was raised by a rich Irish-Catholic uncle who cut her off without a cent when she eloped with a Protestant, and when the novel opens Myra and her husband Oswald have returned to their hometown for a visit. A few months later the narrator, Nellie Birdseye, and her aunt visit New York and the Henshawes, who live comfortably but not affluently. Myra already regrets her marriage and hates not being rich. In this section the evocation of New York in 1904, at the time Cather first knew the city, is remarkably effective.

The bitter denouement of the novel takes place ten years later in San Francisco where the Henshawes are living in a cheap apartment, and Oswald, who has been destroyed by Myra, has been reduced to a minor position with the street railway company. Nellie by this time is teaching in a college in San Francisco and looks in on the Henshawes from time to time. Myra tells Nellie, as she is dying, that the mistake of her life was in marrying for love: "I am a greedy, selfish, worldly woman. I wanted success and a place in the world." Oswald, meantime, ministers devotedly to Myra, who tells Nellie: "Perhaps I can't forgive him for the harm I did him." When her end comes, she hires a cab and goes off to die alone under a tree facing the sea.

This novel, which is written in the "unfurnished" manner, apparently drained the last bit of gall from Cather's system and cleared the way for the serene historical novels of her next decade and a half. The "unfurnished" manner is especially appropriate for this astringent portrayal of defeat and death, and the novel is Cather's final comment on the destructive power of money in a society that worships material values. Perhaps Cather saw in Myra Henshawe the person she might have become if she had not had her art to sustain her.

Cather actually had been preparing to write *Death Comes for the Archbishop* ever since she first visited the Southwest in 1912. The enchantment of Arizona and especially New Mexico had gotten into her bloodstream, and it was inevitable that

Dust jacket for Cather's 1927 novel, which won the William Dean Howells Medal of the American Academy of Arts and Letters

one day there would be a novel about the area. The fascination of the Southwest even antedates her first visit, as one notes in "The Enchanted Bluff," a story written in 1909. Also one of the memorable scenes in *My Ántonia* is the picnic by the river in which Jim Burden tells Ántonia and her friends Lena and Tiny about Coronado's search through the area looking for the seven golden cities. Finally, one remembers Cather's use of the Southwest in *The Song of the Lark* and *The Professor's House*. Professor St. Peter's life work was a study of the Spaniards in North America.

The story of *Death Comes for the Archbishop* is the fictionalized life of Archbishop Lamy, the first bishop appointed for the territory of New Mexico after its annexation to the United States. The story begins in the mid nineteenth century with the Vatican's appointment of a French missionary priest, Jean Latour, to the new bishopric. He and his boyhood friend Joseph Vaillant, who becomes his vicar, take up their posts in Santa Fe. The story is episodic in form and details the lives

of the bishop and his vicar until the old prelate, later the archbishop, dies in 1889 at the end of a long and successful episcopate.

What plot there is concerns itself with the gradual organization of the vast diocese and the bringing under central control, after decades of neglect, all the parishes scattered over hundreds of miles of mountains and deserts. There is plenty of variety and contrast in the novel–from the opening scene in Rome where the appointment of the bishop is discussed to the bishop's lonely journey to Durango in Old Mexico to establish his authority with the former bishop of both Old and New Mexico; from the amusing account of how Father Vaillant separates Manuel Lujon from his two prized white mules to the story of the murderer Buck Scales and his abused Mexican wife; from the chilling account of the night Father Latour and his Indian guide spend in a cave used by the Indians for the secret practice of their ancestral snake worship to the contest between the bishop and Father Martinez of Taos, an old reprobate who is the last holdout of the old regime.

Cather knew that she had accomplished something remarkable in this novel, and when she sent the manuscript off to Knopf she was convinced that long after she and the publisher were gone, Alfred Knopf's son would be paying royalties to her niece. She was right about the book's long life, and it continues to sell and to be read widely. Some of the reviewers were puzzled about whether or not it was a novel since it is a historical reconstruction, loosely episodic, covering forty-one years in the life of its protagonist. Cather preferred to call it a narrative and thought of it as moving along a straight line on the backs of the two white mules that the bishop and his vicar ride during their ministry. Her definition of a novel, however, covers this work, for she describes a novel as "a work of the imagination in which a writer tries to present the experiences and emotions of a group of people by the light of his own." Although the real-life letters of Bishop Lamy's vicar gave her the inspiration for the novel, about ninety percent of the book is fiction. This is a large work of the creative imagination.

Cather wrote an interesting letter to *Commonweal* after the book's publication. The longer she stayed in the Southwest, she said, the more convinced she became that the story of the Catholic church in that country was the most interesting of all its stories. Then while visiting Santa Fe she happened on the vicar's letters and experienced one of those epiphanies that preceded her best fictions. But she said that she also had wanted to do something in the style of legend, the very reverse of dramatic treatment. For this her inspiration was Puvis de Chavanne's frescoes depicting the life of Saint Genevieve, which she first had seen in Paris in 1902. Thus her concept for the novel is that of a series of tableaux. Finally, her title comes from Hans Holbein's woodcut *The Dance of Death*, one of a series in which death comes for an archbishop. This title is instructive, for in the novel death comes for a great many more people than the old archbishop–Indians, Yankees, Mexicans, as well as the French priests.

In *Shadows on the Rock* (1931) Cather retreats further into the past to lay her story in Quebec toward the end of the seventeenth century. The novel testifies to her lifelong love of French culture and the discovery of Quebec during an enforced stay there when her traveling companion Edith Lewis got sick. She was particularly interested in the sense of arrested time she got in Quebec. Built on a rock that Cather treats metaphorically as well as physically, the French city in America had retained its cultural and ethnic integrity into the twentieth century. While the rest of the world was in turmoil, the city on the Saint Lawrence seemed still the city of Count Frontenac and Bishop Laval, both of whom are characters in her novel. Cather celebrates in *Shadows on the Rock* the durability of this Canadian outpost of French civilization. For a moment at least she could stop the clock and pretend that the good old days would last forever.

There is little action in the novel, and it makes no effort to tell a story, though there are narrative vignettes inserted here and there. It mostly recounts one year in the life of the people of Quebec on their rock where nothing really changes. The chief characters are Euclide Auclair, a widower who owns an apothecary shop, and his twelve-year-old daughter Cécile with whom he lives. We follow the characters through the fall, the long winter, the spring, and into the summer when the annual supply fleet arrives from France. The author's knowledge and understanding of French culture give this book distinction in its detail, but the entire work is static and inferior to *Death Comes for the Archbishop*. Although it was a best-seller and the reviewers treated it kindly, Carl Van Doren's judgment is a fair statement: he found the book dramatically thin but pictorially rich.

Again Cather had to work up much of the material and visited Quebec three times during the writing. Her historical knowledge came from extensive reading, but she approached her research with some preconceived ideas. She took her characterization of Count Frontenac from Francis Parkman, a historian she had long known, but when Parkman's view of Bishop Laval did not suit her, she got her data for his fictional portrait from a sympathetic Canadian historian. She treats some of her familiar themes in this novel: the New World versus the Old, stability versus mutability, the virtues of friendship, and the perpetuation of tradition. Although Cather was not yet sixty when the book appeared, it is an old woman's book and has a valetudinarian flavor. But it was written at a distressful time in her life, after the death of her beloved father and during the lingering death of her mother following a stroke.

Cather returned to her Nebraska material for the first time since *A Lost Lady* appeared in 1923 in *Obscure Destinies* (1932), a collection of stories in her best vein. In the late 1920s her father's death and her mother's stroke, which brought long return visits to Red Cloud, turned her mind back to her own past. The results were extraordinarily rich and effective–perhaps the last great fiction she wrote. The first story is "Neighbor Rosicky," a long tale that stands as a sequel to *My Ántonia*. Cather's feelings about her father give the tale its emotional impact, but the prototype of Rosicky is the Czech farmer that Ántonia married. Anton Rosicky is shown in the last few months of his life, and the story is elegiac and retrospective. The reader recognizes the family as Ántonia's some ten years after the end of her novel. The doctor tells Rosicky at the outset that he has a heart condition and must let his sons take over the hard labor of the farm. The relationship between father and sons, husband and wife is devoted and sympathetic, and the human equation in the Rosicky family always takes precedence over the economic one. At the end Rosicky dies and is buried on his own land that he has worked hard to buy and to develop. The doctor pronounces a mute benediction as he passes to the burial ground, thinking that "Rosicky's life seemed to him complete and beautiful."

The second story in the group is "Old Mrs. Harris," a memorable fictional re-creation of Cather's Grandmother Boak, who had lived with the Cathers during their early years in Nebraska. Grandma Harris is a three-dimensional character, and the ambience of the Cather home in Red Cloud is highly evocative. The selfless old woman dies at the end of the tale not wanting to be a burden to anyone, while her daughter and granddaughter (Willa Cather) are absorbed in their own lives. The daughter is preparing to have another baby, and the granddaughter is worrying about getting ready to go to college. The third story of the collection is "Two Friends," the story of the effect that the adult conversation of two men friends in Red Cloud had on a young girl who listened to them on summer evenings.

Lucy Gayheart (1935) returns to Cather's interest in the career of an artist, but it is a rather conventional novel written in the third person and containing a great deal more plot than is characteristic of Cather's best fiction. More than half of the novel takes place in Chicago where Lucy is a piano teacher and piano student. She meets a famous baritone who engages her as his accompanist and falls in love with her despite the fact that he has a wife in Europe. At the end of a summer concert tour in Europe, however, her singer is drowned in an accident at Lake Como, and Lucy goes back to Haverford (Red Cloud) with her broken heart. After four months at home she picks herself up and plans to return to her teaching in Chicago, but while skating on the river she falls through the ice and drowns.

Cather knew that *Lucy Gayheart* was not up to her usual mark and privately admitted as much to close associates. But the novel made the best-seller lists and stayed there for weeks. The reviewers, however, mostly ranked the novel low among her productions. The reviewer for the *Christian Science Monitor* wrote: "One does not get the impression that the hand of the potter shook, but only that it grew weary, and rounded off its work in haste." There was no faulting Cather's narrative skill or her competent prose; the difficulty lay elsewhere. She wrote an old friend that she had lost patience with her silly young heroine–a surprising statement to come from a novelist who knew that she only wrote at her best when she dealt with characters she loved and admired. The story does not grip the reader, as do the tales of Marian Forrester or Ántonia Shimerda, because Cather herself could not kindle an emotional response toward her character.

Cather's last novel, *Sapphira and the Slave Girl* (1940), marks a return to her origins. It is a historical reconstruction of the area around Winchester, Virginia, where she was born, and the time is before the Civil War. The story draws on family history, for the central episode of the novel is the escape of a slave named Nancy, an event Cather's Grandmother Boak helped bring about in 1856. In an epilogue to the novel Cather dramatizes the most exciting event of her young childhood, the return of Nancy from Canada after the war. In a moving scene Cather as first-person narrator describes the reunion of Nancy with her mother some quarter of a century after her escape.

The bulk of the novel concerns the events leading up to the escape. Sapphira Dodderidge Colbert is an imperious old woman, a semi-invalid, who is married to Henry Colbert, a miller. The marriage has been one of form mostly, with Sapphira managing the farm, worked by the slaves she brought with her dowry, and Henry running the mill. Sapphira wants to sell Nancy, but Henry will not hear of it. From this situation develops a tense relationship with Nancy as the pawn. Sapphira sets about to get rid of Nancy and invites her wastrel nephew to visit, expecting that if given the opportunity he will seduce or rape Nancy. With Henry's aid, Rachel Blake, Sapphira's daughter, spirits Nancy away from the farm one night and arranges for her escape to Canada via the Underground Railroad.

Sapphira and the Slave Girl is a very good novel in which setting, plot, and character all are developed skillfully and blended together to reinforce each other. The delight that Cather felt in revisiting the Shenandoah Valley during the writing of this novel is keenly communicated in the effective rendering of place. The house where Cather lived as a small child, the mill, the road up Timber Ridge, the woods, and the wild flowers spring to life under the author's sensuous prose. The characterization, especially that of Sapphira, the cool, crafty, antiheroine, is effective and believable. She is capable of having Nancy debauched to get rid of her, but she also knows how to manage her slaves and feels a sense of noblesse oblige toward them. The plot, which could easily have become melodrama like *Uncle Tom's Cabin* (1852), is keyed low, and the action never runs away with the development of character. The narrative technique is third person, which Cather always believed was the proper method for a story of action. Reviewers in general praised the book, the *Nation* calling it one of her five best–a judgment that many of Cather's admirers find reasonable.

Cather's last novel was published on 7 December 1940, her sixty-seventh birthday, and one year later, as the United States plunged deeper and deeper into World War II, Cather watched with increasing horror the destruction of the world she had known. She felt old and tired and not much like writing. She had a happy reunion, however, with her favorite brother, Roscoe, in California in the summer of 1941 and during the war wrote a beautiful story, "The Best Years," which evokes in her best manner her memories of Nebraska, her youth, and her brothers. But soon after completing this story she received a telegram announcing Roscoe's death, and that event, she said, broke the last spring in her.

Physical infirmities also plagued her in her final years. An inflamed tendon kept her right hand in a brace for eight months and prevented her from writing. Later her vitality was sapped by a gall bladder operation from which she never fully recovered. The habits of a lifetime, however, did keep her writing to a limited degree in these years. She produced one other excellent story, "Before Breakfast," and started another novel. The latter was to have been laid in medieval Avignon, and had she finished the work, it would have continued her fictional retreat into the past begun with *Death Comes for the Archbishop*.

During her last years she lived quietly in her Park Avenue apartment with her longtime companion Edith Lewis. She never again visited Nebraska, and the war kept her from summering in her cottage on Grand Manan Island in the Bay of Fundy. She entertained relatives from time to time, and she greatly enjoyed her warm relationship with Yehudi Menuhin and his sisters that had begun when Yehudi was fourteen. In 1945 she wrote an old friend that she had gotten a good deal of what she had wanted out of life and above all had escaped the things she most violently had not wanted, such as too much money, noisy publicity, and the bother of meeting lots of people. She was reasonably satisfied with her career, and her last letters do not suggest that she felt unfulfilled. She had worked hard and knew that her accomplishments were significant. Her death came quickly from a massive cerebral hemorrhage on 24 April 1947, and she was buried at Jaffrey, New Hampshire, on a hillside spot that she had selected.

Although Cather's refusal to become involved in causes brought her criticism in the socially active 1930s, no one ever questioned her artistic integrity or her literary skill. From *My Ántonia* on, her carefully crafted fiction gathered a steadily increasing following, and since her death her reputation has continued to grow. She was one of the writers selected for inclusion in *Sixteen Modern American Authors* (1973), a volume that generally establishes the canon of our most important writers of the first half of this century, and in that work she is the only woman represented. The scholarly attention to her writings in recent years suggests that her stubborn devotion to her art created a body of work that has enduring value, and the delighted response of successive generations of students to a first reading of her novels makes it clear that Cather's works will go on attracting enthusiastic readers into the indefinite future.

Bibliographies:

Bernice Slote, "Willa Cather," in *Sixteen Modern American Authors,* edited by J. R. Bryer (Durham: Duke University Press, 1973), pp. 28-73.
  A bibliographical essay discussing bibliographies, editions, manuscripts and letters, biographies, and criticism. A second edition is promised for late 1987.

Margaret O'Connor, "A Guide to the Letters of Willa Cather," *Resources for American Literary Study,* 4 (Autumn 1974): 145-172.
  This is a calendar of about 1,000 Cather letters with locations.

Joan Crane, *Willa Cather: A Bibliography* (Lincoln: University of Nebraska Press, 1982).
  This is the definitive bibliography of primary works: novels, stories, articles, poetry.

Biographies:

E. K. Brown, *Willa Cather: A Critical Biography* (New York: Knopf, 1953).
  The first Cather biography, superseded for biographical data but still good for criticism.

Elizabeth Shepley Sergeant, *Willa Cather: A Memoir* (Philadelphia: Lippincott, 1953).
  A memoir by an old friend, especially useful for Cather's work down to *My Ántonia*.

Edith Lewis, *Willa Cather Living* (New York: Knopf, 1953).
  Unobjective memoir by Cather's companion for the last thirty-nine years of her life.

Sharon O'Brien, *Willa Cather: The Emerging Voice* (New York: Oxford, 1987).
A feminist biography of Cather down to *O Pioneers!*

James Woodress, *Willa Cather: A Literary Life* (Lincoln: University of Nebraska Press, 1987).
A full-length biography and, for the present, the definitive life.

References:

Mildred Bennett, *The World of Willa Cather* (Lincoln: University of Nebraska Press, 1961).
A pioneering work when it first appeared; it relates Cather's fiction to the people and places she wrote about in Nebraska.

Edward and Lillian Bloom, *Willa Cather's Gift of Sympathy* (Carbondale: Southern Illinois University Press, 1962).
Clearly written essays on Cather's fiction, especially good on the background of *Death Comes for the Archbishop*.

David Daiches, *Willa Cather: A Critical Introduction* (Ithaca: Cornell University Press, 1951).
The first book appraising Cather's entire career–thoughtful, perceptive, and still useful.

Philip Gerber, *Willa Cather* (Boston: Twayne, 1975).
A brief but reliable introduction to Cather's life and work.

Richard Giannone, *Music in Willa Cather's Fiction* (Lincoln: University of Nebraska Press, 1968).
A thorough survey of Cather's use of music in her work, important because of the large impact music had on her.

John Murphy, ed., *Critical Essays on Willa Cather* (Boston: G. K. Hall, 1983).
A collection of fairly recent critical essays on Cather, including several not published elsewhere.

John H. Randall III, *The Landscape and the Looking Glass: Willa Cather's Search for Value* (Boston: Houghton Mifflin, 1960).
Approaches Cather from a sociological point of view, often dogmatic and critical, but offering an opposing stance to offset the usually enthusiastic comments of most critics.

Susan Rosowski, *Perilous: Willa Cather's Romanticism* (Lincoln: University of Nebraska Press, 1986).
An important recent study of Cather that places her squarely in the tradition of romanticism.

James Schroeter, ed., *Willa Cather and Her Critics* (Ithaca: Cornell University Press, 1967).
A collection of essays, reviews, and excerpts from books from early notices to the 1960s.

Bernice Slote and Virginia Faulkner, eds., *The Art of Willa Cather* (Lincoln: University of Nebraska Press, 1974).
Essays delivered at the Cather centennial in Lincoln in 1973.

David Stouck, *Willa Cather's Imagination* (Lincoln: University of Nebraska Press, 1975).
A significant study of Cather's entire canon arranged under the topic headings of "Modes," "Forms," and "Themes."

Papers:

There are no collections of manuscripts, but there are many letter collections (see O'Connor above), the chief ones being at the Willa Cather Pioneer Memorial in Red Cloud, Nebraska, the University of Nebraska, the Nebraska State Historical Society, the Newberry Library in Chicago, and the libraries of the University of Vermont, the University of Virginia, and Harvard University.

Kate Chopin

This entry was updated by Sara deSaussure Davis (University of Alabama) from her entry in DLB 12, American Realists and Naturalists.

Places	St. Louis, Mo.	New Orleans	Natchitoches Parish and the Cane River Area, La.
Influences and Relationships	Guy de Maupassant Henry James Walt Whitman	Gustave Flaubert George Sand Henrik Ibsen	Emile Zola William Dean Howells
Literary Movements and Forms	Realism	Local Color	
Major Themes	Self-discovery and Autonomy Woman's Role in Society Marriage	Conflict between Self and Society Woman's Sexual Nature Miscegenation	Conflict between Nature and Society Dangers of Sentimentality
Cultural and Artistic Influences	The Americanization of European Culture in Louisiana	Decline of Religious Orthodoxy	Music French Literature and Language
Social and Economic Influences	The Changing Role of Women	Evolution Theories of Charles Darwin, T. H. Huxley, and Herbert Spencer	

BIRTH: St. Louis, Missouri, 8 February 1850 or 1851, to Thomas and Eliza Faris O'Flaherty.

MARRIAGE: 9 June 1870 to Oscar Chopin; children: Jean, Oscar, George, Frederick, Felix, and Lelia.

DEATH: St. Louis, Missouri, 22 August 1904.

BOOKS: *At Fault* (St. Louis: Privately printed, 1890);
Bayou Folk (Boston & New York: Houghton, Mifflin, 1894);
A Night in Acadie (Chicago: Way & Williams, 1897);
The Awakening (Chicago & New York: Herbert S. Stone, 1899);
The Complete Works of Kate Chopin, 2 volumes, edited by Per Seyersted (Baton Rouge: Louisiana State University Press, 1969).

Kate Chopin introduced to the reading public a new fictional setting: the charming, somewhat isolated region along the Cane River in north central Louisiana, an area populated by Creoles, Acadians, and blacks. Beginning in the 1960s, her fiction was also recognized for its new psychological terrain, especially in her depiction of women who experience the power of passion that often brings them into conflict with society. Instead of comparing Chopin to the Louisiana local colorists–George Washington Cable, Ruth McEnery Stuart, or Grace King; or even to Mary E. Wilkins Freeman and Sarah Orne Jewett, the local colorists of New England–critics now compare her exploration of new themes to the innovations of other daring writers of the 1890s: Stephen Crane, Hamlin Garland, and Frank Norris. It is true that her first published novel, *At Fault* (1890), and her two published collections of short fiction, *Bayou Folk* (1894) and *A Night in Acadie* (1897), are set in or refer to the Cane River area and convincingly portray the distinctive customs, language, and atmosphere of the region. The popularity in her own time of such local-colorist qualities, combined with the condemnation of her frank depiction of female sexuality in *The Awakening* (1899), have somewhat obscured Chopin's other achievements. Literary historians of the first half of this century perpetuated some important misjudgments or misinformation about her fiction and her career, typically praising her as the author of "Désirée's Baby" (a short story about, among other things, the tragic ef-

Kate Chopin in 1894

fects of miscegenation) while seldom mentioning *The Awakening,* now considered her masterpiece. On occasion the plot of the short story has been attributed to the novel. A corrective to the stale second- or thirdhand assessments of her work came in 1946, when the French critic Cyrille Arnavon called attention to Chopin's place in the realistic tradition of France and America. Although she treats in *The Awakening* what are basically naturalistic ideas of heredity and environment, the essence of her work remains best described as realistic. Since Arnavon's work a Chopin revival has taken place, in part stimulated by the work of another European scholar, Per Seyersted, who wrote the definitive biography and edited *The Complete Works of Kate Chopin* (1969).

Most of the important experiences that shaped Kate Chopin's temperament and subject matter occurred in the first thirty-four years of her life, before she began to write professionally. Katherine O'Flaherty was born in St. Louis on 8 February to secure and socially prominent parents, Eliza Faris O'Flaherty, of French-Creole descent, and Thomas O'Flaherty, an Irish immigrant and successful commission merchant. Until recently the year of her birth was believed to be 1851, but this has been disputed for the past several years, and many Chopin scholars now believe that she was born in 1850. A forthcoming biography of Chopin by Emily Toth cites evidence, based upon baptismal and census records, that suggests 1850 is the correct date. She attended the St. Louis Academy of the Sacred Heart, graduating in 1868, and then participated in the social life of a belle for two years before she married a Creole, Oscar Chopin of Louisiana, in June 1870.

Kate O'Flaherty's great-grandmother Mme Victoria Verdon Charleville lived in the O'Flaherty household and directed young Kate's mental and artistic growth until her death when Kate was eleven. She cultivated in the young girl a taste for storytelling, a relish for the intimate details about such historical figures as the earliest settlers of the Louisiana Territory, and an unabashed, unhesitant, even nonjudgmental intellectual curiosity about life. Additionally, she superintended the girl's piano lessons and her French, the language especially important in their bilingual home. Chopin's interest in music was lifelong, as was her willingness to explore unconventional ideas. The young Kate was known in St. Louis as the town's "Littlest Rebel" for having taken down and hidden a Union flag from her home where "the Yanks tied it up." A Unionist neighbor managed to keep her from being arrested, but the severity of her offense may be judged by the fact that in New Orleans a man was shot for the same violation.

During her childhood Kate Chopin endured the death of her father, as well as several other family deaths. Although she always recovered, the depth of her grief may be sensed by her reaction as an eleven-year-old to the deaths (that occurred within a month) of both Mme Charleville and her half brother George, who fought on the Confederate side during the Civil War. For about two years Chopin withdrew from school, from friends, even somewhat from her family, and spent much of the time reading in the attic. Yet in her fiction—"Ma'ame Pélagie," for example—as in her life, she stressed the moral and psychological value of living in the present.

In 1869, before she had met her future husband, she met a German woman in New Orleans who combined fame as a singer and actress with a respectable place in society and a wealthy, loving husband. This meeting exhilarated the recently graduated Kate Chopin. She also began smoking during this trip, a pleasure she indulged with relish and humor all her life.

Kate and Oscar Chopin lived for almost a decade in New Orleans, until his cotton factoring business failed in 1879, whereupon they moved to Cloutierville, Natchitoches Parish, in north central Louisiana. In both New Orleans and Cloutierville she absorbed impressions that she would later employ in her fiction. The combination of her gift as a mimic with her talent as a musician—she played by note and by ear and had a remarkable memory for music—allowed her to capture the distinctive cadences, nuances, gestures, and diction of the residents of Louisiana who would, years later, people her fiction. She was at home in New Orleans and Cloutierville society, partly because of her personal magnetism but also because of her faultless French and her southern sympathies.

In the fertile cotton land around the Cane River the Chopins lived on inherited property, with income from the management of several small plantations and the ownership of a plantation store. Although they were not living on a plantation themselves, they were intimately involved in the festive plantation society. By 1879 Kate Chopin had borne her sixth child and only daughter, and by December 1882 she was a widow, her husband dead of swamp fever. For a year she successfully managed his business duties but in 1884 returned with her family to St. Louis to live with her mother. Her mother's death followed shortly afterward in 1885, leaving Chopin without family—except for her six children—and with a small, diminishing income.

Her only close friend during this time was Dr. Frederick Kolbenheyer, her mother's neighbor and her own obstetrician for three of her children, a learned man whose encouragement is believed to have led her to study contemporary science, to give up her religious beliefs, and to start writing professionally. Following a visit to Natchitoches in 1887, she wrote a poem, "If it might be," published 10 January 1888 in *America*, a progressive Chicago magazine; this publication marked her first appearance in print. She also began working on two pieces of fiction, one titled "Euphrasie," which was much later revised and published as "A No Account Creole" in *Century* (1894), and one she referred to in a notebook as "An Unfinished Story—Grand Isle—30,000 words," which she later destroyed. In an unpublished draft of an essay written in 1896, she describes herself as she struggled initially to shape her personal self into a fictive one and credits Guy de Maupassant with helping her find a vision as well as technique and theme: "It was at this period of my emerging from the vast solitude in which I had been making my own acquaintance, that I stumbled upon Maupassant. . . . Here was a man who had escaped from tradition and authority, who had entered into himself and looked out upon life through his own being and with his own eyes." She particularly responded to his spontaneity and his ability to create genuine impressions "without the plots, the old fashioned mechanism and stage trapping that in a vague, unthinking way I had fancied were essential to the art of story making."

Her first two stories to reach print, "Wiser than a God" and "A Point at Issue!," were written and published in 1889; both concern the unconventional attitude of the heroine toward marriage as a reflection of her unconventional attitude toward herself. This subject would become a persistent but not single-minded theme in Chopin's work, culminating in *The Awakening* as well as in the unpublished short story "Charlie," written in 1900. She came to the theme naturally, not ideologically, partly at least through the strong influence of her great-grandmother, Mme Charleville. In "Wiser than a God" Paula Von Stolz chooses a musical career rather than a loving, wealthy husband; she explains to him that music "courses with the blood through my veins. . . . it's something dearer than life, than riches, even than love." Paula's devotion to art is humanized somewhat by her association of musical success with love for her dead parents. The pianist's independence, her renown, her German origin as well as her triumph in Leipzig reveal Chopin's debt to her first visit to New Orleans.

In the other 1889 story, "A Point at Issue!," Eleanor Gail and Charles Faraday begin with a modern, emancipated marriage; they share a "free masonry of intellect." The test of their freedom occurs as a result of her year in Paris (why not *Hades*, say their friends) to study French, while he remains in the United States. During this separation each becomes jealous because of false appearances. She attenuates her rational conception of marriage to accommodate jealous passion; he comforts himself with "my Nellie is only a woman, after all." And Chopin's satiric comment closes the story, "With man's usual inconsistency, he had quite forgotten the episode of [his own jealousy]." Chopin also includes a reference to the woman's suffrage movement's busying itself with the question of clothes, "which while stamping their wearer with the distinction of a

quasi-emancipation, defeated the ultimate purpose of their construction by inflicting a personal discomfort that extended beyond the powers of long endurance." In contrast to such superficial attempts at creating equality is the integrity of Eleanor and Charles's struggle to maintain individual freedom while dealing with essentials like passion.

Chopin's first novel, *At Fault*, was written after "Euphrasie," the first draft of "A No Account Creole." These works are the first to employ the region, families, concerns, and ambience of Natchitoches Parish. Written between July 1889 and April 1890, *At Fault* presents the intertwined questions of divorce and moral idealism and announces a number of Chopin's future themes: the relation of the individual to change and to society, the problems of romantic love and unrestrained passion, and the dilemma of the modern woman. Like many first novels, *At Fault* does not satisfactorily balance its various themes; furthermore, the resolution as well as two major premises of the work seem contrived. The main character, Thérèse Lafirme, who initially seems somewhat like Kate Chopin after the death of her husband, is a young Creole widow who takes over the management of her husband's plantation as a way to cope with her grief. Her healthy accommodation to that painful change in her life is characteristic of her ability to accept such other changes as the new railroad that causes her to move her house, and the sawmill that, because of the allure of money, she permits to alter the landscape she loves; yet she is unable to change or even to question her religious and moral views. Her belief in moral absolutes leads to her attempt to shape the lives of those who work for her. When she discovers that the man she loves, David Hosmer, the sawmill owner, is divorced, she sacrifices their happiness to her rigid morality. If it is nearly incredible that Thérèse asks Hosmer to remarry his alcoholic wife, it is even harder for the reader to believe that he does and returns with her to live on the Lafirme plantation. When Thérèse's interference in the lives of Fanny and David Hosmer, as in the lives of others, begins to produce questionable results, she finally asks herself, "What reason had she to know that a policy of non-interference in the affairs of others might not after all be the judicious one?" Despite her startled discovery that Fanny might not be worth the sacrifice that she and David have made and despite a dream that suggests she is killing David while rescuing Fanny, the solution to her dilemma comes arbitrarily when Fanny is drowned in a surging river, which she is crossing in search of whiskey. Her death renders moot the question of her worth and allows David to marry Thérèse. Thérèse's final realization suggests her growing awareness of moral complexity and personal change: "I have seen myself at fault in following what seemed the only right. I feel as if there were no way to turn for the truth. Old supports appear to be giving way beneath me." David responds, "the truth in its entirety isn't given to man to know–such knowledge, no doubt, would be beyond human endurance." Divorce is neither condemned nor openly endorsed, yet it serves as an appropriate metaphor for those social realities that refuse to be contained within absolute beliefs.

The question of woman's role in society is related to the problem of divorce, though the connection is only tangentially made in the novel. Nevertheless, Chopin creates several psychologically astute vignettes that suggest the varied uses and misuses of a woman's freedom. Fanny's St. Louis friends Belle and Lou are "finished and professional time-killers," who squander their time on matinees, gossip, and, in Lou's case, on an extramarital affair. After their marriage Thérèse will continue to run the plantation and David will operate the sawmill, a division of labor that suits their interests and abilities. This happy ending, which implies the fulfillment of personal, sexual, and social ideals, seems at odds with many of the antiromantic qualities of the novel.

Contemporary reviews of *At Fault* praised its author's characterizations, style, and humor, while complaining about its breaches of respectability in diction and action. By and large, *At Fault* was seen as a promising first novel. Now the novel's refusal to condemn divorce is recognized as a first in fiction, and Chopin's willingness to describe a female alcoholic is also a departure from conventional expectations.

In 1890 Chopin worked primarily on her second novel, "Young Dr. Gosse," which was finished in January 1891 and sent to several publishers but was never accepted. She then returned to shorter fiction, completing about forty pieces in the next three years. Twenty-three of these stories, four previously unpublished, were collected in *Bayou Folk*, published by Houghton, Mifflin in March 1894. By then, Chopin had broken out of the local St. Louis periodicals and children's magazines that first published her work and into the eastern literary market,

though the subject matter of several of the stories caused delays as she searched for more tolerant forums. In 1894 her stories appeared in *Century*, *Atlantic*, and *Vogue*. *Vogue*, in fact, published nineteen of her stories from 1893 to 1900, among them her most provocative and outspoken on the themes of a woman's sexual nature and her situation in marriage, including "Désirée's Baby," "La Belle Zoraïde," "A Respectable Woman," "The Story of an Hour," "The Kiss," "Her Letters," "An Egyptian Cigarette," and "The White Eagle."

Bayou Folk depicts more fully the Louisiana milieu of *At Fault*. The tales are unified by setting, recurring characters, a prevailing theme, and the author's tone–cool and distant but with humor and insight. The setting is occasionally New Orleans but predominately Natchitoches Parish, whether the village of Natchitoches, the plantations along Cane River, the small farms and squalid cabins, or the houses on the bayous. Chopin reveals herself here as a practitioner of Howellsian realism–portraying ordinary people in their everyday concerns. Except for two stories set during the Civil War, the tales take place after the war, the effects of which are apparent in the narratives. The war indirectly provides the main plot in four of the twenty-three stories, but in each the family at home supplies the angle of vision.

The major theme of the *Bayou Folk* collection is love, whether loyal devotion, romantic love, love of honor, sexual passion, or some combination of these. Love is a positive force for the individuals involved and for their community. Devotion to another takes many forms. Yet even devotion has complexity when examined from Chopin's ironic perspective. For example, in "A Lady of Bayou St. John" a childlike wife whose husband is fighting with Beauregard falls in love with a neighboring Frenchman and plans to flee to Paris with him. But before she does, word comes that her husband is dead. Instead of marrying the Frenchman she devotes herself to the memory of her husband. Is devotion to an ideal more satisfying than love itself, and is a dead husband more capable of inspiring fidelity than a living one, or has the passion she experienced with the Frenchman enabled her, ironically, to sacrifice as well as to love? Chopin leaves the enigma unresolved.

Chopin convincingly portrays the simplicity of romantic love in Natchitoches Parish, partly through her use of setting. In such stories as

Manuscript for "The Storm," written in July 1898. The story was not published in Chopin's lifetime.

"Love on the Bon-Dieu," the act of falling in love at first sight is given plausibility by the characters' rootedness in a small, homogenous community, where everyone's knowing one another lays the groundwork for what only seems an impetuous act.

Sexual passion as the basic force in love is wrought with complexity and sometimes with tragedy. The tragic effects of miscegenation loom in the background of two stories of passion, "Désirée's Baby" and "La Belle Zoraïde." The justly famous "Désirée's Baby" dramatizes the rage of a planter, Armand, whose name is one of the oldest and proudest in Louisiana, when he discovers that his infant son has negroid features. Blaming his wife, whom he has loved passionately, and sending her away, he "thought that God had dealt cruelly and unjustly with him; and felt somehow that he was paying him back in kind when he stabbed thus into his wife's soul." She walks into the bayou, carrying her baby, while Armand, in burning all her possessions, discovers a letter from his mother telling of her own Negro blood. In "La Belle Zoraïde" preventing the marriage of a young mulatto girl and the black man for whom she has a spontaneous erotic attraction ends in the girl's insanity.

Reviewers of *Bayou Folk* were enthusiastically favorable, praising its freshness, charm, realistic subject matter, and unpretentious style. Chopin was perceived as more than a local colorist, with the *Atlantic Monthly* reviewer commenting, "Now and then she strikes a passionate note, and the naturalness and ease with which she does it impress one as characteristic of power awaiting opportunity." Modern reaction is in accord with these early appraisals. *Bayou Folk* was reprinted by Houghton Mifflin in 1895, 1906, 1911, and 1968.

The success of *Bayou Folk* no doubt contributed to Chopin's continuing to write short stories. She was not receiving much encouragement for her still-unpublished second novel, "Young Dr. Gosse"; in 1895 it was rejected again, and in 1896 she destroyed it. Her working methods and living conditions probably also influenced her to write shorter fiction. Valuing spontaneity in art as in life, she often composed a story in one sitting, and most of her stories were printed as they were first written. She said of her own writing, "I am completely at the mercy of unconscious selection. To such an extent is this true, that what is called the polishing up process has always proved disastrous to my work, and I avoid it, preferring the integrity of crudities to artificialities." Chopin worked in the living room, subject to the demands of her family. Her children remember her sitting in their midst with a lapboard and writing materials, refusing to exclude them, even though she wished to at times. The youngest of her six children was eighteen when Chopin began her next novel, *The Awakening*. Throughout her career she wrote only one or two days a week, leaving the rest of the time for such activities as musicales, concerts, and the theater. She also presided over the equivalent of a French salon, which attracted St. Louisians of various intellectual interests.

Chopin's second collection of tales, *A Night in Acadie*, which came out in 1897, contains twenty-one stories, all but one of which had first been published in a periodical. Way and Williams, the book's Chicago publisher, was not well known, and this work received less notice than *Bayou Folk*. The milieu and some of the characters are the same as in *Bayou Folk*, but the themes of this second volume are more diverse. The number of stories about devotion falls to two. In place of charmingly depicted romantic love is a more complicated sexual passion. The demands of passion, the reconciliation of public with private self, and the resurrection from a static life are interrelated themes in this collection and point toward Chopin's next book and finest achievement, *The Awakening*. Fifteen tales are equally divided among these three topics; three of the remaining four are miscellaneous sketches, brief insights into character.

In *A Night in Acadie* love is an overwhelming force, irrational in its demands; impervious to caste, class, honor; and dangerous to physical well-being. In "Azélie" the plantation-store manager, 'Polyte, first gives Azélie whatever she wants for her shiftless father so that she will not steal the items; then he falls desperately in love with her, gives up his job as well as his notion of honor, and follows her helplessly to Little River, a place which, he says, "always make me sad–like I think about a graveyard. To me it's like a person mus' die, one way or otha, w'en they go on Li'le river. Oh, I hate it!" When in "At Cheniere Caminada" a clumsy island fisherman falls desperately in love with a wealthy New Orleans girl, his whole life is radically altered, and his despair is so intense that he finds himself glad that she is dead rather than married to someone else. His passion is depicted as inevitable, natural: "He obeyed [this powerful impulse] without a struggle, as naturally as he would have obeyed the dictates of hunger and thirst." A tantalizingly ambiguous story, "A Respectable Woman," shows the dilemma of a married woman who becomes physically attracted to her husband's friend, Gouvernail. As she would later do in *The Awakening*, Chopin details the physical aspects of the wife's attraction: "Her mind only vaguely grasped what he was saying. Her physical being was for the moment predominant. She was not thinking of his words, only drinking in the tones of his voice. She wanted to reach out her hand in the darkness and touch him with the sensitive tips of her fingers upon the face or the lips. She wanted to draw close to him and whisper against his cheek–she did not care what–as she might have done if she had not been a respectable woman." To avoid seeing him again, she leaves to visit the city before his stay has ended. Later she dissuades her husband from inviting him again; but by the end of the year she proposes that he visit, and when her husband is pleased that she has overcome her dislike for him, she replies, "Oh, . . . I have overcome everything! you will see. This time I shall be very nice to him." This ending was ambiguous enough for her audience not to take offense, as they would with Chopin's treatment of passion and adultery in *The Awakening*.

One of Chopin's best stories, "Athénaïse," suggests the degree to which love and passion sometimes go against the demands of the self for both husband and wife. The childlike, passionate, willful bride of two months, Athénaïse, runs away from her husband twice, not because he is in any way objectionable but because marriage does not suit her: "It's jus' being married that I detes' an' despise. I hate being Mrs. Cazeau, an' would want to be Athénaïse Miché again. I can't stan' to live with a man; to have him always there; his coats an' pantaloons hanging in my room. . . . " In spite of his deep love for her, Cazeau does not go after his wife the second time because doing so reminds him of his father's bringing home a runaway slave: "the loss of self-respect seemed to him too dear a price to pay for a wife." He would have her return voluntarily or not at all. Yet passion also reconciles the couple. After a month of hiding out in a New Orleans pension, missing her home and family and nearly beginning an affair, Athénaïse discovers she is pregnant; then, thinking of Cazeau, she experiences "the first purely sensuous tremor of her life." Chopin's astute characterization makes Athénaïse's joyous return home credible.

"The dual life," as Chopin called it in *The Awakening*, "that outward existence which conforms, the inward life which questions," touches five stories in *A Night in Acadie* but is most powerfully realized in "Ozéme's Holiday" and "Nég Créol." Unlike Edna Pontellier in *The Awakening*, who in totally shedding her social self leaves herself nowhere to go but death, the main characters in these stories strike a balance between the two worlds, accommodating self to society in a way that does not extinguish the self; Chopin ironically suggests that some portion of society's demands in fact nourishes some aspect of the self. In five other stories an adult frozen in a kind of emotional or social isolation (or both) is rejuvenated by an encounter with a child, or in the case of "Regret," several children. Chopin uses the symbolism of spring and, sometimes, of Easter to reinforce the awakenings, but the religious motifs in "After the Winter" and "The Lilies," as in "Odalie Misses Mass," serve only to heighten the significant experiences that take place in the natural rituals of life, not in those of the church.

The few reviews *A Night in Acadie* attracted praised Chopin as a local colorist but reacted against the book's sensual themes. The collection is now praised both for its success in the local-color genre and for its indication of Chopin's maturing artistry.

From 1897 to 1900 or 1901 Chopin tried unsuccessfully to market a third collection of stories, called "A Vocation and A Voice." It contained in its final version twenty-one stories, one written before 1894, sixteen written between 1894 and 1897, and four written after 1897. About half of the stories had been published in *Vogue*, a number had been difficult to place because of their subject matter, and five were not to see print until many years after Chopin's death. *Vogue* was clearly aware that Chopin's themes were often daring, and its editors gave her her most consistently tolerant forum.

The variation of themes begun in *A Night in Acadie* increases in this collection, and Chopin moves away from her usual Louisiana setting. Moreover, the characters and themes establish themselves authentically without the Louisiana dialect or setting (present in only three tales), and for the first time Chopin experiments effectively in several pieces with first-person narration. Among these stories are three brief sketches that concern nature as a means of knowledge, specifically a knowledge of God. The remaining tales are almost equally divided: about half deal frankly with the imperatives of passion; the rest can be grouped together not so much by theme as by their most salient quality–an ironic tone, closest in spirit perhaps to Stephen Crane's irony.

Many of the stories treat extramarital sex as a subject of interest for what it reveals of human psychology, not as a subject of lament or moralizing, anticipating Chopin's handling of the theme in *The Awakening*. Furthermore, in the title story, "A Vocation and A Voice," as well as in "Lilacs," "Two Portraits," and "Juanita," she suggests in a Whitmanesque fashion that to obey erotic impulses is to participate in the natural rhythms of life itself. Eschewing all moralizing, Chopin leaves herself free to explore as well the varied consequences within society of such sexuality; they might be painful, tragic, humorous, dangerous, joyous, or pleasurable; they are not, however, wrong. As she implies in "A Vocation and A Voice" and in "Two Portraits," frequently the ardor that makes a good member of a religious order is the same that makes a good lover, and vice versa.

One of the ironic stories, "The Story of an Hour," now frequently anthologized because of its commentary on marriage and its relationship to *The Awakening*, turns on a series of artfully modulated ironies that culminate in a somewhat contrived ending. After an outburst of grief over the news that her loving husband has been killed in a train accident, Mrs. Mallard, who has a heart condition, goes to her room alone, where she fearfully tries to ward off the realization that she is glad to be free, and then becomes intoxicated with the vision of freedom: "she would live for herself. There would be no powerful will bending hers in that blind persistence with which men and women believe they have a right to impose a private will upon a fellow-creature. A kind intention or a cruel intention made the act seem no less a crime as she looked upon it that brief moment of illumination." When her husband returns unharmed (he did not even know of the accident), Mrs. Mallard has a fatal heart attack, her shock emphasizing the completeness of her new commitment to freedom. The final irony comes from the physician, who declares that she died "of joy that kills."

It is unfortunate that "A Vocation and A Voice" has never been published as a collection, because it would confirm what has been generally recognized by critics, that Chopin was interested in universal human nature; Natchitoches Parish or New Orleans merely provided a specific setting for many of her works. This setting was no doubt fresh and piquant to her as to her contemporary audience, but it is not the major basis for her achievement as an artist. "A Vocation and A Voice" offers convincing evidence that her insights into character, her narrative voice, and her prose style are her finest achievements.

In addition to some forty poems and several translations (including seven of Maupassant's tales), Chopin also wrote and had published a small number of essays, among them literary reviews. With the exception of one piece that appeared in the *Atlantic Monthly*, most of the essays were published in St. Louis journals from 1894 to 1897. Not surprisingly, she proves as a critic to be consistent with her own practice of art. For example, in two 1894 essays she chastises Hamlin Garland for dismissing "from the artist's consideration such primitive passions as love, hate, etc.," and she criticizes Emile Zola's method in "Lourdes" because the story is "more than two-thirds of the time swamped beneath a mass of prosaic data, offensive and nauseous description and rampant sentimentality." While her criticism was often acute, Chopin's major achievement remains her fiction, particularly *The Awakening*.

Now often republished and acclaimed as a masterpiece, *The Awakening* was during Chopin's lifetime the subject of scandal and censure. Certain contemporary reviews of the novel depicted the moral and literary biases of her critics, who termed the book "moral poison," "sordid," "unhealthy," "repellent," and "vulgar" with "disagreeable glimpses of sensuality." Accusing Chopin of "out Zola-ing Zola," reviewers were offended because the author did not condemn her adulterous heroine, Edna Pontellier, or, worse, that she seemed at times to sympathize with Edna. In spite of the moral outrage it engendered, the novel also drew some reluctant praise for its artistry and insight. Typical was the comment of her friend, writer C. L. Deyo: "It is sad, and mad and bad; but it is all consummate art." Acquaintances and even some friends cut Chopin socially, and, in fact, reactions to the novel were later credited with paralyzing Chopin's creativity.

The vehemence of the hostile reviews of *The Awakening*, which assuredly contributed to its half century of neglect, is attributable to the novel's special power. That power derives not so much from Chopin's violation of several nineteenth-century principles of womanly and literary decorum, although that violation raised indignant protests, as from the novel's intense poetic unity: the prose style, the characterization of the heroine, and the symbolism all lead inevitably to the novel's tragic resolution. Indeed, Chopin's contemporary reviewers often seem to protest loudest against their own sympathy with Edna.

The poetic beauty of *The Awakening* derives from its organic unity of symbolism and plot, traceable in part to Chopin's methods of composition and in part to Chopin's mature mastery of form and theme. Just as she tended to write a short story in a burst of concentrated writing, Chopin worked on *The Awakening* from about mid 1897 until 21 January 1898, during which time she probably wrote only one other work, the short story "A Family Affair"; thus she gave the novel her full creative effort. The manuscript was submitted to Way and Williams, but when they went out of business, they transferred it in November 1898 to Herbert S. Stone and Company, and the novel was published 22 April 1899. According to the author's notebooks, *The Awakening* earned $145 between 1899 and 1901.

The Awakening was in many ways–despite all the 1890s' celebration of the New Woman–a novel ahead of its time. At a Louisiana summer resort, Edna Pontellier, a native of Kentucky, gradually and unexpectedly discovers the possibilities for a life outside her safe but dull marriage of convenience. At Grand Isle, not far from New Orleans, she is exposed to the sophistication, the sensuality, and the customs of the Europeanized Catholic Creoles, whose values are much different from those of her own Protestant heritage of Kentucky. The lush, languid, and tropical ambience of the island provides the right setting for Edna's awakening to her sensual and psychic needs, as she falls in love with a young Creole, Robert Lebrun. Robert, concerned for their honor and frightened that his dalliance is taken seriously, leaves abruptly for Mexico. Returning to New Orleans, Edna begins to change her life in accordance with her summer discoveries, moving toward a free and independent existence. To her husband's great astonishment, she gives up her day for receiving guests, neglects housekeeping activities and her children (though they continue to flourish), refuses to share her husband's bed, resumes her painting, and, finally, moves out of her husband's house into a small cottage around the block.

Léonce Pontellier has been advised by the family physician that Edna's "peculiarities" will "pass happily over . . . if you let her alone." Léonce is no villain; he is considerate and loving in his way, as Edna recognizes; but he regards his wife, Chopin indicates, much as he would a valuable piece of furniture in his house. The irrevocable split between the Pontelliers is suggested by their inverse actions: as she turns resolutely away from society toward inner realities, he scrambles feverishly to keep up social appearances. He represents the conformity of society, believing his wife is crazy: "He could see plainly that she was not herself. That is he could not see that she was becoming herself and daily casting aside that fictitious self which we assume like a garment with which to appear before the world." Because he believes the changes in Edna are a passing mood he is unconcerned about leaving her alone while he goes to New York on business.

Edna's circle of friends changes too. She spends time with an eccentric musician, Mlle Reisz, imbibing her passionate music along with her perorations on individuality and noncomformity; but she also visits her friend Adèle Ratignolle, one of the "mother-women" who typify Creole culture. Very much as Kate Chopin delighted in doing, Edna wanders the streets unescorted, finding out-of-the-way retreats, exploring the city, observing its people. Most significantly, she succumbs to the seductions of a roué, Alcée Arobin, without shame or remorse, only with regret that he is not Robert.

In spite of her quest Edna finds no complete or lasting realization of her desires. She is not a first-rate artist; she despairs of the value of the Ratignolles' intimate but boring domesticity; nor does she love Alcée, though he meets her sexual needs. Nowhere does she find "the taste of life's delirium," though she seems to have the chance when Robert returns from Mexico. After expressing her feelings openly, in an "unwomanly" fashion, and initiating the caresses between them, she announces, "I am no longer one of Mr. Pontellier's possessions to dispose of or not. I give myself where I choose." In the middle of her declaration of love to him, she is summoned to help with the birth of Adèle Ratignolle's child. She leaves, proclaiming, "Now you are here we shall love each other, my Robert. We shall be everything to each other. Nothing else in the world is of any consequence." He begs her to stay with him, but upon her return he has gone, leaving a farewell note: "Good-by—because I love you." Shattered both by the "scene of torture" at Adèle's and by Robert's second desertion, Edna goes to Grand Isle, strips off her clothing, and swims out to sea to drown.

Two crucial scenes—the delivery of Adèle's child and Edna's suicide—dramatize the novel's major themes. Through the description of the delivery and the subsequent conversation between the physician and Edna, Chopin expresses the idea that children (and by implication, marriage) control the lives of women because of the imperatives of biology as well as of society. Dr. Mandelet observes, "The trouble is . . . that youth is given up to illusions. It seems to be a provision of Nature; a decoy to secure mothers for the race. And Nature takes no account of moral consequences, or arbitrary conditions which we create, and which we feel obliged to maintain at any cost." Edna, though stunned by what she has seen, replies, "perhaps it is better to wake up after all, even to suffer, rather than to remain a dupe to illusions all one's life." Earlier Edna has commented to Adèle that for her children she would "give up the unessential . . . my life . . . ; but I wouldn't give myself." What she realizes after her conversation with the doctor is at least partly responsible for the fact that she does give her life.

Edna's idealized love for Robert sustains her in the face of her disillusionment, but after she finds him gone, she seems to believe it inevitable that she will never find such compensation again. After a long night's meditation she journeys to Grand Isle, where the only embrace and comfort she finds are those promised by death as both lover and self-realization. An evocative, musical refrain that recurs throughout the book has foreshadowed this paradoxical symbolism of the waters at Grand Isle:

> The voice of the sea is seductive; never ceasing, whispering, clamoring, murmuring, inviting the soul to wander for a spell in abysses of solitude; to lose itself in mazes of inward contemplation.
> The voice of the sea speaks to the soul. The touch of the sea is sensuous, enfolding the body in its soft, close embrace.

The original title of the novel, "The Solitary Soul," points to the essential, radical aloneness of Edna, whose transcendent self is only realized in death, a "defeat," as Donald Ringe says in his autumn 1975 article for *Studies in American Fiction*, "that involves no surrender." Chopin's sympathies were no doubt engaged by Edna's tragic dilemma, yet she refrains from all moralizing about Edna's suicide, content to examine with courage and honesty without reaching for easy moral judgments.

The treatment of eros in *The Awakening* has rightly been compared to Greek tragedy, to George Sand's romances, to Walt Whitman's poetry, and to D. H. Lawrence's novels, while in its analysis of woman's role in marriage and society, the novel bears a strong though not derivative resemblance to Gustave Flaubert's *Madame Bovary* (1856), Henrik Ibsen's *A Doll's House* (1879), and Henry James's *The Portrait of a Lady* (1881). The public outcry stirred by *The Awakening* makes it comparable to *Sister Carrie*, published in 1901; Chopin, like Theodore Dreiser, was unwilling to compromise her artistic vision.

The effect of the unfavorable reviews for *The Awakening* was compounded in 1900 by another rejection of Chopin's third collection of stories, as well as by the return of her piece "Ti Démon" from the *Atlantic*, which termed the story "too sombre." Nevertheless, she did not completely cease writing as a result of these disappointments, as has been popularly maintained. She wrote some nine stories after April 1899, three of which were published before her death.

Of the works unpublished in her lifetime, two deserve special mention: "The Storm" was written in July 1898, before the reviews of *The Awakening* appeared; "Charlie" was written afterward, in April 1900. In "The Storm" Chopin portrays the momentary sexual ecstasy of two lovers–although they are married to others, to call them adulterers violates the spirit of the story–who, caught together accidentally in a violent storm, move in their passion as naturally as the rhythms of the storm. Two qualities of the tale are noteworthy: its explicitness for its day in describing the beauty and power of sexuality; and the amoral, happy way the event is described, concluding with, "So the storm passed and every one [both the lovers, their respective spouses, and their children] was happy." Chopin's view of the possibilities for such fulfillment is indicated unobtrusively in the comparison of the lovers' passion with the storm itself, a cyclone, relatively rare in Louisiana; and in the fact that this exquisite pleasure, a first for both lovers, occurs outside of marriage.

"Charlie," a tale of a tomboy-poet's development into a woman, is also one of Chopin's best (and longest) stories. The main character has much in common with the author herself, and more significantly the sustained power of the writing–complex, ironic, ambiguous–bespeaks an artist in control of her talent.

Although she had not been in good health since 1903, and had not written anything since then, Kate Chopin became an enthusiastic daily visitor to the 1904 St. Louis World's Fair. Following one day at the fair she suffered a cerebral hemorrhage and died two days later, on 22 August 1904.

Lacking a good editor who might have provided encouragement or simply good editing for her sometimes artless diction, Kate Chopin did not accomplish what she might have during a career shortened by her death. Nevertheless, she is distinguished for the frankness with which she approached sexuality, the amorality with which she described such problems as divorce and adultery, and for the serious consideration she gave to the restrictions of marriage and childbearing and the uses of freedom. Freed from conventional American male viewpoints by an inheritance that came naturally to Chopin–her French culture and her female perspective–and possessed of a graceful wit and an intelligent honesty, Kate Chopin spoke of woman's condition in American society in a way that her contemporaries could not or would not. But she also, in both male and female characters, explored that persistent American concern, the relationship between self and society.

Biographies:

Daniel S. Rankin, *Kate Chopin and Her Creole Stories* (Philadelphia: University of Pennsylvania Press, 1932).
> The first biography of Chopin, valued particularly for its insights based in part on interviews with people who knew her.

Per Seyersted, *Kate Chopin: A Critical Biography* (Baton Rouge: Louisiana State University Press, 1969).
> The standard biography, it places Chopin fully in the realistic tradition and marks her attention to woman's "sexual and spiritual self-assertion."

References:

George Arms, "Kate Chopin's *The Awakening* in the Perspective of Her Literary Career," in *Essays on American Literature in Honor of Jay B. Hubbell*, edited by Clarence Gohdes (Durham: Duke University Press, 1967), pp. 215-228.
> Examines the unity between the novel and many of her short stories.

Cyrille Arnavon, Introduction to *Edna* (Paris: Le Club bibliophile de France, 1952); translated and republished in *A Kate Chopin Miscellany*, edited by Per Seyersted and Emily Toth (Natchitoches & Oslo: Northwestern State University Press and Universitetsforlaget, 1979), pp. 168-188.
> The French critic who rediscovered *The Awakening* assesses the novel's distinctions in relation to other American literature between the Civil War and World War I.

Robert Arner, "Kate Chopin," *Louisiana Studies*, 14 (Spring 1975): 11-139.
> A lengthy literary analysis of Chopin's artistic development.

Kenneth Eble, "A Forgotten Novel: Kate Chopin's *The Awakening*," *Western Humanities Review*, 10 (Summer 1956): 261-269.
> The first major American attempt, following Arnavon's rediscovery of *The Awakening*,

to appraise the literary significance and power of *The Awakening*.

Barbara Ewell, *Kate Chopin* (New York: Ungar, 1986).
> A comprehensive study of Chopin's life and canon, placing emphasis on late-nineteenth-century social conditions.

Winfried Fluck, "Tentative Transgressions: Kate Chopin's Fiction as a Mode of Symbolic Action," *Studies in American Fiction*, 10 (Autumn 1982): 151-171.
> Examines the short fiction as Chopin's "laboratory of creative fantasy" in which female self-assertion and social and sexual transgressions can be tested.

Sandra Gilbert, "Introduction: The Second Coming of Aphrodite," in *Kate Chopin: The Awakening and Selected Stories* (New York: Penguin, 1984), pp. 7-33.
> Drawing on fin de siècle culture, the study analyzes *The Awakening* as "Kate Chopin's . . . fantasy of the second coming of Aphrodite," "an alternative to the patriarchal myth of Jesus."

William Schuyler, "Kate Chopin," *Writer*, 7 (August 1894): 115-117.
> In the wake of the success of *Bayou Folk*, Chopin's friend provides biographical and anecdotal details.

Emily Toth, "Kate Chopin's *The Awakening* as Feminist Criticism," *Louisiana Studies*, 15 (Fall 1976): 241-251.
> Argues for Chopin's transformation into art of nineteenth-century feminist ideas.

Cynthia G. Wolff, "Thanatos and Eros: Kate Chopin's *The Awakening*," *American Quarterly*, 25 (October 1973): 449-471.
> A provocative psychological reading of Edna as a regressive personality.

Papers:

The major collection of Chopin's papers is held by the Missouri Historical Society, St. Louis. Among other items, it includes manuscripts, a commonplace book, a diary, and two notebooks. A few letters are available in the Century Collection of the New York Public Library and in the Houghton Library, Harvard University.

Samuel Langhorne Clemens
(Mark Twain)

This entry was updated by Howard Baetzhold (Butler University) from the entry by Hamlin Hill (Texas A&M University) in DLB 12, American Realists and Naturalists.

Places	Hannibal, Mo. Buffalo, N.Y. Redding, Conn.	Virginia City, Nev. Quarry Farm, Elmira, N.Y.	San Francisco Hartford, Conn.
Influences and Relationships	Artemus Ward (Charles Farrar Browne) Charles Dudley Warner	Bret Harte W. E. H. Lecky	William Dean Howells Albert Bigelow Paine
Literary Movements and Forms	Romanticism Tall Tale and Southwestern Humor Lecturing	Realism Travel Narrative Journalism	Satire and Burlesque Local Color
Major Themes	Boyhood Freedom and Independence Anticolonialism	Society and the Individual Political Corruption	Slavery Determinism
Cultural and Artistic Influences	The Far West of the Bonanza Mining Days Travel at Home and Abroad	Antebellum South	The Mississippi River During Its Golden Days
Social and Economic Influences	Industrialism and Technology The Gilded Age	Speculation	Aftermath of the Civil War

See also the Clemens entries in DLB 11, American Humorists, 1800-1950, DLB 23, American Newspaper Journalists, 1873-1900, *and* DLB 64, American Literary Critics and Scholars, 1850-1880.

BIRTH: Florida, Missouri, 30 November 1835, to John Marshall and Jane Lampton Clemens.

MARRIAGE: 2 February 1870 to Olivia Langdon; children: Langdon, Olivia Susan (Susy), Clara, Jane Lampton (Jean).

DEATH: Redding, Connecticut, 21 April 1910.

SELECTED BOOKS: *The Celebrated Jumping Frog of Calaveras County, and Other Sketches* (New York: C. H. Webb, 1867; London: Routledge, 1867);
The Innocents Abroad, or The New Pilgrims' Progress (Hartford, Conn.: American Publishing Company, 1869); republished in 2 volumes as *The Innocents Abroad* and *The New Pilgrims' Progress* (London: Hotten, 1870);
Mark Twain's (Burlesque) Autobiography and First Romance (New York: Sheldon, 1871; London: Hotten, 1871);
"Roughing It" (London: Routledge, 1872);
The Innocents at Home (London: Routledge, 1872);
Roughing It, augmented edition (Hartford, Conn.: American Publishing Company, 1872)—comprises *"Roughing It"* and *The Innocents at Home;*
A Curious Dream; and Other Sketches (London: Routledge, 1872);
The Gilded Age: A Tale of Today, by Twain and Charles Dudley Warner (Hartford, Conn.: American Publishing Company, 1873; 3 volumes, London: Routledge, 1874);
Mark Twain's Sketches, New and Old (Hartford, Conn.: American Publishing Company, 1875);
The Adventures of Tom Sawyer (London: Chatto & Windus, 1876; Hartford, Conn.: American Publishing Company, 1876);
Old Times on the Mississippi (Toronto: Belford, 1876); republished as *The Mississippi Pilot* (London: Ward, Lock & Tyler, 1877); expanded as *Life on the Mississippi* (London: Chatto & Windus, 1883; Boston: Osgood, 1883);
An Idle Excursion (Toronto: Rose-Belford, 1878); expanded as *Punch, Brothers, Punch! and Other Sketches* (New York: Slote, Woodman, 1878);

Samuel Langhorne Clemens in 1880

A Tramp Abroad (London: Chatto & Windus/ Hartford, Conn.: American Publishing Company, 1880);
"1601" Conversation, As It Was by the Social Fireside, in the Time of the Tudors (Cleveland, 1880);
The Prince and the Pauper (London: Chatto & Windus, 1881; Boston: Osgood, 1882);
The Stolen White Elephant (London: Chatto & Windus, 1882); republished as *The Stolen White Elephant, Etc.* (Boston: Osgood, 1882);
The Adventures of Huckleberry Finn (London: Chatto & Windus, 1884); republished as *Adventures of Huckleberry Finn* (New York: Webster, 1885);
A Connecticut Yankee in King Arthur's Court (New York: Webster, 1889); republished as *A Yankee at the Court of King Arthur* (London: Chatto & Windus, 1889);
The American Claimant (New York: Webster, 1892; London: Chatto & Windus, 1892);
Merry Tales (New York: Webster, 1892);
The £1,000,000 Bank-Note and Other New Stories (New York: Webster, 1893; London: Chatto & Windus, 1893);

Tom Sawyer Abroad by Huck Finn (New York: Webster, 1894; London: Chatto & Windus, 1894);

Pudd'nhead Wilson, A Tale (London: Chatto & Windus, 1894); augmented as *The Tragedy of Pudd'nhead Wilson and the Comedy of Those Extraordinary Twins* (Hartford, Conn.: American Publishing Company, 1894);

Personal Recollections of Joan of Arc by the Sieur Louis de Conte (New York: Harper, 1896; London: Chatto & Windus, 1896);

Tom Sawyer Abroad, Tom Sawyer, Detective, and Other Stories (New York: Harper, 1896);

Tom Sawyer, Detective, as told by Huck Finn, and Other Stories (London: Chatto & Windus, 1896);

How to Tell a Story and Other Essays (New York: Harper, 1897);

Following the Equator (Hartford, Conn.: American Publishing Company, 1897); republished as *More Tramps Abroad* (London: Chatto & Windus, 1897);

The Man That Corrupted Hadleyburg and Other Stories and Essays (New York & London: Harper, 1900); enlarged and republished as *The Man That Corrupted Hadleyburg and Other Stories and Sketches* (London: Chatto & Windus, 1900);

A Double Barrelled Detective Story (New York & London: Harper, 1902);

A Dog's Tale (New York & London: Harper, 1904);

King Leopold's Soliloquy: A Defense of His Congo Rule (Boston: P. R. Warren, 1905);

Eve's Diary Translated from the Original Ms (London & New York: Harper, 1906);

What Is Man? (New York: De Vinne Press, 1906); enlarged and republished as *What Is Man? and Other Essays* (New York & London: Harper, 1917);

The $30,000 Bequest and Other Stories (New York & London: Harper, 1906);

Christian Science with Notes Containing Corrections to Date (New York & London: Harper, 1907);

A Horse's Tale (New York & London: Harper, 1907);

Is Shakespeare Dead? (New York & London: Harper, 1909);

Extract from Captain Stormfield's Visit to Heaven (New York & London: Harper, 1909);

Mark Twain's Speeches, compiled by F. A. Nast (New York & London: Harper, 1910);

The Mysterious Stranger, a Romance, edited by Albert Bigelow Paine and Frederick A.

Duneka (New York & London: Harper, 1916); enlarged and republished as *The Mysterious Stranger and Other Stories*, edited by Paine (New York & London: Harper, 1922);

The Curious Republic of Gondour and Other Whimsical Sketches (New York: Boni & Liveright, 1919);

Mark Twain's Speeches, edited by Paine (New York & London: Harper, 1923);

Europe and Elsewhere, edited by Paine (New York & London: Harper, 1923);

Mark Twain's Autobiography, 2 volumes, edited by Paine (New York & London: Harper, 1924);

Sketches of the Sixties, by Twain and Bret Harte (San Francisco: Howell, 1926);

The Adventures of Thomas Jefferson Snodgrass, edited by Charles Honce (Chicago: Pascal Covici, 1928);

Mark Twain's Notebook, edited by Paine (New York & London: Harper, 1935);

Letters from the Sandwich Islands Written for the Sacramento Union, edited by G. Ezra Dane (San Francisco: Grabhorn, 1937);

The Washoe Giant in San Francisco, edited by Franklin Walker (San Francisco: Fields, 1938);

Mark Twain's Travels With Mr. Brown, edited by Walker and Dane (New York: Knopf, 1940);

Mark Twain in Eruption, edited by Bernard DeVoto (New York & London: Harper, 1940);

Mark Twain at Work, edited by DeVoto (Cambridge: Harvard University Press, 1942);

Mark Twain, Business Man, edited by Samuel Charles Webster (Boston: Little, Brown, 1946);

Mark Twain of the ENTERPRISE, edited by Henry Nash Smith (Berkeley: University of California Press, 1957);

Traveling with the Innocents Abroad: Mark Twain's Original Reports from Europe and the Holy Land, edited by Daniel Morley McKeithan (Norman: University of Oklahoma Press, 1958);

Contributions to the Galaxy, 1868-1871, by Mark Twain, edited by Bruce R. McElderry, Jr. (Gainesville, Fla.: Scholars' Facsimiles & Reprints, 1961);

Letters from the Earth, edited by DeVoto (New York: Harper & Row, 1962);

Mark Twain's "Which was the Dream" and Other Symbolic Writings of the Later Years, edited by John S. Tuckey (Berkeley: University of California Press, 1967);

Mark Twain's Satires and Burlesques, edited by Franklin R. Rogers (Berkeley: University of California Press, 1967);

Clemens of the "Call": Mark Twain in San Francisco, edited by Edgar M. Branch (Berkeley: University of California Press, 1969);

Mark Twain's "Mysterious Stranger" Manuscripts, edited by William M. Gibson (Berkeley: University of California Press, 1969);

Mark Twain's Hannibal, Huck, and Tom, edited by Walter Blair (Berkeley: University of California Press, 1969);

Mark Twain's Fables of Man, edited by Tuckey (Berkeley: University of California Press, 1972);

Mark Twain's Notebooks and Journals, volume 1, 1855-1873, edited by Frederick Anderson, Michael B. Frank, and Kenneth M. Sanderson; volume 2, 1877-1883, edited by Anderson, Lin Salamo, and Bernard L. Stein; volume 3, 1883-1891, edited by Robert Pack Browning, Frank, and Salamo (Berkeley: University of California Press, 1975, 1979);

Mark Twain Speaking, edited by Paul Fatout (Iowa City: University of Iowa Press, 1976);

Mark Twain Speaks for Himself, edited by Fatout (West Lafayette: Purdue University Press, 1978);

The Devil's Race-Track: Mark Twain's "Great Dark" Writings, edited by Tuckey (Berkeley: University of California Press, 1979);

The Adventures of Tom Sawyer by Mark Twain: A Facsimile of the Author's Holograph Manuscript, 2 volumes (Frederick, Md.: University Publications of America/Washington, D.C.: Georgetown University Library, 1982);

Adventures of Huckleberry Finn (Tom Sawyer's Comrade) by Mark Twain: A Facsimile of the Manuscript, 2 volumes (Detroit: Gale Research, 1983).

Collections: *The Writings of Mark Twain*, Autograph Edition, 25 volumes (Hartford, Conn.: American Publishing Company, 1899-1907);

The Writings of Mark Twain, Author's National Edition, 25 volumes (New York & London: Harper, 1899-1917);

The Writings of Mark Twain, Definitive Edition, 37 volumes, edited by Paine (New York: Wells, 1922-1925).

Editions prepared by the University of California Press in cooperation with the University of Iowa: *Roughing It*, edited by Franklin

R. Rogers (Berkeley: University of California Press, 1972);

"What Is Man?" and Other Philosophical Writings, edited by Paul Baender (Berkeley: University of California Press, 1973);

A Connecticut Yankee in King Arthur's Court, edited by Bernard L. Stein (Berkeley: University of California Press, 1979);

The Prince and the Pauper, edited by Victor Fischer and Lin Salamo (Berkeley: University of California Press, 1979);

Early Tales & Sketches, volume 1 (1851-1864), volume 2 (1864-1865), edited by Edgar M. Branch and Robert H. Hirst (Berkeley: University of California Press, 1979, 1981);

The Adventures of Tom Sawyer; Tom Sawyer Abroad; Tom Sawyer, Detective, edited by John C. Gerber, Baender, and Terry Firkins (Berkeley: University of California Press, 1980);

Adventures of Huckleberry Finn, edited by Walter Blair and Fischer, with the assistance of Dahlia Armon and Harriet Elinor Smith (Berkeley: University of California Press, 1980).

OTHER: Letter to Edgar W. Howe (1884), in C. E. Schorer's "Mark Twain's Criticism of *The Story of a Country Town*," *American Literature*, 27 (March 1955): 109-112.

PERIODICAL PUBLICATIONS: "Report to the Buffalo Female Academy," *Buffalo Express*, 18 June 1870; republished in *Mark Twain on the Art of Writing*, edited by Martin B. Fried (Buffalo, N.Y.: Salisbury Club, 1961);

"Post Mortem Poetry," *Galaxy* (June 1870);

"About Magnanimous Incident Literature," *Atlantic Monthly* (May 1878);

"Unlearnable Things," anonymous, *Atlantic Monthly* (June 1880): 145-180;

"The Private History of a Campaign that Failed," *Century* (December 1885);

"English as She is Taught," *Century* (April 1887);

"Private History of the 'Jumping Frog' Story," *North American Review* (April 1894);

"In Defence of Harriet Shelley," *North American Review* (July-September 1894);

"What Paul Bourget Thinks of Us," *North American Review* (January 1895);

"Fenimore Cooper's Literary Offences," *North American Review* (April 1895);

"How to Tell a Story," *Youth's Companion* (3 October 1895);

"About Play-Acting," *Forum* (October 1898);

"The Man that Corrupted Hadleyburg," *Harper's Monthly* (December 1899);

"My Boyhood Dreams," *McClure's* (January 1900);

"Italian without a Master," *Harper's Weekly* (2 January 1904);

"Italian with Grammar," *Harper's Monthly* (August 1904);

"William Dean Howells," *Harper's Monthly* (April 1906);

"A Fable," *Harper's Monthly* (December 1909).

In the early spring of 1835 John Marshall Clemens and his wife, Jane, loaded up their possessions, their five children, and their single slave in Three Forks, Tennessee, to move to Missouri. It was another in a long series of migrations which the family undertook, seeking the success and affluence which always eluded them. As Dixon Wecter has noted, the Clemenses "appeared to lack the golden touch, even in an age when the riches of inland America hung ripe for the plucking." Their destination, Florida, Missouri, was an unpromising village with two muddy streets, a hundred inhabitants, and the Salt River, which far-fetched optimists predicted would be navigable in the near future; but their family's journey this time would produce a legacy more impressive than all their schemes for wealth and status combined. Along the way, John Marshall and Jane Lampton Clemens conceived their sixth child. At his birth, on 30 November 1835, they named him Samuel, after his grandfather, and Langhorne, purportedly to honor an old-time Virginia friend.

The Clemenses lived–Sam, born prematurely, in precarious health–in Florida for four years. Then the cycle of movement-enthusiasm-disillusionment-movement uprooted them and sent them to the edge of the Mississippi, to Hannibal, thirty miles away. There young Sam spent his youth, living and absorbing the childhood memories that have become a part of American legend and folklore.

His rudimentary formal education lasted only until 1847, when his father died, leaving the family nearly destitute. John Marshall Clemens's steady procession of business failures and the family's frequent moves from house to house in Hannibal undoubtedly impressed upon Sam the goading obsession for success and conspicuous consumption that marked his own mature years.

In addition to his schooling Sam's education continued in the woods outside Hannibal, on the

Clemens as a fifteen-year-old printer's devil (courtesy Mark Twain Papers, The Bancroft Library)

Mississippi River which served as a dangerous playground for the boys of the town, and at his uncle's farm back in Florida, Missouri, where Sam spent most of his summers. Hannibal was a mixture of slaveholding outpost, frontier jumping-off point, and orthodox Calvinist bastion, and infused with the idyllic, pastoral, carefree world he recollected in *The Adventures of Tom Sawyer* (1876) was a layer of violence, horror, and inhumanity that surfaced in his writing only in his middle and old age.

From 1847 until 1853 Sam Clemens served as apprentice and typesetter for various Hannibal newspapers, finally ending up as assistant to his brother, Orion, whose failures were as persistent as John Marshall's. As Orion bankrupted journalism along the Mississippi–with his ownership of the *Hannibal Western Union* and *Journal*, the *Muscatine Journal*, and the *Keokuk Daily Post*–Sam absorbed that brand of frontier humor called the humor of the Old Southwest, a staple as filler for small newspapers along the river. Sam's own first, inept, comic story, "The Dandy Frightening the Squatter," an amateurish version of such humor, appeared in the *Carpet-Bag* in May 1852.

In 1853 Sam Clemens, not yet eighteen, broke loose from the family ties that Jane Clemens struggled to preserve. That year he went to

St. Louis, New York, and Philadelphia; in 1854 he visited Washington, D.C.; in 1855 and 1856 he lived in St. Louis; and in 1857 he lived briefly in Cincinnati. He recorded his compulsive wanderings in travel letters, which Orion published in whatever newspaper he owned at the time.

In April 1857 Sam boarded the *Paul Jones* in Cincinnati, bound for New Orleans as the first stop on a trip up the Amazon to make a fortune growing cocoa, as he later exaggerated. On the way to New Orleans, however, the pilot, Horace Bixby, agreed to take Clemens on as a cub pilot, the profession he later called the "one permanent ambition among my comrades in our village." His apprenticeship to Bixby marked the end of his youthful vagabondage and completed the phase of his life that was later to be transformed into *The Adventures of Tom Sawyer, The Adventures of Huckleberry Finn* (1884), and some of the most poignant recollections in *Mark Twain's Autobiography* (1924).

For almost two years Clemens served as Bixby's "cub," receiving his own license in April 1859 and becoming a pilot, the "only unfettered and entirely independent human being that lived in the earth." Until the outbreak of the Civil War and the closing of the Mississippi River traffic, Clemens wallowed in his prestige, conspicuousness, and grandeur. The only tragedy that interrupted his idyll was the death of his younger brother Henry (fictionalized as Sid in *Tom Sawyer*) in the explosion of the *Pennsylvania*–a death for which Sam was to hold himself responsible for the rest of his life because he had secured his younger brother's passage on the ship.

His profession as effectively closed to him by the war as the river was, Clemens briefly joined an irregular band of Confederate sympathizers who skylarked around the rural surroundings of Hannibal, trying unconvincingly to look like soldiers. Years later Mark Twain was to boast, "I was a *soldier* two weeks once in the beginning of the war, and was hunted like a rat the whole time.... My splendid Kipling himself hasn't a more burnt-in, hard-baked and unforgettable familiarity with that death-on-the-pale-horse-with-hell-following-after which is a raw soldier's first fortnight in the field." But that was embroidery for an escapade (as he described it in "The Private History of a Campaign that Failed," *Century*, December 1885) that was closer to one of Tom Sawyer's "adventures."

Orion Clemens meanwhile had received an appointment as secretary to the governor of the Territory of Nevada but was, embarrassingly but predictably, unable to pay his passage on the overland stage to claim his position. With money from Sam Clemens, the two left St. Joseph, Missouri, on 26 July 1861, headed for Carson City, Nevada. Twenty days later Orion claimed his sinecure and Sam went off, as he later described the opportunities in *Roughing It*, to "maybe go out of an afternoon . . . and pick up two or three pailfuls of shining slugs, and nuggets of gold and silver on the hillside." For a year he tried to cash in on the speculation fever in silver, sending some humorous correspondence to the *Virginia City Territorial Enterprise* for comic relief. In August 1862 he joined the staff of that paper and for two years contributed both "straight" reporting and Far-West humor, wildly improbable hoaxes and burlesque assaults on competing reporters, to its pages. On 2 February 1863 he employed the pseudonym Mark Twain for the first time on one of his contributions.

Virginia City was a boom town, raw and raucous; its first twenty-six graves, Mark Twain was later to claim, were those of murdered men. Its life-style, like its humor, tended to violence, insult, and aggression. Though he was making a name in the Far West as a humorist, Mark Twain overstepped even the liberal tolerance of Virginia City when he accused the wife of the editor of a rival newspaper of collecting money for a society to promote miscegenation. In a town strongly Union in its sympathies during the Civil War, it is no surprise that the husband of the outraged wife challenged Mark Twain to a duel.

Clemens took the stage for San Francisco to avoid the duel and became affiliated with a number of newspapers and magazines on the Pacific Coast. He contributed sketches to the *Golden Era*, the *California*, the *San Francisco Call*, the *Sacramento Union*, and the *Alta California* for two and a half years, from mid 1864 to the end of 1866. Association with Bret Harte and Charles H. Webb during this time helped school him in the art of literary burlesque. Mixed with the humor there was also sufficient moral indignation and editorial outrage that Mark Twain became known as the "Moralist of the Pacific Slope." In late 1864 his attacks on the San Francisco police department produced a libel suit and another hurried departure–this time a three-month vacation at Jackass Hill and Angel's Camp in the California Sierras, which Walter Blair has called "a turning point in the author's career." Between early December and late February 1865 he spent his time pocket mining (seeking small hordes of pure gold, as he describes it in chapter 40 of *Roughing It*) and listening to two raconteurs who wove yarns about a frog filled with shot, a bluejay who tried to fill a cabin with acorns, a cat blown up in an explosion.

Returning to San Francisco after the police had found other diversions, Clemens found a letter from Charles Farrar Browne, the United States' most popular humorist, who wrote under the pen name Artemus Ward and who had spent a riotously liquid three weeks with Mark Twain in Virginia City back in December 1863. The letter requested a contribution for a book of humor; Mark Twain wrote up the story of the frog stuffed with bird shot, "Jim Smiley and His Jumping Frog," later retitled "The Celebrated Jumping Frog of Calaveras County." It arrived on the East Coast too late for inclusion in Ward's book, but it appeared in the *New York Saturday Press* on 18 November 1865 and two years later would be published by Charles Webb as the title piece in Mark Twain's first book, *The Celebrated Jumping Frog of Calaveras County, and Other Sketches* (1867).

The story was an immediate success, and it stretched the western humorist's name and reputation across the continent. Complexly narrated to a humorless listener by a humorless tale teller, the story typified Mark Twain's later dictum that "the humorous story may be spun out to great length, and may wander around as much as it pleases, and arrive nowhere in particular.... The humorous story is told gravely; the teller does his best to conceal the fact that he even dimly suspects that there is anything funny about it."

The following spring the *Sacramento Union* commissioned Clemens to sail for the Sandwich Islands (as the Hawaiian Islands were then called) and to write a series of travel letters from there for the paper. The humorist left San Francisco on 7 March 1866 and remained in the Sandwich Islands for four months. His letters back to the West Coast combined factual and informative writing with the raucous humor his audience expected of him. They also exploited, for the first extended period, the comic contrast between two fictional characters, Mark Twain and Mr. Brown. The Mark Twain character was a sentimentalist and an idealist who went into raptures over the picturesque beauties of the islands; Mr. Brown was a practical, semiliterate vulgarian who undercut Mark Twain's highfalutin rhapsodies by uncouth,

but realistic, evaluations of the identical object. The formula worked so effectively that Mark Twain was to employ it for two more series of travel letters and to continue to use it, with significant modulations, for the rest of his career.

In December 1866, commissioned by the *Alta California* to continue a travel-letter correspondence, Clemens left San Francisco for New York, sailing down the West Coast to Nicaragua, crossing the isthmus, sailing up the Atlantic Coast to New York, and sending twenty-six letters, later collected as *Mark Twain's Travels With Mr. Brown* (1940), back to the *Alta*. Although he was to send another set of letters to the *Alta*, Clemens's departure from San Francisco marked the end of his apprenticeship and symbolized his turning from the wild and extravagant humor of the West to a mode that would capture a national audience.

His background, training, and instinct through the first fifteen years of his writing career made the frontier tradition of humor natural. Vigorous, "masculine" stories, burlesques of wild invention and, quite often, off-color hue, verbal gymnastics which exploited quick laughs by punning and wordplay were his main stock-in-trade. In later years he would call "The Celebrated Jumping Frog of Calaveras County" a villainous backwoods sketch and refer to his letters to the *Alta* as "those wretched, slangy sketches." But when he decided, as he told Orion Clemens on 19 October 1865, that he "had a 'call' to literature, of a low order–*i.e.* humorous," he was already well on his way in exploiting a mode of humor that was realistic in its overtones; as a newspaperman, he was required to report as objectively as possible the mundane world around him; as a travel writer, his function, in part, was to render the unusual in terms which would reproduce an accurate image in his audience's imagination; and as a westerner, he saw a world in which violence determined fate and the frustration of ambitions and goals was more frequent than their realization.

In New York Clemens heard of the impending "pleasure excursion" of the *Quaker City* to Europe and the Holy Land and persuaded the editors of the *Alta* to advance his $1,250 passage in return for a continued series of travel letters. The trip, which Mark Twain was later to call "a funeral excursion without a corpse," was his extended introduction to eastern gentility, sobriety, and decorum; Henry Ward Beecher, the pastor of one of the largest Protestant congregations in the United States, had to back out of the trip, but his spirit was on board. When this excursion was over, Mark Twain wrote for the *New York Tribune*, "The venerable excursionists were not gay and frisky. They played no blindman's buff; they dealt not in whist; they shirked not the irksome journal, for alas! most of them were even writing books. They never romped, they talked but little, they never sang, save in the nightly prayer-meeting. . . . A free, hearty laugh was a sound that was not heard oftener than once in seven days about those decks or in those cabins, and when it was heard it met with precious little sympathy." Nevertheless, Mark Twain joined the mourners and sailed on 8 June 1867 for a five-month sentence in their midst.

Almost immediately he gravitated toward the lunatic fringe on board, a group whose irreverence and devilry matched his own. Delighted to shock the "Pilgrims," as he was later to call the more sedate passengers, the iconoclasts were a slightly older version of Tom Sawyer's gang. They played practical jokes on guides throughout Europe, scoffed at the artifacts of the Old World and its culture, and refused proper reverence at the sacred locations in the Holy Land. Throughout this trip Mark Twain sent his vivid and mocking letters back to the *Alta* and the *New York Tribune*, restrained only by the occasional admonitions of Mary Mason Fairbanks, wife of the owner of the *Cleveland Herald*, and at least briefly Mark Twain's monitor of gentility and propriety.

As he made his way through France, Italy, and the Holy Land, he befriended Charles Langdon, the young and pampered son and heir of Jervis Langdon, a wealthy Elmira, New York, coal magnate. In Charlie's cabin, probably while the *Quaker City* was anchored in the Bay of Smyrna, Clemens spotted a cameo portrait of the young man's older sister, Olivia; and, as legend would have it, he fell immediately in love with the likeness. He was to meet Olivia during that Christmas season of 1867, court her through the end of the decade, and marry her on 2 February 1870.

Meanwhile his career as a newspaper humorist flourished after the return of the *Quaker City*; he contributed humorous articles to newspapers and magazines; he mounted two lecture campaigns during the 1868-1869 and 1869-1870 seasons; and he accepted an offer from Elisha Bliss, of the American Publishing Company in Hartford, Connecticut, to edit his *Quaker City* letters for publication as a subscription book.

The revising, with one eye on a national rather than a western audience and the other on the standards of propriety and decorum that both "Mother" Fairbanks and the Langdon family felt Clemens lacked, attempted to clean up what the humorist himself called "wretched, slangy letters." He added new material that accounted for almost half the published book, eliminated allusions to western personalities and places, removed Mr. Brown as his straight man, but gave some of his lines to other characters, and deleted the coarsest elements of the humor.

The result was an uneven, though still lively, book, with passages of imaginative genius that did much to make up for other passages of tedious statistics and "borrowings" from other travel writers. The many "poses" of its narrator swing from straight, almost "guidebook" description to vitriolic ridicule of the other passengers' "Christian" piety and caustic remarks about American tourists' adulation of European culture, to low comedy and broad burlesque, to humorous anecdote, to purple-prosed reverence before the Sphinx. For many it provided a fresh, new, irreverent look at Europe's tourist attractions. From another point of view it might also be regarded as a case study of a group to become known in the twentieth century as "ugly Americans."

Fortunately, but coincidentally, the audience, which was to make *The Innocents Abroad* a best-seller when it appeared in July 1869, was unconcerned with literary unity or consistency. The American Publishing Company was one, probably the best, of a new kind of publisher which flourished in the three decades after the Civil War. Using veterans as door-to-door salesmen, subscription-book publishers reached a readership for whom a bookstore was unavailable. Late in his life Clemens was to call this audience his "submerged clientele." Bibles and bible commentary, medical and self-help volumes, and Civil War memoirs were their stock-in-trade; but Bliss was convinced that the humor of a Mark Twain would also appeal and sell to the rural and small-town, middle-class audience who were his customers. He was correct; *The Innocents Abroad* sold almost seventy thousand copies in its first year, a record which Mark Twain boasted only *Uncle Tom's Cabin* had beaten.

Still, he considered himself a newspaper humorist rather than an author of books. And after his marriage he and Olivia Clemens moved to Buffalo, New York, where he had purchased a part ownership of the *Express* with money borrowed from his father-in-law. The first few years of the marriage were turbulent ones: his father-in-law died on 6 August 1870; Olivia gave birth prematurely to their son, Langdon, on 7 November; and Mark Twain's writing schedule was a hectic and frenzied one. He wrote columns for the *Buffalo Express*, edited one called "Memoranda" for the monthly magazine the *Galaxy*, and began piecing together the recollections and earlier writings which would become his second book, *Roughing It*, in 1872. In addition he confronted, for the first time in his life, an eastern gentility and decorum which were foreign to his own personality and background.

The Langdons were impressively wealthy, and their standards of propriety were ones which fitted Samuel Clemens uncomfortably. Olivia served as arbiter of taste for his writings throughout most of her life, with Clemens voluntarily seeking her advice and accepting practically all of her suggestions. Her own standards of refinement were enforced in October 1871 when the family moved to Hartford, Connecticut, a stronghold of literary conservatism. Harriet Beecher Stowe and Charles Dudley Warner became neighbors when the Clemenses built their spectacular home on Farmington Avenue in 1874, and William Dean Howells, the editor of the *Atlantic Monthly*, became Clemens's closest friend and literary adviser.

Roughing It appeared from the American Publishing Company's presses in early 1872; and, although it was not the commercial success which *The Innocents Abroad* had been, it marked a significant advance in Mark Twain's literary artistry. He succeeded in adapting the Mark Twain and Mr. Brown dichotomy by having the narrator of *Roughing It* begin as a naive, childish sentimentalist who undergoes an initiation into western and pragmatic ways so that he becomes a wise insider in Nevada culture as the book progresses. As he loses his illusions about silver mining, the Indians, and instant wealth, he becomes a realist about the world in which he lives. That education process was to serve him in most of his later fiction: the cub pilot of "Old Times on the Mississippi," Tom Sawyer, Huckleberry Finn, David "Pudd'nhead" Wilson, and a host of characters in shorter works all begin as "outsiders" and attempt with varying degrees of success to come to terms with a society in which they were originally misfits.

But the book was significantly flawed. Still unable to compose a long narrative with consistency, Mark Twain used old articles from the *Territorial Enterprise* and the *Sacramento Union* to pad out the manuscript to the required length. He embedded anecdotes that rank with his best fiction– "The Mexican Plug," "Bemis and the Bull," "Buck Fanshaw's Funeral," and "Grandfather's Old Ram," for instance–in his book. And he showed, at least briefly, the seamier side of frontier egalitarianism in rigged juries, violence, and rampant speculation.

The Hartford years lasted into the early 1890s, and at first they were idyllic. Langdon's death in 1872 marred an otherwise pleasant domestic scene. Susy was born in 1872, Clara in 1874, and Jean Clemens in 1880. The family summered at Quarry Farm in Elmira, New York, when they were not on trips to Europe. They entertained sumptuously and lived ostentatiously. And Clemens lectured frequently as Mark Twain, and even tried his hand (usually with disastrous results) at writing drama.

His books, always published by the subscription method, poured forth throughout the 1870s: after *Roughing It*, *The Gilded Age: A Tale of Today* in 1873, written in collaboration with his neighbor, Charles Dudley Warner; *Mark Twain's Sketches, New and Old* in 1875; *The Adventures of Tom Sawyer* in 1876; and *A Tramp Abroad* in 1880. He broke into the prestigious *Atlantic Monthly* with "A True Story" in November 1874, following it in 1875 with the series "Old Times on the Mississippi" in seven installments (which became chapters 4 through 15 of *Life on the Mississippi*). These were first collected in an unauthorized Canadian edition which appeared in 1876.

He wrote for a variety of different audiences, and occasionally he made mistakes about them. *The Gilded Age* was one of the earliest uses of the novel in America for political satire. Mark Twain's share of the loosely joined plots brought Col. Beriah Sellers, the ineffectual but constantly optimistic speculator, to life. It included thinly disguised portraits of corrupt senators and representatives, lobbyists, and cabinet members, all of whom Mark Twain expected his audience to recognize. It exposed corruption and greed tainting the nucleus of American government with the firsthand knowledge its author had gained from his own experience in Washington. But it contained chapter mottoes, written by the Hartford savant James Hammond Trumbull, which were pedantic in their display of esoteric and erudite language–inappropriate to his "submerged," middle-class audience.

Both *The Adventures of Tom Sawyer* and "Old Times on the Mississippi" represented an attempt to cultivate the genteel, eastern-seaboard audience currently enthralled by local-color fiction. The "acceptable" literary magazines of the 1870s (and later) wallowed in sentimentality, nostalgia, and pathos brought on–as they believed–by the disappearance of regional distinctions and quirks as a result of the Civil War. By reverting to his own childhood in antebellum Missouri, Mark Twain joined the tidal wave of reminiscers who chose the good old days for their subject. The cub pilot of "Old Times on the Mississippi" was made deliberately younger, more childlike, less perceptive than Clemens had been when he began his course of instruction, perhaps so that he might ignore some of the vulgar realities of steamboat life. But he captured the flavor of the river, however muted and selected he filtered it, with relentless accuracy. The challenge of memorizing the river, both ways, in dark and daylight, in high water and low, with the realization that channels changed, "points" shifted, sandbars built up, landmarks disappeared between trips, was the basic theme of the articles; and Mark Twain achieved his goal so impressively that Howells said, "It almost made the water in our ice-pitcher muddy."

Tom Sawyer was also aimed at the local-color audience, even though it was sold by subscription. Uncertain whether it should be aimed at a youthful or an adult audience, Mark Twain once more submerged in shadow the realistic aspects of puberty, removing portions of the book which might offend younger readers. Like the cub in "Old Times on the Mississippi" Tom undergoes an initiation, learning to act maturely and to gain the adulation of the grown-ups in St. Petersburg. As he takes Becky's punishment, testifies at Injun Joe's trial, saves Becky in the cave, he moves into society rather than out of it. His wealth makes him prominent; his antics, like returning to town in the middle of his own funeral, relieve the boredom of village life; and his rebellions from conformity have none of the subversive quality Huck's were to show just a few years later. Tom is a conformist pretending to be a rebel, with one eye closely on the limits which his society would permit for token assaults on its institutions.

While writing his book, Mark Twain debated about taking Tom into adulthood (to his mid forties, according to one note), but he decided, as he told Howells, that the protagonist of such a novel should not be "Tom Sawyer–he

would not be a good character for it." Perhaps Mark Twain realized that Tom was too socially oriented, too other-directed to accomplish the goals which the author's increasingly pessimistic philosophy required. Clemens had discovered W. E. H. Lecky's *History of European Morals from Augustus to Charlemagne* (1869) in the early 1870s, and it became a favorite whipping boy for his own thought. Lecky had proposed that morality was determined by either altruistic selflessness or by self-serving utilitarianism. Clemens denied the existence of the former and insisted–in a running battle he carried on in the margins of his copy of Lecky–that only the latter existed. Early in 1883 he would embody some of those ideas in a paper he read to a gathering of friends–ideas which he later developed in *What Is Man?* (1906). In a number of the lesser works of the 1870s, he also introduced serious concerns. Partly inspired by Lecky, he questioned human control over conscience in "Facts Concerning the Recent Carnival of Crime in Connecticut" (1876); and partly as a result of his several trips to England (1871-1873) and his resultant approval of the British system, he began questioning universal suffrage ("The Curious Republic of Gondour," 1875) and democracy itself ("The Great Revolution in Pitcairn," 1879).

While seeing *Tom Sawyer* through the press in the summer of 1876, he began work on what he told Howells was "Huck Finn's autobiography. I like it only tolerably well, as far as I have got, & may possibly pigeonhole or burn the MS when it is done" (9 August 1876). Fortunately, he chose pigeonholing and worked sporadically on his masterpiece for the following seven years.

Meanwhile, on 17 December 1877, he committed what he was later convinced was the greatest disgrace of his career. Invited to give an address at the dinner celebration of John Greenleaf Whittier's seventieth birthday, he seriously miscalculated his audience by offering a farcical anecdote about three tramps who invade a miner's cabin, announcing themselves as Ralph Waldo Emerson, Henry Wadsworth Longfellow, and Oliver Wendell Holmes. "Spouting" (and often misquoting) lines from the poetry of these Boston Brahmins, the vagrants eat the miner's food, drink his whiskey, and cheat at cards. Actually, the anecdote was meant to show the abashment of the narrator who was testing his own literary fame–"trying out the virtue of my nom de plume"–for when he informed the miner that his visitors were not really the poets whom all

America revered, the miner replied, "Ah, imposters were they? Are *you?*"

But apparently his audience was not ready for anything that even suggested ridicule of "the literary gods of New England." Later Clemens remembered (erroneously) that a stunned silence greeted the conclusion of his story. There was no doubt, however, that many of the listeners were uncomfortable. Moreover, within a few days a number of newspapers in New England and as far west as Cincinnati and Chicago harshly condemned his flippancy. Devastated, Clemens wrote abject letters of apology to Emerson, Longfellow, and Holmes, all of whom had been present during his speech.

Actually, the Whittier dinner speech might well be seen as signaling the end of the domination of American literature by the New England writers and the freeing of American literature from the restraints that Puritanism and Victorian insistence on "proper" subjects and styles of literature had imposed on it. As Clemens himself later admitted, it is a hilariously funny parody. But he felt humiliated by the reception, even suggesting to William Dean Howells that further publication of his work in the *Atlantic Monthly* might damage the magazine's reputation. Fortunately, Howells did not agree.

Nevertheless, the Whittier dinner was something of a "last straw" on the load of other exasperations and annoyances in the late 1870s, and within three months he fled with his family for a seventeen-month trip to Europe. From April 1878 to September 1879 Clemens wandered through the major cities of Europe–in Germany, Switzerland, and Italy. Of course, a third travel book was the expectation, and *A Tramp Abroad* was the result. Although less lively and energetic than *Innocents Abroad* or *Roughing It* and less profitable to its author, *A Tramp Abroad* was punctuated with such cameo masterpieces as "Baker's Blue-Jay Yarn," "The Awful German Language," and a recounting of a long and placid raft trip down the Neckar River, which has some obvious parallels to Huck's trip down the Mississippi.

Settled back in Hartford, Mark Twain worked on the manuscript which was to become *The Prince and the Pauper.* More important he also decided to become his own publisher and to secure the bulk of the profits from his books. Leaving the American Publishing Company, he set up a subscription-book department for the firm of James R. Osgood, publishing *The Prince and the Pauper* (which had already appeared in Canada

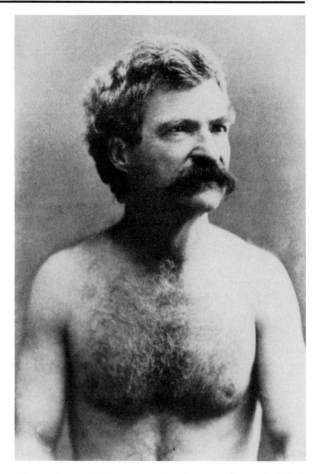

Clemens in an 1885 photograph taken to celebrate his fiftieth birthday and included in his letters to friends (Mark Twain Memorial, Hartford, Connecticut)

and Great Britain in 1881) with its imprint in 1882 and *Life on the Mississippi* in 1883. He secured the New York agency for *The Prince and the Pauper* for his nephew-in-law, Charles L. Webster, and after Osgood went bankrupt, established the subscription-book firm of Charles L. Webster and Company in the early 1880s.

Publishing his own books became only one of a number of extraliterary occupations. He invested in the Kaolatype, an engraving process, began copyrighting and manufacturing children's games, and in late 1881 he became almost obsessively concerned with speculation in the Paige typesetter, an invention in which he was ultimately to invest almost three hundred thousand dollars. Other smaller investments also diverted his time and energy from literature and finally contributed to his bankruptcy in the Panic of 1893. Clemens's mania for speculation and get-rich-quick schemes was an integral part of his personality; so was its predictable corollary, threats of litigation and actual lawsuits against his part-

ners, his competitors, and anyone whom he suspected of cheating him. (It is probably no coincidence that so many of his books use courtroom
scenes and trials for their climaxes.)

His life throughout the 1880s was frenetic.
The Prince and the Pauper appealed to his genteel
audience as an elegant costume piece; but its archaic language, its contrived plot, and its lack of
the anticipated humor defeated it with the subscription audience. Only its satire directed at
legal abuses and its basic plot of mixed identities
command critical attention. Its failure was financial as well as literary.

Life on the Mississippi (1883) fared little better. Clemens took his old *Atlantic Monthly* articles,
"Old Times on the Mississippi," and expanded
them with firsthand reports of the river from a
trip there in 1882. Although the "Old Times" portion involving the cub pilots' learning the river is
more vivid than the later one, *Life on the Mississippi* is an important document, not only in the development of Mark Twain's ideas but in its
depiction of a time that has vanished. Any historian of the Mississippi River should find it indispensable.

For an author who was financing his wildcat
speculations and inventions with anticipated royalties, however, the lack of sales was a disaster. So
Clemens drafted Webster to head a new publishing company, in addition to an overwhelming list
of other chores and duties, and to publish the
American edition of *The Adventures of Huckleberry
Finn.*

The book had moved slowly to its completion. The first four hundred pages had been the
overflow of enthusiasm and energy from *Tom Sawyer,* in 1876. Twain added more chapters in 1879
or 1880, and in 1883, after the river trip, he
wrote the latter half of the novel. The story of
Huck and Jim's raft trip down the Mississippi toward "freedom" has become so imbedded in the
American imagination that it is disconcerting to
the modern reader to realize that its composition
was haphazard, its immediate reception hostile,
and its recognition as a masterpiece delayed until
the twentieth century. Ernest Hemingway's famous judgment that all American literature begins with *Huckleberry Finn* is a relatively recent
one (*The Green Hills of Africa,* 1935).

The opening and concluding chapters of
the novel are burlesque in their main action;
Tom plays the superior, informed romantic who,
in both sections, manipulates Huck into following
his suggestions. It is only when Huck, isolated

from Tom, goes to Jackson's Island, meets Jim,
and heads south on the Mississippi that the book
takes on its serious meaning. Huck and Jim's
search for freedom becomes increasingly somber
and increasingly ominous as they head helplessly
in the exact opposite direction from their goal,
controlled by the flow of the Mississippi until
they can head north only after reaching the Ohio
River at Cairo, Illinois. Moving deeper and
deeper into slave territory, they encounter increasing violence and treachery. Their isolation is violated by the King and Duke, as the raft is com-
mandeered; and Huck's vision of human cruelty
increases as he visits the towns on shore. Mark
Twain used the linear structure of his novel, as
Huck and Jim follow the course of the Mississippi in a straight descending line, to present a
stinging satire not only of the South but of
human nature in general. The characters of the
bogus King and Duke, Colonel Sherburn, the
Grangerford family, the citizens of Bricksville
and of the Wilkses' town, the Phelpses and their
neighbors are not only a panoramic cross section
of the South; their meanness, greed, and violence are universal human traits. In his speech
on mob behavior and human behavior, Colonel
Sherburn condemns "the average all around,"
not merely the southerner; and Huck universa-
lizes that "human beings can be awful cruel."

Beneath the surface conflicts of freedom versus slavery, *Huckleberry Finn* explores whether
any human being can transcend his society, vio-
late his training, and achieve independence from
external pressure and judgment. In his later
years Mark Twain **was** to decide insistently that
he could not. But in *Huckleberry Finn* the issue is
more complex. Huck has wrestled with his conscience three times in the novel, trying to decide
whether to help Jim escape: on Jackson's Island
he concludes that he can help Jim because no
one in St. Petersburg will know about his action;
when he encounters the slave hunters, in chapter
16, he makes an argument on the basis of
expediency—"What's the use you learning to do
right, when it's troublesome to do right and ain't
no trouble to do wrong, and the wages was just
the same." In his final debate with his conscience,
in chapter 31, he must confront the theological implications of his decision . . . damnation. He decides to "go to hell" rather than turn Jim in. As
readers we cheer Huck's ability to loose the shack-
les of convention and conformity.

But the final chapters seem anticlimactic to
many readers. Huck allows Tom to orchestrate

Jim's escape, letting Tom delay it too long with his ornate and ridiculously embellished plans, without protesting Tom's silliness. Huck appears to descend from the height he had reached in chapter 31, allowing Tom to usurp his own role as Jim's liberator. Discovering that Tom knew Jim was "free" all along reduces him and his thrill-seeking even further in readers' estimations.

Much of the continuing critical debate about the final chapters and the ultimate meaning of the novel is a result of Mark Twain's strategy in allowing Huck to narrate his own novel. Huck is not an abstract reasoner; he lacks critical judgment. He admires, for instance, the Grangerfords' house and Emmeline's sentimental poetry, and he fails to perceive the irony in Pap's speech about the "gov'ment." As a result, readers pierce through Huck's literal descriptions and discern a number of value judgments that Huck himself does not make. We hear Mark Twain's voice beneath Huck's and perhaps, with the benefit of that double vision, yearn for more heroism than Huck can possibly achieve.

Contemporary reaction was microscopically small and almost entirely negative. Louisa May Alcott is reported to have decided that "if Mr. Clemens cannot think of something better to tell our pure-minded lads and lasses, he had best stop writing for them." *Life* magazine also condemned it as unsuitable reading for children. The Concord, Massachusetts, public library set the precedent which continues sporadically to the present of banning it from the shelves. Brander Matthews praised it in the London *Saturday Review*, and T. S. Perry was ultimately favorable in the *Century*, but theirs were minority reports.

Fortunately, another book diverted Clemens from concern about his own novel. Former President Ulysses S. Grant, dying of throat cancer, finally agreed to allow Charles L. Webster and Company to publish his *Personal Memoirs* by subscription. The country, knowing of his condition, subscribed for over three hundred thousand volumes of his autobiography; and the Webster marketing apparatus was strained almost to the point of rupture to produce and sell the book. After Grant's death, Clemens delivered to his widow a royalty check for two hundred thousand dollars, which he boasted was the largest one ever paid an author.

But the publishing company had established a network of agents which it was never able to use again. Webster and Clemens began a prodigal publishing campaign, publishing the autobiog-

raphies of other Civil War generals, a biography of Pope Leo XIII, and similar volumes which never managed to attract a fraction of the market Grant's volumes had. In the late 1880s the company was financially overextended and heading precipitously for serious danger.

Before the catastrophe occurred, however, Mark Twain embarked on another important literary project. One of the many influences which inspired it was his anger at Matthew Arnold's supercilious review of Grant's book. But the attack on British monarchy, aristocracy, and the established church, which *A Connecticut Yankee in King Arthur's Court* (1889) ultimately embodied, resulted primarily from a growing sense of the continued presence of social and political oppression into his own day.

The novel did not start out that seriously. The idea had occurred to Mark Twain in December 1884, and he recorded in his notebook, "Dream of being a knight errant in armor in the middle ages." The "dream" was to embody a light-hearted burlesque of the difficulties a modern man would encounter in medieval England. As he worked on the novel over the next four years, however, the tone and theme of the work was to change from lighthearted burlesque to slashing satire.

Hank Morgan, a foreman in the Colt Firearms Factory in Hartford, has been hit in the head during a fight and awakens in sixth-century England at King Arthur's court. With his common sense, inventiveness, and practical knowledge, he sets out to enlighten the kingdom, with its superstitiousness and ignorance most fully embodied in Merlin. Hank strings telephone lines, establishes a newspaper, uses gunpowder and lightning rods to create explosive "miracles." But these trappings of civilization from the nineteenth century eventually become destructive rather than beneficial. Hank's own actions become more and more despotic rather than humanitarian, and his attitude toward the common men of King Arthur's realm, increasingly inhumane. Finally, as a result of manipulations on the stock market which Hank has created, the nation rises against him. At the end of the book he and fifty-two boys destroy twenty-five thousand knights with dynamite, electrified barbed wire, and Gatling guns. Merlin puts Hank in a trance, and he awakens back in the nineteenth century, with "an abyss of thirteen centuries yawning between me and . . . all that is dear to me, all that could make life worth the living!"

On the surface Hank is Mark Twain's spokesman for democracy in preference to monarchy, freedom in preference to servitude and the caste system, a free economy in preference to a controlled one. Indeed, he wanted a twenty-five-cent version of the novel to circulate among the working men in the new labor unions forming in the United States. But beneath that chauvinism there is another message that questions technology and the machine civilization of the late nineteenth century, that confronts the dangers of absolute power, and that ponders whether human beings can ever be enlightened or altered by education.

A Connecticut Yankee in King Arthur's Court infuriated the British; his English publisher even asked for permission to censor some of the more inflammatory passages in the London edition. And even though he refused permission, Mark Twain wrote a curious letter to distinguished English critic Andrew Lang in defense of his novel. He insisted that his audience was not the cultivated reading public but what he called "the Belly and Members" section of society. "I have never tried," he went on, "in even one single little instance to help cultivate the cultivated classes. I was not equipped for it, either by native gifts or training. And I never had any ambition in that direction, but always hunted for bigger game—the masses. I have seldom deliberately tried to instruct them but have done my best to entertain them.... My audience is dumb, it has no voice in print, and so I cannot know whether I have won its approbation or only got its censure." No matter how self-serving that description sounds, it does mark off the major audience for Mark Twain's books.

Neither *A Connecticut Yankee* nor the sumptuous, multivolume Library of American Literature which Webster was publishing on the installment plan produced the revenue necessary to keep the firm afloat. In February 1888 after a series of bitter accusations and recriminations, the ailing Charles L. Webster was replaced as head of the company which bore his name by Fred J. Hall, who managed to keep the foundering organization afloat for five more years, but only by borrowing larger and larger amounts of money from the banks. The Paige typesetter drained funds like an enormous brass leech.

Both of the Clemenses were suffering from rheumatism, and Olivia Clemens had a heart condition, which convinced them that it would be both beneficial and economical to close the Hartford house and spend some time in European health spas. On 6 June 1891 the family left the United States, embarking on a nightmare that was to end only with their deaths and closing the doors of the Hartford residence for what would be the last time as residents.

Throughout the early 1890s, while the girls and their mother lived on the eastern side of the Atlantic, Clemens made frenzied and frequent trips across the ocean to bolster his failing financial condition. His frantic hopscotching was futile: in the depths of the Panic of 1893-1894, Charles L. Webster and Company declared bankruptcy (on 18 April 1894). Eight months later the typesetter failed its trial run and no capital was available for further manufacture. Just turned sixty, Clemens was virtually penniless.

He had just one possible source of substantial revenue—a manuscript for a subscription book on which he had been working for the several years he was in Europe—*The Tragedy of Pudd'nhead Wilson*. Since Webster was bankrupt, Clemens returned to the American Publishing Company with his new volume, and in November 1894 that publisher published the novel together with its burlesque counterpart, *The Comedy of Those Extraordinary Twins*.

After contemplating black slavery in *Huckleberry Finn* and universal slavery to convention and training in *A Connecticut Yankee*, Clemens chose to return to the antebellum South in *Pudd'nhead Wilson*. There a young lawyer, relegated to the status of "pudd'nhead" because of a chance remark he makes when he disembarks at Dawson's Landing, Arkansas, spends most of the next two decades collecting fingerprints of all the residents of the town. Meanwhile, Roxy, a "black" slave whose skin is white and whose eyes are blue, has exchanged her baby with her owner's shortly after their births. As the plot unravels, Tom Driscoll (the black who has usurped the master's position) grows up as the petted heir of a Virginia lineage while Valet de Chambre (the white child relegated to slave status) matures in the slave quarters. Tom gambles, steals to pay his debts, and sells his own mother "down the river" in order to raise cash. Finally, he murders his "uncle" in order to raise cash. At the predictable trial scene Pudd'nhead Wilson uses his collection of fingerprints to reveal that Tom is in fact the slave and Valet the master. And therefore Tom, who was to be executed for murder, is now another man's property and is himself sold down river to settle his "uncle's" estate.

Beneath the contrivance and melodrama of the novel runs the darkest vein of Mark Twain's thought. Neither half of Dawson's Landing is in fact free. Both master and slave are conditioned by generations of slavery to accept white superiority and black inferiority. Even Roxy attributes Tom's inability to live up to his aristocratic expectations to his black blood: "Thirty-one parts o' you is white, an on'y one part nigger, an dat po' little one part is yo' *soul*." The entire town sees "blood" as determining human behavior and fate; but beneath the town's self-deception is Mark Twain's increasingly insistent belief that "training is everything." Not only does Tom revert to property but Valet, now a wealthy white aristocrat, "could neither read nor write, and his speech was the basest dialect of the negro quarter." Moreover, "His gait, his attitudes, his gestures, his bearing, his laugh—all were vulgar and uncouth; his manners were the manners of a slave. Money and fine clothes could not mend these defects or cover them up; they only made them the more glaring and the more pathetic. The poor fellow could not endure the terrors of the white man's parlor, and felt at home and at peace nowhere but in the kitchen. The family pew was a misery to him, yet he could nevermore enter into the solacing refuge of the 'nigger gallery'—that was closed to him for good and all." Most ironic, however, is Pudd'nhead Wilson's fate. It is he who revealed the truth about identity to the town, who should liberate it from its false standards. But he accepts its standards and is elected mayor of Dawson's Landing; "he was a made man for good." Like a series of transcendent strangers in Mark Twain's later works, he should strip the absurdities and vanities from human self-deception and reveal the truth about human character and motivation. Only in Pudd'nhead Wilson's Calendar," epigrams that open each chapter of the novel, does David Wilson reveal those thoughts:

Whoever has lived long enough to find out what life is, knows how deep a debt of gratitude we owe to Adam, the first great benefactor of our race. He brought death to the world.

....

Why is it that we rejoice at a birth and grieve at a funeral? It is because we are not the person involved.

....

All say, "How hard it is that we have to die"–a strange complaint to come from the mouths of people who have had to live.

....

If you pick up a starving dog and make him prosperous, he will not bite you. This is the principal difference between a dog and a man.

Perhaps it is no accident that the novel is called David Wilson's tragedy.

Clemens's own impending tragedies were soon to overshadow Pudd'nhead Wilson's, however. Since September 1893 he had placed almost all of his financial affairs in the capable hands of Henry Huttleston Rogers, a vice-president of Standard Oil and ultimately one of Clemens's closest friends during the last fifteen years of his life. Rogers negotiated the dissolution of the Paige typesetter agreement, arranged for the contracts for editions of Mark Twain's collected works, and oversaw the repayment of the Webster bankruptcy claimants. But Clemens's financial situation was still so complicated that debts, barely alleviated by the sales of *Pudd'nhead Wilson*, plagued both Clemenses. The family returned to the United States in May 1895 to deliver the manuscript of *Personal Recollections of Joan of Arc by the Sieur Louis de Conte* (1896), to deposit Jean and Susy at Quarry Farm, and to embark with Clara for an around-the-world lecture tour intended to get the family debt free.

Clemens, Olivia, and Clara sailed from Vancouver on 23 August 1895; he lectured in Australia, New Zealand, India, and South Africa to throngs of listeners. And when the family arrived in England on 31 July 1896, Mark Twain had materials for his final travel volume, *Following the Equator* (1897).

But the family received first a letter and then a cable advising that Susy was ill; Olivia and Clara boarded a ship for the United States, and while they were in mid ocean, on 15 August 1896, Susy died of meningitis. Clemens, alone in London, unable to reach the United States before the funeral, poured forth his grief and self-blame at having left Susy in the United States, at having separated Olivia from her, and at the loss of the family's "prodigy." The family, reunited in London after Susy's funeral, moved into deep mourning, not celebrating Thanksgiving or Christmas; only furious work on the travel book served, as he told Twichell, as "the 'surcease of sorrow' that is found there. I work all the days, and trouble vanishes away when I use that magic."

*Olivia and Samuel Clemens, circa 1900 (Yale
University Library)*

But additional tragedies were looming: in 1896, Jean's erratic behavior was diagnosed as epilepsy, and she was to undergo almost constant treatments until her death in 1909; Olivia's health, weakened by Susy's death and (Clemens insisted) the lecture tour, seemed fragile.

It is important to notice the elements of pessimism, determinism, and contempt for humanity that formed a part of Mark Twain's belief long before the domestic catastrophes occurred; it is equally important to be aware that the Clemens family was less the Victorian ideal than its head felt it necessary to describe for the public. Nevertheless, after the blows of the late 1890s, the string of pessimism that had been part of his nature all along deepened into an almost persistent misanthropy with fewer interludes of light comedy or optimism. Though he read none of the

major naturalists, his own instincts and beliefs began to parallel theirs. That man was a machine, without free will, whose behavior was determined by biology or environment or chance, incapable of altering his life's course, became Mark Twain's credo at the same time Crane, Dreiser, and Norris were proclaiming it.

Following the Equator was published by the American Publishing Company in November 1897 with a ten-thousand-dollar advance against sales (by the following March all the creditors' claims would be settled). Although, like his earlier travel volumes, this one was basically autobiographical, even it showed Mark Twain's increasing disillusionment with the human race. Attacking imperialism, colonialism, and the torture and exploitation of slave labor by rulers, he turned *Following the Equator*, probably the most un-

79

justifiably neglected of his works, into a preview of his condemnation of imperialism among the early-twentieth-century colonial nations in "To the Person Sitting in Darkness," *King Leopold's Soliloquy* (1905), and "The Czar's Soliloquy." Admittedly, the book is overly long, but it seethes with a sense of injustice and man's inhumanity to man that merits more attention than it has received.

Creditors paid off—Olivia read their letters of appreciation to Mark Twain for making good on his debts and, as Clemens reported to Rogers, experienced "the only really happy day she has had since Susy died"—the family moved to Vienna, and Mark Twain plunged into work on a number of significant manuscripts. Most of them were never finished, and only a few saw publication during his lifetime; but they marked a dramatic turn in the twilight decade of his literary career.

He had tried unsuccessfully to revive Tom Sawyer and Huck Finn in *Tom Sawyer Abroad* (1894) and *Tom Sawyer, Detective* (1896). In 1897 he attempted "Tom Sawyer's Conspiracy" and "Hellfire Hotchkiss" (not published until *Mark Twain's Hannibal, Huck, and Tom*, 1969, and *Mark Twain's Satires and Burlesques*, 1967), using his Hannibal childhood as the skeleton for the stories. In 1898 he attempted to write a Hannibal version of *The Mysterious Stranger* called "Schoolhouse Hill," with Tom and Huck as characters. But the charm, the magic, and the captivation of childhood in Hannibal were gone. Mark Twain wrote in his notebook as the epitaph for the creative inspiration he found in his boyhood,

> Huck comes back sixty years old, from nobody knows where—crazy. Thinks he is a boy again and scans always every face for Tom, Becky, etc.
>
> Tom comes at last from sixty years' wandering in the world and attends Huck and together they talk of old times; both are desolate, life has been a failure, all that was lovable, all that was beautiful is under the mold. They die together.

This plot outline was never converted into fiction. The one major accomplishment of 1898 was the bitter fable "The Man that Corrupted Hadleyburg," published in *Harper's Monthly* in December 1899.

In the summer of 1899 the family stayed in Sanna, Sweden, where Jean underwent treatments for her epilepsy; that winter they spent back in London. And on 15 October 1900 the fam-

ily returned to the United States—to a house in New York City rather than to Hartford. Mark Twain became a social butterfly and a political gadfly, attending banquets, giving after-dinner speeches, delighting in reporters' interviews, and speaking out frequently and forcefully against a wide range of injustices.

He assaulted Christian missionaries in China, the British role in the Boer War, American lynching, the United States' exploitation of the Philippines, King Leopold's butchery in the Belgian Congo, Czar Nicholas's depravity in Russia, New York City politicians, and Mary Baker Eddy's manipulation of Christian Science with particular venom and endurance (perhaps because he believed Susy might have been cured had she not been practicing Mental Science and refused the help of a physician). Between 1900 and 1907 he launched into polemics with equal energy and exhaustion. He even wrote against bullfighting (in *A Horse's Tale*, 1907) and vivisection (in *A Dog's Tale*, 1904).

The intellectual premises of his polemical writing contradicted the themes in his later, usually unfinished, fiction. In "The Chronicle of Young Satan" (written 1897-1900, but not published until 1969 in *Mark Twain's "Mysterious Stranger" Manuscripts*), *What Is Man?* (1906), *Letters from the Earth* (written in 1909, published in 1962), and "The Turning Point of My Life" (collected in *What Is Man? and Other Essays* in 1917) he repeated his refrain that human fate was outside the individual's control, that man was merely a machine, following the "law of his make." Neither blame nor praise, neither vices nor virtues were possible when the universe operated purely on biological law. Thus, in one of his voices and moods he criticized mankind, while in another he absolved it of any alternative and preferable behavior.

Another large body of manuscripts that remained unfinished and unpublished during Mark Twain's lifetime concerned the confusion of dream and reality. "Which Was the Dream?," "The Great Dark," and "No. 44, the Mysterious Stranger" all explored dream and waking selves to question whether external reality existed at all. In small part both this theme and the "man as machine" argument may have been devices for negating the tragedies for which Clemens felt guilty.

Those tragedies were not yet ended. On 12 August 1902 Olivia Clemens suffered a major illness; Clemens was not permitted to see her for long stretches of time—for three months, in late

Clemens at Oxford University, 26 June 1907, in procession to receive his honorary Doctor of Literature degree (Clara Clemens, My Father: Mark Twain, *1931)*

1902. As soon as she improved sufficiently, in the summer of 1903, the family traveled to Florence, Italy, where the climate might improve her health. There, in a sumptuous Villa di Quarto, she continued to fail and died on the evening of 5 June 1904. The remnants of the family returned to New York, Clara to a sanatorium, Clemens and Jean to a house on Fifth Avenue. There he brought to fruition a lifelong project, his autobiography.

Mark Twain had contemplated, and even written portions of, his autobiography earlier in his life; but in 1905 and 1906 (with less frequent additions from 1907 to 1909) he amassed a staggering amount of autobiographical materials. He proposed that, since he intended to withhold the book from publication until after his death, he could speak the absolute truth "as from the grave." Each day a stenographer would record his thoughts, which had no chronological sequence, type them, and have him proofread them. He wandered wherever his fancy led him:

"Start it at no particular time in your life; talk only about the thing which interests you for the moment; drop it the moment its interest threatens to pale, and turn your talk upon the new and more interesting thing that has intruded itself into your mind." This was his plan.

As a result the autobiographical dictations are impressively modern; almost like a patient on a couch talking to a psychiatrist rather than a stenographer, Mark Twain moved by free association, ignoring both chronology and cohesiveness, in order to record the biography of a personality, of a mind at work unrestricted by form. While certainly not the absolute truth he promised, the first several years of the autobiographical dictations capture more convincingly than any other document the spirit, the vanity, the viciousness, and the tenderness which were essential aspects of Mark Twain's personality.

In October 1906 Jean entered the first of a series of sanatoriums which were to separate her from her father for almost three years. Clara pursued a singing career with more perseverance than success. The daughters were replaced by a coterie of admirers–Albert Bigelow Paine, the official biographer; Isabel Lyon, personal secretary; and Ralph Ashcroft, business manager–who insulated Clemens as much as possible from the outside world, and who fought out internecine skirmishes for his attention. In 1907 Clemens was awarded the Litt.D. degree from Oxford University, which he traveled across the Atlantic to accept.

In June 1908 he moved from New York City to an ornate villa outside Redding, Connecticut, which he christened Stormfield after his story "Captain Stormfield's Visit to Heaven," an extract from which, published as a small book in 1909, had helped pay for the building. Jean joined him there in April 1909, and Clara married Ossip Gabrilowitsch there on 6 October 1909 and departed for Germany. On Christmas Eve morning 1909 Jean suffered an epileptic seizure in her bathtub and drowned. Too infirm to accompany the body to Elmira, Mark Twain wandered the huge, empty house, composing "The Death of Jean," which he considered the last chapter of his autobiography. A few days later he made one of the frequent trips of his last years to Hamilton, Bermuda, where he hoped the mild climate might alleviate his worsening angina. In April Paine received reports of his weakening condition, went to Bermuda, and accompanied Clemens back to Stormfield. There, just a few days after Clara and Gabrilowitsch arrived from Germany, Clemens died on 21 April 1910.

Mark Twain's unpublished literary legacy probably almost equaled the works published during his lifetime. Paine, as literary editor, carefully selected manuscripts–a scissors-and-paste version of *The Mysterious Stranger, a Romance* in 1916, two volumes of *Mark Twain's Letters* in 1917, *Europe and Elsewhere*–a collection of essays and sketches–and *Mark Twain's Speeches* in 1923, two volumes of *Mark Twain's Autobiography* in 1924, and a heavily abridged and edited *Mark Twain's Notebook* in 1935. Paine's successors Bernard DeVoto and Dixon Wecter published, along with various miscellaneous pieces, additional passages from the autobiography and several volumes of letters. And, beginning in 1967, under the successive editorships of Henry Nash Smith, Frederick Anderson, and Robert H. Hirst, the University of California Press is publishing the Mark Twain Papers, which will ultimately print all the previously unpublished material by the humorist. There is little chance, however, that the new documents and manuscripts will cause any significant change in Mark Twain's reputation and significance.

Though Mark Twain himself claimed that all of his writings were based on personal experience and several times declared that he knew little or nothing about books, he read widely, if haphazardly, not only in the histories, biographies, travels, and scientific works that he once admitted liking but also in the novels, poetry, and theology that he professed to abhor. Only relatively recently has the extent of his reading and of his debts to other writers been recognized.

Still, he was a unique American writer. His experiences ranged by good fortune through the exact events that captivated the American imagination–the river during the golden age, the Far West of its bonanza days, the first waves of middle-class American tourists to Europe, the mania for material wealth–conspicuous consumption, as Thorstein Veblen was to label it–of the last quarter of the nineteenth century. His chauvinistic pride in democracy and technology began to turn to shame as the United States became a fledgling superpower at the beginning of the twentieth century, as did the pride of many of his countrymen. Because he was a reasonably accurate barometer of their own sentiments and beliefs, he gained acceptance as the spokesman of the common man. And his major voice and prose style–vernacular, commonsensical, pragmatic–struck resonant echoes among his subscription audience. With a mixture of pride and wistfulness, he wrote in his notebook in 1886, "My books are water; those of the great geniuses are wine. Everybody drinks water."

He captured, with amazing fidelity, essential aspects of the American experience and the American stance. The adulation of a highly romanticized childhood, the compulsion of the westward migration, the persistence of the Horatio Alger myth of fame, wealth, and success as somehow synonymous: these he embodied in both his major literature and his spectacularly public life.

From his western background he learned the use of colloquial speech, an egalitarianism only occasionally tarnished by his doubts about human perfidy until his later years, and a love of the lusty, earthy facts of life which New England literature had struggled for a century to ignore. His journalism and his travel writings had compelled him to photographic detail and descriptive accuracy. His honesty–William Dean Howells said after Clemens's death, "At the last day he will not have to confess anything, for all his life was the free knowledge of any one who would ask him of it"–however filtered through Victorian convention, was resolute in every significant way–language, behavior, morality.

If he was a realist in his language and a naturalist in his final philosophy, he was also an archromantic. Neither Howells's smiling aspects of life nor Frank Norris's drama of a broken teacup is a part of Mark Twain's fiction. Wild coincidences (like Tom's unexpected arrival at the Phelps farm at the end of *Huckleberry Finn*), improbable changelings (Edward and Tom Canty in *The Prince and the Pauper*; Tom Driscoll and Valet de Chambre in *Pudd'nhead Wilson*), melodramatic courtroom climaxes, deus ex machina denouements (fingerprints in *Pudd'nhead Wilson*, Tom Sawyer's reappearance in *Huckleberry Finn*), supernatural visitors (in many of the later works), and dream visions (in *A Connecticut Yankee* and many of the unfinished fragments) are the stuff of pure romanticism.

His own personality was predominantly romantic, as well. He abided by most of the domestic conventions of his time; he paraded down Fifth Avenue in his old age in his white suit, simply for its shock value. He needed to be center-stage front in the drama he made of his own life. Perhaps his most endearing quality as a public performer who imposed himself indelibly as an American folk hero was the all-too-human frailty which he refused to camouflage.

His literature explored questions of freedom, independence, identity. In a steady evolution, he moved from the confidence and self-reliance of the brash westerner to the questioning and contradictory stance of the agnostic, until he could write in his notebook in the last years of the century, "The human race consists of the damned and the ought-to-be-damned." It could be argued that, almost singlehandedly, he liberated American fiction from the rigid conventions of the mid nineteenth century–its stilted dialogue, its stereotyped characters, its didactic impulse, its optimistic impetus. At the same time, he lowered American literature to the plane of the mass audience and elevated it to a distinct, indigenous height which no one else has reached.

Letters:

Mark Twain's Letters, 2 volumes, edited by Albert Bigelow Paine (New York: Harper, 1917);

Mark Twain the Letter Writer, edited by Cyril Clemens (Boston: Meador, 1932);

Mark Twain's Letters to Will Bowen, edited by Theodore Hornberger (Austin: University of Texas Press, 1941);

The Love Letters of Mark Twain, edited by Dixon Wecter (New York: Harper, 1949);

Mark Twain to Mrs. Fairbanks, edited by Wecter (San Marino: Huntington Library, 1949);

Mark Twain's Letters to Mary, edited by Lewis Leary (New York: Columbia University Press, 1961);

Mark Twain–Howells Letters, 2 volumes, edited by Henry Nash Smith and William M. Gibson (Cambridge: Harvard University Press, 1966);

Mark Twain's Letters to His Publishers, edited by Hamlin Hill (Berkeley: University of California Press, 1967);

Mark Twain's Correspondence with Henry Huttleston Rogers, edited by Leary (Berkeley: University of California Press, 1969);

Mark Twain's Letters, Volume 1, 1853-1866, edited by Edgar M. Branch, Michael B. Frank, and Kenneth M. Sanderson (Berkeley: University of California Press, 1988-).

Bibliographies:

Merle Johnson, *A Bibliography of the Works of Mark Twain*, revised and enlarged edition (New York & London: Harper, 1935);

Thomas Asa Tenney, *Mark Twain: A Reference Guide* (Boston: G. K. Hall, 1977);

Alan Gribben, "Removing Mark Twain's Mask: A Decade of Criticism and Scholarship," *ESQ: Journal of the American Renaissance*, 26 (1980): 100-108, 149-171;

William B. McBride, *Mark Twain: A Bibliography of the Collections of the Mark Twain Memorial and the Stowe-Day Foundation* (Hartford, Conn.: McBride, 1984).

Biographies:

Willian Dean Howells, *My Mark Twain* (New York & London: Harper, 1910);

Albert Bigelow Paine, *Mark Twain, A Biography*, 3 volumes (New York & London: Harper, 1912);

Minnie M. Brashear, *Mark Twain, Son of Missouri* (Chapel Hill: University of North Carolina Press, 1934);

Ivan Benson, *Mark Twain's Western Years* (Stanford: Stanford University Press, 1938);

DeLancey Ferguson, *Mark Twain: Man and Legend* (Indianapolis & New York: Bobbs-Merrill, 1943);

Kenneth Andrews, *Nook Farm: Mark Twain's Hartford Circle* (Cambridge: Harvard University Press, 1950);

Dixon Wecter, *Sam Clemens of Hannibal* (Boston: Houghton Mifflin, 1952);

Paul Fatout, *Mark Twain in Virginia City* (Bloomington: Indiana University Press, 1964);

Edith Colgate Salsbury, *Susy and Mark Twain* (New York: Harper & Row, 1965);

Justin Kaplan, *Mr. Clemens and Mark Twain* (New York: Simon & Schuster, 1966);

Hamlin Hill, *Mark Twain: God's Fool* (New York: Harper & Row, 1973);

Kenneth E. Eble, *Old Clemens and W. D. H.: The Story of a Remarkable Friendship* (Baton Rouge: University of Louisiana Press, 1985);

John Lauber, *The Making of Mark Twain: A Biography* (New York: American Heritage, 1985).

References:

Howard Baetzhold, *Mark Twain and John Bull* (Bloomington: Indiana University Press, 1970).

Charts the course of Mark Twain's love-hate relations with Britain, his acquaintance with British writers, both personal and literary, and their influence on his works, and also traces the development of his political, social, and philosophical ideas, particularly as influenced by British writers.

Gladys Bellamy, *Mark Twain as a Literary Artist* (Norman: University of Oklahoma Press, 1950).
The first full-length study of Mark Twain's literary artistry, still valuable.

Walter Blair, *Mark Twain & Huck Finn* (Berkeley: University of California Press, 1960).
The fullest and best study of the making of the novel and the influences–personal, social, literary, and philosophical–which helped to shape it.

Edgar M. Branch, *The Literary Apprenticeship of Mark Twain* (Urbana: University of Illinois Press, 1950).
Pioneer study, still extremely valuable, of Mark Twain's writings up through 1867 and their importance in his later development.

Van Wyck Brooks, *The Ordeal of Mark Twain* (New York: Dutton, 1923; revised, 1933).
Influential work which argues that Mark Twain's "later pessimism" and failure to achieve his full potential as artist and satirist resulted from the "repressions" of Victorian prudishness and the necessity to conform to the standards of a commercial and industrial America.

Louis J. Budd, *Mark Twain, Social Philosopher* (Bloomington: Indiana University Press, 1962).
The best study of Twain's political and social ideas and their influence on his works.

Budd, *Our Mark Twain: The Making of His Public Personality* (Philadelphia: University of Pennsylvania Press, 1983).
A stimulating account of the development of the public perception of Mark Twain as one of the best-known and -loved figures in our history, and of the part that the author himself played in the formation of that "image."

Bernard DeVoto, *Mark Twain's America* (Boston: Little, Brown, 1932).
Partly a response to Brooks, arguing that personal tragedies rather than Freudian repressions caused the "later pessimism," but also, although it neglects other significant influences, an important study of the influences of the frontier on Twain's works.

Everett Emerson, *The Authentic Mark Twain* (Philadelphia: University of Pennsylvania Press, 1984).
A dependable survey of Mark Twain's literary career which skillfully integrates discussions of both major and minor works, while expressing a preference for the free-swinging, irreverent humorist of the earlier years.

Paul Fatout, *Mark Twain on the Lecture Circuit* (Bloomington: Indiana University Press, 1960).
Very readable account of Mark Twain's career as a popular lecturist.

Robert L. Gale, *Plots and Characters in the Works of Mark Twain*, 2 volumes (Hamden, Conn.: Archon Books, 1973).
Volume I contains plot summaries of Twain's works, including some not yet published; volume II lists alphabetically the names and nicknames of all characters and the works in which they appear.

William M. Gibson, *The Art of Mark Twain* (New York: Oxford University Press, 1976).
Assesses and analyzes what Gibson considers the "best" in the many types represented by Mark Twain's works–"picaresque" romance, tall tale, burlesque sketch, fable, travel narrative, humorous story, polemic, maxims, and epigrams.

Alan Gribben, *Mark Twain's Library, A Reconstruction*, 2 volumes (Boston: G. K. Hall, 1980).
The fullest record of Twain's reading, listing all identifiable books and periodicals that Twain knew or owned, often with discussion of their pertinence to and their use in Twain's own writings.

Sydney J. Krause, *Mark Twain as Critic* (Baltimore: Johns Hopkins University Press, 1967).
The fullest study of Twain's literary criticism.

Arthur G. Pettit, *Mark Twain and the South* (Lexington: University Press of Kentucky, 1974).
The most detailed study of Mark Twain's attitudes toward the South, slavery, and race, and the effects of those attitudes on his works.

Robert L. Ramsay and Frances G. Emberson, *A Mark Twain Lexicon* (Columbia: University of Missouri Press, 1938; New York: Russell & Russell, 1963).

A dictionary, with a thorough introduction, which vividly illustrates Twain's many contributions to the American language.

Franklin R. Rogers, *Mark Twain's Burlesque Patterns* (Dallas: Southern Methodist University Press, 1960).

Traces Mark Twain's debts to writers of travel burlesques and burlesque "condensed novels" in the development of his own writing up to and including *Huckleberry Finn.*

Arthur L. Scott, *On the Poetry of Mark Twain with Selections from His Verse* (Urbana: University of Illinois Press, 1966).

Presents, with detailed introductory discussion, Twain's various poetic efforts, both comic and serious.

David E. E. Sloane, *Mark Twain as a Literary Comedian* (Baton Rouge: Louisiana State University Press, 1979).

Describes Twain's relationships with and the influence of the so-called "Literary Comedians" or "Professional Humorists" like Artemus Ward, Petroleum V. Nasby, Josh Billings, and others.

Henry Nash Smith, *Mark Twain, The Development of a Writer* (Cambridge: Harvard University Press, 1962).

Discusses the development of Twain as a literary craftsman and thinker, stressing the importance to his art and thought of the conflict between colloquial speech (the "vernacular") and the elevated "language of the official culture" and between attitudes or ideas derived from common experience and the values of the cultural elite.

Albert E. Stone, *The Innocent Eye, Childhood in Mark Twain's Fiction* (New Haven: Yale University Press, 1961).

Traces Twain's changing views, as reflected in his works, of the way the child's imagination operates, comparing and contrasting them with the views of a number of other American authors who have dealt with children, from Nathaniel Hawthorne through Henry James and Henry Adams.

Papers:

The major collection of Mark Twain materials is the Mark Twain Papers at the Bancroft Library, University of California, Berkeley. Other major collections are at Yale University Library, the Henry W. and Albert A. Berg Collection of the New York Public Library, Vassar College, and the Alderman Library of the University of Virginia.

Stephen Crane

This entry was updated by James B. Colvert (University of Georgia) from his entry in
DLB 12, American Realists and Naturalists.

Places	New York City England Syracuse, N. Y.	Greece Cuba	Jacksonville, Fla. Lafayette University
Influences and Relationships	Joseph Conrad William Dean Howells	Leo Tolstoy Hamlin Garland	Harold Frederic Rudyard Kipling
Literary Movements and Forms	Experimental Verse Naturalism	Journalism Realism	Impressionism
Major Themes	Slum Life Village Life	Courage Man's Place in Nature	Indifference of the Universe
Cultural and Artistic Influences	Painting Bohemianism	Environmental Determinism	Methodism
Social and Economic Influences	Urban Poverty Greco-Turkish War	Civil War	Spanish-American War

See also the Crane entry in DLB 54, *American Poets: 1880-1945, Part 1.*

BIRTH: Newark, New Jersey, 1 November 1871, to the Reverend Dr. Jonathan Townley and Mary Helen Peck Crane.

EDUCATION: Lafayette College, 1890; Syracuse University, 1891.

DEATH: Badenweiler, Germany, 5 June 1900.

SELECTED BOOKS: *Maggie: A Girl of the Streets,* as Johnston Smith (New York: Privately printed, 1893); revised edition, as Stephen Crane (New York: Appleton, 1896; London: Heinemann, 1896);

The Black Riders (Boston: Copeland & Day, 1895; London: Heinemann, 1896);

The Red Badge of Courage (New York: Appleton, 1895; London: Heinemann, 1896);

George's Mother (New York & London: Edward Arnold, 1896);

The Little Regiment (New York: Appleton, 1896; London: Heinemann, 1897);

The Third Violet (New York: Appleton, 1897; London: Heinemann, 1897);

The Open Boat (New York: Doubleday & McClure, 1898; London: Heinemann, 1898);

War is Kind (New York: Stokes, 1899);

Active Service (New York: Stokes, 1899; London: Heinemann, 1899);

The Monster (New York & London: Harper, 1899; enlarged, London & New York: Harper, 1901);

Whilomville Stories (New York & London: Harper, 1900);

Wounds in the Rain (New York: Stokes, 1900; London: Methuen, 1900);

Great Battles of the World (Philadelphia: Lippincott, 1901; London: Chapman & Hall, 1901);

Last Words (London: Digby, Long, 1902);

The O'Ruddy, by Crane and Robert Barr (New York: Stokes, 1903; London: Methuen, 1904);

The Sullivan County Sketches of Stephen Crane, edited by Melvin Schoberlin (Syracuse: Syracuse University Press, 1949);

Stephen Crane: Uncollected Writings, edited by O. W. Fryckstedt (Uppsala: Studia Anglistica Upsaliensia, 1963);

The War Dispatches of Stephen Crane, edited by R. W. Stallman and E. R. Hagemann (New York: New York University Press, 1966);

Stephen Crane, 1896 (courtesy of the Lilly Library, Indiana University)

The New York City Sketches of Stephen Crane, edited by Stallman and Hagemann (New York: New York University Press, 1966);

Sullivan County Tales and Sketches, edited by Stallman (Ames: Iowa State University Press, 1968);

The Notebook of Stephen Crane, edited by Donald and Ellen Greiner (Charlottesville, Va.: A John Cook Wyllie Memorial Publication, 1969);

Stephen Crane in the West and Mexico, edited by Joseph Katz (Kent, Ohio: Kent State University Press, 1970);

The Red Badge of Courage: A Facsimile Edition of the Manuscript, 2 volumes, edited by Fredson Bowers (Washington, D.C.: Bruccoli Clark/ NCR Microcard Editions, 1973).

Collections: *The Work of Stephen Crane,* 12 volumes, edited by Wilson Follett (New York: Knopf, 1925-1926);

The Collected Poems of Stephen Crane, edited by Follett (New York & London: Knopf, 1930);

The Poems of Stephen Crane, edited by Katz (New York: Cooper Square, 1966);

The Works of Stephen Crane, 10 volumes, edited by Bowers (Charlottesville: University Press of Virginia, 1969-1976).

A precursor of the imagists in poetry and of the novelists writing the new fiction of the 1920s, Stephen Crane was one of the most gifted and influential writers of the late nineteenth century, noted for his brilliant and innovative style, his vivid, ironic sense of life, and his penetrating psychological realism. Unusually precocious, he wrote his first novel, *Maggie: A Girl of the Streets* (1893), when he was only twenty-one and had his masterpiece, *The Red Badge of Courage* (1895), published before he was twenty-four. When he died in 1900 at the age of twenty-eight, from tuberculosis and the effects of his exhausting life as adventurer and war correspondent, he had written, in addition to his voluminous war reportage and numerous incidental pieces, six novels, well over a hundred stories and sketches, and two books of poems—enough all together to fill ten large volumes in the University Press of Virginia edition of his collected works. Neglected for two decades after his death, he was rediscovered in the 1920s by poets and novelists (such as Amy Lowell, Willa Cather, Sherwood Anderson, and Joseph Hergesheimer) who recognized in his experiments with new subjects, themes, and forms something of the spirit of their own literary aims.

Although these aims were derived originally from such nineteenth-century realists as Hamlin Garland, William Dean Howells, Rudyard Kipling, Leo Tolstoy, and others of perhaps more indeterminant influence, he radically altered their principles and methods to serve his own unique vision and purposes. He eschewed the conventional plot, shifting the focus from the drama of external event or situation to the drama of thought and feeling in the mental life of his subjects. He substituted for the conventional expository, descriptive style a highly metaphorical, imagistic representation of psychological effects. And he denied, in his most telling work, assumptions about norms of reality, often depicting unfolding experience as gradual revelation of its ultimate mystery. A relativist, ironist, and impressionist, he anticipated the modernism of Ernest Hemingway, F. Scott Fitzgerald, Anderson, and William Faulkner by thirty years. Like Hemingway, he was preoccupied with violence, finding in the reaction of his hero under the stress of ultimate crisis the mystery and poignancy of the hero's character and fate. Like Anderson, Fitzger-

ald, and Faulkner, he dramatized the powers of illusion to shape events and destinies. He does, indeed, seem closer to these writers in manner and spirit than to the writers of his own day.

The experience which contributed most importantly to the shaping of Crane's modernist ideas and attitude was probably his early life as a minister's son. He was born 1 November 1871, in Newark, New Jersey, the last of fourteen children of the Reverend Dr. Jonathan Townley Crane, a well-known Methodist clergyman, and Mary Helen Peck Crane. Mrs. Crane, a descendant of a long line of Methodist preachers "of the old ambling-nag, saddle-bag, exhorting kind" (as Crane once described them), was active in church and reform work, serving at one time as an officer in the New Jersey Women's Christian Temperance Union. She was also, like her husband, interested in fiction. Dr. Crane wrote several moralistic little fables for a Methodist Sunday school paper, and Mrs. Crane, as it has been recently discovered, wrote at least two stories in the early or mid eighties for the *Monmouth* (New Jersey) *Tribune.* Her uncle, the Reverend Jesse Peck, a Methodist bishop and one of the founders of Syracuse University, was the author of a minatory religious treatise "redolent with the fumes of sulphur and brimstone," *What Must I Do to Be Saved?* (1858), a copy of which Stephen Crane inherited from his father in 1881. The bishop's view of God as a God of wrath was apparently shared, to some extent at least, by Crane's mother; but his father, who resigned from the Presbyterian church as a young man in protest against the harshness of its doctrine of infant damnation, was apparently of a gentler persuasion, stressing in his milder books on Christian conduct a view of God as a God of mercy and compassion.

The religious poems in Stephen Crane's first book of poems, *The Black Riders* (1895), written about the same time he was writing *The Red Badge of Courage,* reflect the anguish of a spiritual crisis in which he attempted to exorcise the Pecks' God of wrath and, beyond that, to test his faith in general against the moral realities he observed as a young newspaper reporter in Asbury Park, New Jersey, and New York City in the early 1890s. The religious issue haunted Crane's imagination to the end. As Amy Lowell observed, "He disbelieved it and hated it, but he could not free himself from it." The effect of his preoccupation with questions of faith is not only evident in his poetry but appears, more obliquely, in his fiction as well, notably in its striking evocation of man's poignant alienation in a God-abandoned world of menace and violence.

Two years after his father died in 1880, Mrs. Crane moved to Asbury Park, New Jersey, a popular resort town on the coast where one of his older brothers, Townley, operated a news agency for the *New York Tribune.* Left much to his own devices, since Mrs. Crane was often busy with church and reform projects, Stephen roamed the beaches, indulged his passion for baseball (one of the pastimes his father cautioned against in his book *Popular Amusements,* 1869), and, under the influence of his mentor Townley and another older brother Will, who advised him once to ignore the hellfire warnings of his visiting preacher-uncles, began to develop a decidedly secular point of view. In the summers he helped Townley Crane gather news and gossip for his *Tribune* column, "On the Jersey Coast." By 1888, when he enrolled at Claverack College and Hudson River Institute, a quasi-military prep school at Claverack, New York, he was already in full revolt against his Methodist heritage. As one of his classmates reported, he was bohemian in dress and manner, aloof and taciturn except on the baseball field, where he was companionable and "giftedly profane." He violated no rules, but he was known to the faculty for his indifference to the school's official ideals and apparently "enjoyed a certain reputation for villainy." He was even then approaching that break with the current social, intellectual, and literary norms and conventions which H. G. Wells described a dozen years later, after Crane's death, as his "enormous repudiations."

His single year of higher education, at two different colleges, was notably unsuccessful. At Lafayette College, where he enrolled in the fall of 1890, he played baseball and delivered self-assured literary opinions–Tolstoy, whose novel of the Crimean War, *Sebastopol* (1855), he had read, was the world's greatest writer; Flaubert's *Salammbô* (1862) was too long; Henry James's *The Reverberator* (1888) was a bore–but he did no work and at the end of the term was advised to withdraw. At Syracuse University for the spring semester of 1891, he haunted the baseball diamond and, as a part-time reporter for the *Tribune,* scouted the Syracuse tenderloin and police court, studying "humanity," as he explained, rather than the "cut and dried" lessons of the classroom. He was known to his classmates and professors for his unconventionality and undisciplined

brilliance. When the famous reformer Emma Willard visited, he refused to meet her on the ground that she was a fool, and he shocked a professor by declaring in class that he disagreed with St. Paul. Sometime that spring he decided definitely to be a writer and began spending his afternoons in the cupola of the Delta Upsilon fraternity house reading and writing. Classmates recalled that he started a story about a prostitute, perhaps the first draft of *Maggie,* based on his observations in the Syracuse slums. He was also writing stories and sketches in imitation of Twain's tall tales and Poe's satirical hoaxes: a spoof on international politics, a yarn about a swarm of gigantic "electric-light" bugs stalling a locomotive, and a tale about a New York tenor's misadventure on a concert tour in Africa. But he neglected classwork, and by the end of the semester, when only one grade was reported for him, an *A* in English literature, he had already decided not to return.

At Asbury Park he apparently took charge of Townley Crane's *Tribune* column in the summers of 1891 and 1892, gathering news and gossip at the resort hotels, recording events at the Methodist religious conferences at nearby Ocean Grove, and reporting on the annual seminars in the arts and sciences at another neighboring community, Avon-by-the-Sea. During this time he was also working out a theory of art, evidently basing it partly on theories of realism advanced by Hamlin Garland and William Dean Howells, partly on ideas expressed by the realist painter-hero of Kipling's novel *The Light That Failed* (1891), and partly on the practical demonstration of the uses of irony and the handling of psychological realism in Tolstoy's *Sebastopol.* Strolling the beach with a friend who asked his advice about writing, Crane tossed a handful of sand in the air and said, "Treat your notions like that. Forget what you think about it and tell how you feel about it." "I cannot see," he wrote about this same time, "why people hate ugliness in art. Ugliness is just a matter of treatment. The scene of Hamlet and his mother and old Polonious behind the curtain is ugly, if you heard it in a police court. Hamlet treats his mother like a drunken carter and his words when he has killed Polonious are disgusting. But who cares?" This point of view, daring for the times, could have come from the radical-minded Garland, who declared with special emphasis in an 1890 article about Ibsen in the *Arena* magazine that "realism has only one law, to be true, not to the objective reality, but to the objective reality *as the author sees it*." Crane met Garland in August 1891 when the critic was at Avon delivering lectures on Howells, "The City in Fiction" and "Sharpening Social Contrasts." The accuracy of the young reporter's *Tribune* summary of the lecture on Howells called Crane to Garland's attention. Crane's meetings with this pioneer realist in the two weeks of the critic's stay, when they talked literature and pitched baseball, may mark the real beginning of Crane's literary career. Garland's theory of realism ("Veritism"), based on Howells's and modified by his study of Eugene Veron's aesthetics and the theory of impressionism in painting, may have given shape to Crane's ideas; and Garland's stress on the importance of social problems of the city as a subject for the new fiction may have directed him to the slums of New York that fall in search of material.

Meanwhile, he was practicing his literary skills in the satirical sketches of life on the Jersey coast that he was sending to the *Tribune* for Townley Crane's column, probably without his brother's supervision since Townley Crane was apparently more interested in the gambling games at the hotels than in the details of Stephen Crane's newspaper copy. Aware that his bailiwick was a kind of microcosm concentrating tendencies in American religious, cultural, and popular social life, Crane skillfully exploited the potential of its contrasts, picturing its scenes with irreverent irony and enthusiastic hyperbole. Describing preachers congregating at Ocean Grove for a religious conference, he notes that "sombre-hued gentlemen ... are arriving in solemn procession, with black valises in their hands and rebukes to frivolity in their eyes," that "they greet each other with quiet enthusiasm and immediately set about holding meetings." At the resort hotels, in contrast, "pleasure-seekers arrive by the avalanche" and descend on the amusement park where a new "razzle-dazzle" (which is, "of course, a moral machine") is being installed and where an upright wheel revolves "carrying little cars, to be filled evidently with desperate persons, around and around, up and down." Later he reports that the "sombre-hued gentlemen" complained "that the steam organ disturbed their pious meditations on the evils of the world" and that "thereupon the minions of the law violently suppressed the wheel and its attendants." At Avon faculty and students at the School of Biology "are constantly engaged in inspecting great glass jars filled with strange floating growths," and "they

vary this exciting pursuit by taking a boat and going to dig ecstatically for singular things in the mud flats. . . ."

Studying the middle-class vacationers at the hotels, he began to create a character type which would appear more fully developed in his fiction: the poignantly muddled, morally powerless egotist victimized by his sentimental heroic fantasies and delusions. "The average summer guest," he reported, "stands in his two shoes with American self-reliance, playing casually with his watch-chain, and looks at the world with a clear eye." He presumes a vast worldly knowledge even as he foolishly submits to the "arrogant prices" and deceits of the hotel proprietors. "However, deliberately and baldly attempt to beat him out of fifteen cents and he will put his hands in his pockets, spread his legs apart and wrangle in a loud voice until sundown." Crane describes the vain "golden youth," a "rose-tint and gilt-edge" swaggerer who appears on the beach with his narcissistic "summer girl, a bit of interesting tinsel flashing near the sombre-hued waves." And he presents the millionaire owner of the beach, James A. Bradley, as a pompous gentleman who displays signs advertising his principles of piety and gentility and cautioning guests against unseemly conduct on his beaches and who considers it a matter of import that the "ocean of the Lord's" lies "adjacent to the beach of James A. Bradley."

Vain illusion in context of a vast, remote, somber nature is the main theme of his first fiction, written about this time and published in the *Tribune* in the summer of 1892. Based on his hunting and fishing outings in the wilds of Sullivan County, New York, where he often went with friends in the summers, these stories, first collected and published as *The Sullivan County Sketches of Stephen Crane* in 1949, develop elaborately a metaphor of man at war against nature. The hero is the unnamed "little man," an outdoorsman who wanders over the landscape challenging what seems to him its inimical spirit, ludicrously assaulting caves, bears, mountains, and forests. He declares his courage in heroic orations which, as his three mocking companions understand because they share his anxieties, mask an almost hysterical dread of what he perceives as powers of an alien and hostile world. It is the apparent ambiguity, or the indeterminate reality, of the landscape that he finds particularly sinister: it sometimes seems terrifyingly hostile; sometimes serenely Edenic, in harmony with his own visions of the ideal; and sometimes both at once. This uncertainty challenges and enrages him, and when the landscape threatens he assaults it violently in desperate efforts to subdue it to his will. He is moved to explore a cave "because its black mouth gaped at him," he assaults a mountain which he thinks glowered at him, he hurls imprecations at the dreaded dark and kills a bear from ambush "with mad emotions, powerful to rock worlds." But in Crane's perspective, the cave's black mouth is merely "a little tilted hole" on a hillside, the phantom that haunts the night is merely a starving dog, the sinister mountain, once mastered, is after all merely "motionless under his feet," and the dead bear is only a dead bear.

The lurid light the little man's fancy casts on this problematic nature is represented in Crane's remarkable imagery, the impressionistic style he had been developing in some of his "news" reports since 1891. The style transmutes the real Sullivan County landscape into a dreamlike evocation of the little man's distraught fancy, a world curiously animistic, alternately menacing and tender or maddeningly enigmatic. Night masquerades "weird features . . . awfully in robes of shadow" and the sun gleams "merrily" upon waters that hold in their depth "millions of fern branches that quavered and hid mysteries." Religious imagery occurs frequently and often seems faintly facetious, as when tender, sentient pines in a field of snow "huddled together and sang in quavers as the wind whirled among the gullies and ridges," while a "dismal choir of hemlocks crooned over one that had fallen." Crane's irony is directed at the absurdity of his hero's swagger, his pompous oratory, and his outrageous self-esteem–vanities that conjure demons in the landscape.

Perhaps at Garland's suggestion Crane began his firsthand study of city life in the summer of 1891, going into the Bowery from his brother Ed's house in Lake View, New Jersey, within easy commuting distance of New York, to study the color of the city and the effect of the slums on the morals and manners of the poor. A year or so later, in August 1892, his propensity for satire got the Crane brothers in trouble: the owner-editor of the *Tribune*, a Republican candidate that year for the vice-presidency of the United States, fired both Stephen and Townley Crane when the young satirist's graphic and ironic description of a labor-union parade in Asbury Park aroused the ire of the politically influential unionists. His ties with Asbury Park broken

with the sudden demise of Townley Crane's agency, Stephen Crane now moved to the city, taking up precarious residence in the semibohemian quarters of aspiring actors, medical students, and commercial illustrators and beginning his study of tenement life in earnest. He disappeared for days into the Bowery disguised as a derelict, gathering material for sketches and newspaper stories, which he occasionally sold to the *Herald,* and perhaps for his novel *Maggie,* begun either at Syracuse in the spring of 1891 or, more likely, in the late fall after his first excursions into the city. He revised the novel in March 1892 and showed it to Richard Watson Gilder, the editor of the *Century* magazine, who thought it "cruel" and "too honest" in its description of the sordid life of the slums. Crane revised it again that winter, but after it was rejected by editor after editor, Crane gave up. Borrowing money from his brother Will and raising some on the coal-mine stock he inherited from his father, he had the novel privately printed. It appeared in February or March 1893 under the pseudonym Johnston Smith, an ugly, yellow, little book no bookstore would take, except Brentano's, which stocked twelve copies and returned ten.

The novel studies the career of Maggie Johnson, a tenement girl driven by the cruelty, neglect, and selfishness of her family and acquaintances into the streets and ultimately to suicide. Hatred and violence dominate her childhood. She and her brother Jimmie are victims of a brutal, alcoholic mother who alternately beats them and smothers them with sentimental protestations of affection. Their sullen father objects to the beatings only because they disturb his rest. As a young man, Jimmie cultivates the friendship of Pete, a swaggering bartender who at sixteen wears the "chronic sneer of an ideal manhood," and who seems to the blossoming Maggie a man of infinite prowess and sophistication. The abusive mother finally drives Maggie to Pete's protection, and after he has seduced her, the Johnson family, outraged at this affront to their respectability, drive her from the tenement. When Pete abandons her, Maggie drifts into prostitution and finally, in a fit of despair, drowns herself. The book ends with the self-righteous mother shouting to her neighbors, "Oh, yes, I'll fergive her! I'll fergive her!"

The novel's sordid subject, its air of relentless objectivity (despite the implicit editorializing in its irony), and its sense of fatalism have led some historians to claim it as the first American naturalistic novel, a claim supported somewhat by Crane's statement that he intended it "to show that environment is a tremendous thing in the world and frequently shapes lives regardless." But later he noted other forces besides environment at work in the lives of the people he depicted. "I do not think much can be done with the Bowery," he wrote in 1896, "as long as the people there are in their present state of conceit. A person who thinks himself superior to the rest of us because he has no pride and no clean clothes is as badly conceited as Lillian Russell." In his sketch "An Experiment in Misery," a description of slum life published a few months after *Maggie*, he said he "tried to make it plain that the root of Bowery life is a sort of cowardice. Perhaps I mean a lack of ambition or to willingly be knocked flat and accept the licking." His stinging verbal irony constantly chastises the Johnsons and other characters for their moral blindness, which clearly is caused by their absurd and self-indulgent illusions about their world and themselves. This moralistic overtone casts doubt on the theory that *Maggie* is a naturalistic novel. It in fact seems closer to the Sullivan County sketches than it does to Emile Zola's *L'Assommoir* (1877) or other naturalistic novels which have been cited as possible models.

Maggie shares with the Sullivan County sketches the premise that self-aggrandizing conceit is a fundamental human motive and principal source of moral confusion. Like the little man, the swaggering Pete and Jimmie apprehend a world of menace which challenges their assumptions about their special virtues and their dreams of heroic destinies. Pete's manner stamps him as a man who has a "correct sense of his personal superiority," and Jimmie, sitting high on the driver's seat of his delivery truck, turns his sneer on the world below and wonders at the crowd's "insane disregard for their legs and his convenience." The brutish Mrs. Johnson imagines herself "a good mudder," and the father, who complains to bartenders that his "home is a livin' hell," beats Jimmie with a beer pail for amusement. Everywhere in this world is evidence of the power of aggressive conceit to distort reality and twist moral vision.

Like the irony of the sketches, that in *Maggie* marks the contrast between reality and fantasy which is the basis of the novel's structure. In the opening sentence–"A very little boy stood upon a heap of gravel for the honor of Rum Alley"–a mean tenement alley is set against an em-

battled gang's false sense of the heroic. At the theater with Pete, Maggie is transported "by plays in which the dazzling heroine was rescued from the palatial home of her treacherous guardian by the hero with beautiful sentiments." To her these melodramas, with their "pale-green snowstorms," "nickel-plated revolvers," and daring rescues, are "transcendental realism." These sentimental distortions of reality are of course projections from the myths of popular culture, but they are also indications of a more pervasive perceptual distortion. The tenement world is pictured in metaphors which give it an almost surrealistic aura, a displacement of time and space, as, for example, when a looming tenement house is described as having "a hundred windows" and "a dozen gruesome doorways" that "gave up loads of babies to the street and gutter" while "withered persons . . . sat smoking pipes in obscure corners." Descriptions abound in unexpected perspectives and analogies. The inanimate world, like that of the little man, is fantastically alive ("The open mouth of a saloon called seductively. . . ."), and attributes of things observed seem often to be projections of the psychological world of the observer, as when Maggie, plying her trade as a prostitute, encounters "a stout gentleman, with pompous and philanthropic whiskers, who went stolidly by, the broad of his back sneering at the girl." These are the characteristics of style Frank Norris described memorably when he reviewed the novel in 1896, shortly after Appleton gave it, slightly revised, its first commercial publication. "The picture he makes," Norris wrote, "is not a single carefully composed painting, serious, finished, scrupulously studied, but rather scores and scores of tiny flashlight photographs, instantaneous, caught, as it were, on the run."

Impressive as it is, *Maggie* is by no means without flaws. Its unrelieved irony sometimes seems shrill and contrived, and the closing chapters are faulty in pacing and scale, though the saloon scene in which the "woman of brilliance and audacity" fleeces the sorry drunken Pete is as effective as any in the novel. The remarkable vitality of the language, the brilliance of its method, and the originality of its conception point toward the skillful, innovative art of *The Red Badge of Courage* and "The Open Boat."

But hardly anyone noticed it in 1893 except Howells and Garland, both of whom tried to interest editors in the young novelist's work, though without success. Howells invited him to tea and read some of Emily Dickinson's poems, shortly after which Crane himself began writing poems–or, as he preferred to call them, "lines." He continued his study of the tenements, writing a series of three stories about the adventures of a slum child named Tommie and more sketches of the Bowery. He began another novel of the slums, a companion piece to *Maggie,* but he laid it aside to finish a novel about the Civil War he began in the early spring of 1893, taking up the new tenement story in May 1894 when he wrote Garland that his new novel was "a bird." In November he wrote that it was finished and described it enthusiastically as "a New York book that leaves 'Maggie' at the post." Though not published until 1896, after his war novel, *The Red Badge of Courage,* had brought him international fame, the New York book, *George's Mother* (originally titled "A Woman Without Weapons") should be read in the context of *Maggie,* since both deal with similar subjects and themes.

George's Mother is a study of the relationship between a doting widow, Mrs. Kelcey, and her weak, self-indulgent son, George. Although the Kelceys share part of their gloomy tenement building with the Johnsons of *Maggie,* the pious Mrs. Kelcey, who is devoted to religion and her son's welfare, miraculously maintains in this moral chaos a decent, respectable home; and young George, though somewhat spoiled and selfish, is at first a steady and dependable provider. But when he joins an amiable crowd of saloon loafers whose flattery seems to confirm his high opinion of himself, he begins to change for the worse. Resentful of his mother's sentimental moralizing and her criticism of his conduct, convinced that only his saloon friends fully appreciate his moral and intellectual superiority, he rejects her authority, openly expressing his contempt for his religion and abusing her when she upbraids him for neglecting prayer meetings or queries him about his frequent absences. When he loses his job and tries to borrow money from his friends, they become suddenly indifferent. He drifts into a gang of neighborhood toughs and joins them in bullying people in the streets and cadging drinks at the corner saloon. Mrs. Kelcey is convinced almost to the last that these aberrations are temporary and that George is actually a brilliant and devoted son who under her loving care and firm moral guidance will one day make his mark in the world as a great man. When events finally dispel these illusions, she seems to lose her will to live, and as she lies dying from a sudden stroke,

George is in a nearby vacant lot preparing to fight a member of his gang, Blue Billy, to settle a quarrel over a bucket of beer and their relative prowess with their fists.

Although it has been suggested that Crane drew on Zola's *L'Assommoir* for *George's Mother* as well as for *Maggie,* it seems clear enough that its sources are Crane's personal experience and the popular culture of his time. The germ for the mother-son relationship is in his own life, his mother being clearly the model for Mrs. Kelcey and Crane himself for George. One of Crane's nieces gave testimony of the attitude which enabled him to project his mother as the critically contemplated Mrs. Kelcey: "His mother's memory was dear to him, and although he never questioned her ways when he was outside the family portals, he did marvel always that such an intellectual woman, a university graduate . . . could have wrapped herself so completely in the vacuous, futile, psalm-singing that passed for worship in those days." George is a partial, guilt-inspired, self-portrait: "I used to like church and prayer meetings when I was a kid," Crane wrote in later years, "but that cooled off. . . ." Once, he remembered, an Italian on the beach at Asbury Park gave him "a long drink out of a nice red bottle," and arriving home feeling "ecstatic," he amiably agreed, to Mrs. Crane's surprise, to accompany her to a prayer meeting. "Mother was tickled to death. I have frequently wondered how much mothers ever know about their sons."

The literature of the antisaloon movement, in which his mother actively participated and to which his father contributed a book, *Arts of Intoxication* (1870), is also a source for *George's Mother,* as are the views sentimentally dramatized in the popular temperance literature of the time, examples of which are Timothy Shay Arthur's famous *Ten Nights in a Barroom* (1854) and its sequel *Three Years in a Man Trap* (1872). The common elements of these melodramatic fictions are the ruined victim of drink, the blighted career, the impoverishment of the victim's family, and the death of a loved one–child, wife, or mother–from shame or drink-induced poverty. This stereotypical plot Crane merged with elements of his personal history, basing the character of George partly on himself and partly on the swaggering hero he created in the Asbury Park reports and the Sullivan County sketches, the pompous little man. This amalgamation of disparate elements, transmuted by the distancing effect of Crane's critical irony, suggests the undoubted complexity and ambivalence of his feelings about his Methodist heritage and the sentimental heroics celebrated in the popular literature of the 1890s.

Although *George's Mother* is somewhat less dramatic than *Maggie*, more explicitly satirical and more discursive in style, there are passages which are as effective as some of the best parts of its predecessor. The vulgarity of the amiable saloon brotherhood George so much admires–the banality of their talk and interests, their cheap sentiment, and above all their comical swagger and self-congratulatory complacency–are admirably portrayed. In the back room of the saloon, which is their retreat "from a grinding world filled with men who were harsh," these sympathetic comrades "understood that they were true and tender spirits," that they possessed "various virtues which were unappreciated by those with whom they were commonly obliged to mingle." The theme of fraternal order is prominently developed, as it is in much of Crane's work. In *The Red Badge of Courage* and "The Open Boat" it is treated sympathetically, but in *George's Mother*, as in the Sullivan County sketches, comradeship is problematical and uncertain, vitiated by swelling emotions of the self. The description of old Bleecker's party, which satirizes the stereotyped tastes, crippled thought, and vulgar emotions of the guests, of whom George is typical, is especially memorable. Mr. Zeusentell's nervous recitation of "Patrick Clancy's Pig," the comical social helplessness of the timid, the pompous self-confidence of Bleecker, and the ultimate dissolution of the party in an absurd blur of alcoholic violence are brilliantly rendered in Crane's best impressionistic style.

During the years 1893 and 1894, when he was reworking *Maggie* and writing *The Red Badge of Courage*, the poems in *The Black Riders*, and *George's Mother*, Crane continued, apparently by choice, to live in wretched poverty, convinced that suffering was beneficial to his art. This conviction he probably owed to Kipling's *The Light That Failed*, which he most likely read as early as 1891 and which apparently exerted considerable influence on his literary ideas. The hero of the novel, a realist painter who theorizes a good deal about realistic art, advocates poverty as a spur to creativity. "There are few things more edifying unto Art," he says, "than the belly-pinch of hunger," an idea Crane echoed later when he stated that the fact that *The Red Badge of Courage* was "an effort born of pain, despair, almost" made it "a better piece of literature than it otherwise would

have been." Seeking firsthand experience of the bitter life of the poor, he lived in a gloomy, run-down, ill-heated old building, often as cold and hungry as the derelicts he studied in the Bowery. He slept in a tenement-district flophouse and stood in a breadline in a blizzard for the experiences he described vividly in the fine sketches "An Experiment in Misery" and "The Men in the Storm." During this period he wrote three stories about the street adventures of the toddler Tommie Johnson, whose death is mentioned in *Maggie*, and miscellaneous sketches about life in artists' studios, the police court, the saloon, and the amusement park.

But he also wrote during this time, beginning in March or April of 1893, *The Red Badge of Courage*, the novel of the Civil War which made him famous when it was published in 1895 and which has long been regarded as one of the classics of American literature. Unlike *Maggie* and *George's Mother*, which seem to honor a basic tenet of his theory of realism–namely, that truth in art is grounded in actual observation and experience–*The Red Badge of Courage* was apparently a pure invention, written years before its author ever actually saw a battle. But in an important sense real-life experience probably contributed little more to *Maggie* than to the war novel, for although he doubtless observed in the slums most of the particulars of *Maggie*, Crane appropriated the major elements of the novel from the myth of the slum girl, a myth readily accessible in the popular literature of the time–in Edgar Fawcett's *The Evil That Men Do* (1889) and in articles about slum life in the *Arena* magazine, for example. In these writings he found the character types (the pure, betrayed slum girl, the drunken parents, the vicious brother), the attitudes (the scorn of hypocritical respectability, the veneration of purity in women), actions (the fights, the seduction, the suicide of the heroine), and ideas (the powers of vanity and social forces)–all elements which he incorporated in the plot of *Maggie*. *The Red Badge of Courage* apparently originated in much the same way, deriving similarly from a popular myth of war. As Stanley Wertheim has shown, the numerous memoirs of war veterans which appeared in the 1860s, 1870s, and 1880s had established by 1890 "a distinctive literary convention for Civil War narratives, embodied in literally dozens of exemplars," many of which Crane, with his lifelong obsession with war, must have known. He obviously drew upon the common pattern of these chronicles for

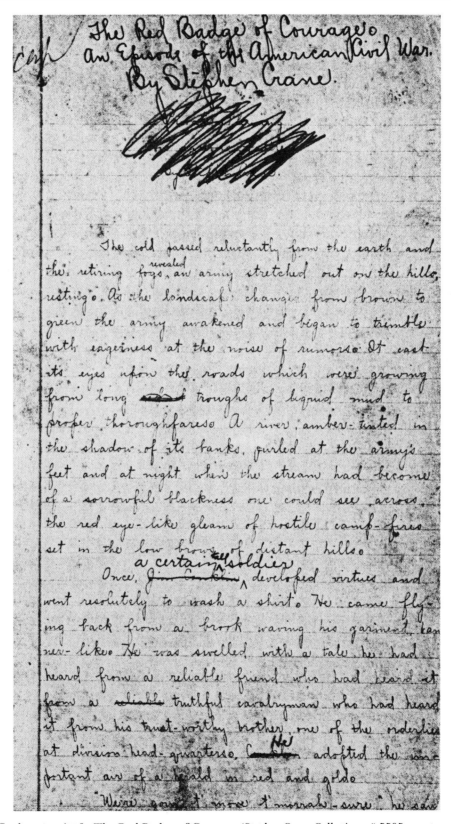

First page of the final manuscript for The Red Badge of Courage *(Stephen Crane Collection, #5505, courtesy of the Clifton Waller Barrett Library, Manuscripts Division, University of Virginia Library)*

the major elements of plot in *The Red Badge of Courage:* the sentimental expectation of the young recruit moved to enlist by patriotic rhetoric and heroic fantasies of war, the resistance of his parents to his enlistment, his anxiety over the apparent confusion and purposelessness of troop movements, his doubts about his personal courage, the dissipation of his heroic illusions in the first battle, his grumbling about the incompetency of generals, and other such motifs, incidents, and situations. H. T. Webster has demonstrated that "everything [except style and execution] that makes up *The Red Badge of Courage* exists at least in germ" in Wilbur Hinman's *Corporal Si Klegg and His Pard* (1887), a story about a raw recruit who, like Crane's Henry Fleming, is given to romantic self-dramatization and anxious worry about his personal courage but who eventually proves himself in battle and is praised for heroism by his colonel.

It is style and execution directed by a powerful imagination which transmutes these commonplace narrative conventions into literature; in a sense, the literary method and the ideas Crane developed in his *Tribune* pieces and New York writings are more relevant to the question of origins than any of these historical accounts. He probably developed his method chiefly on the model of Tolstoy's ironic, impressionistic *Sebastopol,* which demonstrates the powerful dramatic effect of representing reality in the imagery of the hero's psychological life. He may have found in Kipling's *The Light That Failed* an adaptable illustration of the dramatic use of color, as his repetitive use of Kipling's wrathful red-sun image in *The Red Badge of Courage* and other works suggests. The style he shaped from these models was validated theoretically by Howells's concept of realism as the truthful treatment of materials and by Garland's idea that truth is the artist's subjective view of it. Thus when Crane turned to his imaginary war in the spring of 1893, he was in command of formidable literary resources: the plot elements provided by the conventionalized Civil War story, an attitude toward it sanctioned by contemporary theories of realism, a literary character developed in his studies of the little man in his Asbury Park and Sullivan County pieces, and a vivid impressionistic style inspired by Tolstoy and Kipling.

Another force at work in the shaping of the novel was the effect on Crane's imagination of his intense preoccupation at this time with religious questions, the explicit evidence for which is

in his book of poems, *The Black Riders.* More than half of the sixty-eight poems of the volume are on religious themes–the inscrutability of God, man's futile quest for God, God's wrath, the terrors of a Godless universe, and man's pride and impotence–which express Crane's anguished uncertainty about God's character and man's relation to him. Is God dead and man abandoned to an indifferent universe, the questioning runs, or is he, on the contrary, terribly present in the world, a God of wrath breathing hatred and malice on helpless, sinful man? Occasionally he appears in visions of poignant yearning as kindly and compassionate, and again as removed to impossible distances, far beyond the range of human knowledge. Worrying about these puzzling contradictions, the speaker is torn between piety and blasphemy. "I hate Thee, unrighteous picture," he rages against the God of wrath. "So, strike with Thy vengeance/The heads of those little men/Who come blindly./It will be a brave thing." To a man who says the roaring thunder is the voice of God, the speaker says, "not so./The voice of God whispers in the heart/So softly/That the soul pauses." And once he agonizes over the thought that in "the mighty sky" is nothing "But a vast blue,/Echoless, ignorant,–." The God of wrath and the God of indifference often appear in images of hostile or stolidly impassive mountains. In one poem angry mountains appear as an army of vengeance against a defiant little man: "On the horizon the peaks assembled;/As I looked,/The march of the mountains began"; and in still another: "Once I saw mountains angry,/And ranged in battle-front./Against them stood a little man;/Aye, he was no bigger than my finger." And yet another man, "clambering to the house-tops" to appeal to the heavens, finds God, at last, in "the sky . . . filled with armies."

The recurrent motif of the little man against the hostile mountain first appears in expanded form as one of the 1892 Sullivan County stories, "The Mesmeric Mountain," a fablelike narrative of the little man's war against nature which not only outlines the plot of *The Red Badge of Courage* but also explains the symbolic meaning of the motif in the novel, where it occurs a number of times at crucial points in the narrative. The hero of the fable is the little man, who, contemplating the "ecstatic mystery" of a road leading into a pine forest, decides to follow it, certain that "it leads to something great or something." Making his way through the forest, battling "hordes of ignorant bushes" and "obstructing branches," he pauses at sundown to rest near the foot of a mountain. Gazing idly at the mountain in the fading light of "the red silence" of the sinking sun and the "formidable" shadows of the pines, he suddenly perceives that the mountain has eyes and is watching him. It appears about to attack, and the little man springs to his feet and flees in terror. Later, he pauses and, returning cautiously, is horrified to see that the mountain "has followed him" and is now about to crush his head with its heel. In a blind rage he attacks, flinging pebbles against its face and scrambling wildly up toward its summit, which he perceives as "a blaze of red wrath." When he reaches the top at last, he thrusts his hands "scornfully in his pockets" and swaggers victoriously about, confidently identifying distant landmarks. He does not notice that "the mountain under his feet was motionless."

Nearly all of the elements of the war novel are in the fable. Like Henry Fleming in *The Red Badge of Courage*, the little man is motivated to his adventure by heroic expectations of "great things," and like Henry's mother, the little man's camping companion disapproves of the undertaking. Both heroes project their anxieties on the landscape, animating it in their morbid fancies with menacing life. Both are obliged to force their ways against an unfriendly nature, "ignorant bushes" and "obstructing branches." Both are terrorized by perceptions of hostile supernatural forces which seem to threaten their destruction, and both are driven in desperation to attack them. Finally, both entertain illusions of victory and celebrate their delusive triumphs in secret ceremonies of self-congratulation.

The prominence of the imagery of menace and threat in the landscape in *The Red Badge of Courage*, particularly in the images of mountains and hills, clearly shows that the novel, the fable, and the poems all have a common origin in Crane's imagination. Although the novel enlarges the metaphor of the angry mountain to include nature in general, the mountain is nevertheless a central symbol. A passage in chapter 17 describes Henry's reaction when his lieutenant praises him for his violent assault against the attacking enemy: "He had been a tremendous figure, no doubt," Henry thinks complacently. "By this struggle he had overcome obstacles which he had admitted to be mountains. They had fallen like paper peaks, and he was now what he called a hero." Obviously, Henry is symbolically identical with the vainglorious hero of the fable who struts like a victor on the peak of the motionless mountain.

The passage suggests that Henry from the beginning has been as much concerned about how he measures up to nature–and, by extension, to God–as he has about how he measures up to war. For in his imagination, the terror of war–"the blood-swollen god"–and the terror of nature become one. Mountains, fields, streams, the night, the sun, appear in his disordered fancy in guises of living creatures, monstrous and terrible. He sees the "red eye-like gleam of hostile campfires set in the low brows of distant hills" and "the black columns [of enemy troops] disappearing on the brow of a hill like two serpents crawling from the cavern of night." Crossing a little stream, he fancies that the black water looks back at him with "white bubble eyes," and that "fierce-eyed hosts" lurk in the shadows of the woods. When he deserts in his first battle he flees, not the attack of enemy troops alone, but the "onslaught of redoubtable dragons," the approach of the "red and green monsters." Although as these examples show, nature appears in a variety of metaphorical forms–monsters, dragons, ogres, demigods–the figure of the sinister mountain recurs often and crucially, bearing, it would seem, the symbolic meaning given it in the poems in *The Black Riders*.

But the meaning of the landscape shifts with Henry's moods and fortunes: his fear is its hostility, his complacency is its sympathy. Humiliated by his panicky flight from his first battle, he turns to nature for solace and comfort. Wending his way in a peaceful forest, he is gratified to observe that nature is "a woman with a deep aversion to tragedy." He reaches a secluded place where "high arching boughs made a chapel," and he supposes that tender nature has furnished it for his need and convenience. He pushes the "green doors" aside and is suddenly transfixed with horror. Sitting on the "gentle-brown carpet" in the "religious half-light" is a rotting corpse, an abomination in the very nave of peaceful nature. When he tries to flee, it seems to him that nature turns on him in a fury, that the snagging branches and brambles at the threshold of the delusive chapel now try to throw him on the unspeakable corpse. But at a distance the aspect of the horrible chapel seems to change, like the enraged mountain in the fable: "The trees about the portal of the chapel moved soughingly in a soft wind. A sad silence was upon the little, guarding edifice." Earlier, after his company has beaten off an enemy attack, he has glanced upward and felt "a flash of astonishment at the blue sky and the sun gleaming on the trees and fields"; it has seemed to him "surprising that nature had gone tranquilly on with her golden processes in the midst of so much devilment." Such shifts in Henry's perception are signs of his spiritual disorder. A victim of his vain expectations, he can never be certain whether nature is hostile or sympathetic, or merely indifferent.

When Henry is returned to his regiment by the humble and competent "cheery soldier," he finds that his braggart friend Wilson, "the loud soldier," veteran now of a battle, has undergone a remarkable change: he no longer regards anxiously "the proportions of his personal prowess" but shows now a "fine reliance" and "quiet belief in his purposes and abilities." "He was no more a loud young soldier." Henry wonders "where had been born these new eyes" and notes that Wilson "apparently had now climbed a peak of wisdom from which he could perceive himself as a very wee thing." The meaning of the mountain image has clearly shifted: it is no longer the angry mountain driving an exasperated little man to desperate but futile assault, but "a peak of wisdom" from which he is able to perceive correctly his humble place in the scheme of things. Having exorcised his corrupting vanity, Wilson sees himself and the world clearly and truly, as Henry later does also after he yields himself to the larger purposes of the regiment and heroically leads a charge against the enemy.

But the problem with Henry is different. Wilson's conversion is merely given; Henry's must, according to the narrative logic, be demonstrated. Figuratively, he is the little man at war against God as well as against the Confederate enemy, and the war against God he cannot win. When Crane describes Henry's moral transformation in the final chapter, he simply drops the issue of his hero's adversary relation to the landscape. Revising the text before submitting it to Appleton for publication, he deleted in the last chapter all crucial reference to Henry's experience with nature. He struck the sentence "Echoes of his terrible combat with the arrayed forces of the universe came to his ears," and he struck also Henry's thought that the God of wrath could have justly commanded his obeisance–"that he had been wrong not to kiss the knife and bow to the cudgel." He deleted references to the indifference of nature and to Henry's momentary impulse to see himself "once again fraternizing with nature," remembering presumably the harmony he felt with it in the forest before finding the

corspe in the little chapel-like bower. Crane deleted also Henry's reflection that he could "no more stand upon places high and false, and denounce the distant planets." As these cancellations suggest, Crane's attitude toward God was markedly ambivalent, as it is in *The Black Riders,* and his purpose in the revision was apparently to avoid the problem of resolving the whole uncertain issue of Henry's war against God. This evasion is undoubtedly the reason for the diminished vitality of the chapters describing Henry's heroic battlefield exploits: the slackness of the irony, as in the notoriously sentimental description of Henry's feeling about the rescued flag, and the weakening of the symbolic resonance of the imagery.

The irreconcilable tension between Crane's religious and heroic imaginations is clearly revealed in this weakness in construction. If the second half of the novel is much like the conventional heroic war story (expressive certainly of one side of Crane's nature), the first half is powerfully and originally imaginative. The pathos of Henry's alienation in an incomprehensible world, of his helplessness under the spell of his vanity, and of his poignant yearnings for a sign is brilliantly rendered. Generations of readers have found memorable the fantastic descriptions of the landscape, the gay humor of the country maiden's heroic battle to rescue her cow from the fat thieving soldier, the horror of the discovery in the little forest chapel, the awesome death of Jim Conklin, the patient and selfless suffering of "the tattered man," the manliness of the anonymous "cheery soldier," and other scenes, incidents, and characters.

The first publication of *The Red Badge of Courage,* like that of *Maggie,* was irregular and discouraging. *McClure's Monthly* accepted it, presumably intending to publish it as a serial. But after six months of waiting, Crane, doubtful that any such plan would ever be carried out, withdrew it and sold it for ninety dollars to Irving Bacheller, who carved away two-thirds of the text and distributed this abridged version to his newspaper syndicate. It appeared in the *Philadelphia Press,* the *New York Press,* and many other newspapers across the nation (in serial form in many) in early December 1894. Pleased by the favorable response of editors and readers and impressed by Crane's demonstrated powers of description, Bacheller engaged him as a special correspondent and ordered him on a journalistic expedition to Mexico via Nebraska, Louisiana, Arkansas, and Texas. Hastily completing arrangements for the publication of *The Black Riders,* which an editor friend had recommended to a Boston publisher of experimental poetry, and of *The Red Badge of Courage,* the newspaper version of which had attracted the attention of the publisher D. Appleton, Crane departed on his four months' journey west in late January 1895.

The first leg of his trip took him to Lincoln, Nebraska, where he arrived, via St. Louis and Kansas City, in early February 1895. He was already known to the young Nebraskan Willa Cather, a part-time reporter for the *Nebraska State Journal,* who hoped to become a novelist also, and she queried him about writing as he lounged about the newspaper offices, shabby and dispirited, waiting for money from Bacheller. He journeyed into surrounding counties in search of information for an article about Nebraska farmers and their battles against the fury of their weather. In imagery like that he had used in depicting the landscapes of Sullivan County and Chancellorsville, where Henry first encountered "the blood-swollen god" of war, Crane described the agony of a land scorched by a "terrible and inscrutable wrath of nature," a screaming wind, "hot as an oven's fury," that raged over the rich, brown crops "like a pestilence" while the farmers stood by in helpless despair. "It was as if upon the massive altar of the earth, their homes and their families were being offered in sacrifice to the wrath of some blind and pitiless deity." This powerful description he wrote, paradoxically, during a blizzard which brought upon the people another "strange and unspeakable punishment of nature," winds from the north that swept over the devastated country like "wolves of ice." The graphic imagery of tempest-driven snowflakes "fleeing into the south, traversing as level as a line of bullets, speeding like the wind" he adapted nearly three years later in his masterful little tragedy of the Nebraskan plains, "The Blue Hotel": "great whirls and clouds of flakes, swept up from the ground by the frantic winds, were streaming southward with the speed of bullets."

In an article from Galveston, Texas, which he reached in early March after brief visits to New Orleans and Hot Springs, Arkansas, he noted ironically the disparity between the tourist's romantic expectations, conditioned by heroic legends of the West, and the actuality of the city's paved streets, webs of telegraph wires, clamorous trolleys and other such indications of industrial progress. He noted the contrast again in an arti-

cle from San Antonio in which he protested "an eloquent description of the city which makes it consist of three old ruins and a row of Mexicans sitting in the sun" when it is actually "a totally modern" city with "rows of handsome business blocks" and "the terrible almighty trolly car." This diminishment of the mythical Old West by the encroaching reality of civilization is the theme of three of his western stories, "The Blue Hotel," "The Bride Comes to Yellow Sky," and its sequel, "Moonlight on the Snow."

His attraction to the legendary, however, was by no means diminished by his discovery that an "eloquent description" of the Old West is more valuable as a "masterly literary effect" than as a guide to reality. His romantic imagination was profoundly stirred by the heroic legend of the Alamo, "the greatest memorial to courage which civilization has allowed to stand." In recounting the story of a man named Rose, the only member of the Alamo band to refuse Colonel Travis's call for volunteers to defend the mission to the death, Crane's imagination created a poignant movement. Rose stepped forward "with a strange inverted courage" and announced his decision. "He bade them adieu and climbed the wall. Upon its top he turned to look down at the upturned faces of his silent comrades." The suspended moment seems to concentrate the entire question of courage, a question Crane explored more elaborately in "The Five White Mice," a story he wrote in 1896 about a Mexican adventure of a character called the New York Kid. The Kid, facing in a despair of terror a deadly knife-wielding caballero on a gloomy night street in Mexico City, discovers when he at last finds the courage to draw his revolver that his formidable adversary has also been in a kind of despair of terror. His adversary leaps back with a startled cry and melts into the darkness. From a distance he calls, "Well, señor, it is finished?" The story ends: "Nothing had happened."

By mid March 1895 Crane was in Mexico, "hungry for color, form, action," as he noted in one of his articles, and as his dispatches show, the color and movement of Mexican life registered powerfully on his imagination. He found in the mysterious landscape and impassive mien of the people intimations of some alien and impalpable reality and drew once again on the tropes he used to describe Henry's feverish sense of the battlefields in *The Red Badge of Courage.* He was struck by "the inscrutable visage" of a sheepherder, by the "masses of crimson rays" from household fires in a village at dusk "where dark and sinister shadows moved," by the empty, blazing skies of Mexican noons, and by mountains which "stand like gods on the world" and silence the speech of men who "fear that they might hear." Such intimations of menace, he discovered, were not always merely literary or metaphysical. On an excursion in the Mexican backcountry, he and his guide, Miguel Itorbe, were asleep in a primitive village inn when they were awakened by the arrival of a gang of horsemen led by the bandit Ramon Colorado. Crane overheard their discussion of a plan to rob and perhaps murder him, but Colorado was distracted at the crucial moment by the arrival of a band of women. At dawn Crane and his guide fled into the desert on horseback, but the bandits, discovering their flight, gave chase and were gaining steadily on them when a company of mounted police appeared suddenly and drove Colorado and his men away. The hero of the story, which Crane wrote in September 1895 under the title "Horses—One Dash," is the swift little horse which responds to the crisis with supreme courage and determination. It is a masterful evocation of a sense of crisis, furious motion, and rapport between horse and rider.

The best of the stories based on the western adventure, however, are "The Bride Comes to Yellow Sky" (written in 1897) and "The Blue Hotel" (written in 1898). "The Bride Comes to Yellow Sky" introduced some of the themes and situations that later became standard conventions in the plots of commercial Westerns in pulp magazines and cowboy movies: the conflict between gunman and lawman, the climactic "face off" or "walkdown," the yielding of the lawless West to the irresistible influences of civilization. The six-gun wizard Scratchy Wilson, "about the last one of the old gang that used to hang out along the river," periodically goes on drunken rampages and shoots up the little plains town of Yellow Sky, Texas. For years Marshall Jack Potter has restored order on these occasions by facing Scratchy down, but one day when Jack is in San Antonio secretly getting married, the gunman launches an attack. Clad in boots that had "red tops with gilded imprints of the kind beloved in winter by little sledding boys on the hillsides of New England" and a "maroon-colored flannel shirt ... made, principally, by some Jewish women on the east side of New York," he strides up and down the street with revolvers in both hands, firing at everything that moves. The mar-

shall and his bride arrive on the 3:42 from San Antonio, and as they round a corner of the depot, encounter Scratchy face to face. Dropping the revolver he has paused to load, the old outlaw whips the other from its holster like lightning and flings a ferocious challenge at his old adversary. When the marshall advises him that he is unarmed and, moreover, married, Scratchy is paralyzed with astonishment. "Married?" he stammers finally, noticing at last "the drooping drowning woman at the other man's side." Gradually the full meaning of the situation dawns on him. "Well," he says, "I 'low it's all off, Jack." "He was not a student of chivalry," Crane writes; "it was merely that in the presence of this foreign condition he was a simple child of the earlier plains. He picked up his starboard revolver, and placing both weapons in their holsters, he went away."

Scratchy clearly plays—not too seriously—a role created partly by the legend-mongering Eastern imagination, as his costume was created largely by the New York garment industry. In "The Blue Hotel" Eastern influences have dire consequences. The hero, a half-crazed Swede newly arrived in Rompers, Nebraska, his head full of fantasies of violence, is convinced that the blue hotel, where he is the guest of a genial Irishman, old Scully, harbors desperadoes intent on his murder. The terrified Swede's odd behavior leads him finally into a fight with Scully's son, whom the Swede soundly thrashes as Scully and two other guests look on. Flushed with victory, the Swede leaves the hotel, pushing arrogantly through a raging blizzard as if he has defeated it as well as young Scully. In the local saloon he orders whiskey, and blustering and boasting, invites a gambler and his table companions to drink with him. When the gambler refuses, the Swede wrathfully seizes him by the throat. Suddenly a blade "shot forward, and a human body, this citadel of virtue, wisdom, power, was pierced as easily as if it had been a melon. The Swede fell with a supreme cry of astonishment."

"The Blue Hotel" is an ingenious adaptation of the theme of *The Red Badge of Courage* and some of the Sullivan County stories. Like Henry Fleming and the little man, the Swede is at war against nature, and, like them, he can imagine personal victories over it. At one time the vainglorious Henry entertains visions of his triumph over fallen "paper peaks," and once congratulates himself as the deserving recipient of nature's warm sympathy and friendly solicitude. The Swede, having battled his way to the saloon through the blizzard, finds himself likewise equal to this adversary: "I like this weather," he tells the bartender. "I like it. It suits me." Describing this hero's brave progress through the fury of the storm, Crane reflects, more darkly than anywhere in *The Red Badge of Courage,* on man's awesome presumptuousness: "One viewed the existence of man then as a marvel, and conceded a glamour of wonder to these lice which were caused to cling to a whirling, fire-smote, ice-locked, disease-stricken, space-lost bulb. The conceit of man was explained by this storm to be the very engine of life." Like *The Red Badge of Courage,* "The Blue Hotel" is rooted in the deepest sources of Crane's imagination: his radical sense of man's alienation in a problematical universe.

His western adventure contributed significantly to Crane's literary resources, providing not only new subjects and settings but confirmation of the themes and ideas of the earlier fiction. The vast plains of Nebraska and Texas, the awesome mountains of Mexico, the violent western weather, seemed to confirm his convictions about the ways of nature. The primitive, half-lawless settlements like his fictional War Post, Yellow Sky, Rompers, and Tin Can stimulated his sense of the legendary Old West and its theatrical myth of acute crisis and exquisite personal challenge. And tales of courage and commitment in the face of supreme dangers sharpened his ambivalent sense of the heroic ideal which, as in the war novel, he paradoxically both celebrated and ironically mocked.

When he returned to New York City in mid May 1895, he paused to distribute signed copies of *The Black Riders,* which had appeared a few days before his arrival, and then went west to his brother Edmund's house in Hartwood, in Sullivan County, where he lived, with frequent sojourns in the city and other places, for more than a year. Here he received the first reviews of *The Black Riders,* most of which complained of his eccentric disregard for conventional poetic forms, though a few also praised his power and originality. One well-known reviewer, Harry T. Peck of the *Bookman,* praised the poet as "a bold—sometimes too bold—original, and powerful writer of eccentric verse," characteristics which Peck and others thought linked him to Whitman and Dickinson. By early summer his literary reputation among editors and writers such as Richard Harding Davis, Irving Bacheller, S. S. McClure, R. W. Gilder, and Willis Hawkins was well established, and on the strength of it he was invited to

join the Lantern Club, a literary society headed by Bacheller. Crane was apparently searching at this time for a salaried position on some newspaper, for he was in Philadelphia in early September to discuss his possible appointment as drama critic for the *Philadelphia Press;* but he was not hired, despite the editor's personal admiration of the short version of *The Red Badge of Courage* the *Press* had printed in 1894. Crane stayed on in Philadelphia for a while, writing "Horses—One Dash" and basking in his local fame as a war writer. He was in New York when *The Red Badge of Courage* was published in October (1895), then in Hartwood, eagerly following the reviews and pondering his literary situation.

As his letters of late 1895 and early 1896 suggest, his literary situation was somewhat problematic, paradoxically because of the immense success of *The Red Badge of Courage.* It created something of a sensation in late 1895, and before the end of that year Crane was a famous man, an international celebrity known on both sides of the Atlantic for his brilliant and uncompromisingly realistic portrayal of war. But the novel seemed to prove that he was more a realist in theory than in practice, and he was painfully aware that his literary mentors, Howells and Garland, would take it as clear evidence of his abandonment of serious literary purpose, a view Howells more than hinted when he wrote Crane early in 1896: "For me, I remain true to my first love, 'Maggie.' That is better than all the Black Riders and Red Badges." Crane had anticipated the point, however, for in November 1895, about the time he was expressing surprise at his sudden fame and reporting that his incoming mail at Hartwood had "reached mighty proportions," he felt obliged to reaffirm his program as a literary realist: "I decided [in 1892]," he wrote an editor, "that the nearer a writer gets to life the greater he becomes as an artist, and most of my prose writings have been toward the goal partially described by that misunderstood and abused word, realism." He complained about the war novel, as if he blamed it for the predicament it had put him in by making him an authority on war, which he had never seen, and by establishing him as a master of realism, whose first principle he had conspicuously violated. He began in those early months of his fame to derogate the novel: "I suppose I ought to be thankful to 'The Red Badge' but I am much fonder of my little book of poems, 'The Black Riders.' My aim was to comprehend in it the thoughts I have had about life in general, while 'The Red Badge' is a mere episode in life, an amplification" (a comment which may suggest, incidentally, that he was conscious of a significant relationship in the themes of the two books). And he referred to it variously as the "damned 'Red Badge,' " "that damned book," "the accursed 'Red Badge.' "

His belief that a true literary realist ought to write only about what he has experienced first-hand perhaps helps to explain his reluctance to write more war stories, which editors, with their eyes on the success of the novel, were bound to demand. In October 1895 he began a new novel, *The Third Violet,* published in 1897, a thin little comedy of manners based on personal experience which, though in accord with current realistic theory, was, as he realized almost from the beginning, not the kind of realism for which his genius was best suited. In November he reluctantly turned again to war stories. "I am writing a story–'The Little Regiment' for McClure," he complained. "It is awfully hard. I have invented the sum of my invention with regard to war and this story keeps me in internal despair." "The Little Regiment" became the title story of his collection of war stories published late in 1896, and he was still laboring over it in February 1896 when he wrote his friend Nellie Crouse, "I am engaged in rowing with people who wish me to write more war-stories. Hang all war-stories." He referred to "Three Miraculous Soldiers," another war story he was writing at the time, as a "little" story in a note to McClure in January, warning him that the agreement they had made for Crane to write a series of war stories for the Phillip's-McClure Syndicate might not be altogether advantageous to the publisher. "I am perfectly satisfied with my end of it," he advised, "but your end somewhat worries me for I am often inexpressibly dull and uncreative and these periods often last for days"; and again, "I feel for you when I think of some of the things of mine which you will have to read or have read." But by the end of February he had written a total of five new war stories since the publication of *The Red Badge of Courage:* "Three Miraculous Soldiers," "An Indiana Campaign," "The Veteran," "An Episode of War," and "The Little Regiment." He sent at least three–"Three Miraculous Soldiers," "The Veteran," and "The Little Regiment"–to McClure, but only the last two appeared in *McClure's Magazine.* When he finished "The Little Regiment" at the end of that month he described it to the editor of the *Critic* as "a nov-

elette which represents my work at its best," but he felt privately that it showed his failing inspiration as a war writer. He added emphatically that it was "positively my last thing dealing with battle."

The general tendency in these stories, published in late 1896 as *The Little Regiment,* is toward a more conventional realism. Although they draw heavily on the characteristic metaphors and images of *The Red Badge of Courage,* they tend toward a more conventional description, picturing the world not as a projection of the hero's anxieties and fantasies, as in the earlier fiction, but as a world objectively described by a disinterested narrator. The poignantly alienated little man, whose distressed psychological life provides a colorful and dramatic version of reality, appears in none of these stories, and the haunted landscape, though still invested with mystery and menace, is a landscape seen by the narrator, not by the fanciful hero. Thus the radical conflict between the hero and nature which accounts for the intensity and resonance of *The Red Badge of Courage* is abandoned in *The Little Regiment.* The heroes of these stories appear as more or less realistic social types. Unlike Henry Fleming, whose raw perceptions, fantasies, and mercurial emotions are the source of the poetry of the war novel, the heroes of *The Little Regiment* are more normally rational and judgmental. In "A Mystery of Heroism" Fred Collins charges across a field under heavy fire to fetch a bucket of water from a distant well, an action which recalls Henry's desperate charges under fire in the novel. But Collins, unlike Henry, is reflective and critical, conscious of his vanity and its ethical and social significance. The menace in the field is that of Confederate artillery, not a threat born of his guilt or fanciful expectations.

This tendency toward a more objective method and more discursive style is characteristic of the other stories as well. The hallucinatory imagery–the violent colors, the mystical air of menace and dread, the hyperbolic evocation of the monstrous which represents the hero's distraught moral sense–is notably subdued. "An Indiana Campaign" is a comedy of manners gently satirizing old Major Tom Boldin and the folks of Migglesville for their unsophisticated reaction to an idle rumor about a rebel soldier hiding in a cornfield. Although the heroine of "Three Miraculous Soldiers" has certain heroic ambitions, like her very distant fictional cousins Henry and the little man, her homely common sense protects her against fanciful schemes–"gorgeous contrivances and expedients of fiction"–to rescue three friendly soldiers imprisoned in her father's barn. The title story, "The Little Regiment," is an anecdote about two brothers whose deep mutual affection is concealed by their constant bickering, and the function of the war setting, which is profusely elaborated, is merely to provide the moment of danger which tests their true feelings. This story, three months in the writing, engaged Crane in a "daily battle with a tangle of facts and emotions," a difficulty which arose doubtless from his attempt to adapt the reflexive style of the novel to an inappropriate subject.

More successful is "The Veteran," a brief sequel to *The Red Badge of Courage* which tells how Henry Fleming as an old man sacrifices his life trying to rescue two colts from a burning barn and points clearly toward the new style Crane was apparently seeking. The imagery of the familiar metaphysical landscape is much subdued and is largely external to old Henry's thought. The lean, disciplined prose moves the story rapidly from Henry's account of running away from his first battle at Chancellorsville to the narrator's sharp description of his final rush into the blazing barn, just before the roof falls in. The story begins with a brief glimpse of "three hickory trees placed irregularly in a meadow that was resplendent in spring-time green," a faint reminder of that spring long ago when young Henry found the idyllic landscape suddenly filled with "red and green dragons." In the distance, standing now invincible, is another version of the familiar little chapel, "the old, dismal belfry of the village church." Telling the story of his flight, old Henry can now appreciate "some comedy in this recital." The enemy, he recalls, appeared as a "lot of flitting figures," and he remembers thinking at the moment of panic that "the sky was falling down," that "the world was coming to an end." Thus he describes in a serene latter-day recollection the "red and green dragons." The barn in which he meets his death is presented at first glance in "its usual appearance, solemn, rather mystic in the black night," but when he hurls aside the door, "a yellow flame leaped out at one corner and sped and wavered frantically up the old grey wall. It was glad, terrible, this single flame, like the wild banner of deadly and triumphant foes." This picture of satanic fire, "laden with tones of hate and death, a hymn of wonderful ferocity," crosses with the image of demonic war, and old Henry at last challenges the God of wrath he was

permitted to evade at the end of *The Red Badge of Courage*. Thus the story skillfully adapts Crane's familiar symbolic materials to a new style, the style essentially of "The Open Boat," a story "after the fact," as the subtitle notes, but one which, like "The Veteran," is composed of elements drawn obliquely from his mythic imagination.

The Third Violet, which he finished in December 1895, is a romantic comedy of courtship somewhat in the manner of Howells, though without his mentor's consummate mastery of the realism of specification or his grasp of the intricacies of social codes and conventions. Except in "The Pace of Youth," a charming 1893 story about the elopement of two merry-go-round attendants, Crane never wrote successfully about romantic love, and *The Third Violet*, which tells the story of an impressionist painter's wooing of a New York belle, is perhaps the most inconsequential of his efforts to deal with the subject, though his 1899 novel *Active Service* is also a notable failure. For the plot of *The Third Violet* he attempted to tie together two strands of autobiography: his unhappy summer romance with Helen Trent, whom he knew at Asbury Park in 1891, and his life in the gloomy old Art Students' League building he shared with other indigent bohemians in his early years in New York. The courtship begins when Billie Hawker meets Miss Grace Fanhall at a Sullivan County summer vacation hotel and continues in the city after the return of Hawker to his studio and Miss Fanhall to her elegant New York town house. The story ends when Hawker is permitted to understand at last that Miss Fanhall cares for him, an issue addressed somewhat esoterically in Miss Fanhall's manner when she makes her lover a gift, on three different occasions, of a single violet. Except for a vivid portrait of Hawker's awkward and endearing Irish setter, Stanley, and a few happy touches in the characterization of studio life, the novel could hardly be identified on the basis of its style as Crane's. He was aware himself that it was alien to his vision and method. When he mailed the manuscript to Appleton in December, he wrote a friend the same day, "It's pretty rotten work. I used myself up in the accursed 'Red Badge.'" *The Third Violet* is interesting chiefly as evidence of his literary uncertainty at this time and as an indication of the range of his experimentation under the pressure of his sudden recognition as a realist.

Crane aboard the Three Friends *as correspondent for the* New York World *during the Spanish-American War, 1898 (Frances Cabané Scovel Saportas)*

By mid 1896 he had arranged for the publication of all the books he had completed to date. Appleton accepted *The Third Violet* (though somewhat reluctantly, delaying its publication until the spring of 1897) and *The Little Regiment,* which appeared at the end of 1896. The publisher also scheduled a new edition of *Maggie,* which had languished in obscurity since its private publication in the spring of 1893, and Crane began revising it in March 1896, largely by smoothing out some of its doubtful grammar and deleting profanities. Another publisher, Edward Arnold, bought *George's Mother,* and in June both of these companion novels appeared. Although there was the usual carping among the reviewers about the ugliness of war and poverty, the books were on the whole well received, some reviewers finding *The Little Regiment* even better than *The Red Badge of Courage* because the stories admitted more of the spirit of romance. Very few denied the power and originality of the pictures of slum life in *Maggie* and *George's Mother,* evidence perhaps that readers were beginning to come to terms with Crane's innovative methods. He began no more big literary projects after finishing the war

stories, though he considered and rejected McClure's earlier proposals that he write a novel about Washington politics and another book describing some of the major battles of the Civil War. Instead, he arranged with Hearst's *New York Journal* for a series of articles on New York low life and returned once again to the study of the tenderloin which had been interrupted by his western excursion.

That fall (1896), while gathering material for a piece on New York police courts, he became involved in an incident which significantly affected the course of his life, since as a result of it he was never able to live in peace in New York City again. As he was leaving the Turkish Smoking Parlors late one September night with two women to whom he had been talking about their experiences in police courts, a prostitute named Dora Clark approached and joined the group. When Crane stepped aside for a moment to escort one of the women to a cable car, a policemen suddenly appeared and arrested Dora Clark for soliciting. Crane protested, taking the matter as another indication of the notorious brutality and corruption of the police, the very subject he was investigating for his article. The officer threatened to arrest Crane, but the novelist followed him and his prisoner to the station and testified against him in the police-court hearing. Later, he sent a lengthy telegram of protest to Police Commissioner Theodore Roosevelt, and when Dora Clark's suit against the officer came up in court in October 1896, Crane testified again in her behalf. The affair was thoroughly aired in the newspapers, which hailed Crane as a hero for defending the abused Dora, though not without a good deal of sly humor at his expense. The affair cost him the friendship of Commissioner Roosevelt, who had been an early and enthusiastic admirer of *The Red Badge of Courage,* and earned him the lasting hatred of the New York police force, which, as a friend who was with him during the affair observed, "bent all its unscrupulous energies to discrediting him and making New York too hot for him." After he left New York in November 1896, he never lived in the city again; he was harassed by the police as late as January 1899, when he paused there briefly to visit friends on his way home to England from Havana and the Spanish-American War. The policeman he testified against was Charles Becker, who was electrocuted in 1913 for hiring the murder of a gambler who threatened to expose his connections with the underworld.

In November, Irving Bacheller, convinced that Cuba's revolt against Spain would develop into a full-blown revolution, engaged Crane once more as a special correspondent, this time with an assignment far more dangerous and demanding than the one which sent him to the West and Mexico. He was now a war correspondent, a profession he would follow, off and on, for the rest of his life. Arriving in Jacksonville, Florida, in November 1896, with $700 in gold in his money belt, he began his search, in a tense atmosphere of international conspiracy and intrigue, for passage to Havana in one of the filibustering ships running arms and supplies to the Cuban insurgents. He met, fatefully, Cora Taylor, a colorful adventuress who had deserted her husband, a British army and foreign-service officer, to become the proprietress of a discreet brothel, the Hotel de Dream. She later accompanied Crane to Greece as the first woman war correspondent and still later to England as his common-law wife. In late December 1896 he signed on the crew of the filibuster ship *Commodore* as a seaman, and on New Year's Eve, carrying a cargo of cased guns and ammunition and a company of Cuban insurrectionists, the *Commodore* steamed down the St. Johns River, and finally, after delays caused by running aground twice on sandbars in the river, stood to the open sea.

His masterful dispatch to the *New York Press* on 6 January describes vividly the disaster which overtook the *Commodore:* the discovery on the night of 1 January that the groundings had opened her seams, the frantic and futile efforts of the crew to bail the flooded engine room when the pumps failed, the confusion in the management of the lifeboats which resulted ultimately in the stranding of seven crew members on the sinking ship, the horror of abandoning a terrified crewman in the water who threatened to swamp the heavily loaded dinghy Crane shared with the captain and two other crew members, the awesome plunge of the ship as it went down, and the death of the ship's oiler when the dinghy was swamped in the surf in the attempt to land it at Daytona Beach on 3 January. "The history of life in an open boat for thirty hours," Crane wrote at the end of his report, "would no doubt be very instructive for the young, but none is to be told here now." Though physically exhausted and, according to one report, profoundly depressed for days after the ordeal, he must have begun "The Open Boat" almost immediately, for

it was finished and in the hands of his literary agent by the end of February.

For this masterful story Crane drew on literary resources he had been developing since the Sullivan County sketches of 1892. The metaphysical landscapes in these stories and in *The Red Badge of Courage* become in "The Open Boat" the ambiguous seascape which appears to the anxious correspondent, the protagonist of the story, in a bewildering variety of aspects. The sea is nature—"nature in the wind, and nature in the vision of men"—and it appears sometimes cruel, wrathful, and deadly; sometimes wildly beautiful and picturesque; and again merely stolidly indifferent. Like the hero of Crane's poems about God and the hero of his war novel, the correspondent feels that this problematic nature somehow holds the key to the mystery of existence, but unlike these earlier heroes, who confront nature's mystery in helpless and inarticulate confusion, the correspondent is fully conscious and introspective, aware of his egotistical presumptions and of the multifarious ironies in his shifting perceptions of his plight. He knows, as Henry does not, that uncertainty of perception is central to the whole issue. Speaking for himself and the men, he articulates through the narrator their anxiety in the face of uncertainty and mere seeming. To them "the waves *seemed* thrust up in points like rocks." "Viewed from a balcony," their battle against the raging sea "would *doubtless* have been weirdly picturesque." It was "*probably* splendid," it was "*probably* glorious" (italics added). It merely *occurs* to a man that nature does not regard him as important, and for the correspondent the "high cold star on a winter's night" symbolizes nature's attitude toward the men in the boat. Sometimes the correspondent is in the boat, his vision exquisitely narrowed to the threat of the "slaty wall" of waves; sometimes he seems to observe their plight from afar, critically, sadly, even mockingly.

The structure of this powerful story is based on a number of such ironic contrasts, as in, for example, the dramatic antitheses in the exchange among the cook, the correspondent, and the oiler on the difference between a lifesaving station and a house of refuge. The cook's assertion that they will be rescued by the lifesaving crew at the house of refuge near Mosquito Inlet is like a proposition for a debate, challenged, after a balanced question and answer, by the correspondent's statement that houses of refuge have no lifesaving crews. The impasse is addressed by the oiler: "Well, we're not there yet"; but the cook, unwilling to abandon his hopeful illusion, restates his proposition, though allowing now for the correspondent's challenging discrimination between lifesaving stations and houses of refuge. The passage ends with the skeptical oiler's repeated "We're not there yet." The formal design of the colloquy, with its balance and contrast of assertion and the refrainlike comment of the oiler, emphasizes the cook's presumption, an ironic effect powerfully reinforced when the narrator intrudes to say almost casually: "It is fair to say here that there was not a life-saving station within twenty miles in either direction; but the men did not know this fact, and in consequence they made dark and approbrious remarks concerning the eyesight of the nation's life-savers."

Ironic tension is also sustained by the memorable imagery of the contradictory aspects of nature. To the men, the sea gulls seem at different times to be allies or agents of a hostile nature, for "the wrath of the sea was no more to them than it was to a covey of prairie chickens a thousand miles inland." The gull that attacks the captain and threatens to swamp the boat seems malicious. When the birds come close, they seem "uncanny and sinister" and "somehow gruesome and ominous" as they stare at the men with "black bead-like eyes." But later, when they are seen from afar "in slanting flight up the wind toward the gray desolate east," they seem to represent not nature's wrath but the beauty of her order and design.

This ambiguity is suggested also in such phrases as "the terrible grace of the waves," and memorably in the description of the shark, the unnameable "thing" whose "enormous fin" cuts "like a shadow through the water." Like the sea gulls, it strikes the correspondent as an agent of nature's inscrutable malice, and yet he can reflect, as he looks dully into the sea and swears, that "the speed and power of the thing was to be greatly admired."

But in the end, it is the "high cold star" and the desolate distant wind tower which seem to the correspondent to be the true correlatives of nature's significance. The wind tower, "standing with its back to the plight of ants," seems to represent "the serenity of nature amid the struggle of the individual. . . . She did not seem cruel to him then, nor beneficent, nor treacherous, nor wise. But she was indifferent, flatly indifferent." So much has the little man changed since he strutted on the conquered mountain, oblivious to its unconscious neutrality, and since he forlornly, in

one of the poems about God, addressed the sky and found it filled with armies.

In Jacksonville again Crane regained his strength under Cora Taylor's care and set about trying once again to find his way to Cuba. After a month of wading the swamps south of the city, trying to elude U.S. Navy patrol boats, he gave up and signed on with the *New York Journal* to report the fighting between the Greeks and Turks. He was in New York in mid March, where he was joined shortly by Cora Taylor, also going to Greece as a correspondent for the *Journal*. In London he arranged to report the war for the *Westminster Gazette* and then set out for Greece, arriving in Athens about mid April 1897.

He then began a month of hectic chasing after battles and rumors of battles. He was in Arta briefly, then in Athens again to meet Cora Taylor when she arrived under the name Imogene Carter. They joined the *Journal* staff and went north to Volo, where they heard on 4 May about the battle at Velestino. Crane arrived on the second day of the engagement, and from a mountain battery on a ridge overlooking Greek fortifications in the valley below, he witnessed real war for the first time. He followed the slow Greek retreat south and eventually arrived in Athens from Chalcis with a transport of wounded soldiers two days before the armistice was declared on 20 May.

After the Florida experience Crane was never very strong again. He was ill and tired much of the time he was in Greece, and he stayed on until June, resting. He had found Greece and the war disappointing, complaining that observing the battle at Velestino was "like trying to see a bum vaudeville show from behind a fat man who wiggles," though he also told Joseph Conrad later that "The Red Badge is all right. I have found [war] as I imagined it." His fine story "Death and the Child," written that fall in England and the only significant fiction for which he drew on his Greek experience, shows that he described real war and imaginary war in much the same way, shifting events from the real world to the symbolic world of his vision. The hero of "Death and the Child," Peza, is an Italian war correspondent of Greek extraction moved by patriotic sentiment to join the fighting against the Turks. He approaches the front, excited by prospects of battle, and works his way finally to a rifle pit directly in the Turks' line of advance. His enthusiasm is momentarily checked when the officer in charge instructs him to take a rifle and bandolier from a dead soldier, but when he hesitates one of the soldiers performs the task for him and Peza takes his place, with misgivings now, at the parapet with the riflemen. He becomes aware of a rising panic, a sense of being pulled by the dead soldier's bandolier down "to some mystic chamber under the earth." Looking behind him he sees that the corpse's head is turned a little toward him, "as if to get a better opportunity for the scrutiny. Two liquid-looking eyes were staring into his face." Peza is suddenly overwhelmed by panic. Tearing madly at the bandolier–"the dead man's arms"–he bolts toward the rear. Later, a tiny child, deserted in the confusion of war, finds him far behind the lines where he has flung himself to the ground, exhausted and despairing. "Are you a man?" the child asks, and the correspondent, "confronting the primitive courage, the sovereign child, the brother of the mountains, the sky and the sea," knew that "the definition of his misery could be written on a wee grass blade." The story is clearly a version of *The Red Badge of Courage*, which it resembles in the incident of the panicky flight, in its implication of nature in a drama of self-discovery, and in its imagery of the psychological distress that motivates the hero. But it is also like "The Open Boat" in that its protagonist is in a measure–up to the moment of panic–introspective and contemplative. "Death and the Child," "The Open Boat," and the two fine western stories which he also wrote that fall, "The Bride Comes to Yellow Sky" and "The Blue Hotel," show that Crane's powers were most formidable in works treating the crossing themes of man in war and man in nature, themes with which his more discursive, flexible, and reflective style, first developed in the sea story, discovered new and richer significance.

In London in June 1897 Crane decided to settle in England permanently to avoid gossip about his irregular relationship with Cora Taylor and the malice of the New York police, and after a few weeks in the city, moved to Ravensbrook House, Oxted, Surrey, where he plunged into work, writing with astonishing speed "The Monster," "Death and the Child," "The Bride Comes to Yellow Sky," and "The Blue Hotel." He was received cordially by prominent literary men, including Bernard Shaw, Ford Madox Ford, and Joseph Conrad. He discovered especially in Conrad, whose recently published *The Nigger of the Narcissus* (1897) he greatly admired, a kindred artistic spirit, and the mutual regard of the two men

doubtless benefited them both. By the time he finished "The Blue Hotel" in February 1898, he was weary again, suffering poor health, as he had off and on ever since his ordeal in Florida, and the burden of debts he owed publishers and editors for advances. When the *Maine* exploded on 15 February, he seemed hardly to notice, but suddenly in April intimations of war touched his imagination, and "white-faced with excitement," he dragged Conrad about London to help him borrow passage money to New York, where he planned to join the navy. "Nothing could have held him back," Conrad wrote. "He was ready to swim the ocean." He sailed shortly, leaving Cora at Ravensbrook House to deal with their creditors as best she could.

It is regrettable, as John Berryman notes, that he drove himself at the expense of health and energy to those "boring false wars, away from the passionate private real war in his mind." In Cuba as a war correspondent, after failing the physical examination for the navy, he was ill and disconsolate, distracted and reckless. He exposed himself needlessly to Spanish fire at Guantánamo, where he landed with the marines in June, and again at San Juan in July, deliberately attempting suicide, some observers thought. Richard Harding Davis, the dean of war correspondents, who witnessed and reported the incident at San Juan, thought Crane was nevertheless the most successful war reporter in Cuba, citing Crane's "Marines Signalling Under Fire at Guantánamo" as one of the best dispatches of the war. After San Juan Crane was at Old Point Comfort, Virginia, resting, then in New York, where he learned at the *World* offices that he had been fired for filing a report for a wounded correspondent for a rival newspaper. He signed on with the *Journal* and immediately headed south to cover the Puerto Rican campaign, which ended when the armistice was signed in August. He then disappeared for months, burying himself in Havana to write most of the war stories for *Wounds in the Rain* (1900), and to finish his long, tedious novel about a correspondent's courtship in wartime Greece, *Active Service* (1899), begun at Ravensbrook House in 1898.

He was in New York six weeks at the end of the year, and then in England again in January, at Brede Place, an ancient manor house near Rye in Sussex which Cora had rented in his absence. He slowly recuperated from his Cuban adventure, writing little at first, reading mostly, and seeing his numerous literary friends. Henry James, who lived at Rye, was a frequent visitor, and Crane renewed his friendship with Conrad. H. G. Wells and Edward Garnett, both of whom wrote brilliant early critical studies of Crane, also came often, as did the journalist Robert Barr and other writers.

Three books appeared in 1899: *War is Kind,* his second volume of verse, whose title piece is the best, and the most complex, of all his poems; the Greek war novel, *Active Service;* and *The Monster,* whose title story, finished at Oxted in 1897, is a sharp study of community malice, written in a flattened, circumstantial style that moves toward conventional realism. The setting of "The Monster" and "His New Mittens," both in *The Monster,* is Whilomville, a fictional town modeled on Port Jervis, New York, where Crane lived as a young boy. This town is also the setting for the pieces he began writing later in the year, the amusing and often astute anecdotal studies of child life later collected as The *Whilomville Stories* (1900). He also wrote more Cuban war stories to add to those he wrote in Havana, published posthumously as *Wounds in the Rain* (1900), and two, oddly, about an imaginary war, one of which, "The Upturned Face," a grim story about a military burial under sniper fire, is a six-page masterpiece.

There are flashes of his formidable powers in many of these new stories and in the long sketch "War Memories," but consumption gained rapidly on him in the early months of 1900, and he was too weak to undertake major work. In the spring he worked on his swashbuckling romance, *The O'Ruddy* (1903), which he was probably writing as insurance for Cora Crane, but when he became too ill to continue, he turned the manuscript over to Robert Barr, who wrote the last half according to Crane's plot outline. He was hemorrhaging regularly by May, and Cora took him to Dover, and then, desperately, to a sanatorium at Badenweiler, in the Black Forest. There he died on 5 June, five months short of his twenty-ninth birthday.

Letters:

Stephen Crane: Letters, edited by R. W. Stallman and Lillian Gilkes (New York: New York University Press, 1960).

The source of most quotations from and references to Crane's correspondence in writings about him.

The Correspondence of Stephen Crane, edited by Paul Sorrentino and Stanley Wertheim (New York: Columbia University Press, 1988).

Adds many new letters, memoranda, inscriptions, and notes that contribute important details to Crane's biography.

Bibliography:

R. W. Stallman, *Stephen Crane: A Critical Bibliography* (Ames: Iowa State University Press, 1972).

An exhaustive listing of writing about Crane through the late 1960s.

Biographies:

Thomas Beer, *Stephen Crane: A Study in American Letters* (New York: Knopf, 1923).

Though dated and highly erroneous in many details, the source of most of the accepted ideas about Crane.

John Berryman, *Stephen Crane* (New York: Sloane, 1950; revised edition, New York: Farrar, Straus, Giroux, 1962).

This long-standing standard biography offers a well-written but controversial psychological interpretation of Crane's personality and writings.

R. W. Stallman, *Stephen Crane: A Biography* (New York: Brazillier, 1968).

A full-length biography with much detailed information.

Stephen Crane (New York, San Diego, & London: Harcourt, Brace, Jovanovich, 1984).

A brief critical biography designed as an introduction to Crane's life and writings.

References:

Frank Bergon, *Stephen Crane's Artistry* (New York & London: Columbia University Press, 1975).

A good description of Crane's unique style and its relation to his assumptions about the nature of things.

Edwin H. Cady, *Stephen Crane* (Boston: Twayne, 1980).

A good overview of Crane's writings.

Andrew Crosland, *A Concordance to the Complete Poetry of Stephen Crane* (Detroit: Gale Research/Bruccoli Clark, 1975).

Indispensable guide for research on Crane's poetry.

Daniel Hoffman, *The Poetry of Stephen Crane* (New York: Columbia University Press, 1957).
    The earliest significant study of Crane's poetry (and incidentally his fiction) and still a valuable critique of Crane's writings.

Syracuse University Library Associates Courier, 21 (Spring 1986).
    A special Crane edition of new essays based on new biographical materials, new letters, and new writings recently uncovered in the Schoberlin Crane Collection, now a part of the general Crane Collection in the George Arents Research Library for Special Collections, Syracuse University.

Papers:
Most of Crane's manuscripts and papers are in the Special Collection, Columbia University Libraries; the Stephen Crane Collection, George Arents Research Library, Syracuse University Library (which acquired new materials from the collector Melvin Scholberlin in 1984); the Berg Collection, New York Public Library; and the Waller Barrett Collection, Alderman Library, University of Virginia.

Emily Dickinson

This entry was updated by Armida Gilbert (University of South Carolina) from the entry by Ruth Miller (State University of New York at Stony Brook) in DLB 1, The American Renaissance in New England.

Places	Amherst, Mass.		
Influences and Relationships	Samuel Bowles Robert Browning Helen Hunt Jackson	Ralph Waldo Emerson Josiah G. Holland	Thomas Wentworth Higginson
Literary Movements and Forms	Lyrical Poetry	Romanticism	Hymns
Major Themes	Alienation of the Artist Self vs. Society	Death	Nature
Cultural and Artistic Influences	Rejection of Religious Orthodoxy and Revivalism	The Bible	
Social and Economic Influences			

BIRTH: Amherst, Massachusetts, 10 December 1830, to Edward and Emily Norcross Dickinson.

DEATH: Amherst, Massachusetts, 15 May 1886.

BOOKS: *Poems,* edited by Mabel Loomis Todd and T. W. Higginson (Boston: Roberts Brothers, 1890);

Poems, Second Series, edited by Higginson and Todd (Boston: Roberts Brothers, 1891);

Poems, Third Series, edited by Todd (Boston: Roberts Brothers, 1896);

The Single Hound: Poems of a Lifetime, edited by Martha Dickinson Bianchi (Boston: Little, Brown, 1914);

Further Poems of Emily Dickinson Withheld from Publication by Her Sister Lavinia, edited by Bianchi and Alfred Leete Hampson (Boston: Little, Brown, 1929; London: Secker, 1929);

Unpublished Poems of Emily Dickinson, edited by Bianchi and Hampson (Boston: Little, Brown, 1935);

Bolts of Melody: New Poems of Emily Dickinson, edited by Todd and Millicent Todd Bingham (New York: Harper, 1945; London: Cape, 1945);

The Poems of Emily Dickinson, 3 volumes, edited by Thomas H. Johnson (Cambridge: Harvard University Press, 1955).

Emily Dickinson

To be a poet was the sole ambition of Emily Dickinson. She achieved what she called her immortality by total commitment to the task, allowing nothing to deter her or intervene. Contrary to the myth that she would not deign to publish her verse, she made herculean efforts to reach out to a world that was not ready for the poems she offered; her manner and form were fifty years ahead of her time. The lines from James Russell Lowell's poem "The First Snowfall" are typical of popular taste in Dickinson's time; compare them with ones immediately following by Dickinson on the same subject (poem 311):

The snow had begun in the gloaming,
    And busily all the night
Had been heaping field and highway
    With a silence deep and white.

Every pine and fir and hemlock
    Wore ermine too dear for an earl,
And the poorest twig on the elm-tree
    Was ridged inch deep with pearl.

From sheds new-roofed with Carrara
    Came Chanticleer's muffled crow,
The stiff rails were softened to swan's down,
    And still fluttered down the snow.

I stood and watched by the window
    The noiseless work of the sky,
And the sudden flurried of snow-birds,
    Like brown leaves whirling by.

and

It sifts from Leaden Sieves–
It powders all the Wood.
It fills with Alabaster Wool
The Wrinkles of the Road–

It makes an Even Face
Of Mountain, and of Plain–
Unbroken Forehead from the East
Unto the East again–

It reaches to the Fence–
It wraps it Rail by Rail
Till it is lost in Fleeces–
It deals Celestial Vail

To Stump, and Stack–and Stem–
A Summer's empty Room–
Acres of Joints, where Harvests were,
Recordless, but for them–

It Ruffles Wrists of Posts
As Ankles of a Queen–
Then stills its Artisans–like Ghosts–
Denying they have been–

To be understood and appreciated, Emily Dickinson had to wait until a major shift in sensibility and expectation occurred in the decade surrounding World War I, when Imagism, a new school of poetry–precise, stripped of all extraneous verbiage, indifferent to traditional form and content, reaching always for the radical and original image, and wholly unsentimental–had established itself, preparing the way for modern American poetry. Amy Lowell's "Night Clouds," an example of the Imagist school, shows a style far more compatible with Dickinson's verse:

The white mares of the moon rush along the sky
Beating their golden hoofs upon the glass heavens;
The white mares of the moon are all standing on
    their hind legs
Pawing at the green porcelain doors of the remote
    heavens.
Fly, mares!
Strain, your utmost,
Scatter the milky dust of stars,
Or the tiger sun will leap upon you and destroy
    you
With one lick of his vermillion tongue.

Edgar Allan Poe failed in his day; his poems, too, had first to ignite the imagination of the French poet Charles Baudelaire, who opened the way to Symbolism and modern poetry on the Continent, before this country came to read and appreciate Poe. Walt Whitman, too, had a similar fate, although he was of tougher mold, and had the early support of Ralph Waldo Emerson; despite all, Whitman was not accepted, or if read–behind closed doors–not appreciated until our own time. Literary history in America is full of examples of its major writers–Poe, Herman Melville, Nathaniel Hawthorne, Henry David Thoreau, Whitman, Dickinson, perhaps even Henry James–failing in their day, with even a brief success dwindling away; some were driven into isolation and defeat, to be discovered half a century later and given first place. It has been up to modern writers to

choose their influences and ours have chosen the isolates of a former time. Looked at in this way, Emily Dickinson's story is typical of the artist in America: a loner, original in style; a bard, without honor in her own country, until her "letter to the world" reached later generations.

Because the biography of Emily Dickinson is so closely bound up with the meaning and substance of her poetry, a narrative of the events of her life illuminates not only her character and personality, but her poems. Bearing in mind her tendency to self-dramatization and hyperbole, we must read the letters and poems with caution, aware that while she strives to tell the truth, she always tells it "slant." However, there are facts we can be certain of, although much remains mysterious. We know she suffered a traumatic experience between the years of 1858 and 1862, but *what* that was, and whether it took the form of a single event or a cumulative series leading to a sense of loss or failure or rejection, we cannot prove. We know she withdrew into her father's house and for the last seventeen years of her life did not venture beyond the bounds of the "Homestead" with its conservatory and spacious grounds, but *why*, whether out of bitterness, pride, fear, personality maladjustment, or sickness of soul, we are unable, finally, to say. We know she dressed in white but cannot identify the precise meaning of the symbolic color; it may have meant the robe of the martyr, the garment of the virgin, or the mantle of the poet, or all three. She hid from visitors and refused to enter her brother's house, "a hedge away," for fifteen years, until the sudden illness of her beloved nephew brought her sadly to that bedside, but what caused the rupture is conjecture; we do not know if it was a quarrel or a betrayal, whether it was their choice or hers. We know she wrote more than 1,500 poems because we have her manuscripts. We know she copied and recopied 863 of them until they seemed to her perfect and tied them together into 43 separate collections called "fascicles," which she placed into her bureau drawer for posterity to find; we know she put aside another 240 poems, not yet finished, with variant words entered on the manuscripts, to await her final decisions as to word choice and sequence. We know she left approximately 400 poems in various stages of incompletion, on scraps of paper, on the backs of grocery lists, bills, programs, flyers, and used envelopes. But why she discarded some and slaved over others and what principle lay behind her making of the fascicles, we cannot determine. She wrote no essays, and guided only by what she tells us in the many poems she wrote on the creative act, and the cryptic references in her letters, we can only surmise her theory of poetry. There are about 200 poems for which no manuscript has yet been found; whether Dickinson indeed wrote them or whether they were imitations of the poet's style and substance by other people during the time when her poems, published after her death, began to enjoy a huge success, with family quarrels generating new discoveries of poems, altered, bowdlerized, regularized, "improved," is still open to question.

This is the person Richard Sewall predicts will rank with Whitman as one of two major American poets. She is the poet whose influence on modern American poetry has been documented by Amy Lowell, who once planned to write a biography of Dickinson but immersed herself in the new Imagist movement instead. She is the poet about whom the following have written praise: Genevieve Taggard, Marianne Moore, Conrad Aiken, Winfield Townley Scott, John Crowe Ransom, Richard Wilbur, Louise Bogan, Archibald MacLeish, J. V. Cunningham, Galway Kinnell, William Meredith, Philip Larkin, and Ted Hughes. Her poems have been translated into Polish, Hebrew, Japanese, French, and German, to name a few; and studies of her art have occupied scholars in Italy, Germany, Sweden, Japan, and India.

What little is known of her life may be summarized briefly. Emily was born into a household that stood at the center of culture and social activity at Amherst. Her grandfather was the founder of Amherst College; her father, and later her brother, served as the treasurer of that institution for a span of fifty-nine years. Her father, Edward, was a practicing lawyer and well-known, influential public figure. He was the moderator of the town meeting for sixteen years, brought the railroad and telegraph to Amherst, was elected as a representative to the General Court of Massachusetts, served as state senator in 1842-1843, and went to the United States Congress as representative from the Tenth District in Massachusetts in 1854-1855. Edward was admitted to practice law before the Supreme Court and was pressed to run as a candidate for lieutenant governor of Massachusetts in 1869, an offer he declined. In 1873 he was elected to serve on the General Court of Massachusetts and, while there, died suddenly, alone in his hotel room.

Emily's mother was a simple woman, wholly dedicated to her home and family, cheerfully undertaking her domestic duties. After her husband's death she had a stroke and lingered on until 1882, an invalid under the constant care of her daughters. Emily's brother Austin was less respected than his father. Although he, too, practiced law, he was more interested in art and theater, little concerned with politics, but dedicated to the community and the college, though he chafed under the limitations imposed on him by the small town. When he married Susan Gilbert, daughter of a tavern keeper in Amherst, Emily was thrilled to have her dear friend as a sister-in-law. The newlyweds wished to go to Chicago to start a new life, but Mr. Dickinson prevailed on them to stay, building a house next door to the Homestead, and made Austin a partner in his law firm. The marriage soured early and there was always an atmosphere of tension and emotional instability in "The Evergreens." Susan was a social climber and thought of herself as the hostess of Amherst. To her house came Wendell Phillips and Emerson; Samuel Bowles, the editor of the *Springfield Republican*; Judge Otis P. Lord of Salem; and Dr. Josiah Holland, the founder and editor of *Scribner's Magazine*. Bowles and Holland became lifelong friends of Emily's; near the end of her life she was contemplating marriage with Judge Lord.

Lavinia, Emily's younger sister, was not a profound companion but a forthright, active person with a sharp tongue, amiable enough, and practical—even a gadabout compared to Emily. As Austin and Emily succumbed to psychological distress, Lavinia seemed to grow stronger and thrive despite her own disappointment at not being able to find a young man who would marry her. She, too, remained a spinster, and it was Lavinia who was utterly fanatical about having Emily's poems published after her death.

A few good-hearted girls, children of college faculty members or of people well-established in the town, were Emily's friends, joining with her in the usual round of parties, visits, excursions, going to the same school, and, later, sustaining long correspondences. There is little comparable here to the famous friendships that existed between Emerson and Thoreau, Melville and Hawthorne, William Dean Howells and Mark Twain, or Howells and James. But her friends saved her letters and supplied recollections of a loving but demure, shy, and self-demeaning young woman. From her "secret sharing" we begin to find traces of alienation—at first a merely wistful sense of deprivation, carrying hints of a growing discomfort about the religious conversions that were going on about her, gradually darkening into a concern with death and longings for a fulfillment that was denied to her.

Her friendships with the young men of the town were conventional transient affairs—the students or young instructors or law clerks paid court for a time and moved on. There was no fulfilling love affair. She stayed close to home, reading, working in her garden, doing chores, and writing her poetry. There is evidence that a young law student, Ben Newton, encouraged her to become a poet. He died in 1853, which enables us to come close to an early dating of the budding career. The 1850s began as a time of diversions, innocent and ordinary; they concluded with a withdrawn and isolated poet living in growing solitude. The decade started with conventional friendships and ended with the traumatic relationship with Samuel Bowles, whom she first met in 1858.

Dickinson had long made it a practice to send a poem to friends and relatives, tucked inside a letter, hoping it would clarify a point she could not adequately express in prose. Fifty-one poems have been found among the papers of Bowles, and there is no way to tell how many more he received or how many were lost. Her letters to him show an undying hope that he would print one in his newspaper, but he refused. She brooded deeply over his indifference to her verse, noting he easily admitted to the literary columns the sentimental prattle of young lady poets Dickinson knew she transcended in every way. It never occurred to her that that was precisely why he could not print her verse; he himself did not fully understand her poems and was far more interested in politics, in good food and strong drink, in glamorous women. Here is an example from the kind of poem Bowles enjoyed, "A Tender Lay" in the 2 July 1857 *Springfield Republican:*

> Be gentle to the new laid egg,
>   For eggs are brilliant things;
> They cannot fly until they're hatched,
>   And have a pair of wings[.]

Here is what Dickinson did with the image of the hatched egg in poem 956:

> What shall I do when the Summer troubles—
> What, when the Rose is ripe—

> What when the Eggs fly off in Music
> From the Maple Keep?

It is unpleasant to realize the degree to which Dickinson suffered at the rejection of Bowles, but she was a vulnerable woman, albeit an invulnerable poet. Asking for advice, never taking it, asking for assessment, never believing it, she wrote many wistful, pleading, wry, ironic, sorrowful letters with poems to match. They show a changing relationship from supplication to challenge to suffering and despair. In poem 162 she talked of her fear of death, her doubts of salvation, at the same time confessing her great longings to be recognized as a poet, revealing her absolute conviction that she had a supreme gift.

> My River runs to thee—
> Blue Sea! Wilt welcome me?
> My River waits reply—
> Oh Sea—look graciously—
> I'll fetch thee Brooks
> From spotted nooks—
> Say—Sea—Take *Me!*

But her lyrics looked like nothing Bowles had ever seen; her laments did not rhyme; her tribulations were unmetrical; her figures of speech were too original. What else could Bowles do with a poem such as the following (poem 792) except to tuck it away among his papers where it was found in 1893.

> Through the strait pass of suffering—
> The Martyrs—even—trod.
> Their feet—upon Temptation—
> Their faces—upon God—

> A stately—shriven—Company—
> Convulsion—playing round—
> Harmless—as streaks of Meteor—
> Upon a Planet's Bond—

> Their faith—the everlasting troth—
> Their Expectation—fair—
> The Needle—to the North Degree—
> Wades—so—thro' polar Air!

On 7 July 1860 an article appeared in the *Springfield Republican* which Emily construed as a public rebuke and a rejection of all her hopes. Bowles calls attention to "the literature of misery," saying that the writers are "chiefly women . . . lonely and unhappy, whose suffering is seldom healthful." He advises them to wait until the storm is passed: "write not from the fullness of a present sorrow." Their poems reveal "a counte-nance we would gladly brighten, but not by expos-ing it to the gaze of a worthless world." It became at last apparent to Dickinson that there was no more to be hoped for from this quarter.

In the *Atlantic Monthly* of April 1862 she read "Letter to a Young Contributor," written by Thomas Wentworth Higginson, the literary edi-tor and well-known essayist. The article con-tained advice to poets, suggesting what they should write about, how they should train them-selves, what proper style should be, and so on. At once Dickinson sent four poems to ask his opin-ion of her work: "Are you too deeply occupied to say if my Verse is alive?" Higginson was gal-lant enough to write a reply but advised her not to publish. A correspondence ensued, 22 poems coming to the new mentor in the first year and 102 others during her lifetime. She pretends to be unschooled, pretends she is a novice, humble, a willing pupil, and elevates Higginson to the role of preceptor. At no point does he seem ever to have altered his first assessment of her "effu-sions," as he called them. He was gentle in his counsel that she study the craft, but inflexible, re-fusing always to sponsor a single one of her poems.

It was about this time that Dickinson with-drew from the world into a paradise of her own making, where she occupied herself with the writ-ing of verses such as poem 789 to prove to her-self again and again that her mentors were wrong.

> On a Columnar Self–
> How ample to rely
> In Tumult–or Extremity–
> How good the Certainty
>
> That Lever cannot pry–
> And Wedge cannot divide
> Conviction–That Granitic Base–
> Though None be on our Side–
>
> Suffice Us–for a Crowd–
> Ourself–and Rectitude–
> And that Assembly–not far off
> From furthest Spirit–God–

She withdrew into the confines of her house and garden to fulfill her self-appointed mission, work-ing on her poetry–endlessly revising, rewriting, sharpening her observations, and refining the verses. Inside the small room which held a few pieces of furniture–an iron bed, a small writing

table, a painted chair, and a bureau in which she stored her finished work–she allowed her imagina-tion to drift through her window, to wander on vast meadows, climb slopes and mountain peaks, sail on turbulent seas, and soar beyond the skies into the heavens. Her bees flew about, her birds took flight, her horses traversed eternities of space, bearing her spirit to the right hand of God. She never ceased to hope one day her cage door would open, her prison door unlock, her cof-fin lid rise. When she became convinced that the judgment of the world was final, she began to write poems to herself about herself, peering into her soul, traversing a distance between her heart, and her soul, and God. From this period come the poems that pass from self-pity to poise, poems that celebrate the strength of the self, the impregnability of her spirit, the mounting exalta-tion of the soul, all this coupled with an absolute conviction of the ultimate vindication of her poe-try, as poem 530 shows.

> You cannot put a Fire out
> A Thing that can ignite
> Can go, itself, without a Fan–
> Upon the slowest Night–
>
> You cannot fold a Flood–
> Or put it in a Drawer–
> Because the Winds would find it out–
> And tell your Cedar Floor–

Her themes grew more profound, feeding on the visions she had of truths that went far be-yond what she had been taught during her brief schooling at Amherst Academy between 1841 and 1847 and the curtailed year at Mount Hol-yoke in 1848. Her poems talk of affliction and gradual healing and ultimate patience; they ren-der the solitary self as a conscious choice; they con-template the problem of knowing, the experience of death, Jesus or God, the nature of Heaven and Immortality; her poems reflect on nature and regeneration. Using devices such as ellipse, ep-igram, personification, simile, allusion, expand-ing and contracting metaphors, symbolism, allegory, inventing fresh modes of syntax, adapt-ing conventional patterns of prosody to her new use, she created a style that transformed her thoughts into diabolically elusive and exquisite verse, which later generations would cherish, as she predicted in poem 883.

> The Poets light but Lamps–
> Themselves–go out–

115

The Wicks they stimulate–
If vital Light

Inhere as do the Suns–
Each Age a Lens
Disseminating their
Circumference–

The career of Emily Dickinson was without further event. Higginson visited once and found the experience too draining to repeat. She refused medical care when she began to have fainting spells toward the end of her life, saying the doctor might look in on her from the doorway of her bedroom but that was all. She died of Bright's disease on 15 May 1886. Higginson came to her funeral, and it was to him that Lavinia turned, with her young friend Mrs. Mabel Loomis Todd, to ask for his help in the projected publication of Emily's poems.

The publishing history of the poems is complex and warrants a detailed account for there is nothing quite like it in the annals of American literature. In her lifetime Dickinson saw no more than seven poems published, without signature: five in the *Springfield Republican,* one printed by her cousin in an issue of his short-lived journal, and the last slipped into a volume of poetry that was part of the *No Name* series, placed there by Helen Hunt Jackson and generally ascribed to Emerson. Four years after Dickinson's death Mrs. Todd and Higginson brought out a first volume of *Poems* that had to be reprinted twice in two months and ran into eleven editions within two years. A second volume was rushed into print in 1891 to take advantage of public acclaim, and the editing was geared to please public taste. With Mrs. Todd selecting and revising, Higginson organizing, titling, and advising, and because some critics had said that Dickinson was inept, unskilled in the craft, the poems were altered to appear more conventional; words were changed to refine the "harsh exterior," to give her lines "a grace of smoothness," which in an otherwise highly laudatory review Howells had implied she lacked. And the fascicles had long since been broken apart and the poems chosen according to the familiar themes of love, death, nature, friendship, with many of Dickinson's own rejects included, while those in the fascicles were ignored. *Poems, Second Series* went into five editions by 1893.

In October 1891 Higginson wrote an article for the *Atlantic Monthly* featuring the letters he had received from Dickinson during the years they had corresponded. He says it was a deliberate attempt to engage the attention of the potential reader with hints of a love-tragedy, and he made public his impressions of Dickinson as quaint and extravagant, an enigmatic, mysterious, childlike wraith who appeared to be enveloped in a "fiery mist." So successful was this ploy that Mrs. Todd immediately turned her full attention to the task of preparing a collection of Dickinson's letters. Had she not done so, close to the time when there were living friends and relatives to respond to her call, all might have been lost, for it was the custom in New England to burn letters at the death of a loved one unless there were explicit instructions to the contrary. All Dickinson's papers, except for the poems, were burned by her sister Lavinia.

The *Letters of Emily Dickinson* was stimulating and tantalizing, the editor herself removing what might invade "the sanctities" of privacy. Except for Howells, who, consistent to the last, always said the significance of the poet lay in the unique quality of the verse, no critic seemed interested in the poetry at this point. Mrs. Todd's devotion to her task was assuredly part of her long romantic liaison with Austin Dickinson, Emily's brother.

Soon after her arrival in Amherst in 1881, with her husband and infant daughter, Mrs. Todd met the Dickinsons, except for Emily, and after a flurry of friendship with Susan it became clear to all that Susan's nineteen-year-old son, Ned, and her husband were both smitten. Ned was sent packing, but the father was not. By 1883 the affair became a permanent factor in the life of all the Dickinsons, with Mabel, twenty-seven years younger than Austin, meeting her lover regularly in the Homestead. And Emily, well aware of the intrigue, loved her brother enough, and disliked her sister-in-law enough, to accept the circumstances. At Emily's death it was natural to turn to Mrs. Todd, who was already well acquainted with the poems, and solicit her help in the editing. She was paid nothing, Lavinia receiving all the money from the publications. Austin did stipulate that a meadow which he owned, adjacent to the Todd property, be given to Mabel Todd. In 1895, in the midst of the preparation of a third volume of poems, Austin died, and Lavinia agreed to make the transfer but wished to wait until the new volume, *Poems, Third Series* (1896), was in print.

How it was that Lavinia became an ally of Susan is not known, but instead of honoring Austin's will, Lavinia brought suit against Mrs. Todd to prevent the exchange of property. The great scandal of the lawsuit, which Lavinia won, caused Mrs. Todd to end all further association with the poems. She closed the lid of the box containing hundreds of manuscripts, and it was not reopened for nearly forty years. No one knew of her holdings.

The field was left to Susan's daughter. Within the year Lavinia was dead Susan, in sole possession of what she believed to be all of the Dickinson papers, and her daughter, Mrs. Martha Bianchi, worked tirelessly to bring new poems before the public. *The Single Hound* (1914) contained only poems sent to Susan Dickinson during the period when Emily sent copies of her work to "the other house." Mrs. Bianchi steadily refused to use any of the Todd-Higginson versions, and the public was startled to read different versions of familiar verses. Partisans of Dickinson were baffled; dissenting critics were delighted. There was even greater confusion when Mrs. Bianchi collected the poems that had been published in the three series of *Poems,* but in different versions, and combined these with her new discoveries in *The Complete Poems of Emily Dickinson.* More new poems appeared as *Further Poems of Emily Dickinson Withheld from Publication by Her Sister Lavinia* (1929) and *Unpublished Poems of Emily Dickinson* (1935). All that had hitherto been published were combined into a complete edition, *The Poems of Emily Dickinson* (1937).

After Mabel Todd's death in 1932 Mrs. Millicent Todd Bingham, her daughter, took up the battle on behalf of her mother. The box was at last opened, and she was free to publish the manuscripts that had lain hidden for almost forty years. In 1945 *Bolts of Melody: New Poems of Emily Dickinson* presented 668 poems to an astonished world. It was necessary and at last possible to bring all the poems together into a definitive edition based on the original manuscripts. The problems besetting Thomas Johnson, the editor of this massive undertaking, are suggested by the fact that Mrs. Bingham, who lived until 1968, would consent to the microfilming of her manuscripts only in the Library of Congress under the trustworthy eyes of Jay Leyda. Working scientifically, using a microscope to match pinholes and watermarks on the writing paper, a team of scholars restored the fascicles; astute analysis of Dickinson's handwriting by Theodora Ward was the means for establishing approximate dates for the writing of each poem. Since there were no titles, a location number was assigned to each poem and fragment. There was commentary to

describe the letter in which a poem appeared; all formerly published versions and Dickinson's variants were included. Three years later the same patient and careful scholarship produced a definitive edition of all the extant letters. It was a triumph of Richard Sewall's diplomacy and persistence that he persuaded Mrs. Bingham to release her mother's diaries and letters so that he could at last write a biography of the poet that resolves much of the mystery surrounding the poems. Sewall believes there are further poems and more letters that will turn up one day, and perhaps the whole process of discovery will begin again. Meanwhile we have an extraordinary canon of poems.

We know now it was at a very early age that Dickinson became fascinated with the art of poetry and began to practice her craft by rewriting poems she saw printed week by week, in newspapers, magazines, and popular anthologies, an activity she was to continue all her life. She was always stimulated to revise what she read, to pit her skill against that which had won a public stamp of approval. Anyone with patience can find hundreds of examples, not of borrowings or imitations but of revisions of verses, found in sources ranging from the *Hampshire and Franklin Express,* a village paper, to the *Springfield Republican* and the *Atlantic Monthly,* to collections of popular verse in her father's library; she pored over Thomas Bridgman's *Inscriptions on the Grave Stones in the Grave Yards of Northhampton, and of other towns in the Valley of Connecticut* and gradually widened her choices to include the major poets of England and America. She responded, in poetry, to passages in prose works such as *Reveries of a Bachelor* by Ik Marvell (Donald Grant Mitchell) and Henry Wadsworth Longfellow's *Kavanagh.* Poem 675, written in answer to Thomas Wentworth Higginson, is an example of the process:

> Literature is attar of roses, one distilled drop from a million blossoms. (Higginson, "Letter to a Young Contributor")

> Essential Oils—are wrung—
> The Attar from the Rose
> Be not expressed by Suns—alone—
> It is the gift of Screws—

Or, reading a story or news report that interested her, she might write a poem as if she were a character to whom the event had occurred.

"We don't cry–Tim and I" (196) may very well refer to Tiny Tim in Charles Dickens's *A Christmas Carol.* Many of her most provocative lyrics may not have been personal at all but poems assuming diverse personae in the manner of Robert Browning's dramatic monologues, which she admired and studied.

Nothing was banal or trivial to the poet; the poorest verse by Bayard Taylor caught her attention, as did lines from the *Book of Revelation.* She revised Francis Quarles or Mrs. Frances H. Cook. And this is true of the subject matter and form of her poems as well. Anything transient, particular, or small enlivens her imagination and leads to an intuition of a profound truth–regeneration, immortality. Ephemeral phenomena catch her fancy: something she hears, as the song of a bird, the rustle of leaves, the hum of a cricket; or something she sees, a sunbeam, a worm, an emerging crocus, a train, a gravestone, snowflakes, as well as a sunset or a ravishing dawn. Beginning with an observation, a poem moves toward a discovery about the meaning of experience, not logically but by an act of intuition. The reader must be ready to make the leap from one reality to another, from what is on the page to what the poem means. Thus, in poem 6 Dickinson is talking of the miraculous relationship between time and regeneration, not merely of leaves and trees.

> Frequently the woods are pink–
> Frequently are brown.
> Frequently the hills undress
> Behind my native town.
> Oft a head is crested
> I was oft to see–
> And as oft a cranny
> Where it used to be–
> And the Earth–they tell me–
> On its Axis turned!
> Wonderful Rotation!
> By but *twelve* performed!

Dickinson knows that if the only road to knowledge is through sense perception, the mortal person is limited, because senses operate only on corporeal reality. But she wishes to know what lies beyond, to know God and Heaven and what awaits us in the life after death. How does she resolve this dilemma? By relying on intuition, by having faith that the emblem of the unknown world is the literal world: what happens here is a reliable sign of what happens there. Not surety but intuition must content the spirit.

Her faith was often shaken and doubts tormented her, but she joined no church for doctrine and dogma could not convince the soul. Only direct experience leads to spiritual experience. And like experience itself, always unstable, her feelings changed, shifting from terror to complacence, from anger to joy. Her poems are as varied in feeling as they are in metaphor. The same subject is treated with ironic detachment, indignation, melancholy, or despair. The image of herself, too, changes from poem to poem. She is a diminutive being in Nature, a bird–a sparrow–or a flower–the humble daisy. But when Dickinson refers to her poems, they are gems–diamonds, rubies, topaz, pearl, amethyst, beryl–set in diadems or crowns. Many of the funeral poems and the poems of captivity are metaphoric renderings of her living death, although she knew she had walked into her room (cage, prison, coffin) and closed the door. There are as many poems praising her isolation, celebrating her exile, proclaiming the superior quality of the life she has chosen. She is a fearful child; she is a mortal subject to decay; she is a martyr suffering as Christ did; she is a bard whose mission it is to proclaim the truth. What eludes her grasp may be variously a crumb, a leaf, a ducat, a certain kind of light, a sound, a revelation, as well as a beloved person, an editor of a magazine, a neighbor's concern.

There is a striking pattern to the manner in which such poems render the experience of loss. Just as an observation on the known leads to an intuition about the unknown (the unknowable) so deprivation in the real world will be alleviated in a world beyond, either in time (the future) or in place (heaven). If flight, there will be return; the hungry will be fed; a longed for gift will eventually arrive; a separation will lead to ultimate reunion; a loss will be replenished; absence itself guarantees encounter; sunset signifies dawn; snow means spring; decay and disintegration lead to redemption; if there is solitude and isolation on earth, there are promenades in Heaven.

Conventional rhyme schemes or familiar stanza patterns could not serve poems that were documents of revelation. Dickinson's originality did not trouble her but became instead a sign that the poem was true, and therefore good. Nor was she troubled by questions of consistency. A bird in one case may simply be a bird; another time it is the symbol of the song of the poet, singing of heaven; the bird is the ignored poet, or an emblem of the regenerative force in Nature. But the most important emblem for her was her poetry. Just as she must rely on faith that her soul comes from God, so must she believe that her poetic power was God-like and God-given. As her soul was immortal, so must she have faith that the product of her soul, her poems, would achieve lasting fame. Perhaps terrestrial immortality meant more to Dickinson than spiritual immortality; we can only say that her poems testify to both as can be seen in poem 945.

> This is a Blossom of the Brain—
> A small—italic Seed
> Lodged by Design or Happening
> The Spirit fructified—
>
> Shy as the Wind of his Chambers
> Swift as a Freshet's Tongue
> So of the Flower of the Soul
> Its process is unknown.
>
> When it is found, a few rejoice
> The Wise convey it Home
> Carefully cherishing the spot
> If other Flower become.
>
> When it is lost, that Day shall be
> The Funeral of God,
> Upon his Breast, a closing Soul
> The Flower of our Lord.

Bibliographies:
Sheila T. Clendenning, *Emily Dickinson: A Bibliography, 1850-1966* (Kent, Ohio: Kent State University Press, 1968);

Willis J. Buckingham, *Emily Dickinson: An Annotated Bibliography* (Bloomington: Indiana University Press, 1970);

Joel Myerson, *Emily Dickinson: A Descriptive Bibliography* (Pittsburgh: University of Pennsylvania Press, 1984).

Biographies:
Martha Dickinson Bianchi, *The Life and Letters of Emily Dickinson* (Boston: Houghton Mifflin, 1924).
Seemed authoritative because it was a niece's testimony and contained the first full narrative of the sentimental attachment of Dickinson for the Reverend Charles Wadsworth. By now most scholars have come to see the tale as fabrication, although many are reluctant to give up the idea of a romantic love affair.

Genevieve Taggard, *The Life and Mind of Emily Dickinson* (New York: Knopf, 1930).
Believed that the secret attachment was to Leonard Humphrey, principal at Amherst Academy during Emily Dickinson's first year (1847), and then transferred to George Gould, editor of the Amherst College monthly.

Josephine Pollitt, *Emily Dickinson: The Human Background of Her Poetry* (New York: Harper, 1930).
Names Helen Hunt Jackson's second husband, Lieutenant Hunt, as the lost love.

Rebecca Patterson, *The Riddle of Emily Dickinson* (Boston: Houghton Mifflin, 1951).
Guesses that an unfulfilled love affair with Kate Anthon drove Dickinson into a psychic prison.

Millicent Todd Bingham, *Emily Dickinson: A Revelation* (New York: Harper, 1954).
Contains a series of letters conjecturally dated in the late 1870s and early 1880s between Judge Otis P. Lord and Dickinson and suggests their mutual love might have resulted in marriage had not Judge Lord died suddenly in 1884.

Bingham, *Emily Dickinson's Home: Letters of Edward Dickinson and His Family with Documents and Comment* (New York: Harper, 1955).
Focuses attention to the poet's relationship with members of her family, a shift that took hold and persists to the present time.

Thomas H. Johnson, *Emily Dickinson: An Interpretive Biography* (Cambridge: Harvard University Press, 1955).
A documentary biography which attempts to separate the facts about Dickinson from the myths.

Jay Leyda, *The Years and Hours of Emily Dickinson*, 2 volumes (New Haven: Yale University Press, 1960).
A psycho-biography which speculates on the poet's mysterious seventeen years as a recluse.

Clark Griffith, *The Long Shadow: Emily Dickinson's Tragic Poetry* (Princeton: Princeton University Press, 1964).
Argues that the "shadow" was sexual fright

and a neurotic attachment to the poet's austere and repressive father.

John Cody, *After Great Pain: The Inner Life of Emily Dickinson* (Cambridge: Harvard University Press, 1971).
Claims Dickinson's pain originated in an unfulfilled attachment to an indifferent and rejecting mother, made doubly unbearable by a scornful sister-in-law, Susan.

Richard B. Sewall, *The Life of Emily Dickinson*, 2 volumes (New York: Farrar, Straus & Giroux, 1974).
This definitive biography, making use of the diaries and journals of Mabel Loomis Todd, sifts through every conceivable source that may throw light on the life of the poet and renders all prior work obsolete and speculative.

Letters:
Letters of Emily Dickinson, 2 volumes, edited by Mabel Loomis Todd (Boston: Roberts Brothers, 1894);
Emily Dickinson's Letters to Dr. and Mrs. Josiah Gilbert Holland, edited by Theodora Van Wagenen Ward (Cambridge: Harvard University Press, 1951);
The Letters of Emily Dickinson, 3 volumes, edited by Thomas H. Johnson and Ward (Cambridge: Harvard University Press, 1958);
The Lyman Letters; New Light on Emily Dickinson and Her Family, edited by Richard B. Sewall (Amherst: University of Massachusetts Press, 1965).

References:
Charles Anderson, *Emily Dickinson's Poetry: Stairway of Surprise* (New York: Holt, Rinehart & Winston, 1960).
Analyzes Dickinson's theories of art, perception, nature, death, and immortality, suggesting that her greatness as a poet lies in the tension of alternating doubt and belief.

Jack L. Capps, *Emily Dickinson's Reading: 1836-1886* (Cambridge: Harvard University Press, 1966).
Examines Dickinson's use of language, particularly her use of narrative address and of syntactic structure.

Richard Chase, *Emily Dickinson* (New York: Sloan, 1951).
A critical biography that emphasizes Dickinson's use of psychology, suggesting that her main stratagem is "the achievement of status through critical experiences."

Joanne Feit Diehl, *Dickinson and the Romantic Imagination* (Princeton: Princeton University Press, 1981).
Diehl examines Dickinson in the context of the Anglo-American tradition, identifying Dickinson's reactions to Wordsworth, Keats, Shelley, and Emerson and arguing that Dickinson as a female poet is estranged from the Romantic tradition.

Ralph W. Franklin, *The Editing of Emily Dickinson: A Reconsideration* (Madison: University of Wisconsin Press, 1967).
Traces the editing history of Dickinson's manuscripts.

Sandra M. Gilbert and Susan Gubar, *Madwoman in the Attic* (New Haven & London: Yale University Press, 1979), pp. 581-650.
Studies Dickinson's self-dramatization, her Romanticism, her attitude toward the male "other," her self-imprisonment, and her use of the color white.

Inder Nath Kher, *The Landscape of Absence: Emily Dickinson's Poetry* (New Haven: Yale University Press, 1974).
Explores the imagery and symbolism of Dickinson's poems as they relate to such themes as the aesthetics of terror, the paradox of absence and presence, Dickinson's theory of perception, and the interrelationship of love, death, and the quest for identity.

Brita Lindberg-Seyerstad, *The Voice of the Poet: Aspects of Style in the Poetry of Emily Dickinson* (Cambridge: Harvard University Press, 1968).
Analyzes Dickinson's use of language, particularly her use of narrative address and of syntactic structure.

Dolores Dyer Lucas, *Emily Dickinson and Riddle* (DeKalb: Northern Illinois University Press, 1969).
Discusses Dickinson's ritualistic use of riddles to express ambiguity.

Ruth Miller, *The Poetry of Emily Dickinson* (Middletown, Conn.: Wesleyan University Press, 1968).
Examines the effects of Dickinson's publishers and critics upon her poetic reputation, analyzes the Master Letters and the fascicles, and discusses Dickinson's poetic style.

S. P. Rosenbaum, *A Concordance to the Poems of Emily Dickinson* (Ithaca: Cornell University Press, 1964).
Useful guide for tracing patterns of imagery in Dickinson's poems.

Barton Levi St. Armand, *Emily Dickinson and Her Culture: The Soul's Society* (Cambridge: Cambridge University Press, 1984).
Discusses Dickinson's poetry in relation to the literature of her times, equating her intensely personal poetry to the Victorian genre of the portfolio and finding her to be a representative Victorian woman writer. Using previously unpublished Dickinson family documents, St. Armand explores Dickinson's attitudes toward death, romance, immortality, God, nature, and art.

Robert Weisbuch, *Emily Dickinson's Poetry* (Chicago: University of Chicago Press, 1975).
Examines Dickinson's poetic technique, especially her use of the term "circumference."

George Frisbie Whicher, *This Was a Poet: A Critical Biography of Emily Dickinson* (New York: Scribners, 1938).
Examines Dickinson's poetry from a biographical standpoint, arguing that her love poems express an inner devotion that never expressed itself outwardly in a love affair.

Papers:
The manuscripts that led to the Bianchi publications are now in the Houghton Library of Harvard University. Mabel Loomis Todd, having kept all manuscripts that were in her possession at the time she ceased her task of editing the poems, left these manuscripts to her daughter, who gave them to the Frost Library at Amherst College. There are relevant materials in the Margaret Jane Pershing Collection of Emily Dickinson at Princeton University, the Galatea Collection at the Boston Public Library, the Jones Library at Amherst, and the Todd-Bingham Archive at Yale University.

Theodore Dreiser

This entry was updated by J. M. Brook from the entry by Donald Pizer (Tulane University) in DLB 12, American Realists and Naturalists.

Places	Chicago Terre Haute, Ind.	Warsaw, Ind. St. Louis, Mo.	Pittsburgh New York City
Influences and Relationships	Honoré de Balzac Frank Norris	H. L. Mencken Thomas Hardy	Horace Liveright Paul Dresser
Literary Movements and Forms	Naturalism	Journalism	Philosophical Novel
Major Themes	Sex as a Means of Social Advancement Tragedy of the Human Condition	American Success Story Sensual Pleasure vs. Conventional Morality	The Big City as a Place of Opportunity
Cultural and Artistic Influences	Catholicism Quakerism	Hinduism Transcendentalism	Herbert Spencer's Theories of Social Evolution
Social and Economic Influences	Communism Judicial System	Left-Wing Politics Financial Speculation	Censorship

See also the Dreiser entries in DLB 9, American Novelists, 1910-1945 *and* DLB Documentary Series 1.

BIRTH: Terre Haute, Indiana, 27 August 1871, to John Paul and Sarah Schänäb Dreiser.

EDUCATION: Indiana University, 1889-1890.

MARRIAGES: 28 December 1898 to Sara Osborne White; 13 June 1944 to Helen Patges Richardson.

AWARD: American Academy of Arts and Letters Award of Merit, 1944.

DEATH: Los Angeles, California, 28 December 1945.

SELECTED BOOKS: *Sister Carrie* (New York: Doubleday, Page, 1900; abridged edition, London: Heinemann, 1901; Pennsylvania Edition, Philadelphia: University of Pennsylvania Press, 1981);
Jennie Gerhardt (New York & London: Harper, 1911);
The Financier (New York & London: Harper, 1912; revised edition, New York: Boni & Liveright, 1927; London: Constable, 1931);
A Traveler at Forty (New York: Century, 1913; London: Richards, 1914);
The Titan (New York: John Lane, 1914; London: John Lane, 1915);
The "Genius" (New York: John Lane, 1915; London: John Lane, 1915);
Plays of the Natural and the Supernatural (New York: John Lane, 1916; London: John Lane, 1916);
A Hoosier Holiday (New York: John Lane, 1916; London: John Lane, 1916);
Free and Other Stories (New York: Boni & Liveright, 1918);
Twelve Men (New York: Boni & Liveright, 1919; London: Constable, 1930);
The Hand of the Potter (New York: Boni & Liveright, 1919; revised, 1927);
Hey Rub-a-Dub-Dub (New York: Boni & Liveright, 1920; London: Constable, 1931);
A Book About Myself (New York: Boni & Liveright, 1922; London: Constable, 1929); republished as *Newspaper Days* (New York: Liveright, 1931);
The Color of a Great City (New York: Boni & Liveright, 1923; London: Constable, 1930);
An American Tragedy (New York: Boni & Liv-

eright, 1925; London: Constable, 1926);
Moods: Cadenced and Declaimed (New York: Boni & Liveright, 1926; revised, 1928); revised and republished as *Moods Philosophic and Emotional, Cadenced and Declaimed* (New York: Simon & Schuster, 1935);
Chains (New York: Boni & Liveright, 1927; London: Constable, 1928);
Dreiser Looks at Russia (New York: Liveright, 1928; London: Constable, 1929);
A Gallery of Women (New York: Liveright, 1929; London: Constable, 1930);
Dawn (New York: Liveright, 1931; London: Constable, 1931);
Tragic America (New York: Liveright, 1931; London: Constable, 1932);
America Is Worth Saving (New York: Modern Age, 1941);
The Bulwark (Garden City: Doubleday, 1946; London: Constable, 1947);
The Stoic (Garden City: Doubleday, 1947);
Notes on Life, edited by Marguerite Tjader and John J. McAleer (University: University of Alabama Press, 1974);
Theodore Dreiser: A Selection of Uncollected Prose, edited by Donald Pizer (Detroit: Wayne State University Press, 1977);
Theodore Dreiser: American Diaries, 1902-1926, edited by Thomas P. Riggio and others (Philadelphia: University of Pennsylvania Press, 1983).

PLAY PRODUCTIONS: *The Girl in the Coffin*, New York, Comedy Theatre, 3 December 1917;
The Hand of the Potter, New York, Provincetown Playhouse, 5 December 1921.

OTHER: Paul Dresser, *On the Banks of the Wabash Far Away*, first verse and chorus attributed to Dreiser (New York: Howley, Haviland, 1897);
Lieutenant Oswald Fritz Bilse, *Life in a Garrison Town*, introduction by Dreiser (New York: John Lane/London: John Lane/Bodley Head, 1914);
Dresser, *The Songs of Paul Dresser*, introduction by Dreiser (New York: Boni & Liveright, 1927);
Frank Norris, *McTeague*, introduction by Dreiser (Garden City: Doubleday, Doran, 1928);
Harlan Miners Speak: Report on Terrorism in the Kentucky Coal Fields, introduction by Dreiser (New York: Harcourt, Brace, 1932);

Theodore Dreiser, circa 1908, when he was editor-in-chief at Butterick Publications

Henry David Thoreau, *Living Thoughts of Thoreau,* selected, with an introduction, by Dreiser (New York: Longmans, Green, 1938).

Theodore Dreiser is one of the most significant and most problematical of American writers. The acknowledged "trailblazer" for a generation of early-twentieth-century American writers, his rebellious commitment to the honest portrayal of American life and the vagaries of human nature placed him in the forefront of American literature about the time of World War I and earned him a secure place in American literary history. The great popular and critical success of *An American Tragedy* in 1925 solidified his American and international reputations. But from the publication of *Sister Carrie* in 1900, Dreiser was also a byword for all that is inept in fiction and fuzzy in thinking. By the time Lionel Trilling launched his famous attack on him in 1950 (in Trilling's *The*

Liberal Imagination, some five years after Dreiser's death), it was often assumed that Dreiser wrote like a journalist and thought like an adolescent. Yet somehow, despite continuous attack, Dreiser's best fiction continues to hold and move. In recent years, with the appearance of a major biography and a series of perceptive critical studies, the emphasis in Dreiser studies has shifted from defense or condemnation to an effort to come to grips with the elusive and complex nature of his temperament, ideas, and creative power.

It is difficult to overestimate the importance for American literary history of Dreiser's emergence as a major writer out of the special circumstances of his background. Until Dreiser, the typical American author was of Protestant Anglo-Saxon stock. And while not necessarily a college graduate (though many were), he nevertheless grew up either in a bookish setting or in one which permitted easy access to self-education. None of these conditions prevailed for Dreiser. His father, John Paul Dreiser, was a Catholic German immigrant who reached America in 1844 at the age of twenty-three. His mother, Sarah Schänäb Dreiser, was of Bohemian Mennonite background (she became a Catholic on marrying John Paul Dreiser in 1851). The Dreiser family prospered for a time as John Dreiser pursued his career as a wool worker. But then–after the births of six children and after a business failure caused by the burning of an uninsured mill–the Dreisers moved into their permanent condition of poverty and flight. It was into a family at the very bottom of the social scale–poor, large, Catholic, ignorant, and superstitious–that Dreiser was born in late August 1871 in Terre Haute, Indiana. Dreiser's ability to rise out of these conditions (at what cost to his psyche he himself would later document in his autobiography *Dawn*) not only reveals his innate talents and his powerful will to succeed but also anticipates the emergence in following generations of many writers out of similar immigrant stock (the Jewish, for example) and out of similar impoverished backgrounds (particularly the black ghetto).

The character and experiences of the Dreiser family in the years during which Theodore was growing up were later to supply the mature author with many of his themes. The underlying configuration of the family–the warm, forgiving, and loving mother; the narrow-minded, disciplinarian father; and the fun-loving, wayward, and seeking children–became that of Dreiser's fictional families from the Gerhardts of *Jennie Gerhardt* (1911) to the Barneses of *The Bulwark* (1946). And the constant movement of the Dreiser family in search of a better life–in Dreiser's youth from Terre Haute, Sullivan, and Evansville in Indiana, to Chicago, and then back to Warsaw, Indiana–was to suggest to him the centrality of the American life pattern (one pursued by Carrie and Frank Cowperwood and Clyde Griffiths) of pushing on to new worlds as an old world crashes behind one.

In Dreiser's early teens the family settled for some years in the pleasant central Indiana town of Warsaw. There Dreiser had the good fortune to be placed in public schools (he had hitherto been in parochial schools) and to receive the encouragement of sympathetic teachers. But with adolescence there also came–as Dreiser describes in *Dawn* (1931)–the first powerful stirrings of sex and the first sense of the wonder and beauty of life, a wonder and beauty which he could feel in nature, in poetry, and in the face of a girl, but which he as yet could neither understand nor articulate.

Anxious, like Clyde Griffiths, both to experience a wider range of life and to escape the repressive family atmosphere created by his father's religious dogmatism, Dreiser moved to Chicago in 1887, at the age of sixteen. There, living with several of his older sisters who had earlier made their way to the city, he eked out an existence. As Carrie was to be, he was enthralled by the exciting possibilities of the city, its theaters, restaurants, and mansions, but like Carrie on her arrival he was living precariously on the margin of life, with no prospects of change but downward. He was saved for a time by his high school English teacher from Warsaw, Miss Mildred Fielding, who sponsored him for a year at Indiana University. At Bloomington during 1889-1890, he gained little from his classroom work but absorbed from the collegiate setting a drive to somehow achieve the assurance and elegance of the young collegiates around him.

At the end of his year at Indiana, Dreiser returned to Chicago and again held a series of miscellaneous jobs, including one as assistant to a real-estate agent and another as bill collector for an installment firm. During this period the Dreiser family, which had itself resettled in Chicago in the late 1880s, began to break up. Sarah Dreiser died in late 1890; Paul Dreiser (who was to adopt the professional name of Paul Dresser) had long since left the family for a career as an entertainer and songwriter; and Mame, Emma, and

Claire Dreiser had found themselves a series of well-to-do lovers, the prototypes of the Hurstwoods and Lester Kanes who frequent Dreiser's early novels.

Dreiser during these years lacked direction, and the major foundation of his life, the family, was slipping away. And then, in the summer of 1892, at the age of twenty-one, he cut a thin wedge into the kind of life he had been dreaming about and to which he was to devote his life. Completely inexperienced as a newspaperman, he believed nevertheless that the worldliness and excitement of the reporter's life were for him. By dint of luck and perseverance, he was finally taken on by one of the poorer Chicago papers, the *Globe*. There, with the aid of an editor who took an interest in him, he began to learn the trade that was to lead to *Sister Carrie* some eight years later.

By November 1892 Dreiser felt confident enough in his journalistic skills to seek a position with the prestigious *St. Louis Globe-Democrat*. His sixteen months as a reporter in St. Louis, first on the *Globe-Democrat* and then on the *Republic*, played an extremely important role in his development. Assigned to almost every task on a metropolitan daily, he reported murders, robberies, and catastrophes, interviewed visiting personalities, and wrote drama reviews and paragraphs. He saw the life of a late-nineteenth-century American city in all its fullness, and he encountered as well, in the journalistic conventions of the day, the various subterfuges, hypocrisies, and shams present in the late-Victorian representation of that life.

Another significant event of Dreiser's stay in St. Louis was his meeting, in the summer of 1893, Sara ("Sallie") Osborne White, a schoolteacher who was a few years older than himself. Dreiser's relationship to Sallie White (or Jug, as she was familiarly called) dramatized several paradoxes central both to American experience of the time and to Dreiser's own life, paradoxes which were to serve as major themes in his fiction. Although Dreiser and Sallie were passionately in love, her strict moralism prevented any consummation of their love through a six-year engagement. And Dreiser himself found that he was engaged to a girl he wished to possess rather than to marry. Out of these contradictions between the socially required and the felt were to emerge several of Dreiser's early fictional preoccupations.

Increasingly restless in St. Louis, Dreiser in

early 1894 moved on to Pittsburgh and the *Dispatch*. A trip to New York during the summer of 1894 to visit his successful songwriting brother Paul convinced him that it was New York above all which offered a doorway to success, and he moved there in the fall of 1894 in search of a newspaper job. Dreiser's half-year in Pittsburgh, however, completed his education. His work for the *Dispatch* soon settled into the writing of a daily column, and he was therefore free much of the day. Reading deeply at the public library in the philosophical works of Herbert Spencer and the fiction of Balzac, he found in their writing a confirmation of the impressions of experience he had been acquiring the last several years. Spencer's "Synthetic Philosophy"—an amalgam of nineteenth-century social beliefs and evolutionary science—argues that there is no authority in supernaturally sanctioned moral codes, that only that which develops naturally through the struggle for existence, whether this struggle occurs in nature or society, is beneficial. And Balzac's novels, in which "a young man from the provinces" seeks in the urban cockpit of Paris the glories of life, reaffirmed Dreiser's own belief that the seeker will find in the great city not only struggle, degradation, and destruction but also wonder, beauty, and fulfillment.

New York during the winter of 1894-1895, however, offered Dreiser principally hardship and depression. Out of work and almost penniless, he wandered the city as an anonymous stranger in search of warmth, as Hurstwood was to do in his final phase. But in the spring there arose a wonderful opportunity. Paul Dresser had become part owner of a song-publishing firm and was seeking ways to popularize its songs. What better way to do this, Dreiser seems to have suggested to him, than to start a magazine, with Dreiser as editor, which would feature the firm's songs. *Ev'ry Month* appeared initially in October 1895. For two years Dreiser not only edited the magazine but contributed, frequently under a pseudonym, a wide variety of material to it. The most important of these miscellaneous contributions was a monthly column which he called "Reflections" and signed "The Prophet." In his column he tried out the ideas which he had been gathering both from his experience and his reading. (Many of the most significant of his "Reflections" columns were republished for the first time in 1977 in *Theodore Dreiser: A Selection of Uncollected Prose*, edited by Donald Pizer.) A typical reflection would use a current event–an election, a winter storm, or a scandal–as an excuse for a disquisition on the nature of man and life. Dreiser's lifelong Balzacian custom of weaving philosophical commentary into his fiction received initial expression in the analogous form of the journalistic editorial.

After two years of editing *Ev'ry Month*, Dreiser appears to have desired broader and more fully rewarded opportunities. He resigned the editorship in the fall of 1897 and plunged into the expanding and competitive world of free-lance magazine writing. (The "ten-cent magazine revolution" of the 1890s had greatly increased the possibilities for a career as a free-lance journalist.) Writing on a wide variety of subjects (his favorites were accounts of artists and performers of all kinds, lavishly illustrated) and publishing in a large number of journals, Dreiser quickly made his mark in this field. One of the magazines he appeared in most frequently was *Success*, edited by Orison Swett Marden, a prominent promoter during the period of the American cult of success. Beneath the ingenuous optimism of the interviews Dreiser prepared for Marden, however, was his implicit understanding of the vast gulf that separates a Carnegie or a Field from a typical member of the audience of *Success*, a gulf which was to inform his depiction of both Frank Cowperwood and Clyde Griffiths.

Dreiser was aided in much of his free-lance writing by his close friend Arthur Henry. (They had met in Toledo in early 1894 and had cemented their friendship when Henry moved to New York later in the decade.) During the summer of 1899 Henry and his wife Maude Wood asked Dreiser and his wife (Dreiser and Sallie White had at last been married in late 1898) to visit them at their summer house on the Maumee River, near Toledo. It was during this visit that Dreiser began in earnest, at the age of twenty-eight, his career as a writer of fiction. He had made several earlier attempts, notably during his first winter in New York in 1894-1895 and during his years on *Ev'ry Month*. These had all been aborted or had resulted in weak and derivative sketches. But now, encouraged by Henry, who also had aspirations for a career as a novelist, Dreiser wrote during that summer at Maumee four stories, each of which anticipates a major direction in his novels. The most important of these stories was "Nigger Jeff," later collected in Dreiser's *Free and Other Stories* (1918), in which a young reporter views and then comes to understand the lynching of a Negro accused of attacking a white girl. Based on an incident Dreiser had observed while a newspaperman in St. Louis, the story dramatizes Dreiser's realization that the tragic nature of man, whatever his station, lies in his capacity to feel pain, and that the tragic artist seeks to understand and express this capacity—to "get it all in," as the newspaperman exclaims at the end of "Nigger Jeff."

Although none of Dreiser's four Maumee stories was immediately accepted for publication, he was sufficiently stimulated by these new efforts in fiction to respond to Henry's suggestion, once they returned to New York in the fall, that he should undertake a novel. According to Dreiser's recollection, he began his first novel by taking a blank sheet of paper and writing on it, without further thought, its title, *Sister Carrie*. Be that as it may, the title *Sister Carrie* was immediately evocative to Dreiser for several reasons. Carrie in the role of sister has little importance in *Sister Carrie*. But in choosing this title Dreiser was signifying both that he was to tell a story, as did Balzac in his *Cousine Bette* (1846) and *Père Goriot* (1834), of individual failure and success in a great city, and more particularly for Dreiser, that the subject of this story was to be his own sister, Emma.

Emma Dreiser was one of several of Dreiser's sisters who had escaped the Dreiser family for a freer life in the city. In Chicago she had had an affair initially with an architect and then, in 1885, with L. A. Hopkins, a chief clerk for Chapin and Gore, a firm which owned a number of Chicago saloons. Hopkins had a wife and family, and when his wife discovered his adultery in February 1886, he absconded to Canada with several thousand dollars from the firm's safe, taking a compliant Emma with him. Dreiser had met Emma and Hopkins in New York in 1894 and knew their story well. But for *Sister Carrie* he transformed it in several important ways, in particular by "refining" the characters of Carrie and Hurstwood and by giving their lives in New York a direction totally independent of that of Emma and Hopkins.

Dreiser began *Sister Carrie* in October 1899 and, aided by Henry and Jug at various times, completed it in March 1900. (One significant late revision was Dreiser's recasting of the conclusion to provide a Balzacian epilogue in which he effuses over the fate of Carrie.) It was with the completion of the novel that there occurred one of the most famous incidents in American literary history, the so-called suppression of *Sister Carrie* by

Doubleday, Page, and Company, the publisher of the novel.

Doubleday, Page, a new firm, had on its staff as a reader the young novelist Frank Norris, whose own naturalistic *McTeague* had been published the previous year. Norris strongly endorsed *Sister Carrie*, and the firm agreed to publish it, even though its principal partner, Frank Doubleday, was in Europe at the time. On his return, however, Doubleday, Page became much more hesitant about the book and also began to ask for revisions. Dreiser, his back up, refused most of the suggested changes and also refused to consider placing the novel elsewhere. At this point Doubleday agreed to honor the earlier verbal agreement and a formal contract was signed. But the firm failed to push or advertise the book, and it did not sell. In later years, and particularly in Dorothy Dudley's study of Dreiser's career, *Forgotten Frontiers: Dreiser and the Land of the Free* (1932), the actions of Doubleday, Page became to Dreiser and his supporters a major symbol of control of American culture by a puritan ethic, and Dreiser was celebrated as a figure who both suffered from this control and persevered nevertheless. In particular, Mrs. Doubleday, who was rumored to have influenced her husband's attitude toward the novel but whose role is in fact unknown, became a figure epitomizing Victorian prudishness and narrowness. It is now known that the censorship of *Sister Carrie* by Doubleday, Page was minimal (a few changes in profanity and proper names); that Doubleday did not have to agree to a contract after he found the book objectionable, but did so nevertheless; and that Dreiser and his supporters found it useful in later years to picture Dreiser as a martyr to American puritanism. But whatever the factual truth of "L'Affaire Doubleday" (as W. A. Swanberg calls it), the suppression of *Sister Carrie* has had a mythic truth of its own.

One can readily understand why Mrs. Doubleday, or any other proper American of the time, might have objected to *Sister Carrie*. Dreiser's novel begins with an archetypal American scene—the departure of a young girl from her home and family in a small town in order to make her way in the city. By the close of the novel, Carrie has risen, largely by the classic American combination of luck and pluck, to be a musical comedy star on Broadway. But within this traditional pattern of the American success story Dreiser is strikingly innovative. Carrie succeeds in part because at two crucial moments—when she is sick and exhausted after attempting to stay afloat in working-class Chicago, and after she had quarreled with her initial protector, Drouet—she accepts help from a man and then, almost casually and without a full crisis of conscience, sleeps with the man. The implication that sex for a young woman of Carrie's class and background was intimately linked to survival and success, and that a woman using her sex was not necessarily a fallen woman, ran counter to almost every conventional nineteenth-century belief about the nature of women and the inevitability of moral retribution.

Carrie's story is also one which Dreiser was to return to again in The "Genius" (1915), that of the development of the artist. It is this aspect of Carrie—her "emotional greatness" and her capacity to seek "beauty"—which many readers have found less convincing than her career as a "soldier of fortune" armed only with her pertinacity and her sex. For many of these readers, the greater fictional figure in the novel—and for some the greatest in all of Dreiser's work—is Hurstwood, Carrie's second lover and the man with whom she runs away to New York after he has robbed his employers. In the character of Hurstwood Dreiser renders one of the basic fears of middle-class American life. A solid family man who nevertheless is bored by the graspingness and trivialities of his family, Hurstwood reaches out for something finer and richer in the person of Carrie and in doing so sets the stage for his eventual tragic fall into the middle-class hell of disgrace and poverty. This, too, was one of Dreiser's deepest fears, just as Carrie's artistic success reflected his deepest hope. By informing both figures with his most intense personal feelings while maintaining their archetypal relevance to American life, Dreiser created a novel which has seldom failed to interest deeply even those who find major flaws in its form and style.

Dreiser's technical skills as novelist, even at their best, have almost always had their detractors. Sister Carrie, for example, like most of Dreiser's fiction, is marred by an inept prose style in which journalistic cliché, rank sentimentality (the chapter titles in particular), and clumsy syntax compete for attention. It is also a novel in which Dreiser's penchant for authorial philosophizing and commentary both impedes the flow of narrative and muddies characterization. Yet for all its weaknesses, the novel does hold, and in such sections as Carrie's seeking work in Chicago or Hurstwood down-and-out in New York it

achieves the sublimity of expressing with a seeming inevitability the way life is.

Although Dreiser had begun a second novel, Jennie Gerhardt, even before the publication of Sister Carrie in November 1900, he made slow progress with the work. He was disturbed by the "suppression" of Sister Carrie, by money problems now that he was no longer writing for the magazines, and by the deterioration of his marriage. These worries soon began to take the form of frequent periods of depression, debility, and psychosomatic illness. Constant movement among various towns and cities in the Midwest and South in search of a cheap place to live and write did not help, and by early 1903 Dreiser was alone and penniless in New York, living in flophouses and afraid of meeting old friends, much like Hurstwood at the end of Sister Carrie. He was rescued by his brother Paul, who placed him in a health camp for overworked businessmen. This was followed by a period as a day laborer on the railroad, and in late 1903 Dreiser felt himself sufficiently recovered in body and spirit to return to his career as a writer. He began by again undertaking free-lance work; by the summer of 1905 he was installed as the editor of a popular monthly, Smith's Magazine. His success with Smith's and then, during 1906-1907, with the Broadway Magazine was capped in late 1907 when he was asked to become editor of Butterick's Delineator, the most popular magazine for women of its day.

Having reached this peak, Dreiser began to think of returning to fiction. The republication of Sister Carrie in 1907, to considerable critical acclaim, no doubt contributed to his belief that he had lain fallow too long. Another contributing factor was his establishment, also in 1907, of a lifelong relationship with H. L. Mencken. Mencken, who was himself just beginning his career as journalist and editor, shared with Dreiser a good-natured cynicism about the claims of popular taste on a magazine editor. By 1910, after three years at the Delineator, Dreiser had become extremely restless in his role as editor of a popular women's magazine while still relishing the power and wealth which the position entailed. Matters came to a head, as they were often to do for the remainder of Dreiser's life, on the crisis caused by a love affair. Dreiser had become infatuated with Thelma Cudlipp, the young daughter of a contributor to the Delineator. He pursued Thelma in a manner thought unfit for the married editor of a conservative journal and in October 1910 found himself fired. The affair itself soon collapsed, but it nevertheless had an important effect on Dreiser's life and work. It returned him perforce to writing–an effort to complete *Jennie Gerhardt* (1911)–and it was as an author that Dreiser was to spend the rest of his professional life. And it set the pattern for his personal life, a pattern of maintaining a shaky but long-term relationship with one woman (first Sallie White and later Helen Richardson) while pursuing as well many temporary affairs.

Dreiser completed *Jennie Gerhardt* in early 1911. This initial full version of the novel ended with the reconciliation of Jennie and her lover Lester Kane, but after several readers of the manuscript suggested the need for a tragic conclusion to the story, Dreiser revised its final chapters. *Jennie Gerhardt*, like *Sister Carrie*, has its origin in the life of one of Dreiser's sisters, in this instance Mame Dreiser. Jennie, like Mame, is seduced by a well-to-do benefactor of the impoverished Gerhardt family (a family modeled closely on the Dreisers) and has an illegitimate child by him. And again like Mame, Jennie then moves on to a far more satisfying relationship with the son of a prominent commercial family. *Sister Carrie* and *Jennie Gerhardt* are thus similar in centering on the sexual experience of a young girl and in intimating that such experience is not only inseparable from the texture of American life but that it can occur without blemishing the immortal soul of the girl. *Jennie Gerhardt* is dissimilar from *Sister Carrie*, however, in that the characters and fates of Jennie and Lester are considerably different from those of Carrie and Hurstwood.

Jennie is Dreiser's portrait of the woman as giver, of a spirit of feminine plentitude comparable to nature as mother. But as in Thomas Hardy's *Tess of the D'Urbervilles* (1891), a novel which influenced Dreiser deeply, Jennie's natural generosity runs counter both to the mercantile spirit of selling oneself dearly and to the religious spirit of offering oneself only within specific conditions. She gives herself in love, without marriage, and thus suffers rejection first by family and then by the world at large. Yet despite this casting out, she continues to grow in spirit and mind–indeed, and somewhat like Carrie now, she seems to find in her difficulties a form of education of her inner nature.

Jennie's first relationship is with Senator Brander. After his death she begins to live with Lester Kane, who bears a superficial resemblance to Hurstwood in that both men seek love outside of marriage despite prominence and success

in their middle-class worlds. But Kane, unlike Hurstwood, is also an intellectual, and in his brooding, indecisive speculations about the nature of life Dreiser created one of his most moving characters. Loving Jennie deeply yet afraid to surrender the comforts of his position in the world, knowing from his reading the instability of the universe and of man himself, seemingly strong and assertive yet fundamentally insecure and weak, Kane attempts to have it both ways–to keep both Jennie and his "comforts"–and in the end has neither. He is forced to give up Jennie, and he eventually discovers that his old life has lost its savor. Bitterly disappointed, he can only tell Jennie, just before his death, that he has made a mistake. And for Jennie, at the close of the novel, there will only be "days after days in endless reiteration."

H. L. Mencken, who had a surprising weakness for sentiment, always believed that *Jennie Gerhardt* was Dreiser's best novel. Some readers have occasionally felt that Dreiser's earth-mother portrayal of Jennie, particularly in the early chapters, is too cloying. But other critics have found the novel to be a moving and significant portrayal of the nature of tragic pathos in human relations, of the failure of love less because of exceptional major flaws in character or because of extraordinary circumstances than through the steady pressure of social reality and the limitations of human nature upon so fragile a condition as a man and a woman in love.

On the whole *Jennie Gerhardt* was both a critical and a popular success. Dreiser was encouraged sufficiently by its reception to believe that he should continue his literary career rather than return to editorial work. So, at the age of forty, Dreiser for the first time in his life determined that he would try not merely to make a living as a writer but would seek to combine that effort with an attempt to express himself as honestly as possible. Given both Dreiser's financial needs and his immense energy, the result over the next fifteen years (from *Jennie Gerhardt* in 1911 to *An American Tragedy* in 1925) of this full commitment to literature was an outpouring of creative energy seldom equaled in the history of American literature. Dreiser wrote during this period four very long novels (*The Financier*, 1912; *The Titan*, 1914; *The "Genius,"* 1915; and *An American Tragedy*, 1925); four equally lengthy works of travel narrative and autobiography (*A Traveler at Forty*, 1913; *A Hoosier Holiday*, 1916; *A Book About Myself*, 1922; and *Dawn*, 1931); two volumes of plays (*Plays of the Natural and the Supernatural*, 1916, and *The Hand of the Potter*, 1919); most of the contents of four collections of short stories and sketches (*Free and Other Stories*, 1918; *Twelve Men*, 1919; *The Color of a Great City*, 1923; and *Chains*, 1927); and a volume of philosophical essays (*Hey Rub-a-Dub-Dub*, 1920).

Dreiser's personal life was equally active during this period. After the turmoil caused by his affair with Thelma Cudlipp, he and Sallie Dreiser continued to live together in New York for occasional stretches until 1914, when they separated for the last time and Dreiser took up quarters in Greenwich Village. There he had a number of relationships, in particular with the youthful actress Kirah Markham–the Stephanie Platow of *The Titan*–until in 1919 he met an equally youthful and attractive distant cousin, Helen Patges Richardson. They fell in love, and though Dreiser was soon to pursue again his "varietistic" interests (his term for his constant need for different women), he and Helen were to live together for most of the remainder of his life. (They were not married, however, until 13 June 1944.) One immediate consequence of their meeting was Dreiser's move to Los Angeles with Helen in October 1919, since Helen wished to become a film actress. He was uncomfortable in Los Angeles, however, and after three years was happy to return to New York, where he was to live until 1938.

Two other major events of this period in Dreiser's life were the suppression of *The "Genius"* in 1916 and the long and important association with the publisher Horace Liveright, which he established in 1918. Dreiser had come under increasing attack for his depiction of the sex drive in human experience–not for his portrayal of the physical aspect of sex (indeed, he was usually reticent in this matter) as for his amoral acknowledgment of its presence and power. Many reviewers had been scandalized by his depiction of Frank Cowperwood's sexual nature and values in *The Financier* and *The Titan*, and many were outraged even further by the sexual themes in *The "Genius"* on its publication in 1915. Among the most famous and influential attacks of this kind on Dreiser was Stuart P. Sherman's essay, "The Naturalism of Mr. Dreiser," in the 2 December 1915 issue of the *Nation*. Almost inevitably, given the cultural climate of the day, the New York Society for the Suppression of Vice (led by John S. Sumner) brought an action to have the novel banned. This led to a major literary skirmish. H. L. Mencken, who in fact thought the novel banal, organized a campaign in the name of artistic freedom to force the courts to void the censorship of *The "Genius,"* a campaign which a number of more conservative authors and critics supported. Although the case was not to be resolved for several years, it served to confirm in both the public mind and the literary scene the image of Dreiser as at once the champion of artistic freedom and the victim of cultural philistinism.

Of equal importance to Dreiser's career was his association with the flamboyant Liveright. Dreiser had had a series of unsuccessful relationships with publishers–with Doubleday, Page, with Harper, and finally with John Lane–all of whom, he felt, had failed him when they came under pressure from the forces of puritanism. In Liveright he found a publisher who was willing to take risks–who indeed was to publish in 1919 Dreiser's sympathetic treatment of a sex murderer in his play *The Hand of the Potter*. Although theirs was often a stormy association (Dreiser believed all publishers were dishonest), they remained together from 1918, when Boni and Liveright published *Free and Other Stories*, through the great success of *An American Tragedy* in 1925, to the dissolution of Liveright's firm in 1932 after the publication of *Tragic America* (1931).

Although *The "Genius"* was not published until 1915, Dreiser had completed a draft of the novel in the summer of 1911 after finishing *Jennie Gerhardt* and before beginning research on the Cowperwood trilogy. Publication of the novel was delayed because Harper wished to publish *The Financier* and *The Titan* first. Thus, it was not until *The Titan* appeared in 1914 that the firm was ready to go on to *The "Genius."* By this time, however, Dreiser had second thoughts about the conclusion of the work (as he did with almost all his novels, from *Sister Carrie* to *The Stoic*, 1947). In the original version of the novel, Dreiser's autobiographical protagonist Eugene Witla, in an act of fictional wish fulfillment by Dreiser, is reunited with Suzanne Dale, the Thelma Cudlipp of the novel. By 1915 Dreiser recognized the fatuousness of this conclusion and changed it to one in which Eugene has grown beyond the need for Suzanne and has turned fully to his philosophical musings and to his art.

Most readers of *The "Genius"* have held that it was not only the conclusion but the entire novel which reflected adversely Dreiser's excessive closeness to his material. Eugene Witla is Dreiser's most autobiographical fictional figure. Like Dreiser, he becomes an artist (a painter in

40

It seemed as if he thought — awhile for now he arose and turned the gas out, standing calmly in the blackness, hidden from view. After a few moments in which he reviewed nothing, but merely hesitated, he turned the gas on again, but applying no match. Even then he stood there, hidden wholly in that kindness which is night; while the uprising fumes filled the room. When the odor reached his nostrils he quit his attitude and fumbled for the bed.

"What the use" he said wearily, as he stretched himself to rest

The End

Thursday, March 29 - 1900 - 2:53 P.M.

Dreiser's original ending for Sister Carrie *(Henry W. and Albert A. Berg Collection of English and American Literature, New York Public Library, Astor, Lenox and Tilden Foundations)*

Witla's case) after a midwestern boyhood, has a disastrous marriage to a woman who is at once sensual and puritanical, suffers a nervous breakdown, is restored to good health and to a career as an editor, and finally–after a love affair with a young girl–returns to his art. Literalness mars Dreiser's extremely long reprise of his life in *The "Genius"* from the beginning to the end of the novel–both the literalness of external detail and of the details of Eugene's emotional life. Although some sections–such as Eugene's working on the railroad–come to life, on the whole the entire work, in particular its last third, which concentrates on Eugene and Suzanne's affair, exaggerates the reader's interest in a figure as vapid, confused, and self-apologetic as Eugene. The only major area of the novel which still holds is that devoted to the marriage of Eugene and Angela Blue (the Sallie White of the novel). A study in a mismating of temperaments in which only a desperate sexuality and a jealous possessiveness bind the couple, these passages render the deceptions and torments of a destructive marriage with a power equal to that of Edward Albee's *Who's Afraid of Virginia Woolf ?* (1962).

After completing *The "Genius"* in mid 1911, Dreiser plunged into research for the Cowperwood series. Now, after three works which had their source in his family or himself, he was to undertake a novel derived almost entirely from the life and times of a historical figure, the traction magnate Charles T. Yerkes. Yerkes had had a much-publicized career in Philadelphia, Chicago, and London as a traction company organizer, an art collector, and as a womanizer. Dreiser determined to describe Yerkes' life in all its phases through the character of Frank Cowperwood. His intent was to combine a study of the man of power with an epic account of the buccaneering period of American finance from the Civil War to the end of the nineteenth century.

Dreiser worked steadily on *The Financier* until late 1911, when he interrupted his writing for a five-month European tour. His reason for the trip was to gather material on Yerkes' London years, but he was also excited by the idea of going to Europe for the first time. In order to help finance the journey, he wrote for the *Century* magazine a series of travel essays and then, on his return, expanded these into a book. *A Traveler at Forty* is one of Dreiser's most engaging works. A kind of not-so-innocent-abroad travel narrative, the book combines Dreiser's often shrewd comments on European life and institutions with his ingenuous delight at the pleasures of the flesh and spirit (whether in French cafés or Italian galleries) which Europe so amply provided.

On his return from Europe, Dreiser completed *The Financier*. He had realized, by this time, that he would be unable to encompass Yerkes' life in one novel, and he and Harper decided on a trilogy, with each novel to be separately published and titled. The first novel, dealing with Yerkes' early life in Philadelphia, was to be called *The Financier;* the second, with his great triumphs in Chicago, *The Titan;* and the last, with his London years and death, *The Stoic.* After completing *The Financier*, Dreiser went quickly ahead with *The Titan* and was able to have it published in 1914. He then put aside the trilogy until the early 1930s, when he worked on *The Stoic* but did not finish it. This he was unable to do until shortly before his death in 1945. For this reason it has become conventional to discuss the Cowperwood saga principally as *The Financier* and *The Titan* and to consider *The Stoic* as a novel of Dreiser's final years.

The Financier and *The Titan* can be described as antiepics. That is, we follow Frank Cowperwood from his origins in conventional middle-class life to his climactic role as one of the titans of American economic life. Although he has several momentary setbacks during this ascent, including a major one at the conclusion of *The Titan,* his shrewdness, strength, and ruthlessness always carry him on to fresh triumphs. Dreiser's celebration of Cowperwood as an American epic hero is thus inherently ironic, since Cowperwood's success derives principally from his ability to recognize and exploit the difference between the jungle amoralism of American life and the veneer of moral utterance which disguises that reality. What makes Cowperwood so powerful is his willingness to be consciously guided entirely by his own interests. "I satisfy myself " is his motto.

Dreiser also wished in the trilogy to dramatize his belief that the seeking spirit–whether it be a Carrie wishing happiness or a Cowperwood wanting power–almost always desires beauty as well. For Cowperwood, beauty is found in women and art, and much of *The Financier* and *The Titan* are devoted to his pursuit of these. Because Cowperwood has no respect for marriage, casual readers of the trilogy have often missed the "spiritual" nature of his pursuit of women, particularly in *The Titan,* where he has over a dozen affairs. For Cowperwood views sexual gratification not only as a fulfillment, through the "affections," of his desire to possess beauty, but also as communion with his lovers on a higher and higher scale of spirituality. By the close of *The Titan*, he finds in the ethereal and almost sexless Berenice a full expression of woman as spirit.

Neither *The Financier* nor *The Titan* is fully successful as fiction, though both have had their supporters. The two novels—and particularly *The Titan*—are frequently little more than narratives of Cowperwood's alternating successes in the board and bedroom, and for most readers they often contain too much detail of Cowperwood's financial transactions. Indeed, the most compelling portions of the two novels lie less in Cowperwood's epic struggles than in more intimate "family" material. In *The Financier* Cowperwood, while married, falls in love with the young girl Aileen, whose father, Edward Butler, an Irish immigrant, has risen to power in the corrupt Philadelphia political world. The emotional permutations arising out of the "pagan" couple and the old-world protective father reveal Dreiser at his best. And in *The Titan* it is not the largely symbolic figure of Berenice which moves us but the now aging and discarded Aileen whose rages and bitterness have the ring of truth.

With Dreiser's completion of *The Titan* in 1914, and with his decision not to proceed with *The Stoic*, he was free to undertake new fictional projects. But though Dreiser worked sporadically on several long works of fiction during the next decade—principally on his novel of Quaker life, *The Bulwark*—it was not until 1925 that his next novel, *An American Tragedy*, appeared. A good deal of Dreiser's publications during this decade consisted of collections of the various sketches and short stories he had been writing since *Sister Carrie*. His major new writing was in the areas of autobiography, drama, and philosophy.

Dreiser's principal autobiographical works—*A Hoosier Holiday*, *A Book About Myself*, and *Dawn*—were written from approximately 1914 to 1920. *A Hoosier Holiday*, though superficially a record of Dreiser's automobile trip to Indiana in the summer of 1915 with his artist friend Franklin Booth, is more often an evocative account of Dreiser's Indiana boyhood laced with observations about American life. *Dawn* and *A Book About Myself* are more conventional autobiographies. (Although written before *A Book About Myself*, *Dawn* was not published until 1931 because of its frank depiction of Dreiser's youthful sex experiences.)

Dawn takes Dreiser up to about 1890, while *A Book About Myself* (which was entitled *Newspaper Days* on its republication in 1931) is devoted almost entirely to his career as a newspaperman in Chicago, St. Louis, Pittsburgh, and New York. Both works are not only invaluable accounts of Dreiser's early experiences, beliefs, and feelings but also have an aesthetic effect similar to that of Dreiser's best novels. Through a seemingly artless directness and fullness they engage us in the corporal and spiritual adventures of a frequently unattractive "hero" whose life and beliefs are nevertheless absorbing and moving.

Dreiser's plays and philosophical essays of this period—published in *Plays of the Natural and the Supernatural* (1916), *The Hand of the Potter* (1919), and *Hey Rub-a-Dub-Dub* (1920)—reveal his exploration in strikingly different forms of a similar concern. He was increasingly becoming absorbed in what he believed to be the tragic nature of the human condition and was seeking both to explain and dramatize this vision of life. In such realistic plays as *The Girl in the Coffin* (produced in 1917) and *The Hand of the Potter* (produced in 1921), he dealt with the theme by depicting man's inability to shape the direction of his life given his lack of control of his underlying makeup. *The Hand of the Potter*, in its sympathetic portrayal of a sex murderer, is a particularly sensationalistic rendering of this theme. And in a series of one-act plays of the "supernatural" which were heavily influenced by the contemporary expressionistic movement he sought to offer still further examples of the indeterminacy and waywardness of life. The essays of *Hey Rub-a-Dub-Dub*—a work subtitled *A Book of the Mystery and Terror and Wonder of Life*—deal discursively with these themes. Dreiser in his essays was heavily influenced by Herbert Spencer's ideas of "equation," in which individual fates are controlled by the evolutionary force which requires that such unequal conditions in life as poverty and wealth or weakness and strength constantly seek but never fully achieve a balance or equilibrium. The essays are plodding, repetitive, and on the whole unenlightening. Dreiser was the kind of speculative thinker who best expressed his ideas symbolically in the fictional reality of a novel.

The work which climaxed this productive decade and a half in Dreiser's career is *An American Tragedy*. Dreiser in the years after the publication of *An American Tragedy* frequently claimed that from the earliest days of his career as a newspaperman he had had an interest in a certain kind of crime which be believed was significantly expressive of American life. As he encountered this crime on various occasions in St. Louis, Pittsburgh, and New York, it had a single underlying configuration beneath its superficial differences. A young man, poor but anxious to succeed, falls in love with a girl of his own class whom he makes pregnant. There then arrives on the scene a well-to-do young woman who is responsive to the young man and with whose aid he can rise. In one direction lie duty and poverty, in another wealth and power through love. When the young man seeks to solve his dilemma by disposing of "Miss Poor" so that he will be free to marry "Miss Rich," he is discovered and is ultimately punished.

Much of Dreiser's absorption in this kind of crime stemmed from the closeness of its basic characteristics to some of his own most deeply felt motives in life. He, too, as a poor, youthful outsider had dreamed of easily rising to great heights through the favors of a "Miss Rich." And he, too, had felt trapped in dutiful relationships—first with Sallie White (whom he did indeed "kill off" in *The "Genius"* by having Angela Blue die) and later, even while writing *An American Tragedy*, with Helen Richardson.

When Dreiser accompanied Helen to Los Angeles in 1919, he ostensibly was at work on *The Bulwark*, his novel of Quaker life, which he had begun in 1914. But while in California he either discovered or became reinterested in a particular instance of this kind of crime, the famous Chester Gillette-Grace Brown murder case of 1906. In the summer of 1920 he put aside *The Bulwark* and began work on *An American Tragedy*. A lengthy false start, in which he depended too heavily on his own boyhood for the depiction of Clyde Griffiths's youth, delayed his efforts, and it was not until his return to New York in late 1922 that he undertook the novel in earnest. Full use of the accounts of the Gillette trial in the *New York World*, a visit to the North Woods setting where Grace had been killed, and even attendance at a Sing Sing execution supplied some of the material for the million or so words of the novel which Dreiser wrote during the next several years. With the aid of friends and editors, more than half of this manuscript was cut, still leaving the substantial two-volume work which Horace Liveright published in December 1925.

Chester Gillette had gone to the small upstate New York town of Cortland to work in his uncle's skirt factory. There he had seduced and made pregnant a girl from a neighboring village who also worked at the factory. Under pressure from her to marry, he killed her at an Adirondack lake by striking her with a tennis racket until she drowned. Although Dreiser used both the general outline and much specific detail from the Gillette case, he also made several significant changes which suggest the thematic direction he wished to give this material. For example, Clyde Griffiths comes out of a poorer and more limited background than did Gillette, and he is more interested in a specific upper-class girl–the Sondra of *An American Tragedy*–than was Gillette. And Clyde's involvement in the death of Roberta is far more ambiguous than was Gillette's in the murder of Grace Brown. Dreiser in these and similar changes revealed that his intent was less to render literally a sensational crime than to dramatize in fictional form a morally and culturally complex event.

Much of the success of *An American Tragedy* derives from Dreiser's ability to structure his very long novel into three distinctive parts, each with its own setting, pace, and climax, yet with each contributing as well to the powerful tragic effect at the center of the novel. The novel begins with Clyde as a young boy in Kansas City. His parents are ineffectual, self-deluded street evangelists, and Clyde is introduced early in life to the vast difference between their cloudy dreams and the riches and wonders of the metropolis. Although Clyde soon abandons their way of life, he remains—in his own weaknesses and mirages—their son. Clyde's principal initiation into experience occurs at the Green-Davidson Hotel where he works as a bellhop. There he falls in with a group of boys who come to represent all that he wishes in life–girls, clothes, a good time, and little responsibility. *An American Tragedy* thus has from its beginning the character of a simple dramatization of the parable of the prodigal son but for its developing theme that Clyde, because of both his limited equipment and the tawdry nature of the life he so desperately desires, also mirrors some of the essential flaws in the American Dream. Book one ends with an automobile accident which foreshadows the "accident" at the close of book two in which Roberta drowns. Off on a suspect escapade with his chums, Clyde is at once innocent and guilty of contributing to the accident, and he also hesitates in coming to the aid of his companions at a crucial moment.

In book two Clyde makes his way to Lycurgus, in upstate New York, to take a position in his uncle's factory. In Lycurgus he finds himself treated as a poor relation by the Griffithses, while the bulk of the town considers him a member of a wealthy and powerful family. Miserable and lonely, he finds comfort and love with Roberta Alden, who works with him in the factory and who is herself the daughter of poor local farmers. Despite her resistance, he persuades her to become his lover. Soon afterward, however, in a fulfillment of Clyde's wildest hopes, he is taken up by Sondra Finchley and her set. Sondra, the daughter of another Lycurgus manufacturer, is both attractive and rich, and she thus constitutes for Clyde an almost religious manifestation of his dreams. But first Clyde must get rid of Roberta, and as he works up courage to do so, she becomes pregnant. There then follows one of the most harrowing narratives in all of American fiction. Roberta is increasingly insistent that Clyde do something, but because of his ignorance, poverty, and fear, he is incapable of resolving the problem other than in the one way he refuses to accept–to marry Roberta. Sondra, in the meantime, is increasingly warm toward Clyde, and his prospect of marrying her is even brighter. Driven to distraction, Clyde arranges a trip to the North Woods with Roberta. Ostensibly, they are to be married during the trip, but Clyde in fact plans to stage a mock accident at a lake, during which Roberta will drown and he will disappear. (He also plans to disguise his identity during this trip.) On the lake Clyde's nerve fails him. He is so obviously overcome with emotion, however, that Roberta seeks to come to his aid. The boat tips over, and Roberta begins to drown. She calls for help, but Clyde swims away. Has he killed her or has he not?

Book three of *An American Tragedy* demonstrates that this question, as well as similar complex questions concerning moral responsibility and justice, is extraneous within the American legal system. Clyde is soon tracked down, captured, placed on trial, convicted, and sentenced to death. The jury is convinced of his guilt not only because he set out to murder Roberta but because the district attorney persuades them that Clyde, a wealthy Griffiths, seduced and then wished to abandon a poor country girl. Whatever ambiguities are attached to Roberta's death, the case is decided principally on the basis of the jury's class and sex prejudices. In prison, while awaiting execution, Clyde encounters a last dream, that offered by the Reverend McMillan,

who promises forgiveness and salvation in return for confession and an acceptance of God. Clyde again reaches out, but at his death he wonders in his heart if he will find yet another mirage.

An American Tragedy has moved several generations of readers with its compelling power as a narrative of crime and punishment. It has had a more varied history, however, as a view of the tragic nature of experience. As a novel which seeks to dramatize an underlying flaw in American life, *An American Tragedy* reveals the terrible power of American national experience to convince even the weakest and most ineffectual that life is full of promise and that the answer to our dreams lies in wealth. As a work of larger tragic dimensions, the novel forces the reader to share in the fall of a human being who, whatever his limitations, wishes to be understood and finds that he is merely condemned.

An American Tragedy was greeted as a great American novel on its publication. Even one of Dreiser's foremost detractors, Stuart P. Sherman, considered it a major work. The novel was also a financial success, with play and movie adaptations soon augmenting its earnings. So after twenty-five years of struggle for recognition and success as a writer of fiction, Dreiser had at last come into his own. Indeed, for some years it was believed that he would be the first American to be honored with the Nobel Prize.

With the completion of *An American Tragedy*, Dreiser did not turn immediately to another novel, as had been his habit earlier in his career, but rather permitted his increasing absorption in social and philosophical matters to occupy him, as they were to do for almost two decades. Not that there was not a flurry of publication in the five years or so after the appearance of *An American Tragedy* to capitalize on the success of that work. Two editions of Dreiser's poems, a collection of short stories (*Chains*), and a two-volume collection of sketches (*A Gallery of Women*) all appeared between 1925 and 1930.

But for the most part Dreiser's interest during the late 1920s was focused on two fundamental problems–how to make America a better place in which to live, and how to describe the underlying truths of existence. The centrality of these concerns in Dreiser's thought and life of the time is suggested by two events of 1927 and 1928. In November 1927 Dreiser visited the Soviet Union and remained for several months, principally in Moscow. Like most American intellectuals of the day, he was fascinated by the Russian experiment, and like most, he was especially interested in its possible applicability to America. Then, during the summer of 1928, Dreiser spent several weeks visiting the Woods Hole experimental biology station in Massachusetts, where he talked with scientists and observed their work. His interest was less in the details of their experiments than in their beliefs about the fundamental processes of life.

These two personal ventures into knowledge in the late 1920s anticipate Dreiser's almost obsessive preoccupations of the 1930s. During that decade, despite several halfhearted and unsuccessful attempts to work on *The Bulwark* and *The Stoic*, Dreiser's interests were almost entirely limited to the support of left-wing causes and to his own philosophical studies. Out of the first came such volumes as *Dreiser Looks at Russia* (1928); *Harlan Miners Speak* (1932), a record of the investigation by Dreiser and others of the Harlan County miners strike in 1931 for which Dreiser wrote the introduction; and *Tragic America* (1931). Out of the second came a vast collection of notes and a number of muddy and diffuse essays. Several of these essays appeared in the 1930s, but the bulk of his philosophical writing remained unpublished until collected in Dreiser's posthumous *Notes on Life* in 1974.

As some observers have noted, and as Dreiser himself realized, there appears to be a contradiction between these two preoccupations. On the one hand Dreiser's interest in American social problems, in the efforts of the poor and oppressed to gain a better life, posits a belief in man's ability to improve his condition through conscious effort. On the other Dreiser's philosophical speculations had led him to reconfirm his earlier notion that the world was a machine in which the individual had no control over his destiny. To Dreiser, however, these positions were not irreconcilable. He had come increasingly to view the mechanistic foundations of life not so much as imprisoning but as a vast and intricate complex of beauty and wonder in which the destructive effects upon others of extremes in ability and fortune could be lessened through social change. The two positions were, in any case, to be reconciled in Dreiser's life and fiction in the last years of his life. In the period just before his death he was absorbed in the mystical aspects of Hinduism and joined the Communist party. And he sought in the final beliefs of his characters Solon Barnes in *The Bulwark* and Berenice in *The Stoic* to represent his own final equanimity in the face of both the world's pain and beauty.

Dreiser's personal fortunes suffered during the Depression, particularly after the collapse of his longtime publisher, Horace Liveright, in 1932. In 1938 he settled his affairs in New York, where at one time he had had both a country estate at Mt. Kisco and a luxurious apartment on Fifty-seventh Street in New York City, and moved with Helen to a small cottage in Los Angeles. There he became increasingly strident and single-minded in his party-line beliefs and public statements. Unlike most American writers, who had begun to drift away from the Communist party following the Stalinist purges of the mid 1930s and the Nazi-Soviet pact of 1939, Dreiser in the late 1930s and early 1940s became even more convinced that the capitalist countries of the world were engaged in a conspiracy to destroy the Soviet Union. He distributed from Los Angeles a series of privately printed broadsides (often enclosed in letters to friends) supporting his views. He also made these beliefs the center of the last book which he published during his lifetime, the polemic diatribe (largely ghostwritten by a party hack), *America Is Worth Saving* (1941).

Dreiser's major creative effort during the last years of his life was the completion at long last of both *The Bulwark* and *The Stoic*. He had begun *The Bulwark* in 1914, after hearing from Anna Tatum, a young woman of Philadelphia Quaker background, the story of her father's tragic life, and had worked sporadically on the novel for the next several years. (Indeed, Liveright announced the imminent publication of the novel on several occasions during this period.) But though he made extensive notes for the novel and wrote a lengthy draft of its early portion, he failed to complete it, and in 1920 put it aside to work on *An American Tragedy*.

The appeal to Dreiser of the story of Solon Barnes and his family was that it closely resembled both the shape of Dreiser's own family life and that of the families he was depicting in his fiction. A moralistic, disciplinarian father and a warmhearted, generous mother have children whose desire for a fuller, more exciting life breeds rebellion and anger toward the father despite his and their love. The father is thus a bulwark of faith and behavior who nevertheless cannot prevent the tragic consequences of family conflict. This was the kind of story which always moved Dreiser as he responded to its combination of love, blindness, and desire and enveloped the whole in his compassionate understanding.

When Dreiser returned to *The Bulwark* in 1942, he did so with interests which were to give this novel, as well as *The Stoic*, a significant new direction. As has been noted, Dreiser's studies in the 1930s had led him to view the mechanistic design of life as infinitely beautiful and awe-inspiring. He therefore found during these years that such traditional mystic faiths as Hinduism and Quakerism (as well as the transcendentalism of Thoreau, a collection of whose writings he edited in 1938) provided an accommodation of both his mechanistic and his religious beliefs. The world was a complex machine, but a machine so beautiful and complex must have a divine origin, and the man of intuitive insight could recognize the spiritual reality pervading all nature.

It was with this vision of life that Dreiser began to revise *The Bulwark* in 1942, giving now much fuller attention at the beginning and close of the novel to Solon's Quaker beliefs and introducing at the close Solon's conversion to Dreiser's own mystical faith. Increasingly in poor health, however, Dreiser had great difficulty combining his old and new material. In the summer of 1944 he was joined in Los Angeles by Marguerite Tjader Harris, who worked closely with him on *The Bulwark* until the novel was finally completed in May 1945. Dreiser then sent the manuscript to his old friend and editor Louise Campbell, who cut it severely and also smoothed over Dreiser's prose. Although Dreiser's editor at Doubleday, Donald Elder, was later to restore some of Campbell's cuts, *The Bulwark* still reveals the effects of her editing in its uncharacteristic spare form and uncluttered prose.

The Bulwark bears several unfortunate consequences of its long genesis and of Dreiser's changing emphasis within the novel. Its cast and chronology are too expansive for Dreiser's almost chroniclelike treatment of character and event, and the central portion of the novel, much of which deals with Solon's business affairs, is out of key with the tone of the more "religious" sections of the novel. Yet the work also has a moving directness and simplicity in its account of a truly religious man who mistakes moralism and worldly success for God's word and who comes to see, at the end of his life, both the tragedy and beauty of all existence. *The Bulwark* lacks both the density of life and the Dreiserian presence of his most characteristic fiction, but for many readers it has had a fictional quality and appeal distinctively its own.

Almost immediately after completing *The Bulwark*, Dreiser turned his attention to *The Stoic*. He had done most of the research for the volume thirty years earlier, at the time he was working on *The Financier* and *The Titan*. He had also made several attempts to write the novel in the late 1920s and early 1930s and in 1932 had managed to complete a draft of about two-thirds of the book. It was to this draft that he returned in 1945. Now ill and tired, but nevertheless anxious to bring the Cowperwood trilogy to a conclusion, he revised this draft by cutting a good deal of its financial detail and by adding a final section in which Cowperwood dies and Berenice becomes a convert to Yogaism. He had all but finished this task, leaving only the revision of the last two chapters incomplete, when he died in late December 1945.

Even more than *The Bulwark*, *The Stoic* is an anomalous joining of two widely different kinds of fiction. The first portion of the novel is a largely lifeless account of Cowperwood's efforts to win control of the London underground system and of his amorous affairs. The last portion, after his death, deals with the nature of Hindu mysticism and with Berenice's acceptance of its beliefs. Almost all readers have agreed that *The Stoic* is Dreiser's least successful novel. Interest in the work has therefore been confined to its concluding section, in which Berenice's conversion to Hindu mysticism offers a valuable parallel for the historian of Dreiser's ideas to Solon's return to Quaker mysticism at the conclusion of *The Bulwark*.

Dreiser's reputation was at a low ebb for some years after his death. A long period of fictional inactivity in which his political and philosophical ideas appeared either inane or muddy had been followed by the posthumous publication (in 1946 and 1947) of two uncharacteristic novels. No wonder that in 1950 Lionel Trilling viewed Dreiser's earlier stature as a historical aberration. During the past several decades, however, and particularly since the appearance of a number of major studies and appreciations of his work, Dreiser has increasingly been recognized as one of the principal figures in late-nineteenth- and early-twentieth-century American literature. His significance as the one major American naturalist who had a full career and who therefore best exemplifies the character of American naturalism is unchallenged. And the permanent worth and hold of his best fiction—in particular of *Sister Carrie, Jennie Gerhardt,* and *An American Tragedy*—is seen to reside not in some indefinable "power" but in a compelling vision of life expressed through an often brilliant craftsmanship.

Letters:

Letters to Louise, edited by Louise Campbell (Philadelphia: University of Pennsylvania Press, 1959).
Collection of Dreiser's letters to his editor.

Letters of Theodore Dreiser, 3 volumes, edited by Robert H. Elias (Philadelphia: University of Pennsylvania Press, 1959).
Extensive collection of Dreiser's correspondence.

Bibliographies:

Donald Pizer, Richard W. Dowell, and Frederic E. Rusch, *Theodore Dreiser: A Primary and Secondary Bibliography* (Boston: G. K. Hall, 1975).
Comprehensive checklist of Dreiser's works, including pamphlets, leaflets, and broadsides, with an annotated list of works about Dreiser.

Jeanette Boswell, *Theodore Dreiser and the Critics, 1911-1982* (Metuchen, N.J.: Scarecrow, 1986).
Secondary bibliography with selected annotations.

Biographies:

Dorothy Dudley, *Forgotten Frontiers: Dreiser and the Land of the Free* (New York: Harrison Smith, 1932).
Early attempt to place Dreiser and his work in a historical context.

Robert H. Elias, *Theodore Dreiser: Apostle of Nature* (New York: Knopf, 1949; emended edition, Ithaca: Cornell University Press, 1970).
Analysis of the dominant themes in Dreiser's writing and their relationship to his life; emended edition features a survey of secondary materials.

Helen Dreiser, *My Life with Dreiser* (Cleveland: World, 1951).
Dreiser's second wife's account of their relationship, covering the years from 1919 to 1945.

W. A. Swanberg, *Dreiser* (New York: Scribners, 1965).
In-depth study of the life based largely on Dreiser's correspondence and interviews with his friends and colleagues.

Marguerite Tjader, *Theodore Dreiser: A New Dimension* (Norwalk, Conn.: Silvermine, 1965).
Focuses on the political, philosophical, and religious preoccupations of Dreiser's later years.

Richard Lingeman, *Theodore Dreiser: At the Gates of the City, 1871-1907* (New York: Putnam's, 1986).
Exhaustive study of the first thirty-six years of Dreiser's life; first of a projected two-volume biography.

References:

Alfred Kazin and Charles Shapiro, eds., *The Stature of Theodore Dreiser* (Bloomington: University of Indiana Press, 1955).
Collection of personal reminiscences, reviews, and critical essays.

Richard Lehan, *Theodore Dreiser: His World and His Novels* (Carbondale: Southern Illinois University Press, 1969).
Biographical study focusing on the development of Dreiser's ideas and his ability to implement them in his novels.

John Lyndenberg, ed., *Dreiser: A Collection of Critical Essays* (Englewood Cliffs, N.J.: Prentice-Hall, 1971).
Collection of fifteen essays originally published between 1915 and 1964, selected with an emphasis toward controversy and disputation.

F. O. Matthiessen, *Theodore Dreiser* (New York: Sloane, 1951).
Concentrates on the aesthetic aspects of Dreiser's novels.

Ellen Moers, *Two Dreisers* (New York: Viking, 1969).
Lengthy analysis of the composition of *Sister Carrie* and *An American Tragedy.*

Donald Pizer, *The Novels of Theodore Dreiser: A Critical Study* (Minneapolis: University of Minnesota Press, 1976).

Provides a thorough analysis of Dreiser's novels.

Pizer, ed., *Essays on Theodore Dreiser* (Boston: G. K. Hall, 1981).
Collections of previously published critical essays.

Jack Salzman, ed., *Theodore Dreiser: The Critical Reception* (New York: David Lewis, 1972).
Extensive collection of American reviews of Dreiser's books; includes an introduction that presents an overview of the critical response to his work.

Charles Shapiro, *Theodore Dreiser: Our Bitter Patriot* (Carbondale: Southern Illinois University Press, 1962).
Study of Dreiser as a social critic.

Robert Penn Warren, *Homage to Theodore Dreiser: On the Centennial of His Birth* (New York: Random House, 1971).
Critical evaluation of the relationship between Dreiser's life and art seen from the perspective of the centennial of his birth.

Papers:
The Theodore Dreiser Collection of the University of Pennsylvania Library is the principal repository of Dreiser papers. It contains manuscripts of published and unpublished works, including drafts and notes; letters to and by Dreiser; and clippings and scrapbooks. Other important collections of Dreiser papers are in the Cornell University Library, the Lilly Library of Indiana University, the New York Public Library, the University of Texas Library, and the University of Virginia Library.

W. E. B. Du Bois

This entry was updated by Michael D. Senecal from the entry by Addison Gayle, Jr. (Bernard M. Baruch College of the City University of New York) in DLB 50, Afro-American Writers Before the Harlem Renaissance.

Places	New England Ghana University of Berlin	Fisk University, Nashville, Tenn. Philadelphia Harpers Ferry	Harvard University Atlanta University
Influences and Relationships	Booker T. Washington George Santayana	Marcus Garvey William James	Shirley Graham
Literary Movements and Forms	Harlem Renaissance (*Crisis*) Lecturing	Sociological Writing	Historical Essay
Major Themes	Black Contributions to American Society	"The Negro Problem"	International Black Kinship
Cultural and Artistic Influences	Black Revisionist History	Pan-Africanism	Black Colleges and Universities
Social and Economic Influences	Racial Segregation McCarthyism The Depression	American Labor Party NAACP	Black Poverty Communism

See also the Du Bois entry in DLB 47, *American Historians, 1866-1912.*

BIRTH: Great Barrington, Massachusetts, 23 February 1868, to Alfred and Mary Burghardt Du Bois.

EDUCATION: B.A., Fisk University, 1888; B.A., 1890; M.A., 1891; Ph.D., 1896; Harvard University; University of Berlin, 1892-1894.

MARRIAGES: 1896 to Nina Gomer (deceased 1950); children: Burghardt, Yolande Du Bois Williams. 14 February 1951 to Shirley Graham.

AWARDS AND HONORS: Minister Plenipotentiary and Envoy Extraordinary to Liberia, conferred by President Calvin Coolidge, 1923; LL.D. from Howard University, 1930; Spingarn Medal from NAACP, 1932; LL.D. from Atlanta University, 1938; Litt.D., Fisk University, 1938; L.H.D., Wilberforce University, 1940; elected to the National Institute of Arts and Letters, 1943; Lenin International Peace Prize, 1958; honorary degrees from Charles University, 1958 (Prague), Humboldt University, 1958 (Berlin), Moscow University, 1959.

DEATH: Accra, Ghana, 27 August 1963.

BOOKS: *The Suppression of the African Slave-Trade to the United States of America, 1638-1870,* volume 1 of Harvard Historical Studies (New York & London: Longmans, Green, 1896);
The Conservation of Races (Washington, D.C.: American Negro Academy, 1897);
The Philadelphia Negro: A Social Study (Philadelphia: University of Pennsylvania, 1899);
The Souls of Black Folk: Essays and Sketches (Chicago: McClurg, 1903; London: Constable, 1905);
The Negro in the South, His Economic Progress in Relation to His Moral and Religious Development; Being the William Levi Bull Lectures for the Year 1907, by Du Bois and Booker T. Washington (Philadelphia: Jacobs, 1907);
John Brown (Philadelphia: Jacobs, 1909);
The Quest of the Silver Fleece (Chicago: McClurg, 1911);
The Negro (New York: Holt, 1915; London: Williams & Norgate, 1915);
Darkwater: Voices From Within the Veil (New York: Harcourt, Brace & Howe, 1920; London: Constable, 1920);

The Gift of Black Folk: The Negroes in the Making of America (Boston: Stratford, 1924);
Dark Princess: A Romance (New York: Harcourt, Brace, 1928);
Africa: Its Geography, People and Products (Girard, Kans.: Haldeman-Julius, 1930);
Africa: Its Place in Modern History (Girard, Kans.: Haldeman-Julius, 1930);
Black Reconstruction: An Essay Toward a History of the Part Which Black Folk Played in the Attempt to Reconstruct Democracy in America, 1860-1880 (New York: Harcourt, Brace, 1935);
Black Folk, Then and Now: An Essay in the History and Sociology of the Negro Race (New York: Holt, 1939);
Dusk of Dawn: An Essay Toward an Autobiography of a Race Concept (New York: Harcourt, Brace, 1940);
Color and Democracy: Colonies and Peace (New York: Harcourt, Brace, 1945);
The World and Africa: An Inquiry into the Part Which Africa Has Played in World History (New York: Viking, 1947);
In Battle for Peace: The Story of My 83rd Birthday (New York: Masses & Mainstream, 1952);
The Ordeal of Mansart (New York: Mainstream, 1957);
Mansart Builds a School (New York: Mainstream, 1959);
Worlds of Color (New York: Mainstream, 1961);
Selected Poems (Ghana: Ghana University Press, 1964?);
The Autobiography of W. E. B. Du Bois: A Soliloquy on Viewing My Life From the Last Decade of Its First Century, edited by Herbert Aptheker (New York: International Publishers, 1968);
W. E. B. Du Bois Speaks: Speeches and Addresses, edited by Philip S. Foner (New York: Pathfinder Press, 1970);
W. E. B. Du Bois: The Crisis Writing, edited by Daniel Walden (Greenwich, Conn.: Fawcett, 1972);
The Emerging Thought of W. E. B. Du Bois: Essays and Editorials From "The Crisis," edited by Henry Lee Moon (New York: Simon & Schuster, 1972);
The Education of Black People: Ten Critiques, 1906-1960, edited by Aptheker (Amherst: University of Massachusetts Press, 1973);
Against Racism: Unpublished Essays, Papers, Addresses, 1887-1961, edited by Aptheker (Millwood, N.Y.: KTO Press, 1985).

W. E. B. Du Bois (courtesy of Archives, University Library, University of Massachusetts/Amherst)

OTHER: *Atlanta University Publications*, nos. 3-18, edited by Du Bois (Atlanta: Atlanta University Press, 1898-1914);

Haiti, in *Federal Theatre Plays*, edited by Pierre de Rohan (New York: Random House, 1938);

An Appeal to the World: A Statement on the Denial of Human Rights to Minorities in the Case of Citizens of Negro Descent in the United States of America and an Appeal to the United Nations for Redress, edited by Du Bois (New York: National Association for the Advancement of Colored People, 1947).

PERIODICAL PUBLICATIONS: "Strivings of The Negro People," *Atlantic Monthly*, 80 (August 1897): 194-198;

"The Negro and Crime," *Independent*, 51 (18 May 1899): 1355-1357;

"The Atlanta Conferences," *Voice of the Negro*, 1 (March 1904): 85-90;

"Credo," *Independent*, 57 (6 October 1904): 787;

"The Souls of White Folk," *Independent*, 69 (18 August 1910): 339-342;

"Negro In Literature And Art," *Annals of the American Academy of Political and Social Science*, 49 (September 1913): 233-237;

"Editing *The Crisis*," *Crisis*, 58 (March 1951): 147, 213;

"I Take My Stand," *Masses and Mainstream,* 4 (April 1951): 10-16.

"Every intellectual," writes Ignazio Silone, "is a revolutionary," and though this may not be generally true, in the case of W. E. B. Du Bois, the observation is both accurate and fitting. The internationally known scholar and writer, born in Great Barrington, Massachusetts, was one of America's few Renaissance men, contributing to the artistic, social, literary, and political environment of his time as have few men before or since. His dedication to principle and unswerving devotion to truth for over fifty years earned him both the praise and scorn of his fellow countrymen, black and white. When he died on the eve of the March on Washington in 1963, he was lauded from the platform by the executive secretary of the National Association for the Advancement of Colored People (NAACP); yet in 1966 he was excoriated by soon-to-be-President of the United States, Richard M. Nixon, because a group of idealistic, progressive, young Americans had established clubs on the nation's campuses bearing his name. These dual attitudes–praise and scorn–were constants throughout his life, and although, in the latter stages of his career, the scorn seemed excessive, he bore it with that stoic determination that so marked his character. Writing of one trying experience–indictment and trial as a subversive–in 1951, during the infamous McCarthy era, he revealed his attitude toward the numerous crises of his long life: "It was a bitter experience and I bowed before the storm. But I did not break."

If there is something in Du Bois that Americans have come to identify as New England temperament, the stubborn Yankee, spiritual descendant of Henry David Thoreau and Washington Irving, it may well be because Du Bois's character was formed in the same New England clime. Certainly his description of his hometown, written in an essay, "The Pageant Of Seven Decades," rivals some of Thoreau's descriptions in *Walden:* "The town and its surroundings were a boy's paradise . . . there were mountains to climb and rivers to wade and swim, lakes to freeze and hills for coasting. There were orchards and caves and wide green fields; and all of it was the free property apparently of the children of town." Such poetic visions of their hometowns were uncommon to most blacks in America in the 1800s, but Du Bois's family, though not middle-class, was unlike that of most blacks. His mother, Mary Burghardt Du Bois, whom he describes as descending from Dutch-African stock, was a proud woman who encouraged her only son toward hard work and study. His respect for her, evidenced in numerous autobiographical sketches, was perhaps engendered by her condition: she was a single parent whose husband, Alfred Du Bois, had fled almost simultaneously with the birth of their son. Aided now and then by relatives, a close-knit group whom Du Bois was to refer to as "The Du Bois Clan," she inculcated her son with her own New England virtues. She died on the eve of his entrance into college, and for Du Bois her death was both an occasion for grief and a moment for renewal of determination.

This sense of determination had begun to manifest itself earlier, when Du Bois had suddenly realized that here, in this arcadian setting, he was somewhat different from others. The realization was long in coming and exploded with force in a classroom where, during the customary exchange of greeting cards, a white female student refused to accept his. The refusal was registered "preemptorily with a glance. Then it dawned upon me with certain suddenness that I was different from the others . . . shut out from their world by a vast veil." He concluded with angry, defiant words, "I had, thereafter, no desire to tear down that veil, to creep through"; these are sentiments recollected and garnished in the bitterness of later years. For here was the first serious stressful moment of his life, one that fired his determination and imbued his character with such anger that he was propelled forward with almost a singular objective: "That sky was bluest when I could beat them at a foot race or even beat their stringy heads . . . the worlds I longed for, and all their dazzling opportunities were theirs, not mine. But they should not keep these prizes, I said; some, all, I would wrest from them." When he journeyed to the black belt in 1885 to become a student at Fisk University, the wresting time had begun.

Those were memorable years spent in Tennessee at the all-black college founded for the sons and daughters of emancipated slaves, and Du Bois, whose nurturant years were spent in a predominantly white world, was "deliriously happy" in a setting that was black. At Fisk he began writing and public speaking, and, paying obeisance as always to his mother's tutelage, he excelled among his classmates, graduating with honors in 1888. Perhaps the most important days at

Du Bois at the age of nineteen (courtesy of Schomburg Center for Research in Black Culture, the New York Public Library, Astor, Lenox and Tilden Foundations)

Fisk were spent during the summer, when he left the campus to trek out into the hillsides, into the shanties and wood-shack homes of Tennessee's black inhabitants, seeking work as a teacher. Here he glimpsed, despite appalling poverty, a grandeur and heroism that he was later to describe eloquently in the essay "On The Meaning Of Progress." He recalled few such memorable events during his tenure at Harvard, however, where he entered with the junior class in 1888. He remembered the animosity of fellow white students, the friendship and guidance of such influential teachers as William James, Albert Bushnell Hart, George Santayana, and Frank Tausig, and the accolades which greeted his commencement speech on Jefferson Davis as he graduated cum laude with a B.A. degree. "Du Bois, the colored orator," wrote a commentator in *Washington*, a leading periodical, "was the star of the occasion."

A master's degree was awarded to him in the spring of 1891, and though he would not receive his Ph.D. until 1896, he had achieved more

education than most young men in America. Still, he felt unprepared to cope "with the new and extraordinary situations then developing in America." To do so meant more education and this meant, in his mind, training abroad: "Any American scholar who wanted preferment went to Germany to study . . . I wanted then to study in Germany. I was determined that any failure on my part to become a recognized American scholar must not be based on any lack of modern training." With this idea in mind and aided by a fellowship from the Slater fund, he enrolled at the University of Berlin in the fall of 1892.

Like Tennessee before, Berlin provided him with experiences that would last throughout his life. Here more than ever before he felt the dilemma of being black in America. As he traveled across the Continent, sat in classrooms presided over by the intellectuals of the time, formed enduring relationships with whites of both sexes, he experienced for the first time a world unbounded by color restrictions. Not surprisingly then, years after his first experiences abroad he wrote with nostalgia, anger, and sarcasm: "As a student in Germany, I built great castles in Spain and lived therein. I dreamed and wandered and sang; then after two long years I dropped suddenly back into 'nigger' hating America."

He came back to America in 1894, one year before Booker T. Washington, addressing an exposition in Atlanta, was to assume the mantle of "Leader of the Negro People." At that moment, however, Washington was principal of Tuskegee Institute, a black college in Alabama, and his was one of the offers the young scholar received as he began the search for work. In his autobiography, published posthumously in 1968, Du Bois asks sarcastically what the meaning of his life might have been had the offer from Tuskegee arrived before he had accepted the one from Wilberforce College. The small denominational college in Ohio needed a professor of Greek and Latin, and Du Bois took up his duties there in 1894, imbued, he later remembered, with notions of what a university should be. Whether any black university at the time could have met his criteria is doubtful; certainly Wilberforce did not, and his tenure there was somewhat disillusioning. He was chastised by the presiding bishop for refusing to lead students in a prayer and became involved in a patronage dispute concerning the college and the bishop's son. More important, he was denied his request to add sociology to his curriculum, a refusal that led him to conclude that the college was not interested in a scholarly, systematic analysis of "The Negro Problem." Thus he willingly accepted an offer to conduct a sociological study of blacks for the University of Pennsylvania in 1896, the year in which he married Nina Gomer and saw the publication of his dissertation, *The Suppression of the African Slave-Trade to the United States of America, 1638-1870*.

He arrived in Philadelphia to fulfill his mandate, "the study of the social conditions of the Colored People of the Seventh Ward of Philadelphia." What had not been possible at Wilberforce was now offered at the University of Pennsylvania, the chance to test one of his major theories concerning race in America. "The Negro problem," he wrote, "was in my mind a matter of systematic investigation and intelligent understanding. The world was thinking wrong about race, because it did not know. The ultimate evil was stupidity. The cure for it was knowledge based on scientific investigation." Almost single-handedly he sought to provide such knowledge in his study *The Philadelphia Negro* (1899).

The book represented the first systematic study of a large number of blacks in any major city in America. Du Bois studied the racial history of his subjects as well as the history of the city itself. He studied every conceivable group in the community and concentrated on such categories as crime, employment, and education. In the conclusion he offered stern suggestions to blacks throughout the country: "Simply because the ancestors of the present inhabitants of America went out of their way barbarously to mistreat and enslave [blacks] . . . gives those blacks no right to ask that the civilization and morality of the land be seriously menaced for their benefit . . . a nation may rightly demand even of a people it has consciously and intentionally wronged, every effort and sacrifice possible on their part towards making themselves fit members of the community within a reasonable length of time. . . ."

The study abounds with such statements and differentiates the early Du Bois from the latter, the conservative from the radical, who, at this point in his career, is philosophically close to Booker T. Washington in the belief that blacks were unwilling conspirators in their own plight and that through hard work and application their conditions might be readily improved. Thus upon the shoulders of the victim he placed much of the blame for poverty, crime, and lack of progress.

His statements, however, were undercut by the irony of his own situation. He was accomplished, hardworking, diligent; yet, his studies completed, he was not offered a faculty position at the University of Pennsylvania. Thus, because he was black and for no other reason, after one and a half years at Pennsylvania, he was on his way to accept a position as professor of economics and history at Atlanta University, a black college. Later he wrote, "I was going to study the facts, any and all facts, concerning the American Negro and his plight. . . ." He would transfer to Atlanta the methodology he had perfected at the University of Pennsylvania, and his claim that he had developed "during the years 1897 to 1910 . . . a program of study of the problems affecting the American Negro" was justified. University studies concerning blacks were in progress before he arrived at Atlanta, but these, some under the auspices of Tuskegee and Booker T. Washington, concentrated mainly on blacks in agriculture. Under Du Bois's direction, however, the Atlanta conferences became, in effect, a sociological laboratory, a series of "scientific investigation[s]" into social conditions, primarily for social ends. The conferences resulted in the publication of eighteen monographs dealing with such subjects as "Morality Among Negroes in Cities," "The Negro In Business," "The Negro Church," and "The Negro American Family." With these studies, Atlanta became, for years, a resource bank of sociological data for colleges and public and private institutions.

His work at Atlanta was not without some difficulty. He enjoyed cordial relations with President Horace Bumstead, but this relationship would become somewhat strained as a result of Du Bois's increasing criticism of the policies of Washington. Funds to expand and continue his conferences and studies would suffer for the same reason. Yet in 1900 he was the conscientious scholar, using his laboratory to investigate, analyze, measure. He regularly wrote articles for such periodicals as *World Work* and the *Atlantic Monthly*, and in addition to making his first attempt at an encyclopedia of African people, he was elected a member of the American Association for the Advancement of Science. Then, suddenly, cataclysmically, the relatively quiescent life of the social scientist was transformed forever: "I had been studying the American Negro Problem," he writes. "And at the time when these studies were most successful, there cut across this plan which I had as a scientist, a red ray which could not be ignored."

The "red ray" was a metaphor for the circumstances surrounding Sam Hose, an illiterate black, far removed from the environs of Atlanta University. He was charged with having murdered and raped his landlord's wife, a white woman. The facts, however, as Du Bois learned them, were somewhat different. Hose appeared to have acted in self-defense. Armed with these new facts, Du Bois drafted a statement and started for the office of Joel Chandler Harris, editor of the *Atlanta Constitution*. He related the incident in his autobiography: "On the way news met me: Sam Hose had been lynched, and they said that his knuckles were on exhibition at a grocery store. . . . Two considerations thereafter broke in upon my work and eventually disrupted it: first, one could not be a calm, cool, and detached scientist, while Negroes were lynched, murdered, and starved; and secondly, there was no such definite demand for scientific work of the sort I was doing. . . ." In fact the demand seemed to be exactly the opposite of what Du Bois was pursuing at Atlanta, and it was not simply the white world of the early twentieth century that desired no scientific evidence to invalidate the racist machinery of caste distinction; gradually it became clear to Du Bois that such scholarship was not wanted by influential members of the black world either.

Whether this was altogether true of Booker T. Washington is not clear, but what is indisputable is that to speak of the black world after 1895 was to speak first and foremost of Washington, and few programs could be pursued with adequate financial support without his tacit approval. The man, born a slave in 1856, managed through virtue of hard work and application to become principal of Tuskegee Institute and after 1895 became, in the eyes of whites North and South, the accepted leader of black people. His support rested largely on statements he issued at the Atlanta Exposition of 1895 which affirmed the validity of the caste system. He belittled efforts by blacks to gain the right to vote, spoke of the virtues of segregation, and suggested second-class citizenship for America's blacks: "In all things that are purely social we can be as separate as the five fingers, yet one as the hand in all things essential to mutual progress. . . ."

If, as one newspaper later remarked, there were tears in the eyes of blacks in the audience during Washington's speech, Du Bois was not among those so moved. In fact, he lagged behind many black intellectuals whose opposition to Washington was instantaneous. Not only did he not oppose Washington seriously but he praised aspects of the Atlanta Exposition address. When he did speak out, his opposition was reasoned and calculated, and the two men enjoyed, for some time, cordial, if increasingly strained, relations. In 1902, one year before publication of *The Souls of Black Folk*, Washington, in a letter, commended Du Bois upon his work at Atlanta: "Constantly putting such facts before the public cannot but help our cause greatly in the long run." Efforts were made to entice Du Bois from Atlanta to Tuskegee, and several meetings between the two men were held toward this goal.

Du Bois's reticence concerning overt criticism of the Tuskegee principal notwithstanding, chances of a rapprochement were impossible. Though he had accepted much of Washington's program as early as 1890, incidents such as those involving Sam Hose convinced him of its shortcomings. When Du Bois published *The Souls of Black Folk* in 1903, it became apparent to Washington and his supporters, if not to the author himself, that the two men were diametrically opposed. And this despite the fact that the book is not that of an adversary but of a member of an opposition seeking to be loyal. One of the essays, "On Mr. Booker T. Washington and Others," written especially for the book, illustrates this point:

> So far as Mr. Washington preaches Thrift, Patience, and Industrial training for the masses, we must hold up his hand and strive with him . . . glorifying in the strength of this Joshua called of God and of man to lead the headless host. But so far as Mr. Washington apologizes for injustice, North or South, does not rightly value the privilege and duty of voting, belittles the emasculating effects of caste distinctions and opposes the higher training and ambition of our brighter minds . . . we must unceasingly and firmly oppose [him.]

The careful, cool, and detached scholar was barely in evidence in this influential collection of essays, but for the most part his commentary upon men and events bore the unmistakable mark of personal observations and passionate experience. Included among the fourteen essays were autobiographical ones, those that assailed the caste system and those that delineated the dilemma of black folk as few essays have before or

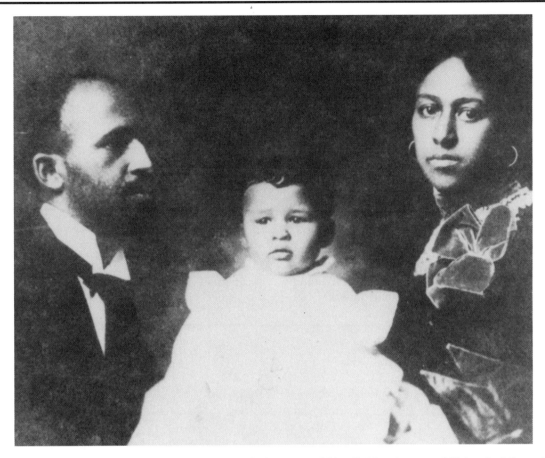

An 1895 photograph of Du Bois, his son, Burghardt, who died young, and his wife Nina (courtesy of University Library, University of Massachusetts/Amherst)

since: "One ever feels his twoness–An American, a Negro; two souls, two thoughts, two unreconciled strivings; two warring ideals in one dark body, whose dogged strength alone keeps it from being torn asunder." Here, clearly revealed, was an intellectual of stature and depth, a formidable potential foe of the policies and programs of Washington. Now, finally, the intellectuals who had opposed the Tuskegan from the beginning had an able champion, and Du Bois's articulate and impassioned voice began to be respected in black America.

It soon became impossible for him to straddle the fence between outright opposition and loyal criticism. He was to discover that Washington considered all criticism destructive, whether from radicals or conservatives, and using the vast resources of the Tuskegee machine, he moved swiftly to demolish it. Du Bois was witness to one dramatic example in the case of William Monroe Trotter. The fiery editor of the *Guardian* magazine had been a staunch Washington critic from the beginning, and some of the most vitriolic at-

tacks on the Tuskegan had come from his pen. Du Bois was not enamored of Trotter's approach, but he considered him a dedicated defender of the race and, above all, a man entitled to have his say. When Washington uncharacteristically addressed an urban, northern, black audience and Trotter rose to speak, he was subdued and arrested. The incident moved Du Bois to words and action: "When Trotter went to jail, my indignation overflowed. I did not always agree with Trotter. . . . But he was an honest, brilliant, unselfish man, and to treat as a crime that which was at worst mistaken judgement was an outrage. I sent out from Atlanta in June 1905 a call to a few selected persons for organized determination and aggressive action on the part of men who believe in Negro freedom and growth." The call resulted in the formation of the Niagara Movement.

The first all-black protest movement in black history, though short-lived, was composed of men and women from fourteen states, most of whom opposed Washington. Their platform advocated voting rights, higher education for blacks, freedom of the press and speech, and first-class citizenship. The group met in 1906, in a symbolic gathering at Harpers Ferry, the scene of John Brown's abortive revolutionary attempt to free slaves, twice more in 1907 and 1908, and was finally eclipsed by a new organization that absorbed many of its members, the National Association for the Advancement of Colored People.

Opposition to Washington's policies had helped to create the Niagara Movement. The NAACP, on the other hand, had a genesis altogether different. In Springfield, Illinois, in 1908 one of the worst race riots in American history occurred. Over 50,000 militia were brought in to quell the disturbance; two blacks were lynched, four whites killed, and over seventy people injured. A white writer, William English Walling, was so appalled by the events that together with Mary White Ovington, a white social worker, and Oswald Garrison Villard, grandson of the abolitionist newspaperman William Lloyd Garrison, he issued a call for "a national conference for the discussion of present evils . . . and the renewal of the struggle for civil and political rights." From this conference sprang the formal organization, chartered in 1910, with one black officer, W. E. B. Du Bois, who became the association's director of publicity and research.

For what can only be described as over two tumultuous decades, Du Bois served the NAACP in this capacity. The only prominent black among the hierarchy for many years, the leading black intellectual of his day, and a man of unswerving principle, he founded the association's official organ, *Crisis* magazine, and became, for black people, the voice of the association. The magazine that began with a circulation of 1,000 in 1910 by 1918 was being read by over 100,000 subscribers. All topics of interest to blacks were covered within its pages: politics, education, culture, art, science. But the most favored sections were the editorials in which the editor, like a Lycurgis, tutored and sometimes cajoled his flock. He inveighed against lynching, disenfranchisement, crimes by and against blacks, and used the pages of the *Crisis* as a fulcrum for the black literary revival known as the Harlem Renaissance.

When Americans went to war in 1914, in a controversial article Du Bois urged blacks to "close ranks" and support the government. After the war he journeyed to Europe to investigate the wartime treatment of blacks abroad and reported his findings of rampant racism and discrimination by the armed services in the pages of the *Crisis*. From 1919 to 1927 he was the leading architect of four Pan-African conferences, and he reported these attempts at international liaison among blacks in the magazine's pages. He penned a denunciatory article on Booker T. Washington when the Tuskegan died in 1915 and took note of the back-to-Africa movement of Marcus Garvey when, under the auspices of a Jamaican black, the mass movement organization began its extraordinary rise in America.

After corresponding with Booker T. Washington, Marcus Aurelius Garvey, who founded the Universal Negro Improvement Association in Jamaica, set out for America in 1915 to meet Washington, who had died earlier in the same year. Garvey stayed on and created an American branch of his organization, appealing primarily to impoverished and uneducated blacks. In less than five years the organization's membership numbered in the hundreds of thousands, and money was available to enable Garvey to attempt many questionable ventures. Through his magazine, the *Negro World*, Garvey openly espoused segregationist policies and attacked the integrationist NAACP and its leadership. Du Bois, who was having his own disagreements with the middle-class leadership of the NAACP, was initially positive toward Garvey. In an editorial in 1920 he wrote that Garvey was "an extraordinary leader of men. Thousands of people believe in him. He is able to stir them with singular eloquence and the general run of his thought is of a high plane."

By 1923 Garvey's business ventures had led to his indictment and arrest by the federal government. As a result he increased his attack upon the Negro leadership. Some prominent blacks, among them members of the NAACP, demanded that he be tried immediately. Though no evidence exists to prove that Du Bois was among them, in the *Crisis* of February 1923 he wrote some of the strongest invective of his journalistic career and in the 24 May issue called Garvey "the most dangerous enemy of the Negro race in America and the world." Du Bois's confrontations with officials in the NAACP, however, are well documented, and these were of a much more serious nature than those involving Garvey.

At the center of this ongoing conflict was Du Bois's control of the *Crisis* magazine, which enabled him to espouse policy, oftentimes antithetical to that of the organization itself. In the January 1934 issue of the magazine he wrote in the editorial "Segregation": "The thinking colored people of the United States must stop being stampeded by the word segregation. The opposition to racial segregation is not or should not be any ... unwillingness of colored people to work with each other, to cooperate with each other, to live with each other." In its entirety the essay, besides being in opposition to the NAACP's stand on integration, illuminated an important shift in his own thinking, brought about by daily events in America and by experience gleaned from travels throughout the world.

In 1924 he admonished blacks to fight for America, declaring that to do so would produce dividends in racial progress in America. Instead, during the Depression years, black progress diminished as whites looked out for the welfare of other whites. The efforts to pass an antilynching bill failed in the Congress of the United States, and the economically hard-hit black population gained less than whites from the programs enacted by the Roosevelt Administration. After his initial trip to Europe when the war ended, Du Bois had traveled extensively in western Europe and Africa, and he had become more extensively involved with the Pan-African conferences and had been a firsthand witness to the Communist experiment in Soviet Russia. The combination of these experiences led him to conceive of black economic cooperatives organized and manned by blacks, underpinned by a quasi-voluntary, segregationist superstructure.

To propound this theory he used the pages of the *Crisis,* often attacking such officials as Walter White in invectives once used to assault the personal character of Garvey. But the *Crisis* magazine was no longer self-supporting and could not be kept as Du Bois's personal vehicle with the acquiescence of the NAACP governing board. During the Depression circulation dropped considerably, and both the magazine and Du Bois's salary were sustained by the NAACP. The organization moved, therefore, in 1934 to exercise censorship over the editorials of the uncompromising editor. The result was that Du Bois tendered his resignation on 11 June 1934 and severed over two decades with the nation's oldest civil rights organization.

At age sixty-six he left the NAACP with an enviable record of accomplishment behind him. In addition to his editorials and articles for the *Crisis* and other magazines, he had lectured widely in America and abroad and published a variety of books. In 1909 he published *John Brown,* a biography of the Kansas hero which he called his best book. *The Quest of the Silver Fleece* (1911) was a

novel in which Du Bois dramatized the economic conflict between southern planters and northern capitalists during Reconstruction. In 1915 he published *The Negro,* a history of African and black Americans, presenting a compendium of facts concerning black people throughout the world. *The Gift of Black Folk* (1924) was a book detailing contributions of blacks to civilization, and he published his second novel, *Dark Princess,* in 1928. The book deals with the international conditions of black people and the worldwide ramifications of racism. His intellectual credentials were unassailable when, accepting an offer from his friend John Hope, who became president of Atlanta University in 1929, Du Bois returned to the school to chair its department of sociology.

He was determined, he later wrote, to resume his role as the dispassionate scholar, and though this was difficult, due to his own activist temperament, between 1935 and 1940 he authored *Black Reconstruction* (1935), *Black Folk, Then and Now* (1939), and *Dusk of Dawn* (1940). In 1941 he held the first of a series of conferences looking forward to "a long time program of Negro economic stabilization after the war." In 1944 he founded *Phylon* magazine, a scholarly journal of "comment and research on world race problems."

Black Reconstruction is a revisionist interpretation of the Reconstruction period. Written with his usual passion and eloquence, Du Bois sought to interpret Reconstruction from a black and Marxist perspective and acknowledged for the first time in American history the impressive role played by blacks in the period. *Black Folk, Then and Now,* like the earlier *The Negro,* traced the continuity between blacks in Africa and America and illustrated varying lines of racial kinship, and *Dusk of Dawn* was his first complete autobiography. Here, in lyrical terms, he presented his life metaphorically and wrote what can only be called a dissertation on race. In 1941, after having gathered the black presidents of the land grant colleges together, he outlined his plan of economic redevelopment and admonished the presidents "that the chief studies of the Negro's condition today are not being done by Negroes and Negro colleges."

His attempts at formulating and carrying out his economic proposals, with the aid of the presidents of the land grant colleges, came abruptly to an end, however, when he was summarily retired from Atlanta University. After the death of John Hope, Du Bois's relations with

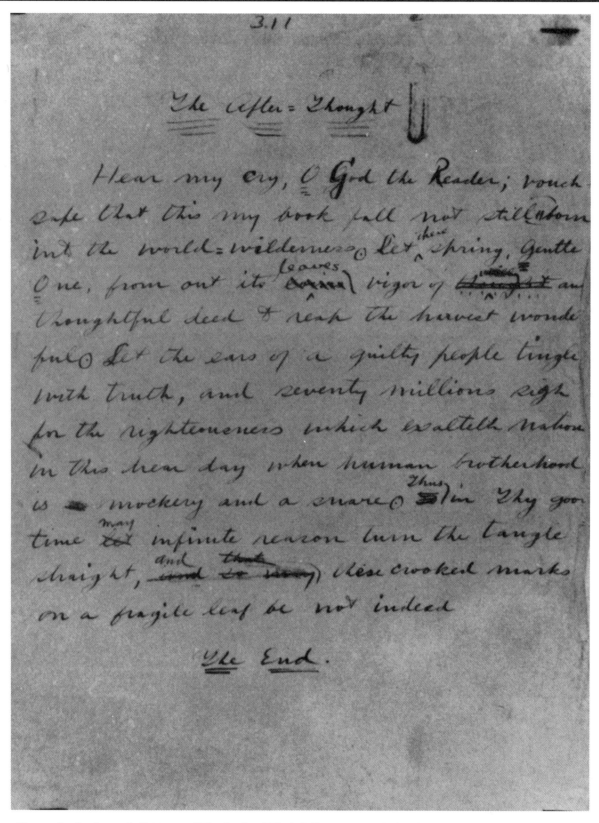

Manuscript for the concluding page of The Souls of Black Folk: Essays and Sketches, *published in 1903 (courtesy of Archives, University Library, University of Massachusetts/Amherst)*

both the new president of Atlanta University, Rufus Clement, and Spellman College's President Florence Reed became strained. Enmity, enviousness, and pettiness all seem to have motivated the sudden decision to retire Du Bois, since he was past the age of retirement when he was hired. More likely his forced retirement rested upon his involvement with the presidents of the land grant colleges, his economic program, and his worldwide reputation. Equally as surprising as his dismissal from Atlanta was his being restored to service by the NAACP.

Two close friends of Du Bois's, Arthur Spingarn and Louis Wright, his personal physician, learned of his dismissal by Atlanta. Without consulting the seventy-six-year-old Du Bois, the two men approached his old adversary, executive secretary Walter White. They arranged a "deal" whereby Du Bois would return, presumably for the rest of his life, to the organization he helped found and in the event White became dissatisfied with him or his performance, he could be terminated. Du Bois's old friends sought protection for their friend in his later years, and White believed that Du Bois would offer prestige and stature to the organization and invaluable help to him as a speech writer. Thus, in 1944 Du Bois returned to the NAACP as director of special research.

In 1945 he attended the sixth session of the Pan-African Conference in England, a session which included future President of Ghana Kwame Nkrumah. In the same year Du Bois worked on proposals for the United Nations Commission on Human Rights, publishing a book, *Color and Democracy: Colonies and Peace*, about his efforts and the organization in general in 1945. However, the possibility of coexistence with White was remote from the outset. Accusations were made early against Du Bois for appearing before a congressional committee without White's consent. Later he was accused of interfering in a school desegregation case as a result of remarks made during a speech. The conflict that led to his expulsion, however, concerned the presidential campaign of 1948. Though the NAACP claimed neutrality during the campaign, White openly campaigned for the election of the Democratic candidate, Harry Truman. When Du Bois privately advocated the candidacy of the Progressive party standard-bearer, Henry Wallace, he was upbraided by White. Du Bois's counteraccusations against White concerning Truman led the secretary to exercise the option granted ear-

lier by Du Bois's friends. For the second time he was removed from the NAACP.

"I would have been hailed with approval, if I had died at age fifty," he recalled later. "At seventy-five my death was practically requested." Yet some of the most tumultuous years of his life lay in the future. After expulsion from the NAACP he became honorary vice chairman of the Council of African Affairs, at a time when the political atmosphere was dense with charges and countercharges of subversion, Communist association, and conspiracy. The role of the organization was to disseminate information pertaining to Africa. Shortly after Du Bois accepted the vice-presidency, the Council was cited by the Attorney General of the United States as a "subversive" organization. Greater consequences of a personal nature, however, confronted Du Bois when he became chairman of the Peace Information Center in 1950.

The avowed aim of the center was to tell "the people of the United States what other nations were doing and thinking about war." In this connection the center issued peace-grams and collected signatures on a petition to abolish the atomic bomb. It sponsored its chairman at meetings abroad, so that Du Bois appeared at conferences in Paris, Mexico City, and Prague. Early on the center was denounced by Secretary of State Dean Acheson as a front for the Soviet Union's propaganda machine, a statement that elicited from Du Bois a summary of his own long involvement with peace, accompanied by questions as to whether or not the sole sponsor of peace in the world was the Soviet Union. In 1951 Du Bois, along with other officials of the center, was indicted for being an unregistered "agent of a foreign principal."

Concurrent with the indictment, Du Bois received a request from the American Labor party, petitioning him to run for the United States Senate as a representative from New York. Hesitant at first, he relented when assured that his candidacy would help that of the progressive congressman from New York, Vito Marcantonio, who faced a difficult reelection fight. His campaign was vigorous and hard-hitting, and though he lost, as expected, he used the platform to further his advocacy of peace, and his untiring effort undoubtedly helped Marcantonio. During this period his first wife, Nina Gomer, died, and in 1951, shortly before arraignment by the government, Du Bois married Shirley Graham, a longtime associate. Together, on 8 November 1951, they sat in the federal courtroom in Washington, D.C. Du Bois wrote of the episode: "nothing has so cowed me as that day . . . when I took my seat . . . as an indicted criminal. I was not a criminal. I had broken no law, consciously or unwittingly." His own judgment concerning his guilt or innocence was validated by the court, which on the first day of trial acquitted the scholar and his associates.

Innocent or not, his passport was still the property of the United States government and remained so for some time, prohibiting him from accepting invitations abroad. Nor did acquittal alter his status among those he believed would be his constituency and defenders in his fight against governmental oppression, the black community. The black churches, the black press, the black educational institutions, and the NAACP were mostly silent during and after the period of his struggle. In his autobiography he expresses his discontent and pain: "the federal government took a determined stand to insure my destruction. . . . The central office of the NAACP refused to let local branches invite me or sponsor any lectures. . . . I found new friends and a wider world than ever before–a world with no color line. I lost my leadership of my race. . . . The colored children ceased to hear my name." In his own recollection of his trial and indictment, which he described in *In Battle for Peace* (1952), he noted one group that supported him during his terrible ordeal and paid tribute to "the communists of the world for their help in my defense."

For whatever the reasons, "the communists of the world" became his ardent supporters and, with progressives in America, his constituency. The organs of the more conservative black press closed to him, he wrote widely for such left-wing periodicals as the *National Guardian*. From 1958 to 1959 his passport, after court action, was finally released by the government, and he traveled extensively throughout eastern Europe and Asia. He received an honorary degree from Prague University and had audiences with the leaders of the Soviet Union and the People's Republic of China. In 1958 he was awarded the Lenin International Peace Prize by the U.S.S.R. In 1961, at the age of ninety-three, he made application for and accepted membership in the Communist party of the United States. Later, during the same year, he accepted an invitation from Prime Minister Nkrumah of Ghana and became a resident of that African nation; shortly before his death in 1963, he renounced his American citizenship altogether, dying as a citizen of Africa.

These actions during the last years of his life do not, as commentators on Du Bois and his biographers assert, amount to either a betrayal of "his" country or his race. Few Americans have defended their right to citizenship as vociferously as Du Bois. In 1903 he extolled an imaginary white audience: "Your country? How come it's yours? Before the Pilgrims landed we were here. . . . Actively we have woven ourselves with the very warp and woof of this nation. . . . Could America have been America without her Negro people?" And few blacks have written so passionately and devotedly about their kinsmen: "Especially do I believe in the Negro Race: in the beauty of its genius, the sweetness of its souls, and its strength in that meekness which shall yet inherent this turbulent earth." Yet the country and the race to which he had given so much offered him little in return. He could and did eventually forgive black people, for he was cognizant of their powerlessness and concerns with their own personal survival. Forgiving the country, however, was another matter altogether.

"I may be a romantic," he once said, "but I am not a damn fool." In time the pragmatist in him consumed the romantic regarding the American society, and he realized what many young blacks were beginning to realize on the eve of his death: that the American Dream would not come true for black Americans, and that at this stage of history one should demand that the nation which asks loyalty from its citizens return loyalty in kind. In articles and lectures near the end of his life, and in his own symbolic exile, Du Bois raised such questions, and the younger, brighter members of the black community, his intellectual heirs, continue to raise them with increasing urgency and consistency.

Letters:

The Correspondence of W. E. B. Du Bois, 3 volumes, edited by Herbert Aptheker (Amherst: University of Massachusetts Press, 1973-1978). Complete collection of Du Bois's personal and professional correspondence, with explanatory notes by the editor.

Bibliography:

Herbert Aptheker, *Annotated Bibliography of the Published Writings of W. E. B. Du Bois* (Millwood, N.Y.: Kraus-Thomson, 1973). Listing of Du Bois's writings and edited works, with helpful annotations by the editor.

Biographies:

Francis L. Broderick, *W. E. B. Du Bois, Negro Leader in a Time of Crisis* (Stanford, Cal.: Stanford University Press, 1959).

Evenhanded summary of Du Bois's life, concentrating on his "great years" as editor of the *Crisis* and as a power in the NAACP.

Elliott M. Rudwick, *W. E. B. Du Bois: Propagandist of the Negro Protest* (New York: Atheneum, 1968).

Anti-Communist interpretation of Du Bois's professional life.

Arnold Rampersad, *The Art and Imagination of W. E. B. Du Bois* (Cambridge: Harvard University Press, 1976).

Laudatory study that views Du Bois's professional life as the consequence of his "essentially poetic vision of human experience."

References:

Franklin E. Frazier, "The Du Bois Program in the Present Crisis," *Race*, 1 (1935-1936): 11-13.

Brief contemporary summary of Du Bois's social and political views at the height of his career.

Gerald Horne, *Black and Red: W. E. B. Du Bois and the Afro-American Response to the Cold War, 1944-1963* (Albany: State University of New York Press, 1986).

Explains Du Bois's increasingly leftist interpretation of international relations after World War II as an outgrowth of his experience of American segregation.

Rayford Logan, ed., *W. E. B. Du Bois: A Profile* (New York: Hill & Wang, 1971).

Ten essays on Du Bois's career (including one by Herbert Aptheker) that present a variety of views and interpretations, especially of his later, pro-Communist years.

Jack B. Moore, *W. E. B. Du Bois* (Boston: Twayne, 1981).

Brief critical introduction to Du Bois's career.

W. M. Tuttle, ed., *W. E. B. Du Bois* (Englewood Cliffs, N.J.: Prentice-Hall, 1973).

Selections from Du Bois's writings with reminiscences of such contemporaries as A. Philip Randolph and Walter White.

Papers:

Papers of W. E. B. Du Bois are at the University of Massachusetts, Amherst.

Paul Laurence Dunbar

This entry was updated by Doris Lucas Laryea (North Carolina State University) from her entry in DLB 50, Afro-American Writers Before the Harlem Renaissance.

Places	Dayton, Ohio Harmon, Colo. The Catskill Mountains	New York City Chicago	Washington, D.C. London
Influences and Relationships	William Dean Howells Frederick Douglass Nathaniel Hawthorne Booker T. Washington	James Whitcomb Riley Richard B. Harrison James Campbell	Alice Dunbar-Nelson Edgar Allan Poe James Weldon Johnson
Literary Movements and Forms	Black Dialect Poetry	Realism	Local Color and Regionalism
Major Themes	Slavery Racial, Political, Economic, and Social Protest	Alienation and Racial Oppression Religion	Migration from South to North The Confidence Man
Cultural and Artistic Influences	Black Folklore	Black Music (blues, spirituals)	Minstrel Tradition
Social and Economic Influences	Slavery	Civil War	Reconstruction

154

See also the Dunbar entry in DLB 54, American Poets, 1880-1945, Third Series, Part 1.

BIRTH: Dayton, Ohio, 27 June 1872, to Joshua and Matilda Glass Burton Murphy Dunbar.

MARRIAGE: 6 March 1898 to Alice Ruth Moore (separated 1902).

DEATH: Dayton, Ohio, 9 February 1906.

SELECTED BOOKS: *Oak and Ivy* (Dayton, Ohio: Press of United Brethren Publishing House, 1893);

Majors and Minors (Toledo, Ohio: Hadley & Hadley, 1896);

Lyrics of Lowly Life (New York: Dodd, Mead, 1896; London: Chapman & Hall, 1897);

Folks from Dixie (New York: Dodd, Mead, 1898; London: Bowden, 1898);

The Uncalled: A Novel (New York: Dodd, Mead, 1898; London: Service & Patton, 1899);

Dream Lovers: An Operatic Romance, music by Samuel Coleridge-Taylor, libretto by Dunbar (New York & London: Boosey, 1898);

Lyrics of the Hearthside (New York: Dodd, Mead, 1899);

Poems of Cabin and Field (New York: Dodd, Mead, 1899);

The Strength of Gideon and Other Stories (New York: Dodd, Mead, 1900);

The Love of Landry (New York: Dodd, Mead, 1900);

The Fanatics (New York: Dodd, Mead, 1901);

Candle-Lightin' Time (New York: Dodd, Mead, 1901);

The Sport of the Gods (New York: Dodd, Mead, 1902); republished as *The Jest of Fate; A Story of Negro Life* (London: Jarrold, 1902);

Lyrics of Love and Laughter (New York: Dodd, Mead, 1903);

In Old Plantation Days (New York: Dodd, Mead, 1903);

When Malindy Sings (New York: Dodd, Mead, 1903);

The Heart of Happy Hollow (New York: Dodd, Mead, 1904);

Li'l' Gal (New York: Dodd, Mead, 1904);

Lyrics of Sunshine and Shadow (New York: Dodd, Mead, 1905);

Howdy Honey Howdy (New York: Dodd, Mead, 1905);

Joggin' Erlong (New York: Dodd, Mead, 1906);

The Life and Works of Paul Laurence Dunbar, edited by Lida Keck Wiggins (Naperville, Ill. & Memphis, Tenn.: J. L. Nichols, 1907);

The Complete Poems (New York: Dodd, Mead, 1913);

The Best Stories of Paul Laurence Dunbar, edited by Benjamin Brawley (New York: Dodd, Mead, 1938);

The Paul Laurence Dunbar Reader, edited by Jay Martin and Gossie H. Hudson (New York: Dodd, Mead, 1975).

OTHER: "Representative American Negroes," in *The Negro Problem: A Series of Articles by Representative American Negroes* (New York: James Pott, 1903), pp. 189-209;

"The Tuskegee Song," in *Selected Songs Sung by Students of Tuskegee Normal and Industrial Institute* (Tuskegee, Ala.: Tuskegee Institute, 1904), p. 3.

PERIODICAL PUBLICATIONS: "Of Negro Journals," *Chicago Record,* 22 June 1894;

"Some London Impressions," *Chicago Record,* 14 April 1897;

"England as Seen by a Black Man," *Independent,* 48 (16 September 1897): 4;

"Our New Madness," *Independent,* 50 (15 September 1898): 469-471;

"The Race Question Discussed," *Toledo Journal,* 11 December 1898;

"The Negroes of the Tenderloin: Paul Laurence Dunbar Sees Peril for His Race in Life in the City," *Columbus* (Ohio) *Dispatch,* 19 December 1898;

"The Hapless Southern Negro," *Denver Post,* 17 September 1899;

"Negro Life in Washington," *Harper's Weekly,* 44 (13 January 1900): 32;

"Is Negro Education for the Negro Hopeless?," *Philadelphia Times,* 10 June 1900;

"The Leader of His Race," *Saturday Evening Post,* 174 (9 November 1901): 15;

"Negro Society in Washington," *Saturday Evening Post,* 174 (14 December 1901): 9;

"The Fourth of July and Race Outrages: Paul Laurence Dunbar's Bitter Satire On Independence Day," *New York Times,* 10 July 1903;

"Is There a Slump in Poetry?," *Literary Digest,* 30 (18 March 1905): 391.

Paul Laurence Dunbar, one of the most popular American poets of his time, was also the first black poet to attain national and international recognition. Booker T. Washington called him the "Poet Laureate of the Negro race," and William Dean Howells lauded him as a Negro dialect poet who studied the Afro-American "objectively and represented him as he found him to be, with humor, with sympathy, and yet with what the reader must instinctively feel to be entire truthfulness." He was a master craftsman not only in his use of dialect but in his standard English poems and in much of his fiction. He captured the humor, pathos, and hopeful spirit of a resolute and struggling people in and out of slavery. His skillful handling of rhythm, satire, narrative, and irony places him among the best poets this country has produced.

Dunbar was born in Dayton, Ohio, to Joshua and Matilda Glass Burton Murphy Dunbar, former Kentucky plantation slaves, who had taught themselves to read and write. Joshua, who was born in 1816, worked as plasterer on a large plantation until he escaped to Canada by the Un-

derground Railroad. During the Civil War he enlisted in the Fifty-fifth Massachusetts Regiment, Company F, under Col. Norwood Penrose Hallowell, and fought in the Union army. After the war he settled in Dayton, where he had lived earlier.

Dunbar's mother was born a slave on the plantation of David Glass near Shelbyville, Kentucky, circa 1844, and she worked as a house servant until the end of the Civil War. As a young woman, she married R. Weeks Murphy, a slave on a nearby plantation, and they had two sons, William and Robert. Following emancipation and Murphy's death (apparently during the war), she and her sons moved to Dayton to be near relatives, and in 1871 she married Joshua Dunbar. When Paul was only one and a half years old, Matilda and Joshua separated, and in 1876 they were divorced. Joshua died when Paul was twelve, and the Murphy boys moved to Chicago. Matilda built a strong bond of affection and understanding between herself and her son that was nurtured throughout his life. She taught him to read, and she shared his interest in literature. When Paul was younger, Matilda and Joshua told him stories of their slave experiences that he later would draw upon as he composed many of his dialect poems and plantation stories.

During his senior year in school Dunbar, the only black in his class, was president of his class, editor in chief of the *High School Times,* president of the Philomathean Society (a literary club), and class poet, writing the class poem and delivering it at graduation in June 1891. Already he had earned recognition in Dayton for his poems, which had begun appearing in the *Dayton Herald* as early as 8 June 1888, and for his ambition in founding the *Dayton Tattler,* a black newspaper printed by his friend and classmate Orville Wright. The first issue appeared 13 December 1889, but the paper folded after about six issues because its advertising revenues failed to cover printing costs.

Following his graduation Dunbar entertained the notion of attending Harvard University to study law, but, aware that his mother's scant earnings as a washerwoman were insufficient to pay his college tuition, he applied for work at newspapers, law offices, and other businesses in Dayton, only to be turned away because of his color. Despite his journalistic experience and creative ability, he was denied all but menial employment.

He went to work in the Callahan Building for four dollars a week as an elevator operator. Between calls, he wrote poems and articles that were published in several midwestern newspapers, although he received little or no pay for them. In the elevator he reread his favorite poets: Alfred Tennyson, William Shakespeare, John Keats, Percy Bysshe Shelley, Edgar Allan Poe, Henry Wadsworth Longfellow, James Russell Lowell, and the regionalist James Whitcomb Riley. Dunbar's biographer Virginia Cunningham suggests that Riley influenced the homely quality of Dunbar's verse, with his "nostalgia for the good old days, love of childhood, a twinkle in one eye and a tear in the other." Dunbar especially imitated Riley's Hoosier dialect and his humor in poems such as "The Ol' Tunes," "A Banjo Song," "The Old Homestead," and "A Drowsy Day."

Not only was Dunbar writing poems at this time but he began writing short stories. For six dollars he sold his first story, "The Tenderfoot," a Western tale, to the Kellogg Newspaper Company, a syndicate firm. "Little Billy," another Western, soon followed. Neither tale added to his reputation, nor did they appear later in his volumes of short stories. Dunbar became convinced that he could get published, however, and that if his works were good enough, he might profit financially.

In June 1892 the Western Association of Writers met in Dayton, and three days before the convention Helen M. Truesdale, a member of the association and Dunbar's former English teacher, asked him to give a welcoming address. For the occasion he composed a twenty-six-line poem, which so stirred the audience that he was invited by James Newton Matthews to become a member. Later, Matthews became one of Dunbar's patrons and friends.

Shortly after the convention Dunbar began experimenting with Negro dialect verse, later becoming the first black American poet to gain national praise for dialect verse, although both white and black writers had used it before. One of his early dialect poems, "Goin' Back," establishes the plantation motif that became a major theme in his work. It is the monologue of a former slave, now residing in the North, who looks with nostalgia to antebellum plantation life as he waits to board a train for a visit to Kentucky. The dialect poems sold, as did Dunbar's poems in standard English, giving him the assurance that poetry could make him famous.

When a letter that Matthews wrote about Dunbar was published in a Mason, Illinois, newspaper and was reprinted in papers across the country, it caught the attention of James Whitcomb Riley, who wrote to Dunbar on 27 November 1892, addressing him as "my chirping friend" and calling his poem "A Drowsy Day" "a superior one." The encouragement from Matthews and Riley furnished Dunbar the confidence he needed to get a volume of poems published. At the suggestion of Orville Wright, he collected fifty-six poems and took them to William Lawrence Blacher, the business manager of the United Brethren Publishing House in Dayton, who agreed to print them for $125, allowing Dunbar to pay him in installments from the proceeds of book sales. Dunbar called his first collection *Oak and Ivy*.

The book came off the press in December 1892, but was dated 1893. Five hundred copies were printed and sold for one dollar a copy, and within two weeks Dunbar had sold enough books to reimburse Blacher for the printing costs. The volume contained the poet's first dialect poems—"A Banjo Song," which had first appeared in the *Chicago News Record*, and "Goin' Back." In the standard-English "Ode to Ethiopia" he affirms his racial loyalty and pride by citing the contributions blacks had made in the building of America and of their achievements during Reconstruction. He tells blacks: "Be proud, my Race, in mind and soul," because they have "the right to noble pride/. . ./No other race, or white or black,/ When bound as thou wert, to the rack,/So seldom stooped to grieving." One of his favorite poems in the volume was "Life": "A Crust of bread and a Corner to sleep in,/A minute to smile and an hour to weep in,/A pint of joy to a peck of trouble,/And never a laugh but the moans come double;/And that is life." Some of the best poems in the collection are "The Ol' Tunes," "A Drowsy Day," "October," "A Career," and "Sympathy," a poem in which he laments, "I know why the caged bird sings, ah me,/When his wing is bruised and his bosom sore,/When he beats his bars and he would be free." "Sympathy" is perhaps Dunbar's most-anthologized poem after "We Wear the Mask."

In early 1893 Dunbar met Charles A. Thatcher, a Toledo lawyer who became a long-time patron and friend. Hearing of Dunbar's strong desire for a college education, Thatcher offered to pay part of his college expenses and to solicit contributions from other philanthropists, but

Dunbar's commitment to becoming a successful poet–after the reception of *Oak and Ivy*–forced him reluctantly to reject the offer. Thatcher later rescued Dunbar when severe financial difficulties arose, lending him money to pay bills and move his mother from Chicago back to Dayton after their sojourn there. Thatcher used his influence, nevertheless, to give the poet literary exposure in Toledo and in other parts of the state by arranging for him to give poetry readings at which Dunbar was able to sell copies of his book and widen his audience.

In the late spring of 1893 Dunbar left Dayton for Chicago in hopes of furthering his writing career, securing more meaningful employment, and thereby, improving his financial situation. This move brought him into contact with other black writers and artists with whom, for the first time in his life, he could discuss his poetic and literary aims. Chief among his new acquaintances was Frederick Douglass, who had been appointed Consul General to the Republic of Haiti, and who gave him work as a clerk at the Haitian Pavilion at the World's Columbian Exposition. In Chicago he met Angelina Grimké, Ida B. Wells Barnett, Hallie Brown, Mary Church Terrell, Alexander Crummell, Rebekah Baldwin, and Wendell Dabney, and he established close friendships with the poets James D. Corrothers and James Campbell, the first black poet to use dialect consistently in his work. His closest friend in Chicago was Richard B. Harrison, an actor who teamed up with him to give dramatic readings and to sell his book. He met composer Will Marion Cook, who would later set "A Negro Love Song" and many of his other poems to music. The Chicago experience provided the poet additional opportunity to write. When the fair was over, he returned to Dayton and ruefully resumed his job as elevator operator.

In 1894 Dunbar suffered critically from financial difficulties; yet he managed to write and survive through the pecuniary assistance of Henry A. Tobey, a Toledo psychiatrist who bought copies of *Oak and Ivy* and who generously sent him money at different points in his life. Tobey offered Dunbar $500 to cover the tuition at Harvard, but Dunbar declined because this sum was not enough to pay college tuition and make mortgage payments on the family house. Fortunately, his financial woes were lessened when in 1895 *Century* magazine published three poems: "A Negro Love Song" (in the April issue), "Curtain" (in May), and "The Dilettante"

(in July). Other popular magazines and newspapers, such as the *New York Times*, the Chicago magazine, *Blue and Gray*, and the *Independent*, also began publishing his poems.

In the spring of 1895 Dunbar fell in love with Alice Ruth Moore when he saw a picture of her in the *Boston Monthly Review*. He began corresponding with this poet from New Orleans, who was also a short-story writer and teacher. During their two-year epistolary romance, they shared each others' works, and in June 1895, while serving as temporary editor of the small black newspaper the *Indianapolis World*, Dunbar published one of Alice's legends of old New Orleans.

Meanwhile, fully determined to help promote Dunbar's career, Tobey collaborated with Charles Thatcher in sponsoring the publication of a second volume of poems with the book's profit to go to the poet. Tobey arranged for Hadley and Hadley Printing Company in Toledo to print and bind the little volume Dunbar called *Majors and Minors*, in an edition of 1,000 copies. The date of its publication was 1895, but it did not appear until 1896. It contains ninety-three poems, some of which had appeared in *Oak and Ivy*, that treat love, nature, race, melancholy, death, and other subjects. At this early stage in his development Dunbar experimented with a diversity of styles, themes, and forms–from the simple language of his dialect poems to the eloquent and more polished diction of the poems in standard English–demonstrating his poetic maturity through his mastery of technically complex poetic forms. *Majors and Minors* includes some of his most serious and most joyful poems and many of the verses that proved most popular at his readings. "When Malindy Sings," inspired by his mother's spontaneous outbursts of singing, became one of his most popular poems.

Tobey brought the volume to the attention of actor James A. Herne, who recognized the genius of its author and notified William Dean Howells, the renowned novelist and critic, of its publication. Howells's review of *Majors and Minors* in the 27 June 1896 issue of *Harper's Weekly* won Dunbar an important place in the literary history of the United States. Howells compared Dunbar with Robert Burns and praised his ear for the southern dialects of blacks and whites. Howells said that in the treatment of his material Dunbar was "able to bring us nearer to the heart of primitive human nature in his race than anyone else has yet done." Finally, Howells noted that he "sometimes fancied that the Negro *thought* black and *felt* black, that they were racially so utterly alien and distinct from ourselves that there could never be common intellectual and emotional ground between us, and that whatever eternity might do to reconcile us, the end of time would find us as far asunder as ever. But this little book has given me pause in my speculation. Here in the artistic effect, at least, is white thinking and white feeling in a black man; and perhaps the human unity, not the race unity, is the precious thing, the divine thing after all." In the review Howells categorized Dunbar as a dialect poet, a label of which the poet was never able to rid himself. Howells was especially effusive in his praise for "The Party," a dialect poem depicting the antics of blacks on a plantation and reflecting the epitome of the "happy darky" stereotype:

> Dey had a gread big pahty down to Tom's de othah
>   night;
> Was I dah? You bet! I nevah in my life see sich a
>   sight;
> All de folks f 'om fou' plantations was invited, an'
>   dey come,
> Dey come troopin' thick ez chillun when dey hyeahs
>   a fife an' drum.

Full of exaggerated manners, the black party goers prance and preen for each other's benefit. They have no cares and concerns; indeed, they are hilariously funny in their dancing, and even churchgoers are tempted to lose their religion:

> Jigs, cotillions, reels an' breakdowns, cordrills an' a
>   waltz er two;
> Bless yo' soul, dat music winged 'em an' dem people
>   lak to flew.
> Cripple Joe, de old rheumatic, danced dat flo' f 'om
>   side to middle,
> Th'owed away his crutch an' hopped it; what's rheu-
>   matics 'ginst a fiddle?
> Eldah Thompson got so tickled dat he lak to los' his
>   grace,
> Had to tek bofe feet an' hol' dem so's to keep 'em
>   in deir place.
> An' de Christuns an' di sinnahs got so mixed up on
>   dat flo',
> Dat I don't see how dey'd pahted ef de trump had
>   chanced to blow.

Howells's praise of such a poem established the pattern for what was expected from Dunbar, for what his primarily white audiences most wanted to read.

Dunbar had higher regard for the sixty-nine poems written in standard English than for his dialect poems, and he demonstrated this preference by grouping them at the beginning of the book under the heading "Majors," and the twenty-four dialect poems at the end under "Minors." Some years later Alice Moore Dunbar wrote that "it was in the pure English poems that the poet expressed *himself*. He may have expressed his racial identities in the dialect poems; they were to him the side issues of his work, the overflowing of a life apart from his dearest dreams."

Later in 1896 Thatcher and Tobey arranged for Dunbar to meet Maj. James B. Pond, a professional manager who had arranged tours for Mark Twain, Frederick Douglass, George Washington Cable, James Whitcomb Riley, and other writers. Pond immediately prepared for Dunbar to visit New York City, where he negotiated contracts for a series of public readings and a contract with Dodd, Mead to become Dunbar's publisher. That December Dodd, Mead brought out *Lyrics of Lowly Life* (1896), which became his best-selling book, introducing him to a national audience and enabling him to devote himself entirely to literature. The publishers were so sure of the book's success that they paid Dunbar $400 in advance and later agreed to pay him a regular monthly income on the understanding they would publish his later works. His reputation increased as groups demanded his poetry readings and newspapers sought out his articles.

Lyrics of Lowly Life, dedicated to his mother, as his other books had been, and to William Dean Howells, who wrote an introduction, contains 105 poems, of which 97 had been published in *Oak and Ivy* and in *Majors and Minors*. Although Dunbar would write three more collections of poetry, none would surpass the achievement of *Lyrics of Lowly Life*.

In February 1897, with his literary reputation firmly established in the United States, Dunbar sailed for London on a reading tour under the management of Major Pond's daughter Edith. In New York, on the eve of his departure, he finally met Alice Ruth Moore at a reception given for him by Victoria Earle Matthews and attended by Booker T. Washington and other prominent people. He and Moore became engaged the same evening.

In London he arranged through Chapman and Hall publishers for an English edition of *Lyrics of Lowly Life*, which appeared in 1897. John Hay, the U.S. Ambassador to Great Britain, scheduled a reading before some of London's most prominent citizens, and he introduced Dunbar to

Samuel Coleridge-Taylor, a black musician who befriended Dunbar and set some of his lyrics to music; Dunbar also wrote the libretto for Coleridge-Taylor's operetta *Dream Lovers* (1898). Dunbar established a friendship with well-known journalist Henry M. Stanley, and for a while he stayed with one of his old friends, Alexander Crummell, and began work on *The Uncalled* (1898), a partly autobiographical novel. By this time Dunbar had become the first black American poet to achieve both national and international acclaim. Despite his popularity he failed to achieve the financial success he had hoped for in England, largely because the celebrations surrounding Queen Victoria's Diamond Jubilee had made poetry readings seem less attractive. His London experiences inspired him to write a poem, "The Garret," and an article, "England as Seen by a Black Man," which appeared in the *Independent* on 16 September 1897.

After spending six months in England, he returned to New York. Through the assistance of Col. Robert G. Ingersoll, he began work on 1 October as an assistant clerk in the reading room at the Library of Congress in Washington, D.C., with an annual salary of $720.

Dunbar's Washington years (1897-1899) were among his most productive, economically successful, and spiritually rewarding. His secret marriage to Alice Ruth Moore–which they kept secret because of her family's objections to his dark skin and to his work in minstrel shows–took place on 6 March 1898. Despite his poor health and the demands of his job, he energetically turned out seven articles (many voiced his racial protest), a musical, two collections of short stories, two volumes of poems, and the novel he had started in London; he also gave innumerable readings. His royalties, fees, and annual salary furnished him the first financial stability he had ever known. In recognition of his achievements, Atlanta University bestowed upon him an honorary Master of Arts degree on 5 June 1899.

The first work that came out of this two-year period was *Folks from Dixie,* a collection of short stories published in April 1898, illustrated by E. W. Kemble, as many of his books were, and dedicated to his patron and friend, Henry A. Tobey. By the end of 1899 it had sold more than four thousand copies, and the J. Bowden Company in London had brought out an edition. Four years would pass before he would publish another collection of poems. Apparently Dunbar turned to fiction to present an enlarged perception of the tragic dilemma of the black American. Prose helped to free him of the yoke that bound him as a dialect poet. He had accommodated his dialect poems to the tastes of his white reading public, but he was also conscious of his black audience and the need to rekindle and reinforce their awareness of the need for solidarity, pride, and above all, dignity.

There were twelve stories in *Folks from Dixie,* five set before emancipation and seven during post-Reconstruction. Dunbar collected the materials for this volume from stories told him by his mother and by freedmen living in Washington, D.C. Although most of them are plantation tales, the second story, "The Ordeal at Mt. Hope," introduces into Dunbar's fiction racial protest against the Jim Crow laws that were implemented and rigidly enforced to prevent blacks from becoming first-class citizens. Dunbar infuses into the story of the Reverend Howard Dokesbury portions of the diverse economic and political philosophies of Booker T. Washington and W. E. B. Du Bois; he traces discrimination against blacks in America and points out that, historically, the black man's plight arose from his association with whites and that this association shaped the world within which he has lived. Dunbar dismisses the belief held by many whites that blacks are shiftless and lazy, and he attacks the grim reality of the system of slavery with little attempt to assume an accommodative spirit.

One of the best stories in *Folks from Dixie* is "Jimsella," Dunbar's first treatment of black migration to the North. Jim and Mandy Mason, who have left the South for New York, discover that while they, and others like them, may enjoy certain social privileges there that they could not enjoy in the South, they cannot secure property, business opportunities, or satisfactory income because of their lack of the necessary skills for jobs in industry and because of their color. Dunbar's antipathy for the city, a major concern in some of his fiction, was shaped by his own experiences and by his observations of transplanted southern blacks in cities such as Dayton, Chicago, New York, and Washington, D.C. He saw the demoralizing effects of racism upon the black urban population. Another post-Reconstruction story, "At Shaft 11," exposes the corruption within labor unions and confirms that labor, when constructively organized, could be one of the major factors in eradicating economic inequality, but when they bar blacks from membership, their action is self-defeating.

Folks from Dixie received generally favorable reviews. The reviewer for *Outlook* (7 May 1898) said Dunbar was "eminently successful in catching the salient traits of southern life, white as well as his own race," and the reviewer for the *Bookman* (7 June 1898) considered the collection "the first expression in national prose fiction of the inner life of the American Negro." Some reviewers pointed to the loose construction of the stories, but the reviewer for *Nation* (21 July 1898) predicted that Dunbar would become a truer chronicler of the folks from Dixie than he had shown in this work.

Dedicated to Alice Dunbar, Dunbar's first novel, *The Uncalled,* appeared in the May 1898 issue of *Lippincott's Monthly* magazine. In September of that year it was published by Dodd, Mead. Although by mid 1899, 3,000 copies had been sold in the United States and editions had been published in Canada and England, it was not as well received as Dunbar had hoped. Reviewers condemned its lack of local color as well as its loosely constructed and implausible plot, found its characters–all white–unrealistic, and differed over the reason Dunbar chose to write about whites rather than blacks. Some critics believed it was for commercial reasons, while others suggested he had not developed enough within himself to write a realistic protest novel about black people.

Set in Dexter, Ohio, *The Uncalled* has characters and themes reminiscent of Nathaniel Hawthorne's classic *The Scarlet Letter* (1850). Dunbar's novel focuses on Frederick Brent, who becomes the ward of Hester Prime, a deeply religious spinster, after his father has become a drunkard and abandoned his family. Convinced, along with the rest of the townspeople, that Freddie will be like his father, Hester rears Freddie strictly by the Calvinistic teachings of her church and insists that he study for the ministry. Eliphalet Hodges, who marries Hester, is less rigid, however, and encourages the young boy to be self-reliant.

Upon graduation from a seminary he returns home to be the respected pastor of Dexter Baptist Church and later becomes engaged to Elizabeth Simpson, whose father is pastor emeritus of the church. However, he frequently goes against the puritanical regulations of the church, and, when the churchgoers insist that he denounce a woman who has given birth to an illegitimate child, he resigns his post, breaks his engagement to Elizabeth, who has sided with her father and the townspeople, and journeys to Cin-

cinnati. There he accidentally meets his father, who now calls himself the "California Pilgrim," since he has undergone a spiritual regeneration. Concealing his identity, Freddie learns of his father's plans to return to Dexter to be reunited with his family. In Dexter the father takes a room by chance in the home of Eliphalet and Hester Hodges and becomes fatally ill, and the Hodges send for Freddie. He returns full of bitterness, but he forgives his father when he learns of his critical condition. After leaving Dexter once more for Cincinnati, he writes the Hodges of his membership in the Congregational church and of his engagement to another young woman, Alice. The story ends when the Hodges arrive for the couple's wedding. The work was important for Dunbar personally because it represented his own meditation over his mother's insistence that he become a minister; however, the novel failed to heighten his literary reputation.

After working about a year and a half at the Library of Congress, Dunbar resigned on 31 December 1898 to devote himself to his literary career and readings. Dunbar had been in delicate health since childhood, but now his health was rapidly failing. He had developed a persistent cough, but he traveled constantly, reciting his poems and giving lectures. His visit to Tuskegee, Alabama, to attend an annual conference on Negro farmers at the invitation of Booker T. Washington was his first physical contact with the South although he had used it as the subject for numerous poems and stories. He wrote the words for the Tuskegee Institute school song, keeping in mind the tune of "Fair Harvard."

A collection of poems, *Lyrics of the Hearthside,* appeared in 1899, sold well, and received favorable reviews. *Lyrics of the Hearthside* contained 110 poems, including 37 grouped under "Humor and Dialect," which Dunbar placed at the end of the book as he had done with the dialect poems in *Majors and Minors.* The range of the poems in this volume illustrates the mature craftsmanship of the poet who presents his broadened perception of art in such poems as "Love's Apotheosis," and "Love," which is a sonnet.

In May 1899, while en route to a poetry recital in Albany, New York, at which Governor Theodore Roosevelt had planned to introduce him, Dunbar fell ill; he later developed pneumonia. For a month he lay near death in a New York City apartment, but his spirit was enlivened by his many visitors, including Howells. After doc-

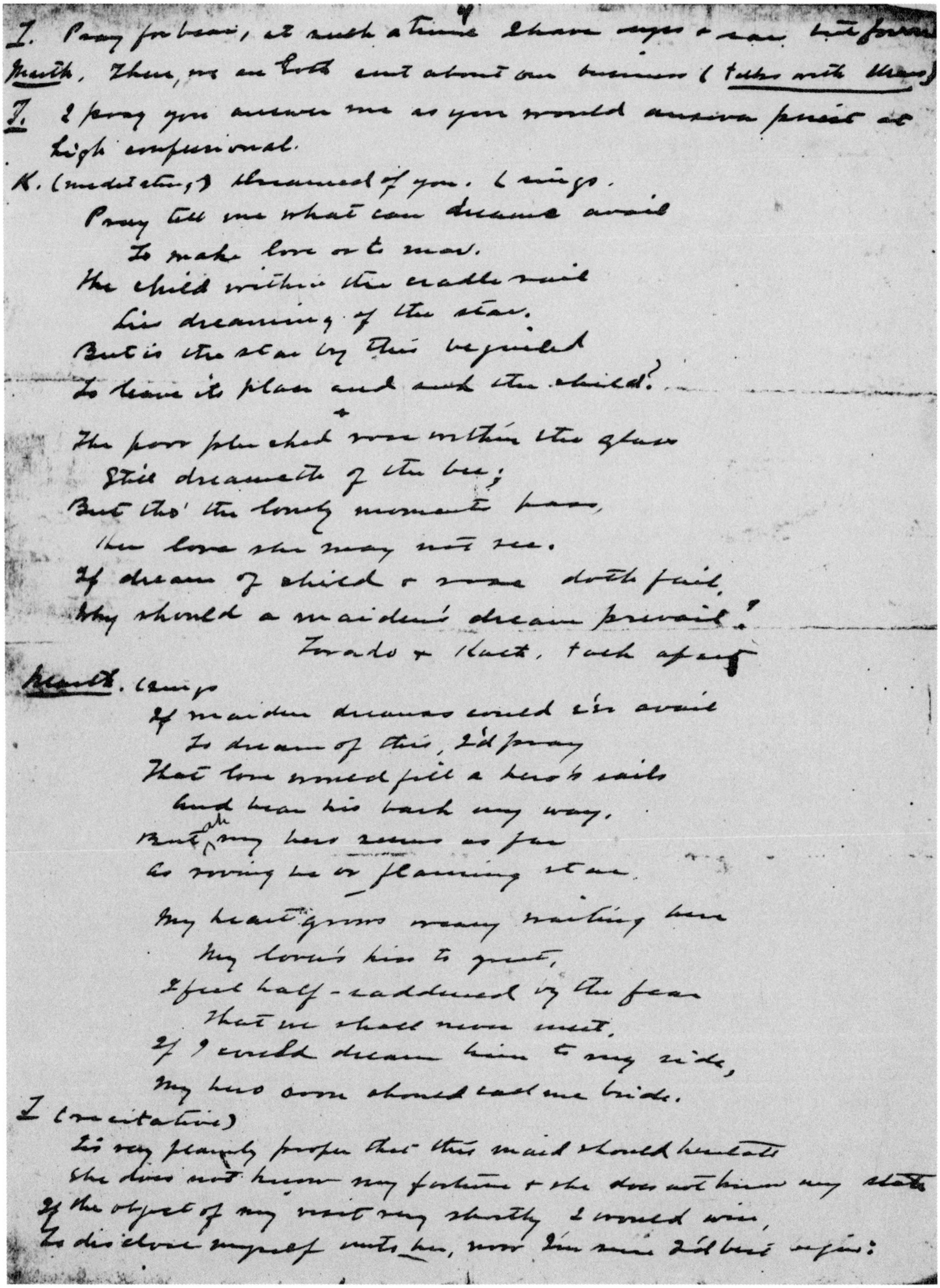

[Handwritten manuscript page — libretto text in cursive, largely illegible. Partial reading follows.]

I. Pray forbear, at such a time I have eyes & ear...
...There, you are both sent about our business *(takes with them)*

I. I pray you answer me as you would answer priest at
high confessional.

K. *(meditating)* I dreamed of you. *(sings)*
  Pray tell me what can dreams avail
    To make love or to mar.
  The child within the cradle rail
    Lies dreaming of the star.
  But is the star by this beguiled
  To leave its place and seek the child?

  The poor plucked rose within the glass
    Still dreameth of the bee;
  But tho' the lonely moments pass,
    Her love she may not see.
  If dream of child & rose doth fail,
  Why should a maiden's dream prevail?

                    Torado & Katt, each apart

Katt. *(sings)*
  If maiden dreams could e'er avail
    To dream of this, I'd pray
  That love would fill a hero's sails
    And bear his bark my way.
  But ah, my hero seems as far
  As roving sun or flaming star.

  My heart grows weary waiting here
    My lover's kiss to greet,
  I feel half-saddened by the fear
    That we shall never meet.
  If I could dream him to my side,
  My hero soon should call me bride.

I. *(recitative)*
  'Tis very plainly proper that this maid should hesitate
  She does not know my fortune & she does not know my state
  If the object of my visit very shortly I would win,
  To disclose myself unto her, now I'm sure I'd best begin:

Page from Dunbar's libretto for Dream Lovers, *the operetta he wrote with black English composer Samuel Coleridge-Taylor (collection of Peter Revell)*

tors diagnosed his underlying ailment as tuberculosis and advised him to move to the mountains, he took Alice to the Catskills for several weeks in hope of recovering. There he wrote an article on the Negroes in Washington, D.C., for *Harper's Weekly*, and several poems and short stories.

In September 1899, at the request of his doctors, the Dunbars left Washington, and along with Dunbar's mother, journeyed to Colorado, where they settled in Harmon, a small town near Denver. He carried letters of introduction from Henry Tobey to friends in Denver and Colorado Springs. For the next few months he contributed stories to the *Denver Post*, the *Independent*, *Lippincott's* and the *Saturday Evening Post*. Some of his poetry appeared in *Century* and *Harper's Weekly*. His special focus at this time, however, was the writing of a Western novel.

By Christmas, Dodd, Mead had published a selection of eight poems from earlier books in an illustrated volume of 125 pages with photographs taken by the Hampton Institute Camera Club of simple, southern, black people in natural settings. Alice Morse decorated each page with light green designs. Dedicated to Bishop Henry C. Potter and friends who had been kind to Dunbar during his illness, *Poems of Cabin and Field* (1899) includes "The Deserted Plantation," "Hunting Song," "Little Brown Baby," "Chris'mus is A-Comin'," "Signs of the Times," "Time to Tinker 'Roun'," "Lullaby," and "A Banjo Song." By the middle of 1900 the book had sold five thousand copies. Reviewers praised these dialect pieces, noting especially Dunbar's sensitive appreciation of nature and human character, his immense sense of humor, and his artistic ability. Over the years Dodd, Mead brought out more illustrated editions of poems from Dunbar's previously published books. After *Poems of Cabin and Field*, these volumes of selections include: *Candle-Lightin' Time* (1901); *When Malindy Sings* (1903); *Li'l' Gal* (1904); *Howdy Honey Howdy* (1905); and the posthumously published *Joggin' Erlong* (1906).

At the turn of the twentieth century Dunbar was America's most notable black poet, and he was quite prosperous. *Lyrics of Lowly Life* alone had sold over twelve thousand copies, and there was a constant flow of requests for his works from such magazines as *Atlantic Monthly*, *Harper's*, *Lippincott's*, and *Century*. On 15 January 1900, in recognition of his literary accomplishments, he was invited to become a member of the Executive Council of the American Social Science Association. By 1900 Dunbar had also made

inroads into a theater career. Ernest Hogan, the comedian who had starred in *Clorindy; or, the Origin of the Cakewalk* (produced in 1898), a musical comedy for which Dunbar had written the book and lyrics, also starred in *Uncle Eph's Christmas* (1900), a one-act musical sketch for which Dunbar had written lyrics in collaboration with Will Marion Cook. "Uncle Eph's Christmas" had been a part of a vaudeville program at the Boston Music Hall but had received very bad reviews, particularly from blacks who objected to Dunbar's stereotyping and his use of minstrel imagery and dialogue. One reviewer went so far as to call him "the Prince of the Coon Song Writers." Dunbar, fearing for his literary reputation, had wished to disassociate himself from the show, but he continued writing musical lyrics for the rest of his career. In early 1900 Dunbar made a few reading appearances in the East and parts of the Midwest, and he and Alice returned to Harmon in March.

In May 1900, just prior to his return to Washington, D.C., for another two-year stay, Dunbar published *The Strength of Gideon and Other Stories*, which contained twenty short stories that treated an assortment of themes, including racial protest. "The Ingrate," one of his best stories, is based on what he knew about his father's slave experiences and of his escape from slavery by the Underground Railroad. "The Finish of Patsy Barnes" and "Silas Jackson" address the black migration theme. There were also three stories that focused on black politicians and two about lynching. "The Tragedy at Three Forks," written at a time when lynchings were quite frequent in the South and other parts of the country, focuses on Jane Hunster. A poor white girl, she is envious of Seliny Williams, who also is white, because Seliny's father is wealthier than hers. Seeking revenge against Seliny, who has embarrassed her at a party, Jane burns the Williams's house and barns. When two black men are arrested and jailed for the crime, the prosecuting attorney forces them to accept the blame. They are denied a trial by jury and are hanged for a crime they did not commit.

The longest short story Dunbar ever wrote is also in *The Strength of Gideon*. Divided into four parts, "One Man's Fortune" gives a rather lengthy yet realistic picture of the experiences of Bertram Halliday, a young black college graduate crippled in employment by racism and prejudice, and it chronicles the corrupt practices of white politicians. Much of Dunbar's own personal experiences of racial discrimination in employment went into his development of Halliday's character. In the story Dunbar demands equal treatment of blacks, and he strongly roots his social protest in the accepted values of American society. He does not argue for the destruction of the white power structure but for an open society for blacks. He regards capitalism as one of the primary causes of racial discrimination and prejudice, and he suggests the need for unity among blacks as the solution for collectively eliminating the major difficulties oppressing them.

"A Council at State" offers a rather vivid picture of the unscrupulous methods of a white party boss and his black deputy. Luther Hamilton, a powerful and corrupt politician, finds it "pleasant and more profitable simply to boss his party" because such a position gives him power and patronage and yet places him under no obligation to constituencies. His greatest pleasure is silencing troublesome dissenters by ruining their careers, driving them out of public life, and forcing their businesses into insolvency. He particularly enjoys harassing black politicians who oppose his political tactics.

Working closely with Hamilton is a black woman who is the only female political spy in Dunbar's fiction. Miss Kirkman, a thirty-year-old mulatto–shrewd, aggressive, and deceitful–is motivated by her desire for financial and social security. Her tragedy is that she does not wish to be black, yet she is constantly and firmly rejected as a social equal by her white associates, who see her as a convenient mediator between the two races. As a political spy, her duty is to disrupt a black political meeting, the purpose of which is to denounce the administration for showing hostile sentiments toward blacks. To achieve her objective, she contacts various blacks and encourages them to reduce their opposition. One of her victims is her own fiancé, Joseph Aldrick, whom she threatens not to marry unless he takes a more conservative stance. In similar fashion throughout the story rebellious sentiment is undercut by concessions made to preserve the security of one's employment or the possibility of social and political elevation. As he does several times in his fiction, Dunbar suggests in one passage that for blacks to obtain justice and equality in America, they must abandon traditional Uncle Tomism and passive resistance. Instead they must adopt violence, which clearly speaks to white America of the deeply rooted anger and dissatisfaction of blacks.

Most early reviewers of *The Strength of Gideon* pointed to Dunbar's crisp style, the quick action of the stories, and his effective use of humor and pathos. Others said he was at his best when he expressed the character, dialect, feeling, and sentiment of southern blacks. In general the public warmly received stories such as "Viney's Free Papers," set before emancipation, "The Case of Ca'line," a humorous kitchen monologue, and "The Fruitful Sleeping of the Rev. Elisha Edwards." The reviewers did not comment on the social, economic, and political protest in stories such as "The Finish of Patsy Barnes," "Mr. Cornelius Johnson, Office-Seeker," and "An Old-Time Christmas." However, recent critics have accorded a number of such protest stories the literary respect they rightfully deserve, and they point to the collection as a demonstration of Dunbar's development as a writer who possessed keen insight into the racial problems of his times and who used his stories to denounce racism. According to Peter Revell, the "unevenness of Dunbar's short story writing has perhaps caused these stories to be underrated by critics.... But Dunbar deserves credit for his attempts to extend the range of the black short story into a wide variety of locales, into various social levels and to use an extensive range of character types."

Later in October of 1900 Dunbar's second novel, *The Love of Landry*, appeared. Most critics agree that this is not Dunbar's best novel. Like those of *The Uncalled*, the characters are not drawn from the rich materials of the black experience. However, Addison Gayle, Jr., wrote in his biography of Dunbar that it is a "remarkable accomplishment" of a "poetic spirit seeking escape, seeking release from the bars and cages of life, of a dying soul attempting to lessen the impact of pain upon the still living." *The Love of Landry* is a short romantic Western tale written while Dunbar convalesced in Colorado. Its plot is slight: Mildred Osbourne, the heroine, comes West to regain her health. She falls in love with cowboy Landry Thaler, and they marry after he saves her during a cattle stampede. One of Dunbar's Denver friends, Maj. William Cooke Daniels, a young merchant and millionaire who frequently sent his carriage for Dunbar, furnished suggestions for the Western mannerisms and customs in the novel, and his stories of cattle stampedes were invaluable. In appreciation of Daniels's assistance, Dunbar dedicated the work to him.

Dunbar's next novel, *The Fanatics* (1901), was the first work to come out of his second Washington stay. It was published in March 1901 and dedicated to Edwin H. Keen, an English friend. Dunbar devoted much time toward its development and was extremely disappointed at its poor reception. As early as September 1899, while he was still in Colorado, he had begun plans for this historical account of the sectional strife in America at the outbreak of the Civil War. Though he rather realistically and objectively captures the spirit of the times, he often fails to furnish accurate historical details. His shallow, incomplete, and unrealistic treatment of many of the black characters is a disappointment, as is his monumental effort to reconcile all parties in the conflict. His sympathies are with the escaped slaves, but he admires the northern copperheads; he respects their courage in voicing their beliefs in a region unsympathetic to their sentiments.

The novel concerns not only sectional chauvinism during the Civil War era, but it also mirrors the conflicts within the lives and thoughts of the main characters, who are white. Two prominent Dorbury, Ohio, families, the Van Dorens and the Waterses, hold dissimilar political views. Bradford Waters sympathizes with the Union, while Stephen Van Doren, a copperhead, sympathizes with the Confederacy. Each finds equal support for his views from the community. Adding to the tension between the two families is the engagement of Bradford's daughter Mary to Robert Van Doren, Stephen's son. When escaped slaves enter town, the two families resolve some of their differences in the common cause of keeping the blacks from settling there. One of the major ironies of *The Fanatics* is the attitude and behavior of the older citizens who are zealous supporters of the Union but do not support the abolition of slavery. The novel shows that Dunbar saw racial injustice not as a regional problem but as a general trend in America.

After the appearance of *The Fanatics* and following a string of strenuous readings, Dunbar, suffering from physical and mental exhaustion, went south in April 1900 to Jacksonville, Florida, where he spent six weeks recuperating in the home of his old friend James Weldon Johnson. By this time he had started drinking heavily to ease his cough and to quench his pain. Although his writing had slackened, he composed several poems and gave a few reading recitals.

Dunbar's last novel, *The Sport of the Gods*, appeared in the May issue of *Lippincott's* magazine and was published by Dodd, Mead in 1902. The English edition, published later that year, was titled *The Jest of Fate; A Story of Negro Life*.

The novel reveals Dunbar's genuine effort to show the forces that prevented black Americans from charting their own destinies, suggesting that by organizing a legal system that denies blacks justice and equal job opportunities—and by generally ignoring the needs of the black man in their political decisions—white Americans set themselves up as "protective guardians" of Afro-Americans.

The plot of the novel follows a straight line of action. Berry Hamilton, the hardworking, thrifty black butler who has remained with his employer, Maurice Oakley, "through thick and thin," is wrongly accused of stealing money from Maurice's weak and dissipated younger brother Francis. Although no evidence supports the charge against him and Berry consistently proclaims his innocence, he is given a ten-year sentence at hard labor, and his wife, Fannie, and two children, Joe and Kitty, are ostracized by both blacks and whites. Unable to find employment, dispossessed by the Oakleys, and robbed of $500 by the police, the Hamiltons are forced to migrate north. In New York, instead of improving economically and socially, they experience physical, mental, and moral decay. The city is "cruel and cold and unfeeling," and corrupt. It is an environment that forces its people to prey upon each other. Nowhere are the characters free agents. Joe is quickly corrupted by the night life, and later he becomes an alcoholic and a murderer. Insincere blacks succeed in spoiling Kitty's character and enticing her onto the vaudeville stage as a dancer and singer. Meanwhile, Fannie is led to believe that Berry's prison sentence automatically grants her a divorce; consequently, she is duped into marrying a man who beats her and reduces her to abject poverty.

In the meantime, in the South, Maurice Oakley has been visited by troubles which weaken him physically and mentally. His brother Francis confesses that he invented the story of the theft and that Berry is innocent. Upon his release from prison after serving five of the ten years (four years of which Maurice Oakley knew of Berry's innocence), Berry travels to New York and discovers his family ripped apart and totally debased by the grim "sport of the gods." Following the murder of Fannie's "husband," Berry remarries her, and they return to Virginia.

"MAMMY PEGGY CAME MARCHING IN LIKE A GRENADIER."

UNCLE ISHAM DYER EXHORTS.

JIM.

HIS BROTHER AND SISTER.

Illustrations by Edward Windsor Kemble for the first edition of The Strength of Gideon and Other Stories

Unlike some of Dunbar's short stories that describe scenes of happy black people on southern plantations, *The Sport of the Gods* becomes social criticism in its exposure of blacks as prey to a white racist society. Maurice Oakley, the genteel southern white liberal, espouses the negative racial attitude that blacks as a race are incapable of intellectual and moral advancement. As a social critic Dunbar condemns racial injustice and stereotyping and argues that blacks have the same hopes, human feelings, and sensibilities as whites and ought to be seen as human kin, not as fearsome criminals and beasts.

The novel further develops Dunbar's vision of the new black man, which he first developed in the strong-limbed twenty-year-old, ragged, barefoot son of a contraband slave he had depicted in *The Fanatics*. In Berry Hamilton, he sees the emergence of this new black man, full of pride and dignity, who recognizes his right to be free and independent, a man struggling against ignorance and white oppression in an effort to offer his children the "best education in town" and his family a "neat cottage." In his concept of this new black man, Dunbar touches upon an idea that is treated more fully by writers of the Harlem Renaissance, who stressed a new black awareness in America nearly twenty years after the appearance of Dunbar's novel.

The Sport of the Gods, Dunbar's major achievement in fiction, was reviewed in the leading newspapers and magazines across the country. Some critics called the story powerful and poignant reality, full of strength, vigor, and timelessness; yet, a few, such as the *Minneapolis Tribune* reviewer, regretted that Dunbar, "whose exquisite darkey stories have delighted the nation, should employ his strength with prose of the sort" found in the book. The *New York Times* reviewer said the New York scenes were the work's strongest part and called the "delineations of the southern gentleman" its weakest. The novel is widely considered to be the first major protest novel by a black American writer and the first significant novel to describe the life of blacks in Harlem.

In January 1902 Dunbar was invited to Charleston, South Carolina, to give a poetry recital. When he returned to Alice Moore in Washington, D.C., they quarrelled as they had done many times before. Under pressure from her family, who objected to Dunbar's blacker complexion, his lack of a college education, and his mother's menial job, Alice, who had become increasingly intolerant of Dunbar's persistent drinking and his moodiness, asked Dunbar to leave. He boarded a train for New York and never returned to Washington.

In New York he wrote three lyrics, "On Emancipation Day," "That's How the Cake-Walk's Done," and "Happy Jim" for *In Dahomey*. Will Marion Cook set the pieces to music, and the show played in Boston, New York, and in England, where it had a command performance at Buckingham Palace in celebration of the Prince of Wales's birthday. After *In Dahomey* Dunbar, who still hoped to achieve a reunion with Alice, living first in Chicago, succumbed to the pressure of the separation and failing health; his creative impulse decreased considerably, and he suffered a nervous breakdown followed by pneumonia. By late autumn, however, with P. R. Reynolds as his literary agent, he was well enough to serve as guest editor of the *Chicago Tribune* and to resume his travels and readings.

Despite his weariness and illness, in 1903 he completed *Lyrics of Love and Laughter, When Malindy Sings, In Old Plantation Days*, and two articles: "Representative American Negroes" and "The Fourth of July and Race Outrages," inspired by the race riots in Wilmington, North Carolina.

Lyrics of Love and Laughter illustrates the poet's full maturity. Dedicated to a friend, Catherine Impey, it includes "The Poet," in which Dunbar laments being praised only as a dialect poet: "He sang of life, serenely sweet,/With now and then, a deeper note./. . ./He sang of love when earth was young,/And love, itself, was in his lays./But ah, the world, it turned to praise/A jingle in a broken tongue." Some of the poems, such as "To a Violet Found on All Saint's Day," allude to his relentless physical and mental pain and suffering. Others reflected his experiences in the Catskills ("Keep a Song Up on de Way," "Joggin' Erlong," "Whip-poor-will And Katy-Did"), in Colorado ("In the Morning," "Dat Ol' Mare O' Mine," "Spring Fever," "A Warm Day in Winter"), and in New England ("Ballade," "To Let," "To Sell"). The long stanzaic poem "The Haunted Oak" treats the theme of lynching. The volume also carries tributes to Abraham Lincoln, Frederick Douglass, Robert Gould Shaw, and Booker T. Washington. It received praise both for the dialect and the nondialect pieces.

In early autumn of 1903 Dunbar left Chicago and returned to Dayton to the home he had bought his mother. Declining health and an unsuccessful reunion with Alice continued to weaken and sadden the poet. In September Dodd, Mead published his *In Old Plantation Days*, dedicated to George H. Lorimer, editor of the *Saturday Evening Post*, "out of whose suggestion these stories were born and by whose kindness they first saw the light." Illustrated by B. Martin Justice, the twenty-five stories are set on Master Stuart Mordaunt's plantation during the time of slavery. Most of the stories give brief accounts of life in the cabins. The slaves appear loyal to their masters, and the masters are benevolent and paternalistic toward them. Such romantic depictions of slavery, coupled with his dialect poems, caused critics for several decades after his death to group Dunbar among writers of the plantation tradition–with writers such as Joel Chandler Harris and Thomas Nelson Page. He was labeled an Uncle Tom by many black scholars and accused of destroying the dignity of black people. Hugh Gloster, for example, saw his fiction as a means of perpetuating the plantation mentality of white America. However, in the 1960s and 1970s black scholars such as Darwin T. Turner and Addison Gayle, Jr., pointed to the literary skill displayed in presenting both elements of accommodation and protest in the stories, and Dunbar's standing as a writer rose. Sometimes a story, such as "Mr. Groby's Slippery Gift," which seems to fit perfectly into an idyllic and romantic treatment of slave life, may ironically focus on the miseries and discontentment among the slaves. As a writer of ironic prose fiction, Dunbar was handicapped by a white reading public, but he devised subtle means to voice his criticism of racism in America and at the same time to get his work published. Not all the stories, however, show elements of protest. "Aunt Tempe's Triumph" is about a forceful and clever house servant, and two stories, "The Walls of Jericho," the most humorous in the volume, and "How Brother Parker Fell From Grace," portray the black plantation preacher.

The collection was a commercial success because it provided the kind of entertainment Dunbar's white audience wanted. The reviewer for the *New York Times* (31 October 1903) expressed the sentiment of most readers of *In Old Plantation Days*, saying these stories were good because they "tend to the encouragement of good feelings between races–black and white.... Dr. Thomas Nelson Page himself does not make 'ole Marse' and 'ole Miss' more admirable nor exalt higher in the slave the qualities of faithfulness and good humor."

The Heart of Happy Hollow (1904), Dunbar's last collection of short fiction, contains sixteen stories and sketches treating a variety of experiences in Happy Hollow, a place "wherever Negroes colonise in the cities or villages, North or South . . . wherever laughter and tears rub elbows day by day, and the spirit of labour and laziness shake hands."

The first story in the book returns to a theme Dunbar had employed in 1900. "The Scapegoat" condemns the corrupt practices of those philanthropists and politicians who use blacks to help them win elections, and it attacks those blacks who willingly participate in any conduct, legal or illegal, that keeps other blacks from increasing their social, economic, and political clout. A shrewd, influential black, who has lifted himself from bootblack to barbershop owner and operator of a private law firm, Robinson Asbury, the main character, is the one man who understands the racial attitudes and political corruption of party leaders, while he is concurrently fully aware of the joys and frustrations of black ghetto dwellers, whose economic status has been determined by politicians unfamiliar with and unsympathetic to their plight.

Dunbar's revelation of the corruption in American politics reaches its peak after a close election which Asbury's party wins. The defeated argue that their opponents won mainly through fraudulent tactics. Perceiving the sudden impulse of reform among the people, Asbury's party members find a scapegoat: Asbury.

Two other stories in the collection develop the theme of the confidence man, which Dunbar introduced in "Aunt Mandy's Investment" in *Folks from Dixie*. In "The Mission of Mr. Scatters," set in Miltonville, Kentucky, the title character is a shrewd, keen-witted, artful master of guile, who seduces and intrigues his listeners with his eloquence and physical appearance. Arrested for swindling the townspeople of their money, he is acquitted after a powerful speech in which he persuades the court that his actions served the worthwhile purpose of teaching "the darkies" not to trust men they do not know.

"The Promoter," set in the North during the Reconstruction, is more than an illustration of criminal conduct in the service of survival, for it shows Dunbar's interest in the confidence man himself and in the forces that motivate him to swindle others. Revealing the proficiency with which the mulatto Jason Buford exercises his profession, the story explores Buford's own response to his experience and captures the quality of Buford's existence in a world full of hatred and racism.

"A Defender of Faith" continues the black migration theme of *Folks from Dixie* and in *The Strength of Gideon*. The only one of Dunbar's stories to describe the physical environment of a northern ghetto and the plight of the poor, it is also the only story to use small children as central characters.

The more popular of Dunbar's two stories on lynching is "The Lynching of Jube Benson," which is included in the volume. The story focuses on Dr. Melville's guilt over having wrongfully accused his loyal servant Jube Benson of having murdered a white woman, whose last words were "That black." Seconds after Jube had been lynched, Jube's brother had dragged in Tom Skinner–"The worst white ruffian in the town"–whose scratched face was smeared with dirt and blackened in order that he might appear black. Melville immediately recognized his mistake and was the first to attempt to resuscitate Jube. Some critics condemn the story because the ending fails to denounce lynching emphatically. But Melville had learned from the experience to protest continuously the injustice of killing a person before his guilt had been established.

Li'l Gal, an illustrated volume of Dunbar's poems published by Dodd, Mead in late October 1904, contains only one poem, "Clarity," that had not appeared in other collections. Apparently the lady in that poem is Alice; the poet reaffirms his love for her and alludes to the pain caused by their separation.

Lyrics of Sunshine and Shadow, which came out in May 1905, contains seventy-eight poems treating such themes as love, sorrow, death, and nature. Dunbar had always wanted children, and the tenderness he had for them can be observed in poems such as "A Boy's Summer Song," "Johnny Speaks," "The Plantation Child's Lullaby," "Puttin' the Baby Away," "The Fisher Child's Lullaby," and "The Farm Child's Lullaby." In general, though, the poems in this volume are weak.

Howdy Honey Howdy, another of Dunbar's illustrated volumes, appeared in October 1905 and was favorably received. Comprised almost exclusively of dialect verse, the volume includes "A Death Song," which later would become Dunbar's epitaph: "Lay me down beneaf de willers in de grass,/Whah de branch'll go a-singin' as it pass./

An' w'en I's a-layin' low,/I kin hyeah it as it go/ Singin', 'Sleep, my honey, tek yo' res' at las'.'"

By the end of 1905 the poet's health had failed, and on 9 February 1906 he died at his home in Dayton, Ohio. Dunbar's last book, *Joggin' Erlong* (1906), published posthumously, contains nineteen previously collected poems, as well as "Sling Long," the last poem Dunbar wrote.

Paul Laurence Dunbar was a poet of genuine imagination who rose to literary fame despite nearly insurmountable obstacles. His fast rise as a widely read poet in little more than a decade is a remarkable phenomenon, especially because of the adverse racial atmosphere in which he lived and wrote, his lack of formal education, financial security, and good health. His poems and stories picture the hopeful, sensuous, and joyous side of working-class black life as well as its sorrows and disillusionments. Few American poets before him attracted such a wide, diversified group of readers and held them for such a long, unbroken period of time. He lifted the black oral tradition to the height of art and looked at his people objectively and with pride.

Twentieth-century critical assessment of Dunbar's poetry largely has followed the course established by William Dean Howells's review of *Majors and Minors*, in which he maintained that Dunbar's genius lay in his dialect verses. James Weldon Johnson said that in these dialect poems Dunbar "not only carried his art to the highest point of perfection, but he made a contribution to American literature unlike what anyone else had made, a contribution which, perhaps, no one else could have made." A modern critical shift toward according Dunbar's standard English poems the recognition they deserve began in 1971 with Allen Fox's article, "Behind the Mask: Paul Laurence Dunbar's Poetry in Literary English," which located the poet's significant contribution to American poetry in his standard English poems rather than in his dialect verse. Darwin Turner in "Paul Laurence Dunbar: The Poet and the Myths" argues that Dunbar's poetic accomplishments have been overlooked because scholars have too often relied upon myths about him, rather than critically examining his works.

Critical reception of Dunbar's fiction has followed a similar course. To Saunders Redding, Dunbar's stories depicted "Negroes as folksy, not-too-bright souls, all of whose concerns are minor, and all of whose problems can be solved by the emotional and spiritual equivalent of sticks of red peppermint candy." According to Sterling Brown, Dunbar's last volume of short stories repeated "the Thomas Nelson Page formula. . . . The harshness of Reconstruction and of Dunbar's own time is . . . conventionally neglected in his other volumes of short stories." In fact Brown claimed that "Dunbar's fiction veers away from anything more serious than laughter or gentle tears. . . . Dunbar in fiction must be considered as one who followed the leader, not as a blazer of new trails." Finally, Robert Bone wrote of Dunbar that whenever he had "something to say which transcended the boundaries of the plantation tradition, he resorted to the subterfuge of employing white characters, rather than attempting a serious literary portrait of the Negro. The effect of his work, therefore, was simply to postpone the main problem confronting the Negro novelist."

Dunbar's fiction, however, deserves reevaluation because much of it is devoted to racial protest against the social, economic, and political conditions of blacks that prevailed in America during the latter half of the nineteenth century and the opening of the twentieth. Dunbar's early stories more often show attitudes of accommodation than of protest, but this approach may have been the only practical way to get them published. Once he became an established writer, he seems to have felt freer to modify his accommodation and to express more openly his condemnation of American racism and prejudice.

Unlike such plantation writers as Harris and Page, whose black men find themselves confused and troubled as freedmen, Dunbar's black man emerges as a new man fully capable of devising the means by which he can ameliorate his social and economic paralysis. Dunbar's depictions depart from the myth that blacks were contented with slavery and that they did not know what to do with freedom once they obtained it. The unwillingness of Dunbar's freedman to remain a laborer or a tenant on the plantation is evident in the behavior of Jeremiah Anderson in "The Wisdom of Silence," Howard Dokesbury in "The Ordeal at Mt. Hope," Bertram Halliday in "One Man's Fortune," and Berry Hamilton in *The Sport of the Gods*. When Dunbar's new blacks are confused and troubled, their condition is mainly attributable to their frustration with white racism in America–not because they lack intellectual capability, or because they are inefficient or dishonest.

In his fiction Dunbar created a skillful mix of accommodation and protest, producing stories designed to offend neither black nor white readers. Seen from this perspective, Dunbar's stories show him to be a skilled spokesman for the racial complexities of his times.

Interviews:
"Solutions of Negro Problem Seen From Two Sides: Bishop H. C. Morrison and Paul Laurence Dunbar Discuss A Subject That is Brought to Notice by Murders in Illinois," *Denver Daily News*, 24 September 1899;
Gilberta S. Whittle, "Paul Dunbar," *A.M.E. Church Review*, 18 (April 1902): 320-327;
Lida Keck Wiggins, "Den of a Literary Lion," *Voice of the Negro*, 3 (January 1906): 50.

Bibliographies:
E. W. Metcalf, *Paul Laurence Dunbar: A Bibliography* (Metuchen: Scarecrow Press, 1975);
M. Thomas Inge, Maurice Duke, and Jackson R. Bryer, eds., *Black American Writers: Bibliographical Essays*, volume 1 (New York: St. Martin's Press, 1978).

Biographies:
Benjamin Brawley, *Paul Laurence Dunbar: Poet of His People* (Chapel Hill: University of North Carolina Press, 1936);
Virginia Cunningham, *Paul Laurence Dunbar and His Song* (New York: Dodd, Mead, 1947);
Jean Gould, *That Dunbar Boy* (New York: Dodd, Mead, 1958);
Addison Gayle, Jr., *Oak and Ivy: A Biography of Paul Laurence Dunbar* (Garden City: Anchor/ Doubleday, 1971).

References:
Davis Wasgatt Clark, ed., *Paul Laurence Dunbar Laurel-Decked* (Boston: Paul Laurence Dunbar Scholarship Fund, 1909).
Contains the addresses presented at the unveiling of the Dunbar Monument in Dayton, Ohio, on 6 June 1909 as well as three poems by Dunbar and various information about him.

Mrs. Paul Laurence Dunbar (Alice Ruth Moore Dunbar Nelson) and others, *Paul Laurence Dunbar: Poet Laureate of the Negro Race* (Philadelphia: Reverdy C. Ransom, 1914).
A pamphlet reprinting articles from the *A.M.E. Church Review* (October) issue contain-

ing Alice Dunbar's account of some of the sources for her husband's poems.

Allen Fox, "Behind the Mask: Paul Laurence Dunbar's Poetry in Literary English," *Texas Quarterly* (Summer 1971).
Shows that while Dunbar mainly "excelled at genteel idealizations of nature and love in his lyrics, he could also deny that such conventions as the pastoral myth of Arcadia had a place in the poetry of the Gilded Age."

Sara S. Fuller, *The Paul Laurence Dunbar Collection: An Inventory to the Microfilm Edition* (Columbus: Ohio Historical Society, 1972).
A microfilm collection in nine reels that contains letters, unpublished works, newspaper clippings and other memorabilia.

James Weldon Johnson, ed., *The Book of American Negro Poetry* (New York: Harcourt, Brace, 1922).
An anthology of Black-American poetry.

Victor Lawson, *Dunbar Critically Examined* (Washington, D.C.: Associated, 1941).
An extended critical study of Dunbar's poetry and prose in an effort to place him in a larger literary setting.

Doris M. Lucas, "Patterns of Accommodation and Protest in the Fiction of Paul Laurence Dunbar," dissertation, University of Illinois, Urbana, 1973.
Takes Dunbar out of the plantation tradition and places him in the protest tradition where he rightfully belongs.

Jay Martin, ed., *A Singer in the Dawn: Reinterpretations of Paul Laurence Dunbar* (New York: Dodd, Mead, 1975).
A book of critical essays about Dunbar delivered at the Paul Laurence Dunbar Centennial Celebration at the University of California at Irvine in 1972.

Peter Revell, *Paul Laurence Dunbar* (Boston: Twayne, 1979).
A standard critical study of Dunbar's works.

James B. Stronks, "Paul Laurence Dunbar and William Deans Howells," *Ohio Historical Quarterly*, 67 (April 1958): 95-108.
Focuses on Howells's "discovery" of Dunbar and on their relationship thereafter.

Darwin T. Turner, "Paul Laurence Dunbar: The Rejected Symbol," *Journal of Negro History*, 52 (January 1967): 1-13.
Suggests that many modern readers have rejected Dunbar as an accommodationist and that such readers have demanded too much of the poet as a symbol.

Jean Wagner, *Black Poets of the United States: From Paul Laurence Dunbar to Langston Hughes*, translated by Kenneth Douglas (Urbana: University of Illinois Press, 1973), pp. 73-125.
A translation of the 1963 Librarie Istra edition of a major critical study of several black poets of the Harlem Renaissance.

Papers:
The largest collection of Dunbar's papers is located at the Ohio Historical Society in Columbus, Ohio. It includes a sizable collection of his prose and poetry manuscripts and several song lyric manuscripts. The Schomburg Collection of the New York Public Library houses a collection of his papers available on microfilm as *The Life and Works of Paul Laurence Dunbar* (St. Paul, Minn.: 3M Company, 1969). Additional letters are scattered among other collections at Houghton Library at Harvard University.

Bret Harte

This entry was updated by Joseph Caldwell from the entry by Ben Merchant Vorpahl (University of Georgia) in DLB 12, American Realists and Naturalists.

Places	Northern California London	Crefeld, Germany	Glasgow
Influences and Relationships	Alexandre Dumas Mark Twain	Shakespeare William Dean Howells	Charles Dickens Edgar Allan Poe
Literary Movements and Forms	Realism Vernacular Verse	Local Color "Pacific Slope" School	Frontier Journalism
Major Themes	Moral Ambiguity Life as Essentially Comic Courage vs. Cowardice	The Physical Environment as an Active Force	Appearances vs. Hidden Meaning
Cultural and Artistic Influences	The Gilded Age	Theater	
Social and Economic Influences	The Westward Movement	California Prospecting	Civil War

See also the Harte entry in DLB 64, American Literary Critics and Scholars, 1850-1880.

BIRTH: Albany, New York, 25 August 1836, to Henry and Elizabeth Ostrander Harte.

MARRIAGE: 11 August 1862 to Anna Griswold; children: Griswold, Francis King, Jessamy, Ethel.

DEATH: Surrey, England, 5 May 1902.

BOOKS: *Condensed Novels, and Other Papers* (New York: Carlton/London: Low, 1867; enlarged edition, Boston: Osgood, 1871);

The Last Galleon and Other Tales (San Francisco: Towne & Bacon, 1867);

The Luck of Roaring Camp, and Other Sketches (Boston: Fields, Osgood, 1870; enlarged, 1870);

Poems (Boston: Fields, Osgood, 1871);

East and West Poems (Boston: Osgood, 1871; London: Hotten, 1871);

Mrs. Skaggs's Husbands, and Other Sketches (London: Hotten, 1872; Boston: Osgood, 1873);

An Episode of Fiddletown and Other Sketches (London: Routledge, 1873);

M'liss. An Idyl of Red Mountain (New York: De-Witt, 1873);

Echoes of the Foot-hills (Boston: Osgood, 1875);

Tales of the Argonauts, and Other Sketches (Boston: Osgood, 1875);

Gabriel Conroy (London: Warne, 1876; Hartford, Conn.: American Publishing Company, 1876);

Two Men of Sandy Bar: A Drama (Boston: Osgood, 1876);

Thankful Blossom, a Romance of the Jerseys, 1779 (Boston: Osgood, 1877; London & New York: Routledge, 1877);

The Story of a Mine (London: Routledge, 1877; Boston: Osgood, 1878);

The Man on the Beach (London: Routledge, 1878);

"Jinny" (London: Routledge, 1878);

Drift from Two Shores (Boston: Houghton, Osgood, 1878);

The Twins of Table Mountain (London: Chatto & Windus, 1879);

The Twins of Table Mountain and Other Stories (Boston: Houghton, Osgood, 1879);

Flip and Other Stories (London: Chatto & Windus, 1882);

Flip and Found at Blazing Star (Boston: Houghton, Mifflin, 1882);

In the Carquinez Woods (London: Longmans, Green, 1883; Boston: Houghton, Mifflin, 1884);

On the Frontier (London: Longmans, Green, 1884; Boston: Houghton, Mifflin, 1884);

By Shore and Sedge (Boston: Houghton, Mifflin, 1885; London: Longmans, Green, 1885);

Maruja (London: Chatto & Windus, 1885; Boston & New York: Houghton, Mifflin, 1885);

Snow-Bound at Eagle's (Boston & New York: Houghton, Mifflin, 1886; London: Ward & Downey, 1886);

The Queen of the Pirate Isle (London: Chatto & Windus, 1886; Boston & New York: Houghton, Mifflin, 1887);

A Millionaire of Rough-and-Ready and *Devil's Ford* (Boston & New York: Houghton, Mifflin, 1887);

Devil's Ford (London: White, 1887);

A Millionaire of Rough-and-Ready (London: White, 1887);

The Crusade of the Excelsior (Boston & New York: Houghton, Mifflin, 1887; London: White, 1887);

A Phyllis of the Sierras and A Drift from Redwood Camp (Boston & New York: Houghton, Mifflin, 1888);

The Argonauts of North Liberty (Boston & New York: Houghton, Mifflin, 1888; London: Blackett, 1888);

Cressy (London & New York: Macmillan, 1889; Boston & New York: Houghton, Mifflin, 1889; London: Macmillan, 1889);

The Heritage of Dedlow Marsh and Other Tales (Boston & New York: Houghton, Mifflin, 1889);

A Waif of the Plains (London: Chatto & Windus, 1890; Boston & New York: Houghton, Mifflin, 1890);

A Ward of the Golden Gate (London: Chatto & Windus, 1890; Boston & New York: Houghton, Mifflin, 1890);

A Sappho of Green Springs and Other Stories (London: Chatto & Windus, 1891; Boston & New York: Houghton, Mifflin, 1891);

A First Family of Tasajara (London & New York: Macmillan, 1891; Boston & New York: Houghton, Mifflin, 1892);

Colonel Starbottle's Client and Some Other People (London: Chatto & Windus, 1892; Boston & New York: Houghton, Mifflin, 1892);

Susy: A Story of the Plains (Boston & New York: Houghton, Mifflin, 1893; London: Chatto & Windus, 1893);

Sally Dows, Etc. (London: Chatto & Windus, 1893); republished as *Sally Dows and Other Stories* (Boston & New York: Houghton, Mifflin, 1893);

A Protegee of Jack Hamlin's and Other Stories (Boston & New York: Houghton, Mifflin, 1894; enlarged edition, London: Chatto & Windus, 1894);

The Bell-Ringer of Angel's and Other Stories (Boston & New York: Houghton, Mifflin, 1894; London: Chatto & Windus, 1894);

Clarence (London: Chatto & Windus, 1895; Boston & New York: Houghton, Mifflin, 1895);

In a Hollow of the Hills (London: Chapman & Hall, 1895; Boston: Houghton, Mifflin, 1895);

Barker's Luck and Other Stories (Boston & New York: Houghton, Mifflin, 1896; London: Chatto & Windus, 1896);

Three Partners or The Big Strike on Heavy Tree Hill (Boston & New York: Houghton, Mifflin, 1897; London: Chatto & Windus, 1897);

Tales of Trail and Town (Boston & New York: Houghton, Mifflin, 1898; London: Chatto & Windus, 1898);

Stories in Light and Shadow (London: Pearson, 1898; Boston & New York: Houghton, Mifflin, 1898);

Mr. Jack Hamlin's Mediation and Other Stories (Boston & New York: Houghton, Mifflin, 1899; London: Pearson, 1899);

From Sand Hill to Pine (Boston & New York: Houghton, Mifflin, 1900; London: Pearson, 1900);

Under the Redwoods (Boston & New York: Houghton, Mifflin, 1901; London: Pearson, 1901);

On the Old Trail (London: Pearson, 1902); republished as *Openings in the Old Trail* (Boston & New York: Houghton, Mifflin, 1902);

Condensed Novels, Second Series: New Burlesques (Boston & New York: Houghton, Mifflin, 1902; London: Chatto & Windus, 1902);

Sue: A Play in Three Acts, by Harte and T. Edgar Pemberton (London: Greening, 1902);

Trent's Trust and Other Stories (London: Nash, 1903; Boston & New York: Houghton, Mifflin, 1903);

Stories and Poems and Other Uncollected Writings, compiled by Charles Meeker Kozlay (Boston & New York: Houghton Mifflin, 1914).

Collection: *The Writings of Bret Harte,* 20 volumes (Boston: Houghton, Mifflin, 1896-1914).

Bret Harte was the first Pacific slope writer to gain an international reputation for his work. As a deft observer of character and conditions, he introduced to a worldwide audience the pictur-esque life of mid-nineteenth-century northern California. Yet his best stories and sketches contain much more than local color. The spectacular settings, the accurate costumes and dialects, even the realistic depictions of character types– ranging from aristocratic hidalgos to scheming women, whores, and bumptious Missourians–are finally subordinate to the questions of courage, cowardice, and moral ambiguity that fascinated Harte as a writer and plagued him as a man. These are also the questions that have occupied literature about the American West throughout the nineteenth and twentieth centuries. Although Harte did not discover them first, he did address them with intelligence, insight, and wit during the four decades of his active writing career. As a writer of short stories, a novelist, an editor, and a critic, he gave the world an image of the West that still prevails.

Francis Brett Harte, as he was christened, was born to Henry Harte and Elizabeth Ostrander Harte at Albany, New York, on 25 August 1836. There were two older children, Eliza, born in 1831, and Henry, born in 1835. A fourth, Margaret, would be born in 1838. Henry Harte operated a private school in the modest family home on Columbia Street. However, the financial panic of 1837 forced the school to close, and the Hartes were plunged into serious financial difficulty. For the next eight years they moved from town to town, setting up a household wherever Henry could find work as a teacher. The lack of permanence, and the anxiety about money and employment, must have been hard on young Frank. He was a quiet, withdrawn child, ill much of the time, who soon took refuge in books. At six, he was reading Shakespeare. By the time he was ten, he had familiarized himself with most of the major British novelists, but Alexandre Dumas's *The Count of Monte Cristo*, which he read at about this time in a translation from the French, remained his favorite novel throughout his life.

Frank was nine years old when his father's death in 1845 left the family destitute. Neither he, his mother, nor his brother and sisters were qualified to earn money. It therefore became necessary for Elizabeth Harte–from all indications a proud woman–to request aid from relatives. Her own family supplied some help, but not enough. Fortunately, her late husband's eighty-one-year-old father, Bernard Hart, was wealthy enough to provide more, but asking him for it must have been difficult. He had secretly married Catherine

Bret Harte at about the time he became editor of the
Overland Monthly

Brett, Henry's mother, in 1799, but their marriage was dissolved in 1800, just after Henry's birth. Henry's chief reason for adding the *e* to the family name had probably been to dissociate himself from the father for whom he felt only bitterness. However, Bernard Hart did provide Elizabeth and her offspring with the means for staying together, at least for a time. They settled in New York City in 1845, where Frank was able to continue school until he was thirteen years old. At eleven he had his first work, a sentimental poem called "Autumn Musings," published in the *Sunday Morning Atlas*. On leaving school he worked briefly in a law office and then a counting-house. Meanwhile, the little family began to break up. Henry Harte went to fight in the Mexican War in 1846, later showing up as an argonaut in San Francisco in 1849. Eliza Harte married in 1851. In 1853 their mother became engaged to Andrew Williams, a California business-

man, whom she married in San Francisco early the next year. Sixteen-year-old Bret, as Frank now began to be called, and his younger sister, Margaret, joined Elizabeth and her new husband in March 1854, after a harrowing passage down the East Coast to Nicaragua, across the isthmus, and up the West Coast to San Francisco. The family settled in Oakland, where Williams enjoyed modest success and prosperity, but Bret was apparently dissatisfied. Late in 1854 he left home to wander in the foothills and valleys about which he would soon begin to write.

Harte probably taught school for a time at LaGrange, on the bank of the Toulumne River, a community that appears as Smith's Pocket in his early short story, "M'liss." He then seems to have drifted north, looking for gold. Acquaintances from this period remember him as a tenderfoot, who came into the country ill prepared for its rigors of climate and terrain. He wore patent leather shoes and a suit of city clothes. Early in 1856 he borrowed an overcoat and money from a friend, returned to his stepfather's house in Oakland, and announced to his family that he intended to become a writer.

He approached his newly chosen line of work in the characteristically calculated and methodical fashion that would become one of his trademarks throughout life. Dickens, he decided, would be his mentor. A recently purchased complete set of Dickens's novels occupied him during the summer of 1856 while he worked at an Oakland drugstore. In the fall he left for a ranch in the Sycamore Valley, at the foot of Mount Diablo, where he tutored the four sons of Abner Bryan, a local rancher and religious enthusiast. In 1857 he briefly took the unlikely position of a Wells Fargo guard on a stagecoach before becoming an apprentice printer on the Humboldt County *Northern Californian* in Arcata the following year. While such meanderings might have led nowhere for someone with less thrifty habits of mind, Harte made them count, drawing from them materials for his writing. From his experience on the Bryan ranch, he wove "A Legend of Monte del Diablo," the story of how a pious Spanish padre is tutored in history by a gentlemanly devil. Out of his experience as a stagecoach "shotgun" came Yuba Bill, the wryly laconic driver in such tales as "Miggles," "M'liss," "Snow-Bound at Eagle's," and "A Niece of Snapshot Harry's." The job on the weekly *Northern Californian*, of course, was a humble beginning at the enterprise that would make him a momentary celebrity, promise him riches, and actually provide him with a competent living over the long term.

Although working in a frontier print shop was probably not what Harte had in mind when he announced in 1856 that he intended to be a writer, newspaper work agreed with him, and he was good at it. He soon found his way out of the back room and into the community, where he covered local news stories with a flair that did him credit. In 1859 Harte was routinely left in charge of the paper whenever S. G. Whipple, the editor, went to San Francisco. Early in 1860, however, he learned for the first time that to have one's work published was not necessarily to be admired, a lesson he would later have many occasions to ponder. On 26 February–a Sunday–a group of whites armed with guns, knives, and axes surprised an Indian camp on Gunther's Island in nearby Humboldt Bay and butchered some sixty inhabitants, mostly women and children. As it happened, Whipple was away. Harte not only reported the incident with outrage, he wrote a stingingly indignant editorial. Not surprisingly, his popularity in Humboldt County evaporated at once. He was probably not seriously threatened with physical violence, but he was certainly made to feel unwelcome. Accordingly, he left the *Northern Californian* the next month and took a steamer down the coast to San Francisco.

Harte found a job as a printer with the *Golden Era*, a respected San Francisco literary magazine, and contributed a number of lively–if somewhat derivative–sketches and stories to that journal. He also completed his first considerable literary effort, the story first published in abridged form as "The Work on Red Mountain." This work created a considerable stir when the *Golden Era* printed it in two installments during December 1860. Superficially, it is the rags-to-riches story of Melissa Smith, the daughter of an indigent gold miner whose claim is discovered, after his death, to be fabulously rich. Even this version raises questions concerning the effects of wealth on M'liss and those around her. However, Harte had written a much longer version of the same story before "The Work on Red Mountain" appeared in print. The longer version, subsequently revised and renamed "M'liss," lacks the economy and easy grace of later tales such as "The Outcasts of Poker Flat," but it is certainly one of the most important stories Harte ever wrote. This dark fable, written when the author was only twenty-four years old, is Harte's prototypical tale of the West. It expresses the wryly be-

mused attitude that characterizes Harte's realism as a whole; it even roughs out the four roles which Harte would spend the rest of his career refining and rearranging. Its lack of artistic finish only emphasizes the quality that would become Harte's trademark–a sense that the play of surface appearances, fascinating in itself, hides some meaning which can never be known.

Harte later wrote that he regarded American life and literature as essentially comic, and "M'liss" is probably a good example of what he meant by comedy. The northern California setting and its rough-hewn but crafty inhabitants express the raffish, accidental grace he could not help recognizing in both himself and his country. Even more important, deceit, surprise, and a peculiar but insistent vitality–qualities in which he delighted, but which he surely knew would get him into trouble–characterize the story and govern the conduct of its four basic roles. One role, played by M'liss herself, is that of the youthful innocent. A second, played by a frontier schoolmaster (whose name, appropriately not revealed until the final chapters, is Gray), is that of the ambivalent observer. A third is that of the attractive but mysterious female, portrayed as a "stunner," who may or may not be M'liss's mother, but who shows up at the close to claim the girl as her daughter, invites schoolmaster Gray to be her lover, transforms the settlement, and acquires a gold mine. The fourth role is that of the physical environment, which continues to assert its manifold and unpredictable powers, despite whatever depredations may be performed against it by settlers, speculators, and others. Murder, lust, greed, suicide, and madness fill out the plot. The action is more or less continuously commented upon by a polyglot chorus, which includes the hypocritical Reverend Mr. McSnagley, the Morpher family–all of whose children bear names drawn from classical lore–and various miners and townspeople. The focus of "M'liss" is on arresting but inscrutable surfaces.

The story opens with a brief description of Smith's Pocket, a settlement located at the base of Red Mountain and named for "Bummer" Smith–presently the town drunk, but formerly a prospector who discovered a small pocket of gold ore near the present town site and triggered a flurry of speculation. The town soon flaunted "its two fancy stores, its two hotels, its one express office, and its two first families." More recent additions include "a Methodist church, and hard by a monte bank, and a little beyond, on the moun-

*A family group, circa 1900. Standing: Bret Harte and his
daughter-in-law Mrs. Francis King Harte. Seated: Ethel
Harte, his youngest child, and Anna Harte, his wife.*

tain side, a graveyard; and then a little schoolhouse." Melissa Smith, Bummer's only offspring,
has grown into a preadolescent ragamuffin with
a reputation for incorrigibility, but she shows up
one evening at the schoolhouse to request that
the master admit her as a student. Shortly after
she enters the school, proving herself to be intelligent, eccentric, and darkly attractive, her father
is found dead on the site of his former claim, presumably a victim of suicide. M'liss is placed as a foster child in the Morpher home, near town, and
soon comes to regard herself as a rival of Clytie
(Clytemnestra) Morpher, a classmate, for the
young schoolmaster's affections. Meanwhile, Aris-
tides Morpher, Clytie's younger brother, discovers that the long abandoned Smith claim is being
worked in secret. At about the same time the
schoolmaster begins to suspect that Bummer
Smith may have been murdered to keep him
from developing the claim. A sinister-looking prospector named Waters also appears, and stories
are told at the hotels and express office about his

having been seen elsewhere in company with a
stunningly beautiful woman. The schoolmaster
then learns that Dr. Dusquene, the local physician, has evidence that M'liss has murdered her
own father.

Waters is eventually arrested—not for the
murder of Smith, but for the murder of the Reverend Mr. McSnagley—and is threatened with lynching, but M'liss, who visits him at the jail on the
night of his arrest, bringing him a bottle of
brandy, mysteriously frees him and in the process sets the town on fire. She then discovers that
he has gone mad, and he wanders off into the
mountains. On the night of McSnagley's murder,
the burning of the town, and the disappearance
of Waters, the schoolmaster visits the Smith claim
and discovers that what everyone has supposed
to be a pocket is actually a lode, studded with
huge nuggets. Although Waters (or someone) has
been secretly removing large quantities of ore, incalculable riches remain. The schoolmaster stakes
the claim out in M'liss's name and the next evening consults with Judge Plunkett, the town lawyer, about establishing the girl's ownership of the
mine. However, a "handsome woman" of undeter-
mined age is already there in Plunkett's parlor,
claiming to be M'liss's mother—the estranged but
undivorced wife of Bummer Smith's youth. She,
rather than M'liss, will presumably be the heiress.
She loses no time in staking her claim to young
schoolmaster Gray, as well, who finds himself wondering whether she has been an actress. With a
"very vivid disclosure of eyes and teeth," she
takes his arm and passes into the night.

Only four weeks later the town is well along
toward being rebuilt on a grander scale, as adventurers and developers pour in to take advantage
of the newly discovered wealth. M'liss has joined
the "handsome woman," who waits in town for
the settlement of her claim to the mine. The
girl's former boisterousness has been replaced by
what seems a guarded stoicism. Schoolmaster
Gray has decided to quit his job, gather his small
assets of some thirty dollars, and see the world.
On the morning of his departure, he first calls
on Clytie Morpher, who, still smitten, insists that
he accept from her a gift he must promise not to
open until his marriage. He then makes his way
to the quarters of M'liss and Mrs. Smith, where
he kisses M'liss goodbye. As Gray leaves town, Aris-
tides Morpher stops the stagecoach to deliver to
him a note from Mrs. Smith informing him that
her legal claim to the mine has been confirmed
and inviting him to visit her in San Francisco.

There have been two supposed murders–not counting a jailhouse guard killed in the fire M'liss set as she freed Waters. Neither murder is solved. Further, each of the fable's four roles has written into it a large measure of guilt. M'liss, the youthful innocent, is clearly not innocent at all–or, if she is, her innocence is catastrophic. Whether accidentally or not, she has killed the jailhouse guard and set fire to the town. Strands of her hair are found on the revolver that killed her father. Concerning McSnagley's murder, she tells schoolmaster Gray that the minister "ought to have been killed long ago." She may, indeed, have conspired with Waters and the "handsome woman" in *both* murders–perhaps to acquire the wealth and respectability she felt might make her more attractive to schoolmaster Gray. Gray, in his turn, cannot observe the events of the community without becoming involved with them. He neither quite succumbs to nor quite resists the charms of adoring Clytie Morpher, an "early bloomer." M'liss, with her "great dark eyes," her fierce passions, her secrets, and her promise of wealth, attracts him in more complicated ways. The "handsome woman," whose looks he cannot fathom, whose age he cannot guess, and whose identity he can never be sure of, affects him in ways that are more complicated still. It is suggested not only that she has been an actress, but that she is the same "stunner" who has been seen consorting with Waters. She may be mother, murderess, mistress, or redeemer–or she may be all of these. As the nexus of feminine sexuality she is both attractive and inscrutable, traits Harte often gave his female characters. The landscape shares these same traits. On one hand it seems to promise gratification of various kinds–from aesthetic enjoyment to treasure. On the other, it yields disfigurement and misery as shafts are sunk into Red Mountain and prospectors suffer agonies of speculation about the direction of "Smith's lead." The fable seems to demonstrate that all appearances are deceptive, all motives questionable, and all speculations fruitless.

Yet "M'liss" is no tale of irrational horror or psychological breakdown, although Harte had read the works of Edgar Allan Poe and admired especially "Ligeia"–which contains, in the title character and Lady Rowena, two women who resemble adult versions of M'liss and Clytie Morpher, respectively. It is told with charm, even gaiety, a characteristic of Harte's realism. Treating dark subjects in a light manner was a trick of frontier journalism that might, had Harte prac-

ticed it in his reports of the Humboldt Bay Indian massacre, have kept him his job on the *Northern Californian*. Harte's fiction had a tone of bantering nonchalance many San Franciscans found attractive, enjoying parodies of their own sentimentalism and chauvinism–as well as their numerous other gaucheries. Harte had a schoolboy's reckless talent for this kind of showing off–but one that was also attached to an adult intelligence. He soon attracted a following of distinguished admirers who involved him in a busy social life. Secession and the outbreak of the Civil War did not diminish his newfound popularity as a regional court jester who often told his jokes without announcing that they were funny and, just as often, shrouded his oracular pronouncements about history and humanity in a veil of farce or melodrama. He had a knack for stating his clear, ironic vision in prophetic terms.

Harte married Anna Griswold on 11 August 1862, just short of his twenty-sixth birthday. She was four years his senior and had been reared in New York City. When Harte met her, she was living with her married sister in San Francisco. Money was a problem for the newlyweds from the beginning. Harte had left his job as a printer for the *Golden Era* in 1861 and accepted the steadier but less exciting position of a clerk in the Surveyor General's office, where he earned $100 per month. He continued to contribute sketches, essays, and verse to the magazine and to participate in the city's increasingly active literary community–enlivened, now, by such people as Charles Warren Stoddard, Robert Newell (Orpheus C. Kerr), Albert Bierstadt, Charles Farrar Browne (Artemus Ward), and later, Samuel Clemens (Mark Twain)–but he was continually short of cash. In 1863, just before the birth of his first child, Griswold, he left the Surveyor General's office for a job in the U.S. Mint, which paid considerably more and required little work. In late 1864 he and Clemens became good friends. He also began having his work published in the *Californian*, a magazine started by Charles H. Webb, a former associate editor on the *Golden Era*. He took an active, if mostly informal, editorial role in the new magazine, leading, more or less directly, to his editorship in 1865 (the year his second child, Francis King Harte, was born) of *Outcroppings*, a volume of verse by California authors. Although the volume was not a success, assembling it probably put Harte in the mood for composing the fifteen "Condensed Novels" he published in the *Golden Era* and the *Californian* and then brought out as a book in 1867. These witty and perceptive parodies of novelists, such as Charles Dickens, Charlotte Brontë, James Fenimore Cooper, and T. S. Arthur, exhibit Harte's surprising skill as a critic and editor. His big break came the next year, in 1868, when he was appointed editor of the newly established *Overland Monthly*.

Anton Roman, the publisher, started the *Overland Monthly* as a regional magazine with national aspirations. He aimed to capture a large audience by emphasizing a positive and sympathetic approach to interests of California and the Pacific slope. Harte, on the other hand, envisioned a more literary magazine, one with less of a tilt toward the local boosterism Roman advocated. The go-between who brought Roman and Harte together on the project was Charles Warren Stoddard, a mutual friend. The first issue of the magazine, which appeared in July, gave little indication that the uneasy alliance of Harte and Roman would succeed, but the second issue, printed in August, carried "The Luck of Roaring Camp," now Harte's most widely acclaimed work and a major step in exploring the dark fable he had begun to compose eight years earlier, in 1860. "The Luck of Roaring Camp" surprised everybody, including the author. At a single stroke the story fulfilled the *Overland Monthly*'s aspirations for a national audience. It also brought Harte instant fame as a master storyteller. Some San Francisco readers were dubious at first—suspecting, perhaps, that the tale made fun of them—but the *Atlantic Monthly* wrote to Harte from Boston requesting a story like "The Luck of Roaring Camp" for its own pages as soon as possible. Some eastern critics even hailed Harte as an American Dickens, doubtless recalling for the thirty-one-year-old author that Dickens had been his model from the beginning.

"The Luck of Roaring Camp" takes place in 1850-1851 at an isolated mining settlement in the California foothills with the self-explanatory name of Roaring Camp. A prostitute known as Cherokee Sal, the camp's only female, dies in childbirth, much to the grief of the miners. But Sal's infant son survives, presenting the camp with an immediate and pressing problem. An impromptu town meeting is called after Sal's slapdash funeral, and the miners arrive at a consensus: they will contrive to somehow raise the child themselves, rather than sending him elsewhere or bringing in a female nursemaid. The child thrives, suckled on ass's milk. John Oakhurst, a dapper gambler, remarks one day that his birth has

"brought 'the luck' to Roaring Camp." The name sticks and is made official at a makeshift christening where a motherly miner named Stumpy announces that "I proclaim you Thomas Luck, according to the laws of the United States and the State of California, so help me God."

Like Cherokee Sal, the miners all bear names that tell something about them—Stumpy and Kentuck, for instance. Tommy thus goes by "The Luck." When the miners bring in a rosewood cradle from Sacramento, they discover that it makes the rest of their furniture—and the rest of the settlement—look crude. They therefore begin a program of general improvement, painting, repairing, and even planting flowers. They wear clean clothes and wash before meals. Profanity and vice are abandoned. The camp no longer roars. As stories about the transformation begin to circulate, mythic elements are added: "They've a street up there in 'Roaring' that would lay over any street in Red Dog. They've got vines and flowers round their houses, and they wash themselves twice a day. But they're mighty rough on strangers, and they worship an Ingin baby." The Luck survives a single "golden summer." The winter of 1851 brings snow to the mountains and torrential rains to the foothills. One night a flash flood inundates Roaring Camp and sweeps away the cabin where The Luck is sleeping. The miner known as Kentuck is found the next morning, barely alive, with The Luck in his arms. Ironically, however, the child is dead, and Kentuck dies as well, proclaiming, "he's a taking me with him. Tell the boys I've got The Luck with me now."

"The Luck of Roaring Camp" is strongly flavored with sentimentalism, but to account thus for its popularity does not do justice to either Harte or his reading public. The story is funny but not laughable, sad but not tearful, palatable but certainly not sweet. That Harte could use sentimentality without succumbing to it is a tribute to his finely calibrated skill. Examining the recurrence in "The Luck of Roaring Camp" of the four roles Harte first identified in "M'liss" shows not so much that he had begun to develop a successful formula for capturing the public imagination as it does that he had discovered a real subject which was worthy of extensive development. The youthful innocent in "The Luck of Roaring Camp" is of course Tommy Luck himself; the female principal is embodied in Cherokee Sal; the physical environment is still the California foothills. However, the ambivalent observer has shifted positions. No longer a character in the story, he has become the narrator who tells the story from the outside. The youthful innocent, the female, and the land are not parts of his direct experience, as they are for schoolmaster Gray in "M'liss," but elements in a story he has heard and which he relates. The difference is subtle but important. The Luck, Cherokee Sal, and Roaring Camp are one step further removed from conventional history than are M'liss, the putative Mrs. Smith, and Smith's Pocket. The story's emphasis is thus shifted away from the events which are said to have happened and toward the processes through which the story is told. The events in "The Luck of Roaring Camp" have relatively little importance, except as they are shown to have become legendary. With "The Luck of Roaring Camp" Harte's dark fable of the West became more fabulous and less historical, which is another way of saying that it came closer to addressing universal themes rather than personal or regional peculiarities. Harte was imprinting the fable with the stamp of his own brand of realism.

"The Outcasts of Poker Flat," published in the *Overland Monthly* for January 1869, some five months after the publication of "The Luck of Roaring Camp," carries forward the development of Harte's realism. Significantly, the mystery of luck again provides a major theme, and John Oakhurst, the gambler whose comment led to Tommy Luck's naming at Roaring Camp, makes a reappearance. The story opens on the morning of 23 November 1850–late in the fall that preceded Roaring Camp's catastrophic flood. Poker Flat, a more pretentious settlement than nearby Roaring Camp, has "lately suffered the loss of several thousand dollars, two valuable horses, and a prominent citizen." Although Oakhurst has not committed a crime, he is victimized by a local "spasm of virtuous reaction quite as lawless and ungovernable as any of the acts that had provoked it." Also caught in the spasm are three other "outcasts": a young prostitute known as The Duchess, an elder prostitute called Mother Shipton, and a profane drunk called Uncle Billy. The four are escorted to the edge of town and told by a member of the vigilance committee that if they return they will be killed.

Sandy Bar, the nearest settlement that might receive them, is a day's journey off, across a high mountain pass, but The Duchess tires by noon and dismounts, refusing to go any farther. Oakhurst protests that they have no food. Uncle Billy produces whiskey instead, and they make

an early camp. Meanwhile, they are joined by a pair of lovers on their way from Sandy Bar to Poker Flat. Young Tom Simson–whom Oakhurst has earlier made a "devoted slave" by returning to him money he lost in a poker game–is known as "'The Innocent' of Sandy Bar." The former waitress at a temperance restaurant with whom he is eloping to Poker Flat is a "stout, comely damsel of fifteen" named Piney Woods. Tom and Piney, who have a mule laden with provisions, sociably decide to join the camp for the night. Piney, says Tom, can sleep with "Mrs. Oakhurst" (The Duchess) and Mother Shipton in a ruined cabin he has discovered nearby. The lovers, who never think to inquire why Oakhurst and the others happen to be camped on the mountainside without provisions, seem to exert a benign influence on the outcasts–one much like the influence on The Luck of Roaring Camp–but Oakhurst awakens toward morning to find that a blizzard has begun and that Uncle Billy has stolen the mules and departed for Sandy Bar.

Innocence prevails, even in the face of terrible ill fortune. Oakhurst has hidden the cards and whiskey; The Duchess and Mother Shipton devote themselves to amusing Piney; Tom produces an old accordion. The evening of the second day is spent singing hymns around the blazing fire. The third day is successfully passed by telling stories–chiefly Alexander Pope's translation of the *Iliad* as remembered by Tom, who had read a copy not long before. However, food soon begins to run out, and the camp is increasingly hemmed in by snowdrifts. Late on the tenth night, Mother Shipton quietly dies, after revealing to Oakhurst that she has been starving herself for the benefit of the others. On the following day Oakhurst fashions a pair of snowshoes from an old pack saddle left behind by Uncle Billy and instructs Tom to go down the mountain to Poker Flat for help. As Tom and Piney part with a kiss, The Duchess anxiously asks Oakhurst whether he is leaving too. The gambler replies, "as far as the cañon," then suddenly kisses her with a passion that leaves her trembling. That night, the blizzard returns, but Oakhurst does not. Piney and The Duchess gradually weaken, die, and are covered over by the drifting snow, where rescuers later find them clasped in each other's arms. Oakhurst has not deserted–at least not in the manner of Uncle Billy. The rescue party finds him–also buried in the snow–at the edge of the canyon, "pulseless and cold, with a Derringer by his side and a bullet in his heart."

Harte in old age (Bret Harte Collection, #5310, courtesy of Clifton Waller Barret Library, Manuscripts Division, University of Virginia Library)

Pinned with a bowie knife to the trunk of a pine tree above his body is a deuce of clubs bearing his penciled inscription:

> Beneath This Tree
> Lies the Body
> of
> JOHN OAKHURST,
> Who Struck A Streak of Bad Luck
> On the 23D of November, 1850,
> And
> Handed In His Checks
> On The 7TH December, 1850

Clearly, there are significant differences between "The Outcasts of Poker Flat" and "The Luck of Roaring Camp," even though the two stories run parallel in some ways. The role of youthful innocent is played in the later story by Tom Simson and Piney Woods; that of the female principal is similarly shared by The Duchess and Mother Shipton. However, the role of the physical environment is considerably enlarged, and

that of the ambivalent observer is rendered both more diffuse and more self-conscious. Harte's realism tends to focus on relationships between the observer and the landscape.

Harte increased the landscape's importance by reducing its scope in "The Outcasts of Poker Flat." Nearly all the events of the story occur at the outcasts' camp on the mountainside—a severely limited scene in which prospect, refuge, and hazard are mingled: "The spot was singularly wild and impressive. A wooded amphitheater, surrounded on three sides by precipitous cliffs of naked granite, sloped gently toward the crest of another precipice that overlooked the valley." Described as "the most suitable spot for a camp, had camping been advisable," this locale offers the outcasts shelter from the blizzard. Yet it also traps them in the drifts of snow that eddy into the three-sided amphitheater from the summits of the upper cliffs. Similarly, it insulates them from hostile Poker Flat and also provides them with a clear view of the valley, where—seen from the "remote pinnacle of . . . rocky fastness"—the hypocritical town seems a "pastoral village." Finally, the environment's threat to life and its nurturing of the humane values of courage, wisdom, and love are curiously intertwined, even to the point of being indistinguishable from each other. Tom's recitations of Homer, Oakhurst's discourses on luck, Mother Shipton's sacrificial fasting, and the final embrace of The Duchess and Piney Woods are all direct consequences of the environment. Just as the "virgin breast" of appropriately named Piney Woods finally cradles the head of the "soiled" Duchess in death, the fatal landscape brings out the best in the flawed outcasts before also bringing about their destruction. "The Outcasts of Poker Flat" is Harte's most skillfully staged story—one in which the physical setting contributes importantly to the action.

It may also be his most carefully directed story—one in which a reader's point of view is carefully and effectively controlled. In the first sentence John Oakhurst is stepping into the street of Poker Flat in the morning, "conscious of a change in . . . moral atmosphere since the preceeding night." The last sentence finds him dead beneath his self-composed epitaph and calls him "at once the strongest and yet the weakest of the outcasts of Poker Flat." Throughout, Oakhurst seems the story's prescient center. While his companions are more or less consistently befuddled, he alone is said to be "aware," to "recognize," to "listen," and "look." When he is resurrected in later stor-

181

ies such as "The Poet of Sierra Flat," or "A Passage in the Life of Mr. John Oakhurst," he seems unrealistic. He is too exotic to be believable save in the spectacular surroundings and among the colorful companions of the outcast camp on the mountain. Although he unquestionably plays the role of ambivalent observer in "The Outcasts of Poker Flat," his bizarre perceptions and insights must be interpreted by an anonymous narrator–the one who glosses the gambler's cryptic epitaph. The paradox framed in this designation deftly sums up the governing mystery of Harte's dark fable of the West: whoever he may be, and wherever he turns his attention, the observer cannot discover any intelligible certainty. Because the face of the world is truly blank, the most a storyteller can hope for is to beguile his audience with some "new diversion" like Tom Simson's rendition of the *Iliad*–which, of course, is both new and old, another paradox. Harte's realism brings this paradox into view and examines it.

Charles Dickens, who read "The Outcasts of Poker Flat" in England, was deeply moved. But Harte's bleak theory of fiction and of life was perilous for Harte as editor of the *Overland Monthly*. Many of those whose manuscripts were rejected thought Harte's manner aloof, overbearing, and arrogant. Anton Roman found his initial plans for the magazine derailed by Harte's abrupt editorial style and by the colorful stories he peopled with attractive but unsavory characters. Both the editorial style and the stories brought attention to San Francisco and the Pacific slope, but not attention of the variety Roman had anticipated. He sold the magazine to John H. Carmany in 1869, before it was quite a year old. Meanwhile, Fields, Osgood and Company of Boston contracted with Harte to publish his early stories as a book which appeared in 1870 as *The Luck of Roaring Camp, and Other Sketches*. This was his first (and last) major collection of short fiction. September 1870 saw publication in the *Overland Monthly* of Harte's humorous dialect verse, "Plain Language from Truthful James," which caught on immediately, nearly everywhere. Popularly known as "The Heathen Chinee," this jingling account of how two white frontier card sharks are outwitted at euchre by a wily Chinese adversary was pirated, recited, quoted, dramatized, and set to music until it seemed that everyone in the country knew it by rote. Harte, who disliked the poem, was astonished. He should not have been. Its immediate and unpredictable popularity proved the theory

of uncertainty he had advanced in "The Outcasts of Poker Flat."

In January 1871, when Harte announced that he was resigning his post on the *Overland Monthly* and leaving San Francisco for the East, he was one of America's most famous writers, a condition to which he could not very well object, but also one with which he was not prepared to deal wisely. The *Atlantic Monthly* had offered him a lucrative one-year contract, which he soon accepted, just to write stories. Representatives of the *Lakeside Monthly*, a new journal being started in Chicago, pressed him with attractive offers to become the first editor. John Carmany proposed to double his salary if he would stay on with the *Overland Monthly* in San Francisco. Friends and admirers suddenly seemed to surround him, each promising some opportunity to which requirements were attached, and Harte–shy, bookish, and withdrawn, as ever–began almost at once to confuse and dismay his new supporters with the same brusque unpredictability of manner that had earned him the dislike of would-be contributors to the *Overland Monthly*. Negotiations with the *Lakeside Monthly* abruptly broke down when he failed to show up at a lavish luncheon in Chicago where the journal's publishers had planned to present him with a $14 thousand bonus in advance. He was slow in meeting his obligations to the *Atlantic Monthly*, and his contract was not renewed after the first year. When he and his family were houseguests of William Dean Howells in Boston for a week, before moving into a country place called The Willows at Morristown, New Jersey, he affected a totally uncharacteristic breeziness that managed to offend such luminaries as Ralph Waldo Emerson, Henry Wadsworth Longfellow, Oliver Wendell Holmes, and Richard Henry Dana. Howells remained unflappable, later declaring that Harte was one of the most charming personalities he had ever met.

For whatever reasons, Harte's output for the *Atlantic Monthly* fell considerably below the standard set by his earlier work for the *Golden Era* and the *Overland Monthly*. Late in 1872 chronic money problems forced him to embark on a lecture tour that took him down the eastern seaboard to Washington, across the American Midwest, and into Canada. Predictably, he found the experience exhausting, depressing, and less rewarding than he had hoped, but he undertook a similar tour the following year, in the fall and winter of 1873-1874, this time into the American South. Collections of his poems and sketches now

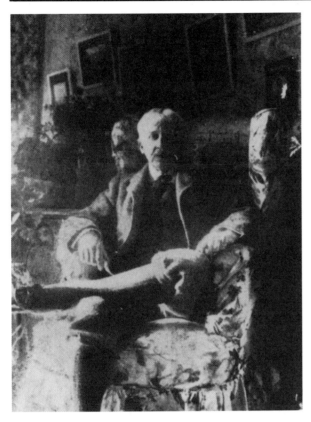

Last photograph of Harte, taken a few months before his death in 1902

appeared often but were not distinguished. Between the two lecture tours he began his first novel, *Gabriel Conroy*, which would be published as a book in 1876, after serialization in *Scribner's* magazine. In many ways this curious work resembles an expanded version of "M'liss," complete with innocence, sex, violence, and the premise of vast wealth, but it is "M'liss" rehashed and warmed over, lacking the vitality and precision that characterized Harte's earlier explorations of his fable of the West in tales such as "The Luck of Roaring Camp" and "The Outcasts of Poker Flat." Criticism of the novel was mostly unfavorable, and–even though it sold moderately well– the royalties were not enough to extricate Harte from his financial difficulties. What had been hailed as new only seven years earlier, when "The Luck of Roaring Camp" appeared in the *Overland Monthly*, had become old hat.

Yet Harte, far from old at the age of forty and with a family to support, could not afford to stop writing. He had fathered two more children– Jessamy, born in 1873, and Ethel, born in 1875. Since he had been fascinated with the theater since childhood, it was perhaps natural that he

should turn to writing plays. *Two Men of Sandy Bar*, his first effort, opened at New York in May 1876 to a mixed, but mostly favorable, audience response. Critics, however, were quick to attack Harte for having the temerity to palm himself off on the public as a playwright. *Ah Sin*, a second play, written in collaboration with Samuel Langhorne Clemens, opened in July 1877. Critics were generally somewhat kinder–probably because of Clemens's part in the project–but the play fell short of real success. It also brought to an end the friendship between Clemens and Harte. Neither man ever revealed the cause of the falling out, but it probably had something to do with Harte's cavalier attitudes toward money, women, and society. Ironically, these attitudes were much like the one Clemens had celebrated in *Roughing It* (1872), but Clemens had become respectable while Harte remained as boyishly irresponsible as ever. Which of the two former friends remained truer to his own version is problematical, but Clemens kept his place as America's literary spokesman while Harte came to resemble the outcasts he had written about in 1869. The mass culture of the Gilded Age, with its casual morality, its technology, its gaudy, shifting enthusiasms, and its taste for new diversions was closing in on the thoughtful, serious clown who had nearly twenty years before begun to publish his observations in San Francisco's *Golden Era*.

When prospective arrangements for him to coedit a new Washington magazine to be called the *Capitol* broke down in 1878, Harte sought and obtained from the Hayes administration an appointment as U.S. Consul at Crefeld, in Germany. After a brief visit with his family at Morristown he sailed on 28 June never to return to the United States again. Anna Harte, with whom his relationship had been strained for some time, remained in Morristown. Harte would continue to write her letters, and to send money, but he would not see his wife again until she arrived at London, unbidden, in 1898. Meanwhile, he disliked Crefeld and spent as little time there as he could manage, making trips to Switzerland and England. London, he found, was more hospitable and less fickle than San Francisco or New York. He managed to be transferred to Scotland in April 1880, where he was assigned the consulate at Glasgow, a post he held until 1885 when Grover Cleveland, a Democrat, ordered his dismissal. He circulated freely in literary circles, creating something of a scandal by his relations with

Marguerite Van de Veldes, the wife of a Belgian diplomat and the mother of nine children. When he lost his consulship in 1885, he elected to stay in England, where he wrote steadily and voluminously, on a free-lance basis, until his death from cancer of the throat on 5 May 1902.

Harte's career as a writer spans a full forty-two years, but his status as a major American realist depends upon the work he completed before leaving San Francisco in 1871. Harte had not exhausted his subject matter. Most of the stories he wrote in England after 1885 concern deserts and mountains, frontiersmen, and bittersweet human relationships–all much like those in the stories he wrote at San Francisco before 1871. Nor had readers lost interest in him. The audience for his later works, especially in England, was steadier and more affectionate than the American Easterners who had earlier received works like "The Luck of Roaring Camp" with surprised excitement. The problem is in Harte's own reluctance to probe the depths of his vision as Clemens and Howells did. He merely rearranged the parts of his initial vision in different combinations. In *The Crusade of the Excelsior* (1887), for instance, contemporary middle-class Americans stranded in a remote Mexican settlement must deal with frontier conditions resembling those of Poker Flat and Sandy Bar. Similarly, Jack Hamlin, Colonel Starbottle, John Oakhurst, and other characters from the early tales, turn up repeatedly in later works–usually unchanged. While Harte's later works satisfied the tastes of readers who liked knowing what to expect, they neither invite nor bear sustained critical attention.

The early works, however, are quite another matter, because they show–in deft, quick strokes–what Harte's realism is about and how it works. Here are no siftings and winnowings of fact to find some kernel of precious speculation about "truth." Here are no moralizings, ironic or otherwise. Above all, here are no attempted explanations. Here, rather, is an array of opaque surfaces arranged to show (rather than tell) the relationships among planes of experience–Mother Shipton's obscurely motivated sacrifice of herself, John Oakhurst's ambivalent suicide, Tom Simson's dubious rendition of the *Iliad*. Harte's greatest achievement was not to indicate how communication among such people might be possible, but to demonstrate that it actually occurs. He did so not by establishing and examining philosophical principles, but by building into his works figurations which paralleled the experience of his

readers. For Harte's realism–founded so much more thoroughly in the vernacular and the current than that of Clemens, Howells, or his other contemporaries–to have remained viable and attractive for as long as it has is itself a delightful and instructive surprise.

Letters:

The Letters of Bret Harte, edited by Geoffrey Harte (Boston & New York: Houghton Mifflin, 1926).

Contains letters written by Harte from 1866 to his death in 1902, both while he lived in the United States and during his residence in Europe, and additional material by Harte's grandson, including an often inaccurate biographical sketch which offers a sentimental, grandiose view of Harte's life and work.

Bibliography:

Joseph Gaer, ed., *Bret Harte: Bibliography and Biographical Data* (N.p., 1935; New York: Burt Franklin, 1968).

An extensive listing of Harte's writings, presented chronologically and categorized by genre, with an accurate biographical sketch and twelve critical essays.

Biographies:

Henry W. Boynton, *Bret Harte* (New York: McClure, Phillips, 1903).

A critical biography that deals chiefly with Harte's years in California; downplays the value of the majority of Harte's work but acknowledges his power, in stories such as "The Luck of Roaring Camp" and "The Outcasts of Poker Flat," to capture the humanity and spirit of his California characters.

Henry Childs Merwin, *The Life of Bret Harte* (Boston & New York: Houghton, Mifflin, 1911).

Contains, as the subtitle *With Some Account of the California Pioneers* suggests, anecdotes and records to show that Harte may have copied his characters from life; extols Harte's genius as a writer but focuses more on San Francisco during Harte's time than on the writer's life.

George R. Stewart, Jr., *Bret Harte: Argonaut and Exile* (Boston & New York: Houghton Mifflin, 1931).

An objective, scholarly biography that focuses almost entirely on Harte's life, with little reference to his skill as a writer.

Richard O'Connor, *Bret Harte: A Biography* (Boston & Toronto: Little, Brown, 1966).
A popular biography made up mostly of anecdotes and gossip concerning Harte's relationship with his contemporaries and his family.

References:

Linda D. Barnett, *Bret Harte: A Reference Guide* (Boston: G. K. Hall, 1980).
A comprehensive chronological bibliography, subdivided into "Books" and "Shorter Writings," of all writings about Bret Harte from 1865 to 1975; features annotated entries and an author-title-subject index for convenience.

Margaret Duckett, *Mark Twain and Bret Harte* (Norman: University of Oklahoma Press, 1964).
A documentary account of the formation and failure of the friendship between Harte and Mark Twain in which Duckett investigates all leads about the final bitter estrangement between the two men in 1878, relates biographical information about both, indulges in conjecture about the character of each, and finally sides with Harte in the dispute.

Patrick D. Morrow, *Bret Harte Literary Critic* (Bowl-ing Green, Ohio: Bowling Green University Popular Press, 1979).
Asserts that greater appreciation of Harte's fiction may be gained by understanding his theories of literary criticism and traces Harte's development and decline as a writer in an attempt to establish him as a transitional figure between romance and realism in American fiction; includes excerpts from Harte's reviews and letters as well as a bibliography of his uncollected critical writing.

Arthur H. Quinn, "Bret Harte and the Moral Contrast," in *American Fiction* (New York: Appleton-Century, 1936).
Explores Harte's ironic juxtaposition of innocence and cynicism in his characters and insists that, despite the inferiority of Harte's later work, had he not been so great an artist Harte would not have been so widely maligned in his decline and that the work that broke him would have enhanced the career of a lesser artist.

Franklin Walker, *San Francisco's Literary Frontier* (New York: Knopf, 1939).
Detailed study of the growth of San Francisco as a literary center between 1850 and 1870, including a general but accurate biography of Harte covering his career as a journalist, his relationships with Charles Warren Stoddard and Ina Coolbrith, his editorship at *Overland Monthly*, and his life in the city.

William Dean Howells

This entry was updated by James Woodress (University of California, Davis) from his entry in DLB 12, American Realists and Naturalists.

Places	Boston Venice and Florence, Italy	New York City Rural New England	Ashtabula and Columbus, Ohio
Influences and Relationships	Heinrich Heine Leo Tolstoy Carlo Goldoni	Miguel de Cervantes Jane Austen Ivan Turgenev	Henry Wadsworth Longfellow Henry James
Literary Movements and Forms	Realism	Antiromanticism	Antisentimentalism
Major Themes	East vs. West Ethics in Business	Europe vs. America Social Justice	Faith vs. Skepticism Egocentrism
Cultural and Artistic Influences	Pragmatism	Foreign Travel	Psychology
Social and Economic Influences	Industrialization Poverty Urbanization	Labor vs. Capital Unequal Distribution of Wealth	Social Climbing Christian Socialism

See also the Howells entry in DLB 64, American Literary Critics and Scholars, 1850-1880.

BIRTH: Martins Ferry, Ohio, 1 March 1837 to William Cooper and Mary Dean Howells.

MARRIAGE: 24 December 1862 to Elinor Gertrude Mead; children: Winifred, John Mead, Mildred.

AWARDS AND HONORS: Honorary M.A., Harvard University, 1867; Litt.D., Yale University, 1901; Litt.D., Oxford University, 1904; Litt.D., Columbia University, 1905; Litt.D., Princeton University, 1912; Academy of Arts and Letters Gold Medal for fiction, 1915.

DEATH: New York, New York, 11 May 1920.

SELECTED BOOKS: *Poems of Two Friends,* by Howells and John J. Piatt (Columbus: Follett, Foster, 1860);
Lives and Speeches of Abraham Lincoln and Hannibal Hamlin, life of Lincoln by Howells and life of Hamlin by J. L. Hayes (Columbus: Follett, Foster, 1860);
Venetian Life (London: Trübner, 1866; New York: Hurd & Houghton, 1866; expanded, New York: Hurd & Houghton, 1867; London: Trübner, 1867; expanded again, Boston: Osgood, 1872; revised and expanded again, Boston & New York: Houghton, Mifflin, 1907; London: Constable, 1907);
Italian Journeys (New York: Hurd & Houghton, 1867; London: Low, 1868; enlarged, Boston: Osgood, 1872; revised, London: Heinemann, 1901; Boston & New York: Houghton, Mifflin, 1901);
No Love Lost, A Romance of Travel (New York: Putnam's, 1869);
Suburban Sketches (New York: Hurd & Houghton, 1871; London: Low, 1871; enlarged, Boston: Osgood, 1872);
Their Wedding Journey (Boston: Osgood, 1872; Edinburgh: Douglas, 1882);
A Chance Acquaintance (Boston: Osgood, 1873; Edinburgh: Douglas, 1882);
Poems (Boston: Osgood, 1873; enlarged, Boston: Ticknor, 1886);
A Foregone Conclusion (Boston: Osgood, 1874; London: Low, 1874);
Sketch of the Life and Character of Rutherford B. Hayes . . . also a Biographical Sketch of William

William Dean Howells

A. Wheeler (New York: Hurd & Houghton/ Boston: Houghton, 1876);
The Parlor Car. Farce (Boston: Osgood, 1876);
Out of the Question. A Comedy (Boston: Osgood, 1877; Edinburgh: Douglas, 1882);
A Counterfeit Presentment. Comedy (Boston: Osgood, 1877);
The Lady of the Aroostook (Boston: Houghton, Osgood, 1879; Edinburgh: Douglas, 1882);
The Undiscovered Country (Boston: Houghton, Mifflin, 1880; London: Low, 1880);
A Fearful Responsibility and Other Stories (Boston: Osgood, 1881); republished as *A Fearful Responsibility and "Tonelli's Marriage"* (Edinburgh: Douglas, 1882);
Dr. Breen's Practice, A Novel (Boston: Osgood, 1881; London: Trübner, 1881);
A Modern Instance, A Novel (1 volume, Boston: Osgood, 1882; 2 volumes, Edinburgh: Douglas, 1882);
The Sleeping Car, A Farce (Boston: Osgood, 1883);
A Woman's Reason, A Novel (Boston: Osgood,

1883; Edinburgh: Douglas, 1883);

A Little Girl Among the Old Masters (Boston: Osgood, 1884);

The Register, Farce (Boston: Osgood, 1884);

Three Villages (Boston: Osgood, 1884);

The Elevator, Farce (Boston: Osgood, 1885);

The Rise of Silas Lapham (1 volume, Boston: Ticknor, 1885; 2 volumes, Edinburgh: Douglas, 1894);

Tuscan Cities (Boston: Ticknor, 1886; Edinburgh: Douglas, 1886);

The Garroters, Farce (New York: Harper, 1886; Edinburgh: Douglas, 1887);

Indian Summer (Boston: Ticknor, 1886; Edinburgh: Douglas, 1886);

The Minister's Charge, or, The Apprenticeship of Lemuel Barker (Edinburgh: Douglas, 1886; Boston: Ticknor, 1887);

Modern Italian Poets, Essays and Versions (New York: Harper, 1887; Edinburgh: Douglas, 1887);

April Hopes, A Novel (Edinburgh: Douglas, 1887; New York: Harper, 1888);

A Sea-Change, or Love's Stowaway: A Lyricated Farce in Two Acts and an Epilogue (Boston: Ticknor, 1888; London: Trübner, 1888);

Annie Kilburn, A Novel (Edinburgh: Douglas, 1888; New York: Harper, 1889);

The Mouse-Trap and Other Farces (New York: Harper, 1889; Edinburgh: Douglas, 1897);

A Hazard of New Fortunes (2 volumes, Edinburgh: Douglas, 1889; 1 volume, New York: Harper, 1890);

The Shadow of a Dream, A Novel (Edinburgh: Douglas, 1890; New York: Harper, 1890);

A Boy's Town Described for "Harper's Young People" (New York: Harper, 1890);

Criticism and Fiction (New York: Harper, 1891; London: Osgood, McIlvaine, 1891);

The Albany Depot, Farce (New York: Harper, 1891; Edinburgh: Douglas, 1897);

An Imperative Duty, A Novel (New York: Harper, 1891; Edinburgh: Douglas, 1891);

Mercy, A Novel (Edinburgh: Douglas, 1892); republished as *The Quality of Mercy* (New York: Harper, 1892);

A Letter of Introduction, Farce (New York: Harper, 1892; Edinburgh: Douglas, 1897);

A Little Swiss Sojourn (New York: Harper, 1892);

Christmas Every Day and Other Stories Told for Children (New York: Harper, 1893);

The World of Chance, A Novel (Edinburgh: Douglas, 1893; New York: Harper, 1893);

The Unexpected Guests, A Farce (New York: Harper,

1893; Edinburgh: Douglas, 1897);

My Year in a Log Cabin (New York: Harper, 1893);

Evening Dress, Farce (New York: Harper, 1893; Edinburgh: Douglas, 1893);

The Coast of Bohemia, A Novel (New York: Harper, 1893; New York & London: Harper, 1899);

A Traveler from Altruria, Romance (New York: Harper, 1894; Edinburgh: Douglas, 1894);

My Literary Passions (New York: Harper, 1895);

Stops of Various Quills (New York: Harper, 1895);

The Day of Their Wedding, A Novel (New York: Harper, 1896); republished in *Idyls in Drab* (Edinburgh: Douglas, 1896);

A Parting and a Meeting, Story (New York: Harper, 1896); republished in *Idyls in Drab*;

Impressions and Experiences (New York: Harper, 1896; Edinburgh: Douglas, 1896);

A Previous Engagement, Comedy (New York: Harper, 1897);

The Landlord at Lion's Head (Edinburgh: Douglas, 1897; New York: Harper, 1897);

An Open-Eyed Conspiracy, An Idyl of Saratoga (New York & London: Harper, 1897; Edinburgh: Douglas, 1897);

Stories of Ohio (New York, Cincinnati & Chicago: American Book Company, 1897);

The Story of a Play, A Novel (New York & London: Harper, 1898);

Ragged Lady, A Novel (New York & London: Harper, 1899);

Their Silver Wedding Journey, 2 volumes (New York & London: Harper, 1899);

Bride Roses, A Scene (Boston & New York: Houghton, Mifflin, 1900);

Room Forty-Five, A Farce (Boston & New York: Houghton, Mifflin, 1900);

An Indian Giver, A Comedy (Boston & New York: Houghton, Mifflin, 1900);

The Smoking Car, A Farce (Boston & New York: Houghton, Mifflin, 1900);

Literary Friends and Acquaintance, A Personal Retrospect of American Authorship (New York & London: Harper, 1900);

A Pair of Patient Lovers (New York & London: Harper, 1901);

Heroines of Fiction, 2 volumes (New York & London: Harper, 1901);

The Kentons, A Novel (New York & London: Harper, 1902);

The Flight of Pony Baker, A Boy's Town Story (New York & London: Harper, 1902);

Literature and Life (New York & London: Harper, 1902);

Questionable Shapes (New York & London: Harper, 1903);

Letters Home (New York & London: Harper, 1903);

The Son of Royal Langbrith, A Novel (New York & London: Harper, 1904);

Miss Bellard's Inspiration, A Novel (New York & London: Harper, 1905);

London Films (New York & London: Harper, 1905);

Certain Delightful English Towns With Glimpses of the Pleasant Country Between (New York & London: Harper, 1906);

Through the Eye of the Needle, A Romance (New York & London: Harper, 1907);

Between the Dark and the Daylight, Romances (New York: Harper, 1907; London: Harper, 1912);

Fennel and Rue, A Novel (New York & London: Harper, 1908);

Roman Holidays and Others (New York & London: Harper, 1908);

The Mother and the Father, Dramatic Passages (New York & London: Harper, 1909);

Seven English Cities (New York & London: Harper, 1909);

My Mark Twain, Reminiscences and Criticisms (New York & London: Harper, 1910);

Imaginary Interviews (New York & London: Harper, 1910);

Parting Friends, A Farce (New York & London: Harper, 1911);

New Leaf Mills, A Chronicle (New York & London: Harper, 1913);

Familiar Spanish Travels (New York & London: Harper, 1913);

The Seen and Unseen at Stratford-On-Avon, A Fantasy (New York & London: Harper, 1914);

The Daughter of the Storage and Other Things in Prose and Verse (New York & London: Harper, 1916);

The Leatherwood God (New York: Century, 1916; London: Jenkins, 1917);

Years of My Youth (New York & London: Harper, 1916);

The Vacation of the Kelwyns, An Idyl of the Middle Eighteen-Seventies (New York & London: Harper, 1920);

Mrs. Farrell, A Novel (New York & London: Harper, 1921);

Prefaces to Contemporaries (1882-1920), edited by George Arms, William M. Gibson, and Frederic C. Marston, Jr. (Gainesville, Fla.: Scholars' Facsimiles & Reprints, 1957);

Criticism and Fiction and Other Essays, edited by Clara Marburg Kirk and Rudolf Kirk (New York: New York University Press, 1959);

The Complete Plays of W. D. Howells, edited by Walter J. Meserve (New York: New York University Press, 1960);

W. D. Howells as Critic, edited by Edwin H. Cady (London & Boston: Routledge, 1973);

Editor's Study: A Comprehensive Edition of W. D. Howells' Column (Troy, N.Y.: Whitson, 1983).

Collection: *A Selected Edition of W. D. Howells*, edited by Edwin H. Cady, Ronald Gottesman, Don L. Cook, and David Nordloh, 22 volumes (Bloomington: Indiana University Press, 1968-1976; Boston: Twayne, 1979-1983).

OTHER: "Novel-Writing and Novel-Reading, an Impersonal Explanation," in *Howells and James: A Double Billing*, edited by William M. Gibson and Leon Edel (New York: New York Public Library, 1958).

William Dean Howells, whose literary career began on the eve of the Civil War and ended after World War I, is one of the three most important American writers of the late nineteenth century. Samuel Langhorne Clemens and Henry James, both of whom were his close friends, may be said to rank higher in the critical esteem of the 1980s, but Howells in his own day was generally regarded as the leading American man of letters. When the magazine *Literature* in 1899 asked its readers to name the ten writers most worthy to become members of an American Academy, Howells's name headed the list. He later was one of the original seven elected to the American Academy of Arts and Letters when it was founded in 1904, and he served as its president from 1908 until his death twelve years later. In 1912 President William Howard Taft, a fellow Ohioan, who attended Howells's seventy-fifth birthday dinner, remarked: "I have traveled from Washington to New York to do honor to the greatest living American writer and novelist." Howells himself, however, assessed his accomplishments more modestly and once wondered in a letter to Clemens if he would not be remembered chiefly because he had been Clemens's friend.

Though his reputation today is neither as high as it was in 1900 nor as low as it fell in the 1920s, it rests solidly on his undeniable merits as a prolific, versatile, and influential author during half a century of American literary life. He not only wrote forty-three novels and story collections, of which a handful have won a permanent place in American letters, but he also was an important editor, critic, and literary arbiter for two generations. Although he was a self-educated midwesterner, he slipped effortlessly into the cultural life of literary Boston, where as editor of the *Atlantic Monthly* he forged a link between the older writers of New England's flowering and his post-Civil War contemporaries. Later, as occupant of the "Editor's Study" and the "Editor's Easy Chair" columns in *Harper's Weekly*, he vigorously promulgated his theories of literary realism and helped shape the course of American literature. He also influenced the taste of a generation of readers by introducing them to little-known foreign authors, and he helped some of the younger generation of writers, such as Hamlin Garland and Stephen Crane, launch their own careers. He wrote a large number of plays in addition to his fiction, about ten travel books, several collections of poetry, several volumes of autobiographies, campaign biographies of two presidents, and about a dozen volumes of literary reminiscence, sketches, and collected essays.

Inevitably, such a vast torrent of writing contained much that was ephemeral, and inevitably its author invited attacks against his commanding position in American letters. Howells had to write steadily throughout his career to make a living in those decades after the Civil War when professional authorship was just becoming possible. Nevertheless, there is integrity, style, and craftsmanship in all his writing, though he rose only sometimes to the highest levels of creative imagination. The denigration of his work in the years after his death is more a commentary on the times and his achievements than an objective appraisal of his career. The battles that he had fought for realism as a young man had long since been won by the time he became an octogenarian and the bête noire of the young Turks.

Howells's chief importance today lies in his leading role as theoretician and practitioner in the movement toward literary realism. Early in his career he committed himself to the cause of realism, which he defined simply as "the truthful treatment of material," and throughout his career he practiced and preached this doctrine. His best works, novels such as *A Modern Instance* (1882), *The Rise of Silas Lapham* (1885), *Indian Summer* (1886), and *A Hazard of New Fortunes* (1889), exemplify his principles and achieve remarkable verisimilitude in their depiction of character and setting. From reading Howells one gets a real sense of what people thought, felt, and did in the late nineteenth century, for his effects are

Howells in Columbus, Ohio, circa 1860

achieved by a careful attention to ample, accurate detail and reasonable motivations. Let fiction "portray men and women as they are," argued Howells; "Let it leave off painting dolls and working them by springs and wires; . . . let it not put on fine literary airs; let it speak the dialect, the language, that most Americans know."

Howells's realism, however, does not embrace an amoral attitude toward its material, as does naturalism, its later progeny. If the object of a novel is "to charm through a faithful representation of human actions and human passions," wrote Howells, the effect can never be solely an aesthetic experience. "Morality penetrates all things, it is the soul of all things." Beauty clothing false morality will corrupt rather than edify: "We cannot escape from this; we are shut up to it by the very conditions of our being." Thus Howells felt a responsibility toward his readers that twentieth-century novelists seldom feel, but the didacticism in his fiction is always subtle, and one does not close a Howells novel feeling that he has listened to a sermon. Howells has a clear vision of the joys and sorrows, the triumphs and trage-dies of life and does not gloss over human imper-fections or avoid painful situations.

There is not, however, the tragic vision of Fyodor Dostoyevski in his work, for his theories re-quired representation of typical American life. In commenting on *Crime and Punishment* (1866), he wrote that American novelists "concern them-selves with the more smiling aspects of life" be-cause "whatever their deserts, very few American novelists have been led out to be shot, or finally ex-iled to the rigors of a winter at Duluth." In a land where "journeymen carpenters and plumb-ers strike for four dollars a day," Howells also wrote, "the sum of hunger and cold is compara-tively small." But he began to have doubts, and when he edited this statement from an 1886 *Harp-er's Weekly* column to include it in *Criticism and Fic-tion* (1891), he added to the opinion that "the wrong from class to class has been almost inappre-ciable" in the United States the conclusion, "though all this is changing for the worse." His so-cial conscience in the late 1880s was profoundly aroused by economic events and the increasingly sharp confrontations between labor and capital. The result of these events and concomitant read-ing of Leo Tolstoy was doubt in the fulfillment of the American promise, a darker note in his fic-tion, and a belief that the salvation of America lay in a kind of Christian socialism.

Howells believed also that the course of liter-ary history was moving toward realism and away from earlier artificial forms. At the beginning of the nineteenth century, Howells said, romanti-cism had to fight its way free from neoclassicism in order to "widen the bounds of sympathy, to level every barrier against aesthetic freedom." Ro-manticism exhausted itself in this struggle, and it remained for realism to "assert that fidelity to ex-perience and probability of motive are essential conditions of a great imaginative literature."

In addition he thought that for the realist nothing in life is insignificant, nothing unworthy of notice. But one has to point out that Howells was a product of the Victorian Age with its ta-boos and delicacies, and he neither could nor would treat sex with the candor allowed the twentieth-century novelist. In fact, he believed that since the novel had been developed in the eighteenth century, its morals had improved along with society's so that both were less inde-cent than they once were. This is not to say that Howells was unaware of man's sexual nature and avoided it. He did not, but one has to read be-

tween the lines. What he could not do himself, however, he defended in others if they were seri-ous writers. Emile Zola's novels, for example, he would not let his daughters read, but he de-fended Zola's art because he saw the Frenchman as a serious moralist.

For Howells there were three ways to repre-sent life in fiction: the novel, the romance, and the romanticistic novel. The novel was the su-preme form of fiction and was represented in work like Jane Austen's *Pride and Prejudice* (1813) or Tolstoy's *Anna Karenina* (1873-1876). The ro-mance, he thought, dealt with life allegorically, in terms of types and ideals, and Nathaniel Hawthorne's novels represented this kind of art. It should be judged as poems are judged and not by the rules that apply to novels. The ro-manticistic novel was a form he deplored because its motives were false. It reveled in the extrava-gant, the extreme, the bizarre and sought effect rather than truth. Charles Dickens and Victor Hugo were practitioners of this kind of novel.

In narrative structure Howells's novels usu-ally take what he called the historical form, which he thought was the greatest way to create fic-tion. By this form he meant a novel written as if it were history. Here the novelist enters into the lives and minds of his characters. As omniscient narrator, he invents speeches for them, gives them their innermost thoughts and desires, and has their confidence in hours of passion or re-morse or even of death. Howells also thought there were two other possible forms for the novel, the first-person narrative point of view, which he believed too narrow in its range and avoided, and the third-person limited, biographi-cal perspective, in which the author's central fig-ure reflects all the facts and feelings involved. This form too he felt was cramping and did not use, though he thought that James was achieving remarkable success with it.

Howells was born in Martins Ferry, Ohio, and spent all of his boyhood in Ohio. His pater-nal ancestors were Welsh and his mother's people Pennsylvania German and Irish. His middle name was the maiden name of his mother, Mary Dean. His grandfather Howells had emigrated from Wales when his father was an infant and after moving about restlessly finally had settled in Hamilton, Ohio, gone into the drug and book business, and become an abolitionist. Howells's fa-ther was a printer and small-town newspaper edi-tor in Hamilton where the family lived from William Dean's third to twelfth year. These were the happy days of his childhood, which he recounts engagingly in *A Boy's Town* (1890), but they did not last, for William Cooper Howells plunged into debt in an unsuccessful effort to become a daily newspaper publisher in Dayton. Formal schooling ended for Howells when this adventure began, for both William Dean and his older brother Joseph had to work cruel hours on the paper. "Until eleven o'clock I helped put the telegraphic dispatches . . . into type and between four and five o'clock in the morning I was up and carrying papers to our subscribers," Howells recalled in *Years of My Youth* (1916). There was a large family to support, seven children in all, four boys and three girls.

The printing shop became Howells's schoolroom, as it also was for Clemens in Missouri and had been earlier for Walt Whitman and Benjamin Franklin. As an adult, Howells could remember when he could not read, but he could not remember when he could not set type. By the time he was ten he was a competent typesetter, and he did not write his first attempt at literature but first set it in type and printed it himself. His father was a cultivated man who owned books and delighted in reading aloud to the family. Howells recalled in *My Literary Passions* (1895) that his home held more books than any other house in town, and while many of the books were devoted to theology (William Cooper Howells was an ardent follower of Swedenborg), there were many volumes of poetry: Lord Byron, Robert Burns, Thomas Moore, Sir Walter Scott, Alexander Pope. But he soon developed an interest in prose and discovered on his own the works of Oliver Goldsmith, Miguel de Cervantes, and Washington Irving. *Don Quixote* (1605, 1615) became the favorite book of his childhood.

The vicissitudes of the Howells family next took them to the countryside where William Cooper Howells tried to become a miller on the Little Miami River near Xenia. Life in the country was good for the children, but after a year of wasted effort Howells's father became a clerk for the Ohio legislature, and William Dean set type on the *Ohio State Journal*, the paper for which he later became reporter, news editor, and editorial writer. When he was fifteen the family moved again, this time for good, to Ashtabula County between Cleveland and Buffalo, and the elder Howells began publishing the *Sentinel*. William Dean Howells's literary career begins at this time with the appearance of his first known publication, a poem printed in the *Journal* on 23 March 1852.

It begins: "Old winter, loose thy hold on us/And let the Spring come forth," conventional newspaper verse, of course, reflecting the romantic poetry he had absorbed, but not bad for a fifteen-year-old. During the next four years he had more poems published and tried his hand at fiction, using mostly the family paper as his medium, but his real job was as printer.

His move to Columbus in 1857 marks his graduation from the compositor's table to journalism. He lived in the Ohio capital, then a city of twelve thousand, corresponded with the *Cincinnati Gazette*, wrote for the *Journal*, contributed occasionally to the *Sentinel*, the *Ohio Farmer*, and the *National Era*, and read omnivorously far into the night. He already had taught himself Spanish, and now he added German so that he could translate Heinrich Heine, a poet "who dominated me longer than any one author that I have known." His interest in the nineteenth-century romantics, which also included a passion for Henry Wadsworth Longfellow, fueled his impulse to write verse. The result was his first book publication, *Poems of Two Friends* (1860), a collaboration with his friend John J. Piatt, in which he included thirty-two poems reflecting the influences of his literary idols.

By this time Howells was aspiring to a literary career. As he remembered in *Literary Friends and Acquaintance* (1900), "I was a poet, with no wish to be anything else." He was contributing to the *New York Saturday Press*, a weekly organ of literary bohemia, and in the same year that his book of poems came out James Russell Lowell, editor of the *Atlantic Monthly*, had accepted four of his verses. This was an exciting event for a young man from the provinces where "the literary theories we accepted were New England theories, the criticism we valued was New England criticism." The *Atlantic Monthly* was the authentic voice of Boston, the literary center of New England. But Howells's verse was so derivative of his models that Lowell had kept his first contribution a long time before acknowledging it in order to make sure it was not a translation. Later he told Howells, "You must sweat the Heine out of you as men do mercury."

The chance to make a literary pilgrimage to Boston came later that year when Howells wrote a campaign biography of Abraham Lincoln and used the money he made from it to finance his journey. The visit was memorable in every way, for Lowell treated him as a young writer of promise whom he had discovered. He arranged a dinner for him at the Parker House, to which he invited James T. Fields and Oliver Wendell Holmes, and during the dinner the witty Dr. Holmes leaned over toward his host and said: "Well, James, this is something like the apostolic succession; this is the laying on of hands." It was a prophetic remark, but the succession did not take place for another six years. Meantime, Howells had to return to Ohio, but before he left Boston Lowell gave him a letter to Nathaniel Hawthorne, and Hawthorne passed him on to Ralph Waldo Emerson. He also looked up Henry David Thoreau while he was in Concord; then he headed for New York and home, but his stop-off in New York was anticlimactic, for the bohemian editors of the *Saturday Press* repelled him, and he was not much impressed with Walt Whitman, whom he met in Pfaff's beer cellar.

When the Civil War began Howells felt no urge to join the Ohio volunteers. Instead he used his campaign biography of Lincoln to secure an appointment as consul at Venice, a position he held from late 1861 until after the war ended in 1865. As Clemens went off to the big bonanza and Virginia City and James sat out the war in Newport, Howells embarked for Europe to begin the pivotal experience of his life. In a real sense Venice was his college education, for his duties as consul were minimal and wartime trade with Venice, never an important port in the nineteenth century anyway, was almost nonexistent. Occasionally he had to look after traveling Americans, but most of his time he could devote to study and writing.

For the first couple of years he persisted in writing poems which he "sent to the magazines in every part of the English-speaking world, but they came unerringly back." Thus it was editorial rejection that turned him from a mediocre poet into a successful prose writer, that and the discovery of Venice as a source of material for prose sketches. As a journalist he already was a trained observer of the world about him, and the exotic setting of Venice supplied material of undeniable interest. Then he discovered the Italian dramatist Carlo Goldoni, who became another literary passion, one whose faithful record of Venetian life in his plays suggested that one's literary objective might well be "the truthful treatment of material." Howells wrote a series of sketches of life in Venice and sent them to the *Atlantic Monthly*, but Lowell was no longer editor, and Fields, who had succeeded him, did not want the pieces. But the *Boston Advertiser*, a newspaper that Lowell and other Boston literati read, did buy them, and during 1864 seventeen appeared in print. The following year Howells revised the sketches for book publication, and *Venetian Life* (1866) became his first literary success, a book that was printed and reprinted throughout his life.

Between the writing of the sketches and the book publication, however, Howells came to what he later called the turning point of his life. After acquiring a fluency in Italian, he had plunged into extensive reading of nineteenth-century Italian writers, and in the spring of 1864 he began writing his first important piece of criticism, an essay on "Recent Italian Comedy." He sent it to Lowell, who was then editing the *North American Review* with Charles Eliot Norton, and awaited its fate. In August he received an electrifying letter from Lowell: "Your article is in print, and I was very glad to get it. . . . Write us another on 'Modern Italian Literature,' or anything you like. I don't forget my good opinion of you . . . I have been charmed with your Venetian letters. . . . They make the most careful and picturesque *study* I have ever seen on any part of Italy. They are the thing itself."

In the months after receiving Lowell's letter, Howells became increasingly restive in Venice and was eager to return to America to get on with his career. During his years in Italy he had acquired a wife and a child, put in four years of study and writing, and prepared himself for the life that was to follow. In 1862 he had gone to Paris to meet and on 24 December to marry Elinor Gertrude Mead of Vermont, who had captivated him during an Ohio visit a couple of years before. He escorted her back to his apartment in a palace on the Grand Canal and Winifred Howells was born a year later. By late 1864 he felt that he had gotten all he could from Venice, and when the war ended the following spring, he asked to be relieved of his consular duties.

The Howells ménage arrived in New York late in the summer of 1865, and while Elinor went to visit her family in Vermont, Howells looked for a job. First he did some free-lance writing for the *New York Times*; then E. L. Godkin offered him a position on the *Nation* at forty dollars a week. He jumped at the job but was barely settled in it before Fields asked him to become assistant editor of the *Atlantic Monthly*. Then he was off like a shot for Boston, the city of his heart's desire, and his subsequent career was inseparably linked with that city for almost a quarter of a century.

With Fields as his employer, Lowell as his sponsor, and Holmes as friend and confidant, Howells settled down in Cambridge as assistant editor of the most influential journal in the literary capital of America. Hawthorne and Thoreau were dead by this time, but he was passing judgment on contributions by Emerson, John Greenleaf Whittier, and a good many others who were established writers when he was a youth in Ohio. Norton took him house hunting as soon as he arrived and introduced him to Longfellow, who became a close friend and not-too-distant neighbor. Within a month Howells was invited to attend the weekly sessions of the Dante Club, which met at Longfellow's home and listened to the poet read the translation he was then making of *The Divine Comedy*. Howells had taken Lowell's advice and studied Dante while in Venice, and his knowledge of Italian literature and culture gave him an immediate entrée into the society of Cantabrigian Italophiles. Lowell wrote of his protégé: "Venice has been the university in which he has fairly earned the degree of Master." The meetings of the Dante Club were among his richest experiences, and he recalled thirty years later that they were the one episode in his life he would most like to live over. The members of the club were "the men whom of all men living I most honored, and it seemed to be impossible that I at my age should be so perfectly fulfilling the dream of my life in their company."

Soon after Howells's settling down in Cambridge, *Venetian Life* appeared in book form and received enthusiastic reviews with Lowell leading the group. Readers of the book found that Howells had avoided the Venice of romance, the Venice of Lord Byron, Samuel Rogers, or James Fenimore Cooper, and he did not try to compete with John Ruskin's study of Venetian art and architecture. What he did was study Venetian life, not high society but everyday life, Venetian customs, Venetian character. He described his apartments on the Grand Canal, his life as a bachelor and later as a married man and father, his servants, walks through the city, trips to islands in the lagoon. He was trying in this work to find a literary form that would break away from the genteel restraints of sentimentality and ideality in the novel of the earlier nineteenth century. Henry Nash Smith sees both Howells in *Venetian Life* and Clemens in *The Innocents Abroad* working toward the same objective. And for Howells there are foreshadowings of the novelist to come, in the narrative voice, the character portrayals, and the self-contained episodes.

The success of *Venetian Life* spurred Howells to continue using his Italian experiences in his next book, *Italian Journeys* (1867). In this work Consul Howells and his wife travel from Venice to Naples and back, going by train, boat, and carriage. The book is nonfiction, but there is continuous narrative and a plot fashioned from the travel framework. He had traveled with notebook in hand, observing and recording the life about him in the manner of the realistic novelist. The material subsequently worked up for the published book departs in many respects from the actual events: it is rearranged, shaped, embellished, dramatized. There are numerous episodes that read like chapters from Howells's later novels, scenes filled with the realistic dialogue that is one of his trademarks. Again reviewers were pleased with his work, and one wrote: "Mr. Howells is, in short, a descriptive writer in a sense and with a perfection that, in our view, can be claimed for no American writer except Hawthorne."

The writer of that review was young Henry James, whom Howells had met in Cambridge soon after joining the *Atlantic Monthly*. James, six years Howells's junior, was just beginning his literary career, having sold his first story to the *Atlantic Monthly* the year before, and the two men began a friendship that ended only with James's death in 1916. As assistant editor, Howells enthusiastically championed James's fiction in the magazine and, as editor, later eagerly solicited his work. Both men were then working out their literary principles and held long, earnest discussions. Howells wrote his New York friend E. C. Stedman on 5 December 1866: "Talking of talks: young Henry James and I had a famous one last evening, two or three hours long, in which we settled the true principles of literary art. He is a very earnest fellow, and I think extremely gifted— gifted enough to do better than any one has yet done toward making us a real American novel."

One of Howells's principal duties as assistant editor of the *Atlantic Monthly* was the writing of book reviews, and one day in 1869 he received a copy of *The Innocents Abroad* for review. Recognizing its quality, he wrote a favorable notice, which appeared in the magazine unsigned, as was the custom. Late in the year when Clemens turned up at the *Atlantic Monthly* office to thank Fields for the review, the editor introduced him to Howells. The two men, only two years apart in age and both from similar Midwestern backgrounds,

William Dean and Elinor Mead Howells in Venice shortly after their marriage (Rutherford B. Hayes Library)

immediately found each other congenial and struck up a friendship that lasted until Clemens's death in 1910. Both writers visited each other back and forth between Cambridge and Clemens's home in Hartford and occasionally collaborated on literary projects. Howells published some of Clemens's best work in the *Atlantic Monthly* during his editorship, and after Clemens's death wrote in *My Mark Twain* (1910) a memoir described by Edmund Wilson as the best "character" of Clemens that readers have.

The two Italian books moved Howells along the path toward his first novel, but he was not quite ready to write it. Meantime he worked prodigiously becoming the de facto editor of the magazine and continuing to write many sketches, stories, articles, and reviews. His expertise in Italian literature brought him an honorary M.A. from Harvard in 1867 and an invitation from the new president, Charles W. Eliot, to be a special lecturer on contemporary Italian literature, an as-

signment that he carried out for two years and interspersed with another series of lectures at the Lowell Institute. Ever since the *North American Review* had published his article on "Recent Italian Comedy," he had been writing essays on Italian poetry. This interest, stimulated both by Lowell's encouragement and a keen sympathy for the Risorgimento, eventually culminated in *Modern Italian Poets* (1887), a critical survey with many translations of a century of Italian verse. Meantime he had managed to find a publisher for a long poem in unrhymed hexameters, *No Love Lost, A Romance of Travel* (1869), that he had written in Venice more than five years before.

In 1871 Howells became editor in chief of the *Atlantic Monthly* and produced another book. This was *Suburban Sketches*, not one of his major productions but his last work before attempting a novel. As the title implies, it is a collection of miscellaneous pieces, all of which had previously been published in the *Atlantic Monthly*. It does for Cambridge what Howells earlier had done for Venice. He describes Mrs. Johnson, the cook, as he had described Giovanna, his Venetian servant, and he relates conversations with Italian scissors grinders and chestnut roasters in Cambridge as he had reported his talks with gondoliers and porters. Howells later recalled that this book was one "where I was beginning to study our American life as I have ever since studied it." Lowell again led the chorus of praise from reviewers, comparing the character sketches to those in Geoffrey Chaucer's *The Canterbury Tales* and finding the style and powers of observation worthy of comparison with Hawthorne.

With such accolades ringing in his ears Howells took the next step and wrote his first novel, *Their Wedding Journey* (1872). As in *Italian Journeys*, the plot is draped on a framework of travel, but unlike the earlier travel book, Mr. and Mrs. Howells now become Basil and Isabel March, fictional characters that Howells was to use nine more times in later novels and stories. In December 1870 he had written his father: "At last, I have fairly launched upon the story of our last summer's travels, which I'm giving the form of fiction so far as the characters are concerned. If I succeed in this—and I believe I shall—I see clear before me a path in literature which no one else has trod, and which I believe I can make most distinctly and entirely my own. I am going to take my people to Niagara, and then down the St. Lawrence, and so back to Boston." The book was serialized in the *Atlantic Monthly* during his first year as editor, and again the critical reception was favorable.

The novel is low-keyed throughout, lacking any sort of melodrama but filled with sharp observation of people and places and authentic dialogue. There is quiet humor, understatement, irony, and the supple style that his readers had come to expect. Henry Adams, who reviewed it for the *North American Review*, found in it "extreme and almost photographic truth to nature, and remarkable delicacy and lightness of touch." He thought the book would have a long life and that "our descendants will find nowhere so faithful and so pleasing a picture of our American existence, and no writer is likely to rival Mr. Howells in this idealization of the commonplace." Howells writes, as Basil and Isabel observe some silly by-play between a young man and woman on the night boat to Albany: "Ah! poor Real Life, which I love, can I make others share the delight I find in thy foolish and insipid face?" Apparently he could, though the novel is flawed if compared with his mature fiction of a decade later; yet it marches toward realism. Howells still had a considerable distance to go, however, in perfecting his narrative technique, in learning how to dramatize his material better, and in keeping out authorial intrusions.

The decade of the 1870s was a time of gathering powers. The *Atlantic Monthly* flourished under his editorship and at one time was simultaneously carrying Twain's "Old Times on the Mississippi" and James's *Roderick Hudson*. Howells also was encouraging and publishing the work of younger writers such as Sarah Orne Jewett, engaging Bret Harte to write for him, and readmitting to the magazine the poems of his older contemporary, southerner Paul Hamilton Hayne. His abilities as a novelist grew steadily as he turned out six works of long fiction in this period, and he tried his hand at play writing, both one-act farces and full-length comedies. As if all this activity were not enough, he still managed to write stories and sketches, introduce works by other authors, bring out a volume of poems, and write a campaign biography of Rutherford B. Hayes.

His second novel, *A Chance Acquaintance* (1873), was a superior performance to *Their Wedding Journey* and introduced into the comedy of manners of the earlier book what was to become a new characteristic dimension, the clash of differing social values. Again the novel's plot depended in part on a travel framework, for the characters are presented as traveling in Canada,

in Quebec, and on the St. Lawrence and Saguenay rivers. Again Howells uses Basil and Isabel March, though they are not the leading figures this time. The real interest lies in the invention of Kitty Ellison, a girl from western New York State, and Miles Arbuton, a Boston snob. Kitty, Howells's best characterization so far, had played a walk-on part in the first novel as one of the passengers on the boat traveling down the St. Lawrence. Now she is the heroine, dramatically presented alone on deck as the novel opens. She is marveling at the lucky chance that has given her the opportunity to travel from Buffalo to Quebec and eventually back home by way of Boston with her Milwaukee cousin and his wife. Howells gives her the same awed respect for Boston that he himself had had as a young man visiting the city for the first time.

The social comedy in the novel develops in the relationship between Arbuton, who is attracted to Kitty but who cannot get over his conviction of social superiority. He falls for her, however, and proposes, but she puts him off, which offends his pride; he had expected her to swoon in his arms. He pursues her further, but when he meets some Boston friends and does not introduce her, she realizes that he is ashamed of her low origin (her father had been killed in a frontier brawl) and rejects him finally.

All this is handled with a light touch and nice irony, and it is interesting to note that Howells has avoided the sentimental ending that his magazine readers would have preferred. He also still is working out his ideas about realism and the use of commonplace material. He has Kitty tell Arbuton: "If I were to write a story, I should want to take the slightest sort of plot, and lay the scene in the dullest kind of place, and then bring out all their possibilities. I'll tell you a book after my own heart: '*Details*,'—just the history of a week in the life of some young people who happen together in an old New England country-house; nothing extraordinary, little, every-day things told so exquisitely, and all fading naturally away without any particular result, only the full meaning of everything brought out." This is a fair description of what Howells was trying to do, though he allowed himself a more exotic setting in his use of French-speaking Quebec than his theory called for.

Howells had to write three novels before he produced one that did not depend on travel to give it movement. His next effort was *A Foregone Conclusion* (1874), a novel that takes place in Venice. The setting is exotic, and the heroine is an American girl sojourning in the Italian city, but the story is worked out within the confines of the *calle*, the palazzi, and the lagoons of Venice. As early as 1866 he had thought of writing a novel laid in Venice, but nothing had come of his idea. Now he had the experience and ability to do it, and the result was his most artistic and best-realized novel so far. At the end of its serialization in the *Atlantic Monthly*, his friend Stedman wrote: "I have read the closing chapters of *A Foregone Conclusion*, having followed it along the *Atlantic*, and like it the best of all your books. Indeed it has been of curious interest to me to see your *gradual* but steady progress in *construction*—invention of plot and management of separate characters.... Each of your books has had a little more *story* to it, and this is a story throughout and therefore the best of all. Of course you had nothing to gain in style or insight of character."

A Foregone Conclusion is the story of an Italian priest who falls in love with an American girl, mistakes her kindness and open American manner for a serious interest, decides to leave the Church and marry her. The girl, Florida Vervain, has encouraged the priest, Don Ippolito, to leave the Church and immigrate to America because she knows he is miscast as a priest and at heart is a frustrated inventor. But when he proposes to her, she is shocked at the idea of a priest's proposition and rejects him summarily. The priest conveniently dies of a fever, and later back in America Henry Ferris, the American consul who had introduced the two, gets the girl. In this novel Howells gave in to his readers' desires for a happy ending, though he felt apologetic about it, but he must have felt that to end with the death of the priest, which he knew was the logical conclusion, would have made the story more tragic than he intended it to be.

A Foregone Conclusion was the most successful of Howells's early novels. Fourteen printings appeared in the next thirteen years, and the book was republished as late as 1916. It was translated into German and put into the English Tauchnitz library for Continental travelers. It also was dramatized and produced both in London and New York, but it was not a hit on the stage. Don Ippolito, suggested by a priest Howells had known during his consulship in Venice, was the most ambitious characterization he had yet tried, and the critics were properly impressed. He came across to James as "a real creation"; Robert Dale Owen, who had been American minister to It-

aly, thought him "an admirable portrait"; John Hay called the priest "the best thing of the sort that has been done." There is a fair amount of anti-Catholicism in the novel, particularly in its criticism of celibacy for the priesthood, and the editor of the *Boston Pilot*, John Boyle O'Reilly, registered a protest against the reflection on the priesthood cast by Don Ippolito. Finally, the novel is Howells's first attempt at the international novel, a genre that both he and James found exceptionally attractive.

Howells's next novel is hardly known at all because it never appeared in book form until 1921, after his death. Published serially in the *Atlantic Monthly* as "Private Theatricals," Howells suppressed its book publication under circumstances that still are mysterious. His biographer, E. H. Cady, reports that Howells was threatened with a lawsuit by the people who ran the "Mountain Farm," where he had taken his family in the summer of 1874. He had vacationed in the White Mountains, as was becoming the custom for affluent Bostonians in the years following the Civil War, near Jaffrey, New Hampshire, and the setting of his novel was apparently too recognizable. If his denigrators of the 1920s had read the novel in 1921, when it finally appeared as *Mrs. Farrell*, they might have been surprised, for its title character is a femme fatale, something of a bitch, and a very well-drawn character.

The action is laid in a summer boardinghouse kept by a retired minister's family. One of the guests is Mrs. Farrell, who is fatally attractive to men and enjoys the fact. She causes the alienation of two young men, both of whom fall in love with her, allows one of them to woo her, but ends up casting him off and going on the stage. When she turns out to be no big hit in the theater, Howells has one of his minor characters comment that perhaps her real talent was for "private theatricals." He also uses the novel as a vehicle to attack the romantic ideals of love and courtship as they existed in sentimental romance. Here the militant realist in him was fully engaged.

After serializing "Private Theatricals," Howells turned to a literary genre that often has had an almost fatal allure for novelists—the drama. His interest in the theater began in his childhood during the terrible year and a half that his father was trying to publish a daily paper in Dayton. A traveling company of players paid for printing handbills with free tickets to their plays, and he remembered going every night to performances of

Macbeth, Othello, Richard III, plus popular dramas now forgotten. Later in Venice Howells made his delighted discovery of Goldoni, whose light-hearted dramatizations of Venetian life left an indelible impression, and he attended the theater there regularly. Back in the United States his interest continued, and once he was well established on the *Atlantic Monthly*, he turned his hand to writing plays. Drama never became a major preoccupation, but Howells is more important as a dramatist than most people know. His pioneering in realistic fiction carried over into his dramatic writing, and Arthur H. Quinn, historian of the American drama, writes: "His example and his critical judgments and inspiration, guided and encouraged [Edward] Harrigan, [James A.] Herne, [Augustus] Thomas, and [Clyde] Fitch, who have expressed their obligation to him directly and implicitly."

His first foray into the theater occurred in 1874 when he translated an Italian play, *Sansone*, by Ippolito d'Aste for Charles Pope. Not much came of this venture, but three years later Lawrence Barrett produced his full-length comedy, *A Counterfeit Presentment* (1877), with considerable success. This is a lighthearted comedy of manners laid in a summer hotel and involving the vicissitudes of young love. Though it is of minor importance among Howells's works, it is full of sharp, witty dialogue and again shows his acute understanding of human nature. When it opened in Boston Howells wrote his father: "The first night was a superb ovation, a gurgle of laughter from the beginning to end, and a constant clapping of hands. They called me up at the end of the third act, and *roared* at me. I never had my popularity at arm's length before, and it was very pleasant." But this never happened to him again, and his only other full-length comedy, *Out of the Question*, also published in 1877, with the same setting and similar action, never was performed professionally. After several later efforts to write for the theater he gave it up and wrote one-act plays, mostly farces and comedies, for his magazine public and amateur theatricals.

Beginning with *The Parlor Car* (1876), Howells turned out twenty-six of these one-act dramas during the next thirty-five years. When he shifted over to *Harper's* in the late 1880s the magazine asked for one of his farces each year for the Christmas issue. "They made me a very amiable public there," he wrote in 1912, "with the youth who played in drawing-rooms and church parlors." Booth Tarkington recalled that "a college

Howells in 1874

boy of the late eighties and 'golden nineties' came home at Christmas to be either in the audience at a Howells farce or in the cast that gave it." On a few occasions these plays were performed professionally as curtain raisers, one of which, *The Garroters* (1886), George Bernard Shaw reported seeing in 1895: "The little piece showed, as might have been expected, that with three weeks' practice the American novelist could write the heads off the poor bunglers to whom our managers appeal."

Shaw was right, and the plays, which are packed with witty dialogue and amusing situations, are still a pleasure to read. When Howells wrote *The Sleeping Car* (1883) seven years after *The Parlor Car*, he invented a group of characters that he carried through a dozen plays. The idea may have been suggested by Goldoni's use of the old commedia del l'arte stock characters in many of his comedies, but wherever the idea came from, it provided Howells with characters who could be expected to amuse from play to play: the garrulous Agnes Roberts and her absent-minded husband Edward, Willis Campbell from

California, and the amiable Amy Somers, a Boston widow who is wooed and won by Willis. Their antics range from slapstick farce to sophisticated comedy of manners.

After his play writing interlude Howells returned to the international theme with *The Lady of the Aroostook* (1879), his most realistic novel yet. Like *A Chance Acquaintance* and *A Foregone Conclusion*, it presents an attractive, independent American girl in situations that test her character and contrast her values. As with Kitty Ellison in *A Chance Acquaintance*, Howells's new character, Lydia Blood, a schoolteacher from South Bradfield, Massachusetts, finds herself confronted with two sophisticated young Bostonians on board a ship sailing for Italy. Then in Italy she encounters, as did Florida Vervain in *A Foregone Conclusion*, the mores of European society. The idea for the story had come from Samuel Langley, the pioneer in aviation, who had visited Howells when he was consul in Venice. There had been an American girl traveling alone as the only woman aboard his ship on her way to visit an aunt in Italy. To the novelist of manners this situation had interesting possibilities, and Howells remembered it fourteen years later.

Nothing much happens in this novel either on board the ship or after Lydia is installed in her expatriated aunt's palazzo on the Grand Canal. The plot is also predictable, boy gets girl, but the novel is extraordinarily interesting and developed with great skill. Again there is superb dialogue and dramatic treatment of incident. Shipboard life is created with excellent use of closely observed detail, and the life of the expatriated American in Venice is vividly rendered. There are excellent minor characters, the captain, the cabin boy, the drunken passenger, the aunt and uncle. Howells was determined to make the novel as realistic as he could, even giving his heroine a name as antiromantic as possible, Lydia Blood. Young James Staniford, the Bostonian who falls in love with her and proposes after they all get to Europe, is a far more attractive and subtle character than the Boston snob Arbuton in *A Chance Acquaintance*. Lydia is as naive as the Bostonians are sophisticated and has no idea that traveling without a chaperon in 1878 is something no innocent girl would do. Her expatriated aunt is shocked by her indiscretion, and the proper Bostonian Staniford has to wrestle with his sense of propriety before proposing.

The novel is a charming period piece that invites comparison with another more famous one, James's *Daisy Miller*, which appeared in the *Cornhill* magazine in London four months before Howells began serializing his novel in the *Atlantic Monthly*. That James and Howells produced similar treatments of the unsophisticated American girl against a European background at the same time is not astonishing, however, given their frequent correspondence, similar literary theories, and common interests. *Daisy Miller* is the greater work of art, but *The Lady of Aroostook* is very good, and one might argue that James gave his story a melodramatic ending by killing off Daisy, whereas Howells wrote a realistic conclusion by letting his main characters get married. James got a lot more critical attention than Howells because some thin-skinned Americans thought he had slandered the American girl, but Howells displeased critics and readers also. Those who liked ideality in their fiction found him too realistic, his characters too clinically studied, despite the happy ending.

The decade of the 1880s opened with the appearance in the *Atlantic Monthly* of *The Undiscovered Country*, Howells's first big novel and one of his best. Called an "American Pastoral" by Kermit Vanderbilt, the novel deals with matters of large scope upon which Howells had brooded a long time: the loss of faith amid nineteenth-century scientific skepticism, the moral and social disorder that he saw in the post-Civil War decade. His readers thought the book was mostly about spiritualism, which had enjoyed a considerable vogue in Boston in the mid 1870s, and the novel sold eight thousand copies in the first month. Then sales dropped off, the reviewers did not recognize the importance of the book, and it has remained for contemporary critics to point out the book's significance as a cultural document.

The story begins with Howells's most extensive use of Boston as a setting, then moves to a Shaker village in the country (where Howells had spent the summer in 1875). In the opening chapters Dr. Boynton, a spiritualist whose daughter Egeria serves as his medium, is conducting a séance, to which comes a Boston journalist named Ford, who wishes to expose the fraud that he thinks is being perpetrated. From this beginning develops a struggle for the possession of Egeria, who immediately senses in Ford's presence a force that opposes her father's hold on her. After the séance is disrupted by Ford, Boynton and his daughter decide to leave Boston and return to their home in Maine, but they take the wrong train and land in the country near the Shaker village. The Shakers take them in, and after an illness Egeria finds that she no longer has the power to act as her father's medium. In the denouncement Ford appears again, claims the girl, Dr. Boynton dies, and the two young lovers are married.

A bare summary of the plot does an injustice to the complexities and subtleties of this novel. The early reviewers who thought the love story was poorly integrated with the exposé of spiritualism missed the overall design. The characters of Boynton, Egeria, and Ford all are lost souls wandering in exile from a rural America and the faith of their fathers. When they stumble into the religious community of the Shakers they undergo a spiritual rebirth. The doctor realizes that he was pursuing a pseudoscience in trying to maintain contact with the wife who died in childbirth; Egeria reawakens after her illness to a normal life and love, and Ford's rough skepticism is softened by his experiences. Thus a regional study of New England character and situation widens to a national analysis of America in an age of transition.

Another aspect of this novel that contemporary reviewers and readers missed is its bold psychological study of sexual passion. The relationship between Dr. Boynton and his daughter is a subtle pre-Freudian description of an Electra complex. Victorian taboos, of course, required sexual matters to be treated so obliquely that readers could ignore them, but Howells is not the timid depicter of sexual relations that he has been accused of being. One of the ironies of Howells criticism in the early twentieth century is that his critics read him so inattentively that they never suspected he was dealing in this novel with an incestuous relationship.

It is also interesting to note that *The Undiscovered Country* is a sort of updated version of *The Blithedale Romance* (1852), Howells's favorite of Hawthorne's novels. Howells and Hawthorne had got on extremely well together when they met that afternoon in 1860, and both Lowell and James had seen affinities between the two. Vanderbilt characterizes this novel as follows: "Egeria is a spiritual Priscilla who blooms into a warm Zenobia and becomes a whole woman. Boynton is a grotesque Westervelt with some of the visionary zeal of Hollingsworth. Ford is a Coverdale with the added good fortune of overcoming skepticism and choosing his ideal lady in time."

The year 1881 was a time of decision,

change, new directions, and serious illness for Howells. By the beginning of the year he was weary of the routine of editing a magazine, reading proof, writing book reviews, corresponding with contributors. Houghton, Osgood, and Company, publishers of the magazine and his books, had split up and were quarreling over his services and literary properties. Because he finally felt able to make a living without the drudgery of his editorial duties, he gave notice to Henry Houghton, now the sole owner of the *Atlantic Monthly*, that he would leave his editorship on 1 March. James Osgood, who was to continue in the publishing business alone, offered him a weekly salary and royalties to write one novel a year. He saw his way clear to a good deal of free time and the chance to travel again and accepted the proposal. But it was a distressing year in his personal life, for his daughter Winifred, whose health was always frail, was sick off and on, and at the end of the year Howells himself was down with a protracted illness from overwork.

That he had worked himself into a sickbed does not seem surprising when one notes that *A Fearful Responsibility* was serialized by *Scribner's* in June and July, *Dr. Breen's Practice* in the *Atlantic Monthly* from August through December, and *A Modern Instance* began in the *Century* in December. The first two works are modest productions, *A Fearful Responsibility* (1881) being a novella that drained the last of his Venetian experiences from his days as consul, and *Dr. Breen's Practice* (1881) being a novel about a woman doctor. The latter is an early study of women in the profession, but Grace Breen studies medicine only to retreat before male hostility and female disapproval and to leave medical practice for matrimony as soon as she can. The former novel was fashioned from a family situation that dated back to Venice in 1863 when Elinor Howells's sister Mary Mead visited Italy.

Professor Elmore and his wife are in Venice during the Civil War so that the professor may write a history of the city. When the professor's sister-in-law Lily comes to visit, the contrast between American and European mores again provides plot. The Elmores' fearful responsibility results from Lily's indiscretion in striking up an acquaintance in a railway car with an Austrian officer and the professor's having to save her from the consequences. The Venetian background is authentic, but Howells had done it better in *A Foregone Conclusion* and *The Lady of Aroostook*. One interesting bit in the novella has the professor expressing remorse over not taking part in the Civil War. Whether Howells felt this way himself, it would be worthwhile to know. The character in the story who most resembles the author is another fictional consul named Hoskins. Howells makes him a war veteran who was wounded early and given a medical discharge.

With the publication of *A Modern Instance* (1882) Howells carved himself a niche among the writers of enduring American classics. This novel, which remains in print and still is widely read, represents Howells at full artistic maturity, a fact that he recognized himself. He told an interviewer in 1893, when asked which of his novels he thought the best: "I have always taken the most satisfaction in 'A Modern Instance.' I have there come closest to American life as I know it." He later elevated *A Hazard of New Fortunes* (1889) to top position, and there is no doubt that this novel is a mature and important work. As the first significant treatment of divorce in American literature, it deals with issues of large and lasting social importance.

Howells had thought about the subject for a long time. In 1875 he had seen a performance of Franz Grillparzer's *Medea*, which had suggested to him the possibility of his own adaptation of the Euripides tragedy to an American divorce case. Although he started work on it the next year, he did not get very far, and nothing remains of that early effort. After he left the editorship of the *Atlantic Monthly*, he settled down to write this story, and the work progressed quickly during the next six months. He had not quite finished by the time he fell sick late in the year, and the serialization began while he was struggling to complete the book. The sure command of the material shown in the first three-quarters of the novel falters toward the end, and the artistry of the whole is marred.

The story traces the course of a deteriorating marriage in the years following the Civil War. Howells's earlier concern with the rise of religious skepticism and the loss of faith and the resultant effect on American society again motivated him to tell this story. Unlike *The Undiscovered Country* with its overt preoccupation with religion, *A Modern Instance* is a completely secular novel. It begins in the small town of Equity, Maine, where Bartley Hubbard, editor of the village newspaper, falls in love with Marcia Gaylord, daughter of a local lawyer. Bartley, though he has had a college education, has no social roots at all and an easygoing, hedonistic nature willing to make com-

promises. Marcia, raised in the circumscribed atmosphere of the small town, is the product of a freethinking father and a self-indulgent and jealous nature. Bartley and Marcia elope and go to Boston where Bartley is hired by a newspaper. The marriage gradually goes to pieces, Bartley begins drinking, loses his job, deserts his wife and child, and the novel moves to an Indiana divorce court many months later. It ends as Marcia returns to a lonely life in Equity, and Bartley drifts off to Arizona where he is killed in a quarrel.

Besides being a splendid study of character, the novel is the picture of an age, what Clemens called "The Gilded Age" or V. L. Parrington "the Big Barbecue," the time of the Grant administration. The novel is told dramatically in one vivid scene after another, the method that both James and Howells had learned from reading Ivan Turgenev. The small Maine village, which in ordinary American mythology is the solid underpinning of national life, is here a town of chaotic liberality in religion. When Bartley and Marcia go to the city, they are aliens, rootless, amid urban religious anarchy. Like Medea in Greek tragedy, Marcia, having left her father, lives in Boston in exile. Finally, the Indiana town where the divorce trial takes place is a copy of the Maine village only "more careless and unscrupulous" in appearance.

The novel made Howells a controversial figure, and the book received mixed reviews. Horace Scudder in the *Atlantic Monthly* hailed it as Howells's greatest achievement so far, "the weightiest novel of the day," but even he hoped that the author would go on to combine the serious matter of his novels with endings of "joyousness." Although the novel sold only six thousand copies in the first six weeks, the sales satisfied the publisher, and Richard Watson Gilder, editor of the *Century*, was happy about the publicity the serial created. Inevitably, some reviewers thought Howells was writing a tract against divorce and charged him with undue polemicism, missing his real concern with larger issues. Scudder's review saw the point of the novel: "a demonstration of a state of society of which divorce laws are the index."

Fuel was added to the controversy the novel created when, a month after the book came out, Howells's article entitled "Henry James, Jr." appeared in the *Century*. In this essay he hailed James as the chief luminary of a new school of fiction, one in which "fiction had, in fact, become a finer art in our day than it was with Dickens and

Thackeray," and he went on to add that "we could not suffer the confidential attitude of the latter now, nor the mannerism of the former, any more than we could endure the prolixity of Richardson or the coarseness of Fielding. These great men are of the past." These remarks raised a storm in England and no doubt tinctured some of the unfavorable reviews *A Modern Instance* received there. The essay was one of the opening salvos in the war for realism that Howells waged relentlessly later in the decade.

While the novel was still appearing serially, Howells fulfilled a long-standing desire to revisit Europe. He had written James in 1873 that the longing to return is "almost intolerable with me, and if I could see any way of keeping the bird in the hand while I clutched at those in the bush, I should go." He finally was able to do it, and before he left he arranged with Osgood, who was now both his publisher and his agent, to contract for the publication of a series of articles on Italian cities. He would make "each study as attractive as possible with anecdote and adventure. I should seek rather interest than thoroughness, and I believe I should succeed and make some sketches which people would like. It is the ground I know, and I should work con amore." The proposal resulted eventually in *Tuscan Cities* (1886), a more modest project than the original plan to treat thirteen cities, but the book he did write is a superior travel book. It blends history and reporting with great skill and uses the craftsmanship of the novelist to make history come alive.

The Howells family sailed from Quebec in July and made their first stopover in London where James found them accommodations and was their host. The stay in London was pleasant, and Howells was wined and dined by artists and writers, but he left for the Continent before his essay on James appeared in the *Century*. He settled down in Switzerland for the fall in order to work on another novel, *A Woman's Reason* (1883), which is perhaps the worst novel he ever wrote. He had trouble writing in Europe and after leaving Switzerland took his family to Florence where they spent the winter and he finished the novel. The story sets out to study the life of a woman, who has no proper education with which to cope with life, trying to make her way after her father's death leaves her destitute. Howells keeps the heroine, Helen Harkness, separated from the man she eventually will marry by sending him off to China and then shipwrecking him for two

years on a coral atoll in the South Seas. The novel is more romance than realism, and Howells's control of the material was at best faltering. He wrote Osgood while he was working on this book: "I find the strain of working out plots and characters amidst new and distracting scenes is awful."

Italy seemed older and dingier than when Howells was consul in Venice. His affection for the country remained unshaken, but he was unable to recapture the youthful charm. In April he took his family to Venice to show Winifred where she had been born, and to introduce his other children, Mildred and John, to Italy. He also wanted to look up old friends and former haunts and to roam the *calle* and canals of the city where he once had been "more intensely at home than in any other, even Boston itself." But the city was strangely shrunken, the churches and palaces shabbier than he remembered. Winifred, however, was enchanted by the city, but he took care not to let her get far from St. Mark's Square, where there was a little "galvanic gaiety," and kept her away from the poverty and misery on the back *calle*.

After nearly a year in Europe Howells retraced his steps north toward England, stopping off again in London, this time to visit Lowell, American minister to England for whose appointment he had been responsible. Lowell took him to a reception at the home of the prime minister and then invited a roomful of titles to meet him. Howells could not do any writing in London because of the incessant round of socializing that made him "acutely miserable," and he was glad to board ship again to return to America. Once back home he settled down to write one of his best, but neglected, novels, *Indian Summer* (1886), the most important product of his return to Italy.

Indian Summer is an excellent example of the international novel, the genre that Howells and James both excelled in. Like James's *The American*, Howells's novel takes an American to Europe where he falls in love. In *Indian Summer*, however, the American Colville traveled in Europe as a young man, became a newspaper editor, and he returns to Italy in order to write a book like *Tuscan Cities*. He is living in Florence when he meets the American Mrs. Bowen, who is his own age, and her young ward, Imogene Graham. He at first falls in love with Imogene but in the end realizes that it is Mrs. Bowen he really wants. This plot provides Howells with the oppor-

The Howells family, circa 1875 (Howells Collection, Houghton Library, Harvard University)

of *The Rise of Silas Lapham*, written later, almost had been completed.

He was disappointed in its reception, however, because he thought it one of his most mature and artistic creations. He remembered in his old age that J. W. Harper had been somewhat dismayed to receive a manuscript which opened on the Ponte Vecchio in Florence when he had expected to get a Boston story. He wrote a friend: "To tell the truth, I like the story altogether, and I enjoyed doing it better than anything since *A Foregone Conclusion*. But our people don't want one on foreign ground, and I shall hardly venture abroad again in fiction." He did not quite stick to his resolve, but he never again placed a story completely in a foreign setting. This was, however, his last major use of Italy except for *Ragged Lady* (1899), a mediocre novel that again takes a New England girl to Venice where she meets her future husband.

While the reviewers found the book clever and neat but lacking in drama, Howells's friends read the novel with pleasure. Among the letters he received, none pleased him more than Clemens's: "You are really my only author; I am restricted to you; I wouldn't give a damn for the rest. . . . It is a beautiful story, & makes a body laugh all the time, & cry inside, & feel so old & so forlorn; & gives him gracious glimpses of his lost youth that fill him with measureless regret." He ended his letter saying that he would rather "be damned to John Bunyan's heaven" than read James's *The Bostonians*, which appeared the same year. And despite Harper's disappointment, the editor of *Harper's*, Henry Mills Alden, wrote that he was "much delighted with the novel. It seems to me to be in your best vein."

The Boston story that Harper had wanted to inaugurate Howells's new relationship with *Harper's* magazine and his publishing firm was *The Rise of Silas Lapham*, but it was promised to the *Century*. Howells wrote it in the spring and summer of 1885, and it began appearing in the magazine in November. By the time it came out he had developed a large following, and a new Howells novel was eagerly awaited. Booth Tarkington remembered that he, at fifteen, was one of "a 'coast-to-coast' network of readers [who] hung upon every issue of the fortunate magazine that printed it." When one particular installment came, he waited at the door for the postman "so that I should be the first of the household to learn what happened to 'Silas Lapham' at the catastrophic dinner." Roswell Smith, publisher of the

tunity for a neat comedy of manners in his best manner. It also gave him a chance, as he wrote to Edmund Gosse, to study the "feelings of middle-life in contrast with those of earlier years." Howells had thought his return to Italy would renew his youth, but he found that impossible. Colville, who is just three years younger than Howells, reflects the author's realistic reassessment of middle age.

The novel has good unity of time, place, and character and creates a singleness of effect that often is lacking in Howells's novels. He liked the foreign setting for fiction because "you can segregate your characters so nicely, and study them at such long leisure." He worked over his manuscript carefully and for once had time to revise adequately. The novel did not begin appearing serially until eighteen months after he had completed the first draft, a unique experience for him, and when it did come out, the serialization

Century, told Howells that an estimated one million people were reading the story as it appeared in the magazine, and tourists in Boston began asking to see where the Laphams lived. The novel represents Howells at the peak of his creative powers in the middle of his most fruitful decade.

In this novel Howells combines a study of business and a study of society in a skillful interlocking narrative. Writing a pioneering novel of business, he creates Silas Lapham, a self-made paint manufacturer who has returned from the Civil War, discovered a paint mine on the family farm in Vermont, gone into business, and prospered. Lapham is not a Carnegie or Rockefeller but reasonably rich and successful. The reader first sees him in a vivid dramatic scene in which he is being interviewed for the "Solid Men of Boston" series by journalist Bartley Hubbard. Lapham is brought down, in the course of the novel, however, through the accidental burning of his new house on Back Bay into which he has poured a fortune, foolish stock speculations, and financial reverses in a time of economic dislocation. After his fall in fortunes, his "rise" takes place when he refuses to save his business through unethical means, and at the end he is back in Vermont starting over.

Coupled with the business story is a social plot in which the Laphams attempt to get into Boston society. The house is the symbol of their striving, and its burning ends their hopes. To bring the two plot threads together Howells invents the Corey family, Boston Brahmins who live on inherited wealth. Young Tom Corey, however, wants to do something with his life and gets a job in Silas's office. This brings Tom into contact with Silas's daughters, Irene and Penelope. Howells combines the business plot with a comedy of manners in the mix-up over which daughter Tom is in love with.

On the social side of the novel Howells wrote one of the great scenes in nineteenth-century American literature. This is the dinner party scene over which young Tarkington cried when Silas got drunk. The socialite Coreys, after Tom enters the paint business, feel they must invite the nouveau riche Laphams to dinner, but the Laphams neither know how to dress nor how to conduct themselves. Silas, who drinks water at home with his meals, allows his wine glass to be refilled far too often, and the result is disaster—a painful scene for Silas and the readers alike.

The novel has a great many attractive elements. The abundance of closely observed detail makes this novel an authentic picture of Boston in the later 1870s. The Laphams' house in unfashionable Nankeen Square, the Coreys' house, the summer cottage at the beach, particularly the new house that Silas builds, the details of Silas's business, the sights and sounds of Boston—all these are rendered superbly and give the novel verisimilitude. In fact the work has sociological interest quite apart from its artistic merits. The only weakness in the novel is its ending, in which Howells has to blend the social comedy of the love story, in which Tom and Penelope finally get together, with the business plot, which requires Silas's financial smash. The two elements do not mix very well, and the reader is left with the feeling that it all did not quite come off at the end.

The reviewers of *The Rise of Silas Lapham* were not very happy with the novel, and it has remained for later readers and critics to give it a high place in American letters. As Howells was the most prominent novelist of his day, the critics spent much of their energy finding flaws in the work. The ending came under attack, but the general tenor of the criticism was directed against Howells's uncompromising realism. As the reviewer for the *New York Herald* put it, Howells "always pleases, often charms us, but he never inspires." In short, Silas was neither a tragic figure whose downfall could bring catharsis, nor a noble character whose career fitted the stereotypes of the American success story. He was just an ordinary kind of person, and Howells, in creating him, seemed too clinically detached from his material.

The years from 1886 to 1891 were a crucial half decade in Howells's career. The appearance of *Indian Summer* in *Harper's Weekly* marked the beginning of an association with the magazine and the publishing firm that lasted the rest of his life. Not only did Harper and Brothers begin to publish his books, but Howells created the "Editor's Study" column in the magazine, where he carried on a vigorous battle for literary realism. At the time his first column came out he wrote Edmund Gosse that "it's fun having one's say again, and banging the babes of Romance about." Also in this quinquennium Howells became deeply involved in social issues, found himself leaning more and more toward socialism, and grew sharply critical of the social and economic injustice suffered by working people. He was so outraged over the miscarriage of justice that followed the Haymarket riot in Chicago in 1886 that he wrote a public letter of protest. This brought him nationwide ridicule in newspapers and magazines.

Not only the deepening struggle between labor and capital changed his thinking but also he had recently discovered the writings of Tolstoy. He wrote his sister that Tolstoy's "heart-searching books" were "worth all the other novels ever written," and in *My Literary Passions* he said that Tolstoy had influenced him not only in aesthetics but in ethics also, "so that I can never again see life in the way I saw it before I knew him." It bothered him a great deal that his creature comforts conflicted with his belief in Tolstoy's Christian socialism. He wrote James that "after fifty years of optimistic content with 'civilization' and its ability to come out all right in the end, I now abhor it, and feel that it is coming out all wrong in the end, unless it bases itself anew on real equality. Meantime, I wear a fur-lined overcoat, and live in all the luxury my money can buy."

The final shaping events of this half decade were the death of his daughter Winifred and his move to New York. Both Howells and his wife watched helplessly as Winny's health deteriorated, and no medical skill of the time was able to stop her decline. When she died in 1889 both parents were devastated, and Mrs. Howells lapsed into semi-invalidism for the rest of her life. Soon after that event Howells decided to edit a magazine again and accepted a coeditorship of the *Cosmopolitan* when his contract with Harper and Brothers expired in 1891. He was unable to endure the grind of editorial duties, however, and resigned after six months. In 1900 he went back to writing a column, "The Editor's Easy Chair," for *Harper's*, but in the meantime the firm had continued to publish his novels. The editorship of the *Cosmopolitan* had necessitated his move to New York where he lived, except for summers, for the rest of his life. New York was the place for a writer to be by 1891, for it had become the literary capital of the nation and the center of the publishing industry.

It is not surprising that three out of the next four novels that Howells wrote reflect his social concerns and his feeling that civilization was coming out all wrong. The first, *The Minister's Charge or, The Apprenticeship of Lemuel Barker* (1886), which at one point he called "The Country Boy in Boston," develops for the first time his doctrine of complicity. Stated by the Reverend Mr. Sewell, it holds that "no one for good or evil, for sorrow or joy, for sickness or health, stood

apart from his fellows, but each was bound to the highest and the lowest by ties that centered in the hand of God." The minister, who is a major character along with his charge Lemuel Barker, arrives at this realization through having been responsible for Barker's coming to the city. The story begins during a summer vacation when Sewell praises the poetry of Barker, a country boy, while really believing the lad has no talent. Barker subsequently comes to the city to seek his fortune and becomes the minister's charge. Barker comes to terms with his predicament, takes whatever work he can do, ends up trying to drive a horsecar, is badly injured, and ultimately returns to Willowby Pastures.

Although Howells always denigrated polemical novels, he skates close to writing one here. He explores the life of the working people in order to prick the consciences of the rich whom he felt should be more concerned with problems of unemployment, bad working conditions, and poverty. The novel is saved from didacticism, however, by good characterization and dramatization of social conditions rather than authorial moralizing, and the complicity doctrine comes at the end in one of Sewell's sermons. The reviewers sharpened their knives when the novel appeared and slashed at Howells for his treatment of "scenes of common and sordid life." The *Nation*'s reviewer asked: "Are the qualities in men that we know to be fine not real? Are trivial baseness, petty viciousness, the only truths?" In short the antirealists rose to the challenge presented both by the novel and by Howells's monthly columns in *Harper's*. Howells had turned upside down the American success story of the poor country boy seeking his fortune in the big city.

April Hopes (1887) was a change of pace, for it posits no social theories and grinds no axes. Set in Cambridge, Boston, Campobello, Washington, and Old Point Comfort, it is an excellent novel of manners in which boy gets girl. The characters are people from Howells's own social class. Of all Howells's work this is the most like the novels of Jane Austen, one of his oldest and greatest literary passions. In starts at Harvard Class Day where Dan Mavering meets Alice Pasmer, then moves to Campobello where Dan and Alice both vacation; Dan proposes and is rejected. When the couple accidentally meet again in Boston in the fall, they become engaged, but there are more vicissitudes before they finally get married.

Again Howells is the thoroughgoing realist. With consummate skill he mangles all the clichés of love and courtship in showing two unsuited temperaments sexually attracted going through an on-again, off-again romance. As they drive off together from the church after the marriage ceremony, Howells makes it perfectly clear that this couple will not have an easy time making the compromises necessary for a successful marriage. Howells later said that this novel was the first he wrote "with the distinct consciousness that he was writing as a realist." By this he meant that it was the first written after he had begun his monthly columns in *Harper's* "banging the babes of Romance about." Reviews of *April Hopes* were decidedly mixed, and the novel never has attained the status of a major work, but reading it today one is inclined to agree with Cady that it is a "neglected little masterpiece."

In *Annie Kilburn* (1888) Howells returned to social themes, writing a story laid in a New England mill town and creating characters that include a female philanthropist, a minister who expounds Tolstoy's Christian socialism, a greedy hypocritical businessman, an alcoholic lawyer who defends the mill workers, and a sensible, non-political doctor. Annie, who returns to her native Hatboro after living abroad for eleven years, is determined to help the people in her hometown. She sees herself as Lady Bountiful, but in the course of the novel she discovers that creating a social club for mill workers is not going to solve the problems of social injustice. While Annie learns a few things about the real world, she ends up marrying the doctor and substituting a happy marriage for philanthropy.

Although this novel is a tract for the times, it does not pose solutions for the problems it treats. Howells's socialist minister Peck sees the ultimate salvation of society in Christian brotherhood, but he has no solution for getting to that utopia, and Howells finishes him off by having him step absentmindedly in front of a locomotive, symbol of the industrialization that no one knows how to control. What Howells has done superbly in this novel is to dramatize the social and economic problems of the late nineteenth century. In this way he hoped to move his readers to compassion and understanding. Edward Everett Hale wrote him a letter of thanks for being willing "to attack such problems" and to do so in a manner "so wise–so kind–so direct." He added: "It is a pulpit indeed–to write such a book for a million readers." Many of the reviewers again savaged his novel, but he did indeed have a pulpit in *Harper's* from which to reach a large audience.

A Hazard of New Fortunes (1889) is Howells's longest novel and his largest canvas. Previously he always had selected a small group of characters and shown them in their relationships to one another. This time he was inspired by having recently read *War and Peace* to write a "big" book with many characters and a wide-angled view of society. His setting was also a first, New York, where he had spent the winter of 1888-1889 before moving to the metropolis permanently and where most of the writing was done. The novel continues his concern with social issues and makes significant use of his growing interest in socialism. His lifelong habit of work enabled him to begin the novel during the agonies of Winifred's failing health and to finish it after her death. The despair he felt over this loss undoubtedly tinctures the novel and heightens its sobering impact. For many Howells critics this is his most important work.

Basil and Isabel March appear in this novel again as two of the fifteen major characters in the story. At the outset Basil, who is in the insurance business in Boston, is persuaded by Fulkerson, promoter of a newspaper syndicate, to come to New York to edit a new magazine that he proposes to launch. The angel of the venture is Dryfoos, a former farmer from Indiana who has struck it rich in gas wells and now is in New York with his family looking for investments. The starting of the magazine requires the hiring of a staff and the recruiting of contributors, and this device allows Howells cleverly to bring together his large cast and to involve them in each other's lives.

One of them is Lindau, a German immigrant who has lost his hand in the Civil War. He is an ardent socialist whose linguistic competence makes him an ideal translator for foreign contributions. His socialism brings him into conflict with old Dryfoos, arch conservative who equates socialism with anarchy and violence. In a crucial episode in the center of the novel Lindau expresses his radical views at a dinner being held to celebrate the success of the magazine. Dryfoos orders March to fire Lindau, but March refuses on principle, and Fulkerson, who is more interested in the magazine than in Lindau's right to his opinions, has to back his editor. The crisis ends when Lindau refuses to have anything to do with Dryfoos. The old man's son, Conrad, who is a Christlike Tolstoyan socialist and a worker among the poor, is installed as business manager at his father's insistence, though he would like to become a minister. The novel reaches its climax when Conrad is killed in a futile effort to stop mob violence during a streetcar strike.

Other important characters are the Dryfoos women, the mother who is hopelessly out of place in New York and two daughters who want to get into society, and Alma Leighton and her mother, who come to the city so that Alma can study art. Alma supplies artwork for the magazine and is courted by Angus Beaton, the hedonistic art editor whom she rejects. There also is Colonel Woodburn and his daughter Madison, the former an anachronism whose solution for social ills is a return to a patriarchal agrarian society and the latter a witty girl who is wooed and won by Fulkerson. Finally, Margaret Vance, rich socialite who shares Conrad's social work and his Tolstoyan opinions, provides a glimpse into the lives and homes of New York's very rich. All the characters are well drawn and clearly differentiated.

Although Howells dramatizes the ideas and issues of 1890 in this well-structured novel, he does not try to solve the problems of society. Indeed he does not know the answers. Lindau often speaks for Howells in expressing his socialist philosophy, but he clearly carries his principles too far when they impel him to taunt the police as they club the strikers, an act that leads to Conrad's death. Conrad's Christlike martyrdom does not solve any problems either and is a needless sacrifice, though March, who speaks for Howells, says, "it was his business to suffer there for the sins of others." His death softens the father, however, but March does not believe that old Dryfoos really has changed. Yet March must believe something and concludes: "*I* don't know what it all means, Isabel, though I believe it means good." At the end of the novel the Dryfoos family, who not only have lost their son but also have been frustrated in their efforts to get into society, go off to Europe leaving Fulkerson and March as proprietors of the magazine. Margaret Vance, who feels responsible for Conrad's death, enters a religious order. Meantime, the life of New York, depicted with all Howells's skill and with all its color and movement and variety, flows endlessly on.

Howells's career also flowed on for another thirty years during which his creative imagination diminished only gradually. In these final three decades he wrote an astonishing number of novels and story collections–twenty-six in all–and continued his steady production of critical essays,

plays, travel books, introductions, and memoirs. At least eight of his novels written after he was fifty-three are important enough to deserve attention, and a few more are worth brief mention.

Two short novels written about the same time and now published in one volume of the Indiana Howells Edition, *The Shadow of a Dream* (1890) and *An Imperative Duty* (1891), are extraordinarily good novels that deserve to be better known. The first is Howells's most Hawthornesque fiction, and the second is a powerful pioneering study of black segregation and miscegenation. *The Shadow of a Dream* is also experimental in form for 1890, for it examines its story from three different points of view. Howells wrote it immediately after he finished *A Hazard of New Fortunes* while his creative energies were strong and his speculations about the meaning of life and death were insistent. Was the realist's demand for empirical fact enough? Was there substance beyond reality in our unconscious lives? Winifred's death and suffering no doubt inspired this fine pre-Freudian study of dreams and their impact on his characters.

Basil March is a first-person narrator in this story, which has three parts, each devoted to one of the three main characters. March visits an old friend Douglas Faulkner, who is slowly dying of a hopelessly incurable disease, and finds him living in a ménage à trois with his wife Hermia and a clergyman friend James Nevil. In part one, which is devoted to Faulkner, the dying man confesses to March that he is obsessed with a recurrent dream. March realizes that this obsession is one of the things killing him, and Faulkner dies soon after. Part two examines the wife's story, in the course of which the reader learns what the dream was when Hermia and Nevil become engaged, and Hermia insists that her deceased husband's doctor tell her. The dream was that Faulkner saw his wife and Nevil in love and waiting for him to die, and he further saw his funeral and the marriage taking place in the same church at the same time. Part three deals with Nevil and the working out of the impact of this revelation. Both lovers are destroyed by this knowledge, and the novel ends with Howells leaving the reader to decide whether the dream was a dying man's illusion or an intuitive glimpse into reality.

An Imperative Duty, a surprisingly early and bold treatment of race relations, is compact, tightly structured, and well executed. There are only three main characters: Dr. Olney, Mrs. Mere-

Howells at work

dith, and her niece Rhoda, all of whom have just returned from living abroad. Dr. Olney is called from his hotel room to treat Mrs. Meredith, who has come to a crisis in her life. Following a proposal of marriage to Rhoda by a white minister, she feels it her imperative duty to reveal a secret, until now concealed, that her niece's grandmother was a slave. When Rhoda learns her history, she writes a letter dismissing her suitor and rushes off into the night. The aunt is so distraught' that she takes an overdose of sleeping medicine. Dr. Olney takes charge of the girl, sees that she is cared for, and after his initial reaction of disgust over the girl's origin, which he recognizes as irrational prejudice, talks Rhoda out of her self-pity, proposes, and marries her. Early in the novel before the secret is revealed, Dr. Olney had reacted to the blacks he saw in Boston on his return as "the only people left who have any heart for life here." "They all alike seemed shining with good-nature and good-will," and he felt that segregation was one of the "the most monstrous things in the world." At the end of the novel Howells adopts a realistic solution for an interracial marriage in 1892 by sending his couple back to Italy to live.

About the time Howells was writing this novel he received an offer from S. S. McClure to become editor of a new magazine, suggested perhaps by *Every Other Week*, the fictional magazine in *A Hazard of New Fortunes*. It was a case of life imitating art, for the ebullient McClure, who ran a newspaper syndicate, was a Fulkerson importuning Basil March's alter ego with the same sort of proposition. Howells was not tempted, even though he was to have a free hand in running the magazine and the contract was better than his arrangements with Harper and Brothers. In 1893 McClure started *McClure's* magazine with himself as editor and achieved a phenomenal success, but it is unlikely that Howells had any regrets. McClure's only accomplishment in approaching Howells was to get him to write an extra novel that year. This was *The Quality of Mercy* (1892), one of Howells's best-plotted, liveliest long novels. McClure syndicated it in six newspapers with great success.

Subtitled in the newspaper version "a story of contemporary American life," it deals with a prominent businessman, Northwick, who has embezzled money from his company and been found out by his board of directors. His options are to commit suicide, go to jail, or flee the country. He takes the easy way out and goes to Canada (there are no extradition treaties yet), but after living in exile for a time, he decides to come back to face the music. He dies, however, on the train returning home. The novel takes place in Annie Kilburn's Hatboro and reuses characters from that story. Then it moves to Quebec, which Howells knew well, also to Boston, where Bromfield Corey, the Reverend Mr. Sewell, and other familiar Howells characters appear. The novel also deals at length with the lives of Northwick's children and the impact of the defalcation on them. The novel had contemporary interest, as defaulters were often in the news, but it has perennial interest to anyone following the Robert Vesco case in the 1970s and 1980s.

That Howells wrote too much is perfectly clear; yet even his lesser works contain good characters, well-developed situations, provocative themes. The two novels he turned out in 1893, *The World of Chance* and *The Coast of Bohemia*, and a later one, *The Story of a Play* (1898), are cases in point. While only moderately successful overall, they deal interestingly with art and the marketplace. The first takes a young man from the provinces, Percy B. Shelley Ray, to New York to find a publisher for his first novel. The second brings an Ohio girl, Cornelia Saunders, to New York to study art and make her way in the art world among men. The third novel does for a young playwright what Howells had done for his youthful novelist in *The World of Chance*, and in writing it Howells had his own experiences with actors and theater managers to draw upon.

These lesser performances punctuate an interlude between the economic novels of the late 1880s and Howells's utopian romances, *A Traveler from Altruria* (1894) and *Through the Eye of the Needle* (1907). Here Howells, following the great popularity of utopian fiction generated by Edward Bellamy's *Looking Backward* (1888), tried his hand at the genre. It gave him another chance to put into fiction his social and political ideas by creating Mr. Homos, the traveler from Altruria, which is somewhere in the antipodes, who visits the United States. At a New Hampshire summer hotel, where he is the guest of an American novelist, he is shocked at the social superiority the other guests assume over the hotel employees in a country where he has been told "all kinds of work are honored." Then he cannot understand why the owner of a stand of timber on the lakeshore near the hotel has been allowed to clear-

cut the trees and deface the landscape. He is further appalled to have a manufacturer explain to him the social Darwinism of his business principles. The traveler, in describing his own society, explains that in Altruria the people, by the simple device of the vote, had finally taken control of the country and resolved to form a society based on the idea of the good for all rather than the good of the individual.

Although this novel is a thinly disguised polemic, it is extremely interesting to read today to compare the conditions Howells describes in 1894 with the social and economic evolution this country has undergone since then. Reviewers found *A Traveler from Altruria* to their taste or distaste according to their preconceived philosophies. The *Critic* noted: "The good-will of a gentle man toward his kind, the interesting speculations of Plato, Bacon and Sir Thomas More, the poetic dreams of William Morris and the prosaic nonsense of Mr. Bellamy are all jumbled and shaken up together in Mr. Howells's book." On the other hand, the *Nation* wrote: "Mr. Howells speaks the thought of many men of his time with that clearness, force, and vivacity which have made his fame as a novelist." The sequel to this book, *Through the Eye of the Needle*, which was published serially in the *Cosmopolitan* after the original series, did not come out in book form until 1907 when Howells thought there was a revival of interest in utopian fiction. In it Mr. Homos falls in love with and marries an American; then he takes her back to Altruria, whence she writes letters home describing conditions in the utopian society where altruism is a way of life.

In the year that he was sixty Howells wrote another novel, *The Landlord at Lion's Head* (1897), that compares favorably with his best. It is a study of the selfish, amiable, amoral Jeff Durgin from the age of fourteen to his mid twenties. He is seen through the eyes of a painter, Westover, who boards at the Durgin farm in the White Mountains one summer and becomes involved in the lives of the folks at Lion's Head. Jeff's doting mother converts the farmhouse into a summer hotel to put Jeff through Harvard, and Westover, from his Boston studio, observes the young man's unprincipled progress through life. Jeff gets engaged to Bessie Lynde, Boston socialite, while Cynthia Whirtwell, his fiancée back home, waits for him. When both girls reject him, he goes off to Florence where he woos and marries a rich American. The old hotel at Lion's Head burns down under mysterious circumstances while Jeff is conveniently in Europe, and with the insurance and his wife's money he builds a more elegant establishment.

Although there are half a dozen good characters in this novel, the portrait of Jeff is outstanding. He is a complex figure whom any novelist would be glad to have created. He is a scoundrel in many ways but a likable one, a comical devil Cynthia's father calls him. Westover, who has observed him for a decade, does not fully understand him, but he actually is Howells's most naturalistic character. Howells would have denied that he was writing a naturalistic novel; yet Jeff Durgin is as amoral and egocentric as Theodore Dreiser's Frank Cowperwood. Westover recalls: "He once said to me, when I tried to waken his conscience, that he should get where he was trying to go if he was strong enough, and being good had nothing to do with it."

Of the seven novels that Howells had left in him after the turn of the twentieth century, two belong with his best work, and the third is a near miss. This last, which was produced first, as *The Kentons* (1902), is a story that begins better than it ends. Howells wrote a friend in 1904: "I know how [novels] are done better than ever, but I haven't the intellectual muscle I once had." The inspiration for *The Kentons* lay in Howells's Ohio background and his own family memories. He had had the idea to write an Ohio novel for half a dozen years; the death of his father in 1894 and visits to his brother and sister in Ohio strengthened his resolve. The result, however, is a novel of an Ohio family, which only begins in the village where Judge Kenton, retired from the bench, lives quietly with his wife and children. The family leaves Tuskingnum, Ohio, for New York to get Ellen away from an undesirable suitor and then continues on to Europe for the summer. On board ship Ellen meets a young clergyman who turns out to be the right man. Besides Ellen, the judge's younger daughter Lottie and his adolescent son Boyne are fully realized characters, and the use of Holland as his European setting is an interesting novelty.

Most critics have neglected this novel, and Howells was disappointed by its reception. He wrote Brander Matthews that the book had been killed by the "stupid and stupefying cry of 'commonplace people.' I shall not live long enough to live this down, but possibly my books may." In this hope he was correct, for the Howells revival of the past generation has found the mirror he held up to common human nature well worth preserving. Howells was incapable of compromising his principles of realism, and this novel, like most of his books of the previous decade, sold only about ten thousand copies. Discriminating readers appreciated the novel, however. James ended a letter praising the book: "It is in short miraculously felt and beautifully done."

The Son of Royal Langbrith (1904) is a major novel, the story of a son's delusion and its tragic consequence. James Langbrith cherishes the memory of his father, who died when he was an infant, as a great and good philanthropist, but the reality is that Royal Langbrith was a scoundrel and blackmailer who kept a mistress in Boston and tortured his wife physically and mentally. The son is a headstrong, selfish youth who has tyrannized his mother and insists that she never marry again. She is in love with her old friend Dr. Anther but afraid of her son. The question becomes: who shall enlighten the boy? Mrs. Langbrith finds she cannot, and the doctor also discovers that he cannot. A long-suffering uncle finally blurts out the truth, but it is too late. The doctor has died of typhoid fever contracted from a patient, and James, chastened and humbled, must live with the knowledge of his father's perfidy and his denial of happiness to his mother.

Howells's creative imagination burned brightly when he was writing this novel. The conception is strong and the execution sure. As psychological drama it compares well with *The Shadow of a Dream*. Howells had thought about the idea for a long time, for the notebook that was his "savings bank" for ideas has a paragraph written about 1894 containing the germ of the story. He spent nine months writing the novel, beginning it in his New York apartment and finishing it in his summer home at Kittery Point, Maine. The novel appeared serially in the *North American Review* the month after James's *The Ambassadors* ended and was widely and favorably reviewed. William M. Payne in the *Dial* thought *The Son of Royal Langbrith* one of the finest books that Howells had written.

Howells felt that he had one good novel left in him, and in 1916, a year short of his eightieth birthday, he published *The Leatherwood God*, which Cady describes as "his great unknown novel." It is unique in the canon of his works: his only historical fiction and his only real Ohio novel. Where *The Kentons* began as an Ohio story and ended up in the international category, *The Leatherwood God* plays out its story in Leatherwood Creek, Ohio, in pioneer times. It is a story, based on fact, of Joseph Dylks, who appears one August day in the frontier community and persuades a large number of people that he is God. It is the dramatic tale, full of life and action, of the rise and fall of this charismatic figure. Dylks is so successful at first that he begins to believe he may really be God; but the opposition gradually gathers strength, and when Dylks is unable to produce a promised miracle his downfall is assured.

Howells's success in telling this story lies in the invention of the skeptical Matthew Braile, who is the observer and commentator on the religious fanaticism that sweeps the community. This canny old man, who knows from the start that Dylks is an impostor, says in explaining the phenomenon: "He [God] doesn't want to keep interfering with man, but lets him play the fool or play the devil just as he's a mind to." He tells this to Nancy Billings, who had been married to Dylks and was deserted by him but who is unable to expose him because, thinking him dead, she has remarried. Howells was pleased with this novel, and so were most reviewers. The *New York Times* noticed both Clemens's *The Mysterious Stranger* and *The Leatherwood God* in the same review and found both essentially contemporaneous works in their dealings with "humanity's religious strivings."

Howells felt the winds of change as he grew older and realized that he belonged to an earlier era. He wrote James in 1915 that "a change has passed upon things, we can't deny it; I could not 'serialize' a story of mine now in any American magazines. . . . I am comparatively a dead cult with my statues cut down and the grass growing over them in the pale moonlight." He was partly wrong, however, as the *Century* ran *The Leatherwood God* the next year, but partly right, as the attacks on him swelled to a considerable volume in the iconoclastic 1920s. They had already begun in 1917 with H. L. Mencken's blast in the *Smart Set*, which proclaimed as though Howells were already dead: "His psychology was superficial, amateurish, often nonsensical; his irony was scarcely more than a polite facetiousness; his characters simply refused to live." But Mencken apparently did not bother to read Howells, for out of the five books he listed as forgotten novels, two are plays and a third poetry. In addition, one of the great ironies of American literature history is the attack that Sinclair Lewis made on Howells in accepting the Nobel Prize in 1930. He called him a writer who "had the code of a pious old maid

whose greatest delight was to have tea at the vicarage." That moment was perhaps the highwater mark of Lewis's reputation, and the low point for Howells. During the Depression 1930s Howells began to be rediscovered through his social and economic ideas, which seemed to anticipate the policies of the New Deal. Then after World War II he began to undergo a revival that has never ceased.

After writing *The Leatherwood God*, Howells never tried another novel, but he continued writing up to the time of his death. He turned out an "Editor's Easy Chair" column once a month for *Harper's Monthly* magazine until the month before his death, wrote autobiographical and travel essays, introductions for works by others, and completed an important book, *Years of My Youth* (1916). The Academy of Arts and Letters awarded him its Gold Medal for fiction in 1915, an award now known as the Howells Medal. By 1920, however, he felt like the last leaf on the bough, for his wife was gone, and two of his best friends, James and Clemens, also had predeceased him. He caught a cold in Savannah where he wintered in 1919-1920 and could not shake it, and after returning to New York in April he died quietly in his sleep on 11 May 1920.

Letters:
Life in Letters of William Dean Howells, edited by Mildred Howells, 2 volumes (Garden City: Doran, 1928; London: Heinemann, 1929);
The Correspondence of Samuel L. Clemens and William D. Howells, 1872-1910, edited by Henry Nash Smith and William M. Gibson, 2 volumes (Cambridge: Harvard University Press, 1960);
Selected Letters, 1852-1872, edited by George Arms et al. (Boston: Twayne, 1979);
Selected Letters, 1873-1881, edited by Arms and Christof K. Lohmann (Boston: Twayne, 1979),
Selected Letters, 1882-1891, edited by Robert C. Leitz III (Boston: Twayne, 1980);
Selected Letters, 1892-1901, edited by Thomas Wortham (Boston: Twayne, 1981);
Selected Letters, 1902-1911, edited by William C. Fischer (Boston: Twayne, 1983);
Selected Letters, 1912-1920, edited by Lohmann and Gibson (Boston: Twayne, 1983).

Interview:
Ulrich Halfmann, ed., *Interviews with William*

Dean Howells (Arlington, Tex.: *American Literary Realism*, 1974).

Bibliographies:

George Arms and William M. Gibson, *A Bibliography of William Dean Howells* (New York: New York Public Library, 1948);

James Woodress and Stanley P. Anderson, "A Bibliography of Writing about William Dean Howells," *American Literary Realism*, Special Number (1969): 1-139;

Vito J. Brenni, *William Dean Howells: A Bibliography* (Metuchen, N.J.: Scarecrow, 1973);

Clayton L. Eichelberger, *Published Comment on William Dean Howells through 1920: A Research Bibliography* (Boston: G. K. Hall, 1976).

Biographies:

E. H. Cady, *The Road to Realism: the Early Years, 1837-1885, of William Dean Howells* (Syracuse: Syracuse University Press, 1956).
This is the first part of a standard life by an authority on the subject and covers Howells's life from birth to the midpoint of his career.

Cady, *The Realist at War: the Mature Years, 1885-1920, of William Dean Howells* (Syracuse: Syracuse University Press, 1958).
This continuation of Cady's earlier work follows Howells's later life and career until his death.

Van Wyck Brooks, *Howells: His Life and World* (New York: Dutton, 1959).
An impressionistic portrait written by one of the great literary historians.

Edward S. Wagenknecht, *William Dean Howells: The Friendly Eye* (New York: Oxford University Press, 1969).
Termed by the author a "psychograph," the book is informative and stimulating but a rather detached portrait that doesn't penetrate deeply.

Kenneth S. Lynn, *William Dean Howells: An American Life* (New York: Harcourt Brace Jovanovich, 1971).
Treats Howells as a "man of modern sensibility, whose awareness of life was rooted in radical doubt and anxiety"–a very competent though partial study.

Kenneth Eble, *Old Clemens and W. D. H.: "The Story of a Remarkable Friendship"* (Baton Rouge: Louisiana State University Press, 1985).
A charming account of the long friendship between two of the major writers of the late nineteenth century.

References:

George N. Bennett, *The Realism of William Dean Howells: 1889-1920* (Nashville: Vanderbilt University Press, 1973).
Examines Howells's entire canon with calm reason, good judgment, and clarity of style.

Bennett, *William Dean Howells: The Development of a Novelist* (Norman: University of Oklahoma Press, 1959).
Like his later work on Howells as a realist, this study discusses his growth as a writer of novels.

E. H. Cady and Norma W. Cady, eds., *Critical Essays on William Dean Howells, 1886-1920* (Boston: G. K. Hall, 1983).
A selection of critical material on Howells written during his lifetime.

E. H. Cady and David L. Frazier, eds., *The War of the Critics over William Dean Howells* (Evanston, Ill.: Row, Peterson, 1962).
A collection of criticism ranging from 1860 to 1960 designed to illustrate the controversy that raged over Howells's work both during and after his life.

George C. Carrington, Jr., *The Immense Complex Drama: The World and Art of the Howells Novel* (Columbus: Ohio State University Press, 1966).
Makes Howells a pre-existentialist, a stance many Howells scholars reject, but includes a provocative analysis of the novels.

Everett Carter, *Howells and the Age of Realism* (Philadelphia: Lippincott, 1954).
Puts Howells in the context of the movement toward realism and is especially good in scrutinizing Howells's realism against the background of industrialization and mounting social problems.

John W. Crowley, *The Black Heart's Truth: The*

Early Career of W. D. Howells (Chapel Hill: University of North Carolina Press, 1985). Treats Howells to 1881 in terms of "the evolution of his 'psychological juggle,' the tactic of psychical self-defense that also became the delimiting means of his art."

James L. Dean, *Howells' Travels Toward Art* (Albuquerque: University of New Mexico Press, 1970).
A specialized study that focuses on Howells's nine travel books.

Kenneth Eble, *William Dean Howells* (Boston: Twayne, 1982).
A critical overview of Howells's life and work.

Eble, ed., *Howells: A Century of Criticism* (Dallas: Southern Methodist University Press, 1962).
A collection similar to that by Cady and Frazier.

Oscar Firkins, *William Dean Howells* (Cambridge: Harvard University Press, 1924).
The first important study of Howells; a competent study, though it has been superseded.

Olov W. Fryckstedt, *In Quest of America: A Study of Howells's Early Development as a Novelist* (Cambridge: Harvard University Press, 1958).
The work of a Swedish scholar, this study is particularly useful in charting Howells's intellectual growth and his use of European authors.

William M. Gibson, *William D. Howells* (Minneapolis: University of Minnesota Press, 1967).
An excellent brief (forty-eight-page) introduction to Howells.

Clara M. Kirk, *W. D. Howells and Art in His Time* (New Brunswick: Rutgers University Press, 1965).
A study of Howells's utopian fiction and the social context out of which it came.

William McMurray, *The Literary Realism of William Dean Howells* (Carbondale: Southern Illinois University Press, 1967).
A reading of twelve major novels to support the thesis that Howells's realism resembles William James's pragmatism.

Elizabeth Stevens Prioleau, *The Circle of Eros: Sexuality in the Work of William Dean Howells* (Durham, N.C.: Duke University Press, 1984).
Explores the hidden sexual contents in Howells's novels.

Kermit Vanderbilt, *The Achievement of William Dean Howells* (Princeton: Princeton University Press, 1968).
A significant book–a close reading of four major novels in which Vanderbilt "uncovers a man who was one of truly perturbed spirits of the late nineteenth century."

James Woodress, *Howells and Italy* (Durham: Duke University Press, 1952).
A study of the impact of Italy and Italian culture, one of the major influences on Howells's development.

Papers:
The largest collection of Howells manuscripts is at Harvard, which has more than seven thousand letters to and from Howells plus many manuscripts and journals. There are also significant collections at the Huntington Library, the Library of Congress, Yale and Columbia Universities, and the Rutherford B. Hayes Library in Fremont, Ohio.

Henry James

This entry was updated by Robert L. Gale (University of Pittsburgh) from his entry in DLB 12, American Realists and Naturalists.

Places	Boston Paris	London Italy	New York
Influences and Relationships	George Eliot Nathaniel Hawthorne Robert Louis Stevenson Emile Zola	Gustave Flaubert William Dean Howells Ivan Turgenev	Edmund Gosse William James Edith Wharton
Literary Movements and Forms	Novel of Manners Naturalism	Supernatural Fiction Psychological Realism	Impressionism Symbolism
Major Themes	The Artist's Life High Society Wealth and Power The Psychology of Women	Children International Cultural Relations Travel	Expatriation Moral Responsibility American Innocence vs. European Experience
Cultural and Artistic Influences	Architecture Travel Pre-Raphaelitism	French Impressionist Painting Renaissance Italian Art	Pragmatism Sculpture
Social and Economic Influences	American Materialism The Feminist Movement	British Imperialism Expansionism	Civil War

BIRTH: New York, New York, 15 April 1843, to Henry James, Sr., and Mary Robertson Walsh James.

EDUCATION: Harvard Law School, 1862-1863.

AWARDS AND HONORS: Honorary degrees, Harvard University, 1911; Oxford University, 1912; Order of Merit, 1916; James Memorial Stone, Poet's Corner, Westminster Abbey, London.

DEATH: London, England, 28 February 1916.

BOOKS: *A Passionate Pilgrim, and Other Tales* (Boston: Osgood, 1875);
Transatlantic Sketches (Boston: Osgood, 1875);
Roderick Hudson (Boston: Osgood, 1876; revised edition, 3 volumes, London: Macmillan, 1879; 1 volume, Boston & New York: Houghton Mifflin, 1882);
The American (Boston: Osgood, 1877; London: Ward, Lock, 1877);
French Poets and Novelists (London: Macmillan, 1878);
Watch and Ward (Boston: Houghton, Osgood, 1878);
The Europeans (2 volumes, London: Macmillan, 1878; 1 volume, Boston: Houghton, Osgood, 1879);
Daisy Miller: A Study (New York: Harper, 1878);
An International Episode (New York: Harper, 1879);
Daisy Miller: A Study. An International Episode. Four Meetings, 2 volumes (London: Macmillan, 1879);
The Madonna of the Future and Other Tales, 2 volumes (London: Macmillan, 1879);
Hawthorne (London: Macmillan, 1879; New York: Harper, 1880);
Confidence (2 volumes, London: Chatto & Windus, 1880; 1 volume, Boston: Houghton, Osgood, 1880);
A Bundle of Letters (Boston: Loring, 1880);
The Diary of a Man of Fifty and A Bundle of Letters (New York: Harper, 1880);
Washington Square (New York: Harper, 1881);
Washington Square, The Pension Beaurepas, A Bundle of Letters, 2 volumes (London: Macmillan, 1881);
The Portrait of a Lady (3 volumes, London: Macmillan, 1881; 1 volume, Boston & New York: Houghton, Mifflin, 1882);
The Siege of London, The Pension Beaurepas, and

The Point of View (Boston: Osgood, 1883);
Daisy Miller: A Comedy in Three Acts (Boston: Osgood, 1883);
Portraits of Places (London: Macmillan, 1883; Boston: Osgood, 1884);
Tales of Three Cities (Boston: Osgood, 1884; London: Macmillan, 1884);
A Little Tour in France (Boston: Osgood, 1885; revised edition, Boston & New York: Houghton, Mifflin, 1900; London: Heinemann, 1900);
The Art of Fiction (Boston: Cupples, Upham, 1885);
The Author of Beltraffio, Pandora, Georgina's Reasons, The Path of Duty, Four Meetings (Boston: Osgood, 1885);
Stories Revived, 3 volumes (London: Macmillan, 1885);
The Bostonians: A Novel (3 volumes, London: Macmillan, 1886; 1 volume, London & New York: Macmillan, 1886);
The Princess Casamassima: A Novel (3 volumes, London: Macmillan, 1886; 1 volume, New York: Macmillan, 1886);
Partial Portraits (London & New York: Macmillan, 1888);
The Reverberator (2 volumes, London: Macmillan, 1888; 1 volume, New York: Macmillan, 1888);
The Aspern Papers, Louisa Pallant, The Modern Warning (2 volumes, London: Macmillan, 1888; 1 volume, New York: Macmillan, 1888);
A London Life, The Patagonia, The Liar, Mrs. Temperly (2 volumes, London: Macmillan, 1889; 1 volume, New York: Macmillan, 1889);
The Tragic Muse (2 volumes, Boston & New York: Houghton, Mifflin, 1890; 3 volumes, London: Macmillan, 1890);
The American: A Comedy in Four Acts (London: Heinemann, 1891);
The Lesson of the Master, The Marriages, The Pupil, Brooksmith, The Solution, Sir Edmund Orme (New York: Macmillan, 1892; London: Macmillan, 1892);
The Real Thing and Other Tales (New York: Macmillan, 1893; London: Macmillan, 1893);
Picture and Text (New York: Harper, 1893);
The Private Life, The Wheel of Time, Lord Beaupré, The Visits, Collaboration, Owen Wingrave (London: Osgood, McIlvaine, 1893);
Essays in London and Elsewhere (London: Osgood, McIlvaine, 1893; New York: Harper, 1893);
The Private Life, Lord Beaupré, The Visits (New York: Harper, 1893);

The Wheel of Time, Collaboration, Owen Wingrave (New York: Harper, 1893);

Theatricals, Two Comedies: Tenants, Disengaged (London: Osgood, McIlvaine, 1894; New York: Harper, 1894);

Theatricals, Second Series: The Album, The Reprobate (London: Osgood, McIlvaine, 1895; New York: Harper, 1895);

Terminations: The Death of the Lion, The Coxon Fund, The Middle Years, The Altar of the Dead (London: Heinemann, 1895; New York: Harper, 1895);

Embarrassments: The Figure in the Carpet, Glasses, The Next Time, The Way It Came (London: Heinemann, 1896; New York & London: Macmillan, 1896);

The Other House (2 volumes, London: Heinemann, 1896; 1 volume, New York & London: Macmillan, 1896);

The Spoils of Poynton (London: Heinemann, 1897; Boston & New York: Houghton, Mifflin, 1897);

What Maisie Knew (London: Heinemann, 1897; Chicago & New York: Stone, 1897);

In the Cage (London: Duckworth, 1898; Chicago & New York: Stone, 1898);

The Two Magics: The Turn of the Screw, Covering End (London: Heinemann, 1898; New York & London: Macmillan, 1898);

The Awkward Age (London: Heinemann, 1899; New York & London: Harper, 1899);

The Soft Side (London: Methuen, 1900; New York: Macmillan, 1900);

The Sacred Fount (New York: Scribners, 1901; London: Methuen, 1901);

The Wings of the Dove (2 volumes, New York: Scribners, 1902; 1 volume, Westminster: Constable, 1902);

The Better Sort (London: Methuen, 1903; New York: Scribners, 1903);

The Ambassadors (London: Methuen, 1903; New York & London: Harper, 1903);

William Wetmore Story and His Friends, 2 volumes (Edinburgh & London: Blackwood, 1903; Boston: Houghton, Mifflin, 1903);

The Golden Bowl (New York: Scribners, 1904; London: Methuen, 1905);

The Question of Our Speech, The Lesson of Balzac: Two Lectures (Boston & New York: Houghton, Mifflin, 1905);

English Hours (London: Heinemann, 1905; Boston & New York: Houghton, Mifflin, 1905);

The American Scene (London: Chapman & Hall, 1907; New York & London: Harper, 1907);

Views and Reviews (Boston: Ball, 1908);

Italian Hours (London: Heinemann, 1909; Boston & New York: Houghton, Mifflin, 1909);

The Finer Grain (New York: Scribners, 1910; London: Methuen, 1910);

The Outcry (London: Methuen, 1911; New York: Scribners, 1911);

A Small Boy and Others (New York: Scribners, 1913; London: Macmillan, 1913);

Notes of a Son and Brother (New York: Scribners, 1914; London: Macmillan, 1914);

Notes on Novelists with Some Other Notes (London: Dent, 1914; New York: Scribners, 1914);

The Ivory Tower, edited by Percy Lubbock (London: Collins, 1917; New York: Scribners, 1917);

The Sense of the Past, edited by Lubbock (London: Collins, 1917; New York: Scribners, 1917);

The Middle Years, edited by Lubbock (London: Collins, 1917; New York: Scribners, 1917);

Gabrielle de Bergerac, edited by Albert Mordell (New York: Boni & Liveright, 1918);

Within the Rim and Other Essays, 1914-15 (London: Collins, 1918);

Travelling Companions, edited by Mordell (New York: Boni & Liveright, 1919);

A Landscape Painter, edited by Mordell (New York: Scott & Seltzer, 1919);

Master Eustace (New York: Seltzer, 1920);

Notes and Reviews (Cambridge, Mass.: Dunster House, 1921);

The Art of the Novel: Critical Prefaces, edited by Richard P. Blackmur (New York: Scribners, 1934);

The Notebooks of Henry James, edited by F. O. Matthiessen and Kenneth B. Murdock (New York: Oxford University Press, 1947);

The Art of Fiction and Other Essays, edited by Morris Roberts (New York: Oxford University Press, 1948);

The Scenic Art: Notes on Acting & The Drama: 1872-1901, edited by Allan Wade (New Brunswick: Rutgers University Press, 1948; London: Hart-Davis, 1949);

The Complete Plays of Henry James, edited by Leon Edel (Philadelphia & New York: Lippincott, 1949; London: Hart-Davis, 1949);

Eight Uncollected Tales, edited by Edna Kenton (New Brunswick: Rutgers University Press, 1950);

The American Essays, edited by Edel (New York: Vintage, 1956);

The Future of the Novel: Essays on the Art of Fiction, edited by Edel (New York: Vintage, 1956);

The Painter's Eye: Notes and Essays on the Pictorial

Arts, edited by John L. Sweeney (London: Hart-Davis, 1956; Cambridge: Harvard University Press, 1956);

Parisian Sketches: Letters to the New York Tribune, 1875-1876, edited by Edel and Ilse Dusoir Lind (New York: New York University Press, 1957);

Literary Reviews and Essays, edited by Mordell (New York: Twayne, 1957);

The Complete Notebooks of Henry James, edited by Edel and Lyall H. Powers (New York: Oxford University Press, 1987).

Collections: *Novels and Tales of Henry James,* 14 volumes (London: Macmillan, 1883);

The Novels and Tales of Henry James, selected and revised by James, New York Edition, 26 volumes (New York: Scribners, 1907-1918);

The Novels and Stories of Henry James, edited by Lubbock, 35 volumes (London: Macmillan, 1921-1923);

The Complete Tales of Henry James, edited by Edel, 12 volumes (London: Hart-Davis, 1962-1964; Philadelphia & New York: Lippincott, 1962-1964);

The Tales of Henry James, edited by Maqbool Aziz (London: Oxford University Press, 1973-   ).

The first important fact in the life of Henry James is the wealth of his paternal grandfather, the Irish immigrant William James (1771-1832), who, when he died in Albany, New York, left a fortune of $3 million (based on salt, tobacco, real estate, and public utilities). A second significant circumstance in the life of the future novelist is his earliest recorded memory: he was less than two years old, was in Paris with his parents, and looked out their carriage window upon an impressive sight, the stately Place Vendôme with "its . . . tall and glorious column." A third fact always to be aware of in trying to come to terms with James is suggested in a passage from a letter which, as an old man, he wrote to his gloomy old friend Henry Adams: "I am that queer monster, the artist, an obstinate finality, an inexhaustible sensibility." These are the ingredients for a unique Jamesian combination: family wealth, travel abroad, and abiding artistic sensibility.

James's father, Henry James, Sr. (1811-1882), revolted against the rigid Calvinism of the family into which he had been born but was happy that the family's money (though split among twelve heirs) enabled him to graduate from Union College (1830) and then study for a couple of years at the theological seminary in

Princeton. He found orthodoxy just as unpalatable and American pedagogical methods thin: so he voyaged to England and was soon influenced by Robert Sandemar., an anti-Calvinist Scotsman whose letters the elder James edited in 1838. A more positive source of religious inspiration for him was Emanuel Swedenborg. James was impressed by the Swedenborgian doctrine that God is a God of love not terror and by the ideas that a spiritual cause lies behind every natural object, that the Trinity is a division of essences only, and that Christ's resurrection is emblematic of man's glorious destiny. As for secular thought, James followed the social philosophy of Charles Fourier, who argued that individualism and competition are immoral, and that true happiness and goodness come from an optimistic expression of passion. Fourier sought to establish small social units–humanistic agricultural communes which would break down the unnatural restraints of so-called civilized society. James associated informally with many like-minded American intellectual leaders, among them Ralph Waldo Emerson, Ellery Channing, Margaret Fuller, Henry David Thoreau, Parke Goodwin, Charles Anderson Dana, Albert Brisbane, and George Ripley. James lectured, traveled, and wrote extensively on his views about Christianity, morality, Swedenborg, social redemption, and God's pervasive power in human affairs.

Today the works of Henry James, Sr., are only of antiquarian interest, but his influence upon his family was enormous. He encouraged free and easy chatter, dinner-table debating, freedom to attend church–any church–or not, reading, travel, and museum attending–in short, an unmethodical, eclectic, intellectual foraging of the most stimulating kind. His father's writings may have influenced Henry James the novelist in some ways, but the influence was probably indirect in the main. After the old philosopher's death, his distinguished son William James edited *The Literary Remains of the Late Henry James* (1884) and sent copies to Henry, who replied with gratitude but added, "how beautiful and extraordinarily individual (some of them magnificent) all the extracts from Father's writings which you have selected so happily. It comes over me as I read them . . . how intensely original and personal his whole system was, and how indispensable it is that those who go in for religion should take some heed of it. I can't enter into it (much) myself–I can't be so theological nor grant such extraordinary premises, nor throw myself into conceptions of heavens and hells, nor be sure that the keynote of nature is humanity, etc. But I can enjoy greatly the spirit, the feeling, and the manner of the whole thing . . . and feel really that poor Father . . . was . . . a great writer."

James's mother, Mary Robertson Walsh (1810-1882), was from a prosperous upstate New York Family, Scottish-Irish in origin and Presbyterian (like her in-laws) in religious persuasion. She accommodated her mind to her free-thinking husband's progressively more mystical thoughts with no evident trauma, and long enjoyed her younger sister Catharine (Aunt Kate) Walsh's loving presence in her household. Mary James was practical, unselfishly devoted to her husband and their five children, fair-minded, and sturdy. Upon her death, her devoted son Henry recorded this tribute to her in a private notebook: "She was our life, she was the house, she was the keystone of the arch. She held us all together, and without her we are scattered reeds. She was patience, she was wisdom, she was exquisite maternity. Her sweetness, her mildness, her great natural beneficence were unspeakable. . . . She is with us, she is of us–the eternal stillness is but a form of her love. . . . Thank God one knows this loss but once; and thank God that certain supreme impressions remain!"

Henry James was the second child. The oldest was William James (1842-1910), who turned out to be at least as brilliant as anyone else in the family. He studied painting under William Morris Hunt at Newport, Rhode Island, then science at Harvard University, then medicine at the Harvard Medical School (M.D., 1869). After a period of physical debilitation and intermittent nervousness, he became physiology instructor at Harvard, a professional experience which soon led him into psychology and then philosophy. Three of his most notable works are *The Principles of Psychology* (1890), which summarizes psychological knowledge to its date and incorporates his discoveries, insights, and hypotheses; *Varieties of Religious Experience* (1902), which insightfully relates religion, science, and common sense; and *Pragmatism* (1907), which persuasively suggests that ideas have meaning only when validated in the world of feeling and action.

After Henry James came Garth Wilkinson (Wilky) James (1845-1883), Robertson (Bob) James (1846-1910), and Alice James (1848-1892). None of these three achieved any sort of intellectual importance, although Alice James might have but for chronic ill health. Wilky and Bob vol-

Henry James at age nine, with his father (photograph by Mathew Brady)

unteered for service during the Civil War. Wilky was wounded at Fort Wagner in 1863; Bob survived the siege of Charleston unscathed and emerged a captain. After the war, the two young brothers went to Florida and became unsuccessful cotton farmers for a time; then they headed west, to railroad jobs in Milwaukee. Wilky remained there, improvident and irresponsible, dying of a weakened heart and Bright's disease in his late thirties. Bob soon returned to the East, settled in Concord, Massachusetts, inveighed against railroad fortunes, considered becoming an actor, suffered from alcoholism, and flitted from religion to religion without finding solace. Alice suffered under the lifelong disadvantages of being the youngest child and the only daughter. She was neurasthenic, fainted often during her adolescence, and recorded in her remarkable diary that from the time she was twenty she felt dead. When she asked her indulgent father for permission to commit suicide and he freely gave it, she decided instead to confront the world's evils with him. Traveling a little, she lived with her parents until they died, then went to sanatoriums in southern England, with Henry James usually nearby and devoted to her always. Cancer, compounding the misery of this intensely analytical and witty woman, finally killed her in 1892.

Henry James, Jr., was born on 15 April 1843 at 21 Washington Place (near Waverly Place), on the edge of Greenwich Village, in New York City. Very late in 1843 the parents took William and Henry to Europe. Once in London, James Senior made plans to meet his friend Emerson's distinguished friends Thomas Carlyle and John Sterling, and also the Swedenborgian J. J. Garth Wilkinson (for whom he was to name his third son). In the spring of 1844 the family was comfortably settled in Windsor, outside London, when the father underwent the horrifying experience of imagining that "some damned shape" with a "fetid personality" was "squatting invisible to me" in his room and "raying out . . . influences fatal to life." It was years before the shattered man felt normal, and water cures and doses of Swedenborg helped but little. Early in 1845 the Jameses visited Paris, then returned to New York City and Albany, which were to be their homes for the next decade. One of the most educational of Albany experiences was the presence of at least twenty first cousins, most of them presided over by their exceedingly sweet old paternal grandmother. Young Willy loved school in Albany from the first day, but the younger Harry cried and kicked. This contrast between the two illustrious brothers continued throughout their lives: William James always seemed the more assured and superior; Henry, less in the limelight, more in need of protection. It took Henry years before he struck out for independence.

Late in 1845 the growing James family moved to New York City, where the Fourierite father could be nearer to like-minded colleagues, lecture halls, and sympathetic publishers. The James residence at 58 West Fourteenth Street was to be at the center of many of the future novelist's fondest memories—of parental affection, sibling play, sprightly talk, reading, and forays into the incredibly bustling, noisy city. The boys' education teetered from attendance at a curious sequence of day schools and academies to being taught at home by polyglot governesses and tutors. The boys often dropped in on Grandmother Walsh, who had her home nearby, on Washington Square. In addition, they attended excellent dramatic and operatic performances on Broadway, as well as circuses and sideshows. Their father, meanwhile, was developing a formidable reputation as a lecturer and, to a lesser degree, as an author. Among the notables who visited the Fourteenth Street mansion were Emerson, Gen. Winfield Scott, and William Makepeace Thackeray. Young Henry profited from family sympathy and sincerity early in his life, and his natural expectation that he should move in important intellectual circles in due time must have been fostered quickly; but he fought juvenile shyness and later expressed slight regret at not only too much religious eclecticism but also at too little school discipline. Perhaps the result for a future novelist was generally beneficial, however, since, as James himself later described it, all this regimen constituted an "orgy of the senses and riot of the mind," both of which could only stimulate his imagination.

In the summer of 1855 the James family took a steamer from New York to Liverpool and went to London, where young Henry had to recuperate from malarial fever before the group could get on to its destination this time–Geneva. All along the way, his vivid senses took in the varied scenes–the Channel crossing, a Parisian balcony, the train, the coach, the Alps, and mutedly glorious Switzerland. James remained too sick to attend the rigorous day school which his father had found for the other boys, and this fact only reinforced young James's sense of uniqueness and passivity. After only three months, the educational experiment palled; so the family returned to London, where the children had milder tutors and relished visits to museums, theaters, public gardens, churches, and old London monuments. James later recalled that everything in London at this time was redolent of Charles Dickens, George Cruikshank, William Hogarth, Thackeray, and old issues of *Punch*. Henry Senior, though enjoying his friendships with Carlyle, Thackeray, and Arthur Hugh Clough, among others, was beginning to think more highly of America again, just as Henry Junior, now a teenager, was inexorably if as yet all unconsciously inclining toward the residential preference of his adult life–the Old World.

June 1856 found the Jameses not yet back home but in Paris, which at that historical moment was perhaps artistically the most stimulating city in the world. Young James took full advantage of his opportunities. Tutors did what they could to regulate his study habits. But his real education during the next two years lay in his perfecting his uncanny fluency in the French language, summering and studying in Boulogne-sur-Mer (at the Collège Impérial), and isolating himself from his siblings to read and scribble. Henry Senior wrote home to his mother as follows: "Harry is not so fond of study, properly so-called, as of reading. He is a devourer of libraries, and an immense writer of novels and dreams. He has considerable talent as a writer." Unquestionably the most momentous psychic experience of his life occurred when young Henry first visited the Galerie d'Apollon of the Louvre, during his Parisian residence of 1856-1857. The 200-foot-long gallery is full of paintings on mythological themes, by such artists as Eugène Delacroix, Charles Lebrun, and Joseph-Benoit Guichard, as well as tapestries, mosaics, sculpture, and jewelry, all of which evoked for young James the name Napoleon. James's response was twofold. First the lad regarded the sight as a "bridge over to Style," at the end of which he "inhaled little by little, that is again and again, a general sense of *glory*." But a few years later, memory of that Napoleonic gallery triggered one "summer dawn" what he called "the most appalling yet most admirable nightmare of my life." He dreamed that he was in a room with the door closed, locked, and barred. A "creature or presence" on the other side was trying to force his way in. James had his shoulder against the door, resisting. Suddenly he became the aggressor, burst out of the room, and chased "the awful agent" down a "tremendous, glorious hall" (like the Galerie d'Apollon)—all to the accompaniment of lightning and thunder. Leon Edel theorizes about this pivotal, prophetic dream, "*Sublimity* was indeed the word for it: to resist nightmare, to turn the tables and counterattack, was consonant with the sense of triumph and glory and conquest and power. Attacked, Henry James had fought back. And he had won." It is hardly too much to suggest that the inspiration for the disturbing dream was also the inspiration of James's entire professional life.

In 1858 Henry Senior took the family back to America. His decision was partly owing to his temporary dissatisfaction with European educational methods but also largely due to an income loss after the 1857 panic. In the summer of 1858 the family crossed the Atlantic and settled in Newport, Rhode Island, then a somewhat remote place, not yet the pretentious resort area it became after the Civil War. William and Henry James attended a school run by a Newport minis-

ter, the Reverend William C. Leverett, who relished Latin and fancied his own oratory. At the school Henry met the future painter, watercolorist, and stained-glass expert John La Farge, of French and Catholic background, who persuaded him to read Honoré de Balzac, Prosper Mérimée, Théophile Gautier, and the *Revue des Deux Mondes*. Henry also made another lifelong friend at this school. He was Thomas Sergeant Perry, later an editor, Harvard professor, and literary critic, and the recipient of some of James's most significant personal letters.

Henry James, Sr., uprooted his children once again in October 1859 and took the family to Europe for what was to be his own final foreign residence. His ostensible aim this time was to try yet another and different sort of school for his children, but the unacknowledged cause was more probably a continued intellectual restlessness and a vague fear about the approaching Civil War. This time they went to Germany and soon after to Geneva once more. The children were split up to a considerable extent. The family residence was a pleasant lakeside hotel, and Alice stayed with her parents. The two younger brothers went to a country boarding school nearby. William began to attend courses at the academy (later the University of Geneva), and Henry was required to take classes at the Institution Rochette, a preparatory school for engineers and architects. Henry James, Sr., seems to have hoped that he could wean William from his desire to paint and Henry from scribbling. It was not until spring that Henry was permitted to drop physics and mathematics, staying only with language classes until it was time for the family to go to Bonn for somewhat irregular study and then to wander in the Rhineland during the summer of 1860.

It was William's continued desire to paint that took the family back home for what was to be their longest American sojourn since 1845-1855. In September 1860, before the outbreak of the Civil War, they returned to Newport, so that William could formally study art at the Newport studio of William Hunt, who had followed his years at Harvard with study in Düsseldorf and Paris. While William worked hard at painting for a good six months, Henry tried sketching a while but soon turned back to more French literature, even translating Alfred de Musset's *Lorenzaccio* (1834) and Mérimée's *La Vénus d'Ille* (1841). Musset's work he adapted rather freely; he came to admire Mérimée inordinately for the firmness of his narrative structures. James did not know it then, but even before the Civil War he was beginning to prepare himself for a life of creativity. Already he spoke French and German, and he knew some Latin as well. He had had the mixed blessing of a dozen cosmopolitan homes and schools. His powers of observation were incredible. He had several brilliant young friends who would in differing ways make their mark in the arts. Also, family fortune and parental devotion would permit him to indulge himself for some years yet and to take his own slow time getting through a long postromantic apprenticeship.

With the outbreak of war early in 1861, the James brothers had decisions to make. Now abandoning art, William decided on a scientific career and enrolled at Harvard. Wilky and Bob joined the Union army in due time. Henry wavered uncomfortably; then in October 1861 he suffered what he later called a "horrid even if an obscure hurt," which he added was "subsequently neglected." In trying to help extinguish a raging fire in a group of Newport stables near some houses, he manipulated a rusty water pump and, wedged between two fences, injured himself severely. Although some earlier scholars suggested that he castrated himself, Edel says that the hurt was in all likelihood a slipped disc or a strained back. Whatever it was, the injury provided a valid reason for remaining on the sidelines during the war and was later a source of chronic pain for the man of letters who spent uncounted hours with his back bent over a desk. James, in his leisure after the fire, must have recalled that his father at the age of thirteen was so severely burned while trying to put out a stable fire that he lost a leg and spent two years convalescing in bed. The father had turned spectator and writer; now so might the son.

First Henry James, Jr., unaccountably entered Harvard Law School. He seems to have had no intention of becoming a lawyer. He later branded himself "a singularly alien member" of the place and attended for only a single academic year, 1862-1863. His enrollment there enabled him to attend James Russell Lowell's lectures on literature at Harvard College, to avail himself of Harvard's library, and—most important, perhaps—to make still more literary friends. Among them, in addition to Lowell, were Charles Eliot Norton, a distinguished professor of art history at Harvard and also a fine translator, biographer, editor, and letter writer; his knowledgeable, sensitive sister Grace Norton, to whom James later

wrote some delightful letters; and Oliver Wendell Holmes, Jr., by then a dashing, wounded Civil War officer and later the eccentric, liberal associate justice of the U.S. Supreme Court.

From 1864 to 1869, James stayed mostly with his parents, first in Boston and, for the last three years, in Cambridge. Now determined to become a man of letters, he broke into print with an unsigned, melodramatic short story called "A Tragedy of Error" in the *Continental Monthly* for February 1864 and eight months later had an unsigned review of a forgotten book published in Norton's *North American Review*. James's first signed piece was "The Story of a Year," which appeared in James T. Fields's *Atlantic Monthly* the following March and which is a disquieting piece about a wounded Civil War lieutenant and his confused fiancée. Fields and his vivacious wife, Annie Adams Fields, maintained a kind of Old World salon to which James soon quietly reported. But it was Fields's young assistant editor, William Dean Howells, appointed shortly after he returned from spending the war years as consul in Venice, whom James ultimately came to treasure as his single most important American professional friend.

Howells became an editor and critic of incalculable influence, in addition to being a distinguished realistic novelist. He was an intimate friend of contemporary literary personalities as diverse as Henry Adams, John Hay, and Samuel Clemens, as well as Hamlin Garland, Stephen Crane, and Frank Norris later. He encouraged young James tremendously. James much later recalled somewhat inaccurately that it was Howells who first accepted his work: "You held out your open editorial hand to me at the time I began to write—and I allude especially to the summer of 1866—with a frankness and sweetness and hospitality that was really the making of me, the making of confidence that required help and sympathy and that I should otherwise . . . have strayed and stumbled about a long time without acquiring." In truth, by mid 1886 James had had twenty-two reviews, four short stories, and a couple of short critical notes published in five different journals, including the *Galaxy* and the *Nation,* the latter founded the year before by E. L. Godkin, a close personal friend of Henry James, Sr. The stream of Jamesian prose was gathering force, even though at this time James the critic, admiring the theory and practice of his French idols Charles Augustin Saint-Beuve, Balzac, and Gustave Flaubert, was ahead in theory of James the practicing story writer, whose early tales often display an apprenticeship fumbling with too much sentiment. All the same, within two years a reviewer in the *Nation* would define James as, within his own established limits, "the best writer of short stories in America."

By the time James went to Europe early in 1869, for his first adult trip abroad, he had written at least ten more short stories, in addition to twice that many reviews. The stories are still technically unsure and more moody than plotted. Two deal with the Civil War. They are "Poor Richard," in which the hero cannot compete with soldiers for the heroine, opts for alcohol, and then goes to war himself; and "A Most Extraordinary Case," which features a hero, already wounded in the war, who cannot compete with a civilian rival and opts for psychic, then real, death. Three other tales hint at the masterly James of the future. In "The Story of a Masterpiece" a painting seems almost alive, and the hero must stab it to assure his future tranquillity. With "De Grey: A Romance" James introduces his sacred-fount motif: in any intimate relationship, one, giving vitality to the other, is sucked dry in the vampiric process. In addition, "De Grey" concerns American travelers abroad. So does "A Light Man," the purpose of which, however, is to dramatize the corrosive effects of prospective money on friendship. James even wrote an unimportant little play called "Pyramus and Thisbe," involving talk in a boardinghouse, before leaving for Europe.

His fourteen months in England and on the Continent, ending late in April 1870, established what was to become his lifelong pattern: travel, observation, and writing; much solitude, decorous friendships with men and women of the arts, homesickness, and mellow letters to loved ones. Bearded now and armed with a £1,000 letter of credit from his parents, James arrived in dingy Liverpool in February 1869 and went on to London, where friends introduced him to John Ruskin, William Morris and his wife, one of Dickens's daughters, Dante Gabriel Rossetti, Edward Burne-Jones, George Eliot, and Charles Darwin, among still other important Britishers. After brief treatment at a Malvern spa to try to set his chronically troubled digestive system in better order, James continued to France and Switzerland, both familiar countries from his childhood, and in September to Italy. Seeming incomparable from his first moments there, Italy soon became and always remained his favorite country. Ger-

many was too harsh to suit him, although his parents wanted him to go straight there and although his brother William, home again after a year of study there, sternly recommended it. Swiss nature appeared raw and overly vigorous, and the country seemed barren of much art. By comparison, the Italian air and vineyards were soft; moreover, Italy had picturesque old ruins, incense-laden cathedrals, and art treasures in the galleries of Venice, Florence, and especially Rome. When James arrived in the Eternal City for the first time, on 30 October 1869, he became delirious with delight. "I went reeling and moaning thro' the streets, in a fever of enjoyment," he wrote home, adding at once, "In the course of four or five hours I traversed almost the whole of Rome and got a glimpse of everything . . . In fine I've seen Rome, and I shall go to bed a wiser man than I last rose. . . ." He felt wiser because, as he said about Rome, "I have caught the keynote of its operation on the senses." As a result, he was soon able to cast much fiction there–notably *Roderick Hudson* (1876), *Daisy Miller* (1878), and *The Portrait of a Lady* (1881)–and in addition to write many superb travel pieces about Italy.

Sick again, James made his way back north and west, to Genoa, Nice, Marseilles, Avignon, Paris, Boulogne, and still-wintry London. He was again at Malvern for the water cure when the saddest news of his life up to that time reached him. His beloved cousin Minny Temple, whom he had known since the old Albany days and adored for her spontaneity, wit, and radiance, had died of tuberculosis back home on 8 March 1870. She was only twenty-four. James was stunned, having thought that she was getting better even while he was slipping into poorer health himself. He vowed to immortalize the lithe, spirited girl in future fiction and later did so in his complex characterizations of Isabel Archer in *The Portrait of a Lady* and then Milly Theale in *The Wings of the Dove* (1902). Still later, he closed the second volume of his autobiography, *Notes of a Son and Brother* (1914), with the poignant cry that Minny's death was "the end of our youth." Perhaps his problem was psychosomatic, but in Malvern James became quite sick. So after meeting his Aunt Kate in London, he returned gloomily to what he then called his "dear detestable . . . Cambridge" in May, in part to be examined by his brother William, now a medical doctor. James found New England culturally thin and uninspiring. His best new fiction to emerge at this time is

"A Passionate Pilgrim," which concerns an American traveler much like James, exclaiming over Europe, specifically Oxford, which James always loved. His longest fictional effusion of this period is his first novel, *Watch and Ward* (not published in book form until 1878); later its author so little admired its thin plot, in which an older man rears an adopted child to be his bride, that he excluded it from the New York Edition of his selected fiction. "A Passionate Pilgrim," his sixteenth short story, is the earliest one to be included. Both of these works first saw print in Howells's *Atlantic Monthly* in 1871.

By 1872 James was again tired of America and was close to a decision to expatriate himself permanently. However, he was financially unable to do so. Nonetheless, he went to Europe again–this time, starting in May, as escort to his debilitated sister, Alice, and their Aunt Kate. Alice James soon grew not better but sicker; James took his charges from Paris over to the Liverpool dock, saw them off on a steamer headed west, and was free to take rooms back in Paris and write so steadily that he could reimburse his parents for their unceasingly generous allowance. *Nation* took five of his charming notes on England, Switzerland, and Italy, based on his travels in 1872. When fall came, James went to Rome again and made friends among the American expatriate community, of whom many were destined to become devoted to him for life. Among them were Fanny Kemble, a British actress, and her dazzling daughter Sarah Wister, the mother of Owen Wister, future author of *The Virginian* (1902). James also renewed his friendship with Francis Boott and his daughter, Lizzie. Their relationship may have partly inspired James's treatment of Gilbert Osmond and his pallid daughter, Pansy, in *The Portrait of a Lady*. Boott was a rather effete, Europeanized American widower, and Lizzie later married the talented American expatriate painter-sculptor Frank Duveneck, whom James also knew.

In 1873-1874 James produced no less than fifty-eight pieces, mostly reviews and travel essays, but also some art gallery notes, items on Renaissance Italian art and Italian architecture, and seven short stories. The best fiction is "The Madonna of the Future" (published in *Atlantic Monthly*, 1873), a haunting fable of a procrastinating artist, his fading model, and his dusty, tattered canvas; "The Last of the Valerii" (*Atlantic Monthly*, 1874), a parable of the competing attractions of past and present; and "Madame de Mauves" (*Galaxy*, 1874), whose ambivalent heroine has recently been attracting and repelling readers of different critical persuasions. Now widening his outlets beyond the *Atlantic Monthly*, the *North American Review*, the *Nation*, and the *Galaxy* to include the *Independent* and *Scribner's Monthly*, James was quick to report home that his annual income approached $3,000–more than enough to support him in Europe indefinitely, independent at last of his indulgent parents.

When William, sick again with another of his periodic nervous disorders, descended in November 1873 upon his younger brother in Florence, Henry could now take the position of the more experienced: he wrote steadily through the morning hours, showed off his increasing knowledge of Italian to William (who was visiting Italy for the first time and did not know the language), and escorted him through museums and galleries. The two brothers were better for each other at a distance: when they were together, one seemed strong while the other waned; but when apart, they praised each other's professional efforts more fondly, although William tended to criticize his brother's increasingly complex fiction.

In the spring of 1874 James began work in Florence on *Roderick Hudson*, the first of his novels to be published as a book and the one he later enumerated as his first, and in September he returned to America to finish it. *Roderick Hudson* opens with a wealthy American named Rowland Mallet offering to become patron to a talented New England sculptor, Roderick Hudson. Once the two men are in Rome, Hudson learns quickly and even displays genius, but he is unstable and egocentric as well. He gambles in Germany, insults a rich would-be buyer, forgets Mary Garland–his fiancée back home–and falls in love with enigmatic Christina Light. Mallet urges her to stay away from Hudson, and her mercenary mother forces her to marry Prince Casamassima of Naples. Despondent in the romantic Swiss Alps, even though his mother and Miss Garland have come to visit him, Hudson leaps or falls to his death. Roderick may be the titular hero, but Rowland is the central consciousness and, though perhaps too certain that everyone's will is free, an admirable force in the action. Christina Light is the first of many deadly females in James, who found her so intriguing that he made her the heroine of *The Princess Casamassima* a decade later. *Roderick Hudson* was respectfully reviewed in America, but James R. Osgood's first printing of 1,500 copies was enough to satisfy

223

American sales. The book was far more popular in England. Roger Gard reports that it sold about 10,500 copies there and in America in James's lifetime.

After a few months in Cambridge, James went in January to live on East Twenty-fifth Street, near New York's old Madison Square, away from his parents and older brother. He worked hard at his varied writing, and in the winter of 1874-1875, as he ground out the concluding chapters of *Roderick Hudson* (which began to appear serially in the January 1875 issue of the *Atlantic Monthly*), he also contributed reviews to the *Nation* (at the rate of more than one a week through 1875), did other writing as well, and readied two books—*A Passionate Pilgrim, and Other Tales* and *Transatlantic Sketches* (twenty-five travel essays)—for publication in 1875 by James R. Osgood and Company, Boston. James tried conscientiously to secure a niche for himself among the Manhattan literati but could not, and found instead that he was both worried by the high cost of living in New York and homesick for Europe. So after staying under the parental roof in Cambridge a final time, from July until October, he made what his biographer F. W. Dupee calls "the great decision" and crossed the Atlantic yet again. James aspired to make Paris his residence for some years. By November 1875 he was there.

His long apprenticeship clearly behind him, James would strike for a position of equality among the literary titans of Europe and for financial independence. His French was as fluent as his English. Rather effortlessly he began to meet and associate with Ivan Turgenev (the influential émigré Russian novelist and ultimately his closest professional friend abroad), Flaubert (whom he defined as "kindly, and touchingly inarticulate"), Guy de Maupassant, Ernst Renan, the naturalists Edmond de Goncourt and Emile Zola, and Alphonse Daudet. James was sufficiently accomplished to appreciate their literary style but New Englander enough yet to decry their moral laxity. He soon began to feel like an unwanted outsider. Nor could he seem to please the *New York Tribune*, whose assistant editor John Hay, soon to become another of James's closest friends, had obtained for him an assignment to write travel, society, political, and art notes from France. When the *Tribune* people urged James to make his efforts more chatty and gossipy, he replied, "they are the poorest I can do, especially for the money!," and quit. In December 1876 James moved from Paris to an apartment at 3 Boulton

Street, near Piccadilly, in London, and eased into a productive pattern in that "great grey Babylon" for the next several years.

A list of the illustrious Britishers whom James met for the first time or with whom he renewed acquaintance is almost unbelievable. His father's books, even if not widely read, were a topic of conversation with many in London and helped to gain his son an entrée into the highest circles. A list of James's old and new friends at this time would include Robert Browning, Sir Charles Dilke, George Eliot, G. H. Lewes, James Anthony Froude, William Ewart Gladstone, Alexander William Kinglake, Andrew Lang, Richard Monckton Milnes (Lord Houghton), John Morley, William Morris, John Ruskin, Dr. Heinrich Schliemann, Herbert Spencer, Leslie Stephen, Alfred Tennyson, and Anthony Trollope. The son, however, already had a reputation which was beginning to eclipse that of the father. This young man of thirty-four years, serious, polyglot, of impeccable taste and formidable professional ambition, was known for his many short stories published in American journals, for his three books, which had been imported from Boston by Trübner, and for his latest novel *The American*, installments of which had started to appear in the *Atlantic Monthly* the previous summer. It was published in Boston by Osgood in May 1877, and an unauthorized English edition appeared later that year.

The hero of *The American*, Christopher Newman, is a Civil War veteran and a rich former businessman, who brashly comes to Paris to buy the best wife on the market. Through an expatriated American matchmaker Newman meets a young widow, Claire de Cintré, whose proud French family, the Bellegardes, accept his suit but then squeeze the outsider back out, much as James was made to feel alienated a year earlier in Paris. Although Newman protests and lashes back, Claire's widowed mother and older brother remain inflexible. But Claire's younger brother is so ashamed of them that on his deathbed after a melodramatic duel he tells Newman that a family servant can tell him a secret he may use to extort permission to wed. James depicts the villainous French pair—mother and older son—as so defiant as almost to compel admiration. Claire enters a convent, and Newman, too noble to carry out his plan, burns the evidence. The main focus of the romantic novel is the contrast of American innocence and Old World experience, and it is hence the first substantial international novel.

In his preface to the revised version of *The*

American, James said that the novel "unfurled . . . the emblazoned flag of romance," that it was a balloon with its cable wrongly detached from the real earth below, and that in real life the Bellegarde family "would positively have jumped . . . at my rich and easy American." Romantically inclined contemporary readers were sad when James's lovers were kept apart, but their creator privately opined that "they would have been an impossible couple." James was paid $1,350 for serial rights to *The American,* but it sold poorly thereafter in book form.

For the next four years James solidified his position as a sophisticated American writer in London. He wrote steadily and had his work published in rapid-fire order. *French Poets and Novelists* (1878) collected several of his sensitive periodical essays on such figures as Charles Baudelaire, Balzac, and *Théâtre Français* dramatists. *The Europeans* (1878) is a winsome study of the adventures of a Europeanized brother-and-sister combination visiting cousins back home in New England, judging their Puritanical strictures but also being quietly judged in return. New World innocence and moral rectitude come off rather well here.

Daisy Miller: A Study (1878), James's most popular success, was serialized in England and promptly pirated in two American periodicals before it was published as a book; the novelist thus lost much in royalties. In the story, expatriate American Frederick Forsyth Winterbourne meets attractive, enigmatically naive Daisy Miller, an American traveling with her vapid, gauche mother, while they are at Vevey. The two young people "improperly" go boating to the Château de Chillon. They meet again in Rome; but Daisy's free and easy if harmless strolling with an opportunistic Italian named Giovanelli causes the girl to be cut socially by the American colony. After this, Daisy rashly visits Rome's miasmal Colosseum with thoughtless Giovanelli, becomes ill, and dies. Having discovered that Daisy was totally innocent after all, Winterbourne regrets his doubts about her virtue and admits, fatally late, that he has "lived too long in foreign parts." James's baffling little "study" of a modern American girl of the 1870s has taken on new meaning with the advent of women's liberation.

Washington Square (1881) brilliantly sets wealthy, widowed Dr. Austin Sloper of Washington Square, New York City, in opposition to his stolid daughter Catherine. When she meets Morris Townsend and is swept off her feet, her fa-

ther judges (correctly) that Morris is a fortune hunter and volubly disapproves. Dr. Sloper's widowed busybody of a sister espouses the couple's cause even as the physician takes his daughter off to Europe. She remains passive but also determined; once home again, she declines Morris's selfish suggestion that she placate her father to avoid disinheritance. Catherine's misery, as caused by both father and "lover," is both poignant and lasting. *Washington Square* enjoyed what Gard calls a "good average sale (for James)," but the novelist excluded it from his New York Edition.

For occasional relaxation during this time, James traveled on a regular basis to France, Scotland, and Italy. Moreover, he maintained a dizzy social pace in London. He wrote to Grace Norton in June 1879 of "having dined out during the past winter 107 times!" No wonder he entitled one of his stories "The Siege of London" (1883).

Next came a monumental professional success followed by family sorrows. James found his income sufficient to permit him to plan and execute his longest novel, *The Portrait of a Lady,* on which he pinned hopes for great renown. The novel concerns an American woman, from Albany, whose inherited wealth would make it possible for her sensibilities to be expanded by European travel and residence, but would also make her the prey of a serpentlike suitor in gardenlike Italy. Beginning the task of composing it in England in mid 1879, James worked on it in Florence in the spring of 1880 and in London from the summer of 1880 until February 1881, finishing it in Venice in the early summer of 1881. By this time it was appearing serially on both sides of the Atlantic: in England the first installment had been published in *Macmillan's Magazine* in October 1880, while the *Atlantic Monthly* began publishing it in November. These serializations, which ran into 1881, earned James about $5,000; book publication of the novel in England and the United States in late 1881 brought in still more money.

The Portrait of a Lady, James's first undisputed masterpiece, has a big cast of characters, several of whom might be construed as partly autobiographical. For example, James, like his heroine Isabel Archer, knew Albany as a child, traveled abroad on money which he had not earned, relished Europe enormously, and feared his own possible American provinciality. Like Isabel's cousin Ralph Touchett, James felt debarred from much normal activity through mysterious physical debility. And like Henrietta Stackpole, James sent journalistic travel letters from Europe, was loyal to America, but succumbed to the Old World at last. *The Portrait of a Lady,* however, is much more than veiled autobiography. Its simple, fairy-tale plot presents a callow, willful, charming American girl who is approached by three attractive suitors in Europe: Caspar Goodwood, a rich American manufacturer; Lord Warburton, aristocratic, ruddy, and political; and the successful Gilbert Osmond, fatally suave, superficially cultured, and as deeply corrupt as any villain in Hawthorne, Herman Melville, or William Faulkner. This rich and subtle novel is a study of deception and conceit, but also a portrayal of social and familial responsibility, and the possibility of triumph through renunciation of self, as Isabel chooses to remain with Osmond for the sake of his daughter, Pansy.

Once the first chapters of this great novel were being printed for book publication, James began to relax a good deal. He traveled in the British Isles and then in October returned, half fearfully, to America to see his aging parents in Cambridge. Independent now and enjoying the profits of *The Portrait of a Lady,* he took residence in a Boston hotel, where on 25 November 1881 he sat down and took stock of his life, recording his thoughts in a notebook: "I am glad I have come–it was a wise thing to do. I needed to see again *les miens,* to revive my relations with them . . . Such relations . . . are a part of one's life, and the best life . . . is the one that takes full account of such things. . . . Apart from this . . . it was not necessary I should come to this country. . . . I have made my choice, and God knows that I have now no time to waste. My choice is the old world–my choice, my need, my life. . . . the problem was settled long ago, and . . . I have now nothing to do but to act on the settlement." During his ample leisure, James went to New York, which seemed dull, and then paid his first visit to Washington, D.C., calling on Henry Adams, whom he knew well by now, and on Adams's wife, Marian. On the evening of 29 January 1882 James was urgently called home from Washington; before he reached Cambridge, the greatest sorrow of his middle years had already happened: his beloved mother had died.

James recorded his impressions of winter in New England during his mother's funeral, later incorporating some of them in a weak short story called simply "A New England Winter" (1884). He stayed on at home, offering what comfort he could to his feeble old father, bereft but gently stoical. James piquantly wrote a family friend that "My father . . . has a way of his own of taking the sorrows of life–a way so perfect that one almost envies him his troubles." Then in May James went back "home" to Europe–first to Ireland, then to Bolton Street, London. His father sent a touching letter after him, "Good-bye then again, my precious Harry! . . . We [he and Alice James] shall rejoice in you in our several way [*sic*] as you plough the ocean and attain to your old rooms, where it will be charming to think of you as once more settled and at work."

And work he did. He went carefully through familiar France and new spots in the fall in preparation for *A Little Tour in France* (1885), one of his most remarkable books of travel. Ensconced back in London again for what he thought would be a winter of much writing, James was called to Massachusetts a final time. His father, no longer desirous of living, was slipping fast, and he died and was buried before the novelist docked in New York. Alice James seemed in somewhat better health at this time. Her friendship with Katharine Peabody Loring, later her traveling companion and private nurse, was a distinct help. The father had named Henry James rather than William James (then on research abroad) as executor of his will. Only the novelist's combination of tact and generosity prevented a family squabble, since William–now married and with a family–thought he should have more than an equitable fraction of their father's $95,000 estate.

After a stay in Cambridge, visiting his unsuccessful younger brothers in Milwaukee, and seeing old friends and familiar haunts in the Boston environs, James in August 1883 resolutely turned his face toward Europe once again. This time he was to remain abroad for the next two decades and more. He had found leisure to write a good deal while in America. Now his pace became fantastic. In 1881 he had no fiction published except *The Portrait of a Lady.* In 1882 he produced one story. In 1883 he had published two stories and an ill-starred dramatic version of *Daisy Miller* with a new and incongruous happy ending. But in 1884 he had six stories published, including the splendid "Lady Barbarina," "The Author of Beltraffio," and "Pandora." In addition, in November 1883 his friend Frederick Macmillan brought out the first collected edition of James's fiction in fourteen inexpensive little volumes. The first ten volumes republished *The Portrait of a Lady,*

Roderick Hudson, The American, Washington Square, The Europeans, and, oddly, one of his weakest novels, *Confidence* (1880). The last four volumes contained thirteen short stories, which illustrate international sexual relations, the contrast of American social gaucherie and European suavity, sad heroines, and what might be called societal incongruities in general. It must have gratified the forty-year-old expatriate American to see this selection of nearly 3,000 pages (well over 900,000 words) of his best fiction; excluded from it are some twenty-seven stories and his apprentice novel *Watch and Ward.*

James solidified his growing reputation with a significant manifesto of literary realism called "The Art of Fiction" in 1885. Started as a rebuttal to a recent lecture by critic and novelist Walter Besant, who had said that novels should have moral purpose and that novel writing can be taught like harmonics and perspective in other art forms, James's essay contends persuasively that fiction, like the best history and painting, should project a direct impression of real life, indeed, that the most artistic fiction competes with reality and–more–makes life worth living. James notes that saccharine fiction, with happy endings, is a base falsification of the real world, in which lives do not end thus. Rules for writing fiction injuriously restrict experiment. Far from limiting himself to his immediate range of experience, the writer should be allowed to project himself by his imagination, which "takes to itself the faintest hints of life, . . . converts the very pulses of the air into revelations." And far from being urged to decide whether to write novels of character or novels of incident, a new writer should be encouraged to make the most of reality seen all around him from his unique point of view. Finally, far from wanting novels to be didactic, James begs critics to let the writer freely choose his subject–his donnée–to find fault only with craftsmanship and execution, and to agree that "no good novel will ever proceed from a superficial mind." In addition, James argued for the theory, later very popular, that a piece of fiction is a living, organic entity with interdependent parts. James's own fiction generally practices what is preached in "The Art of Fiction."

The later years of the 1880s start James's middle period, during which the novelist continued to visit the Continent regularly, remained a loving brother, and worked hard. His mentor Turgenev had died in Paris in 1883; now James seemed to appoint himself mentor in his turn to talented novices. At about this time, in Paris and elsewhere, he made the acquaintance of the younger French writers Pierre Loti and Paul Bourget, the sickly Robert Louis Stevenson, and the expatriate American painter John Singer Sargent, among others. Late in 1884 Alice James voyaged to England, with Katharine Loring and that energetic woman's invalid sister. James, who had made over to Alice $1,200 per year from his patrimony, met the group in Liverpool and helped them settle in London and then Bournemouth. Alice's arrival reinforced Henry's belief that England was now his home; so the novelist leased larger quarters, at 34 De Vere Gardens, in Kensington, London, early in 1886. Meanwhile, 1885 and 1886 saw perhaps the most remarkable publishing event of his life. Appearing at about the same time were American serializations of two of his longest novels, *The Bostonians* and *The Princess Casamassima. The Bostonians* appeared in the *Century* (formerly *Scribner's Monthly*) February 1885 to February 1886; *The Princess Casamassima,* in the *Atlantic Monthly* September 1885 to October 1886. Both novels were published in book form in 1886.

These two novels represent substantive though not stylistic departures for James. *The Bostonians* concerns the post-Civil War feminist movement in New England, particularly Boston. It features an oratorically dazzling heroine named Verena Tarrant, who, somewhat stunted by wretched parental influences, becomes a passive object of contention between an old-fashioned, graciously sensual Confederate army veteran, Basil Ransom, now living in New York (and occasionally visiting Boston), and a possible lesbian, well-to-do Bostonian political activist, Olive Chancellor. The novel also depicts many other female types, including a no-nonsense physician, a rich widow on the prowl, a vociferous organizer, and a dottering old reformer–Miss Birdseye–with memories as hoary as those of Elizabeth Peabody (Hawthorne's reform-minded sister-in-law), whom James too loudly denied using as his model. The male characters in *The Bostonians* are stereotypically chauvinistic, sinister, or foolish. It was as unpopular in book form as it had been when it was serialized. James earned less than £500 in all, from serial and book rights, but it has recently engaged the attention of many fine critics, especially feminist ones. Moreover, most readers now praise it for its evocation of old Boston, for its murky depiction of the eternal battle of the sexes, and especially for its prescience with respect to aspects of women's liberation–for example, the misery of male parental dominance, the victimizing of women by women, marriage as cop-out, and the need for radicalism among reformers.

Political also is *The Princess Casamassima,* which is set in poverty-stricken sections of London, in the manner of Dickens. It deals with international anarchism. Its hero is illegitimate Hyacinth Robinson, whose parents–a French adventuress and a British lord whom she stabbed to death–symbolize his psychic schism. An artistic little bookbinder in early manhood, Hyacinth pledges to assassinate a parasitic aristocrat, but then he is enabled by a small inheritance to have a taste of cultured Paris and Venice. Also wrenching him this way and that are the two loves of his brief life: the cultured but politically radical Princess Casamassima (who proved fatal to Roderick Hudson a decade earlier) and the grandly vulgar shopgirl Millicent Henning, James's most sensual female. Ultimately both women and other friends prove inconstant to Hyacinth; and so, unable to strike a blow against European aristocracy–rotten though it is–which produces sumptuous art, he puts a bullet through his own heart.

In book form *The Princess Casamassima* did not earn the advance of £550 which James received, and contemporary critics ridiculed it on the grounds that its author could not personally know about European anarchists. But in recent years the novel has perhaps been too extravagantly acclaimed for its exciting portrayals of would-be dynamiters and Dickensian have-nots.

Italy called James yet again. Feeling fatigued, without new ideas, and depressed by his books' lack of popularity, he went to Venice at the very end of 1886, stayed a couple of months, then moved on to Florence, where he shared a villa in the gentle hills outside town with Constance Fenimore Woolson, an unmarried expatriate American writer whom he had long known and who evidently cared for him more than he did for her. Here James wrote much of "The Aspern Papers," one of his most beautiful long short stories, inspired by the image of Claire Clairmont, the dead Lord Byron's aged former mistress, clinging to his letters. Wending his way north, James visited Venice again and returned to London after eight months, thoroughly refreshed. His publishing record for 1888 proves as much; in addition to "The Aspern Papers," the short novel *The Reverberator* (satirizing gossip columnists), six short stories (including "The

Liar" and "The Lesson of the Master"), and some critical and travel items.

The unpopularity of his last two lengthy novels had turned James against that form for the next couple of years. But in 1888 he started yet another piece of extended fiction, which he called *The Tragic Muse* (1890) and serialized in the *Atlantic Monthly* in seventeen installments, January 1889 to May 1890. Its complex plot concerns a successful British politician who gives up his promising political career to study painting and a talented Jewish actress who, after studying in Paris, gives up marriage to a dashing British diplomat for success on the London stage. Art has its muse, says James, while politics and diplomacy do not, but serving the muse can be tragic for an artist's personal life.

James had long been a devotee of the theater–in America, London, and especially Paris–and he knew many actors and actresses. His next step was a new, daring, and partly damaging one. He vowed to write successful plays and spent five long years trying to do so. The lack of immediate popular or critical success of *The Tragic Muse* served only to push James harder toward playwriting. First, he accepted the invitation of an actor named Edward Compton to turn his melodramatic novel *The American* into a play. He did so in 1890, and it opened just outside Liverpool, with Compton in the leading role, with James's young American friend Elizabeth Robins (famous for her Ibsen roles in England) as Claire de Cintré, and with a happy ending. After Compton moved the troupe to London, the play was not well received, played only seventy nights, earned James a moderate sum, but did not deter him from further efforts. By 1892 he had completed four new plays. He was led to believe that the famous American theatrical wizard Augustin Daly would convert one of them, called *Disengaged,* into a successful vehicle for his popular actress Ada Reham. But so many troubles ensued that James, refusing to compromise with excessive production changes, demanded his script back and quit Daly. Never one to waste his materials, James had the four plays published in pairs as *Theatricals* (1894) and *Theatricals: Second Series* (1895). Meanwhile, in 1893 he completed yet another drama, this one entitled *Guy Domville.* The popular actor and producer George Alexander took it on. It opened on 5 January 1895; and, although James ultimately netted £750 on the play, it was a dismal failure. The play is set in the year 1780 and pits religious conviction against family

James in Rome, 1899

he was superior as a playwright to such popular contemporary dramatists as Oscar Wilde, noting of himself that "you can't make a sow's ear out of a silk purse." During his playwriting period James had published a number of splendid short stories: "The Pupil," about young male friendship and possible betrayal within a seedy expatriate family from America; "Sir Edmund Orme," a sophisticated ghost story; "Nona Vincent," about a playwright and an actress; "Owen Wingrave," about nonmilitary courage in a military family and the closest James ever came to writing naturalistic fiction; "The Middle Years," about second changes for aging novelists; "The Death of the Lion," about society's lionizing writers but ignoring their work; and "The Coxon Fund," about the risk of subsidizing an unstable genius–among other less distinguished pieces. Now James turned to writing more and possibly even greater fiction.

The half-decade now past had brought him personal sorrows enough to make more profound his sharp probing of psychological reality. His old friend James Russell Lowell died in 1891. James's much-loved sister Alice died in London of breast cancer in 1892, with the novelist at her side. (She left a diary which was so personal and frank that James destroyed his copy of the privately printed edition.) Constance Fenimore Woolson, long sick in Venice, died there early in 1894 under curious circumstances, indicating the possibility of suicide; the news and then subsequent details alarmed James profoundly. (He avoided her funeral in Rome but obtained her family's permission to sort through the dead woman's private papers.) Late in 1894 Robert Louis Stevenson, whose vital personality and adventuresome fiction James relished, died in faraway Samoa, in the South Seas. On top of these losses, the blow to his professional vanity occasioned by the collapse of his play *Guy Domville* was a heavy one.

A badly needed lift to his spirits came in the summer of 1896, when James vacationed in Rye, a little coastal town in Sussex, southeast of London, saw Lamb House there, and the following year took a long lease on the solid, cozy early eighteenth-century mansion. When he had the opportunity to purchase the delightful place two years later, he willingly paid the £2,000 asked. He quickly made it his home, entertained a succession of illustrious guests there, and fashioned some of his finest literary efforts in his adjacent garden-house studio. Numerous photographs show James in his well-manicured garden, alone

responsibility, features melodramatic villainy, and rings with hollow lines (curiously James's fiction is filled with intensely dramatic dialogue). James's friends in the first-night audience–including William Archer, Burne-Jones, Edmund Gosse, Sir Frederic Leighton, Sargent, and George Bernard Shaw–gave the opening a certain tone but could hardly save the play. When James appeared onstage at final-curtain time, he was booed. The play closed after one month.

It took James almost no time to recover his composure from this blow and to return to writing fiction, which, indeed, he never had abandoned during his dramatic years. Late in January 1895 he confided in his private notebook, "I take up my *own* old pen again–the pen of all my old unforgettable efforts and sacred struggles. To myself–today–I need say no more. Large and full and high the future still opens. It is now indeed that I may do the work of my life. And I will." At about the same time he found confidence enough to boast in a letter to William James that and happy, or strolling with relatives and other visitors. Lamb House remained his residence for the remainder of his life. The aging James continued to visit old locales and many friends on the Continent, particularly in summer, and to participate in London social and theatrical seasons. He retained rooms in the London Reform Club for London visits and often went there to avoid Rye's damp and isolated winters or its muggy summers. But Lamb House was home now.

Much of the fiction which James wrote during this time is challenging and technically daring. He was now approaching the end of his so-called middle phase. The titles of two of his collections of short fiction, written before his move to Lamb House–*Terminations* (1895) and *Embarrassments* (1896)–may be an enigmatic comment on the wretched dramatic years of the author, who then plunged ahead with *The Spoils of Poynton* (1897), *What Maisie Knew* (1897), "The Turn of the Screw" (1898), and *The Awkward Age* (1899)–his first work written entirely at Lamb House. These fictional productions are remarkable, each in a different manner.

The Spoils of Poynton turns on an unfortunate British law: when a man dies, his widow must release his property to his oldest son. Not content to use this donnée merely to occasion a fictive family squabble, James dramatizes a brilliant development: have the widowed mother a fighter and her property include a dazzling collection of art objects, make the son bumbling and uncertain, and have a pair of contrasting young women both interested in him. The action continues mostly through the consciousness of Fleda Vetch, a somewhat impoverished young woman with taste enough to appreciate "the spoils." She is gently enamored of young Owen Gereth, but ruinously high principled and hence a match for neither her materialistic rival nor Owen's vindictive mother. The nature of Fleda's sexuality has puzzled readers and critics to this day. Does the young woman have good taste in men? Is she fatally negative, perverse? Does she allow too rigid scruples to make her seem inconsistent? Does she fear profound sexual arousal? Is "Victorianism" responsible for her final desolation?

What Maisie Knew centers in the emerging moral consciousness of an adolescent girl named Maisie Farange whose parents get divorced, marry others, and always treat the child selfishly. What Maisie gradually gains knowledge of is the baseness of some adults, the morality of one eccentric governess, and something which ought to be called love for her father's second wife's lover, who has become Maisie's mother's second husband. Poignant ambiguity results from innocent little Maisie's inability to verbalize her bewildering conceptions.

"The Turn of the Screw," perhaps the world's finest ghost story, is the most satisfying, ambivalent, and provocative piece of fiction James ever wrote. In it, an unnamed governess, who narrates the main action with at least initial credibility, accepts the challenge of tutoring and overseeing the well-being of two young children, Miles and his little sister Flora. Their parents are dead, and their well-to-do uncle is altogether indifferent to them, except financially. He hires the governess (who seems immediately enamored of him and anxious to impress him) and dispatches her to stay with the children at his estate, Bly, in the remote English countryside. The governess is bright but possibly unstable. Suddenly one ghost, and then another, appears before her. One is that of the absent uncle's deceased valet; the other, that of the governess's (presumably) dead predecessor, who may have known the valet intimately. Curiously, only the governess sees the ghosts. Or is that the case? Are the ghosts real? Are they figments of the governess's imagination? Are they projections from her reading, or from her unrequited passion for the children's uncle? James himself is uninformative in critical comments on the puzzling work, which, in his preface to it in the New York Edition, he labels "a piece of ingenuity pure and simple, of cold artistic calculation, an *amusette* to catch those not easily caught. . . , the jaded, the disillusioned, the fastidious." The critical battle is still raging, and it is likely to do so indefinitely, since James seems consciously to have salted his text with veins leading in different directions.

In *The Awkward Age*, which also deals with children, two girls "come out" together in London society, which is a veritable horse fair parading marriageable young females before potential customers. James chose to write the story mostly in dialogue–complete with tersely narrated entrances and exits–and with a minimum of authorial explanation. The technique evidently puzzled early readers of *The Awkward Age*, which sold poorly in James's lifetime, but James's young protégé Percy Lubbock later praised the novel for its "pure drama."

In 1900, at the start of the century whose literature he was to influence so spectacularly, Henry James shaved off his beard, thus greeting the new age more openly, and then proceeded to launch himself into what may well be the most impressive siege of writing, lasting through 1904, in the annals of American literary history. A collection of twelve short stories, *The Soft Side* (1900), was followed by *The Sacred Fount* (1901), *The Wings of the Dove* (1902), eleven more short stories in *The Better Sort* (1903), *The Ambassadors* (1903), a two-volume biography, *William Wetmore Story and His Friends* (1903), and *The Golden Bowl* (1904). This unprecedented burst of creativity, amounting to more than 3,000 pages, is all the more remarkable when one considers that James, from his earliest Lamb House days, had been in the habit of dictating most of his "writing" to a typist, not only because of a slight weakness in his right wrist but also because the volume of his personal correspondence had become almost unmanageable.

The Soft Side includes an innocuous ghost story about decorous smuggling, "The Third Person," set in and near Lamb House. *The Sacred Fount* fictionalizes the theory that in any interpersonal relationship one partner takes while the other is tapped dry of vitality. It is told in the first person by a possibly unreliable narrator who may not be sane, and it has been seen as a parable of the artistic life. To some readers, it is needlessly long-winded and otherwise unsatisfactory; others, however, feel that probing it successfully is tantamount to fathoming James himself. *The Better Sort* includes "The Beast in the Jungle," which, incredibly, James could not place in any journal before its book publication. This matchless story deals with John Marcher, who keeps himself aloof from life because he fancies that life plans to spring something uniquely special on him eventually. He insufficiently commits himself to May Bartram, who guesses the nature of "the beast" in Marcher's life but agrees to wait with him to see. Too late the foolish egoist learns that he is fated to be the one man on earth to whom nothing happens. The story has compelling imagery of masks, fire, and ice, and its syntax is as sluggish as its absurdist hero.

Entering what is now known as his major phase, James, with *The Wings of the Dove, The Ambassadors,* and *The Golden Bowl,* wrote a Dantesque commedia, a monumental triptych, three incomparable novels of expatriate Americans in England, Italy, and France. These tangled fables tell us much about renunciation and generosity, the value of studying new modes of moral behavior, and the price of love; the backgrounds of these ac-

tions inspire James to some of his best pictorial effects, especially when he limns glittering Paris and mouldering Venice.

Milly Theale, heroine of *The Wings of the Dove,* is like James's long-dead cousin Minny Temple, "heiress of all the ages," in the sense of being sensitive, cultured, bright, and well-to-do. And Milly is also dying. When British journalist Merton Densher is encouraged by his materialistic, egocentric fiancée Kate Croy to woo Milly for an eventual legacy, he agrees. Milly eventually finds out from the young man's rival, "turns her face to the wall," and dies–leaving Merton a vast sum. Meanwhile, her dovelike generosity changes him, although Milly's bequest may have been a subtle form of revenge. The conscience-stricken Densher tells Kate he will marry her only if he refuses the bequest, but she refuses to marry him unless he takes it. The first part of the novel is cast in England, with beautiful late Victorian settings in and near London. Later, as Milly grows sicker, the scene shifts to sinister Venice.

The Ambassadors, which James called "quite the best, 'all round,' of all my productions," was inspired by his hearing that Howells, while in the painter James Whistler's Parisian garden, had cautioned a young acquaintance, "I'm old. It's too late. It has gone past me–I've lost it. You have time. You are young. Live!" From that "wind-blown seed," as he often called the inspiration of a plot, James nurtured his finest, most artistically integrated novel. Lambert Strether, a partly autobiographical New England editor, undertakes an ambassadorial mission to Paris for his domineering, widowed fiancée. He is to learn why her son Chad Newsome is dallying abroad and to bring him home to the family business. Strether finds the young man much improved in appearance, manners, and intellect, and soon wonders whether Chad loves married Marie de Vionnet (a bit too old for him) or her little daughter Jeanne (too young). Since everyone is evasively genteel, it takes Strether so long to make a determination that a squad of new "ambassadors" is dispatched by the absent mother. By this time, Chad has grown willing to detach himself, but Strether has now espoused not only the Vionnets' cause but Gallic ethical relativism in general. Strether begins to change for the better, as Chad must have done for a while earlier. Strether's discovery that Chad and Marie are lovers is so beautifully orchestrated that it is a high point in American fiction, complete with French impressionistic backdrop. Character balances render the entire novel as modulated as a minuet: Strether learns graceful Old World steps, as Chad backs away into American awkwardness again; Chad advances toward little Jeanne, then minces away with her mother. James's high opinion of *The Ambassadors* is fully justified–by all evidence, that is, except initially poor book sales. A notable stylistic element in the novel is the manner in which the reader is permitted to learn, which is largely by seeing what and as Strether does, by tentatively concluding with him: as Strether sympathizes with others, so the reader empathizes.

Many critics regard *The Golden Bowl* as its author's finest novel. It offers the reader a plot of mathematical neatness wrapped in Jamesian syntax at its most difficult. A rich American widower and art collector named Adam Verver is traveling with his young adult daughter Maggie, who marries suave Prince Amerigo of Rome, formerly the lover of Charlotte Stant, whom Maggie once knew as well. Sensing her father's loneliness, Maggie throws Charlotte in his path, and Adam and Charlotte soon marry. But father and daughter remain too close. So Amerigo and Charlotte resume their sexual liaison. Earlier, Amerigo and Charlotte, while shopping for a wedding present for Maggie, rejected a beautiful golden bowl because it was flawed. Later Maggie happens upon it and learns indirectly through the shopkeeper of the intimacy of her husband and the young woman who is now her stepmother. Maggie now has an awesome moral problem. She wants her husband, but she also wishes to hurt neither her father nor her rival. James shows the intimacy of Adam and Maggie and depicts the adultery of the prince and Charlotte with what must be called sympathy by resorting to the technical device of the confidante. He gives Maggie a sympathetic ear in the person of Fanny Assingham, an old family friend. Long-winded Fanny in turn makes a patient confidant of her husband Colonel Bob. But mainly James manages difficulties through indirections and even silences in dialogue, ambiguities in narration, and operatic inner scenes first in the prince's mind and later in Maggie's. That James could keep these gossamer-fine subtleties in mental suspension as, month after month, he dictated this 192,000-word novel in his Lamb House chambers, is amazing. *The Golden Bowl* enjoyed a modest success in England, outselling every other one of his London-published books except his controversial *Hawthorne* (1879).

Next James reluctantly agreed to put to-gether *William Wetmore Story and His Friends* from masses of papers which his friend's family made available to him. Story (1819-1895), who had given up his position as a lawyer at Harvard and Boston for expatriation in Rome, where he was sculptor, painter, poet, musician, and travel writer, seemed to James a dilettante; but he nonetheless strung together his subject's papers with fascinating narrative commentary, valuable today only because in it James discusses his own memories of Rome in Story's day.

With his symphonically sustained fiction of the last five years now behind him, James turned his thoughts to rest, travel, lecturing, and note taking in the United States. He projected a travel book on his American sightseeing. Late in August 1904 he sailed from England and was soon enjoying a New England autumn with William James and his family. James stayed with them first in their summer home at Chocorua, New Hampshire, and then at Cambridge. During the Christmas season he went to New York, which seemed to him deplorably altered by tall buildings and noisy commerce. While there, he attended a Harper and Brothers banquet, where the guest list also included Samuel Clemens and Hamlin Garland. Next he went to Philadelphia, where he read his paper called "The Lesson of Balzac" to a culture club for $250. (He later commanded even higher fees–up to £1 per minute, as he once gloated.) He continued on to Washington, D.C., where, through the influence of his old friends John Hay (now secretary of state under President Theodore Roosevelt) and Henry Adams, he had dinner at the White House. (Roosevelt privately regarded James as "a miserable little snob," while the novelist privately called the wielder of the Big Stick "a dangerous . . . Jingo.") After a visit to Virginia, blanketed by late snows which spoiled James's hope of seeing a southern spring there, the traveler returned to the Philadelphia area to lecture at Bryn Mawr College and then went on to Richmond, Charleston, where he called upon Owen Wister, and Florida. James capitalized on his unexpected podium popularity by lecturing successfully in St. Louis, Chicago, Notre Dame, Indianapolis, and Los Angeles. He reveled in California, seeing it from the point of view of one familiar with Mediterranean coastal regions and noting resemblances. Soon he headed north to Oregon and Seattle, then traveled east as quickly as possible early in the spring, going through St. Paul and Chicago, loathing most of what he saw and heard–the clatter, aliens, unpleasant ghettos, and what he regarded as the mangling of the English language.

For the 1905 commencement at Bryn Mawr, James was the principal speaker, and he tactlessly chose "The Question of Our [American] Speech" as his subject. He attacked the natives for their slipshod speech patterns and was counterattacked in return for his syntactical complexities. Soon he ran up to Boston–though not again to see William James, who had mysteriously avoided him by going to Greece. The two had drifted apart since the death of their parents. Curiously, while William was in Greece he was elected to membership in the American Academy of Arts and Letters, but he was elected two months after his younger brother Henry had been. Learning this only upon his return home, William declined the honor, writing the Academy that the James family was sufficiently represented by "my younger and shallower and vainer brother."

Henry James went on to Maine, to enjoy a reunion with the vacationing Howells. Moving south again, James spent a while with Edith Wharton in her American home at Lenox, Massachusetts, and conferred with representatives at Charles Scribner's Sons for a sumptuous selected edition of his best fiction. July found him steaming east to Liverpool. His ten months back in America had been refreshing, impressive, enervating, and lucrative. He was now ready for his real home again, in Sussex. While still aboard the ship, he began the task of revising *Roderick Hudson* for the New York Edition. At the same time his memory was teeming with impressions which he was impatient to focus into a book on America.

Once back at Rye, James had to assert his authority in Lamb House, where problems arose with two of his servants. More happily, he soon reestablished his British friendships after his long absence. Next he began converting his American travel notes into *The American Scene* (1907). He also started rereading the bulk of his enormous fictional productions, eventually selecting sixty-seven novels and tales as suitable, with revision, for inclusion in the New York Edition and rejecting the rest. At the same time he planned to write a series of critical prefaces for the edition. Minor publishing ventures distracted him a trifle: early in October 1905 he put together his lectures on Balzac and American speech patterns in a small book. Later in the same month he gathered fourteen old essays and two new ones on English scenes in *English Hours* (1905).

The American Scene is James's most penetrating travel book, and one of the best of its genre in world literature. James limited himself to his observations of the Eastern seaboard. (He hoped to write a follow-up volume on his western travels but did not live to do so.) He reveals uncanny powers of visual perception in the present and with it tender sensory memories of his fading past. Since the purpose is personal evocation, the book usually lacks the social background normally found in an effort, as James puts it, to depict "a society reaching out into the apparent void for the amenities . . . after having earnestly gathered in so many of the . . . necessities." From New England to Florida James ranges, sees, and records his impressions. He is at his depressing best in describing New York City, which he found so grossly, energetically materialistic that it would take a potent Zola, not a squeamish James, to embody it in fiction. As they disturbed Howells earlier, the slums dismayed James, and in his book he therefore contents himself with commenting on the threat to spoken English there and then the charm of adjacent stores. Better far is his treatment of Manhattan architecture, the eclectic clutter of which symbolizes the city as explosive chaos.

Pathetic nostalgia combines with an implicit admonition in James's eloquent description of his lost Newport: "it had simply lain there like a little bare, white, open hand, with slightly-parted fingers, for the observer with a presumed sense for hands to take or to leave. The observer with a real sense never failed to pay this image the tribute of quite tenderly grasping the hand, and even of raising it, delicately, to his lips. . . . The touchstone of taste was indeed to operate, for the critical, the tender spirit, from the moment the pink palm was turned up on the chance of what might be 'in' it. For nine persons out of ten, among its visitors, its purchasers of sites and builders. . . , there had never been anything in it at all–except of course an opportunity . . . The pink palm being empty, in other words, to their vision, they had begun . . . to put things into it, things of their own, and of all sorts, and of many ugly, and of more and more expensive, sorts; to fill it substantially, that is, with gold, the gold that they have ended up heaping up there to an amount so oddly out of proportion to the scale of nature and of space."

The sections on the South in *The American Scene*, though gracefully composed and predictably observant of architecture and setting, lack the sociological acumen demonstrated in those few chapters on regions James knew best and dreamed of most fondly: New England, New York, and the Hudson River region. The book is valuable today for its timeless warning to all Americans: treasure old local color, avoid ravaging the land, resist placing commerce above all else, respect your best art, look about, look out. The often gloomy message is lightened by glints of Jamesian humor and decidedly resembles the prophetic admonitions of Henry David Thoreau.

Preparing the splendid New York Edition cost James about four years. In his short story "The Real Thing" (1893) he had described tardy justice finally rendered to a neglected writer by means of a well-illustrated *édition de luxe*. Here was James's own chance. The aging novelist extensively revised earlier tales, making them more subtle in the eyes of critics who prefer his major-phase style, but veiling their romantic crispness according to those who like the early James best. He rejected works which neither could be cleaned by "the tentative wet sponge" and then "varnish[ed] . . . anew" (as he puts it in his preface to *Roderick Hudson*, the edition's first volume) nor could be fitted into Balzacian thematic units. James collaborated with a pioneering young American photographer, Alvin Langdon Coburn, for frontispieces which might hint at fictive contents without being blatant and delimiting. Best of all, James wrote eighteen prefaces in which he discusses individual works as to their inspiration and compositional difficulties, includes relevant personal anecdotes, and mentions laudable successes and technical aspects where germane. His self-evaluation, sparkling with fine imagery, amounts to subjective literary criticism of the very highest order.

Twelve volumes of the New York Edition were devoted to six of James's best novels: *The Portrait of a Lady, The Princess Casamassima, The Tragic Muse, The Wings of the Dove, The Ambassadors,* and *The Golden Bowl. Roderick Hudson, The American,* and *The Awkward Age* took another volume each. Other novels and also long short stories and shorter tales accounted for the rest, bringing the total edition to twenty-four volumes. (In 1917, the year after James's death, his unfinished novels *The Ivory Tower* and *The Sense of the Past* were added, in a volume each.) James labored hard to group the shorter works he had selected into fiction about English life, international manners, artists and writers, and things supernatural. Omitted therefore were *The Europeans, Washington Square,* and *The Bostonians* (all set in America), most of the American-based short stories, the weak novels *Watch and Ward, Confidence,* and *The Sacred Fount,* and dozens of early tales.

Volumes of the New York Edition appeared regularly from late 1907 until mid 1909. James had such high hopes for good sales that low royalty reports—as little as £85 in all!—plunged him into gloom. He had worked frantically on revisions and prefaces alike, allowing himself only one good-sized vacation, in 1907, when he traveled by automobile with Edith Wharton and her husband through southern France, and then went on alone to Italy for a final time. During the same year he had made the mistake of dabbling in more playwriting, with no more success than in the early 1890s. He collected a volume of his critical essays, *Views and Reviews,* in 1908 (but some of these pieces were forty years old). *Italian Hours* (1909), James's last travel book, gathers more than a dozen previously published essays and adds five new ones. The volume is beautifully illustrated by Joseph Pennell and is one of the most delightful literary works on Italy by any American.

As for writing new fiction, in the next few years James slowed down but was never idle. Despite his other work and then his depression over poor sales of his New York Edition, he wrote eight more tales. Three were in time for inclusion in that edition. One, "The Jolly Corner," is a captivating story of an expatriate's return to the Manhattan neighborhood of his childhood. The hero wonders with such intensity what he might have been like had he remained at home that he actually sees his alter ego. Among the last five tales that James wrote are "The Bench of Desolation," a surreal fable recently evoking splendid readings, and "A Round of Visits," a story about betrayal, crime, and suicide, set in New York City. James included these last five stories in *The Finer Grain* (1910)—an appropriate choice of title for the master of fictive subtlety.

James suffered through a long period of nervous sickness beginning in 1909. William James, though sick himself—with severe heart trouble—and his wife, Alice, came to Lamb House in the summer of 1910 to be of moral support. The three journeyed to Germany and Switzerland in search of health. But William became worse; so, sick though he was, Henry decided to return with him and his wife to New Hampshire, where William died in August. Henry was now the only survivor of the five children. He was deso-

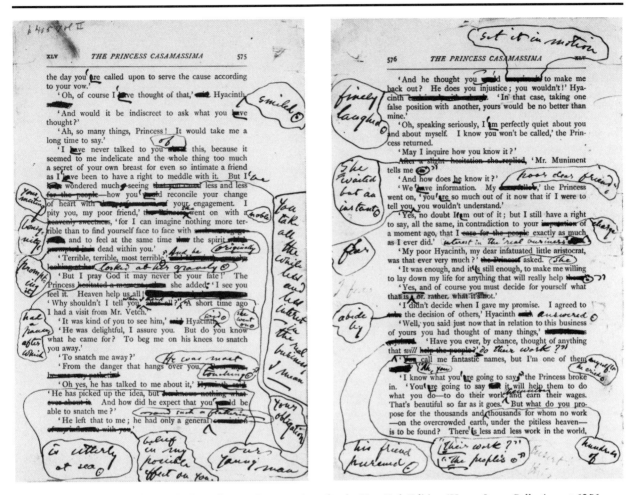

Pages from James's revision of The Princess Casamassima *for the New York Edition (Henry James Collection, #6251, Clifton Waller Barrett Library, Manuscripts Division, University of Virginia Library)*

late and wrote his old friend T. S. Perry, "I sit heavily stricken and in darkness—for from far back in dimmest childhood he had been my ideal Elder Brother, and I still, through all the years, saw in him, even as a small timorous boy yet, my protector, my backer, my authority and my pride. His extinction changes the face of life for me. . . ."

James remained in America for a year, during which time he accepted an honorary degree from Harvard University (Oxford University followed suit in 1912), consulted physicians in the hope of curing his partly psychosomatic disorders, and evidently tried, while staying in dead William's Cambridge house, to communicate with his brother's spirit. He also saw Edith Wharton and Howells again. August 1911 found James steaming back to England. His traveling days were over.

His widowed sister-in-law, Alice James, was so impressed by his ability to evoke the distinct

family past through tender reminiscences that she persuaded James to write them down. Finding Lamb House something of a cage that aggravated his depression, he let his secretary engage him a room or two in her apartment building in Chelsea, London, near the Reform Club, where he slept; soon he was pouring forth an almost unstoppable stream of autobiography at her. It was great therapy. In *A Small Boy and Others* James shares his earliest recollections, then slowly describes his teens to the point where he suffered from typhoid at Boulogne. By the time the book was published in 1913, James was well into *Notes of a Son and Brother,* which draws on masses of old family letters, portrays his father and favorite brother, and brings the author into his mid twenties. It was published in 1914, during which year James also gathered *Notes on Novelists with Some Other Notes,* an important collection of eighteen critical and travel pieces, all of which had previously appeared in journals. His subjects include

Balzac, George Sand, Stevenson, Zola, the new generation of novelists (most of whom James "prize[d] not"), and London.

James had now reached seventy years of age. He was living in an apartment at 21 Carlyle Mansions, Chelsea, with three servants, staying at Lamb House only during the summer. His poor royalties were slipping even more; so Edith Wharton, with more good intentions than good sense, tried secretly to make up a birthday purse for him through friends. James got wind of the plan and furiously stopped it. However, he accepted, as a seventieth-birthday gift, an expensive silver bowl and dish plated with gold (a Golden Bowl) from 300 distinguished friends; he also sat for a portrait by John Singer Sargent, and donated it to the National Portrait Gallery, London.

The publication of *Notes of a Son and Brother* carried James by its momentum into further autobiographical dictation. The book was to be followed by a third volume and possibly two more. But *The Middle Years* (1917), starting with his first adult trip to Europe, remains a fragment of only 120 pages because in the summer of 1914 World War I crashed into James's tenuously cohering world and wrenched it irretrievably. Describing the war, James wrote a close friend about "the appalling blackness of it all, and the horror of having lived to see it!" He threw himself into what war work he could manage, given his age and his now weakened heart. He visited hospitals and comforted the wounded, made his quarters available to soldiers in transit, supported an American ambulance corps, and wrote to denounce German atrocities and to praise British and French courage. On 26 July 1915 James became a British citizen (sponsored by Prime Minister Herbert Asquith), not only to put a stop to the inconvenience of having to get permission from the police to go to Lamb House in coastal Rye as an alien but also to protest his native country's continued neutrality.

Not even the war could silence James the writer. Curiously, he had begun his professional writing during the Civil War; he was destined to end it during another war. He had started a new long novel some years earlier, perhaps in 1908. Set in gracious Newport, it was to dramatize the reconciliation of rich, disputatious former business partners and also to concern a Europeanized American returning to an inheritance and quickly becoming entangled in financial betrayal and sexual intrigue. Early in 1914 James felt well enough to resume work on this novel to which

he had given the title *The Ivory Tower*. If completed, it might have been an almost Theodore Dreiser-like study of wealth, culture, and temptation. But the war came; James, now back in Lamb House, found it impossible to address a contemporary problem, and so he abandoned the work when it was about thirty percent complete. But he still did not quit. Instead, he turned to another long-delayed project, a historical novel to be called *The Sense of the Past*, begun about fifteen years before in his excitement following the success of "The Turn of the Screw." This new long fiction would combine James's interest in extrasensory phenomena, international social relations, and the past. In it a young New York historian named Ralph Pendrel writes a book which so pleases an English relative that he wills the American an eighteenth-century mansion in London. Taking possession of it, Pendrel is deeply stirred by evidence of the past in its portraits, furniture, appointments, and very atmosphere–so much so that one day as he steps across the threshold he finds himself in the eighteenth century communing with his eighteenth-century alter ego, whose picture has been on the wall. Later he becomes that earlier Pendrel and converses with his fiancée, Molly Midmore, who is also exactly like her portrait. He meets his prospective sister-in-law Nan Midmore and quickly feels an affinity to her because of her–their–modernity. Rivalry starts between Pendrel and Nan's suitor, at which point the fragmentary novel breaks off.

Two unpleasant circumstances intervened to disturb James while he was writing the early parts of *The Sense of the Past*. In *Boon* (1915) H. G. Wells made a stinging attack on James's mannered style. He compared a Jamesian novel to "a church lit but without a congregation..., with every light and line focused on the high altar. And on the altar, very reverently placed, intensely there, is a dead kitten, an egg-shell, a bit of string.... [James] splits his infinitives and fills them up with adverbial stuffing. He presses the passing colloquialism into his service. His vast paragraphs sweat and struggle ... And all for tales of nothingness.... It is leviathan retrieving pebbles. It is a magnificent but painful hippopotamus resolved at any cost ... upon picking up a pea which had got into a corner of its den."

A second unpleasantness came in the form of violent denunciation in America of James for his supposed disloyalty in giving up his American citizenship to become a British citizen. He did not trouble to explain. He might have reminded his Yankee readers of his Christopher Newman, Daisy Miller, Isabel Archer, Milly Theale, Lambert Strether, and Adam and Maggie Verver–Americans all, and mostly innocent, decent, attractive, and eager to confront reality, and probably all moral victors in their clashes with smooth Europeans. But James let his fiction debate in his stead.

To Wells, however, James wrote a pair of epistolary rejoinders, at first protesting, then explaining, and finally theorizing that "It is art that *makes* life, makes interest, makes importance, . . . and I know of no substitute whatever for the force and beauty of its process."

On 2 December 1915 James was in his apartment on 21 Carlyle Mansions when he sustained a stroke, which paralyzed his left side. His maid heard him say that the beast in the jungle had sprung. He later told a friend that as he fell he thought, "So here it is at last, the distinguished thing." The next day, he had another stroke. William James's widow, Alice James, received the news and crossed the wintry Atlantic at once to be with James until the end. Delirium upset his sense of place, and he grew frantic, but by mid-January he had improved. In moments of confusion, he dictated rambling thoughts of Robert Louis Stevenson and Henry Adams. James was mentally wandering and sometimes spoke of cities in Ireland and Italy. But more awesome and suggestive were letters which James in his delirium dictated from Napoleon Bonaparte to relatives, concerning renovations of the Louvre and the Tuileries. The Louvre was again on James's mind, decades after his momentous dream of its Galerie d'Apollon.

Meanwhile, regal machinery of another sort was being set in motion. Prime Minister Asquith recommended to King George V that James be granted the Order of Merit. The award was announced on 1 January 1916, and James was lucid and delighted when his old friend the historian-diplomat James Bryce brought the insignia from the king. Through February James rambled much about William. During the afternoon of 28 February 1916, Henry James quietly died, technically of edema. After a funeral service in Chelsea Old Church and subsequent cremation, his ashes were transported to the United States and placed in the James family plot in Cambridge, Massachusetts.

After James's death, his works continued to decline in popularity for about a quarter of a cen-

tury. But roughly with the outbreak of World War II, a new generation of readers began to see the value of his psychological profundity and of his perceptions about international manners. During the early 1940s, and especially in 1943, on the occasion of the centenary of his birth, the so-called James boom began. It has shown no letup in the succeeding decades. Some of the important commentators on James in his lifetime and shortly after his death are William Dean Howells, Joseph Conrad, Ford Madox (Hueffer) Ford, Ezra Pound, T. S. Eliot, Joseph Warren Beach, and Percy Lubbock. Contributing to the James boom were R. P. Blackmur, Philip Rahv, Stephen Spender, Edna Kenton, Edmund Wilson, and F. O. Matthiessen. In the last third of a century more than 125 books and over 2,500 chapters and journal essays have added to the ongoing boom. It would be impossible to name the best five or ten modern Jamesian critics without committing a tasteless sin of omission. Perhaps it should be added that in addition to H. G. Wells, two voices raised against the chorus of praise for James are those of Van Wyck Brooks and Maxwell Geismar. In truth, James left a legacy which is well worth the most serious, varied, and conscientious study.

James's literary production was staggering. His fiction alone amounts to 22 novels and 114 short stories. In addition, he wrote enough critical essays to fill about ten books, seven books of travel, three of autobiography, fifteen plays, and two critical biographies. On an average, one item by James was published every three weeks for more than half a century, in total volume possibly not much short of eight million words. Fifteen thousand of his personal letters are extant.

Of more lasting importance than prodigious quantity and selective popularity, however, are the high quality of James's work and its influence on other writers. James wrote on a limited range of themes but with subtlety and charm. He frequently depicts the clash of American inexperience and European sophistication. Often the American is an innocent person of wealth and intelligence, traveling in Europe and seeking to penetrate its cultural, social, and ethical mysteries. James sometimes complicates his conflicts by making his representatives of European culture Americans living abroad–hence at times trying to be more European than their native friends and neighbors. James's American naifs usually fail to achieve personal and social happiness and success, but they gain in moral esteem, in their eyes and those of their friendly readers. James always combines the international theme with other themes. He may stage with international overtones a drama which illustrates not only the virtue of a forgiving consideration for others but also the vices of meddling, coercion, or revenge. Or he may have the clash of personalities from different countries and social milieus effectuate in an exposure of such false values as social ambition, patriotism, exertion for fame, and pride—pride in one's pedigree, appearance, social renown, or connections. Sometimes these fictive dramas involve only Americans; sometimes, only Englishmen and Englishwomen. James constantly placed his faith in art, rather than in formal religion, political power, wealth, or possessions; and he preferred professional independence rather than personal "love," involvement rather than smug aloofness, or fear of variety, or secondhand living. James was steadily unromantic and individualistic.

James's work is stylistically complicated, demanding much of the reader. He is verbally subtle and delicately comic. His use of the restricted point of view, especially in his later, more realistic work, makes his plots hard to follow but exciting because the reader shares the same delusions, limited perceptions, and dawning awarenesses as the character through whose consciousness the story is filtered. James's imagery adds a poetic dimension to his prose, and individual similes and metaphors cluster into patterns which elucidate human conduct. James's plots are precise and usually quite simple. His purpose is not to tell a story so much as it is to show the interaction between character and character and between character and setting, which is often presented pictorially and usually has symbolic import.

James's fiction is like life. It presents challenges, not answers. It deals in tension resulting from the collision of personalities having different backgrounds and degrees of decency. His endings are almost always unhappy and often unjust, and readers used to final wrap-ups often complain. But James once said that an entire story can never be told, that the novelist should therefore present only what harmonizes.

James's heroines are better than his heroes, more vibrant as artistic creations and finer models for the reader to emulate. James's settings and props are impressionistically painted in, and appreciating his artistry here sharpens the reader's vision for the appreciation of his own surrounding reality. James's concomitant love of fiction, poetry, drama, biography, painting, and sculpture inspires his devotees to try to see for themselves the unity of all art. Awareness of James's sturdy defense of his profession, his craft, is noble and worthy of emulation.

James was forward-looking, and hence his work wears well. He tentatively explored eroticism (especially in the young), imaginative quests through time, nihilism, and absurdist disorientations. James disliked shapeless novels, bulky with social or personal protest and holding up a mirror to chaotic reality; he preferred those with balanced parts and a tidied appearance that please through subjective probing and unusual artistic tension and balance. He has a character in *The Tragic Muse* say, "The book of life's padded, ah but padded—a deplorable want of editing." James sought to edit and thus order the reality he knew. Nearly every artistically shaped novel in English since James, and perhaps many not in English too, have probably been at least indirectly influenced by his example. What James ignores in his fiction would make a long list. Among many other things, a James character rarely works for a living or grabs a quick breakfast. His characters are usually rich enough, instead, to indulge their imaginations more sedately. Joseph Conrad once said that James is "the historian of fine consciences."

Henry James has frequently been compared to other writers. He belongs in a distinguished company which includes Nathaniel Hawthorne, Mark Twain, William Dean Howells, Edith Wharton, George Eliot, Joseph Conrad, Ivan Turgenev, Marcel Proust, Anton Chekhov. He lacks the sweep of Tolstoy, the humanitarianism of Dickens, the animal energy of Balzac. In the American Pantheon, he belongs with Hawthorne as a moral fabulist, Melville as a tragic-comic stylist, and Twain as a painter of innocents at home and abroad.

Letters:

The Letters of Henry James, edited by Percy Lubbock, 2 volumes (London: Macmillan, 1920; New York: Scribners, 1920);

Henry James and Robert Louis Stevenson: A Record of Friendship and Criticism, edited by Janet Adam Smith (London: Hart-Davis, 1948);

Virginia Harlow, *Thomas Sergeant Perry: A Biography and Letters to Perry from William, Henry, and Garth Wilkinson James* (Durham, N.C.: Duke University Press, 1950);

Selected Letters of Henry James, edited by Leon Edel

(New York: Farrar, Straus & Cudahy, 1955);

Henry James and H. G. Wells: A Record of Their Friend-ship, Their Debate on the Art of Fiction, and Their Quarrel, edited by Edel and Gordon N. Ray (London: Hart-Davis, 1958);

Henry James: Letters, edited by Edel, 4 volumes (Cambridge: Harvard University Press, 1974-1984).

Bibliographies:

Richard N. Foley, *Criticism in American Periodicals of the Works of Henry James from 1866 to 1916* (Washington, D.C.: Catholic University Press, 1944);

Robert L. Gale, "Henry James," in *Eight American Authors: A Review of Research and Criticism,* revised edition, edited by James Woodress (New York: Norton, 1971), pp. 321-375;

Kristin Pruitt McColgan, *Henry James 1917-1959: A Reference Guide* (Boston: G. K. Hall, 1979);

Dorothy McInnis Scura, *Henry James 1960-1974: A Reference Guide* (Boston: G. K. Hall, 1979);

Leon Edel, Dan H. Laurence, and James Rambeau, *A Bibliography of Henry James,* third edition, revised (New York: Oxford University Press, 1982);

John Budd, *Henry James: A Bibliography of Criticism, 1975-1981* (Westport, Conn.: Greenwood, 1983);

Nicola Bradbury, *An Annotated Critical Bibliography of Henry James* (New York: St. Martin's Press, 1987).

Biographies:

Theodora Bosanquet, *Henry James at Work* (London: Hogarth Press, 1924);

Pelham Edgar, *Henry James: Man and Author* (London: Richards, 1927);

Clinton Hartley Grattan, *The Three Jameses: A Family of Minds: Henry James, Sr., William James, Henry James* (New York: Longmans, Green, 1932);

Simon Nowell-Smith, *The Legend of the Master: Henry James* (New York: Scribners, 1947; revised edition, Oxford: Oxford University Press, 1985);

F. W. Dupee, *Henry James* (New York: Sloane, 1951; revised edition, Garden City: Doubleday, 1956);

H. Montgomery Hyde, *Henry James at Home* (London: Methuen, 1969);

Leon Edel, *Henry James: The Master, 1901-1916*

(Philadelphia & New York: Lippincott, 1972);

Harry T. Moore, *Henry James* (New York: Viking, 1974);

Norman Page, ed., *Henry James: Interviews and Recollections* (New York: St. Martin's Press, 1984);

Katherine Weissbourd, *Growing Up in the James Family: Henry James, Sr., as Son and Father* (Ann Arbor: UMI Research Press, 1985);

Edel, *Henry James: A Life* (New York: Harper & Row, 1985).

References:

Charles R. Anderson, *Person, Place, and Thing in Henry James's Novels* (Durham: Duke University Press, 1977).
Analyzes James's use of places and things to symbolize people in six representative novels.

Osborne Andreas, *Henry James and the Expanding Horizon: A Study of the Meaning of James's Fiction* (Seattle: University of Washington Press, 1948).
Discusses ten basic themes in James's fiction—for example, the past and false values.

Michael Anesko, *"Friction with the Market": Henry James and the Profession of Authorship* (New York: Oxford University Press, 1986).
Explores James's efforts to be artistically independent and at the same time to sell widely.

Paul B. Armstrong, *The Challenge of Bewilderment: Understanding and Representation in James, Conrad and Ford* (Ithaca: Cornell University Press, 1987).
Discusses the epistemology of representing in works by James, Joseph Conrad, and Ford Madox (Hueffer) Ford.

Armstrong, *The Phenomenology of Henry James* (Chapel Hill: University of North Carolina Press, 1983).
Shows how James's understanding of experience, learning, and writing coincides with phenomenological and existential theories.

John Auchard, *Silence in Henry James: The Heritage of Symbolism and Decadence* (University Park: Pennsylvania State University Press, 1986).
Analyzes James's awareness and use in representative fiction of silence in positive, anti-

materialistic symbolism and in negative, nihilistic decadence.

Joseph Warren Beach, *The Method of Henry James* (New Haven: Yale University Press, 1918).
Pioneering study of James's stylistic techniques–for example, scene, dialogue, and point of view.

Millicent Bell, *Edith Wharton and Henry James: The Story of a Friendship* (New York: Braziller, 1965).
Details James's personal and professional relationships with one of America's finest women novelists.

Ralph F. Bogardus, *Pictures and Texts: Henry James, A. L. Coburn, and New Ways of Seeing in Literary Culture* (Ann Arbor: UMI Research Press, 1984).
Discusses James's general dislike of illustrations for fiction but also his helping photographer A. L. Coburn obtain photographs to illustrate the 1907-1918 edition of James's novels and tales.

Van Wyck Brooks, *The Pilgrimage of Henry James* (New York: Dutton, 1925).
Theorizes wrongheadedly but fascinatingly that James's deracinating expatriation ruined his art.

Peter Buitenhuis, *The Grasping Imagination: The American Writings of Henry James* (Toronto: University of Toronto Press, 1970).
Studies James's fiction, essays, and travel literature having American settings.

Henry Seidel Canby, *Turn West, Turn East: Mark Twain and Henry James* (Boston: Houghton Mifflin, 1951).
Compares and contrasts the lives, attitudes, and writings of James and Samuel Langhorne Clemens.

Oscar Cargill, *The Novels of Henry James* (New York: Macmillan, 1961).
Analyzes all of the novels, stressing previous criticism and James's sources.

Susan Carlson, *Women of Grace: James's Plays and the Comedy of Manners* (Ann Arbor: UMI Research Press, 1985).
Places James's dramatic women in the tradi-

tion of the post-Restoration British comedy of manners.

Seymour Chatman, *The Later Style of Henry James* (Oxford: Blackwell, 1972).
Probes technical elements of James's style to show how they serve his artistic intentions.

Sarah B. Daugherty, *The Literary Criticism of Henry James* (Athens: Ohio University Press, 1981).
Discusses all of the extensive criticism written by James.

Leon Edel and Adeline R. Tintner, *The Library of Henry James* (Ann Arbor: UMI Research Press, 1987).
Lists 1,404 books now known to have been in James's personal library (which at his death numbered more than 4,000), and discusses its history and significance.

Daniel Mark Fogel, *Henry James and the Structure of the Romantic Imagination* (Baton Rouge: Louisiana State University Press, 1981).
Examines the dialectic of spiral return in selective fiction by James which shows the inexperienced hero questing, learning by experience, and returning on a higher plane to his origin.

Virginia C. Fowler, *Henry James's American Girl* (Madison: University of Wisconsin Press, 1984).
Theorizes that American women in James's fiction, abandoned and betrayed by their men, are emotionally crippled.

Robert L. Gale, *The Caught Image: Figurative Language in the Fiction of Henry James* (Chapel Hill: University of North Carolina Press, 1964).
Analyzes water, flower, animal, war, art, religious, and other categories of similes and metaphors in James's fiction.

Gale, *Plots and Characters in the Fiction of Henry James* (Hamden, Conn.: Archon, 1965).
Summarizes every plot and identifies every character in James's fiction.

Roger Gard, ed., *Henry James: The Critical Heritage* (London: Routledge & Kegan Paul, 1968).
Reprints reviews of and essays on James from periodicals and books, letters from

and concerning him, memoirs of his friends, and much else.

Maxwell Geismar, *Henry James and the Jacobites* (Boston: Houghton Mifflin, 1963).
Savagely attacks advocates of James for creating a James cult.

David Gervais, *Flaubert and Henry James: A Study in Contrasts* (London: Macmillan, 1978).
Contrasts the differing theories of tragedy held by James and Gustave Flaubert, and defends Flaubert from James's adverse criticism of him.

Philip Grover, *Henry James and the French Novel: A Study in Inspiration* (New York: Barnes & Noble, 1973).
Shows the influence on James of French novelists, especially Honoré de Balzac, Alphonse Daudet, and Gustave Flaubert.

Richard A. Hocks, *Henry James and Pragmatistic Thought: A Study in the Relationship between the Philosophy of William James and the Literary Art of Henry James* (Chapel Hill: University of North Carolina Press, 1974).
Theorizes that William James's philosophy is actuated in the art and idiom of Henry James's work.

Alan Holder, *Three Voyagers in Search of Europe: A Study of Henry James, Ezra Pound, and T. S. Eliot* (Philadelphia: University of Pennsylvania Press, 1966).
Studies the consequences of expatriation, disaffection, and criticism of the United States in the works of three Americans.

Marcia Jacobson, *Henry James and the Mass Market* (University: University of Alabama Press, 1983).
Discusses James's 1883-1898 efforts to improve his sales by writing on such current pop-literature subjects as women's liberation, the working class, actresses, and children.

Granville H. Jones, *Henry James's Psychology of Experience* (The Hague: Mouton, 1975).
Shows how James in his fiction presents heroic individuals moving from innocence to experience, initiation, responsibility and renunciation.

Vivien Jones, *James the Critic* (New York: St. Martin's Press, 1985).
Shows how James the critic moved from American idealism through French aesthetics to British moralism.

James J. Kirschke, *Henry James and Impressionism* (Troy, N.Y.: Whitston, 1981).
Traces the possible influence of impressionistic painters and writers on James's fiction and criticism.

James Kraft, *The Early Tales of Henry James* (Carbondale: Southern Illinois University Press, 1969).
Discusses James's first thirty-seven short stories (to 1879) to show how his fiction started and began to evolve.

Dorothea Krook, *The Ordeal of Consciousness in Henry James* (London & New York: Cambridge University Press, 1962).
Explores James's notion of being and seeing as presented in seven representative fictional works, and relates consciousness to his moral, social, and philosophical concerns.

Ellen Douglass Leyburn, *Strange Alloy* (Chapel Hill: University of North Carolina Press, 1968).
Shows the relationship between comedy and tragedy in James's fiction.

Robert Emmet Long, *The Great Succession: Henry James and the Legacy of Hawthorne* (Pittsburgh: University of Pittsburgh Press, 1979).
Shows how James transformed Nathaniel Hawthorne's romantic plot patterns and themes into his own brand of realism.

Anne T. Margolis, *Henry James and the Problem of Audience* (Ann Arbor: UMI Research Press, 1985).
Shows how James wished to sell well, tried to compete with commercially successful writers, and compromised to a degree by trying to adapt pop-literature themes and devices.

F. O. Matthiessen, *Henry James: The Major Phase* (New York: Oxford University Press, 1944).
Probes James's major work from 1902 forward.

Bruce R. McElderry, Jr., *Henry James* (New York: Twayne, 1965).
Treats James's life briefly, considers all aspects of his literary production, and traces his artistic evaluation.

George Monteiro, *Henry James and John Hay: The Record of a Friendship* (Providence: Brown University Press, 1965).
Details the long friendship of James and John Hay, and reveals the opinions of each concerning the other's writings.

Elsa Nettels, *James & Conrad* (Athens: University of Georgia Press, 1977).
Discusses the friendship of James and Joseph Conrad, and compares and contrasts their respective works.

Dale Peterson, *The Clement Vision: Poetic Realism in Turgenev and James* (Port Washington, N.Y.: Kennikat Press, 1975).
Shows how Ivan Turgenev as man and writer influenced James's behavior and fiction.

Richard Poirier, *The Comic Sense of Henry James: A Study of the Early Novels* (New York: Oxford University Press, 1960).
Treats comic elements in six early novels through *The Portrait of a Lady*.

Ross Posnock, *Henry James and the Problem of Robert Browning* (Athens: University of Georgia Press, 1985).
Discusses the consequences in James's writing of his belief that Browning had a dual personality (social and creative).

Lyall H. Powers, *Henry James and the Naturalist Movement* (East Lansing: Michigan State University Press, 1971).
Examines the influence of experimental and naturalistic French fiction, especially that of Emile Zola, on James's fiction, mainly *The Bostonians*, *The Princess Casamassima*, and *The Tragic Muse*.

Strother B. Purdy, *The Hole in the Fabric: Science, Contemporary Literature, and Henry James* (Pittsburgh: University of Pittsburgh Press, 1977).
Theorizes as to James's influence on modern literature dealing with horror, time, sex, and nihilism.

S. Gorley Putt, *A Reader's Guide to Henry James* (Ithaca: Cornell University Press, 1966; London: Thames and Hudson, 1966).
Offers a systematic commentary, organized chronologically and thematically, on all of James's fiction.

John Carlos Rowe, *Henry Adams and Henry James: The Emergence of a Modern Consciousness* (Ithaca: Cornell University Press, 1976).
Contrasts the ways James and Henry Adams showed awareness of and responded in their writings to some of the religious, historical, social, and artistic problems of their times.

Rowe, *The Theoretical Dimensions of Henry James* (Madison: University of Wisconsin Press, 1984).
Shows how James has been interpreted by critics using the psychology of literary influences, feminism, Marxism, psychoanalysis, phenomenolgical hermeneutics, and reader-response theory as their respective approaches.

Ora Segal, *The Lucid Reflector: The Observer in James' Fiction* (New Haven: Yale University Press, 1969).
Traces the evolution of the Jamesian observer from outside onlooker to central intelligence caught up in the action.

Mark Seltzer, *Henry James & the Art of Power* (Ithaca: Cornell University Press, 1984).
Shows that James, far from being nonpolitical, demonstrates in his writings, notably *The Princess Casamassina*, *The Golden Bowl*, and *The American Scene*, the interrelationship of art and power.

Sister M. Corona Sharp, *The "Confidante" in Henry James: Evolution and Moral Value of a Fictive Character* (Notre Dame: University of Notre Dame Press, 1965).
Explores the technical functions of the confidante as she evolves in James's fiction.

Muriel G. Shine, *The Fictional Children of Henry James* (Chapel Hill: University of North Carolina Press, 1969).

Explores James's fictional representation of troubled and perceptive children and adolescents.

Tony Tanner, *Henry James: The Writer and His Work* (Amherst: University of Massachusetts Press, 1985).
Provides a brief introduction to James and his major works.

Tintner, *The Book World of Henry James: Appropriating the Classics* (Ann Arbor: UMI Research Press, 1987).
Shows how James's creative reading of books by the dozens, especially those of Honoré de Balzac, John Keats, Guy de Maupassant, William Shakespeare, and Robert Louis Stevenson, is reflected in his own writings.

Tintner, *The Museum World of Henry James* (Ann Arbor: UMI Research Press, 1986).
Demonstrates the extensive influence of pictorial art (painting, illustration, caricature, photography), sculpture, architecture, furniture, jewelry, and vehicle design, on aspects of James's fiction.

William Veeder, *Henry James—The Lessons of the Master: Popular Fiction and Personal Style in the Nineteenth Century* (Chicago: University of Chicago Press, 1975).
Shows James's awareness of the popular fiction of his time and his 1871-1881 use of some of its techniques.

Edward Wagenknecht, *Eve and Henry James: Portraits of Women and Girls in His Fiction* (Norman: University of Oklahoma Press, 1978).
Analyzes James's female characters–portrayed as innocent, victimized, assertive, or self-sacrificing–and relates them to persons James knew.

Wagenknecht, *The Novels of Henry James* (New York: Ungar, 1983).
Surveys previous criticism of and offers insights on all of James's novels.

Wagenknecht, *The Tales of Henry James* (New York: Ungar, 1987).
Surveys previous criticism of and offers insights on all of James's short stories.

J. A. Ward, *The Imagination of Disaster: Evil in the Fiction of Henry James* (Lincoln: University of Nebraska Press, 1961).
Discusses James's dramatization in his fiction of good versus evil in modern society.

Christof Wegelin, *The Image of Europe in Henry James* (Dallas: Southern Methodist University Press, 1958).
Explains the evolution of James's fictional treatment of international themes from conventional to complex.

Joseph Wiesenfarth, *Henry James and the Dramatic Analogy* (New York: Fordham University Press, 1963).
Applies James's own theories concerning the dramatic novel to four middle-phase novels by James.

Ruth Bernard Yeazell, *Language and Knowledge in the Late Novels of Henry James* (Chicago: University of Chicago Press, 1976).
Analyzes James's major-phase syntax, dialogue, and power language (especially in *The Golden Bowl*).

Papers:
Most of James's manuscripts and other papers are deposited in the Houghton Library at Harvard University. Other materials are in the Collection of American Literature, Yale University, and in the Library of Congress. The libraries of the following institutions also have notable collections: the University of Leeds, Colby College, the University of Rochester, the University of Chicago, the University of California at Los Angeles, the British Museum, the archives of Charles Scribner's Sons at Princeton University, the Huntington Library, the Morgan Library, the New York Public Library, the Buffalo Public Library, and the Century Association in New York City.

Vachel Lindsay

*This entry was updated by Dennis Camp (Sangamon State University) from his entry in
DLB 54, American Poets, 1880-1945, Third Series, Part 1.*

Places	Springfield, Ill. New York Boston	Hiram College, Ohio Gulfport, Miss. Glacier National Park	Chicago Spokane, Wash.
Influences and Relationships	Floyd Dell Sara Teasdale William Marion Reedy	Harriet Monroe Louis Untermeyer Edwin Arlington Robinson	Abraham Lincoln William Butler Yeats Edgar Lee Masters
Literary Movements and Forms	New Poetry Regionalism Performance Poetry	Chicago Renaissance Pre-Raphaelites	Popular Modernism New Localism
Major Themes	Vagabondism Pacifism	Social Reform "Inspiration Girls"	Alienation of the Artist
Cultural and Artistic Influences	Art/Illustration Dance Jazz	Ash Can School of Painting Egyptian Hieroglyphics	Vaudeville Film
Social and Economic Influences	Midwestern Traditions Buddhism Utopianism	Socialism Campbellite Ecumenism Populism	World War I 1920s Culture

244

BIRTH: Springfield, Illinois, 10 November 1879, to Vachel Thomas and Esther Catharine Frazee Lindsay.

EDUCATION: Hiram College, 1897-1900; Chicago Art Institute, 1901-1903; New York School of Art, 1903-1904.

MARRIAGE: 19 May 1925 to Elizabeth Conner; children: Susan Doniphan, Nicholas Cave.

AWARDS AND HONORS: *Poetry* magazine prize, 1913; Levinson Prize (*Poetry* magazine), 1915; Phi Beta Kappa Poet, Harvard University, 1922; *Poetry* magazine prize, 1928; Honorary doctorate, Hiram College, 1930.

DEATH: Springfield, Illinois, 5 December 1931.

BOOKS: *The Tree of the Laughing Bells* (New York: Privately printed, 1905);
God Help Us to Be Brave (New York: Privately printed, 1908); revised as *The Heroes of Time* (Springfield, Ill.: Privately printed, 1909);
The Last Song of Lucifer (New York: Privately printed, 1908);
War Bulletin: Number One (Springfield, Ill.: Privately printed, 1909);
War Bulletin: Number Two (Springfield, Ill.: Privately printed, 1909);
War Bulletin: Number Three (Springfield, Ill.: Privately printed, 1909);
The Tramp's Excuse and Other Poems [*War Bulletin: Number Four*] (Springfield, Ill.: Privately printed, 1909);
War Bulletin: Number Five (Springfield, Ill.: Privately printed, 1909);
The Spring Harbinger (Springfield, Ill.: Privately printed, 1910);
The Village Magazine (Springfield, Ill.: Privately printed, 1910; enlarged, 1920; two revised editions, 1925);
Rhymes to Be Traded for Bread (Springfield, Ill.: Privately printed, 1912);
The Soul of the City Receives the Gift of the Holy Spirit (Springfield, Ill.: Privately printed, 1913);
General William Booth Enters into Heaven and Other Poems (New York: Kennerley, 1913; London: Chatto & Windus, 1919);
Adventures While Preaching the Gospel of Beauty (New York: Kennerley, 1914);
The Congo and Other Poems (New York: Macmillan, 1914);

The Art of the Moving Picture (New York: Macmillan, 1915; revised, 1922);
A Handy Guide for Beggars, Especially Those of the Poetic Fraternity (New York: Macmillan, 1916);
A Letter About My Four Programmes (Springfield, Ill.: Privately printed, 1916);
The Chinese Nightingale and Other Poems (New York: Macmillan, 1917);
A Letter for Your Wicked Private Ear Only (Springfield, Ill.: Privately printed, 1920);
The Golden Book of Springfield (New York: Macmillan, 1920);
The Golden Whales of California and Other Rhymes in the American Language (New York: Macmillan, 1920);
The Daniel Jazz and Other Poems (London: G. Bell, 1920);
Collected Poems (New York: Macmillan, 1923; enlarged, 1925);
Going-to-the-Sun (New York: Appleton, 1923);
Going-to-the-Stars (New York: Appleton, 1926);
The Candle in the Cabin: A Weaving Together of Script and Singing (New York: Appleton, 1926);
Johnny Appleseed and Other Poems (New York: Macmillan, 1928);
The Litany of Washington Street (New York: Macmillan, 1929);
Every Soul Is a Circus (New York: Macmillan, 1929);
Rigamarole, Rigamarole (New York: Random House, 1929);
Selected Poems of Vachel Lindsay, edited by Hazelton Spencer (New York: Macmillan, 1931);
Selected Poems of Vachel Lindsay, edited by Mark Harris (New York: Macmillan, 1963);
Adventures: Rhymes & Designs, edited by Robert F. Sayre (New York: Eakins, 1968);
Springfield Town Is Butterfly Town and Other Poems for Children, edited by Pierre Dussert (Kent, Ohio: Kent State, 1969);
The Poetry of Vachel Lindsay, 3 volumes, edited by Dennis Camp (Peoria, Ill.: Spoon River Poetry Press, 1984-1986).

OTHER: "What It Means to Be a Poet in America," *Saturday Evening Post*, 198 (13 November 1926): 12-13, 45-47;
"The Buggy-Breaking Doctor," *Macmillan News Review*, 1 (2 March 1931): 4; republished as "To Vachel Thomas Lindsay," in *What I Owe to My Father*, edited by Sydney Dix Strong (New York: Holt, 1931), pp. 99-108.

Vachel Lindsay's considerable loss of reputation in American letters is a continuing theme in critical evaluations published during the 1970s and 1980s. Ironically, the theme is illustrated, in part, not only by the meager number of articles written about Lindsay but also by their lack of inclusion in leading journals. Several scholars have lamented the fact that Lindsay's work is not represented in such widely used college text surveys as Grosset & Dunlap's *American Tradition in Literature*, *The Norton Anthology of American Literature*, and Macmillan's *Anthology of American Literature* (in spite of the fact that Macmillan published most of Lindsay's important books). Although one critic (Donald Wesling) has defended Lindsay's exclusion from current anthologies, Lindsay's contemporaries, even detractors such as Ezra Pound and critic Gorham B. Munson, would likely be surprised to learn that scholars in the 1980s consider Lindsay not worth mentioning in purportedly comprehensive surveys of American letters. In 1932, for example, just months after Lindsay's death, Edwin Arlington Robinson admitted that it is "extremely difficult, and at present probably impossible," "to give to Vachel Lindsay his place." Robinson suggested that the greater part of Lindsay's work, "as the greater part of most men's work," would be forgotten. However, Robinson concluded that "in the best of Lindsay there appears to exist a nameless quality that vanished cave-dwellers would have understood, and that unborn sophisticates will accept."

Publications from Lindsay's own years consistently demonstrate that, from the time of his first trade volume, *General William Booth Enters into Heaven and Other Poems* (1913), to the publication of his *Collected Poems* (1923), few if any other American poets, Pound included, could have presented a serious challenge to Lindsay's stature and popularity. That reputation, of course, was not based solely on the published poetry: Lindsay performed his poetry in lecture halls across the United States and Canada, and, for a few weeks in 1920, in England as well. He wrote two popular books that were largely prose: *Adventures While Preaching the Gospel of Beauty* (1914) and *A Handy Guide for Beggars, Especially Those of the Poetic Fraternity* (1916). He also published the world's first study of film as an art form: *The Art of the Moving Picture* (1915; revised, 1922), a work that earned him the friendship of Mary Pickford, Douglas Fairbanks, Anita Loos, D. W. Griffith, and others among the motion-picture world's elect.

Nevertheless, Lindsay's poetry received high praise from the leading literary figures of his age: editors such as Floyd Dell, William Marion Reedy, Harriet Monroe, and Louis Untermeyer, as well as fellow poets such as William Butler Yeats, John Masefield, Amy Lowell, and Christopher Morley. Yale professor William Lyon Phelps, in his *The Advance of English Poetry in the Twentieth Century* (1918), paired Lindsay with Robert Frost, giving twenty-two pages to Lindsay and only ten to Frost. Phelps placed Lindsay in a class with Walt Whitman, Rudyard Kipling, and Masefield. Indeed, for every voice that criticized Lindsay's poetry–generally calling it something like puerile fustian–ten or more voices proclaimed him to be one of America's foremost poets, not just for his own era but for all time.

According to Edgar Lee Masters, Lindsay's first major biographer (1935), "G. K. Chesterton called Lindsay the most national poet, and the one with most normal energy of literary genius since Walt Whitman." Masters also credited Ludwig Lewisohn with describing Lindsay's poetry as "the purest in America since Poe." Masters himself asserted that Lindsay's poems "constitute the most considerable body of imaginative lyricism that any American has produced." Fellow poet James Stephens praised Lindsay's poem "The Chinese Nightingale" as "the greatest written since the Pilgrims came over on the one subject that poetry has any true concern with, the soul of man and its meaning and destiny." Amy Lowell claimed she would "never forget" the song of the nightingale "because I know it/By heart." Harriet Monroe, reminiscing at the close of a long life of writing, editing, and publishing poetry, conjectured that Lindsay was "perhaps the most gifted and original poet" whose work appeared in *Poetry: A Magazine of Verse*. More recently, John T. Flanagan, in his *Profile of Vachel Lindsay* (1970), concluded: "Lindsay's verse has earned him a permanent place in American literature, and future anthologists who deny him that place will reflect only their own myopic vision."

Controversy and contradiction are central in Lindsay's life from his earliest years. He was the son of a Democratic father, Vachel Thomas Lindsay, a Kentuckian who accused Abraham Lincoln of destroying the family property. Dr. Lindsay delivered his own children, and he expected his only son to follow him in his profession. Lindsay's mother, Esther Catharine (Kate) Frazee Lindsay, challenged her husband's views of Lincoln and destined her son, "from the beginning," as

Vachel Lindsay, about age fifty, reciting his poetry

he believed, "to be an artist." Lindsay later claimed that the Mason-Dixon line, "deep-dyed and awful," ran through the middle of his heart, through the middle of his home, and through the middle of Springfield, Illinois, his beloved native city.

The house at 603 South Fifth Street in Springfield, where Nicholas Vachel Lindsay was born on 10 November 1879, at 5:00 A.M.–and where he finally died–had once belonged to the sister-in-law of Abraham Lincoln. The family knew that the Great Emancipator had been welcomed in their home many times and that the front parlor had been the scene of "one grand party" given the night before the president-elect had left for Washington. Several Lindsay poems reflect admiration for the North's great president ("Abraham Lincoln Walks at Midnight," "The Soul of Lincoln," "Litany of the Heroes"), but the poet also emphasized that the family "fathers" came from Kentucky: "No drop of my blood

from north/Of Mason and Dixon's line" ("Alexander Campbell"). Lindsay portrayed himself as an "intrusive Kentuckian" in a Republican state capital, and the belief that he was a displaced "rebel" is latent in much of his writing. "The Moon's the North Wind's Cooky," for example, is apparently an innocent children's poem, until Lindsay's political inclinations are considered in his description of a "South Wind" whose creative efforts are devoured by a *"greedy/North . . . Wind"* (Lindsay's emphasis).

The Lindsay and Frazee families were proud of their heritage. Family historians, such as Lindsay's aunt Frances Frazee Hamilton and his cousin Eudora Lindsay South, traced their ancestral history to Jane Austen and to Sir David Lindsay, the distinguished Scottish bard mentioned in Sir Walter Scott's *Marmion*. The family also believed that Spanish blood and Indian blood flowed in Lindsay and Frazee veins, a conviction that plays an important role in such Lindsay poems as "Billboards and Galleons," "Doctor Mohawk," and "The Indian Girl–My Grandmother." Although Lindsay asserted that his forefathers came from Kentucky, he placed his great-grandfathers in Virginia, as evidenced by the late poems "Virginia" and "The Virginians Are Coming Again." Time and time again, Lindsay alluded to his heritage in his poetry: "I was stuffed," he explained, "with family history in my helpless infancy."

One pertinent family story relates the origin of the poet's unusual middle name. According to cousin Eudora South, "at some far-away time there were twins born, the boy being called Vachel to accord with the girl's name of Rachel." Lindsay himself, who was named Nicholas Vachel after his paternal grandfather, advised that his middle name does not rhyme with "satchel," "rock hell," "hash hell," or "bottle": "My name is just the same as Rachel,/With V for R;/Please call me Vachel" ("My Middle Name").

Ironically, the poet who in maturity was frequently described as "childlike" (or as "childish" by his critics) weighed ten pounds at birth "and looked as if he had the experience and wisdom of age," according to his mother. Writing her memories of her son in February 1916, she added: "He had over his face what 'old-wives' fables' have called 'a prophet's veil,'" an auspicious birth omen that Lindsay often referred to with pride. His first four months were normal, but from March to October 1880, according to his mother, "his life was often despaired of. For many weeks he was a breathing skeleton carried on a pillow by his mother." Figuratively, Kate Lindsay continued to carry her son for the rest of her life, remaining a powerful influence even after her death. To Sara Teasdale and to others, Lindsay admitted that his perception of his mother was the basis for his evaluation of women in general and of wives in particular.

Lindsay's sickliness impaired his normal growth. He was held back from school and his mother taught him to read, using the Grimms' fairy tales. Young Lindsay's Springfield, his sister Olive remembered, was characterized by "mud and books": "Outside all was mud. Inside all was books–books and pictures." The family library boasted not only the brothers Grimm but Hans Christian Andersen, the *Arabian Nights*, editions of the major English poets, the novels of Sir Walter Scott and Charles Dickens, and the work of one American poet, Edgar Allan Poe, who soon became youthful Lindsay's favorite. Dr. Lindsay

gave his son a two-volume edition of George Rawlinson's history of Egypt, the pictures and the substance of which Lindsay claims to have known by heart "when I was very young indeed." His mother especially enjoyed poets whose work "dealt also in art," and, Lindsay stated, she "filled me full of the Brownings and the PreRaphaelites."

Lindsay's first years of formal education were in three private schools, at least one of which (the Bettie Stuart Institute) specialized in training children in English, the classics, and the arts. Kate Lindsay recalled in 1916 that her son "drew many little sketches as soon as he could hold a pencil, usually illustrating some idea," and she regretted not having saved any. At one point Dr. Lindsay, still planning to have his son join him in his profession, gave young Lindsay a medical-school skeleton and ordered him to learn to put the bones together. Years later, however, Lindsay's sister Olive disclosed: "He never succeeded in putting that skeleton together, but he was interested in the varied shapes of the bones, and drew pictures of them." When Lindsay was in high school his teacher and lifelong friend Susan Wilcox was impressed with his "passionate interest in drawing." In botany, she noted, "His plates were so beautifully done that they drew high grades regardless of the explanations that accompanied them." Reinforced by his mother's artistic knowledge and accomplished abilities (she was a superb copyist), this early exposure to art developed into a lasting passion. Lindsay often stated that his poems were normally written to accompany his drawings and paintings. By the 1920s he was determined to emphasize his artistic interests and generally refused publication of new books of poetry unless publishers agreed to include his pen-and-ink drawings as well.

The Bible was central in Lindsay's young life. Both parents were active members in Springfield's First Christian Church, Disciples of Christ, commonly known as the Campbellites. The Lindsay children were given daily Bible lessons before breakfast, and scripture readings before the evening meal were an established family ritual, even thirty or more years after Lindsay's grammar-school days when poet Jessie Rittenhouse visited Springfield.

Once, when Lindsay was "six or seven," his mother produced two "miracle plays" for the benefit of the church missionary fund. Entitled *Olympus*, one play featured the Greek gods, with Lindsay's uncle as Neptune and his Sunday school teacher as Venus. Lindsay himself was Cupid, a picture of splendor with long blond curls, dressed in a pink slip with "dove's wings" sewn on it and carrying a pasteboard bow and arrows and quiver. Kate Lindsay described the second play, *The Colloquy of Nations*, as "a highly symbolic representation of all the leading countries, and what they had accomplished." This play was clearly meant to dramatize Campbellite ecumenism. Kate Lindsay remembered in 1916 that her son "attended every rehearsal, and was simply *carried away* [her emphasis] by the entire performance." Lindsay himself credited his mother's efforts with providing the inspiration for his "Litany of the Heroes," a poem that he labored over for almost two decades of his life. The ecumenical theme is apparent in many other Lindsay poems: it is the essential element in his plans to make Springfield, and afterward the United States and the world, a better place in which to live (see especially "On the Building of Springfield").

Lindsay's lifelong zeal for social reform was largely based on Campbellite traditions, but it also reflects the particular tone of his mother's joyous and somewhat unorthodox ecumenical efforts. "My mother," he recalled in 1923, "was a riot in those days." This emphasis on mirth provides the structural key to one of Lindsay's typical reform works, "The Village Improvement Parade," which began as a series of six drawings (published in 1910). The parade's opening banner reads: "To begin, we must learn to smile." The final banner completes the formative circle: "To begin, we must have a sense of humor and learn to smile." The overall shape of the work, according to Lindsay, is echoed by the sun, "drawn with a compass" in the background of the plates. The circular form, he added, is the "central design" of the "Litany of the Heroes" and is the "central symbol" of Egyptian hieroglyphics. He attributed his many moon poems and drawings to this same hieroglyphic symbol, including a reminder of the proper attitude: "No man should stand before the moon/To make sweet song thereon/With dandified importance,/His sense of humor gone."

The supreme dramatic moment in Dr. Lindsay's life occurred in late 1892, when John Peter Altgeld was elected the first Democratic governor of Illinois after the Civil War and Democrat Grover Cleveland was elected for a second term as President of the United States. With his children looking on, the doctor rode "in the ratifica-

tion parade in a silk hat and big sash," his son reminisced in 1922. Conversely, Altgeld's defeat in 1896, along with the defeat of the national Democratic ticket led by "that Heaven-born Bryan," was considered a disaster, not only by the doctor but also by his son. More than twenty years later, Lindsay described the 1896 election results as "Defeat of my boyhood, defeat of my dream" ("Bryan, Bryan, Bryan, Bryan"). Dr. Lindsay's despair over the election of "Mark Hanna's McKinley," "The man without an angle or a tangle," is reflected in the sarcasm at the close of "Bryan, Bryan, Bryan, Bryan."

Politics was as close to the Lindsays as the Illinois governor's mansion, located just across the street from the Lindsay home. Fifteen years after Altgeld's defeat, Lindsay memorialized the late governor in "The Eagle That Is Forgotten," a poem written in 1911, just three blocks from Lincoln's home. In 1914 Lindsay depicted Lincoln as an emblem of hope for a world at war in "Abraham Lincoln Walks at Midnight." Catharine Lindsay's admiration for Lincoln continued to influence her son in spite of the glories of the Democratic torchlight parades.

In school Lindsay was modestly successful, winning several prizes for his essays and skipping the seventh grade because of his high marks. His promise was evident early: his first private-school teacher, "old Mrs. Brooks," once expressed the desire to live "twenty years more" because she longed, according to Kate Lindsay "to know what that little boy of yours will be: he asks so many and such strange questions. Where does he get such ideas?" At one point in the fifth grade, Lindsay managed to place at or near the top of his class, not because he was enamored with studies but because seating arrangements were dictated by academic excellence, and he wished to sit next to one of the prettiest girls in the room, who was also very bright. Though this schoolboy incident may seem trivial, it is entirely representative of Lindsay's later relationships with women. Throughout his life, there were many "inspiration girls," as his family called them. These love interests obsessed Lindsay and seemingly compelled him to write, to draw, to "revel" (his term), and, finally, to despair, as one by one each girl renounced him in order to pursue other attractions.

Though the girls changed, female inspiration remained an essential requirement in Lindsay's life. The need is perhaps best illustrated in "The Map of the Universe," a detailed expression of his personal mythology, the first version of which Lindsay completed in 1904. The "Palace of Eve" stands in the map's east, the direction of beginnings, and symbolizes the place "where all the bright beautiful girls come from." Also in 1904 he finished the first version of the poem and drawing entitled "The Tree of Laughing Bells," which presents another aspect of the map and helps to illustrate this side of Lindsay's thinking. The poem depicts a desperate Miltonic flight on "the Wings of the Morning" above "the Chaos roar." The flight is undertaken to attain two "blood-red" bells (symbols of happiness, beauty, success), which are the "fruit" of the "Tree of Laughing Bells." The tree is rooted on the "Star of Laughing Bells," which Lindsay locates in the far west of his map, opposite to the "Palace of Eve." The expedition for the bells is predictably inspired by a member of the palace sorority, a beautiful "Indian Maiden." All ends happily, as the valiant aviator returns, bells in hand, and his "inspiration" maiden rewards him with a kiss.

One of Lindsay's first poems (written when he was seventeen), "How a Little Girl Sang," reflects the influence of his high-school classmate and early "inspiration girl," Mary Tiffany. Many of the poems in *The Chinese Nightingale and Other Poems* (1917), including the title poem, were written for Sara Teasdale, who was the most important "inspirational girl" of Lindsay's bachelor days. Before and after Teasdale, however, there were many others–Octavia Roberts, Isadora Bennett, and Elizabeth Wills–and all prompted numerous Lindsay poems. Indeed, Lindsay apparently found it impossible to think of significant male endeavor that was not female inspired. In the mature poem "Daniel," the imagined "tender sweetheart" who spurs Daniel's bravery even boasts the added attraction of middle-western qualities: "she was as fine as a melon in the cornfield." Predictably, Lindsay's late poetry (1925-1931) is replete with praise for Elizabeth Conner, who was to be not only his wife but also his ultimate "inspiration girl."

The early prose poem "The Faces That Pass" (1909) perhaps best captures Lindsay's particular feelings of awe and respect in regard to women. The narrator claims to be "on my knees to woman," asking never to forget "that woman is holy." More than twenty years later, in an unpublished letter to a Springfield friend written just after her husband's death, Lindsay's wife revealed that she felt as though she were "on an altar" during their marriage and added that, al-

though she initially felt honored, the excessive attention was finally annoying and wearisome.

James Hurt has noted that all the "inspiration girls," as represented in Lindsay's work, reflect the distinctive features that he attributed to his mother. After Lindsay's graduation from high school, therefore, his personal feelings about his mother accentuated his sense of betrayal when Kate Lindsay concurred with her doctor husband that their only son should be sent to Hiram College to study in the scientific curriculum that would prepare him for medical school. According to Susan Wilcox, young Lindsay stated he would be an artist were he an orphan, and there is little doubt that he had expected his mother to support his artistic inclinations. Nevertheless, Lindsay's weekly letters written to his parents from Hiram reveal that he tried valiantly during his first two years. He was, Susan Wilcox commented, "a dutiful son."

Lindsay's troubles at Hiram began early, when he was dropped from his physics class because he did not have an appropriate high school background in trigonometry. For a year or more, he tried in vain to learn anatomy and physiology, studying many extra hours with the assistance of his friend and future brother-in-law, Paul Wakefield. For Lindsay, though, a scientific understanding of anatomy remained elusive, reminiscent of his earlier failures with his father's medical-school skeleton and also a foreshadowing of his future difficulties in art school, where he was advised that he could not draw the human figure.

Socially, Lindsay thoroughly enjoyed the Hiram tradition of "perching," that is, sharing a "perch" and talking with a person of the opposite sex, usually in an open and entirely innocent fashion. He also enjoyed athletics: he had been a champion walker on his high-school track team (a skill that later proved useful in his tramps and in his living arrangements while he was an impoverished art student). The lack of intercollegiate athletic competition at Hiram disturbed him. With his friends he made several attempts to establish an interest in track and in football, although he played football very badly. Indeed, a scar on his chin, the result of an injury in a Hiram game, remained a lifelong reminder of his gridiron ineptitude. In addition he was a vigorous proponent of the usual freshman/sophomore rivalries, actively participating in various antics and pranks. He made at least one of his escapades the subject of an anonymous short story that was published in the college literary paper, assuring his nervous parents that some of the story was fiction.

Hiram did provide Lindsay with the invaluable opportunity of sharing his imaginative creations, in poetry and in drawing, with an interested group of fellow students and with a concerned faculty. He contributed crude illustrations to the college annual, and he participated, rigorously albeit unsuccessfully, in several college orations. Two terms of oratory were required of all Hiram sophomores, and this training was of obvious benefit to the later Lindsay of "the Higher Vaudeville," as he referred to his performances.

Although he had trifled with verse in high school ("How a Little Girl Sang," "The Battle"), Lindsay's first concerted efforts at writing poetry date to his Hiram years (1897-1900). He sent several results, at times with explanations, to his parents, but their responses were far from encouraging. His mother admonished him not to divide his industry and attention. (Much earlier, her father had told young Lindsay that poets "were clever men": "But almost all of them had a screw loose somewhere.") Lindsay claimed to have read one Hiram poem, "The Last Song of Lucifer" (written in 1899) "to fifty fellow-students throughout the year, correcting immediately by their suggestions, making it all casual and conversational." He continued this practice during much of his creative life, submitting manuscripts to friends and accepting nearly all suggested changes. One of Lindsay's frequent critical confidants, Louis Untermeyer, remarked in his *From Another World* (1939): "My letters from Vachel are full of thanks for what any other poet would have considered effrontery."

In a short preface to "The Last Song of Lucifer," Lindsay warned that he was not depicting Satan but rather "the first singing creature weary of established ways in music, moved with the lust of wandering." In early manuscripts the leading figure is named "Israfel," rather than "Lucifer," manifesting Poe's influence on young Lindsay. Israfel/Lucifer is obviously Lindsay's perception of himself as the artistic "rebel." He struggled with his frustrations and with his sense of alienation, much of which was caused by a devotion to aesthetic traditions while being forced to wrestle with a practical, scientific curriculum, with the added pressure of great parental expectations. Lucifer's "lust of wandering" adumbrates Lindsay's future tramps, and Lucifer's failure reflects what Lindsay terms "the usual Middle West crucifixion of the artist." In the "Map of the Universe," Luci-

fer is buried in the deep South, covered over with the "River of Hatred." There is little doubt that young Lindsay saw himself as an artist/Christ figure and fully expected, perhaps even looked forward to, some kind of crucifixion (see "I Heard Immanuel Singing"). For all his merry pranks and his emphasis on a sense of humor, Lindsay's happy disposition was more than balanced and threatened by bone-marrow feelings of despair and rejection. As early as his college years, he was a person of conflicting emotional extremes.

After Lindsay had spent two and a half years at Hiram, it was apparent to everyone that he would not join the helping professions as a doctor. With assistance from his sister Olive, he persuaded his parents to send him to art school, ostensibly to learn Christian cartooning. In other words he would learn to use humor and art to develop his own helping profession. His personal notebooks from this time contain entries such as: "My art should contain Beauty, and love and goodness"; and "There is one thing infinitely better than art for art's sake, and that is art for love's sake." His final semester at Hiram was spent in recording these and similar thoughts in at least seven notebooks, in reading English poetry, in drawing, and in not attending classes. He left Hiram in June 1900, without a degree and with only enough credits to be ranked as a sophomore.

In early January 1901 Lindsay began his studies at the Chicago Art Institute, keeping a detailed date book for his parents, who were paying his bills. The date book relates his early successes and failures in his classes and also manifests his legendary propensity for candy, cakes, cookies, and pies. He was, he admitted, "fond of sweets." His first living quarters were at 224 South Paulina, where he shared a room with Springfield friend Fred "Bogie" Bogardus. In addition to attending classes, he was reading William Morris, John Ruskin, Algernon Swinburne's study of Blake, and the poetry of Sidney Lanier. He also began submitting poetry to the nation's top magazines, including *Century*, *Life*, *McClure's*, and *Outlook*. He recorded editors' rejections in his date book, usually adding that he agreed with their appraisals. A 12 April 1901 entry in his date book summarizes a rejection statement he had just received from William Dean Howells of *Harper's*: "Howells said my work was frantic frenetic and obscure. Went home to eliminate obscurity."

When Bogardus left the Paulina address in

order to take up residence at his medical school, Lindsay was forced to find more affordable lodging. He finally selected a room on Kenwood "near 50th," a two-hour walk from the Art Institute. The hike was often necessary, as Lindsay was unable to resist spending his limited funds on theater performances and books. At times his plight was desperate, and he borrowed money for meals from various friends. One stark date-book entry (12 August 1901) reads: "First Paste Breakfast." On 23 September he overcame his contempt for what he called the tragedy of the dollar bill and took full-time employment with Marshall Fields Wholesalers, in the top-floor toy department, from 8:00 A.M. to 5:30 P.M. Now on his own, he stopped writing daily entries in his date book. The pages are largely blank until 5 December, when he noted that he had quit Marshall Fields because the late hours were interfering with his art studies and with his desire to spend two weeks revising several poems. One of these is the well-known "Star of My Heart," written at Christmas in 1901.

After more study and struggle in Chicago, including more rejection slips and different rooms, Lindsay persuaded his parents to send him to William Merritt Chase's New York School of Art. He left Chicago in June 1903, not able, according to his instructors, to draw the human figure adequately. (His nudes, however, were realistic enough to cause a major conflict with his parents, who felt the drawings were "immoral.") The summer of 1903 was the first of many that Lindsay spent at home alone, reading, drawing, writing, napping, and house-sitting, while the rest of the family was on an annual camping trip in Colorado. From the time he left Hiram, he had corresponded regularly with one of his "perch" mates, Ruth Wheeler. On the way to New York in fall 1903 he stopped in Akron, Ohio, to visit Ruth and left believing that they were informally engaged.

In New York Lindsay studied under Robert Henri with fellow students George Mather Richards, Rockwell Kent, George Luks, and George Bellows. The curricular emphasis on realism is apparent in that Henri and several of his students would soon be considered a part of the so-called "Ash Can school." As in Chicago, Lindsay sought to publish his poetry while he was studying art. But unlike in Chicago, he finally experienced an exhilarating though modest success when Jeannette Gilder of the *Critic,* upon the advice of associate editor Ridgely Torrence, accepted two poems

with accompanying drawings. "The Queen of Bubbles" appears in the *Critic* for March 1904; it is Lindsay's first published work. The nude figure in the original drawing was omitted in the published version, since apparently Gilder, as Lindsay's parents before her, felt that his artistic depiction of the human anatomy was adequately realistic. The theme of the poem reflects Lindsay's faith and his Keatsian despair: all that is beautiful is born to die, to break like a bubble, but thankfully beauty's births are endless. A second expression of faith, "At Noon on Easter Day," poem and drawing, was published the following year (April 1905). Lindsay expected as many as ten more acceptances, but there are no subsequent *Critic* publications.

During summer 1904, under protest, Lindsay returned home for his sister Olive's wedding to Paul Wakefield. He was the best man, and Ruth Wheeler was the maid of honor. After the wedding and during the family vacation, Lindsay again remained home alone, enjoying several months of intense creativity and, for the first time in his life, experiencing "visions," both at night and in broad daylight. Typically, he was not overawed or intimidated by these apparent visitations from the spirit world, attributing them to his art-school training, where he was taught to imagine that which was not present. He resolved to make the visions "the servants, not the masters" of his religious thought, using them as the basis for the personal mythology expressed in "The Map of the Universe," the pen-and-ink drawing largely completed during summer and fall 1904. He added a number of related poems at the same time: "The Soul of the Spider," "The Soul of the Butterfly," "A Prayer in the Jungles of Heaven," "Heart of God," and an early version of "The Tree of Laughing Bells." The drawing from "The Queen of Bubbles" is placed in the map's northeast corner.

The center of "The Map of the Universe" pictures earth connected to heaven, not by Milton's golden chain, but by an amaranth vine, a symbol of eternal beauty. Beauty is also depicted as the soul of the butterfly, which lies within the boundaries of Lindsay's universe. Mammon, as the soul of the spider, lurks without. Heaven is a "jungle," since anyone worthy of eternal bliss is not content to rest in peace but instead manifests a "lust of wandering" among the stars for the purpose of saving others. Similarly, the jagged "Throne Mountains" of the Trinity loom desolate. Heaven is allowed to grow unchecked, and the resulting

Lindsay, about age thirty

"jungle" hides many treasures, including Aladdin's lamp. The "boats of the prophets," which are sprinkled across the map, constitute the means of transportation for all the missionary angels. The boats also contain wine jars of the transubstantiated "blood of the crucified angels," wine/blood that "is poured as a purple mist in the paths of men." The mist, Lindsay explains, "becomes the light that never shone on sea or land, the gleam, the still small voice, the cloud of glory." For Lindsay, the mist guides a knowing observer to salvation. The mist is visible only to those who know artistic principles and appreciate beauty; it is not visible through science. As late as 1925, Lindsay credited the map with dominating "all my verses since [1904]."

Many of Lindsay's works related to the "Map of the Universe" and to his visions are included in his first "book," "Where Is Aladdin's Lamp," three handmade volumes with yellow pasteboard covers, "written, invented, illustrated, designed, decorated and bound," he writes modestly in his preface, "by me!" Poems and drawings are loosely tied together by a prose narrative involving three figures who represent different aspects of Lindsay himself: the Painter, the Evangelist, and the Counselor. All search for Aladdin's Lamp, guided by Tennyson's "gleam," what Eleanor Ruggles calls "that magic or unknown quantity in spiritual life proposed by seers, like Blake and Poe, and denied by the scientists." Although Lindsay claimed to have destroyed his book, fragments are extant, and the essential idea underlies such poems as "The Sorceress!" and "Aladdin's Lamp."

With his new book Lindsay returned to New York in January 1905, not as an art student but as an artist in search of a publisher and a job. He was bold, since Robert Henri had told him to start at the top: "You'll find as many fools there as anywhere else." His reception in publishers' offices was cordial but unproductive. His book was praised but politely refused with comments such as the "house didn't handle that line of goods," in the words of a Scribners business manager. Lindsay was also unable to find satisfactory employment and was forced to continue asking his father for money, with increasing stress for both father and son. One noon, in early 1905, he impulsively recited "The Tree of Laughing Bells" for Robert Henri and his wife, and a somewhat stunned Henri urged Lindsay to focus his creative effort on poetry. Many years later in 1926, Henri recalled his immediate thoughts after Lindsay's recitation: "This fellow is a poet—he is a singer of songs."

Unable to find a publisher and believing himself to be a poet with a message, Lindsay borrowed enough money from his friends to print two broadside poems and drawings with a social message: *We Who Are Playing Tonight* (later titled "Sweet Briars of the Stairways") and *The Cup of Paint*. On 23 March 1905 he attempted to give away copies of *We Who Are Playing Tonight* on the streets of New York. When his gifts were refused, he sold several copies for two cents apiece, demonstrating to his own logical satisfaction that Americans value Mammon above art. *We Who Are Playing Tonight* evidences Lindsay's distress at the hopeless plight of Chicago and New York slum children. *The Cup of Paint*, which was sold on subsequent nights, is an early Lindsay reaction to vaudeville, a style of entertainment that he rejected in 1905 but attempted to use for his own purposes by 1915, when he was engaged in promulgating "the Higher Vaudeville." Both poems, and the drawing for *We Who Are Playing Tonight*, exhibit

Lindsay's strained response to the New York school's emphasis on realism. His own artistic propensities were far more imaginative.

Meanwhile Lindsay's inability to secure a living wage discouraged him enough so that he felt obligated to break his informal engagement to Ruth Wheeler. By October 1905 he was desperate and accepted a menial job in a New York manufacturing firm, the Nicholls Gas Tubing Works. He also volunteered to teach a class in art appreciation at the New York West Side YMCA. When the YMCA classes proved popular and profitable, Lindsay was paid a modest salary, and he quit Nicholls. His notebooks show that his preparation for his classes was meticulous and that his consistent theme was the value of past art in respect to understanding and solving current social issues and problems. He continued to experience pictures in the air, as he called his visual phenomena, including an apocalyptic vision of New York on the evening of 23 December 1905. The great city Babylon, as Lindsay commonly called New York, was, after all, merely a bubble.

In March 1906, "with malice aforethought," he asserted later, Lindsay joined his friend Edward Broderick on the tramp steamer *Iroquois*, sailing from New York's Pier 36 to Jacksonville, Florida. After tramping in Florida for a time, Broderick returned to New York, but Lindsay begged rides on trains and walked some six hundred miles across Florida and on north to Grassy Springs, Kentucky. Here he wrote "The Flower of Mending," after "certain dire adventures." These adventures are reported in the first half of *A Handy Guide for Beggars* a work that features, prose stories interspersed with poems. Since the book was not published until a decade after the fact, *The Tree of the Laughing Bells* (1905), which Lindsay carried with him in pamphlet form and traded for food and lodging, is not included; it had been published in *Gen. William Booth Enters into Heaven and Other Poems* (1913).

One poem in *A Handy Guide for Beggars*, "The Would-Be Merman," is crucial for understanding Lindsay's purposes, especially his purposes for tramping the country as a poet/artist. He believed that the sophisticated saw the masses, for the most part, as "Crude, ill-smelling voters,–/Herds," mobs "like the Gulf Stream./Like the vast Atlantic." In contrast, he would be a merman, a deep-sea "diver," sharing the lives of and bringing hope to the common people in the depths. Lindsay's tramps convinced him that "Wisdom waits the diver/In the social ocean." Through-

out his life he was fond of proclaiming his faith in the ninety million Americans, as he informed Sara Teasdale in 1914. The missionary intent that lies at the heart of the tramps helps to explain why Lindsay's poetry shifts from an early emphasis on Poe and aesthetics to an increasing emphasis on Whitman and democracy. It also explains his admiration for General William Booth, who was, in Lindsay's mind, the merman of mermen, in the social ocean.

After leaving Grassy Springs, Lindsay walked farther north to his mother's girlhood home in Rushville, Indiana, where he joined his parents to leave for a tour of European art galleries in summer 1906. The tour was an important part of his preparation for a series of art history lectures that he delivered at New York's Metropolitan Museum of Art during the winters of 1906-1907 and 1907-1908. During the return trip from Europe, on the night of 4 September 1906, he dreamed of Christ, "his work done, singing to free his heart in Heaven." Soon after, Lindsay used his dream for the poem "I Heard Immanuel Singing," in which Immanuel is depicted as a laughing/weeping shepherd singing in a minor key: "No chant of gilded triumph– /His lonely song was made/Of Art's deliberate freedom." The song is an "hour of sorrow" for neglected and transient beauty, for bubbles, "For flowers and Arts of men." The poem itself is another expression of young Lindsay's identification with the Christ figure.

Back in New York, Lindsay continued to lecture on poetry and art at the YMCA, as well as at the Metropolitan Museum. The *Outlook* accepted one of his short stories from his southern tramp ("The Man under the Yoke," 1 June 1907). With a group of friends, he decorated the Pig and the Goose restaurant with a series of murals that reflected his museum course on the "Dominating Personalities of History." The course and the murals provided the basic subject matter for his "Litany of the Heroes," a poem first entitled "God Help Us to Be Brave" and, subsequently, "The Heroes of Time," before assuming its final title. Typically, missionary Lindsay portrays the great figures of the past as archetypes for present well-being.

By April 1908 Lindsay was ready to return home, ready to "give" his ideas and his art, he wrote in one of his many notebooks, to those who were "dearest" to him. His intentions were to blossom into the primary credo of his "Gospel of Beauty," something he called the "New Localism." Art students are lured to Chicago and New York, but in the end, due to "lack of funds," they return to the "old home." Here they must renew their war for civilization and taste, a war as vital for the continuance of American democracy as the Civil War itself. Art student soldiers are to undertake "any cherished beauty-enterprise" where they are, as they *"will find no better place in all America"* (his emphasis). Although forced on him by circumstances and economics, the "New Localism" developed into a major theme in Lindsay's work, whether he was located in Springfield; in Gulfport, Mississippi; or in Spokane, Washington. During the years 1908-1912, he especially emphasized the Illinois village crossroads, including Springfield, as the hope of America: "There we meet the real citizen, three generations before he is ironed out into a mechanical toy," like a "Hart, Schaffner and Marx" Chicagoan or New Yorker. As a unique individual, the artist has a missionary responsibility to bring beauty to modern man, who otherwise is "Dominated by a switchboard civilization" and "moves in grooves from one clock-work splendor to another." Dr. Lindsay brought health to Springfield bodies; his son came home in 1908 for the purpose of bringing health to Springfield souls and minds.

Lindsay's return was accomplished in his own inimitable way. He borrowed money to print *The Last Song of Lucifer* (1908) and *God Help Us to Be Brave* (1908) and tramped across New Jersey, Pennsylvania, and Ohio, joining his young sister Joy at Hiram College. His many adventures, including a miserable night in a Presbyterian Mission in Morristown, New Jersey, are recorded in the second half of *A Handy Guide for Beggars*. With Joy, he arrived in Springfield by train, determined to "keep laughing" and to be "true to democracy" and "true to grand-father's log cabin," while remembering the artistic principles and education that he had acquired while away.

In August 1908, at the very time his missionary zeal for his hometown stimulated great plans for reform and righteousness, Lindsay suffered through one of the North's first race riots. Unruly mobs rampaged just blocks from the Lindsay and Lincoln homes, and several Springfield blacks were murdered. The centennial of Lincoln's birth (12 February 1909) was only months away, and city fathers were already planning a substantial celebration. Lindsay was deeply distressed, but instead of fulminating in letters to the newspaper, he arranged to give a series of ten lectures at the local YMCA. Beginning the

night of 14 October 1908, he focused each of the first nine weekly lectures on an individual race or ethnic group living in Springfield. Each lecture emphasized the group's great heritage and then contrasted that heritage with its menial role in contemporary Springfield. On 11 November 1908, with great courage, he lectured on "The Negro. His Native Genius:–Sorrow Songs; Folk Lore; Oratory; Sense of the Picturesque; Minstrelsy." Then Lindsay contrasted this "Native Genius" with the race's contemporary role: "American Calling: Professor of the Whisk Broom."

For the tenth lecture, "The Future of Springfield" (16 December 1908), Lindsay recited his new poem, "On the Building of Springfield," arguing in his lecture that the various races offer the potential for a unique and rare opportunity: "All cities in America are much alike. Why not make Springfield different?" In later years Lindsay asserted that the race riot and the lectures were part of the background of "The Congo," but the idea also underlies his other racially oriented poems, such as "The Jingo and the Minstrel," "The Chinese Nightingale," "Shantung," and "A Rhyme for all Zionists."

During the years 1908-1912 Lindsay tried his hand at painting on commission, harvesting corn, hauling bricks for the local waterworks, lecturing for the Anti-Saloon League, teaching English and art at a local mission, writing poetry, and publishing and giving away a large number of broadsides, many paid for by his parents. His frustrations surfaced in the summer of 1909, when he published a series of pamphlets he called *War Bulletins*, informing his Springfield neighbors: "I have spent a great part of my few years fighting a soul battle for absolute liberty, for freedom from obligation, ease of conscience; independence from commercialism." He announces that he feels freer than most people, but he regrets that he still finds himself "taking counsel to please the stupid, the bigoted, the conservative, the impatient, the cheap." The *War Bulletins* will publish, he warns, only what pleases him: *"To the Devil with you, average reader"* (his emphasis). It did not seem to occur to him that the *War Bulletin* announcements contradicted his merman philosophy.

Lindsay first tried to sell the *War Bulletins* for a nickel but at last had to give them away. *War Bulletin: Number Three*, published 30 August 1909, opens with "The Creed of a Beggar," in which he catalogues his personal beliefs. Several of these may be described as heterodox at best:

"I believe in Christ the Socialist, the Beautiful, the personal savior from sin, the Singing Immanuel." Many Springfieldians were shocked, including some of Lindsay's closest friends, and he was asked to resign from his work at the local mission. In continuing defiance, he wrote such poems as "Why I Voted the Socialist Ticket."

War Bulletin: Number Four is different from the others. Entitled *The Tramp's Excuse and Other Poems*, it is a booklet of some seventy poems and drawings, including a sampling of Lindsay's early aesthetic poetry, "The Map of the Universe" and related poems, several rhyme sheets that he printed privately and distributed in Springfield, and poems reflecting the 1906 and 1908 tramps, such as "Upon Returning to the Country Road." Floyd Dell was told that *The Tramp's Excuse and Other Poems* presented the poet's system "at one fell swoop"; Sara Teasdale was informed that the book is "crude autobiography." Actually, the booklet is comprised of poems and drawings that date from Lindsay's high school days up to and just beyond the 1908 race riot.

At Christmas 1909 Lindsay ended his unilaterally declared war, distributing a series of poems under the title *The Sangamon County Peace Advocate*, including "Springfield Magical" and "The Springfield of the Far Future." In "Springfield Magical" he admits his ambivalence in regard to the "City of my Discontent," although he also emphasizes his frustrations over his city's baffling ways: "No picture-palace in a picture-book/ Such webs of Friendship, Beauty, Greed and Fate!" Another poem in *The Sangamon County Peace Advocate*, "The Shield of Lucifer," depicts a defeated Lucifer/Lindsay but concludes with "a sign" that he "shall rise at last from out the tomb," "a warrior fit to own that glimmering perfect shield." The 1909 peace was only for an interim.

At the time of the *War Bulletins* and *The Sangamon County Peace Advocate*, Lindsay was hopelessly in love with a Springfield girl ten years his junior, Nellie Tracy Vieira. At first Lindsay courted Nellie in an avuncular manner, stressing his age and experience and praising her youth and innocence. While Nellie was a student at the Cumnock School of Oratory at Northwestern University, Lindsay sent almost daily letters, some of which were to instruct her in philosophy and art history. His intention, he admitted, was Pygmalion-like: he wished to have her develop into a suitable mate. As Nellie increasingly pulled away from him, however, the tone of Lindsay's letters changed dramatically. He reversed the age disparity, pleading with Nellie as a boy who needs a mother figure to guide and inspire him. He was deeply hurt when she rejected the role, as she had rejected the role of sweetheart before. By early 1910 Nellie succeeded in ending the relationship but only after several attempts in which she argued the necessity of doing her duty as a daughter and as a student. A hurt but proud Lindsay recorded his curious perspective on the break in his poem, "Why I Fled from Duty."

The Lindsay letters to Nellie Vieira (edited by Elizabeth Fowler in 1968) provide important biographical information, and they also manifest a pattern that is repeated several times in Lindsay's life. He would court a young girl as an experienced, avuncular male, fall in love, and be inspired to write large quantities of poetry and prose; the girl would at first welcome but finally reject his courtship; he would become a young boy, pleading for motherly love and protection; the girl would exit, and he would be left in despair. With only slight variations, the scenario was played out with Octavia Roberts, Mary Johnson, Sara Teasdale, Eleanor Dougherty, Isadora Bennett, Elizabeth Mann Wills, and other, more shadowy women in Lindsay's life. Elizabeth Conner, Lindsay's wife, was half his age when they married in May 1925. She was attracted, in part, to his stature in the world of letters. After Lindsay's death in 1931, however, Elizabeth Lindsay informed Sara Teasdale that her husband depended upon her as a mother figure, an expectation that Teasdale certainly could have predicted.

In the final days of his relationship with Nellie Vieira, in early 1910, Lindsay conducted his first lecture tour of the East. He was sponsored by the Eastern Lyceum Bureau (Boston), and the program was largely a synopsis of his old Metropolitan Museum course on the "Dominating Personalities of History." Returning to Springfield, he privately printed a small booklet of verses and drawings entitled *The Spring Harbinger* (1910), characteristically handing the work out for free on various Springfield street corners. *The Spring Harbinger* is a humorous view of male/ female relationships, with both the verses and the drawings highly suggestive of the later work of James Thurber.

Lindsay meanwhile continued to lecture for the Anti-Saloon League on weekends. In summer 1910 he prepared a collection of poems and drawings with the title *The Village Magazine*, the first of four editions. His scheme was to leave this 1910 version of *The Village Magazine* in various Illinois villages while touring for the league. The word "magazine," he explained in the second edition (1920), means "arsenal": the work was to be ammunition for his localized war on behalf of beauty and decency. The war motif is evident in the poem "On Reading Omar Khayyam" but also underlies poems such as "What the Great City Said" and "The Airship of the Mind." One poem in *The Village Magazine*, "Genesis," is an early example of Lindsay's daydream poetry, a kind of "Walter Mitty" poetry, as it were. In these works a male figure demonstrates bravery and ingenuity in extreme circumstances, inspired by love for a desirable and vulnerable woman. "The Tree of Laughing Bells" is another example, although "The Chinese Nightingale" stands as the most polished of the Lindsay daydream poems.

Lindsay mailed copies of *The Village Magazine* to several important writers and editors and was rewarded with a substantial review by Edward J. Wheeler in *Current Literature* (March 1911). Hamlin Garland read the review, wrote for a copy of *The Village Magazine*, and then invited Lindsay to Chicago, expenses paid, to address the Cliff Dwellers. Floyd Dell published an occasional Lindsay poem in the *Chicago Evening Post Friday Literary Review*, and the *Outlook* had accepted more of his prose. *Collier's Weekly* published two prose sketches: "The Factor in the Village" (13 August 1910) and "The Education of Aladdin" (18 March 1911). Still, during 1910 and 1911, Lindsay's pile of rejection slips far outweighed his acceptance letters and checks.

Octavia Roberts was Lindsay's sometime "inspiration girl" during the years 1910-1913, and she also had minor successes as an author. Her contact with *American Magazine* was rewarded in April 1912, when an *American* editor asked for a sketch of Lindsay for the department "Interesting People." The *American* also accepted two of Lindsay's poems, "The Knight in Disguise" (a poetic portrait of O. Henry) and "The Proud Farmer" (a portrait of Lindsay's maternal grandfather). Both Octavia Roberts's article and the poems were published in summer 1912, while Lindsay was in the midst of his third and last tramping trip. At the same time *Twentieth Century Magazine* published four of his 1908 tramping stories.

On the 1912 tramp Lindsay walked west along the Santa Fe trail to Colorado (where his parents and Octavia were camping) and then south-

west to Wagon Mound, New Mexico. He carried with him a collection of poems, *Rhymes to Be Traded for Bread* (1912), a series of drawings ("The Village Improvement Parade"), and a leaflet entitled *The Gospel of Beauty*. Lindsay's account of his journey is recorded in *Adventures While Preaching the Gospel of Beauty* (1914), first published as a series of six articles and poems in the *Forum* (Winter 1913-1914). *Adventures While Preaching the Gospel of Beauty* includes "The Kallyope Yell," Lindsay's vivid re-creation of the noise and fanfare of the Illinois State Fair (held in Springfield), when "Popcorn crowds shall rule the town." The book also features a poetic portrait entitled "Kansas" and an impressionistic self-portrait of a "ne'er-do-well" who would rather play music than weed his garden ("The Flute of the Lonely").

The avowed purpose of the 1912 tramp was to carry his "gospel of beauty" across the country, "penniless and afoot," "returning home in due time." The gospel is ecumenical: it "does not say 'no' to any creed." The gospel proclaims " 'the church of beauty' or 'the church of the open sky' " and has two main tenets: "the love of beauty and the love of God." The heart of the gospel is the "New Localism": children should "wander over the whole nation in search of the secret of democratic beauty with their hearts at the same time filled to overflowing with the righteousness of God. Then they should come back to their own hearth and neighborhood and gather a little circle of their own sort of workers about them and strive to make the neighborhood and home more beautiful and democratic and holy with their special art."

Rhymes to Be Traded for Bread, another privately published booklet, was printed, according to the preface, "expressly as a substitute for money." The forty-six poems are organized according to themes: fantasy and desire, religion, politics and current issues, and future utopias, including tramping and begging as a utopian way of life. Nellie Vieira's poem, "Why I Fled from Duty," is included among "Verses of Fantasy and Desire." Additional examples of Lindsay's male daydream poetry appear as "Eden in Winter" and "The Master of the Dance." "The Tower Builder" manifests Lindsay's views on female inspiration, as the narrator, touched by "Venus the holy," now knows "why strong men toil,/And why bright cities rise" and describes this "power" as "the key to life." "The Hearth Eternal" is an impressionistic portrayal of Lindsay's mother, while the justly well-known elegy for Peter Altgeld, "The Eagle That Is Forgotten," is included under "Rhymes of the Day and Hour," along with Lindsay's protest against white slavery, "The Trap." "The Pilgrims from Asia" presents Lincoln as the continuing exemplar of "sweet freedom," and to be like Lincoln is thus the final goal of all freedom-seeking pilgrims. Several poems in *Rhymes to Be Traded for Bread* counsel those who may despair, as Lindsay did on occasion, in their missionary efforts: "The Missionary Misgiving," "To Those That Would Mend These Times," and "To Reformers in Despair."

At Wagon Mound Lindsay "lost his nerve," he told Sara Teasdale. In the poem concerning his capitulation, "I Went Down into the Desert," he states that he went "To meet my God" but instead *I met the devil in red*" (his emphasis). He wired his long-suffering father for $40 in order to take the train to Los Angeles. Here, at the home of his cousin Ruby, he wrote "General William Booth Enters into Heaven" and mailed the manuscript to Harriet Monroe. The verses appeared as the lead poem in the January 1913 issue of *Poetry: A Magazine of Verse*, and Lindsay's contemporary fame as a leading figure in the New Poetry Movement was assured. On 6 September 1913 Peter Clark Macfarlane published an extensive account of Lindsay's life and work in *Collier's Weekly*, and soon after Mitchell Kennerley published Lindsay's first trade volume, *General William Booth Enters into Heaven and Other Poems* (1913).

Well over half the poems included in *General William Booth Enters into Heaven and Other Poems* had already been printed in private publications or in magazines–from the Booth-as-merman title poem to the moon poems in the middle to the "Gospel of Beauty" poems at the close. Two poems reflect the end of the 1912 tramp, when Lindsay walked from Los Angeles to San Francisco: "God Loves a Gambler Lady" and "The Wedding of the Rose and the Lotus." Both poems reflect Lindsay's excitement over the opening of the Panama Canal and San Francisco's gala Panama-Pacific Exposition organized to celebrate the event. Meanwhile, *Poetry* awarded Lindsay a special one-hundred-dollar prize for "General William Booth Enters into Heaven."

About the time of the Macfarlane article, Octavia Roberts bid Lindsay farewell and destroyed his letters in her possession. A distressed Lindsay, finding it difficult to be creative without an

"inspiration girl," soon started a new personal relationship with a friend of his sister Joy, Mary Johnson, whom he playfully named "the daughter of Lyssipus," in apparent reference to her lovely "Greek" body. Lindsay also redoubled his recently begun correspondence with St. Louis poet Sara Teasdale. By January 1914 he was writing to Teasdale almost daily, gossiping about his problems with Mary Johnson, his daily activities, and his new poems. On 18 February he traveled to St. Louis and met Sara Teasdale face to face. He had already written her more than fifty letters, several of which can only be described as intimate.

Just prior to his one-day visit with Teasdale, Lindsay had recited his new poem, "The Congo," at Springfield's annual Republican dinner, an event that he described to Harriet Monroe as "the big fat-sides Lincoln Banquet." His fellow townspeople, some one thousand strong, were amused and embarrassed by the performance, but Lindsay himself remained typically unabashed. Proudly, he informed Monroe that he "boomed it to the very back of the building."

On 1 March 1914 he performed "The Congo" again, this time at a Chicago poetry banquet in honor of William Butler Yeats. Lindsay was warmly praised by the distinguished visiting poet, who cited the American's work as an example of "earnest simplicity" and "strange beauty." Lindsay's missionary purpose, however, seems to have escaped Yeats, judging from the Irish poet's remarks as they are reported by Harriet Monroe. Yeats used "General William Booth Enters into Heaven" as a pretext for a short talk on poetry, in which he recommended Lindsay as an example of a contemporary writer who is "simple" and "humble," one who avoids "rhetoric" and Victorian "moral uplift." Although Lindsay was exultant, Yeats's commendation reflects the same lack of understanding that finally drove Lindsay to despair. Audiences were carried away with his voice and gestures, praising him lavishly and paying him handsomely. But he soon learned, to his dismay, that people totally missed or only tolerated his moral intentions and "rhetoric."

Back home Lindsay worked hard to complete two poems, "The Santa-Fé Trail" and "The Firemen's Ball," the latter based on a Springfield event that he had attended. He recited "The Santa-Fé Trail" for Sara Teasdale at their second meeting in April 1914. Teasdale did not care for the poem's noisy depiction of automobile horns, although she did profess admiration for the contrapuntal song of the bird, the "Rachel-Jane." Typically receptive to a friend's criticism, Lindsay labored to reduce the noise and to expand the bird's song. He must not "frighten the ladies," he informed Harriet Monroe, although he added: "still I must roar." "The Firemen's Ball," yet another recitation piece, extols the Buddha's philosophy of conquering desire through self-denial. According to Olivia Dunbar, one roaring Lindsay performance of the poem, at the Chicago home of Harriet Moody, "actually made people congregate in front of the house, thinking there was a fire inside."

When the relationship with Mary Johnson soured, Lindsay attempted to follow the philosophy expressed in "The Firemen's Ball," denying himself any emotional interest in women. In a matter of weeks, however, his letters to Teasdale began to "burn." Although they had had but two brief meetings, by summer 1914 Lindsay was in love once again. He flooded Teasdale with love poems, praising her eyes, her hair, even her writing pen. He speculated on how to make enough money to support her as his wife, and several recital successes in early 1914 seemed to offer the answer. Determined to marry, he purchased a ring (which Teasdale refused) and spent July 1914 living in Harriet Moody's New York apartment; working with his new publisher, Macmillan; and courting Teasdale. In August he returned to Springfield to complete the manuscript for his second trade volume of poetry, *The Congo and Other Poems* (1914).

After the three major recitation poems in the opening pages (the title poem, "The Santa-Fé Trail," and "The Firemen's Ball"), *The Congo and Other Poems* features many of the poems inspired by Sara Teasdale. As with his other "inspiration girls," Lindsay initiated the relationship in the role of the avuncular, experienced male, liberally giving advice to a young female poet (in his words, lecturing as "a Dutch uncle"). But when Teasdale was about to reject him, Lindsay reversed their roles and, like a frightened boy, begged for her maternal care. This characteristic Lindsay reversal is the key to understanding the epilogue poem in *The Congo and Other Poems:* "Under the Blessing of Your Psyche Wings," in which the distressed narrator seeks refuge against the breast of the very girl whose head once drooped on his shoulder. Two poems in the volume, "Darling Daughter of Babylon" and "Two Easter Stanzas," reflect Lindsay's anger at the earlier rejection by Octavia Roberts. In fact, "Two Easter Stanzas" establishes a Lindsay for-

mula for dealing with female rejection: the girl may successfully end the relationship in this life, but she will still have to deal with him in heaven (see also "A Kind of Scorn," "Harps in Heaven," and "The Celestial Circus").

Six poems at the end of *The Congo and Other Poems* were added in feverish haste in August 1914. All manifest Lindsay's abhorrence for war, an abhorrence sparked by the opening salvos of Europe's "Great War." The best of the six, "Abraham Lincoln Walks at Midnight," is a good example of another Lindsay theme. Lindsay himself was something of a merman or deep-sea diver in time, as well as in social affairs. When faced with a disconcerting present, such as war in Europe, Lindsay's inclination was to plunge backward in time to an Edenic past, such as Lincoln's Springfield, or to plunge forward to a utopian future, such as the coming "spirit-dawn" envisioned at the close of "Abraham Lincoln Walks at Midnight." One or the other propensity is evident in many Lindsay works. Each of the three parts of "The Congo" begins with a brief depiction of a current scene but then plunges into other times, including the imaginative picture of a future Congo paradise in the final part of the poem. In "The Chinese Nightingale," laundryman Chang irons "the night away" in modern San Francisco but "is satisfied" through his daydream visions of past glories and adventures with "a Chinese lady of high degree."

On 30 August 1914 Sara Teasdale announced her engagement to Ernst Filsinger, a shoe manufacturer, just four days after Lindsay had begun a daily poetry column, "Rhymes from Sangamon County," in the *Chicago Herald.* Lindsay's subsequent distress was intense, as he had come to consider poet Teasdale the only possible "inspiration girl" for his own creativity. He was unable to write much of anything for several weeks, and the *Herald* poetry column ground to a halt after he had used his poems in hand. By late 1914, however, he was able to complete "The Chinese Nightingale." He had begun the poem after Teasdale expressed her fondness for the "Rachel-Jane" in "the Santa-Fé Trail." If Teasdale liked singing birds, she should have more of them.

In late 1914 Lindsay was also struggling to express his artistic theories in regard to the new popular entertainment medium, the movies. The result was published by Macmillan as *The Art of the Moving Picture* (1915; revised, 1922), the world's first study of film as an art form. The book was widely praised and soon imitated, and

Lindsay and Stephen Graham in Springfield, Illinois, 1921

Lindsay felt especially honored (and vindicated) when it was adopted as a text in Victor Freeburg's film-production class at Columbia University. In succeeding years Lindsay lectured on film at Columbia and elsewhere, including Los Angeles and the University of Chicago. He also published some of the nation's first film reviews, several of them in the *New Republic*. He had already completed poems for actresses Mary Pickford and Blanche Sweet, and he continued to write poems reflecting his movie interests ("Mae Marsh, Motion Picture Actress," "Epitaph for John Bunny," and "A Doll's Arabian Nights"). In time Lindsay became friends with many early film stars and producers, receiving a personal invitation from D. W. Griffith to attend the New York debut of *Intolerance* (1916).

Lindsay's life followed much the same pattern during the years 1915-1920: a combination of recital tours interspersed with periods at home

writing poetry and prose. By June 1916 his platform popularity was such that he published *A Letter about My Four Programmes,* an impressively printed, sixty-eight-page brochure that includes prose statements concerning each of the four recitals that he was willing to offer. The letter was mailed to people who inquired about a Lindsay performance. It features a generous sampling of his poems and drawings, as well as a brief history of his publications. The four "Programmes" are the old "Gospel of Beauty" lecture, theories on the "Art of the Moving Picture," "An Evening of Higher Vaudeville and Orthodox Verse," and "The Chinese Nightingale and Dramas for Impromptu Actors." The "Higher Vaudeville" program opened with Lindsay's well-known recitation poems: "General William Booth Enters into Heaven," "The Santa-Fé Trail," and "The Congo," but then continued with a selection from the less noisy works that he himself preferred:

moon poems, love lyrics, and political verses such as "The Eagle That Is Forgotten" and "Abraham Lincoln Walks at Midnight."

Lindsay's fourth program, the poetic dramas for impromptu actors, manifests a new element in his platform life. He chanted several older poems ("The King of Yellow Butterflies," "The Potatoes' Dance"), repeating many lines, and a fellow performer, usually a young girl, danced the poem onstage. Lindsay finally called these exercises the "Poem Games," and his first experiments were with Lucy Bates, a local "inspiration girl," in Springfield in 1914. The poem games received general exposure and mixed reviews in late 1916, when another Lindsay inamorata, Eleanor Dougherty, danced his poetry in rhythmic accompaniment to his chanting at the University of Chicago's Mandel Hall and at Maurice Browne's Chicago Little Theatre.

The poem games were successful enough so that Lindsay wrote several new poems to encourage audience participation in the dance-chants, including "King Solomon and the Queen of Sheba" and "A Visit to Palestine." His interest in the "experiments," as he often called the poem games, lasted for the rest of his life. In his final trade volume of poetry, *Every Soul Is a Circus* (1929), he argues that poetry set to music "is the destruction of poetry." But, he continues, "poetry carefully read and set to dancing is recreated, made social and troubadourish, raised from the dead golden treasuries into life again." In fact, Lindsay and his young wife arranged poem games in their home on a regular basis during the late 1920s, both in Spokane and in Springfield, and Lindsay advised the public in 1929: "If you want mental stimulus and a new basis for speculation, try this out in your parlor. Always after an hour of these experiments, however awkward they seemed at the time, we all had our heads in a whirl of speculation, reconstruction, and poetical music for two days."

The theory of the poem games developed into an early weapon in Lindsay's futile war against his widespread reputation as a strident platform entertainer. Typical newspaper articles reporting his performances are headlined: "Women Yodel Vagabond Airs" (Detroit, February 1919) and "Hear Banging Drum? 'Tis Poetry" (Cleveland, March, 1919). Audiences clamored for "The Congo," "General William Booth Enters into Heaven," "The Kallyope Yell," and other "Higher Vaudeville" verses. Initially, Lindsay was flattered with the attention: he had, after all, suffered neglect for many years. He made a concerted effort to keep performances original, continually adding new works: "The Ghosts of the Buffaloes," "Niagara," "Simon Legree," and "How Samson Bore Away the Gates of Gaza." But to his increasing sorrow and frustration, Lindsay realized early that he was a failure as a social missionary and reformer. Audiences listened to but did not hear his message. People loudly demanded "General William Booth Enters into Heaven," but they had no intention of joining either merman Booth or merman Lindsay at the bottom of any social ocean. "Night after night," he asserted, "I step forth, a gently but altogether misrepresented stranger." By 1929, his war against his reputation essentially lost, a desperate Lindsay defended the poem games as mentally stimulating, offering audiences the opportunity to grasp the intended meaning of a literary work. Even more important, the games accomplish their purposes without "thumping, drumming, and musical notation and any imitations of singing, and orchestras." The poem games are not strident.

Lindsay's early essay, "The Poem Games," is included in his third trade volume of poetry, *The Chinese Nightingale and Other Poems* (1917), along with the new game poems named above. The volume also contains new performance pieces (such as "Two Old Crows"), motion picture poems (such as "Mae Marsh, Motion Picture Actress"), poems from his tramping days (such as "The Flower of Mending"), and at least one poem dating back to "The Map of the Universe" ("How I Walked Alone in the Jungles of Heaven"). As already noted, the title poem was written for Teasdale, and the book is dedicated to "Sara Teasdale, Poet." Meanwhile, "Our Guardian Angels and Their Children" reflects a typical Lindsay response to the loss of an "inspiration girl," perhaps Teasdale, perhaps Eleanor Dougherty.

The controlling theme of *The Chinese Nightingale and Other Poems* is not love, however, but war. The book is a record, Lindsay states, of the transformation of a Tolstoy/Jane Addams pacifist into a supporter of Woodrow Wilson's decision to bring the United States into the European war. An early poem in the book, "The Tale of the Tiger Tree," depicts the drunkenness of war emotions and argues the ancient Greek concept that no side wins a war. Subsequently the book, "The Bankrupt Peace Maker," reflects Lindsay's feelings of hypocrisy and ineptitude when he considers what to do about the war. Finally, "This, My

Song, Is Made for Kerensky" portrays the Russian as an exemplary hero who has Lindsay's nonpacifist approval in "Enforcing with a bayonet the thing that ages teach–/Free speech!"

One poem in *The Chinese Nightingale and Other Poems,* "The Broncho That Would Not Be Broken," parallels a Lindsay prose account of an experience during his western tramp, as related in *Adventures While Preaching the Gospel of Beauty.* On a farm two miles north of Great Bend, Kansas, on 8 July 1912, he witnessed the brutal beating of "a broncho colt" that had been hitched to a reaper, in spite of its youth and in spite of its propensity for "dancing." Lindsay's description of the colt's life and death is obviously empathic, and he concludes: "I think I want on my coat of arms a broncho, rampant." Of all his poems, "The Broncho That Would Not Be Broken" may best portray those transitory moods in which Lindsay felt that his defiance and "boyish heart," like that of Dick the broncho, could overcome frustrations and despair. But the cost, he believed, was persecution and alienation, ending finally with an inevitable but unjust death.

After *The Chinese Nightingale and Other Poems,* Lindsay expended much of his creative effort on *The Golden Book of Springfield* (1920), his imaginative prose account of Springfield in the year 2018 (the bicentennial of Illinois statehood). *The Golden Book of Springfield* was to be his magnum opus, and he worked on the concept intensively from 1917 to 1920, although he conceived the idea as early as 1913. The several extant manuscript versions reveal Lindsay's immense struggle to express his dreams and ideas. Curiously, although utopian in vision, *The Golden Book of Springfield* does not portray a perfect Springfield. Prejudice, snobbery, strife, and even war (including an airplane dogfight) are all part of the 2018 scene. Perfection, Lindsay believed, is attainable only in the far-distant future: "It will be longer to our goal than from Adam to Mary of Bethlehem. If we are millennialists, we must be patient millennialists." But we must "begin to-day as though the Millennium were tomorrow"; otherwise no reform can occur. *The Golden Book of Springfield* is a beginning, not, as several critics have described it, an end. Indeed, critical misconceptions concerning the work reflect its fundamental problem. In spite of Lindsay's intentions, his many attempts at explanation, and his expectations, the book that he describes as "the great effort of my life" was and still is largely unread. The heroine of the work, Avanel Boone, was

based on "inspiration girl" Isadora Bennett, to whom it is dedicated. She had married another man by the time the book was published.

When he was not at work on *The Golden Book of Springfield* or performing, Lindsay wrote the majority of the poems in his second "golden" book for 1920: *The Golden Whales of California and Other Rhymes in the American Language.* The title poem continues his sarcastic views concerning worldly wealth, but the majority of the book's poems reflect his personal feelings as he approached and passed his fortieth year (1919). Characteristically, the somewhat traumatic birthday that punctuated the arrival of middle age caused Lindsay to plunge backward into a comparatively idyllic past, primarily his own remembered past, as in the poems "John L. Sullivan," "Bryan, Bryan, Bryan, Bryan," "The Last Song of Lucifer," "The Lame Boy and the Fairy," "In Memory of My Friend, Joyce Kilmer," "When the Mississippi Flowed in Indiana," and "My Fathers Came from Kentucky." The publication of an expanded edition of *The Village Magazine* this same year should be recognized as another indication of the emotional need to resurrect the past. *The Golden Whales of California and Other Rhymes in the American Language* also demonstrates an interest in the future, as the volume contains some of Lindsay's best poetry for children, most of it written for his own nieces ("Davey Jones' Door-Bell," "The Little Turtle," and "The Sea Serpent Chantey").

The year 1920 was the high point in Lindsay's literary life and fame. In late summer and fall he toured England, performing at Oxford, Cambridge, Westminster Central Hall, and less distinguished places. He met for the first time or renewed his acquaintance with England's best-known poets: John Masefield, Robert Graves, Robert Bridges, Robert Nichols, J. C. Squire, and John Drinkwater, all of whom praised his work. London publishers George Bell & Sons published a generous selection of his poetry, *The Daniel Jazz and Other Poems* (1920). Although the volume contains no new poems, it did provide occasion for a new label and new distress. Various English newspapers and periodicals began to describe their American visitor as "the jazz poet," an epithet then echoed in the American press. Lindsay grew to hate the new label as much as he hated his reputation as a strident entertainer. When "The Daniel Jazz" appears in later Lindsay volumes, the title is simply "Daniel"; poems such as "The Modest Jazz-Bird" are not included at all.

262

Lindsay in 1930 or 1931

After his annual spring recitation tour in 1921, under the aegis of Baylor University professor A. J. Armstrong, Lindsay spent the summer hiking in Glacier National Park with English writer Stephen Graham. Lindsay felt that Graham's subsequent book, *Tramping with a Poet in the Rockies* (1922), illustrated by artist Vernon Hill, portrayed the mountains as "not sufficiently perpendicular," and he began to think of a "sequel and a reply" to Graham and Hill. Lindsay's version, drawings and poems, was finally published as *Going-to-the-Sun* (1923), with the title poem based on the name of the park's famous mountain. The dominant poem in the book, "So Much the Worse for Boston," depicts a Rocky Mountain cat who cannot comprehend Boston blue bloods and Harvard professors. Lindsay's satire reflects his experience in June 1922, when he delivered the Harvard Phi Beta Kappa poem. He recited "Bob Taylor's Birthday," a distended poetic portrayal of the Tennessee governor as a he-

roic political figure and another expression of Lindsay's love for the past. The poem was not well received, and Lindsay, who seldom experienced public failure, was apparently embarrassed, perhaps for the first time in his professional life. "So Much the Worse for Boston" is clear evidence, however, that he was not about to apologize to any "big-eared" Boston rats.

During the 1922 recitation tour, Lindsay's mother died (1 February). He was in the Pacific Northwest at the time and made the long, sad trip home by train in order to attend the funeral. After eight days he returned to his tour, very much at a loss, but he never quite recovered from the death of his archetypal "inspiration girl." The following January he suffered a severe mental and physical collapse, canceled the rest of his scheduled tour, and began a slow recovery at Gulf Park College in Gulfport, Mississippi, where a friend from his Hiram days was president. He underwent a sinus operation in April 1923, and Paul Wakefield, his doctor brother-in-law, felt that Lindsay was never quite himself after the surgery. Certainly there is ample evidence of increased moodiness, irascibility, and paranoia.

In addition to *Going-to-the-Sun*, the year 1923 saw the publication of the first edition of Lindsay's *Collected Poems*, complete with a lengthy autobiographical preface. *Collected Poems*, in spite of the title, is only a selection of the previous work, albeit a generous one. None of the *Going-to-the-Sun* poems is included. At Gulf Park Lindsay taught a single class in the new poetry and fell deeply in love with one of his students, Elizabeth Mann Wills. She loved to dance and flirt, and she was less than half his age. There is no doubt that she offered encouragement, but Lindsay's nature was such that encouragement took very little effort on her part. She also aroused his jealousy and intensified his despair. Lindsay captured the essence of their relationship in the poem, "The Rhinoceros and the Butterfly," where Elizabeth Wills, of course, is the graceful butterfly. The poem "Doctor Mohawk," moreover, a work that portrays Dr. Lindsay's toughness of mind, should be read in the context of his son's hopeless love for Elizabeth Wills. In his wishful thinking Lindsay imagined that he had inherited his father's strength of character and that he therefore could control his feelings, alluding to his love for Elizabeth Wills. In the poems that concern his own emotions, however, Lindsay's art rarely imitates life. Seldom if ever did he manifest the strength necessary to control his emotions for any length of time.

In July 1924, while under contract at Gulf Park, Lindsay visited Spokane, Washington, and decided to accept an offer to be the city's informal poet laureate. He was given room 1129 on the top floor of the Davenport Hotel, and he undertook his role with the enthusiasm that characterized so many of his beginnings, including his initial days at Gulf Park. However, his correspondence reveals that, in succeeding months, he suffered increasingly from debilitating loneliness. He wrote regularly to Elizabeth Wills, with little or no satisfaction. In early 1925, in obvious desperation, he attempted to renew a regular correspondence with Sara Teasdale, intimating darkly that he was contemplating suicide. When he was able, he was working on the third edition of *The Village Magazine* and on an illustrated and expanded edition of his *Collected Poems* (both published in 1925). He also renewed his studies in Egyptian hieroglyphics.

Within a few days of writing a particularly desperate love letter to Elizabeth Wills, Lindsay met and married Elizabeth Conner, a young Spokane woman who taught English and Latin at the local Lewis and Clark High School. Following the day of their wedding on 19 May 1925, the *Spokane Daily Chronicle* announced: "ENGAGED ONE DAY, POET WEDS NEXT." The couple is reported to have omitted the word "obey" from the ceremony, after which they donned hiking clothes for a honeymoon tramp in Glacier Park.

Lindsay's new edition of *Collected Poems* was released on the very day of his wedding. At his insistence the book features nearly fifty of his drawings, although he was disappointed in the quality of the reproductions. A second lengthy autobiographical essay appears at the beginning and several new poems are added at the end, including "Doctor Mohawk" and a few poems written for Elizabeth Wills. One of the poems for Elizabeth Wills, "Bob Taylor's Birthday," is a full revision of the Harvard Phi Beta Kappa poem, making Elizabeth Wills the heroine of the state of Tennessee. The revised *Collected Poems* closes with "The Trial of the Dead Cleopatra," Lindsay's longest poem and a reflection of his Egyptian studies. The publisher, Macmillan, selected a new version of "The Map of the Universe" as a frontispiece. The dedication reads: "To Sara Teasdale, Poet."

In May 1926, a year after his wedding, Lindsay's last bachelor poems were published in *Going-to-the-Stars*, a book reflective of his varied in-

terests in the 1920s. Now over forty-five, Lindsay emphasized the attraction of "the young," "the darlings of my heart," in the lead poem ("These Are the Young"). His love for the past, for youthful America, is expressed in "Old, Old, Old, Old Andrew Jackson," "Nancy Hanks," and "The Flower-Fed Buffaloes." Pride in his personal, ancestral past underlies the poem "Virginia." Meanwhile, his continuing hatred for the jazz epithet is manifested in "The Jazz of This Hotel" and in "A Curse for the Saxophone" ("None but an assassin would enjoy this horn"). The poem and drawings entitled "Hieroglyphics on the Gulf of Mexico" offer a detailed explanation and illustration of the personal hieroglyphic signature that Lindsay used liberally in his work from the earlier *Going-to-the-Sun* volume to the end of his life. Finally, the little poem "Three Hours" is Lindsay's impressionistic account of the impact of his first sexual experience with his wife. Indeed, the poem is a striking example of his characteristic openness in regard to his personal affairs. He was anything but shy, announcing on several occasions that he was a virgin when he finally married.

In fall 1926 Lindsay published the collection of poems and drawings largely completed in Glacier Park during the summer of 1925. *The Candle in the Cabin* is best viewed as a honeymoon poetry/picture album, with all the weaknesses and strengths of any personal disclosure. Several poems, such as "Begging Pardon" and "The Writhing, Imperfect Earth," indicate that the adventure was not entirely blissful, but such poems are in a distinct minority. The book's final poem, "One More Song," punctuates the fact that Elizabeth Lindsay was not only Lindsay's new wife but his new "inspiration girl" as well.

Lindsay's married life commenced in great happiness. The contrast with his despairing and lonely bachelor days was even more extreme than the contrast between his many years of neglect followed by his sudden fame in 1913. He celebrated his love in a flood of verses that can only be described as mediocre at best. Financial difficulties, however, surfaced almost immediately. Elizabeth Lindsay was fired from her teaching position because of her marriage, and Lindsay characteristically demonstrated little talent or interest in managing funds. He published a fourth, elaborate edition of *The Village Magazine*, at his own (and now his wife's) expense, just months after the marriage, and he insisted on costly summer vacations. At first, Elizabeth Lindsay allowed him to

Vachel, Nicholas, Elizabeth, and Susan Lindsay, 1931

direct their affairs, advising Sara Teasdale that the desperate situation would soon take care of itself. Her prediction proved entirely correct, and Lindsay was finally compelled to return to the platform. His hatred for performing was at first extenuated by his proud sense of responsibility and by the fact that Elizabeth Lindsay was able to be with him. But after the birth of their first child, Susan Doniphan, on 28 May 1926, Lindsay was forced to tour alone. His hatred for the "Higher Vaudeville" and his loneliness soon caused major difficulties, including outright verbal battles with audiences.

In December 1928 he published *Johnny Appleseed and Other Poems,* a selection of his poetry for children. The book is illustrated with drawings by his friend from his New York art school days, George Mather Richards. Meanwhile, Lindsay grew less and less enamored with Spokane's hospitality, and by the winter of 1928-1929, now with two children (Nicholas Cave was born on 16 September 1927), he was determined to return to Springfield. After overcoming the legal problems involved in evicting renters, he moved his new family into his boyhood Springfield home in

April 1929, just after the publication of his final prose volume, *The Litany of Washington Street.* The book constitutes yet another statement of Lindsay's democratic principles, delineated this time in the affirmation of Washington Street (representing past American patriotism) against Babbitt's Main Street. To reinforce his point, Lindsay includes lengthy excerpts from the poetry of Walt Whitman, democracy's great poetic spokesman.

By the late 1920s and early 1930s Lindsay was back on the road for the majority of the year. In October 1929, with Elizabeth Lindsay's help, he published *Every Soul Is a Circus,* a volume of poems and drawings "for precocious children, twelve or fifty years of age." The title poem appeals to youth and imagination: "For every soul is a circus,/And every mind is a tent,/And every heart is a sawdust ring/Where the circling race is spent." Now nearing his fiftieth birthday, and very much aware of his age, Lindsay included poems that typically plunge backward in time to his personal and ancestral past: "A Christ Child Book," "What Is the Mohawk?," "The Virginians Are Coming Again," "The Song of My Fiftieth Birthday," and "Twenty Years Ago." Many of the shorter lyrics are children's verses, most of them written for his own children. In the same light vein there are new poem games: "A Swan Is Like a Moon to Me," "The Chipmunk," and " 'How' and 'How.' " A few of the lyrics reflect the family's last years in Spokane. At least one poem directly praises his "inspiration girl" wife: "My Lady, Dancer for the Universe."

Several additional honors yet awaited Lindsay. Toward the close of his early years in New York, he had written to Hiram College, asking to be considered for a degree on the basis of his art lectures and studies. He was curtly informed that no degree would be forthcoming until he had completed "further resident work." More than twenty years later, however, on 10 October 1930, his beloved alma mater awarded him an honorary doctorate. Lindsay recited "The Ezekiel Chant," a poem written expressly for the occasion, as part of the ceremony. Soon after, in January 1931, the poet's voice and more than thirty of his poems were imperfectly captured for posterity on a series of 78-RPM recordings that were completed with the assistance of Professor William Cabell Greet of Columbia University. In the same month the *Selected Poems of Vachel Lindsay,* edited, with an introduction, by Johns Hopkins professor Hazelton Spencer, was published as part of the Macmillan Modern Readers' Series.

After further struggles on the platform and with mounting problems in his marriage, Lindsay endured a brief "vacation" (August 1931) at a Wisconsin resort, largely at the direction of his wife, who felt that he needed to be away. He was back on the platform through the fall months, not returning home until November. By the time of his homecoming, Lindsay's marriage, at least in his perception of it, was in difficult straits, and his single method of earning an income had seriously jeopardized his health. On 30 November 1931 he gave an impressive and moving performance of his work in his family church, undoubtedly with a few elderly people in the audience who recalled his mother's great successes many years previous. But the resulting euphoria did not last; indeed, there are ominous indications that he had already decided to take his own life.

On the night of 5 December 1931, Lindsay's conflicts and despair ended in great mental and physical pain, as he swallowed the contents of a bottle of old-fashioned "Lysol," that is, lye. Although there are several published theories concerning Lindsay's final act, personal difficulties with his marriage were almost certainly the primary cause. The official report was death by heart failure. The suicide was not general knowledge until the publication of Edgar Lee Masters's biography, *Vachel Lindsay: A Poet in America* (1935).

In spite of occasional voices to the contrary, the critical perspective on the poetry of Vachel Lindsay is unlikely to change in the foreseeable future. Much of his contemporary fame was earned through his performances for crowds who refused to buy his books, let alone read them, as he often complained. Nevertheless, Lindsay's revised *Collected Poems* was reprinted for the twenty-fourth time in 1980, and a three-volume variorum edition of his poetry and his drawings has been published (1984-1986). Although Lindsay's work is largely ignored in schools, at least part of the public has continued to exhibit an obvious interest in his verse. The great variety alone must attract some readers; others are aware of Lindsay's historical significance, not only in his life's activities but also in his many topical poems. Romantics will always be attracted by his enthusiasm, emotional candor, and extreme idealism. More reserved readers will be repelled for much the same reasons.

Lindsay himself would not likely be disturbed by his present lack of stature in official statements concerning American letters. In "What It Means to Be a Poet in America," an essay he published in the *Saturday Evening Post* (13 November 1926), Lindsay blamed school assignments and textbooks for what he called the general American hatred for poetry: "poems have been used to punish students in grammar and high school; and as they grow up, in college and university." Poems "are rubbed in like salt." Poetry, Lindsay maintained, will be hated until it is thrown out of school, until it "becomes a volunteer game, as baseball and football are." Textbook anthologies give "the general impression that poetry is cold soup. It is indeed cannibal soup—one man's eye and another man's liver. If you are not willing to read all of a man and then pick his seven best for yourself with your own taste, you had better let him alone forevermore." The number of printings for Lindsay's *Collected Poems,* if nothing else, indicates that the public, in spite of the schools and the textbooks, has not left him alone.

Letters:

"Letters of Nicholas Vachel Lindsay to A. Joseph Armstrong," edited by Armstrong, *Baylor Bulletin*, 43 (September 1940): 1-121.
  Collects Lindsay's letters to Armstrong from 1918 to 1925–before, during, and after the period that Lindsay toured the United States under Armstrong's direction.

"Letters of Vachel Lindsay in the Lilly Library at Indiana University," edited by Doris M. Reed, *Indiana University Bookman*, 5 (December 1960): 21-63.
  Collects and comments on several Lindsay letters, dating from 1913 to 1930, most of them to Frederic G. Melcher.

"Vachel Lindsay Writes to Floyd Dell," edited by G. Thomas Tanselle, *Journal of the Illinois State Historical Society*, 57 (1964): 366-379.
  Important commentary on Lindsay's relationship with Dell, including six Lindsay letters to Dell, dating from 1909 to 1912.

Letters of Vachel Lindsay, edited by Marc Chénetier (New York: Burt Franklin, 1979).
  Generous selection of Lindsay's letters, dating from 1904 (the first letter is misdated "1903") to 1931; the notes, however, contain several factual errors.

Bibliographies:

Cecil K. Byrd, "Check List of the Melcher Lindsay Collection," *Indiana University Bookman*, 5 (December 1960): 64-106.
  Excellent bibliographical description of Lindsay's publications, including most of the private publications.

William White, "Lindsay/Masters/Sandburg: Criticism from 1950-1975," in *The Vision of This Land* (Macomb: Western Illinois University Press, 1976), pp. 114-119.
  Comprehensive and reliable listing of critical literature (from 1950 to 1975) on Lindsay and his work.

Biographies:

Albert Edmund Trombly, *Vachel Lindsay, Adventurer* (Columbia, Mo.: Lucas, 1929).
  First biography of Lindsay, brief but useful; written by Lindsay's personal friend.

Edgar Lee Masters, *Vachel Lindsay: A Poet in Amer-* *ica* (New York: Scribners, 1935).
  Limited, as Masters largely skips the years 1914 to 1931; reveals Lindsay's suicide; many errors, especially in the excerpts from Lindsay's notebooks and diaries.

Mark Harris, *City of Discontent: An Interpretive Biography of Vachel Lindsay* . . . (New York: Bobbs-Merrill, 1952).
  Enjoyable, but basically fiction; very unreliable as biography.

Eleanor Ruggles, *The West-Going Heart: A Life of Vachel Lindsay* (New York: Norton, 1959).
  Limited, in that much has been discovered since publication; still the best biography to date and reliably accurate.

Eudora Lindsay South, *From the Lindsay Scrapbook: Cousin Vachel* (Lafayette, Ind., 1978).
  Privately printed biography by Lindsay's cousin that is especially good for understanding family background and Lindsay's 1906 tramp; several important photographs.

References:

Conrad Aiken, "The Higher Vaudeville: Vachel Lindsay," in his *Scepticisms: Notes on Contemporary Poetry* (New York: Knopf, 1919), pp. 155-159.
  Unflattering contemporary account of Lindsay's "Higher Vaudeville" efforts.

Dennis Camp, "Vachel Lindsay and the Chicago *Herald*," *Western Illinois Regional Studies*, 2 (Spring 1979): 70-88.
  Summary of Lindsay's brief career, in 1914, as a newspaper poet.

Margaret Haley Carpenter, *Sara Teasdale: A Biography* (New York: Schulte, 1960).
  Summarizes Lindsay's relationship with Sara Teasdale and includes many excerpts from Lindsay's unpublished letters.

Floyd Dell, *Homecoming: An Autobiography* (New York: Farrar & Rinehart, 1933), pp. 208-211.
  Interesting firsthand account of Lindsay's ebullient behavior.

William Drake, *Sara Teasdale: Woman & Poet* (San Francisco: Harper & Row, 1979).

Useful addition to Carpenter's biography of Teasdale; also includes excerpts from Lindsay's unpublished letters.

Bernard Duffey, *The Chicago Renaissance in American Letters: A Critical History* (East Lansing: Michigan State College Press, 1954).
Surveys Lindsay's position in the Chicago Renaissance.

Olivia Howard Dunbar, *A House in Chicago* (Chicago: University of Chicago Press, 1947).
Summarizes Lindsay's relationship with Harriet Moody and includes many excerpts from Lindsay's unpublished letters.

Elementary English Review, "Vachel Lindsay Memorial Number," 9 (May 1932).
Contains ten articles by persons who knew Lindsay personally, including an essay by his high school teacher and confidante, Susan Wilcox.

John T. Flanagan, ed., *Profile of Vachel Lindsay* (Columbus, Ohio: Merrill, 1970).
Collects fourteen critical articles, most of them written by Lindsay's contemporaries, such as Carl Van Doren, Herbert S. Gorman, and William Rose Benét.

Hamlin Garland, "The Village Magazine," in his *Companions on the Trail: A Literary Chronicle* (New York: Macmillan, 1931), pp. 462-471.
Important firsthand account of one of Lindsay's first literary relationships.

Stephen Graham, *Tramping with a Poet in the Rockies* (New York: Appleton, 1922).
Relates Lindsay's ideas as he expressed them while tramping with Graham in Glacier National Park during the summer of 1921.

Owen Hawley, "Lindsay's 1908 Walking Trip," *Western Illinois Regional Studies*, 2 (Fall 1979): 156-172.
Comments on unpublished Lindsay materials related to his 1908 tramp across New Jersey, Pennsylvania, and Ohio.

Llewellyn Jones, "Vachel Lindsay: Millennialist," in his *First Impressions: Essays on Poetry, Criticism, and Prosody* (New York: Knopf, 1925), pp. 85-96.

Another contemporary account of Lindsay as a poet.

Dale Kramer, *Chicago Renaissance: The Literary Life in the Midwest, 1900-1930* (New York: Appleton-Century, 1966).
Like Duffey's 1954 study of the Chicago Renaissance, surveys Lindsay's position in this movement.

Ann Massa, *Vachel Lindsay: Fieldworker for the American Dream* (Bloomington: Indiana University Press, 1970).
Best account of Lindsay's themes and ideas, including the variety of influences on his thinking.

Harriet Monroe, *Poets & Their Art*, revised and enlarged edition (New York: Macmillan, 1932), pp. 21-28, 268-273.
Interesting thoughts on Lindsay's poetry by his first important publisher.

Monroe, *A Poet's Life: Seventy Years in a Changing World* (New York: Macmillan, 1938).
Useful addition to the above, focusing on Lindsay's role in Monroe's own life.

David Perkins, *A History of Modern Poetry From the 1890s to the High Modernist Mode* (Cambridge: Harvard University Press, 1976), pp. 348-362.
Best overall view of Lindsay's era, although includes a somewhat cursory treatment of Lindsay himself.

William Lyon Phelps, "Vachel Lindsay and Robert Frost," in his *The Advance of English Poetry in the Twentieth Century* (New York: Dodd, Mead, 1918), pp. 213-244.
First important scholarly support for Lindsay and his work.

Max Putzel, *The Man in the Mirror: William Marion Reedy and His Magazine* (Cambridge: Harvard University Press, 1963), pp. 177-192.
Summarizes Lindsay's publications in Reedy's *Mirror* (St. Louis) during 1912-1914.

Jessie B. Rittenhouse, *My House of Life: An Autobiography* (Boston: Houghton Mifflin, 1934), pp. 290-313.
Personal memories by one of Lindsay's first important Eastern supporters.

Shane Quarterly, "Vachel Lindsay Number," 5 (April-July 1944).
Collects eight articles written by Lindsay's contemporaries, including a lengthy account by his sister Olive and an essay by his wife.

Louis Untermeyer, *From Another World: The Autobiography of Louis Untermeyer* (New York: Harcourt, Brace, 1939), pp. 126-158.
Personal account of Lindsay's enthusiasm and intellectual purposes.

Peter Viereck, "The Crack-Up of American Optimism: Vachel Lindsay, the Dante of the Fundamentalists," *Modern Age,* 4 (Summer 1960): 269-284.
Humorous account of Lindsay's fundamentalism.

Edward J. Wheeler, "An Illinois Art Revivalist," *Current Literature,* 50 (March 1911): 320-323.
One of the first literary recognitions of Lindsay.

Ellen Williams, *Harriet Monroe and the Poetry Renaissance; The First Ten Years of Poetry, 1912-22* (Urbana, Chicago & London: University of Illinois Press, 1977).
Summarizes Lindsay's relationship to Harriet Monroe and *Poetry–A Magazine of Verse* during 1912-1922.

Glenn Joseph Wolfe, *Vachel Lindsay: The Poet as Film Theorist* (New York: Arno, 1973).

The only book-length account of Lindsay's film theories.

Michael Yatron, *America's Literary Revolt* (New York: Philosophical Library, 1959), pp. 71-122.
Defines Lindsay as a populist poet.

Papers:
The largest collection of Lindsay papers, including his notebooks and date books, is in the Clifton Waller Barrett Library at the University of Virginia Library. Other important collections are at the Houghton Library, Harvard University; Beinecke Library, Yale University; Firestone Library, Princeton University; Joseph Regenstein Library, University of Chicago; Lilly Library, Indiana University; University Libraries, State University of New York at Buffalo; Armstrong Browning Library, Baylor University; Berg Collection, New York Public Library; Library of Congress; Illinois State Historical Society Library, Springfield; George Arendts Research Library, Syracuse University; Swarthmore College Peace Collection; Abernethy Library, Middlebury College; Newberry Library, Chicago; Henry E. Huntington Library, San Marino, California; Dartmouth College Library; Brown University Library; Rollins College Library; Vachel Lindsay Home, Springfield; Memorial Library, Marquette University; Humanities Research Center, University of Texas; University of Oregon Library; and University of Southern California Library.

Jack London

*This entry was updated by Earle Labor (Centenary College of Louisiana) from his entry
in DLB 12, American Realists and Naturalists.*

Places	San Francisco The Valley of the Moon (Sonoma Valley) East End of London	Oakland The South Seas	The Klondike Hawaii
Influences and Relationships	Rudyard Kipling Robert Browning Upton Sinclair Sinclair Lewis	Joseph Conrad Edgar Allan Poe George Sterling	Herman Melville Horatio Alger, Jr. Herbert Spencer
Literary Movements and Forms	Naturalism	Realism	Personal Journalism

Major Themes	Social, Economic, and
	  Penal Reform
	Environmental Determinism
	Quest for Paradise
		Primitivism
		Anglo-Saxonism
			Atavism
			Myth of the Hero
			Triumph of the
			  Underdog

Cultural and Artistic Influences	The American Dream Freudianism	Darwinism	Jungianism
Social and Economic Influences	Socialism and Marxism Hoboing	Industrialism Mexican Revolution	Poverty Russo-Japanese War

BIRTH: San Francisco, California, 12 January 1876, to William Henry Chaney (?) and Flora Wellman.

MARRIAGES: 7 April 1900 to Bessie Mae Maddern (divorced); children: Joan and Bess (Becky). 19 November 1905 to Clara Charmian Kittredge; child: Joy.

DEATH: Jack London Ranch, Glen Ellen, California, 22 November 1916.

SELECTED BOOKS: *The Son of the Wolf: Tales of the Far North* (Boston & New York: Houghton, Mifflin, 1900; London: Isbister, 1902);

The God of His Fathers & Other Stories (New York: McClure, Phillips, 1901; London: Isbister, 1902);

Children of the Frost (New York: Macmillan, 1902; London: Macmillan, 1902);

The Cruise of the Dazzler (New York: Century, 1902; London: Hodder & Stoughton, 1906);

A Daughter of the Snows (Philadelphia: Lippincott, 1902; London: Isbister, 1904);

The Kempton-Wace Letters, anonymous, by London and Anna Strunsky (New York: Macmillan, 1903; London: Isbister, 1903);

The Call of the Wild (New York: Macmillan, 1903; London: Heinemann, 1903);

The People of the Abyss (New York: Macmillan, 1903; London: Isbister, 1903);

The Faith of Men and Other Stories (New York: Macmillan, 1904; London: Heinemann, 1904);

The Sea-Wolf (New York: Macmillan, 1904; London: Heinemann, 1904);

War of the Classes (New York: Macmillan, 1905; London: Heinemann, 1905);

The Game (New York: Macmillan, 1905; London: Heinemann, 1905);

Tales of the Fish Patrol (New York: Macmillan, 1905; London: Heinemann, 1906);

Moon-Face and Other Stories (New York: Macmillan, 1906; London: Heinemann, 1906);

White Fang (New York: Macmillan, 1906; London: Methuen, 1907);

Scorn of Women (New York: Macmillan, 1906; London: Macmillan, 1907);

Before Adam (New York: Macmillan, 1907; London: Werner Laurie, 1908);

Love of Life and Other Stories (New York: Macmillan, 1907; London: Everett, 1908);

The Road (New York: Macmillan, 1907; London: Mills & Boon, 1914);

The Iron Heel (New York: Macmillan, 1908; London: Everett, 1908);

Martin Eden (New York: Macmillan, 1909; London: Heinemann, 1910);

Lost Face (New York: Macmillan, 1910; London: Mills & Boon, 1915);

Revolution and Other Essays (New York: Macmillan, 1910; London: Mills & Boon, 1920);

Burning Daylight (New York: Macmillan, 1910; London: Heinemann, 1911);

Theft: A Play in Four Acts (New York: Macmillan, 1910);

When God Laughs and Other Stories (New York: Macmillan, 1911; London: Mills & Boon, 1912);

Adventure (London: Nelson, 1911; New York: Macmillan, 1911);

The Cruise of the Snark (New York: Macmillan, 1911; London: Mills & Boon, 1913);

South Sea Tales (New York: Macmillan, 1911; London: Mills & Boon, 1912);

The House of Pride and Other Tales of Hawaii (New York: Macmillan, 1912; London: Mills & Boon, 1914);

A Son of the Sun (Garden City: Doubleday, Page, 1912; London: Mills & Boon, 1913);

Smoke Bellew (New York: Century, 1912; London: Mills & Boon, 1913);

The Night-Born (New York: Century, 1913; London: Mills & Boon, 1916);

The Abysmal Brute (New York: Century, 1913; London: Newnes, 1914);

John Barleycorn (New York: Century, 1913; London: Mills & Boon, 1914);

The Valley of the Moon (New York: Macmillan, 1913; London: Mills & Boon, 1913);

The Strength of the Strong (New York: Macmillan, 1914; London: Mills & Boon, 1917);

The Mutiny of the Elsinore (New York: Macmillan, 1914; London: Mills & Boon, 1915);

The Scarlet Plague (New York: Macmillan, 1915; London: Mills & Boon, 1915);

The Jacket (London: Mills & Boon, 1915); republished as *The Star Rover* (New York: Macmillan, 1915);

The Acorn-Planter: A California Forest Play (New York: Macmillan, 1916; London: Mills & Boon, 1916);

The Little Lady of the Big House (New York: Macmillan, 1916; London: Mills & Boon, 1916);

The Turtles of Tasman (New York: Macmillan, 1916; London: Mills & Boon, 1917);

The Human Drift (New York: Macmillan, 1917; London: Mills & Boon, 1919);

Jerry of the Islands (New York: Macmillan, 1917;

London: Mills & Boon, 1917);

Michael Brother of Jerry (New York: Macmillan, 1917; London: Mills & Boon, 1917);

The Red One (New York: Macmillan, 1918; London: Mills & Boon, 1919);

Hearts of Three (London: Mills & Boon, 1918; New York: Macmillan, 1920);

On the Makaloa Mat (New York: Macmillan, 1919); republished as *Island Tales* (London: Mills & Boon, 1920);

Dutch Courage and Other Stories (New York: Macmillan, 1922; London: Mills & Boon, 1923);

The Assassination Bureau, Ltd. (New York: McGraw-Hill, 1963; London: Deutsch, 1964);

Jack London Reports: War Correspondence, Sports Articles, and Miscellaneous Writings, edited by King Hendricks and Irving Shepard (Garden City: Doubleday, 1970);

No Mentor But Myself: A Collection of Articles, Essays, Reviews and Letters, by Jack London, on Writing and Writers, edited by Dale L. Walker (Port Washington, N.Y.: Kennikat, 1979);

A Klondike Trilogy: Three Uncollected Stories, edited by Erle Labor (Santa Barbara, Cal.: Neville, 1983).

Jack London has been recognized as one of the most dynamic figures in American literature. Sailor, hobo, Klondike argonaut, social crusader, war correspondent, scientific farmer, self-made millionaire, global traveler, and adventurer, London captured the popular imagination worldwide as much through his personal exploits as through his literary efforts. But it is the quality of his writings, more than his personal legend, that has won him a permanent place in world literature and distinguished him as one of the most widely translated American authors. In 1914 Georg Brandes called him the best of the new twentieth-century American writers: "He is absolutely original," said the Danish critic, "and his style is singularly forcible and free from all affectation." Anatole France remarked that "London had that particular genius which perceives what is hidden from the common herd, and possessed a special knowledge enabling him to anticipate the future." More recently, Vil Bykov, comparing London favorably with Leo Tolstoy and Anton Chekhov, has observed that the "life-asserting force" in London's writings and particularly the portrayal of "the man of noble spirit" have "helped London to find his way to the heart of the Soviet reader." Among a number of contemporary European critics, London is considered "pos-

sibly the most powerful of all American writers."

London was, in fact, a writer of extraordinary vitality. He pioneered in the literature of social protest and apocalypse as well as in the fiction of escape and adventure. He excelled in the "plain style": the terse, imagistic prose so well suited to the depiction of physical violence and to the stringent demands of the modern short story. The publication of "An Odyssey of the North" in the January 1900 *Atlantic Monthly* and of his first book, *The Son of the Wolf,* a few months later was like a draft of bracing Arctic air: "Except for the similar sensation caused by the appearance of Mark Twain's mining-camp humor in the midst of Victorian America, nothing more disturbing to the forces of gentility had ever happened to our literature," says Kenneth Lynn, "and it decisively changed the course of American fiction." London was a major force in establishing for fiction a respectable middle ground between the saloon and the salon, and he blazed the way for such later writers as Ernest Hemingway, Norman Mailer, and James Dickey, as well as for George Orwell and Henry Miller. During the first fifteen years of the twentieth century, the golden era of the magazine, Jack London dominated the literary marketplace: scarcely a month passed without the appearance of his name in the newspapers and his stories in popular magazines like *Cosmopolitan* and the *Saturday Evening Post.* In less than two decades he produced some 400 nonfiction pieces, 200 short stories, and more than 50 books, fiction and nonfiction, that treat such varied subjects as architecture, astral projection, economics, gold hunting, penal reform, political corruption, prizefighting, seafaring, and socialism. His vitality seemed inexhaustible; yet he died before reaching his forty-first birthday, his body worn out by exertion and excess. In spirit, his brief career was a dramatic epitome of America's strenuous age; in mythic terms, his spectacular rise from rags to riches was paradigm of the American dream of success.

Jack London was born out of wedlock in San Francisco. His paternity has never been conclusively established. The biographical consensus is that his father was William Henry Chaney, a "Professor of Astrology" with whom his mother, Flora Wellman, was living in San Francisco as a fellow spiritualist and common-law wife in 1875. She named the child John Griffith Chaney—even though Chaney had deserted her in a rage of denial when he learned of her pregnancy. On 7 September 1876 she married John London, a Civil

Jack London (Gale International Portrait Gallery)

War veteran and widower who had been forced to place his two youngest daughters, Eliza and Ida, in an orphanage while he worked as a carpenter. Evidently it was a marriage of convenience rather than of love, providing a father for the infant boy and a home for the two girls.

Out of the circumstances of London's childhood were shaped the essential attitudes of his adulthood, and throughout his mature years he compensated, both creatively and self-destructively, for what he considered to have been a deprived youth. "My body and soul were starved when I was a child," he said; and he never fully outgrew his deep-seated resentment of his boyhood poverty and of his mother's detachment. Flora Wellman London was an unhappy, restless woman whose body had been dwarfed by a girlhood attack of typhoid fever and whose dreams of the genteel life had been aborted by the birth of an unwanted child. Too frail to nurse the infant herself, she had been forced to find a wet nurse, a black woman named Mrs. Vir-

ginia Prentiss, whose own baby had been lost in childbirth. What little maternal affection Jack received as a youngster, he got from his "Mammy Jennie" and from his older stepsister Eliza, not from his mother. One of the most significant factors in London's development was his conscious rejection of the occult, the supernatural, and the mystical–all of which he associated with his mother's cold spiritualism.

London's childhood was insecure financially as well as emotionally. The family moved often from one rented house to another in the Bay Area as John London tried desperately to make a living: contracting, selling sewing machines from door to door, storekeeping, and farming. On Jack's seventh birthday they moved from Alameda to a farm down the coast; as London recollected, "We had horses and a farm wagon, and onto that we piled all our household belongings, all hands climbing up on the top of the load, and with the cow tied behind, we moved 'bag and baggage' to the coast in San Mateo County, six miles beyond Colma." The next year, encouraged by his ambitious wife, John London bought an eighty-seven-acre ranch in Livermore; and they moved once again.

His loneliness led London at a very early age to seek companionship in books. "I always could read and write," he claimed, "and have no recollection antedating such a condition. Folks say I simply insisted upon being taught." Washington Irving's exotically romantic sketches in *The Alhambra* and Ouida's *Signa,* the story of a peasant girl's illegitimate son who rose to fame as a great Italian composer, were among his early favorites–as were Capt. James Cook's *Voyages* and Horatio Alger's success stories. In 1885, when the Londons moved back to the city after an epidemic had destroyed their chicken flocks and forced John to give up his Livermore ranch, Jack found that he could check out books from the Oakland Public Library as fast as he could read them. "It was this world of books, now accessible, that practically gave me the basis of my education," he later wrote.

Other, coarser worlds also played notable roles in his education: the worlds of the gutter, the factory, the saloon, the sea. Although John London was a conscientious provider, his vitality had been sapped by war injuries and poor health, and his efforts to succeed in various business and farming enterprises were repeatedly thwarted by bad luck and by Flora London's instability. Consequently, even as a grade schooler, Johnny, as he was called, had been forced to help support the family, later attesting that "from my ninth year, with the exception of hours spent at school (and I earned them by hard labor), my life has been one of toil." At first the work was part-time: delivering newspapers, setting pins in a bowling alley, sweeping saloon floors, and doing whatever odd jobs would bring a few extra pennies into the family budget. When he finished grade school in 1889, he went to work full-time in a West Oakland cannery, spending as many as eighteen hours a day at ten cents an hour stuffing pickles into jars. It was a traumatic ordeal, impressing upon him a lifelong loathing of physical labor. Years later that trauma was translated into art in one of London's most powerful stories, "The Apostate." Describing the plight of his protagonist–a teenaged factory worker named Johnny–London wrote: "There was no joyousness in life for him. The procession of days he never saw. The nights he slept away in twitching unconsciousness. . . . He had no mental life whatever; yet deep down in the crypts of his mind, unknown to him, were being weighed and sifted every hour of his toil, every movement of his hands, every twitch of his muscles, and preparations were making for a future course of action that would amaze him and all his little world." That "course of action" was escape: just as London himself had done, the hero of "The Apostate" suddenly deserts the tattered army of "work beasts," abandoning the factory in favor of adventure.

The pattern of London's life, reflected in much of his fiction, might be viewed as a series of escapes–first from the drudgery of poverty, later from the monotony of work: a constant alternation between commitment and escape, routine and recreation, work and adventure. At the age of fifteen, after borrowing $300 from Mammy Jennie to buy a sloop from one of the hoodlums who made their living by raiding commercial oyster beds, Jack (by now he had disavowed his childhood name of Johnny) achieved notoriety on the Oakland waterfront as "Prince of the Oyster Pirates." He followed this dangerous career for a year before, apprehensive that like a number of his comrades he would wind up dead or in prison, he switched sides to become a member of the California Fish Patrol. Many of his escapades during these two years were later fictionalized in *The Cruise of the Dazzler* (1902) and *Tales of the Fish Patrol* (1905).

London's maritime adventures continued into the next year when, a few days after his seventeenth birthday, he shipped out as an able-bodied seaman aboard the *Sophia Sutherland,* a sealing schooner bound for hunting grounds in the northwestern Pacific. This seven-month voyage provided the raw materials not only for his novel *The Sea-Wolf* (1904) but also, more immediately, for his first successful literary effort: "Story of a Typhoon off the Coast of Japan," a prizewinning sketch published in the *San Francisco Morning Call* on 12 November 1893.

Subsequent experiences that winter working in a jute mill and at the power plant of the Oakland Electric Railway intensified his wanderlust: "The thought of work was repulsive," he recollected in his autobiographical *John Barleycorn* (1913). "It was a whole lot better to royster and frolic over the world in the way I had previously done. So I headed out on the adventure-path again, starting to tramp East by beating my way on the railroads." At first he rode with the West Coast contingent of Coxey's Industrial Army, a group of unemployed men who went to Washington to petition Congress for relief following the Panic of 1893. After deserting this army at Hannibal, Missouri, on 25 May 1894, he hoboed northeast on his own. Arrested for vagrancy in Niagara, New York, in late June 1894, he served thirty days in the Erie County Penitentiary, then headed back home to Oakland, determined to raise himself out of what he perceived as "the submerged tenth" of American society.

London's tramping experiences, later recounted in *The Road* (1907), were profoundly influential in shaping his career. First, they helped develop his natural talents as a raconteur: "I have often thought that to this training of my tramp days is due much of my success as a story-writer," he said. "In order to get the food whereby I lived, I was compelled to tell tales that rang true. At the back door, out of inexorable necessity, is developed the convincingness and sincerity laid down by all authorities on the art of the short-story." Second, they transformed him from what he termed a "blond-beastly" bourgeois adventurer into a Socialist: "It is quite fair to say that I became a Socialist in a fashion somewhat similar to the way in which the Teutonic pagans became Christians," he recollected, "—it was hammered into me." Finally, they convinced him that to raise himself from "the shambles at the bottom of the Social Pit," he must resume his formal education. Consequently, he wrote, "I ran back to California and opened the books."

By 1895 London was reading Charles Darwin's *Origin of Species*, Herbert Spencer's *First Principles*, and Karl Marx's *Communist Manifesto*. At the first of the year he enrolled in Oakland High School and began contributing essays and sketches regularly to the student literary journal, the *High School Aegis*. The following spring he joined the Socialist Labor party, and his activism won him notoriety as Oakland's "Boy Socialist." In the late summer of 1896, after feverish cramming for the entrance exams, he was admitted to the University of California at Berkeley. Forced to withdraw after one semester for financial reasons, he launched his writing career in earnest: "Heavens, how I wrote!" he recalled in *John Barleycorn*. "I wrote everything—ponderous essays, scientific and sociological, short stories, humorous verse, verse of all sorts from triolets and sonnets to blank verse tragedy and elephantine epics in Spenserian stanzas. On occasion I composed steadily, day after day, for fifteen hours a day. At times I forgot to eat, or refused to tear myself

away from my passionate outpouring in order to eat." But all his efforts earned him nothing but rejection slips, and he was forced to return again to manual labor, this time in the laundry at the Belmont Academy, a private boys' school. Escape came once again in July 1897, when he left for the Klondike gold rush with his brother-in-law, Capt. J. H. Shepard, who had mortgaged his house for their stake.

His experience in the Klondike was the turning point in his career. "It was in the Klondike that I found myself," he confessed. "There you get your perspective. I got mine." Forced by an attack of scurvy to return home the next summer, he took back no gold, but a wealth of experiences—not only his own but also those of the argonauts and sourdoughs with whom he had spent the richest winter of his life, experiences which his artistic genius could then transmute into marketable fictions.

The fall of 1898 was for London a time of furiously intense work—an incredible outpouring of creative energy, subsequently documented in his autobiographical novel *Martin Eden* (1909) as well as in *John Barleycorn*. London had found his métier; and having discovered that, he was able now to find a market for his work. By January 1899 he had broken into print in the *Overland Monthly;* within a year his work was appearing in the most prestigious magazines in the country; and in the spring of 1900 his first book was published by a highly respected Boston publishing house. "Critics have complained about the swift education one of my characters, Martin Eden, achieved," London commented in *John Barleycorn*. "In three years, from a sailor with a common school education, I made a successful writer of him. The critics say this is impossible. Yet I was Martin Eden. At the end of three working years, two of which were spent in high school and the university and one spent at writing, and all three in studying immensely and intensely, I was publishing stories in magazines such as the *Atlantic Monthly*, was correcting proofs of my first book (issued by Houghton, Mifflin Co.), was selling sociological articles to *Cosmopolitan* and *McClure's*, had declined an associate editorship proffered me by telegraph from New York City, and was getting ready to marry."

Bessie Mae Maddern was the woman London was "getting ready to marry" that spring. The daughter of an Oakland plumber, Bessie Maddern was an athletically attractive, quietly intelligent young woman who had graduated from business school and who made her living as a tutor. She had been engaged to London's friend Fred Jacobs, but he had recently died of food poisoning aboard a troopship en route to Manila during the Spanish-American War. London had known her for several years–in fact, she had tutored him in advanced mathematics during his intensive preparations for his university examinations in 1895–but there was evidently no stronger attachment than friendship between them when he decided that marriage and family life should be a part of his new-won success and impulsively proposed to her. They were married on 7 April 1900–the same day *The Son of the Wolf* was published by Houghton, Mifflin.

London's first book was an immediate success. A reading public tired of a cloying diet of sentimental romances welcomed the fresh, meatier fare that London had brought back from the Northland. "Where the 'artisan' Norris failed, London the 'artist' succeeds in giving us 'the real texture' of the Northland," wrote an anonymous reviewer in San Francisco's *Town Topics*. "The Klondike has waited three years for its storyteller and interpreter to set it in an imperishable literary mold," said the *New York Times Saturday Review of Books and Art;* "London catches the life and conflicts of the Far North with a sure touch, strong dramatic power, a keen eye for character drawing and a natural gift for storytelling." George Hamlin Fitch, reviewing *The Son of the Wolf* for the *San Francisco Chronicle*, awarded London "a foremost place among American short story writers," calling him "the Bret Harte of the Frozen North, with a touch of Kipling's savage realism. . . ." "His work is as discriminating as it is powerful," wrote Cornelia Atwood Pratt in the *Critic;* "it has grace as well as terseness, and it makes the reader hopeful that the days of the giants are not yet gone by."

The Son of the Wolf was the first volume of London's fabulous Northland Saga–the largest single facet of his complex literary achievement–comprising seventy-eight stories, most of which were collected in *The Son of the Wolf, The God of His Fathers & Other Stories* (1901), *Children of the Frost* (1902), *The Faith of Men and Other Stories* (1904), *Love of Life and Other Stories* (1907), *Lost Face* (1910), *Smoke Bellew* (1912), *The Night-Born* (1913), *The Turtles of Tasman* (1916), and *The Red One* (1918); four novels–*A Daughter of the Snows* (1902), *The Call of the Wild* (1903), *White Fang* (1906), and *Burning Daylight* (1910); and one play– *Scorn of Women* (1906); along with a half-dozen

nonfiction pieces (two of which, "The Shrinkage of the Planet" and "The Gold Hunters of the North," were collected in *Revolution and Other Essays,* 1910). The major themes of the saga are primitivism, atavism, Anglo-Saxonism, environmental determinism, stoicism, and humanism. What is perhaps most distinctive about the saga is the paradoxical intermingling of naturalism and supernaturalism. Born into an age when the larger religious structures of Western civilization were tottering, reared in a home without any formal religious orientation, and negatively conditioned by his mother's weird spiritualism, London gravitated logically toward the secular doctrines of Karl Marx, Ernst Haeckel, Charles Darwin, and Herbert Spencer, describing himself as a revolutionary Socialist and materialistic monist. But while he remained reasonably true to these convictions in theory, he betrayed himself time and again in fictional practice as an individualist and a philosophic dualist. And notwithstanding his asseverations to the contrary, the best of his creative writing is informed by an instinctive mysticism in what Carl Jung has called the "visionary mode." The following paragraph from "The White Silence," the first story in *The Son of the Wolf,* is exemplary:

> The afternoon wore on, and with the awe, born of the White Silence, the voiceless travelers bent to their work. Nature has many tricks wherewith she convinces man of his finity,–the ceaseless flow of the tides, the fury of the storm, the shock of the earthquake, the long roll of heaven's artillery,–but the most tremendous, the most stupefying of all, is the passive phase of the White Silence. All movement ceases, the sky clears, the heavens are as brass; the slightest whisper seems sacrilege, and man becomes timid, affrighted at the sound of his own voice. Sole speck of life journeying across the ghostly wastes of a dead world, he trembles at his audacity, realizes that his is a maggot's life, nothing more. Strange thoughts arise unsummoned, and the mystery of all things strives for utterance. And the fear of death, of God, of the universe, comes over him,–the hope of the Resurrection and the Life, the yearning for immortality, the vain striving of the imprisoned essence,–it is then, if ever, man walks alone with God.

The modulating of naturalism into supernaturalism through the visionary mode is nowhere better illustrated than in *The Call of the Wild*, written at the bungalow London had rented in the Piedmont hills above Oakland during the winter of 1902-1903 when he had reached his full maturity as a prose craftsman. Read superficially, the story of Buck's transformation from ranch pet to Ghost Dog of the Wilderness is entertaining escape literature, often relegated to the children's sections in libraries. But to read the novel on this level is tantamount to reading *Moby-Dick* as a long-winded fisherman's yarn. Mere escape novels do not become classics—and *The Call of the Wild* has become one of the great books in world literature, published in hundreds of editions in more than eighty languages. In the strictest sense, London's book is not a novel at all but, as Maxwell Geismar has classified it, "a beautiful prose poem, or *nouvelle*, of gold and death on the instinctual level." Its plot is animated by one of the most universal of thematic patterns: the myth of the hero. The call to adventure, departure, initiation through ordeal, the perilous journey to the "world navel" or mysterious life center, transformation, and final apotheosis—these are the phases of the myth—and all are evident in Buck's progress from the civilized world to the raw frontier of the Klondike gold rush, and then through the natural and beyond to the supernatural world. These rites of passage carry him not only through space but also through time and, ultimately, into the still center of a world that is timeless. London's style is modulated to conform to this transformation, becoming increasingly poetic as Buck progresses from the naturalistic world into that of myth. London's opening paragraphs are thoroughly prosaic: "Buck did not read the newspapers. . . . Buck lived at a big house in the sun-kissed Santa Clara Valley. Judge Miller's place, it was called." However, describing the death of one of the sled dogs when Buck arrives at the Dyea beach, London changes to the staccato cadence of violence: "It did not take long. Two minutes from the time Curly went down, the last of her assailants were clubbed off. . . . So that was the way. No fair play. Once down, that was the end of you." And, toward the end of the novel, the quest of John Thornton's gold-seekers into the mysterious "uncharted vastness" of the Northland wilderness is depicted in the softer rhythm of dreams: "In the fall of the year they penetrated a weird lake country, sad and silent, where wild-fowl had been, but where then there was no life nor sign of life—only the blowing of chill winds, the forming of ice in sheltered

places, and the melancholy rippling of waves on lonely beaches."

This land is an appropriate setting for the "call to adventure," which, according to Joseph Campbell in *The Hero with a Thousand Faces*, "signifies that destiny has summoned the hero and transferred his spiritual center of gravity from within the pale of society to a zone unknown." This "fateful region of both treasure and danger," says Campbell, may be represented "as a distant land, a forest, [or as a] profound dream state"; but it is invariably an unearthly place of "superhuman deeds and impossible delight." This weird region in *The Call of the Wild* is a far cry from the pastoral ranch where the novel begins—and is remote as well from the raw frontier of the Klondike gold rush. Buck's party discovers at last a fantastically rich gold deposit at the heart of this "zone unknown," where "Like giants they toiled, days flashing on the heels of days like dreams as they heaped the treasure up."

His role fulfilled as guide, Buck's master John Thornton is killed by a raiding party of Yeehat Indians, thereby releasing the hero to complete his transformation into the awesome Ghost Dog of Northland legend—an incarnation of the eternal mystery of creation and the life force: "When the long winter nights come on and the wolves follow their meat into the lower valleys," London concludes, "a great, gloriously coated wolf, like, and yet unlike, all other wolves . . . may be seen running at the head of the pack through the pale moonlight or glimmering borealis, leaping gigantic above his fellows, his great throat a-bellow as he sings a song of the younger world, which is the song of the pack." London's masterpiece—all rights to which he had sold to Macmillan for a mere $2,000—was an instant hit with the reviewers and the reading public alike. The *Athenaeum* was representative of the general response in calling it "London's best work so far. . . . an enthralling story, told ably, with restraint and artistry." In similar fashion the *Literary World* praised it as "a story of the robust variety which is never the work of any but a strong and original mind . . . first rank as to its conception and purport." J. Stewart Doubleday, in the *Reader*, wrote: "The Territory is brought home to us with convincing vividness; every sentence is pregnant with original life; probably no such sympathetic, yet wholly unsentimental, story of a dog has ever found print before; the achievement may, without exaggeration, be termed 'wonderful.' " "The telling thing in the book is its deep and underlying truth," observed Kate B. Stille in the *Book News Monthly:* "In this little drama we are brought face to face with that which we refuse to confess to ourselves, and are chilled by the realism of *The Call of the Wild,* and bidden by it to listen to the Voice of the Divine, which is also a part of our being."

While London had found the key to literary success in his Northland Saga, he was still searching for the key to domestic happiness during the years between the publication of *The Son of the Wolf* and *The Call of the Wild.* He had impulsively married Bessie Maddern because he believed he needed someone to tame his wildness, to give him a sense of roots and respectability, and to bear him "seven sturdy Saxon sons and seven beautiful daughters." Bessie Maddern, still trying to recover from the death of her fiancé, wanted someone to make a home for. The marriage seemed to make a good deal of sense at the time—except for one fatal flaw: neither partner truly loved the other. Love apparently came to Bessie after the wedding—but not to Jack—and it became evident fairly early in the marriage that their personalities and interests were not, in fact, compatible. He was gregarious and fun loving; she was prudish and humorless. He loved to fill their home with friends; she disliked company. He had counted on a son as their firstborn: instead, she gave him a daughter, Joan, on 15 January 1901, and a second daughter, Bess (Becky), on 20 October 1902. Though he came to love both of the girls, his disappointment in not getting a boy was nonetheless acute.

A year or so after his marriage to Bessie Maddern, London fell in love with Anna Strunsky, a brilliant Stanford University student whom he had first met in San Francisco at a lecture by Socialist Austin Lewis in early December 1899. Two years younger than London, Strunsky had already won considerable notoriety as the "Girl Socialist" of San Francisco—just as London had earlier been called "Boy Socialist" of Oakland. London thought her a "beautiful genius" and quickly struck up a correspondence. "Take me this way: a stray guest, a bird of passage, splashing with salt-rimed wings through a brief moment of your life—a rude and blundering bird, used to large airs and great spaces, unaccustomed to the amenities of confined existence," he wrote to her on 21 December 1899. "And further, should you know me, understand this: I, too, was a dreamer, on a farm, nay, a California ranch. But early, at only nine, the hard hand of

the world was laid upon me. It has never relaxed. It has left me sentiment, but destroyed sentimentalism. It has made me practical, so that I am known as harsh, stern, uncompromising. It has taught me that reason is mightier than imagination; that the scientific man is superior to the emotional man."

Some of the ideas in this early letter—most notably the dichotomy between the rational man and the emotional man—are central to much of London's work and constitute, particularly, the genesis of *The Kempton-Wace Letters,* an epistolary dialogue on love written in collaboration with Anna Strunsky in 1901-1902, and published anonymously by Macmillan in 1903. As Dane Kempton, Strunsky argues for the idealistic conception of love; behind the persona of Herbert Wace, a young economics professor at Berkeley, London contends that romantic love is nothing but "prenuptial madness," an emotional trap set by nature and idealized by man as simply "*a means for the perpetuation and development of the human type.*" A sensible union, he insists, "is based upon reason and service and healthy sacrifice." But these fine qualities, without love, were not enough to sustain a marriage, London subsequently realized. Because of his cold rationality, Herbert Wace's engagement to Hester Stebbins is broken; and by the time Jack and Anna had completed their collaboration on *The Kempton-Wace Letters,* London's marriage was clearly disintegrating. Writing to his friend Cloudesley Johns soon after his separation from Bessie in the late summer of 1903, London observed, "It's all right for a man sometimes to marry philosophically, but remember, it's damned hard on the woman."

Although Anna Strunsky was implicated when Bessie London filed suit for divorce in 1904, there is no real evidence that her affair with London was ever physically consummated; and she had apparently decided to end the romance when London left for England in the summer of 1902. They remained lifelong friends, but there was no passion in their letters after that summer, and Anna subsequently enjoyed a happy marriage to the wealthy socialist William S. Walling.

London went to England presumably en route to South Africa to report the aftermath of the Boer War for the American Press Association; that assignment was canceled, however, and he reported, instead, on the aftermath of the Industrial Revolution that he found in the London slums. Despite warnings from his friends that he would never be seen alive again, he spent ten shillings at a second-hand clothing shop in Petticoat Lane for a change of wardrobe; and, disguised as a stranded-and-broke American seaman, he disappeared into the black heart of the East End. On 16 August 1902 he wrote to Anna Strunsky, "Am settled down and hard at work. The whole thing, all the conditions of life, the immensity of it, everything is overwhelming. I never conceived such a mass of misery in the world before." The next week he wrote to her again, saying that his book was one-fifth done: "Am rushing, for I am made sick by this human hellhole called London Town. I find it almost impossible to believe that some of the horrible things I have seen are really so." When he emerged a month later, he had the vivid record–manuscript with photographs–ready for Macmillan.

The result was *The People of the Abyss* (1903), a pioneering work of creative nonfiction in the method now widely known among such contemporary writers as Tom Wolfe as the "New Journalism." This method involves the writer's total immersion in his subject, not merely as an objective reporter but, rather, as an active, sympathetic participant, so that his work achieves the immediacy of concrete human experience. "Of all my books on the long shelf," London said near the end of his career, "I love most 'The People of the Abyss.' No other book of mine took so much of my young heart and tears as that study of the economic degradation of the poor." What had affected him perhaps most deeply was the hopeless plight of the very old and the inevitable doom of the very young. For example, there were the two pathetic individuals called simply "the Carter" and "the Carpenter": decent, respectable tradesmen now too old to compete with vigorous younger men in a ruthless industrial system; their children dead and with no one left to care for them, they have been set loose without shelter or money, to scavenge for bits of garbage along filthy sidewalks and to drift aimlessly and painfully toward death. At the other end of this awful spectrum were the children, of whom 75 out of every 100 were doomed to perish before reaching the age of five. "If this is the best that civilization can do for the human, then give us howling and naked savagery," London concluded bitterly. "Far better to be a people of the wilderness and desert, of the cave and the squatting-place, than to be a people of the machine and the Abyss."

London returned home from Europe in November 1902, shortly after the birth of his sec-

ond daughter, hoping to make his marriage work; but despite his efforts, it was increasingly obvious that he and Bessie could not live happily together. In May 1903 he took his family to Glen Ellen, California, a picturesque hamlet nestled in the heart of the Sonoma Valley (which London would call the Valley of the Moon in his novel of the same name), fifty-five miles north of Oakland. There he rented a summer cottage from Ninetta and Roscoe Eames, the managing editor of the *Overland Monthly;* and that summer he fell in love with Mrs. Eames's niece Clara Charmian Kittredge. Though she was four years older than he and though she was not beautiful, Charmian Kittredge was a comely, vivacious woman who not only knew how to make the most of her physical charms but also possessed an independent spirit that set her apart from the other young intellectuals, artists, and dilettantes who constituted the crowd of London's acquaintances. The better he came to know her, the more it seemed to him that she was endowed with all the qualities he associated with the ideal comrade and "mate-woman" he had long dreamed about. In late July, without revealing that he was in love with another woman, he announced to his wife that he was leaving her. Shortly afterward he moved his belongings from their Piedmont bungalow into an Oakland apartment rented for him by his boyhood friend Frank Atherton. So discreet were he and Charmian in their affair that it was more than a year before Bessie London discovered the true identity of her husband's lover. In the meantime London was finishing his novel *The Sea-Wolf,* using Charmian as the model for Maud Brewster and putting his own romantic sentiments into the mouth of the narrator-hero Humphrey Van Weyden. In combining the ingredients of the two major genres of the turn-of-the-century novel– the new naturalistic novel and the ever-popular sentimental novel–*The Sea-Wolf* proved to be one of London's most successful productions, rivaling *The Call of the Wild* in reprints and total sales (and even exceeding that classic with seven film versions). Soon after completing *The Call of the Wild* in late January 1903, London had written to George Brett, the president of Macmillan Company, about a new novel he had in mind: "My idea is to take a cultured, refined, super-civilized man and woman, (whom the subtleties of artificial, civilized life have blinded to the real facts of life), and throw them into a primitive sea-environment where all is stress & struggle and life expresses itself, simply, in terms of food &

shelter; and make this man & woman rise to the situation and come out of it with flying colors." By this time fully aware of his market, he shrewdly added: "Of course, this underlying motif, will be *underlying;* it will be subordinated to the love motif. The superficial reader will get the love story & the adventure; while the deeper reader will get all this, plus the bigger thing lying underneath."

Essentially *The Sea-Wolf* is an initiation novel, charting the progress of Humphrey Van Weyden from an effete upper-class sissy to full-blooded manhood. Cast to sea when the San Francisco-Sausalito ferryboat collides with a steamship in a heavy fog, Van Weyden is saved from drowning and pressed into sea duty aboard the sealing schooner *Ghost.* Though he is a highly educated literary critic, thirty-five years old, Humphrey is put to work as a lowly scullery boy and scornfully called Hump. During the course of his ordeal he learns for the first time in his life to stand on his own two feet amidst the rigorous brutalities of the seaman's world and eventually becomes first mate of the ship, earning the title of "Mr. Van Weyden."

The high priest of his initiation is Capt. Wolf Larsen, one of the truly unforgettable characters in American fiction. "It is a rattling good story," wrote Ambrose Bierce in praise of the novel. "But the great thing—and it is among the greatest of things—is that tremendous creation, Wolf Larsen. . . . The hewing out and setting up of such a figure is enough for a man to do in a lifetime." Van Weyden calls Larsen "a magnificent atavism, a man so purely primitive that he was of the type that came into the world before the development of the moral nature." This predatory character is not immoral, but simply amoral. He is a splendid physical specimen, capable of squeezing a raw potato into pulp with one quick grasp of his fist—or of killing a man with one blow of that same fist. Yet he is neither unusually large nor brutish—he is, in fact, quite handsome—and he is remarkably well-read. His personal library includes Shakespeare, Tennyson, Browning, Darwin, and Herbert Spencer. He is a tragically flawed superhuman, doomed despite his intelligence and extraordinary physical strength. Larsen bridges the gap between the Byronic hero and the modern antihero: like the earlier romantic rebel, he is sensitive, arrogant, uninhibited, actively contemptuous of conventional social mores and traditional beliefs, and—above all—alone. He rules alone; he suffers alone. But like the twentieth-century antihero, he lacks purpose and direction. Without a constructive goal or a meaningful quest into which to channel his great personal force, his energies are perverted into senseless brutality, brooding frustration, and finally self-destruction. "I believe that life is a mess," he confesses. "It is like a yeast, a ferment, a thing that moves and may move for a minute, an hour, a year, or a hundred years, but that in the end will cease to move. The big eat the little that they may continue to move, the strong eat the weak that they may retain their strength. The lucky eat the most and move the longest, that is all." A hopeless materialist at home nowhere in the world, this rapacious loner, aptly named Wolf, epitomizes the plight of the naturalistic protagonist. Physically and morally, Larsen is a prototype of Eugene O'Neill's Yank Smith and of T. S. Eliot's ape-neck Sweeney; psychologically, he has more in common with Prufrock and Gerontion: he is cursed with a hyperrational sensibility. In his gradual deterioration—first headaches, then blindness and paralysis, and finally death from a brain tumor—he is symbolic of a modern type: the psychopathic overreacher who is alienated both from nature and from his fellowman by the disease of self. "The superman is anti-social in his tendencies," London observed, explaining Larsen's failure, "and in these days of our complex society and sociology he cannot be successful in his hostile aloofness."

The character best fitted for survival in *The Sea-Wolf* is not the *super* man but the *whole* man. It is a combination of adaptability, moral as well as physical courage, enhanced by a vital optimism and the capacity to love, that enables Humphrey Van Weyden to achieve wholeness in the course of his initiation. If Wolf Larsen is the high priest of his initiation, Maud Brewster—the great American poetess shipwrecked and rescued by the *Ghost* at midpoint in the novel—serves as priestess, or anima figure. It is through her influence and through their valiant escape from Larsen's hell ship that Van Weyden is able to put his new-found manhood to test. That manhood is confirmed when he manages not only to cope with the forces in nature, in the mode of Robinson Crusoe, on Endeavor Island, but also—and most significantly—to restep the masts of the derelict *Ghost* which is stranded there with its dying captain after the crew's desertion. Although the introduction of Maud Brewster midway through the plot has been disparaged by many critics as London's concession to sentimental popularity, such denigration overlooks what London called "the bigger thing lying underneath." A primary reason that his "man and woman rise to the occasion and come out with flying colors," while the great Wolf Larsen passes away in blind, impotent isolation, is that they have found the greater strength that comes from love, idealism, and cooperation. This was the underlying theme of much of London's work and was central to his socialistic beliefs. London "admired, even worshipped, strength," zoologist Conway Zirkle has remarked, "but he had learned that strength was increased by cooperation, by union. . . . Those who cooperated won because they were fit. The social virtues, altruism, cooperation–even self-sacrifice–were justified biologically for they made gregarious living possible and the strength of the strong was the strength of the group."

In early January 1904, leaving the manuscript of *The Sea-Wolf* with Charmian Kittredge and his poet-friend George Sterling to edit and proofread, London sailed on the SS *Siberia* for Yokohama, to report the Russo-Japanese War for the Hearst Syndicate. He managed to get closer to the front than any other reporter but was continually frustrated by the Japanese officials, who had imposed strict censorship on reports of all military activities. "Personally, I entered upon this campaign with the most gorgeous conceptions of what a war correspondent's work in the world must be," London wrote. "I had read 'The Light that Failed.' I remembered Stephen Crane's descriptions of being under fire in Cuba. I had heard . . . of all sorts and conditions of correspondents in all sorts of battles and skirmishes, right in the thick of it, where life was keen and immortal movements were being lived. In brief, I came to war expecting to get thrills. My only thrills have been those of indignation and irritation." After six months of thwarted attempts to get into the action, London returned home with a high opinion of the Japanese soldier's toughness but only disgust for the Japanese military bureaucrat's obtuseness: "The Japanese does not in the least understand the correspondent or the mental processes of a correspondent, which are a white man's mental processes. . . . The Japanese cannot understand straight talk, white man's talk. This is one of the causes of so much endless delay."

The year following London's return from Japan was a crucially important one. In the spring of 1905, after his unsuccessful campaign for mayor of Oakland on the Socialist ticket, he

took up permanent residence in the Sonoma Valley with Charmian Kittredge and in June purchased the 130-acre Hill Ranch, near Glen Ellen. Now happily engaged, they would be married as soon as his divorce became final. During those months he produced some of his best fiction, including "The Unexpected," "The Sun-Dog Trail," "All Gold Canyon," and what some critics consider the most artistically successful of his longer novels, *White Fang* (also, with a first printing of 48,195 copies in October 1906, one of his most commercially successful books).

The genesis of this novel may be found in a letter to George Brett written 5 December 1904: London proposed a "complete antithesis" and "companion-book" to *The Call of the Wild*. "Instead of devolution or decivilization of a dog," he explained, "I'm going to give the evolution, the civilization of a dog–development of domesticity, faithfulness, love, morality, and all the amenities and virtues." Rather than being a true companion piece, however, this work would be, when finished, a completely different kind of book from *The Call of the Wild*. *White Fang* is a sociological fable intended to illustrate London's theories of environmental determinism and is therefore more thoroughly naturalistic than London's mythic classic. "I know men and women as they are–millions of them yet in the slime stage," he wrote to George Wharton James. "But I am an evolutionist, therefore a broad optimist, hence my love for the human (in the slime though he be) comes from my knowing him as he is and seeing the divine possibilities ahead of him. That's the whole motive of my 'White Fang.' Every atom of organic life is plastic. The finest specimens now in existence were once all pulpy infants capable of being moulded this way or that. Let the pressure be one way and we have atavism–the reversion to the wild; the other the domestication, civilization. I have always been impressed with the awful plasticity of life and I feel that I can never lay enough stress upon the marvelous power and influence of environment."

The power of environment is dramatically evident throughout *White Fang*. Born in the wild, the young cub sees his world through the eyes of the predator: "The aim of life was meat. Life itself was meat. Life lived on life. There were the eaters and the eaten. The law was: EAT OR BE EATEN." Later, after his mother has taken him with her from the wilderness back to her former Indian master, Gray Beaver, the young wolf dog is bullied mercilessly by Lip-lip, the leader of the

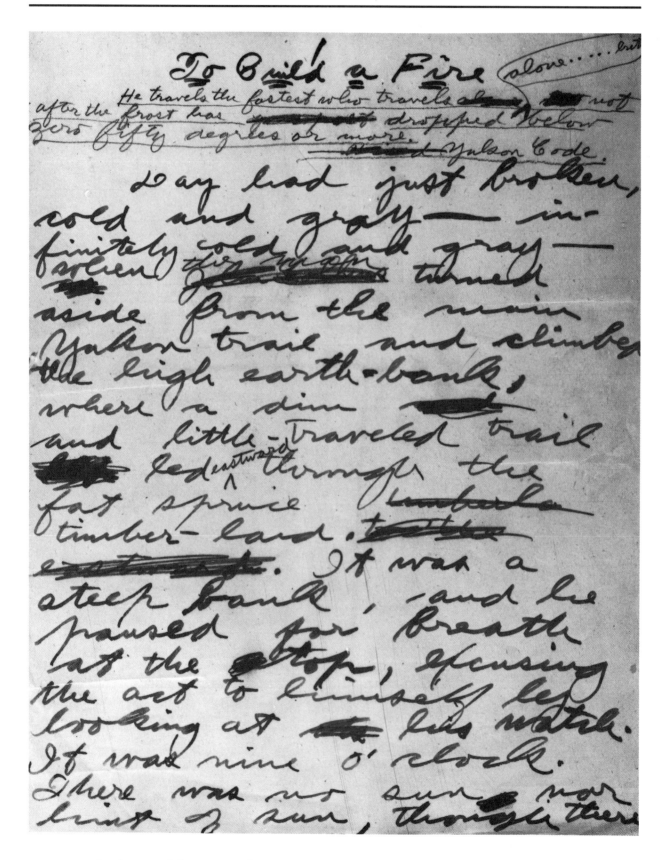

Opening page of the manuscript for "To Build a Fire" (Henry E. Huntington Library and Art Gallery)

camp dogs, and persecuted as an outsider by the other puppies, consequently becoming a fierce pariah. London makes it clear that environmental determinism is a crucial factor in the shaping of White Fang's character: that if Lip-lip had not tormented him, he would have "grown up more dog-like and with more liking for dogs"; and that if his Indian master had been capable of affection, White Fang might have developed "all manner of kindly qualities." Unfortunately, such is not the case; instead, the dog has been perversely molded into a creature of hate, "morose and lonely, unloving and ferocious, the enemy of all his kind."

This hateful ferocity is intensified when Gray Beaver sells White Fang into the bondage of Beauty Smith, under whose sadistic tutelage he becomes the lethal Fighting Wolf. After a bloody and near-fatal career as a dog killer, the hero is redeemed by a new master, Weedon Scott, whose loving kindness converts him from vicious beast into loyal pet. The final stage of his initiation is accomplished when White Fang is taken to Scott's California ranch. Here he becomes properly domesticated; and–after saving the life of Judge Scott, Weedon's father, from the escaped convict Jim Hall (the man transformed into mad-dog killer by harsh social treatment)–he is renamed Blessed Wolf: "Not alone was he in the geographical Southland, for he was in the Southland of life. Human kindness was like a sun shining upon him, and he flourished like a flower planted in good soil."

In October 1905 London started east on tour for the Slayton Lecture Bureau, and on 19 November he and Charmian were married in Chicago. His tour climaxed with his famous lectures on revolution at Harvard and Yale that winter. "I went to the University. . . . but I did not find the University alive," he told his student audience. "If [collegians] cannot fight for us, we want them to fight against us–of course, sincerely fight against us, believing that the right conduct lies in combating socialism because socialism is a great growing force. But what we do not want is that which obtains today and has obtained in the past of the university, a mere deadness and unconcern and ignorance so far as socialism is concerned. Fight for us or fight against us! Raise your voices one way or the other; be alive!" That fall he was also elected first president of the Intercollegiate Socialist Society, with Upton Sinclair as vice-president.

London's socialist enthusiasm reached its peak in 1905 and culminated creatively in his composition of *The Iron Heel* (1908) the following year. This apocalyptic novel purports to be a copy of the "Everhard Manuscript": a fragment written and hidden away by Avis Everhard, widow of the leader of the "Second [unsuccessful] Revolt," and edited seven centuries later by the historian Anthony Meredith in the year 419 B.O.M. (Brotherhood of Man). Mrs. Everhard's document covers the twenty-year period from 1912 to 1932 when the capitalist oligarchy, called "the Iron Heel" by her late husband, Ernest, rises to complete power, grinding all opposing political systems underfoot. In the early stages of the conflict Ernest works against this oppression by use of democratic methods, winning election to Congress, where he is joined by a half-hundred Socialist representatives. This apparent victory is short-lived, however, for the oligarchy quickly consolidates its ranks and moves forcefully to suppress all political opposition. Union leaders are bought off; secret police and mercenaries are employed as terrorists; and political antagonists are arrested or murdered. Everhard's followers are forced to move underground and to fight violence with violence. The narrative reaches a bloody climax when an oppressed mob erupts from the great Chicago ghetto and is methodically slaughtered by the mercenaries of the Iron Heel. Although Ernest survives the holocaust and works to reorganize the forces of the revolution, the manuscript ends abruptly; and the reader is told in Professor Meredith's concluding footnote that Everhard has been mysteriously executed. Meredith says that the oligarchy held its power for another three centuries and throughout numerous revolts before Herbert Spencer's prophecy of socialist evolution was at last fulfilled.

No one seemed to care for *The Iron Heel*. Reviewers called it "pernicious" and "incendiary." The public bought only a few thousand copies. Even the socialist press gave it a mixed reception. "It was a labor of love, and a dead failure as a book," London remarked about *The Iron Heel*. But if the novel was something less than a commercial and artistic success, it was nevertheless an important book, enthusiastically commended later by such noteworthy figures as Eugene V. Debs, Leon Trotsky, and Anatole France. Philip Foner asserts that it is "probably the most amazingly prophetic work of the twentieth century"; Robert E. Spiller calls it "a terrifying forecast of Fascism and its evils"; and Maxwell Geismar suggests that it is "a key work–perhaps a classic work–of American radicalism." Moreover, as a fictional articulation of London's private dreams of revolutionary glory, *The Iron Heel* is one of his most revealing works. The novel's "earnest" and "ever-hard" hero represents London's fantasy about himself, purged of his obsession to win the good life of the American Dream. A "natural aristocrat" and a "blond beast" with blacksmith's biceps and prizefighter's neck, Ernest is the author's exact physical replica; with his Spencerian Weltanschauung and his Marxist rhetoric, he is also London's metaphysical replica; and the love affair between Avis and Ernest Everhard is virtually a carbon copy of that between Charmian and London. "Few of Jack London's books, even those which were consciously autobiographical, are so intensely personal," remarked his daughter Joan London in her biography: "His best knowledge of the class struggle and the socialist movement, his best speeches and essays he gave to Everhard. . . ."

But "intensely personal" as it is, *The Iron Heel* is not so personal as *Martin Eden*, London's next novel, begun the following summer in Hawaii and completed in February 1908 in Tahiti, while he was sailing the South Seas on his much publicized cruise aboard the *Snark*. "Nowhere in London's fiction are the complexities and contradictions of his life and mind more intimately revealed than in *Martin Eden*," Jonathan Yardley has perceptively observed. Even London was not entirely sure how much of himself he was putting into this remarkable Bildungsroman, for in September 1907 he wrote to George Brett: "I am surging along with my new novel, for which I cannot find a name, and which is so totally different a novel from anything I have written, that I do not know quite how to make up my mind about it as I go along." Because of the author's deep personal involvement in the book, *Martin Eden* is an imperfect but powerful work.

The plot, unlike the novel's underlying theme, is fairly straightforward and uncomplicated. In much the same fashion that Jack London had fallen in love with Mabel Applegarth (the lovely sister of Ted Applegarth, the closest friend of his college days), Martin Eden, a husky young sailor, falls in love with Ruth Morse, a fragilely beautiful Victorian lady. Though lacking in manners and formal education, Martin is a sensitive, intelligent young man who possesses extraordinary vitality. Inspired to make something of himself, he accepts Ruth as his cultural tutor and enters upon a rigorous program of self-education. He learns with astonishing rapidity and within a few months has become conversant not only with the best-known literary artists but also with such philosophers as Adam Smith, Karl Marx, and–above all–Herbert Spencer, who becomes his intellectual idol. Gifted with a natural talent for storytelling, Martin determines to make a career as a writer. Renting a typewriter, he sets himself to work in an eighteen-hour-a-day frenzy of creativity, churning out stories, poems, jokes, and articles by the dozens. For several months he gets nothing but rejection slips from the magazine editors and nothing but nagging from Ruth, his family, and his friends, all of whom insist that he get a steady job. His only encouragement comes from his poet-friend Russ Brissenden (modeled after George Sterling). Everything seems to go wrong for Martin. He is falsely publicized in the local newspapers as a notorious revolutionary; under pressure from her mother, Ruth rejects him; a few weeks later he discovers that Brissenden, a world-weary consumptive, has taken his own life. Exhausted by his ordeal and profoundly depressed, Martin lapses into neurasthenic apathy. Ironically, at almost the same time, he starts to receive acceptances for the numerous manuscripts he has already sent out. His success snowballs; he becomes an instant celebrity; the publishers begin to clamor for his work; his friends invite him into their homes again, and even Ruth comes back, begging his forgiveness. But the recognition and the good fortune have come too late. Martin is thoroughly disenchanted. "It was work performed," he keeps repeating to himself. "And now you feed me, when then you let me starve, forbade me your house and damned me because I wouldn't get a job. And the work was already done, all done. And now, when I speak, you . . . pay respectful attention to whatever I choose to say. . . . And why? Because I'm famous; because I've got a lot of money. Not because I'm Martin Eden. . . ." All his dreams of love and success shattered, Martin books passage on a ship bound for the South Seas and, halfway across the Pacific, quietly squeezes through a porthole and drowns himself in the ocean.

"I am Martin Eden," London later professed. "I would not die but I went largely through Martin Eden's experience. Martin Eden died because he was an individualist, I live because I was a socialist and had social consciousness." But this novel was considerably more than an indictment of rampant individualism: a generation before Theodore Dreiser's *An American Tragedy* (1925) and F. Scott Fitzgerald's *The Great Gatsby* (1925), London had revealed the hollow core of the American Dream (his first preference for the title of his book had been *Success*). Ultimately, Martin is destroyed by the delusions that an ideal goal may be attained through material means and that success is synonymous with happiness—and by his failure to realize until too late that in America status derives more from image than from "work performed."

The deeper cultural implications of *Martin Eden* were generally overlooked by contemporary reviewers, who decried Martin's "turbulent egotism" and "defiance of the collective wisdom of mankind," denigrating his suicide as too pessimistic, "inartistic and unnecessary." William Morton Payne, in the *Dial*, remarked that Ruth Morse was "far more worth while than the man who has outgrown her in his own conceit" and concluded that it was "just as well" that Martin dropped out of the porthole at the end. Frederic Taber Cooper, in the *Bookman*, condemned London's "grotesque exaggeration of Martin's difficulties with his publishers," suggesting that the author was "out of his element" in trying to depict respectable social types. A few critics, however, perceived the merits of the novel. H. W. Boynton, in the *New York Times*, observed: "It is not a very sane or well-balanced book, but there is much wholesome truth in it." And Edwin Markham, in the *San Francisco Examiner*, praised it as London's "best novel—his story richest in the wisdom of the heart." More recently, Franklin Walker has concurred that despite its obvious flaws, *Martin Eden* remains an important novel: "Like all his books, it is uneven in structure, sometimes clumsy in expression, at times mawkish in tone. Yet it possesses great lasting power, having more vitality today than it did the day it issued from the press."

Martin Eden was written during the most highly publicized of all Jack London's adventures: the cruise of the *Snark*. The dream of circumnavigating the globe in their own boat had been inspired by Joshua Slocum's *Sailing Alone Around the World*, which Jack and Charmian had read at Wake Robin in summer 1905. London had calculated that the boat would cost him about $7,000, but in his careful planning he had anticipated neither the San Francisco earthquake of April 1906 nor the subtler disasters of twentieth-century production standards. Consequently, the *Snark* cost five times the original esti-

mate, was a half-year late in leaving Oakland, and was so badly botched in the building that extensive repairs were needed when the boat reached Hawaii in May 1907. Moreover, the voyage originally planned as a seven-year around-the-world cruise lasted less than two years. By fall 1908 all seven members of the crew had been stricken with various tropical ailments—malaria, dysentery, Solomon Island sores—and, in addition to these, London himself suffered from a double fistula and a mysterious skin disease that caused his hands to swell and peel so badly that he could use them only with great pain. That December, on the advice of physicians in Sydney, Australia, he called off the voyage; and the following spring he and Charmian London departed for home, via Ecuador, Panama, New Orleans, and the Grand Canyon, arriving in Oakland on 21 July 1909.

While the *Snark* voyage had been disastrous from the standpoint of London's health and finances, it resulted in a book, *The Cruise of the Snark* (1911), and enriched the mythic element in his fiction. The impulse to escape from the dullness of work through travel and adventure, which informs much of London's career, may be seen in his fiction as a revelation of the universal human yearning to recapture the condition of prelapsarian freedom and happiness. This archetypal motif, the quest for Paradise, recurs time and again throughout London's work. Its first significant manifestation is in the Northland Saga. There civilized man might discover gold—and something even more precious than gold: "true comradeship," London called it. Confronted by the cold, implacable laws of the White Silence, those who were unfit—the morally weak, the selfish, the foolhardy—perished. Those who were fit candidates, however, might not merely survive but actually be improved by their adaptation to the Northland Code, which fostered such virtues as "unselfishness, forbearance, and tolerance." Still, the Northland wilderness was a far cry from Eden. Its spiritual wellsprings might be pure—but they were also frozen. Though an agent of moral formation, the region offered neither warmth nor security—and the only serenity it provided was the stillness of death. In short, the Northland, London realized, was a region to escape *from*—not *to*.

On the other hand, the South Seas—particularly Hawaii and Polynesia—held forth the promise of warmth, good health, and life abundant. When he first visited the Hawaiian Islands in 1904 en route to the Russo-Japanese War, London felt as if he had truly found Elysium, a paradise of flower-swept valleys peopled by bronzed youths and golden maidens. "When Hawaii was named the Paradise of the Pacific, it was inadequately named," he wrote afterward in an article for *Cosmopolitan* (October-December 1916). "Hawaii and the Hawaiians are a land and a people loving and lovable. By their language may ye know them, and in what other land save this one is the commonest form of greeting, not 'Good day,' nor 'How d'ye do,' but 'Love'? That greeting is *Aloha*– love, I love you, my love to you. . . . It is a positive affirmation of the warmth of one's own heart-giving." London's further experience taught him, however, that Hawaii was, in truth, Paradise Lost: a lovely land whose economy had been commercialized, whose politics had been usurped, and whose inhabitants had been contaminated by the "civilized" haoles. "They came like lambs, speaking softly," remarks Koolau in London's "Koolau, the Leper": "They were of two kinds. The one kind asked our permission, our gracious permission, to preach to us the word of God. The other kind asked our permission, our gracious permission, to trade with us. That was the beginning. Today all the islands are theirs, all the land, all the cattle–everything is theirs." Also theirs, insidiously shared with the Hawaiians, is the "rotting sickness" of civilization, the leprosy which has metamorphosed a beautiful people into hideous monsters with stumps for arms and gaping holes for faces: "The sickness is not ours," says Koolau. "We have not sinned. The men who preached the word of God and the word of Rum brought the sickness with the coolie slaves who work the stolen land" (*The House of Pride*, 1912). The situation was the same wherever London traveled in Polynesia. Expecting to find the natives of Typee as splendidly vigorous as Melville had described them two generations earlier, he found, instead, nothing but a handful of "wretched creatures, afflicted with leprosy, elephantiasis, and tuberculosis." Bitterly disappointed, he wrote in *The Cruise of the Snark*, "Life has rotted away in this wonderful garden spot, where the climate is as delightful and healthful as any to be found in this world. Not alone were the Typeans physically magnificent; they were pure. . . . When one considers the situation, one is almost driven to the conclusion that the white race flourishes on impurity and corruption." Echoing a similar disenchantment, Prince Akuli, the Oxford-educated narrator of one of

London's Hawaiian stories, mutters, "This is the twentieth-century, and we stink of gasoline" ("Shin Bones," *On the Makaloa Mat*, 1919).

But if Polynesia was Paradise Lost, Melanesia, particularly the Solomon Islands, which the *Snark* reached in the summer of 1908, was an Inferno. "If I were a king, the worst punishment I could inflict on my enemies would be to banish them to the Solomons," London reminisced in *The Cruise of the Snark*. "On second thought, king or no king, I don't think I'd have the heart to do it." He was drawing from firsthand experience when he wrote that in the Solomons "fever and dysentery are perpetually on the walk about, . . . loathsome skin diseases abound, . . . the air is saturated with a poison that bites into every pore, cut, or abrasion and plants malignant ulcers, [and] many strong men who escape dying there return as wrecks to their own countries." It was this region, rather than the Klondike, which inspired London's bitterest naturalistic writing. Here the wilderness-as-Eden symbolism is wholly inverted. Unlike the golden youths of Polynesia, the Melanesians are ugly myrmidons of the Prince of Blackness himself–"a wild lot, with a hearty appetite for human flesh and a fad for collecting human heads." The moral effect of this rotting green hell, unlike the Northland, is to bring out the worst in those who survive. Among the natives the "highest instinct of sportsmanship is to catch a man with his back turned and to smite him a cunning blow with a tomahawk that severs the spinal column at the base of the brain. It is equally true that on some islands, such as Malaita, the profit and loss account of social intercourse is calculated in homicides." The white man is reduced to like savagery: "I've been in the tropics too long," confesses a character in the title story of *A Son of the Sun* (1912). "I'm a sick man, a damn sick man. And the whiskey, and the sun, and the fever made me sick in morals, too. Nothing's too mean and low for me now, and I can understand why the niggers eat each other, and take heads, and such things. I could do it myself." The only salutary effect Melanesia had on London was to convince him that the paradise he sought was not halfway around the globe but at home. "I also have a panacea," he wrote after suffering through a half-dozen hellish ailments inflicted by the tropics. "It is California. I defy any man to get a Solomon Island sore in California."

His ranch in the Sonoma Valley seemed, indeed, to be the panacea London needed after the *Snark* cruise; and for a while after returning home he thrived as he devoted the major time and energy to fulfilling his agrarian dream. "I believe the soil is our one indestructible asset," he said. "I am rebuilding worn-out hillside lands that were worked out and destroyed by our wasteful California farmers. . . . Everything I build is for the years to come." Between 1909 and 1916 he increased the size of Beauty Ranch to 1,500 acres, one of the largest in the Sonoma Valley; and during those seven years he came to be regarded by the agricultural experts as "one of California's leading farmers" whose ranch was "one of the best in the country." By combining modern agronomy with the wisdom of Oriental agriculture (using such techniques as terracing, drainage, and tillage), he succeeded in growing bumper crops of prunes, grapes, and alfalfa on land that had been abandoned by previous owners. He built the first concrete-block silo in California and constructed a "pig palace" which was a model of sanitation and efficiency. His livestock regularly took high honors in the county and state fairs and brought top breeding prizes. One of the finest tributes he ever received was that of Luther Burbank in *The Harvest of Years* (1927): "Jack London was a big healthy boy with a taste for serious things, but never cynical, never bitter, always good-humored and humorous, as I saw him, and with fingers and heart equally sensitive when he was in my gardens."

London's agrarian enthusiasm manifested itself in his literary as well as in his agricultural achievements; in fact, the two fields of interest were reciprocal, each enhancing the other. Four major works—three novels and one play—reflect his agrarian vision. The first of these, *Burning Daylight*—begun in Quito, Ecuador, on 5 June 1909, and finished on the ranch that fall—is the story of a Klondike bonanza king, Elam Harnish, who, having made his fortune in the Northland, seeks new worlds to conquer in the civilized southland, only to discover that the naturalistic laws of survival are no less operative in the jungle of big business than in the Arctic wilderness. Here, as in the Northland, life "was a wild animal fight" in which "the strong trampled the weak," and the strong "were not necessarily the best"—merely the luckiest. Existence was a gamble, and "God was a whimsical, abstract, mad thing called Luck." There was no justice, no fairness, in any of it. "The little men that came, the little pulpy babies, were not even asked if they wanted to try a flutter at the game. They had no choice. Luck jerked them into life, slammed them up against the jos-

tling table, and told them: 'Now play, damn you, play!' "

Harnish, nicknamed "Burning Daylight" because of his tremendous vitality, after being mulcted of $11 million by Wall Street robber barons, decides to match their ruthlessness–and their luck–with his own. He recoups his fortune, consequently amassing even greater wealth as a San Francisco street-railway magnate; but in the process he loses his soul, becoming even more ruthless than those who swindled him. At the end, however, he is redeemed by the love of a woman, his secretary Dede Mason (modeled after Charmian London), who persuades him to renounce his financial empire and to move onto a small ranch in the hills near Glen Ellen, California. The reading public and the critics alike, for the most part, responded favorably to *Burning Daylight*. The novel, with a first printing of 27,108 copies, sold better than any book London had written since *White Fang*, and the reviewers praised both his portrayal of Dede Mason ("a real human being . . . the best woman London has created," wrote Una H. H. Cool in the *San Francisco Sunday Call*) and his morally affirmative ending. A typical review, in the *Nation*, attested that "this is by all odds the most interesting, as well as the most wholesome long story Mr. London has written."

By this time in his career London's socialist enthusiasm had clearly begun to wane, and he envisioned a less violent solution to modern man's woes than social revolution: "Oh, try to see!" he exclaimed: "In the solution of the great economic problems of the present age, I see a return to the soil. I go into farming because my philosophy and research have taught me to recognize the fact that a return to the soil is the basis of economics . . . I see my farm in terms of the world, and the world in terms of my farm." This vision is the central theme of *The Valley of the Moon* (1913), generally considered the best of London's agrarian novels. "I am planning a serial, the motif is back to the land," he wrote to *Cosmopolitan* editor Roland Phillips on 30 May 1911: "I take a man and a woman, young, who belong to the working class in a large city. Both are wage-workers, the man is unskilled–a driver of a brewery wagon, or something of that sort. The first third of the book will be devoted to their city environment, their meeting, their love-affair, and the trials and tribulations of such a marriage in the working class. Comes hard times. The woman gets the vision. She is the guiding force. They start wandering over the country of California. Of course, they have all sorts of adventures, and their wandering becomes a magnificent, heroic detailed pilgrimage. After many hints and snatches of vision, always looking for the spot, they do find the real, one and only spot, and settle down to successful small-scale farming."

The central characters of the novel, Saxon and Billy Roberts, have a stillborn child in the ugly, strike-ridden city of Oakland; but, like Dede and Elam Harnish, they find Eden in the Sonoma hills. The novel concludes with a promise of new life in Saxon's announcement of her pregnancy as she and Billy, standing beside a quiet pool in the heart of their pastoral sanctuary, gaze blissfully upon a doe and a newborn fawn at the edge of the forest.

The reviewers were enthusiastic in their reception of *The Valley of the Moon*, seeing in this novel a departure from the brutality and pessimism of London's earlier, more naturalistic fictions. E. F. Edgett, in the *Boston Evening Transcript,* recommended it as a novel "for all thoughtful readers," especially praising the author for his realistic treatment of industrial turmoil and for his subordination of socialism to art. The *Athenaeum* observed that London had grasped "the essential traits of humanity" in this "essentially American" novel.

London's third agrarian novel, *The Little Lady of the Big House* (1916), was a less happy work. Unlike Elam Harnish and Billy Roberts, who have purified themselves of all exploitive motives before entering the pastoral wilderness, Dick Forrest, the hero of *The Little Lady of the Big House,* is possessed with a mania for efficiency and profit. The wealthy owner of a large California ranch, Forrest is a success as a commercial farmer and as a scientific breeder of prize stock—but he is a failure as a husband and his marriage is barren. He is London's version of the twentieth-century clockwork man whose every hour is governed by his watch. His wife, Paula (the title character), neglected and starved for genuine affection, falls in love with Dick's best friend, the artist-writer Evan Graham, and dissolves the love triangle by committing suicide at the end of the novel.

Contemporary reviewers condemned *The Little Lady of the Big House* as a bad book that immorally portrayed the "erotomania of three persons who fiddle harmonies on the strings of sensualism." Many of London's critics have subsequently agreed that this is his worst novel–cynical, con-

fused, and gratuitously if unconsciously titillating. And several of his biographers have suggested that the book was a mirror of London's own psychological state following the multiple disasters of 1913: an attack of appendicitis and the discovery that his kidneys were badly diseased; the loss of his fruit crop by a false spring and late frost; the accidental killing of one of his prize mares by a hunter; the threatened loss of his motion picture copyrights by the lawsuit of the Balboa Amusement Company; and, on 22 August, the burning of his great new mansion, the Wolf House. Although there is some truth to these allegations, they nevertheless tend to obscure the important thematic implications underlying the tragedy of the Forrests' marriage: While "a return to the soil" is vital, mere scientific efficiency in treatment of the land is not the ultimate answer to the "problems of the present age"–efficiency must be tempered with love; head must be balanced by heart.

This humanistic theme is explicitly dramatized in *The Acorn-Planter* (1916), a play which London began writing on Christmas Day 1914, two weeks after completing the manuscript for *The Little Lady of the Big House.* This play, replete with references to nature but with virtually no naturalism, is a mythopoeic fantasy beginning in "the morning of the world" and concluding with "the celebration of the death of war and the triumph of the acorn-planters," incarnated in Red Cloud, the philosopher-agrarian. California is celebrated as the place of Edenic possibilities, "A sunny land, a rich and fruitful land . . . warm and golden," where "In place of war's alarums . . . The New Day dawns, / The day of brotherhood, / The day of man!"

Jack London was by this time a dying man, stricken with fatal kidney disease. During the next two years, though he tried to maintain a vigorous public image, his body betrayed him: the symptoms of uremia–edema, swollen ankles, bloated body, kidney stones, gouty rheumatism– were increasingly evident. Yet he refused to heed the warnings of his physician that he must restrict his diet and get more rest. He spent several months in Hawaii in 1915 and 1916, trying to recapture his lost health in that benevolent climate; but his body continued to deteriorate.

Coincidentally, while in Hawaii in the spring of 1916, he discovered the recently translated work of Carl Jung and was immediately captivated: "I tell you I am standing on the edge of a world so new, so terrible, so wonderful, that I am almost afraid to look over it," he announced to Charmian London. Suddenly, the Polynesian myths he had listened to with good-natured disbelief over the past several years came to life within the Jungian context of racial memory and the archetypes of the collective unconscious. The literary results of this new discovery were a series of extraordinary stories written during the last six months of his life, published posthumously in *The Red One* and *On the Makaloa Mat*, and signifying not only an advance in his own work but a new dimension in twentieth-century literature: London became the first American fictionist to make use of Jung's theories consciously as well as creatively. "The Water Baby," for example, in *On the Makaloa Mat*, involves a dialogue between the world-weary narrator, John Lakana (the Hawaiian name for London), and Kohokumu, an ancient Hawaiian diver who claims the sea as his true mother. "But listen, O Young Wise One, to my elderly wisdom," the old man admonishes his skeptical listener:

> "This I know: as I grow old I seek less for the truth from without me, and find more of the truth within me. Why have I thought this thought of my return to my mother and of my rebirth from my mother into the sun? You do not know. I do not know. I do not know, save that, without whisper of man's voice or printed word, without prompting from otherwhere, this thought has arisen from within me, from the deeps of me that are as deep as the sea. . . . Is this thought that I have thought a dream?"
>
> "Perhaps it is you that are a dream," I laughed. . . .
>
> "There is much more in dreams than we know," he assured me with great solemnity. "Dreams go deep, all the way down, maybe to before the beginning. . . ."

London himself, the self-avowed materialistic monist, was evidently undergoing a change during the last months of his life, coming to terms at last with those nonrational psychic elements he had so rigorously rejected in his earlier years. He finished "The Water Baby" on 2 October 1916; seven weeks later his meteoric career was ended by a fatal attack of what the attending physicians called "gastrointestinal type of uraemia." In his copy of Jung, Charmian reports, London had underscored the following biblical quotation: "Think not carnally or thou art carnal, but think symbolically and then thou art spirit."

The nation mourned London's death as that of one of its heroes, the newspapers allotting more space to London than to Francis Joseph I, the Emperor of Austria, who had passed away on the preceding evening of 21 November. Yet, despite this enormous popularity, his rating as an artist was negligible among the members of the literary establishment. William Dean Howells, who had encouraged such other young writers as Stephen Crane and Frank Norris, never so much as mentioned Jack London in his hundreds of literary reviews and essays. Joan Sherman has remarked that London's reputation "exemplifies the split between 'high' and 'low' culture," that he was the victim of "critical standards established by the New England Sages and their New York heirs in 'The Age of Innocence,' 'The Age of Decorum,' 'The Genteel Decades,' 'The Purple Cow Period'—as the years from 1870 through the early 1900's were variously called." Those same critical standards were implicit in Arthur Hobson Quinn's attempt to write London's literary epitaph in 1936: "It is almost certain that his vogue is passing, for there is something impermanent in the very nature of the literature of violence." The New Critics of the succeeding generation relegated classics like *The Call of the Wild, The Sea-Wolf*, and *White Fang* to junior-high-school classes, ignoring the rest of his work altogether.

But a change in London's reputation began in the 1960s with the publication of *Letters from Jack London* (1965), edited by King Hendricks and Irving Shepard; Hensley C. Woodbridge, John London, and George H. Tweney's comprehensive *Jack London: A Bibliography* (1966); and Franklin Walker's *Jack London and the Klondike* (1966). At the same time, the publication of the *Jack London Newsletter*, edited by Woodbridge, provided a forum for London scholars. The London "renascence" was readily apparent in the following decade with the publication of book-length critical studies by Earle Labor and James I. McClintock, along with another primary bibliography by Dale L. Walker and James E. Sisson III and a secondary bibliography by Joan Sherman, as well as biographies by Russ Kingman and Andrew Sinclair. In 1976, the centennial of London's birth, three scholarly journals—*Modern Fiction Studies, Western American Literature*, and the *Pacific Historian*—published special Jack London numbers. The subsequent publication of several scholarly studies by university presses in the 1980s indicates that London has at last won the academic respectability so long awaited in his own country.

Letters:

Letters from Jack London, edited by King Hendricks and Irving Shepard (New York: Odyssey, 1965).
> Contains 402 letters by Jack London, along with the correspondence between London and Sinclair Lewis.

The Letters of Jack London, 3 volumes, edited by Earle Labor, Robert C. Leitz III, and I. Milo Shepard (Stanford, Cal.: Stanford University Press, 1988).
> Contains 1,554 extensively annotated letters by London, as well as 112 photographs.

Bibliographies:

Hensley C. Woodbridge, John London, and George H. Tweney, *Jack London: A Bibliography* (Georgetown, Cal.: Talisman, 1966; enlarged edition, Millwood, N.Y.: Kraus, 1973).
> Comprehensive listing of primary and secondary materials by and about London.

Dale L. Walker and James E. Sisson III, *The Fiction of Jack London: A Chronological Bibliography* (El Paso: Texas Western University Press, 1972).
> Annotated descriptive guide to all of London's published fiction.

Joan Sherman, *Jack London: A Reference Guide* (Boston: G. K. Hall, 1977).
> Annotated descriptive bibliography of works about London.

Biographies:

Charmian K. London, *The Book of Jack London,* 2 volumes (New York: Century, 1921).
> Strongly biased but invaluable source of information about London's life, written by his second wife.

Irving Stone, *Sailor on Horseback: The Biography of Jack London* (Boston: Houghton Mifflin, 1938).
> Because of numerous inaccuracies and plagiarized passages from London's own fiction, the subtitle of this best-selling popular book was revised to "A Biographical Novel."

Joan London, *Jack London and His Times: An Unconventional Biography* (New York: Doubleday, Doran, 1939).
> A remarkably objective treatment of London's life by his daughter, particularly useful in providing social, economic, and political background.

Andrew Sinclair, *Jack: A Biography of Jack London* (New York: Harper & Row, 1977).
> An impressively documented but misleading account of London's life and personality, with obsessive emphasis on his medical problems.

Russ Kingman, *A Pictorial Life of Jack London* (New York: Crown, 1979).
> Thoroughly researched and sympathetically written by the executive director of the Jack London Foundation, this amply illustrated volume is the most reliable biography available.

References:

Richard W. Etulain, *Jack London on the Road: The Tramp Diary and Other Hobo Writings* (Logan: Utah State University Press, 1979).
> A scrupulously edited collection of London's hobo writings with a substantial introductory essay.

David Mike Hamilton, *"The Tools of My Trade": Annotated Books in Jack London's Library* (Seattle: University of Washington Press, 1986).
> The detailed description of some 400 of the 15,000 volumes in London's personal library, revealing the sources of many of his ideas; includes a useful introductory essay.

Joan D. Hedrick, *Solitary Comrade: Jack London and His Work* (Chapel Hill: University of North Carolina Press, 1982).
> A controversial psychological analysis of London's career from his early work through *Martin Eden,* emphasizing the conflicts between his humanism, primitivism, and materialism and between his lower-class background and middle-class aspirations; neglects to examine important developments in London's later life and works.

Carolyn Johnston, *Jack London—An American Radical?* (Westport, Conn.: Greenwood Press, 1984).

Definitive study of London's socialism.

Earle Labor, *Jack London* (New York: Twayne, 1974).
Concise critical introduction to London's life and works.

James I. McClintock, *White Logic: Jack London's Short Stories* (Grand Rapids, Mich.: Wolf House Books, 1975).
Perceptive analysis of the major body of London's short fiction, especially strong in treatment of the influence of Jung on the late Hawaiian tales.

Ray Wilson Ownbey, ed., *Jack London: Essays in Criticism* (Santa Barbara, Cal.: Peregrine Smith, 1978).
Contains ten essays on major themes in London's works.

Jacqueline Taverier-Courbin, ed., *Critical Essays on Jack London* (Boston: G. K. Hall, 1983).
Comprehensive collection with twenty-three essays on London, including selections by H. L. Mencken, Carl Sandburg, Ford Madox Ford, Anatole France, and Katherine Mansfield, along with useful essays by recent academic critics and a substantial introductory essay on London as a professional writer.

Franklin Walker, *Jack London and the Klondike: The Genesis of an American Writer* (San Marino, Cal.: The Huntington Library, 1966).
Carefully researched scholarly account of London's Klondike experiences and works.

Charles N. Watson, Jr., *The Novels of Jack London: A Reappraisal* (Madison: University of Wisconsin Press, 1983).
Close analysis of nine of London's most important novels.

Papers:
The Henry E. Huntington Library in San Marino, California, houses the largest collection of Londoniana, comprising some 60,000 items: the major portion of London's manuscripts and letters, as well as scrapbooks, most of London's personal library, and Charmian London's diaries. The Merrill Library at Utah State University in Logan, Utah, has the second largest collection of London materials, including many letters, some manuscripts and notes, along with a significant portion of Charmian London's correspondence. The New York Public Library houses London's correspondence with George P. Brett and the Macmillan Company, as well as some manuscripts. The Clifton Waller Barrett Library at the University of Virginia includes more than 100 London letters (most of them to his agent Paul Revere Reynolds). The Jack London State Historical Park in Glen Ellen, California, houses the Holman Collection of London materials, including important letters to his friend Frederick Irons Bamford. Other smaller but noteworthy collections of London materials are on file at the following libraries: The Bancroft Library at the University of California, Berkeley; Stanford University; the Cresmer Collection at the University of Southern California; the Irving Stone Collection at the University of California, Los Angeles; and the Oakland Public Library.

Edgar Lee Masters

This entry was updated by Herbert K. Russell (John A. Logan College) from his entry
in DLB 54, American Poets, 1880-1945, Part 2.

Places	Petersburg, Ill. Lewistown, Ill.	New York (The Chelsea Hotel)	Chicago St. Louis
Influences and Relationships	William Marion Reedy William Cowper Powys Robert Browning	Theodore Dreiser Vachel Lindsay Percy Bysshe Shelley	Dorothy Dow Carl Sandburg
Literary Movements and Forms	Naturalism Chicago Renaissance	Realism Romanticism	Free Verse *Epigrams from the Greek Anthology*
Major Themes	Revolt from the Village	Agrarianism	Sexuality
Cultural and Artistic Influences	Small Town Life Romanticism	Music The Law	American History
Social and Economic Influences	Populism Spanish-American War	Civil War The 20s	World War I The "Gay Nineties"

BIRTH: Garnett, Kansas, 23 August 1868, to Hardin Wallace and Emma Jerusha Dexter Masters.

MARRIAGES: 21 June 1898 to Helen M. Jenkins (divorced); children: Hardin, Marcia, Madeline. 5 November 1926 to Ellen F. Coyne; child: Hilary.

AWARDS AND HONORS: Levinson Prize (*Poetry* magazine), 1916; Mark Twain Medal, 1936; National Institute and American Academy of Arts and Letters Award in Literature, 1942; Poetry Society of America medal, 1942; Shelley Memorial Award, 1944; Academy of American Poets Fellowship, 1946.

DEATH: Melrose Park, Pennsylvania, 5 March 1950.

BOOKS: *A Book of Verses* (Chicago: Way & Williams, 1898);
The Constitution and Our Insular Possessions (Chicago?, 1900?);
Maximilian: A Play in Five Acts (Boston: Badger, 1902);
The New Star Chamber and Other Essays (Chicago: Hammersmark, 1904);
The Blood of the Prophets, as Dexter Wallace (Chicago: Rooks, 1905);
Althea: A Play in Four Acts (Chicago: Rooks, 1907);
The Trifler: A Play (Chicago: Rooks, 1908);
The Leaves of the Tree: A Play (Chicago: Rooks, 1909);
Eileen: A Play in Three Acts (Chicago: Rooks, 1910);
Songs and Sonnets, as Webster Ford (Chicago: Rooks, 1910);
The Locket: A Play in Three Acts (Chicago: Rooks, 1910);
The Bread of Idleness: A Play in Four Acts (Chicago: Rooks, 1911);
Songs and Sonnets: Second Series, as Webster Ford (Chicago: Rooks, 1912);
Browning as a Philosopher (Chicago?, 1912?);
Spoon River Anthology (New York: Macmillan, 1915; London: Laurie, 1915; enlarged edition, New York: Macmillan, 1916; London: Laurie, 1916);
Songs and Satires (New York: Macmillan, 1916; London: Laurie, 1916);
The Great Valley (New York: Macmillan, 1916; London: Laurie, 1916);
Toward the Gulf (New York: Macmillan, 1918);
Starved Rock (New York: Macmillan, 1919);

Courtesy of the Harry Ransom Humanities Research Center, University of Texas at Austin

Mitch Miller (New York: Macmillan, 1920; London: Cape, 1921);
Domesday Book (New York: Macmillan, 1920; London: Nash, 1921);
The Open Sea (New York: Macmillan, 1921);
Children of the Market Place (New York: Macmillan, 1922; London: Hodder & Stoughton, 1923);
Skeeters Kirby (New York: Macmillan, 1923);
The Nuptial Flight (New York: Boni & Liveright, 1923);
Mirage (New York: Boni & Liveright, 1924);
The New Spoon River (New York: Boni & Liveright, 1924);
Selected Poems (New York: Macmillan, 1925);
Lee: A Dramatic Poem (New York: Macmillan, 1926);
Kit O'Brien (New York: Boni & Liveright, 1927);
Levy Mayer and the New Industrial Era (New Haven: Yale University Press, 1927);
Jack Kelso: A Dramatic Poem (New York & London: Appleton, 1928);
The Fate of the Jury: An Epilogue to Domesday Book (New York & London: Appleton, 1929);

Gettysburg, Manila, Ácoma (New York: Liveright, 1930);

Lichee Nuts (New York: Liveright, 1930);

Lincoln: The Man (New York: Dodd, Mead, 1931; London: Cassell, 1931);

Godbey: A Dramatic Poem (New York: Dodd, Mead, 1931);

The Serpent in the Wilderness (New York: Sheldon Dick, 1933);

The Tale of Chicago (New York: Putnam's, 1933);

Dramatic Duologues: Four Short Plays in Verse (New York, Los Angeles & London: French, 1934);

Richmond: A Dramatic Poem (New York, Los Angeles & London: French, 1934);

Invisible Landscapes (New York: Macmillan, 1935);

Vachel Lindsay: A Poet in America (New York & London: Scribners, 1935);

Poems of People (New York & London: Appleton-Century, 1936);

The Golden Fleece of California (Weston, Vt.: Countryman, 1936);

Across Spoon River: An Autobiography (New York: Farrar & Rinehart, 1936);

Whitman (New York: Scribners, 1937; London: Scribners, 1937);

The Tide of Time (New York: Farrar & Rinehart, 1937);

The New World (New York & London: Appleton-Century, 1937);

Hymn to the Unknown God (Brown City, Mich.: New Age Ministry of Religious Research, 1937?);

Mark Twain: A Portrait (New York & London: Scribners, 1938);

More People (New York & London: Appleton-Century, 1939);

Illinois Poems (Prairie City, Ill.: James A. Decker, 1941);

The Sangamon (New York & Toronto: Farrar & Rinehart, 1942);

Along the Illinois (Prairie City, Ill.: James A. Decker, 1942);

The Harmony of Deeper Music: Posthumous Poems of Edgar Lee Masters, edited by Frank K. Robinson (Austin: Humanities Research Center, University of Texas, 1976).

OTHER: Ralph Waldo Emerson, *The Living Thoughts of Emerson*, edited, with an introduction, by Masters (New York & Toronto: Longmans, Green, 1940).

PERIODICAL PUBLICATIONS: "What is Poetry?," *Poetry*, 6 (September 1915): 306-308;

"The Artist Revolts," *Poetry*, 22 (July 1923): 206-209;

"What is Great Poetry?," *Poetry*, 26 (September 1925): 349-351;

"Days in the Lincoln Country," *Journal of the Illinois State Historical Society*, 18 (January 1926): 779-792;

"Poetry Revival of 1914," *American Mercury*, 26 (July 1932): 272-280;

"The Genesis of *Spoon River*," *American Mercury*, 28 (January 1933): 38-55;

"Literary Boss of the Midwest," *American Mercury*, 34 (April 1935): 450-455;

"To the People of Petersburg and Menard County," *University Review*, 3 (Winter 1936): 107-108;

"Dreiser at Spoon River," *Esquire*, 11 (May 1939): 66, 146, 151, 152, 154, 156, 158.

Beginning in May 1914 Edgar Lee Masters, then an eminently successful Chicago lawyer, published in the St. Louis magazine *Reedy's Mirror*, under the pseudonym Webster Ford, some two hundred poems about talkative ghosts in a midwestern cemetery. His identity was revealed the following November, and in 1915 the poems were collected in book form as the *Spoon River Anthology*. The volume became an international popular and critical success and introduced with a flourish what has since come to be known as the Chicago Renaissance. Readers had never before seen anything quite like these poetic monologues, or "epitaphs." Literary critics accused Masters of showing too little respect for poetic rules; a wide variety of people felt that he had written too realistically about subjects which heretofore had been regarded as inappropriate for verse. Yet for these very reasons Masters's book soon became what Percy Boynton described in his *Some Contemporary Americans* (1924) as "the most read and most talked-of volume of poetry that had ever been written in America." It also became Masters's only lasting success; although he eventually published more than fifty other volumes, he was never able to duplicate his one-time phenomenal achievement. As Louis Untermeyer said of the writer's dramatic rise and subsequent decline in *American Poetry Since 1900* (1923): "With *Spoon River Anthology*, Masters arrived–and left."

The son of Hardin Wallace Masters, a lawyer, and Emma Jerusha Dexter Masters, Edgar Lee Masters was born in Garnett, Kansas, in 1868, but grew up in the Illinois towns of Petersburg (on the Sangamon River) and Lewistown (near the Spoon River)–two corn-belt county seats which provided him with models for his literary village of "Spoon River." After graduation from the Lewistown high school, Masters attended "the preparatory school" of Knox College at Galesburg for one year (1889-1890), but, instead of enrolling as a freshman the following year, he read law in the office of his father and was admitted to the Illinois bar in 1891. Following a brief partnership with his father, Masters moved in 1892 to Chicago, his home for the next thirty years. He thrived in the city, marrying Helen M. Jenkins, the daughter of a wealthy transportation magnate, on 21 June 1898 and working as a law partner with Clarence Darrow from 1903 to 1911. By 1912 Masters had taken time from his attorney's duties to write a book of political essays, seven plays, and four volumes of verse.

Little in his early poetry anticipated the Spoon River poems. *A Book of Verses* (1898) is a collection of conventional juvenilia and poems written in his early days in Chicago. Its form is traditional, as are its subjects of love, fellow poets, mythical heroes, and the seasons. "A Dream of Italy" illustrates:

> In our rough clime where skies are gray
> > O'er leafless trees in winter's clime
> We dreamed of a serener day
> > Through books of rhyme.

Although Masters long retained a fondness for portions of this book, his publisher had second thoughts (declaring bankruptcy on the day it was to be released), and the few reviews, though friendly, were the result of Masters's circulating copies.

Nor did his second volume of miscellaneous poetry, *The Blood of the Prophets* (1905), attract much attention. Published under the pseudonym Dexter Wallace (two family names), the poems serve primarily as vehicles for expressing Masters's political sympathies–and in the process they illustrate what would become his chief problem of authorship: his willingness to publish as finished works books that were inartistically cluttered with his own highly subjective viewpoints. As an old friend of his, Gertrude Claytor, once remarked, "Opinions were convictions with Masters."

For five years following the appearance of *The Blood of the Prophets*, Masters attempted no

new volumes of poetry but concentrated on the publication and circulation of his plays. When none of these was produced, he turned again to poetry in 1910 and 1912, publishing under the pseudonym Webster Ford (the names of two British dramatists) miscellaneous verses entitled *Songs and Sonnets* and *Songs and Sonnets: Second Series.*

These pre-*Spoon River* poems are of little interest except for those which reflect his serious extramarital love affair with the artist Tennessee Mitchell (later to be Mrs. Sherwood Anderson). Masters had "contracted madness in her kiss" (as he put it) and in 1909 had asked his wife for a divorce. In order to soothe his conscience (and perhaps to prepare for the inevitable), he presented Helen Masters with a three-story Georgian brick house at 4853 Kenwood Avenue in Chicago. She accepted the house but refused the divorce, and Masters found himself frustrated at home and at work (he had a bitter falling out with Clarence Darrow over the division of a legal fee). His personal and professional lives remained without major changes until the spring of 1914, when several factors coalesced to launch the epitaphs of the *Spoon River Anthology.*

The chief factor behind the book's success was the drive and desire of Masters himself. From late adolescence he had dreamed of making his mark as a writer, and, as early as 1906, he had contemplated a novel about the towns of his boyhood, explaining to his father his plans for someday writing such a book: "I told him that my life in Chicago had shown me that the country lawyer and the city lawyer were essentially the same; that the country banker and the city banker had the same nature; and so on down through the list of tradespeople, preachers, sensualists, and all kinds of human beings." It was such a gallery of many different types of people which ultimately served to universalize the people of Spoon River–but in 1906 Masters did not think to express his thoughts in poetry, and so what he characterized as this early "germ" of the *Spoon River Anthology* was for a time dormant.

A year later, in 1907, Masters met William Marion Reedy, the editor of the St. Louis magazine *Reedy's Mirror*. In the course of a long relationship Reedy published many poems and letters by Masters, including most of the Spoon River poems (which Masters first published under the pseudonym Webster Ford for fear they would hurt his law business). But Reedy's most important act was to make Masters aware of *Epigrams from the Greek Anthology*. These highly compressed, ancient writings did much to shape Masters's book, a fact he publicly acknowledged shortly after the publication of the *Spoon River Anthology:* "It was you," Masters wrote to Reedy, "who pressed upon my attention in June, 1909, the Greek Anthology. It was from contemplation of its epigraphs that my hand unconsciously strayed to the sketches . . . of The Spoon River Anthology."

A second literary acquaintance of considerable influence was novelist Theodore Dreiser. He had introduced himself to Masters about 1912 while researching his trilogy on the life of the Chicago streetcar baron C. T. Yerkes. Dreiser by then had solid plans to trounce the tenets of the so-called genteel tradition in American literature, and he was in fact already doing for the American novel what Masters would shortly do for poetry–forcing its re-evaluation, especially with respect to its content. The two soon became lifelong friends, with Dreiser visiting with Masters in the Spoon River country just a short time before Masters began his famous epitaphs.

The real catalyst to *Spoon River Anthology,* however, the one which actually started Masters writing, was a May 1914 visit by his mother. In the course of this visit the two of them reminisced about the towns of his boyhood: "We went over the whole past of Lewistown and Petersburg," Masters wrote in his autobiography, *Across Spoon River* (1936), "bringing up characters and events that had passed from my mind. . . . The psychological experience of this was truly wonderful. Finally on the morning she was leaving for Springfield we had a last and rather sobering talk. It was Sunday, too, and after putting her on the train at 53rd Street I walked back home full of strange pensiveness. The little church bell was ringing, but spring was in the air. I went to my room and immediately wrote 'The Hill,' [the introductory poem,] and two or three of the portraits of Spoon River Anthology." Unsure of just what he was on to, he proceeded to write a total of eight poems before sending these to Reedy for publication on 29 May. By 11 July, however, he had discovered the uniqueness of his work, writing to Dreiser that he was at work on the "Spoon River stuff into which I am pouring divers philosophies–taking the empty tomato cans of the rural dead to fill with the waters of the macrocosm."

Finally the times themselves contributed to Masters's literary success. When he sat down to write the poems in *Spoon River Anthology* the country was in a transitional period in which prewar America, "courthouse America" (or "old America," as Masters called it), would soon give way to more dynamic times. The country's literary tastes were changing too, with the controversial free verse movement at last gaining some acceptance.

This verse form proved to be just right for Masters, for its plainness complemented the matter-of-factness with which his Spoon River inhabitants told of their lives and deaths. In speaking their own epitaphs, most of them confronted eternity armed with only a simple truth or two, a few lines distilled as the essence of their existence. Had Masters used conventionally rhymed and metered verse, it would have added a melodious quality inconsistent with the somber truths spoken on the graveyard hill. The epitaphs of two of the better-known characters are representative:

KNOWLT HOHEIMER

I was the first fruits of the battle of
    Missionary Ridge.
When I felt the bullet enter my heart
I wished I had staid at home and gone to jail
For stealing the hogs of Curl Trenary,
Instead of running away and joining the army.
Rather a thousand times the county jail
Than to lie under this marble figure with wings,
And this granite pedestal
Bearing the words, "*Pro Patria.*"
What do they mean, anyway?

The following epitaph serves to make Hoheimer's pitiful story a little worse.

LYDIA PUCKETT

Knowlt Hoheimer ran away to the war
The day before Curl Trenary
Swore out a warrant through Justice Arnett
For stealing hogs.
But that's not the reason he turned a soldier.
He caught me running with Lucius Atherton.
We quarreled and I told him never again
To cross my path.
Then he stole the hogs and went to the war–
Back of every soldier is a woman.

The effect of such verses on the literary community was remarkably varied. To nineteenth-century traditionalists such as William Dean Howells (the editor of *Harper's* magazine), Masters was not writing poetry at all but only "shredded prose" (*Harper's*, September 1915). Genteel innovators, such as poet Amy Lowell, were also of-

Ellen, Hilary, and Edgar Lee Masters in Charlotte, North Carolina, spring 1946 (courtesy of the Harry Ransom Humanities Research Center, University of Texas at Austin)

fended: "Spoon River is one long chronicle of rapes, seductions, liaisons, and perversions," she wrote in her *Tendencies in Modern American Poetry* (1917). "One wonders, if life in our little Western cities is as bad as this, why everyone does not commit suicide." In Chicago newspaper reporter and struggling poet Carl Sandburg was quick to recognize the unique qualities of the *Spoon River Anthology:* "The people whose faces look out from the pages of the book are the people of life itself " (*Little Review,* May 1915). But Sandburg was not nearly so exuberant as was Ezra Pound, then in London: "AT LAST!," Pound shouted in the pages of the *Egoist* (January 1915); "At last America has discovered a poet." Enjoying the literary storm occasioned by *Spoon River Anthology,* Masters noted later, in an article for the January 1933 issue of the *American Mercury,* that "it was called the greatest American book since Whitman, and on the other hand one of the evilest books of all time." What Masters had begun (as novelist Sinclair Lewis said in his 1930 Nobel Prize speech) was "a new school of native American poetry."

His literary reputation established, Masters was soon confronted with a new set of problems. His troubles began in January 1915, after he had completed the last of the epitaphs for *Reedy's Mirror.* He had put so much energy into the composition of his poems that his health broke. He suffered a severe bout with pneumonia, nearly died, and, when he returned to his law office in May, was so weak that he could work only a few hours a day. Meanwhile the number of those seeking legal assistance from his office had greatly declined, both because of his enforced absence and because of the notoriety caused by the epitaphs as they appeared in serial form. With his reputation as a lawyer damaged by this unfavorable publicity, and with his literary career on the ascendency, he needed to decide–at age forty-six, with a wife and three children–whether to continue as a lawyer or to break with the law and try to survive as a poet. It was to be one of the major decisions of his life–but he failed to make a clean choice. Instead he compromised, continuing half-heartedly in law for five more years, until 1920, while also publishing a great deal, thereby giving full-time attention to neither career while severely damaging both.

Complicating both vocations was Masters's unhappy home life. In 1919, while involved in what he characterized as one of those "lighthearted adulteries that do no harm," Masters fell in love, this time with the widow of an Indiana banker. Her name was Lillian Pampell Wilson; she was beautiful, wealthy, and cultured; and Masters was determined to marry her. Helen Masters was determined that he would not, and, as had resulted a decade before (when Tennessee Mitchell threatened), Mrs. Masters had her way. The Masterses were separated for more than two years before Helen Masters succeeded in forcing her husband home by tying up his finances in a receivership. (For legal counsel she chose two of Masters's former law partners, one of whom was Clarence Darrow.) By the time Masters's relationship with Lillian Wilson ended in the spring of 1922, his reputation in Chicago was ruined and with it any hopes of ever again earning his livelihood as a lawyer. What vestiges of respectability lingered on vanished the following year when the Chicago press recorded on page one the proceedings of his messy and prolonged divorce.

During these same years Masters also battered his literary reputation through an injudicious approach to his publications. In 1916-1921 he published an augmented edition of *Spoon River Anthology* (with thirty-two new poems) as well as his first novel (*Mitch Miller*, 1920); a long narrative poem (*Domesday Book*, 1920); and five volumes of miscellaneous verses: *Songs and Satires* (1916), *The Great Valley* (1916), *Toward the Gulf* (1918), *Starved Rock* (1919), and *The Open Sea* (1921). He achieved this phenomenal output only by padding his post-*Spoon River* miscellanies with early and inferior writings and by seldom revising his new efforts. Critics were quick to note the archaic form and style of some of the early poems and the lapses in artistic taste in some of the later ones, with the result that poor reviews and sluggish sales attended several of these books. But such was the strength of *Spoon River Anthology* that Masters in the early 1920s was still one of the best-known poets in America. As one of his contemporaries, Dorothy Dow, put it, he was "an authentic lion" in the literary world.

He could not long retain this title, however, without some new success. He hoped to realize it through his 1920 epic of the American involvement in World War I, *Domesday Book*, a work he often referred to as his "finest achievement." In its ten thousand lines of blank verse he tells of Elenor Murray, an Illinois charmer who does Red Cross work during the war and then comes home, where she dies unexpectedly of heart failure. Masters meant her story to be a "census spiritual/Taken of our America," but reviewers as diverse as Edmund Gosse, Harriet Monroe, and Louis Untermeyer found Masters's allegory too ambitious and the book too long and dull. They also questioned its originality, citing similarities between it and Robert Browning's *The Ring and the Book* (1868-1869). For reasons that are not clear, Masters denied having read this long poem before beginning his work–although he had in 1912 published a pamphlet, *Browning as a Philosopher*, in which he discussed *The Ring and the Book*. As to his frequent insistence that *Domesday Book* was his finest achievement, the general consensus is that he was simply trying (for a good many years on end) to avoid the stigma of being known as "a one-book author." In any event, in *The Fate of the Jury: An Epilogue to Domesday Book* (1929) he suddenly ended his tale in midstory: the sequel to his finest achievement did not interest him enough to complete it.

Stymied in his efforts to produce a poetic equal to *Spoon River Anthology*, Masters turned to fiction, publishing five novels in the period 1920-1924. When his law practice dwindled he had more time to devote to his writing, and he also had an economic incentive to experiment with a more lucrative art form: his 1923 divorce cost him everything–money, town house, and farm, as well as his good name in Chicago. He was left with only the royalties from his books, which he now had to publish in quick succession in order to survive.

Masters was never to be very honest with himself about his failures–literary, legal, or domestic– but instead used his artistic creations to blame others for his problems. He was especially bitter about his expensive divorce and the unhappy conclusion to his affair with Lillian Wilson (who soon married another), as well as with other people (such as Clarence Darrow), and ultimately with anyone he suspected of siding with a growing circle of enemies. He closed out his literary career in the Midwest by publishing in the September 1923 issue of *Poetry* an angry sonnet sequence damning his former wife and then moved to New York City, where in 1924 he published a novel, *Mirage,* damning his former mistress.

In the same year, a decade after his initial success, Masters turned back to the hill of Spoon River and published his second book of epitaphs, *The New Spoon River.* Due to Masters's temperament, personal experiences, and changing times, he could not again journey home as successfully and artistically as he had done earlier. The *Spoon River Anthology* concentrates on a specific part of the national scene, the midwestern village; its subject is the individual in that village, and the objective treatment made the book successful. In contrast, the treatment in *The New Spoon River* came across as highly subjective: with his polemics and prejudices clearly showing, Masters seems to wander in and out of his book, pausing to tell his readers what to think and making the same points so often that his characters lose their individuality. As in the epitaph "Martin Venable," there is often a sense of loss, mutability, or dislocation, phenomena which Masters himself had by 1924 experienced in the extreme:

> Did you ever destroy a bird's nest,
> So there was not a vestige of it left in the tree?
> Then have you watched the bird when it returned,
> And flew about and about the place where the nest
>   had been,
> Wondering what had become of the nest,
> Or wondering if this be the tree of the nest?
> It was even so with me and Spoon River:
> I returned to find the old town
> And found it not;
> And drifted about wondering   -
> If Spoon River had ever been my home,
> And if so what had become of Spoon River!

In spite of several problems, *The New Spoon River* was more successful than many literary sequels and is today considered Masters's second-most-important book, preceding *Domesday Book* and *Selected Poems* (1925) in the list of his best volumes of verse.

Following a cross-country tour early in 1925, Masters paused to prepare for publication of his *Selected Poems,* in the course of which he had the opportunity to gather his best verses past and present and put together an attractive volume. He followed an ambitious plan, remarking in his headnote that his aim was to demonstrate both "the variety and the quality of the themes, and the measures in which I have expressed myself." He succeeded at this aim and in the process brought new critical attention to some of his fin-

est poems which had been published and virtually forgotten in one miscellany or another, among them the following lines from "Silence," first collected in *Songs and Satires:*

> I have known the silence of the stars and of the
>   sea,
> And the silence of the city when it pauses,
> And the silence of a man and a maid,
> And the silence for which music alone finds the
>   word,
> And the silence of the woods before the winds of
>   spring begin,
> And the silence of the sick
> When their eyes roam about the room.
> And I ask: For the depths
> Of what use is language?

Thirty-eight epitaphs from the *Spoon River Anthology* and *The New Spoon River* concluded the volume of 158 poems.

This 1925 volume marked the end of Masters's major phase as a practicing poet. It did not by any means mark the end of his writing, and it certainly did not mark the end of his influence–indeed, he would spend the rest of his life famous as "the *Spoon River* poet" (a designation which both pleased and galled him)–but he achieved no new poetic sensation, though he lived by his pen and published verse (or hoped to publish it) for another quarter of a century.

The mid 1920s also signaled a turning point in his personal life. After 1923 he was for many years a resident of New York, where he remarried on 5 November 1926. His bride was Ellen Coyne, a twenty-six-year-old University of Chicago graduate whom Masters had known for several years. They lived together until 1930, after which her teaching duties (in English) often separated them. During these years of separation Masters established residence at New York's Hotel Chelsea (a hangout for artists), where he spent the remainder of his literary career.

As he neared and passed his sixtieth year, he continued to publish a great deal and "at a prodigious rate, to the consternation even of his admirers" (as midwestern scholar John T. Flanagan once put it). In the twelve-year period following his 1925 *Selected Poems,* Masters averaged a book of verse per year; the best of these volumes rivaled none of his previous best while the worst was likened to "so much cast-iron" (by a reviewer for the *New Republic,* 17 November 1926). During this same time he also published his sixth and seventh novels, a history of Chicago, a book of

Masters as the guest of honor at the Petersburg, Illinois, centennial celebration, 3 September 1936 (courtesy of the Harry Ransom Humanities Research Center, University of Texas at Austin)

four plays, as well as his autobiography and four of his five biographies (of Abraham Lincoln, Walt Whitman, Vachel Lindsay, and Chicago lawyer Levy Mayer).

Of these twenty-one volumes, only three of the prose works had any lasting effect on his literary reputation. *Lincoln: The Man* (1931) was intended to dispel several myths about the former president, and on the surface at least, Masters seemed well qualified to handle this subject: his hometown of Petersburg was but two miles from Lincoln's New Salem; he knew personally William Herndon (Lincoln's law partner), the Armstrong family (one of whom Lincoln had defended), and John McNamar (the man who jilted Ann Rutledge before her story became entwined with Lincoln's). But Masters, a Jeffersonian Democrat, was so unfair to his Republican subject that *Lincoln: The Man* drew some of the most hostile criticism ever leveled at an American biography. According to *Literary Digest* (28 February 1931), "A bill was introduced into Congress to bar it from the mails," and in the end its publication hurt Masters with his public.

A second biography somewhat offset the effects of the Lincoln book. In *Vachel Lindsay: A Poet in America* (1935) Masters announced that he would write "biography as truth" and succeeded so well that his book remained the finest life study of Lindsay a half century after his death.

Masters's autobiography, *Across Spoon River* (1936), is trickier to assess. He once remarked to Gertrude Claytor that he felt most autobiographies were "fakes because no one can really penetrate the web of motive in himself." Certainly this quirk manifests itself in *Across Spoon River*, which is both self-serving and incomplete: Masters ended his story in mid 1917 at a time when he was still a successful lawyer and *Spoon River* was still "in flood" (as a popular saying once had it). Although he was said to have the second portion of his autobiography in progress as early as 1938, this continuation of his life story has never been published. Because there is no full-length biography of Masters, the incomplete state of his autobiography represents an important stumbling block to understanding him.

In his seventieth year Masters published a biography of Mark Twain (1938) and then concluded his career with three poetic miscellanies, an edited collection of Emerson (*The Living Thoughts of Emerson,* 1940), and a history of the Sangamon River (1942), the river flowing by his "heart's home" of Petersburg.

In these later years he was the recipient of several literary prizes, among them an award from the National Institute and American Academy of Arts and Letters (1942) for "the timeless verse in which his people are remembered," the Shelley Memorial Award (1944), and an Academy of American Poets Fellowship (1946). These complemented his earlier Mark Twain Medal (1936) for the Lindsay biography and the Helen Haire Levinson Prize (1916) awarded him by *Poetry* magazine.

Following a seven-year period of increasing debility, Masters died in his sleep far from Spoon River in a Melrose Park, Pennsylvania, nursing home in March 1950. He was buried on "the hill" in Petersburg among the pioneer dead, some of whose stories he had made famous through his epitaphs. The epitaph on his own tomb, chosen by his wife Ellen, who cared for him during his final years, is from a poem called "To-morrow is My Birthday." He first published it in *Toward the Gulf* and selected it as his "best." The epitaph reads as follows:

Edgar Lee Masters
1868-1950

Good friends, let's to the fields . . .
After a little walk, and by your pardon,
I think I'll sleep. There is no sweeter thing,
Nor fate more blessed than to sleep.

I am a dream out of a blessed sleep–
Let's walk and hear the lark.

As a voice prominently and permanently associated with that literary coming-of-age known as the Chicago Renaissance, Masters is one of the few American poets ever to achieve and keep both a popular and a critical audience. His position in American letters might have been much greater had he not vitiated the quality of much of what he wrote through hasty publications revealing his own intrusive, authorial voice. It was this lack of artistic restraint which largely determined his literary reputation both before and after his death. But Masters was also the victim of the success of his one enduring achievement,

Spoon River Anthology: no matter what he published after it, he could never produce a rival to it, and so each ensuing volume represented a decline. *Spoon River Anthology* made him famous, but it also contributed to some of the sadness in his life, and it is (to borrow from it) his "true epitaph, more lasting than stone."

Interviews:
"Spoon River Poet Called Great," *New York Times,* 4 April 1915, V: 7, 9;
"True Marriage, a Beautiful Monogamy, to be the One Great Fruit of Freedom for Women, says Edgar Lee Masters," *New York Tribune,* 9 August 1915, p. 5;
Walter Yust, "Edgar Lee Masters: An Interview," *Double Dealer,* 2 (August-September 1921): 79-83;
Frank Waller Allen, "With Edgar Lee Masters in the Spoon River Country," *Springfield* (Illinois) *Sunday Journal,* 1 January 1922, pp. 22, 27;
Rose C. Feld, "Spoon Rivers with the Full Quality of America," *New York Times Book Review,* 7 September 1924, p. 2;
Walter Tittle, "Glimpses of Interesting Americans," *Century,* 110 (August 1925): 447-448;
David Karsner, *Sixteen Authors to One: Intimate Sketches of Leading American Storytellers* (New York: Lewis Copeland, 1928), pp. 123-142;
"New Book Assails the 'Lincoln Myth,'" *New York Times,* 6 February 1931, p. 28;
Mary Bell Sloan, "Edgar Lee Masters–A Portrait," *University Review,* 1 (Summer 1935): 4-7;
Selig Greenburg, "Edgar Lee Masters, Poet Who Looks Like, and Is, Lawyer, Doubts U.S. Likes Poetry," *Providence Evening Bulletin,* 4 May 1936, p. 9;
Georges Schreiber, ed., *Portraits and Self-Portraits* (Boston: Houghton Mifflin, 1936), pp. 91-94;
A. M. Sullivan, "Spoon River Twenty-five Years After," *Dun's Review and Modern Industry,* April 1940, pp. 18-22, 42-44;
Robert Van Gelder, "An Interview with Mr. Edgar Lee Masters," *New York Times Book Review,* 15 February 1942, pp. 2, 28.

Bibliography:
Frank K. Robinson, *Edgar Lee Masters: An Exhibition in Commemoration of His Birth* (Austin: Humanities Research Center, University of Texas, 1970).

A bibliography of Masters's major works; includes many pictures.

Biographies:

Josephine Craven Chandler, "The Spoon River Country," *Journal of the Illinois State Historical Society,* 14 (October 1921-January 1922): 252-329.
The place to begin research on Masters.

Gertrude Claytor, "Edgar Lee Masters in the Chelsea Years," *Princeton University Library Chronicle,* 14 (Autumn 1952): 1-29.
Discusses Masters's later life in New York City.

Herb Russell, "Edgar Lee Masters' Final Years in the Midwest," *Essays in Literature* (Macomb), 4 (Fall 1977): 212-220.
Focuses on the end of Masters's first marriage.

Hardin W. Masters, *Edgar Lee Masters: A Biographical Sketchbook about a Famous American Author* (Rutherford, N.J.: Fairleigh Dickinson University Press, 1978).
A useful volume by Masters's eldest son.

Hilary Masters, *Last Stands: Notes from Memory* (Boston: David R. Godine, 1982).
This memoir by his youngest son sheds much light on Masters's second marriage.

References:

Percy H. Boynton, "The Voice of Chicago: Edgar Lee Masters and Carl Sandburg," in his *Some Contemporary Americans* (Chicago: University of Chicago Press, 1924), pp. 50-62.
Discusses the two major Illinois writers of the 1920s.

Charles E. Burgess, "Edgar Lee Masters: The Lawyer as Writer," in *The Vision of This Land: Studies of Vachel Lindsay, Edgar Lee Masters and Carl Sandburg,* edited by John E. Hallwas and Dennis J. Reader (Macomb: Western Illinois University, 1976), pp. 55-73.
Shows how Masters's legal career is reflected in his writings.

Bernard Duffey, *The Chicago Renaissance in American Letters: A Critical Study* (East Lansing:

Michigan State College Press, 1954), pp. 143-170.
Provides useful background reading.

Hugh Dalziel Duncan, *The Rise of Chicago as a Literary Center from 1885 to 1920: A Sociological Essay in American Culture* (Totowa, N.J.: Bedminster Press, 1954), pp. 130-140.
Discusses problems faced by Masters and other Chicago writers of his generation.

Ernest Earnest, "Spoon River Revisited," *Western Humanities Review,* 21 (Winter 1967): 59-65.
Compares Masters and poet T. S. Eliot.

John T. Flanagan, *Edgar Lee Masters: The Spoon River Poet and His Critics* (Metuchen, N.J.: Scarecrow Press, 1974).
An exhaustive critical overview.

Lois Teal Hartley, *Spoon River Revisited,* Ball State Monograph no. 1 (Muncie, Ind.: Ball State University, 1963).
Makes sense of Masters's life and work, by one who knew him.

Ima Honaker Herron, *The Small Town in American Literature* (Durham: Duke University Press, 1939), pp. 353-366.
An excellent discussion of Masters's achievement.

Dale Kramer, *Chicago Renaissance: The Literary Life in the Midwest, 1900-1930* (New York: Appleton-Century, 1966), pp. 263-277.
A useful study of the early-twentieth-century Chicago literary scene.

Amy Lowell, *Tendencies in Modern American Poetry* (New York: Macmillan, 1917), pp. 130-200.
First extended analysis of *Spoon River Anthology,* by a hostile critic.

Ronald Primeau, *Beyond Spoon River: The Legacy of Edgar Lee Masters* (Austin: University of Texas Press, 1981).
Discusses Masters's literary influences.

Max Putzel, *The Man in the Mirror: William Marion Reedy and His Magazine* (Cambridge: Harvard University Press, 1963).
Excellent discussion of the St. Louis editor

who helped shape *Spoon River Anthology* and then published it serially.

Louis Untermeyer, *American Poetry Since 1900* (New York: Holt, 1923), pp. 113-132.
  Deals with Masters and his times.

John H. Wrenn and Margaret H. Wrenn, *Edgar Lee Masters* (Boston: Twayne, 1983).
  A useful overview of Masters's life and writings.

Michael Yatron, *America's Literary Revolt* (New York: Philosophical Library, 1959).

Explores Masters's political preferences and intellectual background.

Papers:
The University of Texas at Austin has more than twelve thousand items of Mastersiana–personal papers, manuscripts, and letters, as well as the writer's library. The Newberry Library in Chicago has some three hundred items, and the University of Chicago's Regenstein Library has some 250 items concerning Masters. Masters was a voluminous letter writer, and much of his correspondence has not been critically analyzed or described.

Frank Norris

This entry was updated by Joseph R. McElrath, Jr. (Florida State University) from his entry in DLB 12, American Realists and Naturalists.

Places	Cuba San Francisco	South Africa Chicago	Paris New York City
Influences and Relationships	Honoré de Balzac William Dean Howells Sir Walter Scott	Emile Zola Stephen Crane Anthony Hope	Guy de Maupassant Robert Louis Stevenson
Literary Movements and Forms	Romanticism Muckraking Fiction Nineteenth-Century Interest in Medieval Culture	Naturalism Anti-aestheticism	Impressionism Western Regionalism

Major Themes	Survival of the Fittest
	Life as "Romantic" in
	  Nature
		Need for Humane
		  Moral Values
		Amorality of Modern
		  Economic Life
			The American Dream
			The "Ideal Woman"

Cultural and Artistic Influences	Social Darwinism
	The Breakdown of
	  Victorian Values
	The American Success
	  Myth
		Distrust of Metaphysical
		  Philosophies
		The Rise of Psychology
		  as a Science
			"Social Conscience" Art
			Academic and Impressionist
			  Painting

Social and Economic Influences	Boer War
	Emergence of the U.S.
	  as a World Power
		Spanish-American War
		Laissez-faire Capitalism
			Growth of Trusts
			Populist Reform
			  Movements

BIRTH: Chicago, Illinois, 5 March 1870, to Benjamin Franklin and Gertrude Doggett Norris.

EDUCATION: University of California at Berkeley, 1890-1894; Harvard University, 1894-1895.

MARRIAGE: 12 February 1900 to Jeannette Black; child: Jeannette.

DEATH: San Francisco, California, 25 October 1902.

BOOKS: *Yvernelle: A Legend of Feudal France* (Philadelphia: Lippincott, 1892);
Moran of the Lady Letty: A Story of Adventure off the California Coast (New York: Doubleday & McClure, 1898); republished as *Shanghaied* (London: Richards, 1899);
McTeague: A Story of San Francisco (New York: Doubleday & McClure, 1899; London: Richards, 1899);
Blix (New York: Doubleday & McClure, 1899; London: Richards, 1900);
A Man's Woman (New York: Doubleday & McClure, 1900; London: Richards, 1900);
The Octopus: A Story of California (New York: Doubleday, Page, 1901; London: Richards, 1901);
The Pit: A Story of Chicago (New York: Doubleday, Page, 1903; London: Richards, 1903);
A Deal in Wheat and Other Stories of the New and Old West (New York: Doubleday, Page, 1903; London: Richards, 1903);
The Responsibilities of the Novelist and Other Literary Essays (New York: Doubleday, Page, 1903; London: Richards, 1903);
The Joyous Miracle (New York: Doubleday, Page, 1906; London: Harper, 1906);
The Third Circle (New York & London: John Lane, 1909);
Vandover and the Brute (Garden City: Doubleday, Page, 1914; London: Heinemann, 1914);
Collected Writings Hitherto Unpublished in Book Form, volume 10 of *Complete Works of Frank Norris* (Garden City: Doubleday, Doran, 1928);
Frank Norris of "The Wave": Stories and Sketches from the San Francisco Weekly, 1893 to 1897, edited by Oscar Lewis (San Francisco: Westgate Press, 1931);
The Literary Criticism of Frank Norris, edited by Donald Pizer (Austin: University of Texas Press, 1964);
A Novelist in the Making: A Collection of Student Themes and the Novels Blix *and* Vandover and

Frank Norris

the Brute, edited by James D. Hart (Cambridge: Harvard University Press, 1970).

Collection: *Complete Works of Frank Norris*, 10 volumes (Garden City: Doubleday, Doran, 1928).

Frank Norris is a central figure in American literary history mainly because of three novels, *McTeague* (1899), *The Octopus* (1901), and *The Pit* (1903). But he is also important because of what he indicates to the cultural historian: his works mirror changes occurring in his milieu during a remarkable period of intellectual and artistic transition at the end of the nineteenth century and the beginning of the twentieth. The need to redefine man's situation in the "new world" revealed by scientists, by antitraditional social theorists, and by modern schools of philosophical inquiry was a primary motivation for Norris as he shaped his more serious writings. Conventional Judeo-Christian "certainties" about man, God, nature, and society had waned. Norris realized just as dramatically as Henry Adams that the useful and comforting truths of traditional culture had become either defunct or dubious. In the cultural crisis resulting, Norris was one of many writers who sought to clarify the troubling questions of the age and to provide new explanations of life in their descriptions of characters and environments. What is unique about Norris, however, is that he ultimately transcended the iconoclastic attitudes popular among the turn-of-the-century avant-garde—as sardonically expressed by Stephen Crane and Ambrose Bierce when they ruminated over how little their unsophisticated contemporaries understood life's complexities. After some similar flourishes of rebellion against his parent culture, he went on to anticipate, in his own fashion, T. S. Eliot's manner of dealing with the "modern predicament" by synthesizing what seemed to remain valid in the old thought and artistic methods and what seemed important in the new. The blending of the modern and the Victorian in his works once caused some confusion among literary historians: Norris's fiction was identified as a puzzling mixture of pessimism and optimism, realism and romanticism, progressive philosophy and regressive thought. The apparently paradoxical yoking of Charles Darwin and St. Paul and the blending of Emile Zola and William Dean Howells, however, was purposeful. Whether Norris always succeeded is debatable, but his intention was clearly that of a synthesizer attempting to wed the traditional and the modern in distinctive novelistic statements on the nature of life.

Born in Chicago on 5 March 1870, Benjamin Franklin Norris, Jr., was the son of a self-made businessman who prospered as the head of a jewelry business and who sought to improve his fortunes by moving the family to California in 1884. San Francisco provided new opportunities, and this entrepreneur flourished in his realm of interest. At home, Norris's mother, the one-time actress Gertrude Doggett Norris, pursued the genteel life, leading Frank and his younger brother Charles (1881-1945), who also became a novelist, down Victorian cultural byways. While Benjamin Franklin Norris, Sr., speculated in land acquisition and rental properties, Gertrude Norris shared the polite delights of Sir Walter Scott, Robert Browning, and Alfred Tennyson, with her children. Frank was given the appropriate upper-middle-class education: private schooling at the Belmont Academy south of San Francisco and then at the Boys' High School in the city; Episcopal Sunday School; some athletics (he broke his arm playing football); and training in art at the San Francisco Art Association. The well-to-do family made the socially requisite grand tour in 1887, and Frank remained in Paris at the Atelier Julien to study painting when the rest of the family returned to San Francisco.

As would later happen during his college years, Norris did not seriously apply himself. Subsequently eclectic in his literary style, he early demonstrated his aversion to formality, consistency, and specialization by turning from sketch pad and canvas—too often—to delight in the potpourri of varied experience provided by Paris. Like the largely autobiographical hero of his novel *Blix* (1899)—who suffers from a lack of focus in his personal life and career—Norris was preoccupied with fencing, the opera, Jean Froissart's *Chronicles,* and the composition of tales about a character named Robert D'Artois, which he mailed in installments to brother Charles in San Francisco. None of these Paris tales, later described by Charles Norris, has survived, but Frank Norris's strong fascination with things medieval and romantic is indicated in the 31 March 1889 issue of the *San Francisco Chronicle.* He had turned from the one ambitious painting project that he is known to have undertaken—an enormous, Froissart-inspired canvas devoted to the Battle of Crecy—to write an article on knightly appurtenances, "Clothes of Steel." It was his first publication, and Norris was clearly still under the spell of *Ivanhoe.* While progressive writers such as Honoré de Balzac, Zola, Gustave Flaubert, brothers Edmond-Louis-Antoine and Jules-Alfred Huot de Goncourt may have come within the range of Norris's varied interests, the Paris experience mainly heightened his romantic view of life and art, which would soon come to dominate the character of his early poetry and fiction.

While Norris went on to do pen-and-ink illustrations for some of his later published writings, he failed as a painter, possibly because of a lack of talent but almost certainly because of a lack of self-discipline and personal commitment. (*Blix* suggests that such was Norris's personal predicament as late as 1897.) Details are sparse, but it would seem that the early choice of a career was largely one made by his parents and that Frank Norris had much in common with the undirected and weak-willed hero of another autobiographical work, *Vandover and the Brute* (1914), at this very self-indulgent stage of his life. Moreover, Norris's romantic imagination was hardly suited to the academic atmosphere of the late 1880s. His riotous delight in the dramatically forceful and the sensationally colorful, as evidenced in his writings, was hardly a trait of the sensibility encouraged by the French academy. The drama of Eugéne Delacroix's canvases—which were *not* held up as models for imitation then—reflected Norris's tastes, while the academicians' preference was for a subdued, pre-impressionistic "realism" expressive of ideal concepts in tones of cool clarity. At the Atelier Julien there were the bohemianism of the students, the nude models of whom Gertrude Norris may not have been aware, and the fleshly fantasies of Adolphe William Bouguereau's canvases for stimulation. Norris described these conventional aspects of the offbeat world of art study in "Student Life in Paris" (1900); by 1900 the experience seemed to have mellowed in memory. In 1889, though, he yearned for something else, the "days of old/ When swords were bright and steeds were prancing." Like Miniver Cheevy, Norris "missed the medieval grace/Of iron clothing." Finally he returned to San Francisco.

Although scholastically unprepared, Norris entered the University of California at Berkeley in 1890, initially playing the Parisian artiste and appearing the dandy. He maintained a position as one of the attractive young men in the better class of San Francisco society. He also associated with local artists–some decidedly in the decadent tradition. He was something of a fellow traveler with a group dubbed Les Jeunes, which came to publish its own "Yellow Book," the *Lark,* in 1895-1897. Norris began to develop in new ways, though. It was not long before he became a boisterous fraternity man, a sworn foe of literary preciosity and effete cultural pretension in any form. He also turned his back on his one notable but commercially unsuccessful publication of the early 1890s: a Scott-like verse romance published in late 1892, *Yvernelle: A Legend of Feudal France,* which he gladly allowed to remain in oblivion when he began writing his quite different novels at the end of the decade. One may turn to any passage in *Yvernelle* and, with some surprise, note the difference between Norris's juvenilia and the typically less "literary" writing of his maturity. The substance of *McTeague* and *The Octopus* bears little resemblance to

> Time there was when squire, page and knight,
>   Portcullis, keep and barbican were real;
> When tournaments were things of daily sight,
>   And chivalry arrayed in flashing steel;
> And time there was when the brave errant-knight
>   Was not a fancy of a minstrel's tale,
> But fought in very earnest for the right,
>   Or wandered wide to find the Holy Grail.

The kind of artist and thinker who created that genteel piece of fine writing was the type that Norris would later lampoon with considerable spleen in five of his novels, especially in *The Octopus.*

The highly romantic short fiction that Nor-

ris produced during the early Berkeley years will disappoint readers looking for signs of originality or traces of genius: "Les Enerves de Jumieges" (1890), "The Son of the Sheik" (1891), "Le Jongleur de Taillebois" (1891), and "Lauth" (1893) are, at best estimation, pulp fiction in the sensational vein. Norris gave himself over somewhat lamely to the marvelous during the early years of his apprenticeship. "Le Jongleur de Taillebpos," for instance, recalls Edgar Allan Poe and Nathaniel Hawthorne in their most spectral, and slickly Gothic, moments. And poems such as "Crepusculum" (1892) did not indicate any great advance over the verse of *Yvernelle.* Of more significance and promise, however, were fictional sketches and dialogues which were drawn from Norris's personal experiences among the San Francisco debutantes and young gentlemen; the polite society comedies of Anthony Hope and Richard Harding Davis had a potent effect on Norris as he adopted their mannerisms to depict life among the swell set. The farcical play *Two Pair* (1893), and short stories such as "Travis Hallett's Halfback" (1894) and "She and the Other Fellow" (1894) featured the urbane and witty characters of Hope's and Davis's society tales. Norris was clearly paying attention to the magazines and the stage to determine what worked and sold in the literary marketplace. By 1895, however, Norris was beginning to imitate other voices, such as those of Balzac and Zola, perhaps because he felt he had something more worthwhile to declare than did the popular drawing-room satirists. The turn toward the grimly realistic may also have been determined or accelerated in 1894 by the second great personal failure in Norris's life.

While Norris was trying his wings as a writer, he seemed to have little time for or interest in his studies. *Yvernelle* and the several short stories appearing in West Coast magazines counted for naught in academic life at Berkeley, nor did his prominent role in fraternity high jinks, his participation in amateur theatricals, and his work for school newspapers and yearbooks. Berkeley had admitted him as a special student and expected him to make up for his shortcomings. But he did what he wanted rather than what was required. After some unsuccessful petitioning for even more special status on the grounds that he had chosen to prepare himself for a career as a writer rather than a scholar, he had to leave Berkeley in 1894, carrying away a dislike for Thomas Babington Macaulay, mathematics, and academic life in general. Only the evolutionary idealist Prof. Joseph LeConte seems to have left a positive and deep impression upon his imagination.

LeConte was the exceptional professor for Norris: like Delacroix and two other influences, Robert Louis Stevenson and Victor Hugo, Le-Conte was an artist at vividly dramatizing concepts in a fully engaging manner. To the excitable imagination of his student he presented a grand spectacle in his interpretation of the evolutionary process and man's place in it. Like Stevenson, he acknowledged the brutal side of man, the animalistic inheritance transmitted from generation to generation. Allusion to the "foul stream" of hereditary evil in *McTeague* would later recall this concept. LeConte also pictured the other side, demonstrating an inclination toward morality, spirituality, and the "upward movement" of man, a propensity for improvement of the individual and the race, which Ralph Waldo Emerson had described in his idealistic essays. To the melodramatically inclined Norris the tension between the two sides–the Dr. Jekyll versus Mr. Hyde dilemma–seemed confirmed by his own tendency toward self-indulgence and his simultaneous desire to live up to the "finer fabric" of his personality. In all of his novels Norris mined the concept of man's dual nature as a source of story material, as is demonstrated in Donald Pizer's *The Novels of Frank Norris* (1966). LeConte's lectures, then, were the most important and positive intellectual experiences during Norris's largely negative Berkeley period.

He emerged from these troublesome years of 1890 to 1894–during which his parents' marriage failed–with one emotionally sustaining conviction: that he could make his mark as a writer. He then went to Harvard University for a final flirtation with the academy, and in 1894-1895 he wrote under the direction of Prof. Lewis E. Gates and his assistants as a special student.

By this time he was already under the spell of Zola, whose work he viewed as a large step beyond the romanticism of Scott, Alexandre Dumas, and Victor Hugo toward a progressive kind of romantic realism (or realistic romanticism). Norris was at this time taking the same step, away from *Yvernelle* and "Le Jongleur de Taillebois" toward *McTeague*. Gates, it seems, helped him to make the move forward by suggesting a more realistic aesthetic than the one he had been following. Gates's pronouncements in *Studies and Appreciations* (1900) are revelatory in this connection. When considering the failures of one

of Gertrude Norris's saints, Tennyson, and charging him with an inability to relate literature to life, Gates articulated a literary criterion which remained at the front of Norris's mind and on the tip of his tongue throughout his career. Gates encouraged writers not to shrink from the "commonplace and from the crude" but to "interpret into fine significance life's puzzling complexities of motive, character, and passionate action." He proposed the achievement of a "renovating imaginative realism," and Norris's writing thenceforth was largely based on such an aesthetic foundation.

The immediate result was the forty-four known themes Norris wrote as a course requirement, now collected in edited form in James D. Harte's *A Novelist in the Making* (1970). *McTeague, Blix,* and *Vandover and the Brute* were, in effect, begun by 1894-1895, for many of the sketches became sections of those novels. Indeed, chapter 2 of *Vandover and the Brute* is set in Cambridge, Massachusetts.

Another stage of apprenticeship completed, Norris returned to San Francisco, apparently expecting a rapid rise to national prominence. His envy-tinted comments about Stephen Crane in 1896 and 1897 suggest that he was very much aware of that young writer's leap to fame in 1895 with *The Red Badge of Courage;* and jaded allusions to another "boy wonder," Richard Harding Davis, indicate his full awareness of Davis's near overnight success when he was twenty-six years old. Norris–almost twenty-six–was ready for his turn, and he took the path that had led to Davis's *The West from a Car Window* (1892), *The Rulers of the Mediterranean* (1894), *Our English Cousins* (1894), and *About Paris* (1895)–impressionistic travel writing. Norris made arrangements with the *San Francisco Chronicle* and was off to exotic lands.

In November 1895 he traveled to South Africa, and the Davis luck, initially, seemed to be his too. The Jameson Raid, an attempt to overthrow the Boer government of Transvaal, occurred while he was there. It was a story that filled newspaper columns throughout the Anglo-American world. Unfortunately, Norris failed to capitalize on the event. Only one of eight articles–"Street Scenes in Johannesburg During the Insurrection of January, 1896"–was placed in a national publication, *Harper's Weekly;* the rest, which appeared in the *San Francisco Chronicle* and the *Wave,* were undistinguished local-color pieces, such as "A Zulu War Dance" and "A Californian in the City of Cape Town." Norris could write *up* an event–sensationalize it in the manner of Davis and Zola to near-yellow journalism proportions–by this time. But he failed to draw much attention. He returned from his South African adventure to a dubious reward: two years as a copywriter for the *Wave,* a San Francisco weekly of small and local circulation.

Much of Norris's 1896-1898 writing for the *Wave* was worthy of a larger readership–a fact not yet obvious to many because the texts are still unavailable in collected form. He produced more than 150 prose pieces, many of which would have gained him a following had they been published in newspapers such as the *New York Evening Sun* or magazines such as *Harper's Weekly* or *Scribner's,* as were Richard Harding Davis's during his early days. Quantitatively and qualitatively Norris's work was frequently superior to Davis's; and perhaps if he had enjoyed the kind of familial connections afforded to Davis his pieces would have been appearing in *Century* and *Harper's Monthly* rather than the *Wave.* Norris, however, was on his own. He conducted interviews, wrote sophisticated book reviews, theorized about literary movements and trends in pieces such as "Zola as a Romantic Writer" (1896), translated several tales from the French, and reported on many cultural, athletic, and civic events in the environs of San Francisco. His short fiction was largely in step with current fashions: a series entitled "The Opinions of Leander" (1897) wittily approximated Anthony Hope's *Dolly Dialogues* (1894); "The Heroism of Jonesee" (1896) and "Bandy Callaghan's Girl" (1896) were cut from the Davis cloth; and "The Third Circle" (1897) was a Stevensonian thriller. His originality manifested itself mainly in two ways. First, in journalistic pieces such as "On a Battleship" (1896) and "A Strange Relief Ship" (1897) he displayed considerable polish as an impressionist capable of vitalizing his subjects with a tone of awe and wonderment. His was the talent of making the ordinary seem extraordinary and thus interesting. Second, he displayed a de Maupassant-like sense of mordant humor, producing several noteworthy comic plunges into the bizarre. "A Salvation Boom in Matabeleland" (1896) is a near-bantering account of the crucifixion of a Salvation Army officer on a telephone pole. "Judy's Service of Gold Plate" (1897) anticipates the sometimes grotesquely comical characterizations of Zerkow and Maria Macapa in *McTeague.* "Fantaisie Printaniere" (1897) is a Dickensian sketch dealing

with the niceties of the fine art of wife-beating–directly related to Trina and Maria's discussion of the same subject in *McTeague.* In 1897, as Norris was moving toward the completion of *McTeague,* he was developing a point of view and tone of his own, together with an interest in what may be termed the eccentric or, in 1897, the "improper" in literature. While the influences on his work would always remain clear, he dramatically declared his independence in the Christmas 1897 issue of the *Wave:* in "Perverted Tales" he parodied his masters with a skill equal to that of Bret Harte in his *Condensed Novels and Other Papers* (1867). His victims, predictably, were Rudyard Kipling, Stephen Crane, Bret Harte, Richard Harding Davis, Ambrose Bierce, and Anthony Hope. Then in January 1898 he once again attempted to break into the *real* world of publishing, centered in the East; and, finally, he succeeded, with *Moran of the Lady Letty: A Story of Adventure off the California Coast* (1898).

He turned to *Moran of the Lady Letty,* though, after two more failures: a plan for a collection of short stories fell through; and *McTeague* was not accepted by a publisher. Late 1897 was marked by his depression. Norris felt that he had patiently served the appropriate apprenticeship, that he knew his craft from the critic's and the practitioner's points of view, and that he had something significant to say to the public–if he could only create a readership. Finally, he analyzed the market with his father's entrepreneurial eye, and he shrewdly chose a move that made a real career in writing possible. He stooped to conquer with a made-to-order thriller for the American audience then reveling in the melodramatic delights provided by Hope's *The Prisoner of Zenda* (1894) and Stevenson and Lloyd Osbourne's *The Wrecker* (1892). *Moran of the Lady Letty* began its serialization in the *Wave* in January 1898–with Norris sending the installments, as they appeared, to the S. S. McClure Syndicate in New York City. This sensational and luridly violent tale of Ross Wilbur's shanghai experience, blatantly echoing Davis's *Van Bibber and Others* (1892), Kipling's *Captains Courageous* (1897), and Stevenson's *Treasure Island* (1883), brought Norris to New York and a position with McClure. By the end of February he was living in a flat at 10 West Thirty-third Street, where he finished writing the final installments for the *Wave* at the end of March. McClure, in late spring, sent him to Cuba to cover the Spanish-American War. Like other journalists, he was stalled at Key West. He finally made it to Cuba, but while Crane and Davis enjoyed their finest, highly paid hours, Norris proved invisible. He returned to New York on 5 August with no publications to his credit except for two newspaper serializations of *Moran of the Lady Letty*. Malaria necessitated a lengthy recuperation in San Francisco. It was not until mid October that he returned to New York, moving into a new apartment on Washington Square. Two articles about Cuba, "Comida" and "With Lawton at El Caney," were published in two first-rate magazines, *Atlantic Monthly* and *Century*, but too late to create a sensation—in March and June 1899. It was another lost opportunity and a setback. Still, *Moran of the Lady Letty* was trimmed and bowdlerized for book publication in September 1898; it proved a modest success with the reviewers, and Norris was on his way. Doubleday and McClure next published *McTeague: A Story of San Francisco* in February 1899; and *Blix* was readied for serialization beginning in the March issue of a ladies' magazine, *Puritan*, and published by Doubleday and McClure in September 1899. The reviews—positive and negative—resulted in considerable visibility. None was a best-seller, but the adventure romance, the naturalistic novel, and the Howellian love idyll—appearing almost simultaneously—made Norris look so versatile a writer that heads turned and eyebrows were raised.

These books were the work of a young man. While *McTeague* is accounted a masterpiece, all three were the products of his apprentice years. He could have written *Moran of the Lady Letty* before the 1894-1895 sojourn at Harvard, so facile was the surface adherence to the adventure-romance formula as it had developed from Walter Scott to Robert Louis Stevenson. *Blix* is a pleasant boy-loves-girl romance cast in the genteel mold and it passed muster in the rigorously idealistic book-review section of the *Chautauguan*. Both did raise serious notions: *Moran of the Lady Letty* brutally rejects Judeo-Christian values and revels in post-Darwinian "survival of the fittest" thinking and "might makes right" sloganeering; *Blix* rejects hypocritical social conventions for the sake of more honest and thus more natural and ideal ways of living. But both fail to dramatize modern questions and predicaments in universally relevant and engaging fashion. Although William Dean Howells praised *Moran of the Lady Letty* in what were for him tones of marked enthusiasm, critics have typically viewed this novel and *Blix* as either youthful larks or potboilers. *McTeague* is different. It

richly blends a de Maupassant-like fascination with the grim, a Dickensian sense of the ridiculous, a Zolaesque understanding of life's determinisms, and even a Bret Harte-inspired sense of "Western" color. It is a varied tapestry in which the "novel of degeneration" narrative structure and theme stand in relief. As such, it is a masterfully worked counterpart to Zola's *L'Assommoir* (1877). In *McTeague* Norris makes what may be termed his first truly significant statement: he expresses an American truism emerging among the intellectual elite of the 1890s, that man is not the free creature whom Emerson described in "Self-Reliance." Rather, he is more like the pathetic creature described by Emerson in the essay "Fate"—a pawn of environmental determinisms, chance, and genetically inherited traits.

The composition of *McTeague* merits some special consideration in light of the long span of years some biographers have attributed to the process, extending back to late 1893 and the notorious murder of Sarah Collins by her husband in a San Francisco kindergarten, the setting for Trina McTeague's death. Donald Pizer's "The Genesis of *McTeague*" in *McTeague: A Norton Critical Edition* (1977) describes the long evolution of the work in as much detail as is now possible. Specific dates are difficult to determine with certainty; but three states of mind and thus, in effect, three aspects of Norris's development from the mid 1890s through February 1899 seem preserved in *McTeague*. Norris begins it on Lewis E. Gates's serious and realistic note regarding the "commonplace and the crude." A day in the life of Polk Street, San Francisco, is rendered in a vital, detailed, colorful, and panoramic manner recalling (and surpassing) the first chapter of Zola's *L'Assommoir*. The crude dentist-hero McTeague is established in his milieu as a subject for study; he is the low-life character of limited intelligence suited to naturalistic treatment, and Norris is quick to provide an intellectual frame of reference within which the plot may develop with naturalistic significance. As chapter 2 progresses, though, the comic sensibility that emerged in Norris's *Wave* writings of 1896-1897 comes to the fore. Through chapter 10 the stage is carefully set for the grim and inexorable developments typical of a degeneration tale; but much of the writing is comedy at the expense of McTeague, his friend Marcus Schouler, a maid named Maria, and the junkman Zerkow, who loom large as bumpkins and grotesques. There is a good inimical deal of the vaudeville spirit in Norris's handling of his characters' antics. Like Zola in *Nana* (1880), Norris did not see comedy and pathos as inimical. The drolleries cease and another sensibility comes to dominate, however, as Trina McTeague's latent, self-destructive traits are activated by worsening economic conditions and as McTeague's genetically inherited tendency toward alcoholism is triggered by his loss of occupation and disintegrating marriage. As McTeague begins his descent to what a LeContean would describe as his bestial state, Norris adopts a more sympathetic tone toward his character. Gradually McTeague becomes a pathetic victim of heredity, environment, and chance. When McTeague beats Trina to death and steals her hoarded wealth, he seems as much a "victim" as the woman lying in a pool of blood.

By late 1897, just prior to the beginning of the *Moran* project, Norris had apparently taken the work this far, to chapter 20. In the fall he left San Francisco for Placer County in the Sierras where he finished the novel, transporting his hero in flight from legal authorities to that mountainous locale. The flight is sensationally and, in the conclusion, melodramatically handled as a piece of regional writing in the adventure-romance tradition. His former friend, Marcus Schouler, pursues McTeague through Death Valley. Just before McTeague kills his nemesis, Marcus finds enough strength to handcuff their wrists. We last see McTeague chained to the dead man in Death Valley.

William Dean Howells and others noted this turn from the realistic and complained accordingly. Norris's eclectic mind of the Paris period was still in evidence; and when he was called upon to explain the long leap from the realistic to the romantic at the end of *McTeague,* he was unrepentant. He was convinced that the ending belonged. As he explained in conversation and indicated in "A Plea for Romantic Fiction" (1901), the conclusion was not the result of what would be termed today a "mood swing." While the various sensibilities informing *McTeague* do make that term seem most relevant to the actual situation, Norris argued that the romantic seemed an essential in the most effective art. He never changed his mind on this point; and his later novels illustrate the conviction. What remained constant from 1896 and "Zola as a Romantic Writer" through 1902 and his death was Norris's allegiance to what he defined as the romantic.

Vandover and the Brute, although not published until 1914, was actually a fourth product of Norris's youthful phase. It was most certainly begun by 1895 when Norris was at Harvard and most probably finished before 1900. More relentlessly than *McTeague,* and without any leavening element of comedy, it pictures a young San Franciscan driven by forces–social, cultural, moral, commercial, and temperamental–toward a calamitous end. It was an end, some interpreters have suggested, toward which Norris feared he was moving before he attached himself to Jeannette Black in 1897 and enjoyed her stabilizing influence. The novel is largely intimately familiar with the drawing rooms, barrooms, and places of assignation that the hero frequents. Vandover is a weak, maladapted individual bewildered by conflicts between instinctive appetites and social mores (particularly in regard to sexual matters). He cannot resolve conflicts between conclusions about life derived from practical experience and metaphysical "certainties" proffered by conventional society. The LeContean "brute" in him is constantly at odds with his "better self," and he is totally incapable of designing a rational balance between the two. While Norris indicates that the self-indulgently lazy and dismayingly unanalytical Van is largely responsible for his degeneration and that society cannot be totally blamed, the novel is a critical "Study of Life and Manners in an American City at the End of the Nineteenth Century" (the subtitle in the manuscript). Norris was critical of society's "laws"–again, sexual mores in particular–when they did not correspond to the actualities of human nature and human experience. That is, he was just as hostile toward morality unrelated to life as he was toward literature standing in the same relationship. Social criticism was minimal in *McTeague;* but in *Vandover and the Brute* Norris broadened his scope to picture San Francisco as representative of an entire society worthy of criticism. As Van degenerates and moves downward from the highest echelons of society to the lowest, the reader is presented with a total picture; and with this city as a metaphor for modern life, Norris offered a more widely relevant conclusion than that found in *McTeague.* The theme is that late-nineteenth-century American experience is fraught with social, moral, and intellectual complexities not amenable to any available solutions or even traditional explanations. Although Norris did not craft Van as the representative American, he did posit a disoriented and bewildered response to the world which recalls that of the correspondent in Crane's "The Open Boat," published in 1898 as the title story for a collection of Crane's short fiction. "The Open Boat" seems to have met with Norris's approval and may have both shaped the shipwreck episode of chapter 9 and informed its theme. This theme would be expanded and elaborated in the first work of Norris's mature phase, *The Octopus;* but before he wrote *The Octopus* between the spring of 1899 and the late winter of 1901, Norris involved himself in a project which the sympathetic critic would kindly term an experimental or transitional piece. Most critics simply label *A Man's Woman* (1900) Norris's worst.

By mid 1899 Norris turned from *Blix* to the composition of *A Man's Woman* (or possibly its completion, since at least one scholar has concluded that it was begun in 1898). Once again, as with *Blix,* he was writing for the popular market; he exploited public interest in the quest to reach the North Pole; a fashionable new figure in the popular mind, the Nurse, was brought in as heroine; the horrors of physical suffering in the Arctic and a vivid description of a surgical technique provided sensation; and the muse of melodrama was called upon frequently. One reviewer noted that the novel contained enough crises to serve several novels. The novel also has a "serious" subject, however. Norris provides a psychological analysis of two American character types which is both profound and detailed. Less than enthusiastic about what he had done, Norris himself later termed it a "niggling analysis."

Ward Bennett is the opposite of the unfocused and unmotivated Vandover. A man of single ideas and absolute determination, he sets goals and brooks no opposition to reaching them. Although his field of action is Arctic exploration, he is essentially the self-reliant American cast in the heroic frontiersman mold. Lloyd Searight is the female counterpart, the "New Woman" of the 1890s, who pursues her vocation in the field of nursing with Brunhild-like tenacity. Lloyd is Norris's opportunity to examine the social consequences of the newly "liberated" professional woman's emergence—a subject with which he had flirted in several *Wave* pieces and in *Blix.* But, while sympathetic to Lloyd, his response to her was distinctly traditional. Once Lloyd resolves her own psychological problems and feels fulfilled, she sees it as her duty to help her husband, Ward, realize his potential for greatness as an explorer. As the reviewer for the *Argonaut* observed, Lloyd ends up playing an updated version of the "angel in the house" role.

The most important focus of the novel, however, is on interpersonal relationships. In a post-Darwinian age, survival, success, and the positive evolution of the Anglo-American type (the spearhead of evolution in Norris's mind) depend upon the personality and accomplishments of "the fittest." In this class, unfortunately, one usually finds the most highly individuated and selfish types of humanity, such as the equally egotistical Ward and Lloyd. They are tough-minded achievers callous to the more tender-minded concerns that inform much of the nature of humane society, the family, and marriage—the essential institutions fostering sensitivity and countering the "laws of the jungle." The refrain of *Moran of the Lady Letty* was "To hell with the weak!" Ross Wilbur and Moran Sternersen derided Victorian sentiments regarding the value of Judeo-Christian civilization, and Norris appeared to condone the piratical behavior of the barbarically "fit." In *A Man's Woman,* though, the essentially Victorian thinker reemerged in Norris, and he puzzled over the problem of humanizing his Darwinian exemplars. On the one hand, he saw the evolutionary vanguard, "the fittest," as absolutely necessary to the positive historical process in which he wanted to believe; on the other, he realized that the future of Anglo-American society was imperiled by the amorality and insensitivity manifested in the behavior of those in that category. True to the principles of Prof. Joseph LeConte, Norris tried to demonstrate the need to synthesize vigor and fitness with ethicality and humaneness. He hoped to fashion his hero and heroine as instructive models of what may be involved in taking the difficult steps upward on the evolutionary ladder.

Unlike Ross and Moran, then, Ward and Lloyd are made to suffer the negative consequences of extreme self-interest and to temper their selfishness with concern for others' needs. Both overcome egotism and its debilitating effects; both move beyond the paralysis of self-pity in the face of failures; and both learn a new and constructive kind of sympathy. In their own ways, they become social creatures able to see beyond self. Needless to say, the novel ends happily.

Unfortunately, the unbridled melodrama, bombastic language, irritating anticlimaxes, and overwrought allegorical characterizations of *A Man's Woman* obscured the new and intellectually worthwhile theme. The author lamented in a letter to one reviewer that the novel was too "theatrical" and "slovenly put together." The central

Page of the manuscript for McTeague. *A leaf of the 245-page manuscript was included in each copy of the 1928 Argonaut Manu-script Edition of Norris's works.*

concept was most progressive: rather than accept the antisocial implications of Darwinism, Norris had tried to reconcile man's "animal" heritage (energy and endurance being requisite for positive evolutionary action) with the best consequences of civilization. Norris seemed to hold as a point of faith that someone, at some time, should show how sensitivity to human needs had an essential place in the post-Darwinian Western world. To him the paramount question of the age was: how can Judeo-Christian values best exert their mollifying effects on a harsh world? In *The Octopus* he returned to this question—with much greater success. What he pictured was a Darwinian world, like that in Zola's *Germinal* (1885), crying out for humanizing influences.

As Zola had moved from an interest in objectively reporting the grimness of life in *L'Assommoir* to the more moralistic point of view and tone of *Germinal,* Norris was moving away from the largely amoral, naturalistic perspective of *McTeague* to a more traditional kind of fiction in which the author seeks to suggest a pragmatic solution to social and personal problems. The friendship he began in 1898 with the Reverend W. S. Rainsford, of St. George's Episcopal Church in New York City, is significant in this regard. Rainsford, as Pizer relates, held views similar to Joseph LeConte's; he was a social activist, and he may have encouraged Norris to strive for more constructive ends in his fiction. In one piece of literary criticism, "The Novel with a 'Purpose' " (1902), Norris advised against overt didacticism in novel writing, but in *The Octopus* he did not hesitate to raise the question of what one ought to do in regard to the social injustices and economic abuses typical of the late nineteenth century.

While *Blix* was in press and *A Man's Woman* was running as a newspaper serial, Norris visited California and began research on the Trilogy of the Wheat, the first volume of which was *The Octopus.* The trilogy was to be the most ambitious work of his career, and Norris became obsessed with its concept. After Norris's death, Frederic Taber Cooper recalled: "His friends are still fond of telling of the day he came to his office trembling with excitement, incapacitated for work, his brain concentrated on a single thought, his Trilogy of the Wheat. 'I have got a big idea, the biggest I ever had,' was the burden of all he had to say for many a day after." On 7 May 1899 he wrote to his old friend Ernest Peixotto, with whom he had studied in Paris, telling him how

his research for *The Octopus* in California was proceeding: "The Wheat stuff is piling up BIG. Everybody is willing to help. . . . I may be here longer than I first expected. Mebbe til late in the fall, and I dunno why I should not write my immortal worruk at a wheat ranch any way. Tell [Gelett] Burgess I'm full of ginger and red pepper and am getting ready to stand up on my hind legs and yell big. . . ."

By the close of 1899 he was back in New York City with his notes in hand, ready to produce his prose epic. The focus of the California research was on socioeconomic conditions in the San Joaquin Valley and particularly the Southern Pacific Railroad's abuse of the wheat growers, which had triggered the infamous gun battle, the Mussell Slough Affair, of May 1880. The railroad trust provided all the material that a muckraker might want: it had attracted farmers with the promise of cheap land ceded to it by the government. It was to sell the land at unimproved prices at some future date; but once the growers developed the properties agriculturally, the railroad priced the land at improved rates. This change of policy, together with the railroad's high freight charges, meant economic ruination for the growers. Norris, however, did not resort to moral melodrama by pitting the noble husbandman of the soil against the malevolent trust. As a notebook-carrying Zolaist who had performed his field research—including an interview with C. P. Huntington, the head of the Southern Pacific—he sought instead to compose a trilogy representatively picturing the complexities of modern economic life, the unifying motif of which was the production, distribution, and consumption of an essential commodity. As a commentator he sought to shed some light on a lamentably junglelike society characterized mainly by rapacious interactions.

In late 1899 Norris began work as a reader for Doubleday, Page, a welcome position, making financially possible his marriage to Jeannette Black on 12 February 1900 in New York City. He seems to have spent little time at the office. In the spring he was hard at work on *The Octopus.* Reflecting on his data and writing at Greenwood Lake, New Jersey, in the summer of 1900, Norris maintained a nonsentimental point of view—in spite of the obvious temptations provided by the subject matter. Continuing the composition after he moved to Roselle, New Jersey, in October, Norris saw both the growers and the representatives of the trust as dominated by the same fixation:

an insatiable mania for profit and self-aggrandizement. Wealth and power are the prime motivations in a dog-eat-dog order; it is a Darwinian world order that Norris sternly fashions. *The Octopus* graphically and unshirkingly lays out the apparently insuperable problem confronting the social ameliorist who might dare to offer a proposal for macrocosmic reform. As in *Vandover and the Brute,* Norris presents a harsh world defying any mollifications.

Norris, of course, attempts an enlightening response. Which is *his* response, however, has been a matter of heated debate for decades because some critics have perceived confusion in the novel regarding point of view. Adhering to the principles later enunciated in "The Novel with a 'Purpose,' " Norris did not commit the literary sins of intruding upon the story and declaring his message to the world. Rather, he set up various characters, each with his own response to the central dilemma of the story–planning, most likely, to clarify his major theme in the never-written final volume of the trilogy. That is, *The Octopus* is not a fully independent work but a part of an intended but incomplete whole. When one reads the novel as an integral, separate work, with the expectations that naturally accompany such an approach, disappointment with Norris and disagreements with other interpreters may–and do–result.

Thus, a few critics have seen Shelgrim, the head of the railroad, as Norris's spokesman. This apologist for social Darwinism declares that events are beyond his control and that the economic order governs itself toward necessary and ultimately natural ends. "You are dealing with forces, young man, when you speak of Wheat and Railroads, not with men," he tells the character named Presley. "Complications may arise, conditions that bear hard on the individual–crush him maybe–*but the Wheat will be carried to feed the people* as inevitably as it will grow. If you want to fasten the blame . . . on any one person, you will make a mistake. Blame conditions, not men." Others have argued that the poet Presley and his mentor, Vanamee, a shepherd with mystical propensities, are more proximate to Norris's point of view. Both make what may be termed metaphysical responses to the disaster in the San Joaquin Valley and to life's problems in general: Vanamee asserts the illusory character of evils such as death, privation, and the abuse of the individual; Presley leaps to an Emersonian faith that the good produced by events compensates for evils

and in the end, or "larger view," always dominates. Since these characters' thoughts and comments close the volume, critics judge that Norris was making a "transcendental" response to the human predicaments pathetically described in *The Octopus.*

There is yet another interpretive possibility remaining–that Norris experiments with a traditional assertion of Judeo-Christian values through the example of Annixter, one of the leaders of the growers in their fight against the railroad. Like Ward Bennett of *A Man's Woman,* Annixter is the epitome of selfishness in the first half of *The Octopus.* Like Ward, he is extraordinarily competent, fiercely competitive, and markedly insensitive toward others. He is famous for using and abusing everyone–until he experiences love for Hilma Tree. The consummation of his love requires a nearly total personality transformation, and that change occurs. He gradually becomes oriented toward others and develops an acute awareness of others' needs. Hilma and Presley are astounded at the emergence of the new man; and Annixter himself is surprised at the joy that comes with caring for his fellows. He is killed by railroad agents shortly after he begins to act as a new man, but during his brief experience of concern for Hilma and the other members of his immediate society, Annixter demonstrates what may have been the only pragmatic possibility for even minor social amelioration that Norris could imagine as of 1901. Annixter makes life better for those immediately around him; he is the only principal character in the whole of *The Octopus* to succeed in humanizing his environment.

Actually, the interpretive crux involves the choice of Vanamee, Presley, or Annixter as Norris's true hero. The choice of Vanamee or Presley involves positing an optimistic metaphysical response on Norris's part. The choice of Annixter implies that Norris was tentatively proposing a practical revival of Judeo-Christian values (relatively selfless living directed toward the end of love for one's neighbor). If one chooses Vanamee or Presley, though, he must deal with the fact that both are self-absorbed individuals; and Norris had identified that state as a negative condition in *A Man's Woman.* Moreover, in his next novel, *The Pit,* he would again make the same point.

With *The Octopus* in press by the early spring of 1901, Norris gave up his house at Roselle, New Jersey, and traveled with Jeannette to Chicago, where he worked up the technical details and local color for the second stage of the trilogy. He was also writing short stories, contributing literary essays to the *Chicago American,* and dealing with the interruptions resulting from the critical and commercial success of *The Octopus.* By May he was in California, where he stayed for two months; then three months of privacy followed at Greenwood Lake, New Jersey. In September 1901 he was back in New York City, living in a West Side apartment, hard at work on *The Pit.* One year later it began its serialization in the *Saturday Evening Post,* and in 1903 it was published in book form. The flow of wheat eastward is the background for the drama of *The Pit;* but, once more, it is human relationships on which the limelight is focused.

Curtis Jadwin is closely related to Ward Bennett and Annixter. Having made a fortune in real estate and occasional speculative sallies into the Board of Trade, Jadwin is a commanding figure whom Norris adorns with much chivalric imagery, and whom he elevates to near-epic stature as the archetypal, achievement-oriented American. (Norris, too, was interested in writing the "Great American Novel," and the best-selling *The Pit* was his second attempt–as reviewers immediately recognized. Most praised it as an undeniably great novel.) Jadwin is not one who fails, and, when he competes for Laura Dearborn's hand in marriage, he ignores rejection, routs his opponents, and wins the field. When he decides to speculate seriously in wheat futures, his relentless determination leads him to attempt a cornering of the entire wheat harvest. Obsessed with his goal, he wreaks havoc in a global population dependent upon reasonably priced wheat for its survival. In his personal life with Laura calamitous consequences occur as well. With his marriage on the rocks because of his neglect, Jadwin suffers financial disaster and a nervous breakdown.

Laura is also an egotist with very grand expectations for herself. While Jadwin is the Darwinian exemplar, Laura is the epitome of another variety of a self-absorbed way of life–romantic narcissism, the other nineteenth-century manifestation of the "cult of the self." She requires a courtly lover who will dote upon her and see her as she views herself, as the grand heroine at center stage in the romantic drama that is life. Like the melodramatically self-conscious Lloyd Searight, she lives as though she is following the script provided by an operatic librettist. When Jadwin's obsession with the "battle" at the Board of Trade disqualifies him as the necessary idol-

izer, the spurned heroine turns to another gallant and toward the traditional end of romantic love, adultery.

Laura comes very close to leaving Jadwin and, indeed, to going insane. Jadwin loses his immense future in his wheat speculations and discovers that he has ruined his life. With his two exaggerated symbols of nineteenth-century egotism on the brink of absolute tragedy, Norris stops the degeneration process and kindly allows them a second chance. Jadwin is not an intellectual, but he does realize that the path he has followed was the wrong one. His Titan-like energies were mischanneled. Laura, while not much clearer in her comprehension of what went wrong, is more conscious of the point that Norris wishes to convey to the reader. It is Ward's, Annixter's, and Lloyd's movements beyond self-absorption that come to mind when Norris relates Laura's final thoughts to the reader: "Self, self. Had she been selfish from the very first? . . . Whither had this cruel cult of self led her?" Familiar with Tennyson's *Idylls of the King*–to which there are overt allusions in *The Pit*–Norris allows his Guinevere time for reflection and reform. His Lancelot, Sheldon Corthell, is sent packing. And his Arthur escapes total defeat. It is to new possibilities in life that Jadwin, Laura, and Norris turn as *The Pit* closes.

Egotism, as encouraged by social Darwinism and fin de siècle romantic narcissism, was the villain of Norris's mature fiction. The world is harsh in all of Norris's novels, except in *Blix* wherein a clever heroine deftly checks the consequences of the hero's immaturity. This harshness Norris could accept as a hard fact. He could recognize the complexities and irremediable aspect of a world not especially amenable to positive change. What he could not accept or sanction was the way in which human beings regularly worsened conditions by engaging in destructive and self-destructive behavior. The laws of the universe could not be changed, and the socio-economic order could not be immediately redesigned, but individuals could alter and improve their lots, especially if they asked the question that occurred so late to Ward, Annixter, and Laura: what is *really* important? The answer demonstrated explicitly and implicitly in the last three novels was relationships characterized by benign, mutual concern. As an evolutionist the young Frank Norris echoed the "hard Darwinism" of Herbert Spencer; but as his thought matured, he gravitated toward the view of Peter Kropotkin in

Mutual Aid (1902), which chastised Spencer for overlooking the "instinct of human solidarity and sociability" and its positive consequences. It was, possibly, an old-fashioned answer that Norris came to when examining modern conditions. He echoed the positive theme in the final stanza of Matthew Arnold's "Dover Beach" (1867). But, to Norris's credit, he also anticipated the only hope for man seen by John Steinbeck and Albert Camus.

Norris died of appendicitis in San Francisco in October 1902, before the serialization of *The Pit* was concluded. He had not begun the final volume of the trilogy, "The Wolf." He might have planned to elaborate in "The Wolf" upon the negative effects of culturally sanctioned selfishness on the macro- and microcosmic levels; perhaps he would have clarified the situation in *The Octopus* and explained whether Presley's and Vanamee's transcendental visions of a good universe or Annixter's "helping hand" response to an imperfect world represented his final position.

When the reader turns from the novels of 1898 through 1902 to the post-*Wave*, nonnovelistic works for indications of what Norris may have planned to do in "The Wolf," he will meet with disappointment in this regard–and in other regards as well. While Norris dramatically improved as a novelist after he wrote *Moran of the Lady Letty* and earned a permanent place in literary history as a result, he did not fare so well in other types of writing. While *The Pit* was easily adapted by Channing Pollock for the stage in 1904, Norris never exploited his penchant for melodrama in this way. Writing poetry, like his banjo playing, he wisely allowed to remain something associated with his fraternity days. Indeed, his last poem was a bit of comic doggerel, "The Exile's Toast," addressed to his Phi Gamma Delta brothers when he could not attend the November 1900 reunion in San Francisco. He did continue to write short fiction, but it is obvious that his talent and energy were directed principally into novelistic writing. It is difficult to identify individual stories representing any advance over the quality of his 1896-1898 work. In fact, there is a falling off in quality and a frequent resort to easy formula.

There were two posthumous collections of short fiction, *A Deal in Wheat and Other Stories of the New and Old West* (1903), which includes stories published in periodicals between 1901 and 1903, and *The Third Circle* (1909), made up of magazine stories mainly from the mid 1890s. Neither of these books impressed contemporaneous reviewers. Viewing both collections one sees no growth of any sort in the early 1900s: all that is apparent is experiment with various formats, all of which have more in common with the features of pulp fiction than high art. The substance of *Yvernelle* became "The Riding of Felipe" (1901) with the hero saving the heroine at the last moment "from a fate worse than death." The lurid mystery of "The Third Circle" and "The House with the Blinds" (both 1897) anticipate "The Ship That Saw a Ghost" (1902) and "The Ghost in the Crosstrees" (1903)–two truly lifeless pieces in the Gothic vein. The earlier, pleasant humor of "This Animal of a Buldy Jones" (1897) proves superior to the heavy-handed comedy in "A Bargain with Peg-Leg" (1902), "The Passing of Cock-Eye Blacklock" (1902), and "Two Hearts That Beat as One" (1903). The 1900s stories, then, tell little about Norris's career except that he wrote twenty pieces, seemingly for pocket money. That the two collections were assembled and published was mainly the result of the enormous success of *The Pit* and the marketability of Norris's name.

"A Deal in Wheat" (1902) is, unfortunately, Norris's best-known short story. Frequently anthologized because of its relationship to *The Pit*, it delineates the chicanery allegedly common in the daily activities of Chicago wheat speculators. Like Norris's later attempts at comedy in the short fiction, it is nothing more than a lengthy set-up for a snappy, surprise conclusion–one, in fact, borrowed from Richard Harding Davis's *The West from a Car Window*. Norris was not at his best when writing short stories; but he was better than "A Deal in Wheat" suggests, as a perusal of *The Third Circle* will indicate.

In his literary essays of the post-*Wave* period Norris may have spent the greater part of the energies he had left over from his novelistic enterprises. Today Norris is identified as "the most vocal expounder" of naturalistic critical theory at the end of the nineteenth century in America, according to Hugh Holman. But a study of his critical canon reveals something else. During the *Wave* period, he wrote only one essay truly "expounding" the virtues of "naturalism," and Norris did not even stress that term when he chose the title, "Zola as a Romantic Writer" (1896). If anything, Norris indicated that he did not find that term a useful one, especially since it was then synonymous with "dirty books" and "the

French school" in the American reader's mind. The point of "Zola as a Romantic Writer" was that so-called naturalism "is a form of romanticism, not an inner circle of realism" as reviewers and essayists were then claiming. Norris wrote that in Zola's works everything "is extraordinary, imaginative, grotesque even, with a vague note of terror quivering throughout like the vibration of an ominous and low-pitched diapson. It is all romantic . . . closely resembling the work of the greatest of all modern romanticists, Hugo." To Norris in 1896, naturalism or Zolaism was romanticism set in the milieu of actual social conditions. And he allied himself with this school because it seemed the one most truthfully depicting the full "drama of the people" in real life.

In December 1901 he again held forth on the subject. By then he had in mind not only Zola's example but his own practice in five published novels–each a romance, or romance-novel (to use the term employed by Richard V. Chase in *The American Novel and Its Tradition*, 1957). The still-young novelist was extremely close to his own works, and many of his literary essays are explanatory glosses on the volumes he had so recently completed. "A Plea for Romantic Fiction" further diminishes the emphasis on the term naturalism and more heavily emphasizes the Zolaesque-Norrisean concept of a romanticism transcending realism (as defined by Howells's practice) and popular romance writing (as exemplified by the cut-and-thrust and moonlight-and-golden-hair traditions). Norris's romanticism was a synthetic concept: by vitally blending a Hugoesque choice of remarkable incidents and characters with a Flaubertian concern for the specifics of actual human experience in the present, the truest kind of art became possible. For Norris, romanticism at its best was the ultimate form of realism in literature. The term denoted a full examination and presentation of the whole of experience from the trivial to the profound.

With such a redefinition of terms and concepts, Norris confidently entered the arena of American literary debate, somewhat unkindly hoisting William Dean Howells by his own petard. In the second chapter of *Criticism and Fiction* (1891), the dean of American letters warned of how realism might degenerate as a movement. "When realism becomes false to itself," Howells wrote, "when it heaps up facts merely, and maps life instead of picturing it, realism will perish." Norris saw Howells as guilty of such literal-

mindedness and shallowness, and he damned the Howellsian tradition: "Realism stultifies itself. It notes only the surface of things." Romanticism, as practiced by Zola (and Norris), attended to surfaces in a documentary way, but it also penetrated to the depths of human nature and finally to Truth. As indicated in another essay, "The True Reward of the Novelist" (1901), Norris was as fixated on "the Truth" as Zola in his later years; and he celebrated Zola as *the* artist who knew how to use "romance" properly, as "an instrument with which [one] may go straight through the clothes and tissues and wrappings of flesh down deep into the real, living heart of things. . . . the unplumbed depths of the human heart, and the mystery of sex, and the problems of life, and the black, unsearched penetralia of the soul of man."

When Norris signed himself the "Boy Zola" in letters, he identified with a romantic. He does not even use the word *naturalistic* in "A Plea for Romantic Fiction." While historians will continue referring to Norris as a naturalist (especially when viewing his thoughts in *McTeague* and *Vandover and the Brute*), it is necessary to acknowledge Norris's self-perception and his view–which was, ironically, anticipated by Howells in *Criticism and Fiction*–that the best literary art of the late nineteenth century is a manifestation of the noblest impulses of the romantic movement. That is, both Howells and Norris viewed remoteness from real life, which the romantics had found in neoclassicism, as negatively as Wordsworth did. Both championed greater fidelity to the natural and true–Howells declaring that at the beginning of the century "romance was making the same fight against effete classicism which realism is making to-day against effete romanticism." Norris too lamented degenerate romanticism, "the misuse of a really noble and honest formula of literature," and argued for the recognition of romance as "a teacher sent from God." In theory Norris was, perhaps unwittingly, in harmony with Howells; but in practice, of course, their differences were as obvious to Norris as they are to the modern reader.

Between 25 December 1897, when his last book review for the *Wave* was published, and 25 May 1901 Norris wrote no literary essays except for "The Unknown Author and the Publisher," published in the *World's Work* in April 1901 and signed "A Publisher's Reader." One of the main reasons it is attributed to him is because of his work as a reader for Doubleday, Page and Company. The little time he actually spent at the office gave him enough experience to provide in "The Unknown Author" the first of several peeks-behind-the-curtains by one who was there in the New York publishing world.

One month later he had better credentials as a literary man and was sought after for essays on many topics. The homage generated by *The Octopus*, which was published in April, made all the difference. Norris was now a bona fide celebrity engaged by the *Chicago American* to write a series of articles entitled "Literature in the East" for its Saturday literary supplement. The feature ran from 25 May through 28 August 1901, missing only the 27 July issue. In the October issue of the *World's Work*, "The True Reward of the Novelist"–his most idealistic assessment of the artist's role in society–appeared. Then, on 6 November the *Boston Evening Transcript* welcomed him for twelve essays published through 5 February 1902. An as yet unidentified firm contracted with Norris for syndicated distribution of his work in January 1902, and he wrote at least eight essays for that company. A plateau was soon scaled: *The Critic* began a "Salt and Sincerity" series comprising seven essays published between April 1902 and February 1903. In November it printed his best-known essay, "The Responsibilities of the Novelist."

Norris had become an authority. Yet, while he was clearly aspiring toward the status of Howells, he most often reached only the level of Hamlin Garland and frequently fell short of that. Many of the essays respectfully ushered into print were no better than what many Sunday supplement paragraphers were providing: inside scoops on what is really going on in the literary world, as in "New York as a Literary Centre" (1902) and "What Frank Norris Has to Say About the Unknown Writer's Chances" (1902); casual chat about "Why Women Should Write the Best Novels" (1901); and gossip about luminaries such as Richard Harding Davis in "It Was a Close Call" (1902). Cultural analysis such as "The Frontier Gone At Last" (1902) exalts the Anglo-Saxon spirit in sincere tones but also in a manner designed to please the Rooseveltian mentality.

There were, of course, several truly interesting essays. As one who had tried to write the "Great American Novel" in *The Octopus* and had been praised for coming very close to it, his "The National Spirit: As It Relates to the 'Great American Novel'" (1902) makes a good deal of sense in regard to how the regional orientation fostered by the local-color tradition might be transcended.

"A Neglected Epic" (1902) notes the closing of the frontier chapter in American cultural history and laments the fact that no one had successfully responded to the epic subject matter of the frontier experience in the West–a notion touched upon through Presley in *The Octopus*. "The Novel with a 'Purpose'" (1902) addresses the difficulties of enlightening the public while avoiding the overt didacticism of genteel-ideal literature–another problem dealt with in *The Octopus*. It is especially clear in these essays that Norris was too close to his own work to develop the trait of catholicity in his expository prose. They are relevant to the cultural history of the United States, but they are more revelatory of the concerns that the author of *The Octopus* then had in mind.

Two essays stand apart. "Simplicity in Art" (1902) is a truly sophisticated statement of an aesthetic. Norris restates his detestation of the gingerbread style of late-Victorian architecture and the overly ornate in all forms. He had originally expressed this point of view in the *Wave*, and he had laced *The Octopus* with similar commentary. In the essay he argued that elaborate phrasing, rhetoric, metaphor, and allegory–"rococo work"–too often disguise the "innate incompetence" of the writer. Quoting the narrative exposition in the King James translation of Luke 2: 6-7, he identified "the bare dignity of the unadorned" as the finest artistic trait. The essay is a curiosity among the others since its thesis seems to have nothing to do with Norris's own writing, which may fairly be termed "baroque"–with the Vanamee sections of *The Octopus* verging toward the "rococo" itself. Norris buttresses his argument with these questions: "Does exclamation and heroics on the part of the bystanders ever make the curbstone drama more poignant? Who would care to see Niagara through colored fire and calcium light?" The irony is that, in January 1902, Norris was depicting the "Niagara" of wheat which would crush Curtis Jadwin in language which was colored, fiery, and sometimes too dazzlingly brilliant. Autobiographically viewed, then, the essay seems to speak of the writer's future: that Norris was planning, distantly, for a change of voice and method; that the author and redactors of Luke might someday join Norris's long list of literary influences.

The other essay of enduring value and interest is "The Mechanics of Fiction" (1901). It expresses a Poe-like concern for the particulars of effective craftsmanship in art. Recalling the mechanics of planning and execution described in

"The Philosophy of Composition," Norris portrays the capable writer as one who behaves as a mosaicist–carefully choosing, shaping, and fitting into place the individual pieces of his picture. He intelligently proceeds with a plan, moved not by the frenzy of inspiration, but directed by practical intelligence and the knowledge that comes with experience. Norris's final revisions of *Blix* and *A Man's Woman* prior to book publication– the former especially indicating the degree to which Norris was a craftsman–make "The Mechanics of Fiction" seem more autobiographically significant than "Simplicity in Art." "The Mechanics in Fiction" also helps one to appreciate Norris's intentions in regard to the episodic structure of *McTeague* and the panel-like or framelike arrangements of parts in *The Octopus.* Moreover, the essay is also relevant to modern critics because of the emphasis Norris placed upon fine craftsmanship. His points are ones that still have current value.

Donald Pizer's arrangement of the literary essays into thematically similar groups brings a good deal of coherence to the corpus. *The Literary Criticism of Frank Norris* (1964) identifies these main concerns: how the novelist might prepare for his profession; the need for literature to embody life rather than merely imitate prior "literary" portraits of the same; the methods of literary creation; and the role of the artist in society. The topics are worthy ones; but, again, Norris seemed a newcomer to the field, lacking in objectivity and breadth of vision. In 1903, when Doubleday, Page sought to cash in on the success of *The Pit* and gathered twenty-eight pieces for *The Responsibilities of the Novelist and Other Literary Essays,* American and English reviewers panned it as derivative, contradictory, and sophomoric.

When appendicitis struck in October 1902, Norris was a successful novelist and had been invited a few weeks before to give a reading at Berkeley, honored at the university he had attended but from which he never received a diploma. At thirty-two he had risen to the prominent position of one addressing a national audience on literary matters through the *Critic.* Having moved to 1921 Broderick Street in San Francisco in July 1902, after he had finished writing *The Pit,* he was financially secure and was enjoying a stable marriage. He delighted in his daughter, born in February 1902; and it seems that he planned to proceed with his career at a less hectic clip. For instance, he canceled a planned trip around the world during which he was to gather data for

"The Wolf." Friends related after his death that his new ambition was to settle down for good in the part of the country he loved and among the people whose friendship he cherished. According to Franklin Walker, Norris was thumping his chest as he announced to his friends, "*Maintenant je suis bon bourgeois, moi-père de famille!*" The enfant terrible who shocked the reviewers with a vengeance in *McTeague* was no more. Norris had become a vested member of the establishment.

Norris planned to build a country home in Gilroy, California. With "The Wolf " completed, he would write short stories set in that locale and begin a second trilogy dealing with the Battle of Gettysburg. As a literary critic he did not make any astounding contributions. As a short-story writer he rarely rose above the rank of adequate in his later years. But, as a novelist who finished seven novels before his death, he made a distinctive mark, and as a thinker increasingly interested in individual and social psychology, he offered some truly unique insights, graphic delineations, and–true to his Victorian background– relevant "morals" grounded in the realities of human behavior.

Letters:

Frank Norris: Collected Letters, edited by Jesse S. Crisler (San Francisco: Book Club of California, 1986).
  Presents all of the known letters by Norris as well as inscriptions in books he gave to friends, along with full explanatory notes which include much new biographical information.

Bibliographies:

Kenneth A. Lohf and Eugene P. Sheehy, *Frank Norris: A Bibliography* (Los Gatos, Cal.: Talisman Press, 1959).
  A description of Norris's book publications and listing of his newspaper and magazine publications.

Joseph Katz, "The Shorter Publications of Frank Norris: A Checklist," *Proof,* 3 (1973): 155-220.
  Focuses on Norris's shorter works and supplements the earlier work of Lohf and Sheehy.

Jesse S. Crisler and Joseph R. McElrath, Jr., *Frank Norris: A Reference Guide* (Boston: G. K. Hall, 1974).

A chronologically arranged checklist of writings about Frank Norris, supplemented by the "Current Publications" features in each issue of the journal *Frank Norris Studies*.

William B. Dillingham, "Frank Norris," in *Fifteen American Authors Before 1900*, revised edition, edited by Robert A. Rees and Earl N. Harbert (Madison: University of Wisconsin Press, 1984), pp. 402-438.
Presents an overview and evaluation of scholarship on Norris.

Biography:
Franklin Walker, *Frank Norris: A Biography* (Garden City: Doubleday, Doran, 1932).
The only biography of Norris published in book form.

References:
Lars Ahnebrink, *The Influence of Emile Zola on Frank Norris* (Uppsala, Sweden: A. B. Lundequistska Bokhandeln, 1947).
Observes many instances in which Norris appears to have been influenced directly by the French novelist who was "The Father of Naturalism."

Richard Allan Davison, ed., *The Merrill Studies in The Octopus* (Columbus, Ohio: Merrill, 1969).
Reprints noteworthy articles on and reviews of *The Octopus*.

William B. Dillingham, *Frank Norris: Instinct and Art* (Lincoln: University of Nebraska Press, 1969).
Analysis of Norris's writings emphasizing the anti-intellectual character of Norris's thought and his emphasis upon the centrality of instinct in human behavior.

Warren French, *Frank Norris* (New York: Twayne, 1962).
A biographical and critical study emphasizing Norris's debt to both American romantic thinkers and to late-nineteenth-century evolutionary theorists dealing with various aspects of the "survival of the fittest" ideology.

W. M. Frohock, *Frank Norris*, University of Minnesota Pamphlets on American Writers, no. 68 (Minneapolis: University of Minnesota Press, 1969).
A critical analysis and evaluation of Norris's writings emphasizing his debt to Emile Zola.

Don Graham, *The Fiction of Frank Norris: The Aesthetic Context* (Columbia: University of Missouri Press, 1978).
A revisionist interpretation of Norris's career focusing upon the artful way in which he developed his major themes and characterizations via a significant use of cultural allusions.

Graham, ed., *Critical Essays on Frank Norris* (Boston: G. K. Hall, 1980).
A collection of reviews of Norris's works and a representative selection of the most significant articles and sections of books on Norris.

Ernest Marchand, *Frank Norris: A Study* (Stanford, Cal.: Stanford University Press, 1942).
The first book-length interpretation of Norris's writings, which explains the major themes that he developed and particularly those having to do with philosophical naturalism and the need for social and economic reform in America.

Joseph R. McElrath, Jr., and Katherine Knight, eds., *Frank Norris: The Critical Reception* (New York: Burt Franklin, 1981).
Presents reviews of Norris's book publications.

Donald Pizer, *The Novels of Frank Norris* (Bloomington: Indiana University Press, 1966).
Interprets Norris's novels as shaped in their themes and characterizations by the thought of Berkeley evolutionary thinker Prof. Joseph LeConte.

Papers:
The Frank Norris Collection at the Bancroft Library, University of California at Berkeley, contains the largest collection of letters and manuscripts, as well as Franklin Walker's notes for *Frank Norris: A Biography*. The Barrett Collection of the Alderman Library, University of Virginia, also contains manuscript material.

William Sydney Porter
(O. Henry)

This entry was updated by Eugene Current-Garcia (Auburn University) from his entry in DLB 12, American Realists and Naturalists.

Places	Greensboro, N. C.
	New Orleans
	Columbus, Ohio, Federal
	  Penitentiary
		Texas-Mexican Border
		Central America
		New York City
			Austin, Houston,
			  San Antonio

Influences and Relationships	William Shakespeare Franklin P. Adams Gilman Hall Rudyard Kipling	Greek and Roman Classic Writers Edgar Allan Poe	Witter Bynner Henry Peyton Steger Guy de Maupassant

Literary Movements and Forms	Growth of Sunday
	  Newspaper Supplements
	Arabian Nights Romance
		Southwestern Frontier
		  Humor
			Local Color
			Vernacular Literature

Major Themes	Misplaced Devotion
	Alienation of Artist
	White-Black Racial
	  Attitudes in the South
		Nobility in Disguise
		Poverty and Wealth
		Initiation Through
		  Adventure
			Irony of Fate
			Unrecognized Virtue
			Wheel of Fortune

Cultural and Artistic Influences	Bohemianism
	"Old South" vs.
	  "New South"
		Broadway Glitter	Cowboys and the
			  Wild West

Social and Economic Influences	European Immigration
	Colonialism in Central
	  American "Banana
	  Republics"
		Reconstruction
		  Movement in the South
		Sweatshop Labor and
		  Tenement Housing
			Rise of Big-Business
			  Tycoons

BIRTH: Greensboro, North Carolina, 11 September 1862, to Algernon Sidney and Mary Jane Virginia Swaim Porter.

MARRIAGES: 5 July 1887 to Athol Estes Roach (deceased 25 July 1897); children: unnamed son, Margaret; 27 November 1907 to Sara Lindsay Coleman.

DEATH: New York, New York, 5 June 1910.

BOOKS: *Cabbages and Kings* (New York: McClure, Phillips, 1904; London: Hodder & Stoughton, 1916);
The Four Million (New York: McClure, Phillips, 1906; London: Nash, 1916);
The Trimmed Lamp (New York: McClure, Phillips, 1907; London: Hodder & Stoughton, 1916);
Heart of the West (New York: McClure, 1907; London: Nash, 1916);
The Voice of the City (New York: McClure, 1908; London: Nash, 1916);
The Gentle Grafter (New York: McClure, 1908; London: Nash, 1916);
Roads of Destiny (New York: Doubleday, Page, 1909; London: Nash, 1916);
Options (New York & London: Harper, 1909; London: Nash, 1916);
Strictly Business (New York: Doubleday, Page, 1910; London: Nash, 1916);
Whirligigs (New York: Doubleday, Page, 1910; London: Hodder & Stoughton, 1916);
Sixes and Sevens (Garden City: Doubleday, Page, 1911; London: Hodder & Stoughton, 1916);
Rolling Stones (Garden City: Doubleday, Page, 1912; London: Nash, 1916);
Waifs and Strays (Garden City: Doubleday, Page, 1917; London: Hodder & Stoughton, 1920);
O. Henryana (Garden City: Doubleday, Page, 1920);
Postscripts, edited by Florence Stratton (New York & London: Harper, 1923);
O. Henry Encore, edited by Mary S. Harrell (Dallas: Upshaw, 1936; New York: Doubleday, Doran, 1939; London: Hodder & Stoughton, 1939).
Collections: *The Complete Writings of O. Henry*, 14 volumes (Garden City: Doubleday, Page, 1917);
The Biographical Edition, 18 volumes (Garden City: Doubleday, Doran, 1929);
The Complete Works of O. Henry, 2 volumes (Garden City: Doubleday, 1953).

When William Sydney Porter had his first book, *Cabbages and Kings* (1904), published he had only six more years to live. But, with his identity hidden beneath the legendary pen name O. Henry, the fame of his short stories was already firmly established in New York. By then he had written and published in several magazines at least half of the nearly three hundred stories that would fill eight more volumes before he died– and still another seven published within the two decades after his death. These collections of stories, however, were only a prelude to the avalanche of later editions, authorized and pirated, that would bring his works, in English and translated into dozens of foreign languages, to readers throughout the world as well as in the United States and other English-speaking countries. Since this process of dissemination is still going on, there is no way of estimating how many separate editions, let alone copies, of O. Henry's tales have been printed and distributed to date, but they have probably brought O. Henry's appealing image of America, however outdated, to tens of millions of foreigners. Yet, paradoxically, despite the worldwide popularity that O. Henry's writings still enjoy, the experiences and reputation of their author, William Sydney Porter, remain shrouded in pathos and mystery. Porter's life was fraught with pain, grief, and humiliation– ironic opposites to that joyous response to life's hardships which typifies so many of O. Henry's surprise endings. It can be argued, indeed, that O. Henry's enchanting fictive world offered a welcome refuge from Porter's unhappy life. Yet the psychic wounds of his childhood and his adult follies enriched his fiction.

Born in 1862, the second son of Dr. Algernon Sidney and Mary Jane Virginia Swaim Porter, Will (as he was known to everyone) spent the first twenty years of his life in Greensboro, North Carolina. Shortly after the birth of a third son in 1865 his mother died, and with her death his father's world collapsed. Dr. Porter gave up his home, moved to his widowed mother's house, and gradually abandoned his practice. The discipline of his two sons, Shirley and Will (the youngest, David, had died in infancy), was taken over by his mother and his maiden sister Evelina. "Miss Lina" was a forceful disciplinarian who served not only as Will's surrogate mother for the next seventeen years but also as the best teacher he ever had.

In the private primary school that Miss Lina kept as one means of providing the family in-

William Sydney Porter

come, young Will learned respect for the written word. She inculcated in her young charges a love of learning by making them active participants in the learning process: among the devices she employed was that of beginning an original story herself and then calling upon each of her pupils in turn to contribute a part. And regularly throughout the school year she read to them, guiding and stimulating their minds through the example of good literature. Without question, her enthusiasm and discipline were the primary forces that aroused Porter's youthful passion for reading and his later desire to write.

Porter left his aunt's school at age seventeen to work in his uncle William Clarkson Porter's drugstore, where he found an educational resource second only to that of Miss Lina. During his three years as a pharmacist's apprentice, Porter mastered pharmaceutical techniques sufficiently to earn a state license as a practicing pharmacist in 1881. But most important for his future career as a writer, during these drugstore years he was meeting people and storing up countless impressions of their personal oddities, man-

nerisms, gestures, and modes of speech which were later to be reflected, along with his expert use of professional terminology, in many of his stories, notably such well-known tales as "Let Me Feel Your Pulse," "At Arms With Morpheus," "A Ramble in Aphasia," and "The Love-Philtre of Ikey Schoenstein."

In 1882 Porter left Greensboro and went to Texas, where he spent the next fifteen years, first on a cattle ranch near the Mexican border; then he served briefly as a bookkeeper and drug clerk in Austin. Here he gained the reputation among his acquaintances as a voracious reader and it was rumored that, for lack of other reading matter, he read Noah Webster's Unabridged Dictionary, pages at a time. Following his marriage to nineteen-year-old Athol Estes Roach on 5 July 1887, he worked as a draftsman in the Texas Land Office for four years. Porter's years in the land office were probably his happiest, for his wife was a young woman of wit and high spirits, who is said to have stimulated and encouraged him in his ambition to become a writer and who shared his joys on receiving the first small checks

Porter in his teller's cage at the First National Bank of Austin, from which he embezzled funds to subsidize his humorous weekly, the Rolling Stone

his published skits occasionally brought in. But Athol Porter was not physically strong: her first child, a son born in 1888, lived but a few hours; and she herself survived the birth of her second child, Margaret, in 1889 by only seven years of steadily declining health. Soon after Porter's job at the land office folded in January 1891, he went to work as teller in the First National Bank.

While Porter worked as a bank teller he continued writing skits and short sketches, and in March 1894 he fulfilled a long-felt aim to publish them in his own humor paper by buying a cheap printing press and the rights to a local scandal sheet, the *Iconoclast*. Porter renamed the paper the *Rolling Stone*, changed it from a monthly to a weekly, and, while holding down a full-time job, managed to fill its eight pages each week with humorous squibs and satirical barbs on persons and events of local interest, most of them written, even set in type, by himself. Though never a commercial success, the *Rolling Stone* survived a full year, attaining a peak circulation of fifteen hundred but as Porter worked tirelessly to keep it rolling, the little paper gradually dragged him deeper into debt. Striving to shore up its sagging prospects, he borrowed heavily

from his father-in-law and other friends; sometime during the year he also began taking funds he needed from the bank and altering his accounts with the hope that he could readjust them later upon replacing the money. When the shortages were discovered, Porter was obliged to give up his job in December 1894 and ordered to appear before a grand jury the following July on charges of embezzlement.

While awaiting trial Porter still tried futilely to keep the *Rolling Stone* alive, but the last issue of the humor sheet appeared on 30 March 1895 and was soon forgotten until O. Henry's fame a few decades later made it a collector's item. In this ephemeral little paper are to be found the origins of his later themes, plots, methods, and style. Porter continued developing these talents later in 1895 when, the grand jury having apparently closed the case in his favor, he took a job as a fill-in writer for the *Houston Post* and soon began running a daily feature column, "Some Postscripts," which resembled the kind of anecdotal humor he had written for the *Rolling Stone*. For the *Post* he also wrote longer sketches, many of them embryonic foreshadowings of his later, more famous stories. In the nearly sixty pieces identified as Porter's work, his facility for ringing changes on the familiar O. Henry themes of mistaken identity, false pretense, misplaced devotion, nobility in disguise, and the bitter irony of fate are plainly visible, along with such sentimental character types as the sensitive tramp, the ill-starred lovers, the starving artist, and the gentle grafter. Both the basic structure and tone of his stories, as well as the attitudes responsible for them, were being shaped in the *Post* sketches.

In February 1896 the embezzlement case was reopened. He was arrested in Houston and obliged to face trial within six months. Despite the goodwill and support of his friends in both Houston and Austin, he prepared no defense but instead fled the country, pausing first for a few weeks in New Orleans and then sailing to Honduras, where he remained for the rest of the year. His experiences in Honduras, like his others elsewhere, are veiled in legend and myth, the most romantic versions of which are presented in his own stories. Nearly thirty of these stories, written later, appeared in various popular magazines. It was at the suggestion of Witter Bynner, then employed by McClure's as a first reader, that about twenty of them were reworked and tied together loosely, to be published in 1904 as his first book, *Cabbages and Kings*. As a record of

Athol, Margaret, and William Porter, circa 1895

what actually happened to Porter they are wholly unreliable; but one of their special artistic merits, shared by most of his other stories as well, is their high concentration of realistic detail, captured chiefly in descriptive and dialogue passages. It is possible that Porter planned to remain in Honduras indefinitely and hoped to bring his wife and child to live with him, at least until the statute of limitations might dispel his troubles at home. But he had to acknowledge the hopelessness of this plan when news that Athol Porter was dying obliged him to return in January 1897 and to face trial.

Ironically, it was also the year that first brought Porter a foretaste of the national fame to come when in December the McClure company accepted his story "The Miracle of Lava Canyon"; but Athol would not live to know of this good fortune. She died on 25 July 1897. In February 1898 Porter was convicted of embezzling over $5,500 and of having attempted through flight to evade prosecution. He was given the lightest sentence possible under the prevailing terms of the law—a term of five years, which his good behavior as Prisoner Number 30664 in the Ohio Penitentiary at Columbus would reduce to three.

Humiliated by his imprisonment, Porter kept up an elaborate pretense in a long series of

charming letters to young Margaret Porter (who was never told the real reason for his absence), and he also produced fourteen tales that bear the unmistakable stamp of the O. Henry style. While there are various versions of how and when Porter took his famous pen name, "O. Henry" was born during Porter's three-year stretch in prison. Besides the fourteen stories written and published in periodicals during this period (beginning with "Georgia's Ruling" in 1900), many others published later grew out of anecdotes and yarns Porter heard from his fellow prisoners. The Jeff Peters stories in *The Gentle Grafter* (1908), as well as many others involving the exploits of Texas outlaws and Mexican bandits in *Heart of the West* (1907), *Roads of Destiny* (1909), *Options* (1909), and still other volumes, came from the same sources. The most famous of them was "A Retrieved Reformation," the tale of a light-fingered safecracker, Jimmy Valentine, first published in *Cosmopolitan* in April 1903. The story was dramatized with phenomenal success in 1910 at Wallack's Theatre in New York with Norman Hackett playing the lead. Hackett later took the play on the road; eventually *Alias Jimmy Valentine* appeared in many motion-picture versions.

Porter entered the Ohio Penitentiary an amateur, but thanks to dedicated effort he emerged three years later as O. Henry, the professional literary artist. When he left the prison he had but nine more years to live, years that would be packed with personal triumphs, bringing him to the pinnacle of success as the self-anointed "Caliph of Bagdad-on-the-Subway." Yet, they were also to be years of suffering, loneliness, want, and guilt-ridden fear, as he tried vainly to elude the shadow of his past and to meet, through writing, his insatiable need for money to provide an expensive private education for Margaret Porter and to support a second, unsatisfactory marriage, hastily undertaken in 1907; as well as to satisfy his spendthrift indulgence in easy living, lavish gratuities, gambling, and alcohol.

After a brief hitch in Pittsburgh, during which he published nearly a dozen stories in such popular magazines as *Ainslee's*, *Munsey's*, and *Smart Set*, Porter went to New York in the spring of 1902. Quickly becoming an anonymous habitué of hole-in-corner hangouts and garish restaurants, he secluded himself in out-of-the-way hotels and prowled endlessly through New York streets to savor the varied color and texture of the city's life; but, fortified by his two-bottle average daily intake of alcohol, he also turned out the many stories (often six or more appeared simultaneously in different magazines) that soon made everyone wonder who O. Henry was. Porter's background had provided him a great variety of colorful types and adventures which, along with many new ones, he now swiftly transformed into the even more beguiling exploits of a multitude of fictive characters in O. Henry's glittering tales. The range of Porter's experience, from the provincial limitations of boyhood in an embittered Reconstruction South to ultimate triumph in New York, seemed limitless as more and still more of O. Henry's stories appeared in print—113 of them in the weekly *New York Sunday World* alone between 1903 and 1905, and at least 25 longer ones published during the same period in monthly magazines such as *Everybody's*, *McClure's*, and *Munsey's*.

Appropriately enough, Porter's fame—as O. Henry—is most widely associated with his tales of New York's "four million," roughly the population of the metropolis in 1906, and shrewdly chosen as the title of his second collection of tales in response to Ward McAllister's claim in 1892 that "there are only about 400 people in New York society." Porter's assertion that four million New Yorkers were well worth noticing in print touched a democratic chord that appealed to people everywhere. During his residence in New York he produced more than 140 stories (virtually half his total output), based on the appearance and behavior of the throngs he observed daily in shops and offices, restaurants and theaters, on street corners, park benches, and tenement fire escapes. He could select two or three individuals who had caught his fancy, invent imaginary situations and predicaments for them, and work out ingeniously unexpected solutions for their problems which rarely failed to satisfy his grateful readers. New York challenged the adventurous author to record its true voice and to penetrate its mystery and also to show others that real worth and beauty were to be found even beneath Coney Island's spangled temples, since they too "offered saving and apposite balm and satisfaction to the restless human heart." O. Henry eagerly accepted the challenge and thus captured the essence of New York in story after story, quintessentially in such a pair of perennial favorites as "The Gift of the Magi" and "The Furnished Room," representing the polar opposites of joy and sadness with which his imagination clothed the domestic life of average New Yorkers.

When *The Four Million* appeared in 1906, Por-

Sara Lindsay Coleman, who became Porter's second wife in 1907

ter's fame was assured; besides strong public acceptance, this collection of twenty-five stories also received some favorable notice from serious critics in the *Atlantic Monthly* and the *Bookman*, who began comparing O. Henry to Guy de Maupassant and other eminent writers. Porter could be sure that further volumes of his stories would be noticed, and these, indeed, appeared fairly regularly during his remaining years and after his death. In 1907 and 1908 *The Trimmed Lamp* and *The Voice Of The City* brought to seventy-five his total of New York stories in book form. Also published during these same years were *Heart of the West* and *The Gentle Grafter*, containing the tales based on Porter's experiences in Texas and in prison. In 1909 two volumes of stories with various settings, *Roads of Destiny* and *Options*, appeared, and another, *Strictly Business*—containing twenty-two more New York stories plus "A Municipal Report"—was published in 1910 shortly before Porter's death. More collections were published after his death.

Toward the end of 1907, however, though Porter's stories were in great demand, he was on the verge of a breakdown. Only 11 new stories were published in 1907 compared with 19 in 1906 and 120 in the two years before that. Since his need for money was greater than ever following his marriage to Sara Lindsay Coleman, he drove himself remorselessly, producing 29 new stories in 1908 for an income of about $14,000; but the income was insufficient for his lavish lifestyle. The strains and tensions in his marriage deepened as his health and energies declined. During this period he devoted much of his energy to working with Franklin P. Adams on lyrics for a musical comedy based on his story "To Him Who Waits." The production, entitled *Lo!*, opened in August 1909 but was abandoned as a failure by the following December. As well, it was in the summer of 1909 that all attempts to maintain a normal family life were abandoned, and, his health shattered, Porter could no longer summon enough energy in a week to finish a short story which, a few years before, he could have written in several hours. Virtually an invalid during the spring of 1910, he kept on trying to write until he collapsed on 3 June and was taken to the Polyclinic Hospital, where he succumbed two days later to cirrhosis of the liver. Owing thousands of dollars advanced to him by his father-in-law and his publishers, he died a pauper.

The "O. Henry Story," as it came in time to be recognized and admired, owed much of its popular appeal to Porter's sophisticated updating of two types of short fiction which had flourished in magazines and newspapers during the decades immediately preceding and following the Civil War: namely, the boisterous tall tale of the Old Southwest frontier, and the more sentimental, romantic adventure story of the postwar local-color movement. During his long apprenticeship in Texas, Porter taught himself how to combine the most attractive features of both types by imitating and writing parodies or burlesques of other well-known writers' works and by turning his own personal encounters into farfetched legends. Experimenting with techniques and developing an individual style, he worked over in these sketches familiar old chestnuts like the disguise or imposter motif, and he presented such motifs in conjunction with the theme of disparity between rich and poor and the idea that destiny or fate imposes inescapable roles on the individual.

This sense of determinism is treated, both seriously and comically, in many of his early pieces.

During Porter's three years in prison and the next two while getting his bearings in Pittsburgh and New York, he wrote about half of his eighty Western stories (excluding those published earlier in the *Houston Post* and *Rolling Stone*) that he produced throughout his career. Some two-thirds of the total number are settings in Texas and Latin America, but virtually all of them reflect the conventional images associated with the "wild West." Despite realistic, specific details, the colorful characters presented in these stories are invariably romanticized: their actions are governed by a few basic passions–love, hate, fear, greed–as befitting a simplistic dichotomy of "good guys" and "bad guys." The prevailing situation in most of them is a variant of the boy-meets-girl problem, involving either rivalry between two men for the possession of a woman, or barriers between a man and a woman which, until removed by an unforeseen turn of events near the end, prevent a satisfactory resolution of the problem. Other situations concern the reformation or rehabilitation of criminals, or the opposing forces of crime and authority. O. Henry became increasingly skilled in setting up tightly knit plots with breathless tensions relieved in last-minute, quick reversals.

In his Western stories O. Henry brilliantly shifted and rearranged pieces of his "cops-and-robbers" pattern, sometimes humorously, as in "A Call Loan" and "Friends in San Rosario," both of which dramatize the lax banking laws that victimized Porter himself by showing how they could be circumvented through the collusion of friendly bankers. And sometimes the pattern could be brutal, as in "The Caballero's Way," which combines the revenge and infidelity motifs in a gruesome plot involving the deadly Cisco Kid, O. Henry's most attractive villain, who "killed for the love of it–because he was quick-tempered–to avoid arrest–for his own amusement–any reason that came to his mind would suffice." The Cisco Kid must avenge the insult his honor has suffered from his mistress, Tonia Perez, who has conspired to turn him in to her new lover, Sandridge, the Texas Ranger who has been pursuing him, but his method of paying off her unfaithfulness is the "caballero's way" of tricking Sandridge into performing the dirty work instead. Coldly narrated, and almost totally free of sticky sentimentality, "The Caballero's Way" is a brilliant performance. Despite the liberal doses of "Western corn" in most of these tales, the plotting in them is often admirable, even more impressive because O. Henry repeatedly reworks hackneyed situations based on primitive forms of conflict and adventure.

The basic themes dramatized in all his later stories are fundamentally the same as those underlying the earlier ones. The four themes that recur most often have to do with pretense and reversal of fortune, discovery and initiation through adventure, the city as playground for the imagination, and the basic yearning of all humanity. The theme of pretense–the desire to pose as what one is not, if only for a few brief moments, and regardless of the price exacted–is the most persistent in nearly all O. Henry's stories from the earliest to the last few he left unfinished at his death. Yet in his later stories, O. Henry occasionally managed to tie it in brilliantly with the other three themes, as in his subtle response in "The Duel" to the implications of the city's glowing lights seen at midnight from a hotel window high above: "There arose the breath of gaiety unrestrained, of love, of hate, of all the passions that man can know. There below him lay all things, good or bad, that can be brought from the four corners of the earth to instruct, please, thrill, enrich, despoil, elevate, cast down, nurture, or kill. Thus the flavor of it came to him and went into his blood."

Within the decade after his death O. Henry's popularity had soared to unprecedented heights, and even scholarly critics such as Carl Van Doren, Archibald Henderson, and Hyder Rollins were praising him as one of the great masters of modern English literature. His writings became the norm against which other short stories were judged. Thanks to such mounting praise, his name was the inevitable choice when in 1919 Doubleday began publishing a selection of the year's best stories by American writers in American periodicals. To have a story published in *O. Henry Memorial Award Prize Stories* symbolized preeminence in the field, because his work stood– for the time being at least–as the highest standard of what the short story was meant to be.

By the mid 1920s, however, the O. Henry vogue began to wane as critics such as F. L. Pattee and N. Bryllion Fagin denounced the superficiality and falseness in his stories and his failure, as they saw it, to take himself and his art seriously. They felt, and subsequent generations of critics have agreed, that O. Henry's brilliant technical skills were misapplied. Overall in his

work, Fagin wrote, "there is the unmistakable charm of the master trickster, of a facile player with incidents and words," but while O. Henry has been ignored by academics, his stories are still read.

What contemporary critics tend to ignore is that O. Henry's techniques in isolated instances are less important than his technique as a whole; his individual imperfections and inadequacies are less significant than his pervasive literary personality. Moreover, his individual techniques, however limited and tricksterish, turn out to be quite impressive; carefully examined, they reveal a subtle artistry that Poe himself would have admired. The element of surprise or wonder that lies at the core of O. Henry's art, the motivating power instilled in virtually all his tricky endings even when shamelessly based on sheer coincidence, is more than just facile legerdemain. More often than not the surprise endings are logically contrived within the framework of the narrative. While the extraordinary compression of O. Henry's dialogue and descriptive details often trips the unwary reader into making wrong assumptions, his wit and verbal trickery, his fondness for puns, word coinages, sophistries, slang, and malapropisms of all sorts, appropriately sprinkled in the speech of all his romanticized types–even the dregs of humanity–make the characters seem authentic, funny, and important at the same time. Like Shakespeare and Sheridan, he enjoyed tampering with standard idioms, and his familiarity with their works, as well as with the ancient classics, is evidenced in the hundreds of sly allusions to them casually dropped into his stories.

O. Henry's typically romantic approach to life willfully chooses to ignore many sordid facts, yet there is something indestructibly appealing in the romanticist's creed which the world cherishes and clings to, and that is what explains O. Henry's hold on the world's reading public. The reader knows very well that things do not work out in real life as they do in O. Henry's stories, but often he would like to believe they might. Porter knew that too; he expressed it best, ironically, with a tribute to Milton's *Lycidas* in "Let Me Feel Your Pulse," the last story he completed before he died. Based on Porter's own search for relief during his final months, the story recounts the narrator's ordeals as physicians thumped and probed and prescribed medications for him to no avail, until at length in the Blue Ridge Mountains of North Carolina he learned of a magic flowering plant, amaryllis, as a possible cure for all human ills. Almost imperceptibly O. Henry has shifted the focus of his tale into the realm of allegory and fantasy, ending it with a question that delicately implies the essence of all that he had learned about himself and the world, and about his relationship to the world as an artist: "What rest more remedial than to sit with Amaryllis in the shade, and, with a sixth sense, read the wordless Theocritan idyll . . . ?" The question subtly reminds the attentive reader that in the next few lines following that familiar allusion the poem speaks of hard-won fame and invokes a grim image of "blind Fury [who comes] and slits the thin-spun life." Death was much on O. Henry's mind at this point; yet with impeccable artistry he fused comedy and pathos in this story to show how well he understood–and endorsed–Milton's caveat to the artist, not to expect his meed of fame in the world of his contemporaries, but in Heaven as "all-judging Jove" decrees.

The ups and downs of Porter's fame since his death nearly eighty years ago support the wisdom of Milton's judgment. Although absurdly overpraised by critics and reviewers at first and just as thoughtlessly repudiated by them later, O. Henry's stories maintained a respectable place among the reading public, growing in popularity as new editions of them were translated into nearly a hundred foreign languages. The pen name O. Henry thus became a byword both at home and in faraway places, and gradually a more evenly balanced assessment of his achievement has come about. He can now be seen, for example, as a true regionalist whose inherent good humor and fine-tuned ear enabled him to capture and record with uncanny accuracy the imagery, tones, and speech rhythms of American men and women on many social levels.

O. Henry's lasting and wide appeal was demonstrated by the citizens of Greensboro in April 1985, when a group of them gathered to pay homage to the memory of their native son. They came to witness an impressive ceremony: to hear and see spoken plaudits at the unveiling of a life-sized bronze statue erected in his honor in the heart of the city's commercial center. It was a ceremony carefully planned to initiate a week-long O. Henry Festival. Surely, if the ghost of Will Porter's alter ego hovered nearby on this seventy-fifth anniversary of his demise, he must have relished the occasion.

Letters:
Letters to Lithopolis, from O. Henry to Mabel Wagnalls

(Garden City: Doubleday, Page, 1922).
Examines O. Henry's correspondence with Mabel Wagnalls.

Clarence Ghodes, "Some Letters by O. Henry," *South Atlantic Quarterly*, 38 (January 1939): 31-39.
A group of nine letters, previously unpublished, throwing significant light on O. Henry's predicament shortly before his death.

Bibliographies:
Paul S. Clarkson, *A Bibliography of William Sydney Porter* (Caldwell, Idaho: Caxton, 1938).
Though incomplete, this was the most exhaustive listing of works by and about O. Henry up to the 1960s; hence an invaluable aid to the student.

Richard C. Harris, *William Sydney Porter (O. Henry): A Reference Guide* (Boston: G. K. Hall, 1980).
Invaluable chronological listing of titles and sources of all important books and articles on O. Henry's life and works.

Biographies:
C. F. Richardson, "O. Henry and New Orleans," *The Bookman*, 39 (May 1914): 281-287.
Useful biographical data concerning O. Henry's brief sojourn in New Orleans and his use of that city as background in some of his stories.

C. Alphonso Smith, *O. Henry Biography* (New York: Doubleday, Page, 1916).
The first full-length, authorized biographical treatment of Porter and, although outdated by subsequent findings, still an authoritative source.

Sara Lindsay Coleman, *Wind of Destiny* (New York: Doubleday, Page, 1916).
A fictionalized treatment of O. Henry's second courtship and marriage, written by his wife.

Al Jennings, *Through the Shadows With O. Henry* (London: Duckworth, 1923).
A colorful but not wholly trustworthy account of O. Henry's Latin-American and prison experiences.

Frances G. Maltby, *The Dimity Sweetheart* (Rich-

mond, Va.: Dietz Printing Company, 1930).
Contains intimate biographical data about
both Athol Estes and William Porter.

Robert H. Davis and Arthur B. Maurice, *The Caliph of Bagdad* (New York: Appleton, 1931).
An engaging but unscholarly memoir based
on personal recollections.

William Wash Williams, *The Quiet Lodger of Irving
Place* (New York: Dutton, 1936).
An informal portrait of Porter in New York,
based on personal recollections of an intimate friendship.

J. A. Lomax, "Henry Steger and O. Henry," *Southwest Review*, 24 (April 1939): 299-316.
Chatty reminiscences of Steger's anecdotes
about his relations with O. Henry.

Trueman O'Quinn, "O. Henry in Austin," *South-
western Historical Quarterly*, 43 (October
1939): 143-157.
An impartial discussion of Porter's activities
in Austin prior to and during his trial.

E. Hudson Long, *O. Henry, The Man And His
Work* (Philadelphia: University of Pennsylvania Press, 1949).
Competent scholarly dissertation, but largely superseded by Langford's 1957 biography.

Gerald Langford, *Alias O. Henry: A Biography of
William Sydney Porter* (New York: Macmillan,
1957).
The most carefully documented and, on controversial matters, the most evenly balanced
treatment of Porter's life as a whole available to date.

Ethel Stephens Arnett, *O. Henry from Polecat Creek*
(Greensboro, N.C.: Piedmont Press, 1962).
Contains previously undisclosed facts about
Porter's birthplace and childhood envi-
ronment.

Eugene Current-Garcia, *O. Henry* (New York:
Twayne, 1965).
Updated biographical and critical full-
length study of O. Henry's life and works
based on most recent trustworthy scholarship at that date.

Richard O'Connor, *O. Henry: The Legendary Life
of William S. Porter* (Garden City: Doubleday,
1970).
Conventional biographical treatment which
adds nothing significant to earlier scholarly
biographies.

References:
Deming Brown, "O. Henry in Russia," *Russian Review*, 12 (October 1953): 253-258.
An exploration of the reception of O. Henry's short stories in Russia.

Brown, *Soviet Attitudes Toward American Writing*
(Princeton, N.J.: Princeton University Press,
1962), pp. 230-238.
Excellent summary and interpretation of
O. Henry's popularity in Russia during the
preceding forty years, both among literary
critics and general readers.

Paul S. Clarkson, "A Decomposition of Cabbages
and Kings," *American Literature*, 7 (May
1935): 195-202.
An important scholarly analysis showing
how original stories were cut and spliced together to produce O. Henry's first book.

L. W. Courtney, "O. Henry's Case Reconsid-
ered," *American Literature*, 14 (January
1943): 361-371.
First scholarly proof that Porter received a
fair trial and was unquestionably guilty of
embezzlement.

Edward C. Echols, "O. Henry and the Classics–
II," *Classical Journal*, 44 (October 19-May
1949): 209-210.
A continuation of Echols's exploration of
the mythological bases in O. Henry's work.

Echols, "O. Henry's 'Shaker of Attic Salt,'" *Classical Journal*, 43 (October 1947-May 1948):
488-489.
Concise demonstration of O. Henry's broad
knowledge and use of standard Greek and
Roman myths in his stories.

B. M. Ejxenbaum, *O. Henry and the Theory of the
Short Story*, translated, with notes and a post-
script, by I. R. Titunik (Ann Arbor: University of Michigan Press, 1968).
Most thorough foreign criticism of O. Henry's literary artistry, published in Russian in

1925, but not available in English translation until 1968.

N. Bryllion Fagin, *Short Story Writing: An Art or a Trade?* (New York: Seltzer, 1923), pp. 36-42.
Valuable as an example of early adverse critical reaction to O. Henry's work in the United States.

H. J. Forman, "O. Henry's Short Stories," *North American Review*, 187 (May 1908): 781-783.
Important as first serious critical recognition in America of O. Henry's artistry.

Joseph H. Gallegly, "Backgrounds and Patterns of O. Henry's Texas Bodman Stories," *Rice Institute Pamphlet*, 42 (October 1955): 1-32.
Scholarly proof that the real-life desperados were more brutal than O. Henry's fictional versions of them.

Gallegly, *From Alamo Plaza to Jack Harris's Saloon: O. Henry and the Southwest He Knew* (The Hague: Mouton, 1970).
Detailed full-length treatment of the general area and specific sites in Texas with which O. Henry was closely associated.

William B. Gates, "O. Henry and Shakespeare," *Shakespeare Association Bulletin*, 19 (January 1944): 20-25.
Traces O. Henry's familiarity with and use of well-known Shakespearian phrases in his stories.

Archibald Henderson, "O. Henry—A Contemporary Classic," *South Atlantic Quarterly*, 22 (July 1923): 270-278.
Typical example of excessive praise lavished upon O. Henry by critics of the 1920s.

F. M. Kerchville, "O. Henry and Don Alfonso: Spanish in the Work of an American Writer," *New Mexico Quarterly Review*, 1 (November 1931): 367-388.
Useful discussion of O. Henry's intimate knowledge of and fondness for using Spanish vernacular in his stories.

Stephen Leacock, "O. Henry and his Critics," *New Republic*, 9 (2 December 1916): 120-122.
Good example of heated controversy stirred up by early attacks on O. Henry's influence.

Dan McAllister, "Negligently, Perhaps; Criminally, Never," *South Atlantic Quarterly*, 51 (October 1952): 562-573.
Strong but obviously biased defense of Porter's innocence of embezzlement; intemperately brushes aside all contradictory evidence.

Gilbert Millstein, "O. Henry's New Yorkers and Today's," *New York Times Magazine*, 9 September 1962, pp. 36-38, 132-138.
Lucid, informative comparison of similarities and differences between typical New Yorkers of the early 1900s and those of the 1960s.

Raoul Narcy, "O. Henry Through French Eyes," *Littell's Living Age*, 303 (11 October 1919): 86-88.
Good example of the earliest favorable reception of O. Henry's stories among European critics.

F. L. Pattee, *The Development of the American Short Story* (New York & London: Harper, 1923), pp. 357-376.
Biased, but vigorously expressed argument that O. Henry's lack of seriousness and his trickery have cheapened literary standards in the United States.

Pattee, "The Journalization of American Literature," *Unpopular Review*, 7 (April-June 1917): 374-394.
Some of the earliest unfavorable criticism of O. Henry's methods and techniques.

L. W. Payne, Jr., "The Humor of O. Henry," *Texas Review*, 4 (October 1918): 18-37.
Excellent early critical analysis of basic sources of O. Henry's humor and of his humorous devices.

H. T. Peck, "The American Story Teller," *The Bookman*, 31 (April 1910): 131-137.
A discriminating discussion of the strengths and limitations of O. Henry's humorous American slang.

Hyder E. Rollins, "O. Henry," *Sewanee Review*, 22 (April 1914): 213-232.
Excellent biographical and critical treatment of O. Henry and his writings, showing care

for scholarly accuracy and for impartial judgments.

William Saroyan, "O What a Man Was O. Henry," *Kenyon Review*, 24 (1967): 671-675.
A brief but charming and generous tribute from one innovative master of short fiction

writing of another who had obviously influenced him.

Papers:
Greensboro Public Library, Greensboro, North Carolina, contains the most complete collection of Porter's papers.

Edwin Arlington Robinson

This entry was updated by Robert Gilbert from the entry by Nancy Carol Joyner (Western Carolina University) in DLB 54, American Poets, 1880-1945, Third Series, Part 2.

Places	Boston MacDowell Colony, Peterborough, N.H.	Gardiner, Maine	New York City
Influences and Relationships	William Cullen Bryant Witter Bynner	Theodore Roosevelt	Alanson T. Schumann
Literary Movements and Forms	Narrative Poetry	Dramatic Monologue	

Major Themes	Material Wealth vs.
	  Spiritual Health
	Arthurian Romance
		Freedom of the
		  Individual
			Artistic Failure

Cultural and Artistic Influences	Calvinism	Opera	The Bible
Social and Economic Influences	Industrial Revolution	World War I	

BIRTH: Head Tide, Maine, 22 December 1869, to Edward and Mary Palmer Robinson.

EDUCATION: Harvard University, 1891-1893.

AWARDS AND HONORS: Pulitzer Prize for *Collected Poems*, 1922; D.Litt., Yale University, 1922; Levinson Prize (*Poetry* magazine), 1923; Pulitzer Prize for *The Man Who Died Twice*, 1925; D.Litt., Bowdoin College, 1925; Pulitzer Prize for *Tristram*, 1928; Gold Medal, National Institute and American Academy of Arts and Letters, 1929.

DEATH: New York, New York, 6 April 1935.

SELECTED BOOKS: *The Torrent and The Night Before* (Cambridge: Privately printed, 1896);
The Children of the Night (Boston: Richard G. Badger, 1897);
Captain Craig (Boston & New York: Houghton, Mifflin, 1902; London: A. P. Watt, 1902; enlarged edition, New York: Macmillan, 1915);
The Town Down the River (New York: Scribners, 1910);
Van Zorn (New York: Macmillan, 1914);
The Porcupine (New York: Macmillan, 1915);
The Man Against the Sky (New York: Macmillan, 1916);
Merlin (New York: Macmillan, 1917);
Lancelot (New York: Thomas Seltzer, 1920);
The Three Taverns (New York: Macmillan, 1920);
Avon's Harvest (New York: Macmillan, 1921);
Collected Poems (New York: Macmillan, 1921; London: Cecil Palmer, 1922);
Roman Bartholow (New York: Macmillan, 1923; London: Cecil Palmer, 1923);
The Man Who Died Twice (New York: Macmillan, 1924; London: Cecil Palmer, 1924);
Dionysus in Doubt (New York: Macmillan, 1925);
Tristram (New York: Macmillan, 1927; London: Gollancz, 1928);
Collected Poems, 5 volumes (Cambridge, Mass.: Dunster House, 1927);
Sonnets, 1889-1917 (New York: Crosby Gaige, 1928);
Fortunatus (Reno: Slide Mountain Press, 1928);
Modred (New York, New Haven & Princeton: Brick Row Bookshop, 1929);
Cavender's House (New York: Macmillan, 1929; London: Hogarth Press, 1930);
Collected Poems (New York: Macmillan, 1930);
The Glory of the Nightingales (New York: Macmillan, 1930);
Selected Poems (New York: Macmillan, 1931);

Matthias at the Door (New York: Macmillan, 1931);
Nicodemus (New York: Macmillan, 1932);
Talifer (New York: Macmillan, 1933);
Amaranth (New York: Macmillan, 1934);
King Jasper (New York: Macmillan, 1935);
Collected Poems (New York: Macmillan, 1937);
Selected Early Poems and Letters, edited by Charles T. Davis (New York: Holt, Rinehart & Winston, 1960);
Uncollected Poems and Prose, edited by Richard Cary (Waterville, Maine: Colby College Press, 1975).

One of the most prolific major American poets of the twentieth century, Edwin Arlington Robinson is, ironically, best remembered for only a handful of short poems. Aside from a few that he complained were "pickled in anthological brine"–"Richard Cory," "Miniver Cheevy," and "Mr. Flood's Party"–most of his work is not widely known. The fifteen-hundred-page collected edition of his work (1937) contains the twenty volumes of poetry published during his lifetime, including the thirteen long narratives which critics have ignored or denigrated but which he regarded as among his best work. Indeed, the long poems that occupied his energies during the last dozen years of his life were not designed for popular appeal, and his stubborn insistence on traditional forms at a time of extraordinary technical experimentation led to the critical attitude that his work is anachronistic, a throwback to the nineteenth-century triumphs of Robert Browning, Alfred Tennyson, and Matthew Arnold. Such a view and the concomitant lack of interest in his work is unfortunate, for Robinson was a true innovator within the constraints of the traditional forms; his attitude, tone, and eclectic subject matter genuinely anticipate the main thrust of twentieth-century American poetry. As Robert Frost, in his introduction to *King Jasper*, put it, Robinson was "content with the old-fashioned way to be new."

In an age when other prominent poets were engaged in many other pursuits, Robinson stood alone in his unmitigated devotion to writing poetry. T. S. Eliot with his career in publishing, William Carlos Williams with his medical practice, Wallace Stevens with his executive position in an insurance company, and Frost, seemingly the most "professional" poet, with his teaching jobs and his speaking tours–all had other interests and accomplishments. Robinson, on the other hand, did virtually nothing in his life save write po-

Photograph by Pirie MacDonald

[signature: E. A. Robinson]

something that, for him, should be recognized as the Inner Fire. For him, that is the Gleam, the Vision and the Word! He'd better follow it. The greatest adventure he'll ever have on this side is following where it leads.

The expense of Robinson's single-mindedness was virtually everything else in life for which people strive, but it eventually won for him both fortune and fame, as well as a firm position in literary history as America's first important poet of the twentieth century.

The time and place of Robinson's birth contributed both positively and negatively to that position. Born in the tiny hamlet of Head Tide, Maine, and growing up in the somewhat larger town of Gardiner, he lived in a remote corner of the nation that was nevertheless relatively close to a cultural center, Boston. Also, he had the advantage of a neighborhood that helped to cultivate his literary interests at an early age. Born in 1869, at the threshold of the gilded age, when the industrial revolution was making an irreversible impact on his surroundings, he was deeply aware of and later recorded the dichotomy of material wealth versus emotional and spiritual health as values in his society. Robinson reached his audience in 1890, that decade notorious in American literary history because of its poetic aridity. When he published his first volume in 1896, he could admire no living American poet, much less enjoy membership in a literary community.

Robinson's immediate family also helped and hindered him. Both of his parents, Edward and Mary Elizabeth Palmer Robinson, were of old New England stock, although his mother's family was the more illustrious as well as the more thoroughly traditional in that she had bona fide Puritan ancestors. It is often noted that Robinson is related on the distaff side to Anne Bradstreet, the first genuine American poet. The stronger influence in Robinson's home was his father, Edward, an eminently practical man of Scotch-Irish descent, who had a strong sense of civic responsibility and sufficient business acumen to retire from his mercantile business with a fortune of eighty thousand dollars, in 1870, at fifty-one. It was then that he moved his family from Head Tide to Gardiner, where his three sons could receive a better education. Edward Robinson had nothing against education so long as it enabled a person to improve his financial opportunities. He sent his studious eldest son, Dean, to medical school but prevented his continuing in

etry: he neither married nor traveled; he neither taught nor gave public readings; he neither had professional preparation nor any extended occupation other than the writing of poetry. On the occasion of his fiftieth birthday he was treated to an encomium in the *New York Times Book Review* (21 December 1919), which published comments by sixteen writers, including this statement from Amy Lowell: "Edwin Arlington Robinson is poetry. I can think of no other living writer who has so consistently dedicated his life to his work." Hermann Hagedorn used as the epigraph for the first and still the most valuable biography this quotation from Robinson:

> In the great shuffle of transmitted characteristics, traits, abilities, aptitudes, the man who fixes on something definite in life that he must do, at the expense of everything else, if necessary, has presumably got

medical research; he groomed his affable middle son, Herman, to take up the family business ventures, principally land speculation; and he advised his youngest, Edwin, called Win, to follow the scientific (or non-college-preparatory) track in high school, although he did send him, eventually and somewhat grudgingly, to Harvard as a special student. Although business success was Edward Robinson's chief goal, he was not without cultural interests. He often spent his evenings singing with the others around the family piano or reading excerpts from William Cullen Bryant's *Library of Poetry and Song.* It has been said that memories of childhood constitute a writer's capital. Robinson's memories are generally those of an upper-middle-class, rural, Calvinistic upbringing in which the arts were part of his home environment but secondary to an emphasis on the practical necessities of earning a living. He both represented and rebelled against that background.

Robinson's only published autobiographical account is a magazine piece, "The First Seven Years," which appeared in the December 1930 issue of *Colophon* and is now included in *Uncollected Poems and Prose* (1975). In it he pointed out his early enthusiasm for poetry and his parents' lack of awareness that that interest was developing into a serious career goal. He acknowledged the influence of his neighbor, Dr. Alanson T. Schumann, an amateur versifier who encouraged metrical exercises for Robinson during his high-school years. He reported that when he was seventeen he "became violently excited over the structure and music of English blank verse" and made several metrical translations from Cicero, Virgil, and Sophocles. He went on to say, "It must have been about the year 1889 when I realized finally . . . that I was doomed, or elected, or sentenced for life, to the writing of poetry." The seven years to which the title refers is the period between that realization and the publication of his first book in 1896. In that period he published a few poems in the local newspaper, the *Harvard Advocate,* and in two or three magazines. He also noted that he collected a pile of rejection slips "that must have been one of the largest and most comprehensive in literary history." Eventually he decided to publish his poems on his own and paid fifty-two dollars to the Riverside Press in Cambridge to print 312 copies of a forty-four-page pamphlet "named, rather arbitrarily, from the first and last poem: *The Torrent and The Night*

Before." With that pamphlet Robinson's poetic career was launched.

Ever the restrained New Englander, Robinson did not record the dismal family circumstances of those first seven years. His brother Dean was thwarted in his ambition to become a pathologist and, by dosing himself for facial neuralgia, acquired a drug habit that lost him his medical practice and led to his eventual suicide. His brother Herman met Win's putative fiancée, Emma Shepherd, and married her. Win managed to go to Harvard for two years partially because he needed medical treatment in Boston for his lifelong difficulties with one ear. His father died of a stroke in 1892. Much of the family fortune was lost during the recession of 1893. Finally, in 1896, his mother died of black diphtheria, a disease so contagious that the undertaker would not set foot in the house and her sons were required to make the burial preparations themselves. A few weeks after his mother's death Robinson received in the mail the surprise he had planned for her–the copies of his first book. He did not open the package for a day, he reported to his friend Harry Smith, and when he did the books "looked so small and devilish blue" they made him sick, but, he went on, "now I am feeling better and beginning to foster my same old ridiculous notion that they may amount to something some day." They have.

The forty-six poems in *The Torrent and The Night Before* (1896) present an impressive variety in theme, subject matter, and technique. Consistent with his future practice, all the poems are in rhymed or blank verse. (All his life Robinson strenuously objected to free verse, replying once when asked if he wrote it, "No, I write badly enough as it is.") These early poems, however, are distinguished from his later practice in that there are more examples of elaborate verse forms: villanelles and ballades appear along with the more conventional quatrains and the form of which he was to become a modern master, the sonnet. One of the sonnets is "The Clerks," the poem whose rejection by the editor of the *New York Sun* Robinson cited as the final impetus for him to publish his own book. It is in many ways representative of his early work:

> I did not think that I should find them
> there
> When I came back again; but there they
> stood,

As in the days they dreamed of when
   young blood
Was in their cheeks and women called
   them fair.
Be sure, they met me with an ancient air,–
And yes, there was a shop-worn
   brotherhood
About them; but the men were just as
   good,
And just as human as they ever were.

And you that ache so much to be sublime,
And you that feed yourselves with your
   descent,
What comes of all your visions and your
   fears?
Poets and kings are but the clerks of Time,
Tiering the same dull webs of discontent,
Clipping the same sad alnage of the years.

The deceptive simplicity of the words tends to obscure the artistry of the work, with the commonplace scene of the octet transfigured into a striking metaphor in the sestet, where the tone, subject matter, theme, diction, and technical mastery are all quintessentially Robinsonian. The combination of the realistic, narrative mode and the more romantic, expository mode is deftly indicated by the switch from first-person narration to the generalized address at the end. These two forms are not always in the same poem, but the combination of narrative and expository writing is perhaps Robinson's most characteristic trait. The undeniably gloomy "message," or theme, of the poem, couched as it is in a deliberate matter-of-fact and unpretentious tone, is also typical. The self-consciousness of the climactic line, "Poets and kings are but the clerks of Time," however, is indicative of Robinson's earliest work.

Charles T. Davis, in his introduction to *Selected Early Poems and Letters* (1960), says, "The odd fact about Robinson is that he began, in a sense, as a mature poet, almost immediately conscious of his artistic goals and aware of his own powers and weaknesses." This notion has become a critical commonplace, with some validity. His first brief character sketch of the sort that are now called his Tilbury poems is placed second in *The Torrent and The Night Before:* "Aaron Stark," the miser with "eyes like little dollars in the dark." And the name Tilbury is first mentioned in this volume in "John Evereldown," a dialogue between a man and his wife. Two of his best-known poems, "Credo" and "Luke Havergal," appear in this volume, along with several others that are highly regarded. Nevertheless, this earli-

est collection also contains poems that may legitimately be considered juvenilia, and, while it would be difficult to consider these efforts derivative, some do indicate a dependence on earlier poets that does not appear in Robinson's more mature work. In fact, more individual poems from this volume than any other were omitted from the first *Collected Poems* (1921). To say that Robinson was at the height of his powers in 1896 implies that no development occurred in the remaining forty years of his career. Such a claim is a distinct disservice to the poet and his art.

When Robinson received his packet of pamphlets in December 1896, he literally gave them away, both to local acquaintances and, more important, to editors of journals and to writers who he thought might be sympathetic to his work. Richard Cary, former curator of the Robinson collection at Colby College, included in *Early Reception of Edwin Arlington Robinson* (1974) nineteen reviews from journals which received the volume and named twenty-five other recipients–such as Robert Bridges, Thomas Hardy, and Algernon Charles Swinburne–who did not respond publicly to the book. The nineteen reviews are, if somewhat tentative, generally favorable, since editors rarely take up valuable space by panning an unsolicited, privately printed book of poems. Many of them were noncommittal notices that quoted a sample poem, but some were quite extensive, the most thorough and thoughtful one being that of William Peterfield Trent, in the April 1897 issue of the *Sewanee Review.* Trent suspected that the writer was young and noted some poems that seemed derivative, but he also offered the book "some ungrudging praise."

The most noteworthy review of *The Torrent and The Night Before* was that of Harry Thurston Peck, published in the February 1897 issue of the *Bookman.* Peck found many of the poems too somber for his liking and said that Robinson's "humour is of a grim sort, and the world is not beautiful to him, but a prison-house." In response to that comment Robinson wrote a letter of rebuttal, published in the March 1897 *Bookman,* which has become as well known a critical statement as he was ever to make: "I am sorry that I have painted myself in such lugubrious colours. The world is not a prison house, but a kind of spiritual kindergarten, where millions of bewildered infants are trying to spell God with the wrong blocks."

Certainly Robinson was anything but pessi-

Emma Shepherd Robinson, wife of the poet's brother Herman (courtesy of Edwin Arlington Robinson's Heirs)

mistic regarding his career during this period. As his letters indicate, he was buoyed by the critical success of *The Torrent and The Night Before* and had a second manuscript ready within months of his first publication. A vanity press in Boston, Richard G. Badger and Company, solicited his business and promised promotion and distribution as well as an attractive product, all advantages over the situation of the book he had printed privately. Although Robinson was unable to pay the costs of vanity publishing, he accepted the offer of his friend William Butler to do so. Using a vanity press rather than the "respectable publisher" for which he had originally looked also gave Robinson the advantage of speed. In 1897, almost exactly one year after his first book appeared, *The Children of the Night* was printed attractively in two formats, a five-hundred-copy trade edition bound in light tan cloth with a red and green art nouveau design, as well as a fifty-copy limited edition printed on vellum. The book was designed and marketed for the Christmas trade, and the strategy was successful: three hundred copies

had been sold by January.

Included in *The Children of the Night* are forty-four of the forty-six poems published the previous year as well as forty-three additional poems. The new poems are in much the same vein as the earlier ones, but there are some important additions. One has become Robinson's best-known poem, "Richard Cory," notable for its contrast between the aloofness of the eponymous character and the down-to-earth quality of the unusual narrator who speaks in the first-person plural, "We people on the pavement"; the effectiveness of the surprise ending in which the sensational event is related in understated diction; and the consistent image pattern of royalty. Also added are twenty-seven "Octaves," an eight-line, blank-verse form, usually written as one sentence, that Robinson claimed was more difficult to write than the sonnet. The octaves are somewhat somber philosophical speculations or pronouncements whose generalizations are given force by a striking image or an unusual choice of words. "Octave XVII," for example, uses a quite ordinary travel metaphor but concludes with a startling oxymoron:

> We lack the courage to be where we are:–
> We love too much to travel on old roads,
> To triumph on old fields; we love too
>   much
> To consecrate the magic mix of dead
>   things,
> And yieldingly to linger by long walls
> Of ruin, where the ruinous moonlight
> That sheds a lying glory on old stones
> Befriends us with a wizard's enmity.

Reviews of *The Children of the Night* were mixed, with some critics providing only luke-warm notices, apparently because of the vanity imprint. With a few exceptions the notices were extremely brief and in local newspapers rather than in journals with national circulations. But the prestigious Thomas Wentworth Higginson, writing for the *Nation* in June 1898, found that the poet "does his work deftly and thoroughly." Allen Tate, in an essay collected in his *On the Limits of Poetry* (1948), called this book "little noticed at the time but one which marks the beginning of a new era in American poetry."

Until 1897 Robinson lived in his childhood home in Gardiner, sharing the house, after his parents died, with his two brothers, Herman's wife, Emma, and his three nieces. According to one biographer, Chard Powers Smith, he left the house in the fall of 1897 after a dispute with Herman over Emma, a triangular situation that Smith maintains is the biographical impetus for the predominance of triangular love affairs in Robinson's poetry. In November of 1897 Robinson "discovered" New York, sharing an apartment with a friend and encountering a cosmopolitan society he had not known theretofore. One of his new acquaintances was the erudite derelict Alfred H. Louis, an English Jew with a checkered legal and literary career, a pianist, philosopher, and impromptu orator who had no visible means of support. Louis became the prototype for the title character in Robinson's long poem "Captain Craig."

The story of the difficulties attendant upon the publication of "Captain Craig" is symptomatic of Robinson's early struggle for recognition. In the spring of 1900 he wrote a friend that he had finished the work and was satisfied with it, but that he might not be so pleased after it came back from "six or seven publishers." The comment proved prophetic, for the poem was examined by five publishing houses before it was finally accepted. For three months the manuscript languished in a Boston brothel, having been left there by a reader for Small, Maynard and Company and the thoughtful lady of the house having kept it until the client returned. Robinson almost despaired of ever getting "Captain Craig" into print and wrote a group of shorter poems to be published under the title "Isaac and Archibald." Eventually, however, two of his friends, by agreeing to contribute to the publication costs of the long poem, persuaded Houghton, Mifflin to publish the volume under its imprint. In 1902 *Captain Craig*, a volume comprised of the title poem and fifteen shorter poems, finally appeared.

Originally, "Captain Craig" was just over two thousand lines long, the first of the long narratives that were to dominate his poetry in the last half of his career. In the first of the three sections of the poem, the narrator and his drinking cronies in Tilbury Town meet Captain Craig and presumably save him from starvation. A confessed failure, the captain is unable even to beg:

> There was a time
> When he had fancied, if worst came to worst
> And he could work no more, that he might beg
> Nor be the less for it; but when it came
> To practice he found out that he had not
> The genius.

He has a large capacity for conversation, however, and the narrator is fascinated. When the narrator leaves to go on a six-month trip, the captain writes him voluminous letters, which the narrator saves "for the jokes." Among the jokes are frequent classical and literary allusions, reminiscences of old acquaintances, the recounting of dreams, criticism of poetry, and comments of a vaguely philosophical sort. The third section recounts the narrator's return to Tilbury and the death of the captain, who bequeaths to his benefactors "God's universe and yours." In the funeral procession the Tilbury band "Blared indiscreetly the Dead March in Saul."

As in all of Robinson's long poems, unity in "Captain Craig" is achieved through theme rather than structure, with the personality of the captain far more significant than the action described. In his first speech to his group of admirers he makes what may be considered a thesis statement:

> "You are the resurrection and the life"
> He said, "and I the hymn the Brahmin sings;
> O Fuscus! and w'll go no more a-roving."

This quotation is a pastiche of references to the Bible, Emerson, Horace, and Byron, the juxtaposition of which creates an extraordinarily dense texture and anticipates the early work of T. S. Eliot. It is an illustration of the complexity of this fine poem.

The critics were not kind to *Captain Craig*. Praise was reserved for some of the short poems included in the volume, such as "Isaac and Archibald," "The Klondike," and "Sainte-Nitouche." "Captain Craig" was either ignored, noted as a difficult and puzzling poem, or derogated. Bliss Carman in the December 1902 *Reader* called it "worse than Browning . . . a mistake rather than a failure." And in the March 1903 *Critic* Clinton Scollard suggested that "the volume might have been vastly improved from an artistic standpoint had the author so willed it." According to the biographers, especially Emery Neff, Robinson realized that he was taking a risk in writing so experimental a poem as "Captain Craig," but when the critics did not respond as he had hoped, he was devastated.

The poor critical response to *Captain Craig* is sometimes cited as the reason for the eight-year lapse in Robinson's creative efforts, but other reasons may account for this period of diminished activity. For long periods between 1898 and 1905 he was nearly destitute, living for the most part in a tiny room in a fourth-floor, walk-up apartment house in New York. He held intermittent jobs: as office assistant at Harvard for six months in 1899, as an advertising editor in Boston for two months in 1905, and most notoriously, as time-checker for the construction of the IRT Subway in New York for nine months in 1903-1904. Also, he began to drink heavily; frequenting bars was not only a way to forget his troubles but also a way to get a free lunch, since dispensers of liquor were required by law to provide food with the drink. During this period he came perilously close to falling into permanent dissolution, as both his brothers had done. His whimsical "Miniver Cheevy," the poem about the malcontent modern who yearned for the past glories of the chivalric age and who finally "coughed, and called it fate/And kept on drinking," is presumably a comic self-portrait.

It was President Theodore Roosevelt who almost single-handedly pulled Robinson out of the gutter. In 1904 his son Kermit brought home a copy of *The Children of the Night*. Roosevelt read it, voiced his approval sufficiently for Charles Scribner's Sons to republish it in 1905, and wrote a review for the *Outlook* in which is included the statement "I am not sure I understand 'Luke Havergal'; but I am entirely sure that I like it." He also granted Robinson a sinecure in the New York Customs House, a post he held from June 1905 until Roosevelt stepped down from office in 1909.

The two thousand dollars he received annually for his non-demanding job gave Robinson financial security, but it had a debilitating effect on his writing. He published a few poems in magazines and worked on a new interest, the writing of drama, but he produced no new volume of poetry until after he had resigned his post. In 1910 he at last discharged the debt he felt he owed the former president by producing *The Town Down the River*, named for New York and dedicated to his most prestigious sponsor, Roosevelt.

The Town Down the River is a collection of thirty-three short poems, similar in form to *The Children of the Night* but differing from those in the earlier volume in the predominance of objective, psychological portraits. Some are portraits of public figures: poems to Lincoln and Roosevelt begin and end the volume, and in the middle is a lengthy dramatic monologue, "The Island," spoken by Napoleon on St. Helena. The most prominent theme in the book is one that

has come to be associated with all of Robinson's work, private failure. "Clavering," for example, is one of a group of interrelated poems having to do with a circle of friends. It begins,

> I say no more for Clavering
>   Than I should say of him who fails
> To bring his wounded vessel home
>   When reft of rudder and of sails.

"Miniver Cheevy" appears in this volume, as does the only slightly lesser-known "How Annandale Went Out," the dramatic monologue in sonnet form that deals with euthanasia and probably is based on the suicide of his brother Dean. Other themes represented in this volume are satires on the writing of poetry, "Momus" and "Shadrach O'Leary," and elegiac verse, notably "Leonora" and "For a Dead Lady," whose final stanza is surely an example of what Robinson called "unmistakable" poetry:

> The beauty, shattered by the laws
> That have creation in their keeping,
> No longer trembles in applause,
> Or over children that are sleeping;
> And we who delve in beauty's lore
> Know all that we have known before
> Of what inexorable cause
> Makes Time so vicious in his reaping.

The variety of topics and the artistic control demonstrated in this volume indicate a marked step in Robinson's poetic development.

The Town Down the River received more reviews than any of the preceding volumes. None was negative, but most were only mildly approbative. Joyce Kilmer's review-essay in the *New York Times Book Review* (8 September 1912), is important, however, because it is an overview of Robinson's work. His reputation was growing in England as well as the United States. One of the most interesting opinions was voiced in a *Boston Sunday Post* interview (2 March 1913) with British poet Alfred Noyes. When asked about current American poets, Noyes told the reporters that Robinson was the second-best poet writing in America. (Noyes's nomination for the foremost Yankee poet was somebody named Brian Hooker.)

Ever since Robinson had moved from Gardiner, he had lived in a variety of furnished rooms or made extended visits to friends. In 1911 Hermann Hagedorn persuaded him to try summering at a place where a small group of artists lived and worked, the MacDowell Colony in Peterborough, New Hampshire. In 1911 Robinson reluctantly accepted the invitation, bringing with him a telegram to show as an excuse to leave before the season was over in case he did not find the situation to his liking. The reverse was true, however; he found the place so congenial to his work that he returned to Peterborough every summer until his death, and one of his rare prose pieces is an encomium to the MacDowell Colony entitled "The Peterborough Idea."

Although Robinson had begun to acquire a reputation as a poet, he was still in need of an adequate income, and for a few years he tried his hand at fiction and drama. The fiction has not survived, but two plays, *Van Zorn* (1914) and *The Porcupine* (1915), were brought out by Macmillan after Scribners refused them. The plays were neither popular nor critical successes, but by accepting them, as well as bringing out a new edition of *Captain Craig* in 1915, Macmillan was able to publish his next volume of poetry, the one which established Robinson as a major poet.

The Man Against the Sky, published in 1916, marks the midpoint of Robinson's publishing career and is his most important single volume. Of the twenty-six poems included, fourteen had received prior magazine publication, and almost all of them are representative of Robinson's mature work. Among the most noteworthy are "Flammonde," the brief reworking of "Captain Craig" which opens the volume; "Cassandra," an attack on American capitalism; "Ben Jonson Entertains a Man from Stratford," a lengthy dramatic monologue in which Jonson reminisces about his friend Shakespeare; and the title poem, which describes a variety of ontological stances. Robinson maintained that "The Man Against the Sky" was the most succinct statement of his philosophy, but it is a somewhat unsatisfactory meditation emphasizing transcendental idealism in negative terms. (The final line of the poem, "Where all who know may drown," has frequently been misinterpreted as a straightforward statement; Robinson insisted that it was meant to be ironic.) Four of the eleven short poems which Yvor Winters called Robinson's greatest are in this volume: "Hillcrest," "Veteran Sirens," "The Poor Relation," and "Eros Turannos." Louis O. Coxe has persuasively argued that "Eros Turannos" is archetypically Robinsonian.

The immediate critical response to *The Man Against the Sky* was overwhelmingly positive. Amy Lowell's enthusiastic review for the *New Republic*

(27 May 1916) was republished as the first chapter in her *Tendencies in Modern American Poetry* (1917), the first book of criticism which included a serious discussion of Robinson. Harriet Monroe sanctified him through a strong review in *Poetry* magazine (April 1916). And William Stanley Braithwaite, long a Robinson champion, proclaimed in the *Boston Evening Transcript* (26 February 1916) that "In this man American poetry has its deepest vision, its most enduring utterance." Richard Cary has pointed out that the wide critical acceptance of Robinson after 1916 indicates a change in critical taste rather than a substantive change in Robinson's method or manner. With *The Man Against the Sky*, Robinson arrived.

One year later, in 1917, Robinson published the first of his single, book-length poems, *Merlin*, a twenty-five-hundred-line blank-verse narrative which retells that part of the Arthurian legend involving Merlin's relationship with Arthur and with Vivian. Robinson presents Merlin realistically, as a prophet without magical powers, whose personal interests are in conflict with his public responsibilities as adviser to the king. It was intended to provide a symbolic commentary on World War I.

The critics who had found *The Man Against the Sky* so appealing were dismayed by the new direction Robinson had taken. Harriet Monroe wondered in *Poetry* (July 1917) why Robinson had bothered to use so threadbare a subject as the Arthurian romances, and Odell Shepard in the *Dial* (11 October 1917) objected to the Jamesian quality of the writing. Later critics have given only faint praise to the poem.

While Robinson was preparing *Merlin* for the publishers, he was already working on its sequel, *Lancelot*. Because Macmillan had lost money on *Merlin*, it refused to publish the second Arthurian poem, necessitating the finding of a new publisher. Eventually Samuel Roth, an editor for the Thomas Seltzer Publishing Company, agreed to take it, and the book appeared under the Seltzer imprint in 1920. It was the last time Macmillan was to refuse a Robinson manuscript.

In contrast to their reactions to *Merlin*, critics applauded *Lancelot*, some insisting it was better than *Merlin*, some ignoring the earlier poem altogether. Most later critics have paid little attention to the volume, although Chard Powers Smith, who quoted *Lancelot* in the title for his critical biography of Robinson, *Where the Light Falls* (1965), claims that *Merlin* and *Lancelot* should be considered a single entity representing Robinson's most important work, both in conception and in autobiographical significance.

In 1920 Robinson also published a substantial collection of short and medium-length poems, *The Three Taverns*. Among the twenty-nine poems are sonnets and short, rhymed narratives, the most notable being "The Mill," an often-anthologized piece which conveys to the careful reader the story of a double suicide. The most distinctive quality of this collection, however, is the abundance of biblical references and subjects: the title poem is a dramatic monologue spoken by Paul just before he gets to Rome, and the concluding one, "Lazarus," is principally a blank-verse conversation among Lazarus, Mary, and Martha. Other medium-length poems such as "Tasker Norcross," a Tilbury poem, deal with fictional characters and with characters from American history, as in "John Brown," which concludes with the line that is inscribed on a plaque on Robinson's studio at the MacDowell Colony: "I shall have more to say when I am dead." Reviewers generally wrote favorable notices of *The Three Taverns*; later critics have almost entirely ignored it.

Actually, during the early 1920s reviewers barely had time to review one volume before another appeared. In 1921 Robinson published two more volumes. *Avon's Harvest* is a book-length poem that deals with a macabre situation: Avon believes himself to be haunted annually by the ghost of an old school enemy who had been drowned when the *Titanic* sank; the morning after he relates his story he is found dead, and the narrator says, "He died, you know, because he was afraid." Reviews were scanty but positive. Although John Farrar in the *Bookman* (May 1921) called it "a dime novel in verse," he approved of it. An interesting piece of scholarship is "A Note on 'Avon's Harvest,'" by David Brown in *American Literature* in 1933, in which he explains that substantial revisions in the poem were made after reviewers misinterpreted it.

Robinson had a chance to publish a revised version of *Avon's Harvest* that same year, for his first *Collected Poems* also appeared in 1921. "Captain Craig" was the one other poem that underwent extensive revisions. In *Collected Poems* some forty-three poems were dropped from *The Children of the Night* (including the title poem), and fourteen previously uncollected poems were added at the end of the volume. Otherwise, the title *Collected Poems* means what it says: it is a collection of the poetry which had appeared in nine previous volumes. One curiosity of *Collected Poems* is

that the volumes are not presented in chronological order. *The Man Against the Sky*, his biggest critical success, comes first. Thereafter the volumes are arranged so that the book-length poems are interspersed among the volumes of short pieces.

Among the new poems in *Collected Poems* are three of his best known: "Mr. Flood's Party," "The Tree in Pamela's Garden," and "Rembrandt to Rembrandt." These three represent Robinson's work at the height of his powers: "Mr. Flood's Party," the rhymed narrative dealing with a lonely but valiant old man, is one of the best of the Tilbury poems. "A Tree in Pamela's Garden" is one of the cryptic, perfectly constructed sonnets which demonstrates Robinson's ability to empathize with women, and "Rembrandt to Rembrandt," whose subject is a historical figure and whose theme is a meditation on aesthetic theory, closes *Collected Poems* and is one of Robinson's most celebrated blank-verse poems of medium length. The 592-page volume indicated to those who had been unaware of Robinson the extent of his achievement, and reviewers were duly impressed. In the following year this volume earned for Robinson the first Pulitzer Prize ever awarded for poetry.

The publication of *Roman Bartholow* in 1923 marks the beginning of Robinson's later phase, that period in which he wrote hurriedly and concentrated on book-length narratives almost to the exclusion of other forms. In the last fourteen years of his life he published eleven books, nine of them single poems. *Roman Bartholow*, with more than four thousand lines, is second only to *Tristram* in length and presents the sort of domestic situation that was to intrigue Robinson in his later years. The title character, recuperating from an illness, is visited by his old friend, Penn-Raven. Bartholow's wife, Gabrielle, realizing that Penn-Raven is the more attractive of the two men, commits suicide. The triangular relationship is then discussed at length by the two remaining principals and an outside observer, Umfraville. The poem is flawed by lack of clarity in characterization and a plethora of unrelated images. It is perhaps Robinson's least successful poem, and both reviewers and later critics have written predominantly negative assessments.

The Man Who Died Twice, published in 1924, is different from its immediate predecessor in almost every respect and won for Robinson his second Pulitzer Prize. Here the narrator finds Fernando Nash beating a drum for the Salvation Army. Nash had once been a good musician and

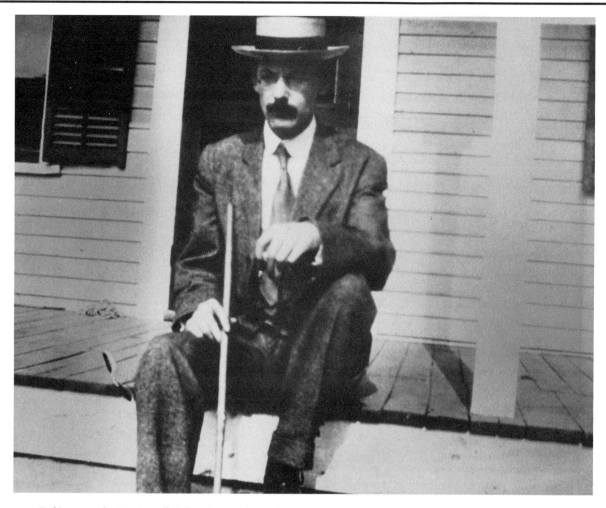

Robinson at the MacDowell Colony in Peterborough, New Hampshire (courtesy of the Watkinson Library, Trinity College, Hartford)

a promising composer, but his career has been cut short by debauchery. One night he hallucinates a symphony performed by rats in his room and shortly thereafter imagines his own magnum opus. He is unable to complete it, however, before his physical collapse, and when he recuperates he is spiritually regenerated and resigned to spend the rest of his days as a street musician. This poem is a variation on the theme of "Captain Craig," although the grotesque imagery is more controlled than in the earlier poem. The combination of down-to-earth diction, classical allusion, and understated humor contributes to its success. Occasionally excerpts from this poem are anthologized, a measure of its acceptance among scholars.

In 1923 Robinson had made his one trip abroad, spending six weeks in England. An impetus for his making the trip at that time was his dismay at the passage of the Eighteenth Amend-

ment. He observed in a letter to Witter Bynner that prohibition should be placed along with free verse and motion pictures as a "triumvirate from hell." He reported having a good time in London and Oxford, but he cut short his trip so he could spend two months at Peterborough, where he began to work on a book of short poems. The result was *Dionysus in Doubt,* published in 1925. The title poem and "Demos and Dionysus" are propagandistic poems decrying the curtailment of individual freedom through the imposition of behavioral standards. Also included are eighteen sonnets, notably "The Sheaves" and "Karma," as well as two poems of medium length, "Genevieve and Alexandra" and "Mortmain." Reviewers generally preferred any of the other poems to the Dionysus ones, objecting to their didacticism.

Robinson's single popular triumph, *Tristram,* appeared in 1927. His longest poem, reminiscent of his previous treatment of the Arthurian legends, received elaborate praise and sold fifty-seven thousand copies in the first year. Robinson's lifetime appreciation of opera, especially those of Richard Wagner, perhaps contributed to his interest in the topic. As he had done with his earlier Arthurian poems, he made his characters' actions realistic rather than the result of their having drunk a magic potion. The poem is tied together with carefully unified imagery, and the portrait of Isolt, looking out over the sea after hearing of Tristram's death, is justly celebrated:

> And white birds everywhere, flying, and flying;
> Alone with her white face and her gray eyes,
> She watched them there till even her thoughts were
>   white,
> And there was nothing alive but white birds flying,
> Flying, and always flying, and still flying,
> And the white sunlight flashing on the sea.

For the only time in his life Robinson was lionized: he agreed to attend a dramatic reading of the poem in New York and allowed a reception to be given for him after it. The royalties made him financially secure at last, and the book earned him his third Pulitzer Prize. Although Robinson was to write seven more volumes, he experienced his final triumph with *Tristram*.

Cavender's House (1929), *The Glory of the Nightingales* (1930), and *Matthias at the Door* (1931) are all reworkings of earlier themes. *Cavender's House* is similar to *Avon's Harvest* in that Cavender speaks with a ghost, in this case the wife he has murdered after he suspected her of infidelity. The other two long poems are principally variations on the theme examined earlier in *Roman Bartholow*—domestic tragedies dealing with flawed friendships, unfaithful wives, and suicides. These later poems are, however, more carefully composed than the earlier ones. Although critics treated them with respect, they almost always compared them to *Tristram* and found them wanting.

Nicodemus, a volume of ten medium-length poems, appeared in 1932. Nine of the ten are character sketches of biblical, historical, or Tilbury figures. Most often noted by the reviewers were "The March of the Cameron Men," "Ponce de Leon," and the title poem. "Annandale Again," the third poem Robinson wrote on the character of Annandale, summarizes his much earlier poem "The Book of Annandale."

With *Talifer* (1933) Robinson attempted a new mode of writing—a domestic comedy rather than a tragedy. Instead of his usual triangular situation, this poem involves two women and two

men who change partners. After an unsuccessful marriage to the intellectual Karen, Talifer weds the more pliant Althea. Talifer's friend, Dr. Quick, then takes Karen as his wife, but he soon leaves her to her books in Oxford and returns to admire the success of Talifer's second marriage. Karen perhaps represents Robinson's opinion of independent women. Most of the reviewers did not like the poem and politely said so. Richard Crowder, however, has written an article in the *Personalist* (January 1962) reassessing the poem and suggesting an allegorical interpretation.

Allegorical interpretations of Robinson's last two poems, *Amaranth* (1934) and *King Jasper* (1935), are inevitable. *Amaranth* is cast in the form of a dream, in which Fargo, a former painter who is now a pumpmaker, visits the "wrong world" guided by his host, Amaranth, "the flower that never fades." The people they meet are primarily failed artists or writers who, when they look into Amaranth's eyes, can see the truth about themselves. Several casually commit suicide, actions which do not detract from the grotesque comedy of the piece. Reactions to his poem were mixed, though many critics greeted it enthusiastically, and several later critics, such as Floyd Stovall in his *American Idealism* (1943) and Dolores Brien in *Research Studies* (June 1968), have presented various interpretations of this ironic and ambiguous poem.

In January 1935 Robinson was diagnosed as having an inoperable cancer. During his stay in the hospital he read galley proofs of his final poem, *King Jasper*, completing the corrections only hours before he sank into his final coma. *King Jasper* is a complex, highly symbolic work which is an appropriate culmination of Robinson's career, for it combines the themes of personal failure, artistic endeavor, materialism, and the inevitability of change. It deals with Jasper and his family—his wife, Honoria; his son, Jasper, Jr.; his son's wife, Zoë; and Jasper's old enemies, a father and son both named Hebron. Jasper's empire comes crashing down on him, but Zoë, so named because she represents the life force, prevails. The same sort of dreams and grotesque images Robinson had used in earlier works appear in this poem, as well as lengthy conversations attempting to analyze motivations. Although the poem is set in modern times, it has a vaguely Arthurian air about it. It has been interpreted as a commentary on American politics as well as a philosophical construct. Although the poem is not entirely successful because it tries to do too many things, it is nevertheless a fitting conclusion to the Robinson canon. Published posthumously, the book was introduced by a now well-known essay by Robert Frost, who wrote in glowing terms of his contemporary and chief rival, commenting particularly on Robinson's profundity, humor, and technical skill. It is a Robinsonian irony that Frost does not mention the poem he set out to introduce.

Magazines and newspapers throughout the country took elaborate notice of Robinson's death, reminding their readers that he had been considered America's foremost poet for nearly twenty years and praising his industry, integrity, and devotion to his art. During his lifetime Robinson suffered the extremes of obscurity and fame, but Robinson the poet maintained a steadfast course in spite of both of those encumbrances. He often said that a poet cannot be definitely placed until he has been dead half a century. While he is no longer considered the brightest star in the poetic firmament, part of his work remains among the greatest American poetry.

In an interview with Joyce Kilmer (*New York Times Magazine*, 9 April 1916) Robinson once defined poetry as "a language which tells us, through a more or less emotional experience, something that cannot be said. All real poetry, great or small, does this. And it seems to me that poetry has two characteristics. One is that it is, after all, undefinable. The other is that it is eventually unmistakable." With his metrical control, precise diction, and keen observation of human triumphs and frailties, Robinson's poetry remains unmistakable.

Letters:

Selected Letters, edited by Ridgely Torrence (New York: Macmillan, 1940);

Letters from Edwin Arlington Robinson to Howard George Schmitt, edited by Carl J. Weber (Waterville, Maine: Colby College Library, 1943);

Untriangulated Stars: Letters to Harry de Forest Smith 1890-1905, edited by Denham Sutcliffe (Cambridge: Harvard University Press, 1947);

Edwin Arlington Robinson's Letters to Edith Brower, edited by Richard Cary (Cambridge: Harvard University Press, 1968).

Bibliographies:

Charles Beecher Hogan, *A Bibliography of Edwin Ar-*

lington Robinson (New Haven: Yale University Press, 1936);

William White, *Edwin Arlington Robinson: A Supplementary Bibliography* (Kent, Ohio: Kent State University Press, 1971);

Nancy Carol Joyner, *Edwin Arlington Robinson: A Reference Guide* (Boston: G. K. Hall, 1978).

Biographies:

Mark Van Doren, *Edwin Arlington Robinson* (New York: Literary Guild of America, 1927);

Hermann Hagedorn, *Edwin Arlington Robinson: A Biography* (New York: Macmillan, 1936);

Rollo Walter Brown, *Next Door to a Poet* (New York: Appleton-Century, 1937);

Emery Neff, *Edwin Arlington Robinson* (New York: Sloane, 1948);

Chard Powers Smith, *Where the Light Falls: A Portrait of Edwin Arlington Robinson* (New York: Macmillan, 1965);

Louis O. Coxe, *Edwin Arlington Robinson: The Life of Poetry* (New York: Pegasus, 1969).

References:

Wallace L. Anderson, *Edwin Arlington Robinson: A Critical Introduction* (Boston: Houghton Mifflin, 1967).
Argues that Robinson's most notable achievement is his perception and depiction of character, coupled with his psychological insight, and studies his reaction to the poetry of the late nineteenth century, which resulted in his rejection of the restrictions on the subjects, language, and form of poetry.

Ellsworth Barnard, *Edwin Arlington Robinson: A Critical Study* (New York: Macmillan, 1952).
Studies Robinson's work from a biographical viewpoint and examines his supposed pessimism as a facet of his personal spiritual search, asserting that "although his characters suffer, they are not thereby destroyed."

Barnard, ed., *Edwin Arlington Robinson: Centenary Essays* (Athens: University of Georgia Press, 1969).
Collection of critical essays with extensive primary and secondary bibliographies.

Richard Cary, ed., *Appreciation of Edwin Arlington Robinson: Twenty-Eight Interpretive Essays* (Waterville, Maine: Colby College Press, 1969).
Selected essays by prominent critics, includ-

ing Hyatt H. Waggoner, David Brown, and Archibald MacLeish.

Cary, ed., *Early Reception of Edwin Arlington Robinson: The First Twenty Years* (Waterville, Maine: Colby College Press, 1974).
Presents and discusses Robinson's critical standing during the first two decades of his career.

Charles Cestre, *An Introduction to Edwin Arlington Robinson* (New York: Macmillan, 1930).
Early critique of Robinson's work; includes selected poems and an introduction by Bliss Perry.

Hoyt C. Franchere, *Edwin Arlington Robinson* (New York: Twayne, 1968).
Clarifies certain argument concerning Robinson's "dark mind dwelling on darker subjects," with refutations against specific critical contentions, and contrasts the accepted story of his career with little known essential details of the "Robinson Myth."

Edwin S. Fussell, *Edwin Arlington Robinson: The Literary Background of a Traditional Poet* (Berkeley: University of California Press, 1954).
Argues that Robinson was essentially a traditional poet and that this was a major factor in his being "the pre-eminent poet of his generation in America"; also traces English, European, Biblical, and early American influences on his work.

Estelle Kaplan, *Philosophy in the Poetry of Edwin Arlington Robinson* (New York: Columbia University Press, 1940).
Explores the philosophical implications of Robinson's poetry, concluding that there is no essential, integrated philosophical thesis underlying his work.

Francis Murphy, ed., *Edwin Arlington Robinson* (Englewood Cliffs, N.J.: Prentice-Hall, 1970).
Collection of critical essays by James Dickey, Warner Berthoff, and others; includes Robert Frost's introduction to *King Jasper*.

Hyatt H. Waggoner, *American Poets: From the Puritans to the Present* (Boston: Houghton Mifflin, 1968), pp. 262-292.
Contains an examination of Robinson's importance as a poet in the context of the historical continuity of American poetry.

Yvor Winters, *Edwin Arlington Robinson* (Norfolk, Conn.: New Directions, 1946).
Studies various influences on Robinson's poetry, including Robert Browning and Rudyard Kipling and discusses the importance of Robinson's literary achievements.

Papers:
Substantial holdings of Robinson papers are in the Colby College Library, the Houghton Library at Harvard University, the New York Public Library, and the Library of Congress.

Carl Sandburg

This entry was updated by Penelope Niven from her entry in DLB 54, American
Poets, 1880-1945, part 2.

Places	Chicago New York City	Milwaukee Lake Michigan (Harbert, Mich.)	Galesburg, Ill. Flat Rock, N.C. Sweden
Influences and Relationships	Walt Whitman William Marion Reedy Alfred Harcourt Ezra Pound Vachel Lindsay Abraham Lincoln	Philip Green Wright Edgar Lee Masters William Morris Amy Lowell Louis Untermeyer	Elbert Hubbard Harriet Monroe and Alice Corbin Henderson Theodore Dreiser Archibald MacLeish
Literary Movements and Forms	New Poetry The Chicago Literary Renaissance Advocacy Journalism	Free Verse Realism Modernism	Imagism The Literature of Democracy
Major Themes	Man's Relation to Man The Struggle of the Common Man Democracy	Social Protest The American Dream The Search for Self Estrangement	The Affirmation of the Human Spirit
Cultural and Artistic Influences	Lyceum and Chautauqua Movements American Slang Platform Entertaining	Edward Steichen and Photographic Art The Arts-Craft Movement	Folk Music and Folklore Humanism
Social and Economic Influences	Socialism The New Deal Era Progressivism The American Labor Struggle	The Life of the American Immigrant World War II The Depression	World War I Civil War Civil Rights

See also the Sandburg entry in DLB 17, Twentieth-Century American Historians.

BIRTH: Galesburg, Illinois, 6 January 1878, to August and Clara Mathilda Anderson Sandburg.

EDUCATION: Lombard University, 1898-1902.

MARRIAGE: 15 June 1908 to Lilian Steichen; children: Margaret, Janet, Helga.

AWARDS AND HONORS: Levinson Prize (*Poetry* magazine), 1914; Poetry Society of America Awards, 1919, 1921; Litt.D., Lombard College, 1923; Phi Beta Kappa Poet, Harvard University, 1928; Litt.D., Knox College, 1928; Litt.D., Northwestern University, 1931; elected to the National Institute of Arts and Letters, 1933; Friends of Literature Award, 1934; Pulitzer Prize for *Abraham Lincoln: The War Years*, 1940; elected to the American Academy of Arts and Letters, 1940; special diploma, Lincoln Memorial University, 1940; Litt.D., Lafayette College, 1940; Litt.D., Wesleyan University, 1940; Litt.D., Yale University, 1940; Litt.D., Harvard University, 1940; Litt.D., Syracuse University, 1941; Litt.D., Dartmouth College, 1941; LL.D., Rollins College, 1941; Phi Beta Kappa Poet, College of William and Mary, 1943; LL.D., Augustana College, 1948; honorary Ph.D., Upsala College, 1950; Pulitzer Prize for *Complete Poems*, 1951; National Institute and American Academy of Arts and Letters Gold Medal, 1952; Commanders Cup of the Order of the North Star (Sweden), 1953; Poetry Society of America Gold Medal, 1953; Tamiment Institute Award, 1953; LL.D., University of Illinois, 1953; New York Civil War Round Table Silver Medal, 1954; Boston Arts Festival Poetry Prize, 1955; Litt.D., University of North Carolina, 1955; Award of Merit, University of Louisville, 1955; humanities award, Albert Einstein College of Medicine, 1956; named honorary ambassador for North Carolina, 1958; Lincoln Day speaker, U.S. Congress, 1959; Litt.D., Upsala College, 1959; Litteris et Artibus medal from King Gustav VI of Sweden, 1959; Roanoke-Chowan Poetry Cup for *Harvest Poems*, 1960; named poet laureate of Illinois, 1962; Presidential Medal of Freedom, 1964.

DEATH: Flat Rock, North Carolina, 22 July 1967.

SELECTED BOOKS: *In Reckless Ecstasy,* as

Carl Sandburg, 1926 (courtesy of the Carl Sandburg Collection, University of Illinois Library at Urbana-Champaign)

Charles A. Sandburg (Galesburg, Ill.: Asgard Press, 1904);
Incidentals, as Charles Sandburg (Galesburg, Ill.: Asgard Press, 1907);
The Plaint of a Rose, as Charles Sandburg (Galesburg, Ill.: Asgard Press, 1908);
Joseffy, as Charles Sandburg (Galesburg, Ill.: Asgard Press, 1910);
Chicago Poems (New York: Holt, 1916);
Cornhuskers (New York: Holt, 1918);
The Chicago Race Riots, July, 1919 (New York: Harcourt, Brace & Howe, 1919);
Smoke and Steel (New York: Harcourt, Brace & Howe, 1920);
Slabs of the Sunburnt West (New York: Harcourt, Brace, 1922);
Rootabaga Stories (New York: Harcourt, Brace, 1922);
Rootabaga Pigeons (New York: Harcourt, Brace, 1923);
Abraham Lincoln: The Prairie Years, 2 volumes (New York: Harcourt, Brace, 1926); repub-

lished in part as *Abe Lincoln Grows Up* (New York: Harcourt, Brace, 1928);

Selected Poems, edited by Rebecca West (London: Cape, 1926; New York: Harcourt, Brace, 1926);

Carl Sandburg, edited by Hughes Mearns (New York: Simon & Schuster, 1926);

Good Morning, America (New York: Harcourt, Brace, 1928);

Steichen, The Photographer (New York: Harcourt, Brace, 1929);

Potato Face (New York: Harcourt, Brace, 1930);

Early Moon (New York: Harcourt, Brace, 1930);

Mary Lincoln: Wife and Widow, by Sandburg and Paul Angle (New York: Harcourt, Brace, 1932);

The People, Yes (New York: Harcourt, Brace, 1936);

Abraham Lincoln: The War Years, 4 volumes (New York: Harcourt, Brace, 1939);

Storm Over the Land: A Profile of the Civil War Taken Mainly from Abraham Lincoln: The War Years (New York: Harcourt, Brace, 1942; London: Cape, 1943);

Home Front Memo (New York: Harcourt, Brace, 1943);

The Photographs of Abraham Lincoln, by Sandburg and Frederick Hill Meserve (New York: Harcourt, Brace, 1944);

Remembrance Rock (New York: Harcourt, Brace, 1948);

Lincoln Collector: The Story of Oliver R. Barrett's Great Private Collection (New York: Harcourt, Brace, 1949);

Complete Poems (New York: Harcourt, Brace, 1950; revised and expanded edition, New York: Harcourt Brace Jovanovich, 1970);

Always the Young Strangers (New York: Harcourt, Brace, 1953); republished in part as *Prairie-Town Boy* (New York: Harcourt, Brace, 1955);

The Sandburg Range (New York: Harcourt, Brace, 1957);

Harvest Poems, 1910-1960 (New York: Harcourt, Brace, 1960);

Wind Song (New York: Harcourt, Brace, 1960);

Honey and Salt (New York: Harcourt, Brace & World, 1963);

The Wedding Procession of the Rag Doll and the Broom Handle and Who Was in It (New York: Harcourt, Brace & World, 1967);

Breathing Tokens, edited by Margaret Sandburg (New York: Harcourt Brace Jovanovich, 1978);

Ever the Winds of Chance, edited by Margaret Sandburg and George Hendrick (Urbana-Champaign: University of Illinois Press, 1983).

OTHER: *The American Songbag,* edited, with introduction and notes, by Sandburg (New York: Harcourt, Brace, 1927);

Edward Steichen, comp., *The Family of Man,* prologue by Sandburg (New York: Published for the Museum of Modern Art by the Maco Magazine Corp., 1955).

American poet and biographer Carl Sandburg sketched a revealing portrait of himself in the preface to his *Complete Poems* (1950): "there was a puzzlement," he said, "as to whether I was a poet, a biographer, a wandering troubadour with a guitar, a midwest Hans Christian Andersen, or a historian of current events. . . ." He was seventy-two in 1950 and "still studying verbs and the mystery of how they connect nouns. . . . I have forgotten the meaning of twenty or thirty of my poems written thirty or forty years ago. I still favor several simple poems published long ago which continue to have an appeal for simple people."

Sandburg wrote a landmark six-volume biography of Abraham Lincoln. A consummate platform performer, he roamed the United States for nearly a half century, guitar in hand, collecting and singing American folk songs. For his own children and children everywhere he wrote *Rootabaga Stories* (1922) and *Rootabaga Pigeons* (1923), some of the first authentic American fairy tales. He was a journalist by trade; his newspaper reportage and commentary documented labor, racial, and economic strife and other key events of his times. But Carl Sandburg was first and foremost a poet, writing poems about America in the American idiom for the American people. The titles of his volumes of poetry testify to his major themes: *Chicago Poems* (1916), *Cornhuskers* (1918), *Smoke and Steel* (1920), *Good Morning, America* (1928), *The People, Yes* (1936).

Louis Untermeyer described Sandburg in 1923 as the "emotional democrat" of American poetry, the "laureate of industrial America." Harriet Monroe, founder and first editor of *Poetry: A Magazine of Verse,* gave Sandburg's poetry its first serious audience in 1914. She believed that this son of Swedish immigrants was particularly suited to write about the "incomplete, but urgent and hopeful" American democracy. She wrote in

Poets and Their Art (1926) that Sandburg was bent on the business, "in the deepest sense a poet's business, of seeing our national life in the large–its beauty and glory, its baseness and shame."

Sandburg's vision of the American experience was shaped in the American Midwest during the complicated events which brought the nineteenth century to a close. His parents were Swedish immigrants who met in Illinois, where they had settled in search of a share of American democracy and prosperity. August Sandburg helped to build the first cross-continental railroad, and in the twentieth century his son Carl was an honored guest on the first cross-continental jet flight. August Sandburg was a blacksmith's helper for the Chicago Burlington and Quincy Railroad in Galesburg, Illinois, when his son was born on 6 January 1878 in a small cottage a few steps away from the roundhouse and railroad yards. Carl August Sandburg was the second child and first son of the hardworking Sandburgs. He grew up speaking Swedish and English, and, eager to be assimilated into American society, he Americanized his name. In 1884 or 1885, "somewhere in the first year or two of school," he began to call himself Charles rather than the Swedish Carl because he had "a feeling the name Carl would mean one more Poor Swede Boy while the name Charles filled the mouth and had 'em guessing."

There were seven children in the Sandburg family, and the two youngest sons died of diphtheria on the same day in 1892. Charles Sandburg had to leave school at age thirteen to work at a variety of odd jobs to supplement the family income. As a teenager he was restless and impulsive, hungry for experience in the world beyond the staid, introverted prairie town which had always been his home. At age eighteen he borrowed his father's railroad pass and had his first look at Chicago, the city of his destiny. In 1897 Sandburg joined the corps of more than 60,000 hoboes who found the American railroads an exhilarating if illicit free ride from one corner of the United States to another. For three and a half months of his nineteenth year he traveled through Iowa, Missouri, Kansas, Nebraska, and Colorado, working on farms, steamboats, and railroads, blacking stoves, washing dishes, and listening to the American vernacular, the idiom which would permeate his poetry.

The journey left Sandburg with a permanent wanderlust. He volunteered for service in the Spanish-American War in 1898 and served in Puerto Rico from July until late August. As a veteran, he received free tuition for a year at Lombard College in Galesburg and enrolled there in October 1898. He was offered a conditional appointment to the U.S. Military Academy at West Point, New York, on the basis of his Spanish-American War service, but in June 1899 he failed entrance examinations in arithmetic and grammar. He returned to Lombard, where he studied until May of 1902, when he left college without enough credits for graduation.

At Lombard, he encountered the first catalyst for his poetry, Prof. Philip Green Wright, economist, scholar, and poet. Wright fostered Sandburg's interest in writing and published the young poet's first small books at his Asgard Press, which he modeled after William Morris's Kelmscott Press and its offspring, Elbert Hubbard's Roycroft Press. On the small handpress in the basement of his Galesburg home, Wright set the type for Charles A. Sandburg's *In Reckless Ecstasy* (1904), *Incidentals* (1907), *The Plaint of a Rose* (1908), and *Joseffy* (1910). The last book was commissioned by Joseffy, a magician, musician, inventor, and wanderer, who wanted an "appreciation" to promote his lyceum appearances. The three other early works, slim booklets which are now rare collectors' items, contain Sandburg's juvenilia, which he viewed in retrospect as "many odd pieces . . . not worth later reprint." They record the tentative and conventionally modeled lyrics of a young poet deeply influenced by Villon, Browning, Kipling, Emerson, and Whitman, as well as idealistic aphorisms in the style of Elbert Hubbard. These early writings are foretokens of the major themes of Sandburg's later poetry, as well of the idealism which led him to become an activist and organizer for the Social Democratic party in Wisconsin from 1907 until 1912.

By the time he was thirty Sandburg had tried a variety of jobs, often supporting himself as an itinerant salesman of Underwood and Underwood stereopticon equipment and pictures. He tried to establish himself as a Lyceum and Chautauqua lecturer, published occasional poems, and worked for a variety of periodicals. In 1908 he married Lilian Steichen, sister of photographer Edward Steichen, who had already achieved some international success with his artistic photographs. Lilian Steichen was a beautiful Phi Beta Kappa graduate of the University of Chicago, a schoolteacher, and an active Socialist. Sandburg said later that the three chief influences in

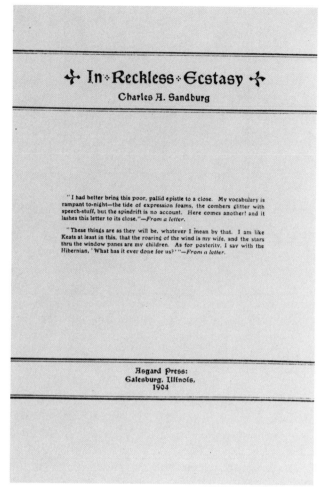

Title page for Sandburg's first book, printed by one of the poet's professors, Philip Green Wright, on the small handpress in Wright's basement

his life were Philip Green Wright, Edward Steichen, and Lilian Steichen Sandburg, his wife for fifty-nine years. He called her Paula, and she urged him to return to his christened name Carl, to affirm his Swedish roots. She also urged him to concentrate on his poetry, and her steady faith in his work undergirded his long struggle to find his own poetic style and a serious audience for his poetry.

From 1910 until 1912 Carl and Paula Sandburg lived in Milwaukee, where Sandburg was instrumental in the Milwaukee Socialists' unprecedented political victory in 1910. When Emil Seidel was elected Milwaukee's first Socialist mayor in that year, Sandburg, then thirty-two, was appointed his secretary. Sandburg left city hall in 1911 to write for Victor Berger's *Social Democratic Herald* in Milwaukee. In June 1911 the Sandburgs' first child, Margaret, was born. A second daughter died at birth in 1913; Janet was born in

1916, and Helga was born in 1918. In 1912 the Sandburgs moved to Chicago, where Sandburg joined the staff of the Socialist *Chicago Evening World,* which had expanded in the wake of a pressman's strike that closed most other Chicago newspapers. Once the strike was settled, the *World* went out of business, and Sandburg found work with small periodicals such as the business magazine *System* and *Day Book,* an adless daily newspaper owned by W. E. Scripps. He contributed occasional articles to the *International Socialist Review,* often using the pseudonym Jack Phillips. Sandburg struggled to find an outlet for his poetry and enough income to support his young family. His fortunes turned in 1914 when Harriet Monroe of *Poetry* published six of his radical, muscular poems in the March issue of her forward-looking journal. This first significant recognition of his work brought him literary friendships with Edgar Lee Masters, Theodore Dreiser,

Vachel Lindsay, Amy Lowell, Alice Corbin Henderson, Floyd Dell, Sherwood Anderson, and others. His poetry also came to the attention of Ezra Pound, who was the magazine's foreign editor. Masters and Dreiser encouraged Sandburg to construct his first book of poetry, and Henderson, then assistant editor of *Poetry*, brought the collection to the attention of Alfred Harcourt, a young editor at Henry Holt and Company, who risked his own job to persuade the firm to publish Sandburg's *Chicago Poems* in 1916.

Carl Sandburg found his subject in the American people and the American landscape; he found his voice, after a long, lonely search and struggle, in the vivid, candid economy of the American vernacular. He worked his way to a rugged, individual free-verse style which spoke clearly, directly, and often crudely to the audience which was also his subject. His poetry celebrated and consoled people in their environments—the crush of the city, the enduring solace of the prairie. In his work for the *Day Book*, the *Chicago Daily News*, and the Newspaper Enterprise Association (NEA), Sandburg had become a skilled investigative reporter with passionate social concerns. He covered war, racial strife, lynchings, mob violence, and the inequities of the industrial society, such as child labor, and disease and injury induced in the workplace. These concerns were transmuted into poetry. *Chicago Poems* offered bold, realistic portraits of working men, women, and children; of the "inexplicable fate" of the vulnerable and struggling human victims of war, progress, business. "Great men, pageants of war and labor, soldiers and workers, mothers lifting their children—these all I touched, and felt the solemn thrill of them," Sandburg wrote in "Masses." "And then one day I got a true look at the Poor, millions of the Poor,/patient and toiling; more patient than crags, tides, and stars; innumer-/able, patient as the darkness of night—and all broken, humble ruins of nations."

Sandburg's themes in *Chicago Poems* reflect his Socialistic idealism and pragmatism, but they also contain a wider humanism, a profound affirmation of the common man, the common destiny, the common tragedies and joys of life. Just as Sandburg's subject matter transcended that of conventional poetry, his free verse form was unique, original, and controversial. Some critics found his forms "shapeless" and questioned whether Sandburg's work was poetry at all. In her *Tendencies in Modern American Poetry* (1917), Sandburg's respected friend and colleague Amy

Lowell called him a lyric poet but stated that "the lyricist in him has a hard time to make itself heard above the brawling of the marketplace." She praised Sandburg's virility and tenderness, his originality and strength, and ratified his importance as a democratic poet. But she objected to the propagandistic overtones she perceived in Sandburg's poetry. In June 1917 Sandburg wrote to Lowell in his own defense that his aim was not to advance social theories, but "to sing, blab, chortle, yodel, like people, and people in the sense of human beings subtracted from formal doctrines."

The reviews for *Chicago Poems* were predictably disparate in their assessment of what the reviewer for the *American Library Association Booklist* (October 1916) called Sandburg's "tradition-shattering poetry," but the criticism which caused him long hours of reflection was Lowell's view that there was too much propaganda in his work. He continued as a journalist, joining the *Chicago Daily News* in 1917 as a labor reporter and editorial writer, but he was a poet by vocation. His newspaper job exposed him to the issues and conflicts of his time. The grim realism of labor conflict, racial strife, and mob violence in Chicago and the growing chaos of World War I led Sandburg to a growing cynicism and pessimism. He struggled for an equilibrium which would help him avoid the confusion of poetic theme and propaganda of action. But Sandburg was becoming the poet of democracy, and he believed that the poet had a public duty to speak to his times.

Cornhuskers (1918) is a celebration of the prairie, the agrarian life, the people living it. The volume includes some revealing autobiographical poems, many gentle, lyrical evocations of his family life, and poignant portraits of American working men and women reminiscent of *Chicago Poems*. The strength of *Cornhuskers* rests in its remarkable war poems. In the concluding section, "Shenandoah," Sandburg sketches with a deceptively gentle irony the phantoms of soldiers who died in past battles of earlier wars. He concludes with a forceful and bitter attack on modern warmongers who use the lives and deaths of "A Million Young Workmen, 1915":

> The kings are grinning, the kaiser and
> the czar—they are alive riding in leather-
> seated motor cars, and they have their
> women and roses for ease, and they eat
> fresh poached eggs for breakfast, new
> butter on toast, sitting in tall water-tight
> houses reading the news of war.
>   I dreamed a million ghosts of the young

Fog

The fog comes
on little cat feet.

It sits looking
over city and harbor
on silent haunches
and then moves on.

Carl Sandburg

Manuscript for "Fog," collected in Chicago Poems *(by permission of Maurice Greenbaum, Trustee for the Estate of Carl Sandburg; courtesy of the Carl Sandburg Collection, University of Illinois Library at Urbana-Champaign)*

workmen rose in their shirts all soaked in crimson . . . and yelled:

God damn the grinning kings, God damn the kaiser and the czar.

Critical reception for *Cornhuskers* was mixed, ranging from the view that Sandburg was in the front rank of American poets to the opinion that his outspoken idealism prevented him from being a poet at all. Some reviewers described him as the first American poet of his generation, revealing the "vitality and strength of the English tongue as it was in its beginnings" (*Review of Reviews,* January 1919), while others, such as the

New York Times reviewer, commented on the melancholy mood of the book, attributing it to "the racial soberness of the Scandinavian" (12 January 1919).

By the time the book appeared in October 1918, Sandburg was in Stockholm, Sweden, for his first closeup view of his parents' homeland, as well as for a brief view of World War I. He stayed on after the November Armistice to continue his work as Eastern European correspondent for the Newspaper Enterprise Association and became entangled with wartime bureaucracy when he brought back to the United States a trunk full of Russian literature and propaganda and some funds intended for the Finnish People's Republic Movement in New York. His good intentions validated, Sandburg was not charged with any violations of the Trading with the Enemy Act, but he was sobered and distressed by the questioning of his loyalty as an American citizen. Back at work at the *Chicago Daily News*, he covered a range of postwar issues, as well as the ongoing racial and labor conflict in Chicago. He was assigned to investigate the background of racial tensions in the city during the summer of 1919, and his thoughtful series of articles proved tragically prophetic when the Chicago Race riots erupted in late July. Alfred Harcourt gathered Sandburg's columns into a book entitled *The Chicago Race Riots, July, 1919* (1919).

Once again, Sandburg transmuted the harsh reality of his times into poetry, and the emerging volume, *Smoke and Steel* (1920), was dedicated to his brother-in-law, Edward Steichen. As in preceding volumes, Sandburg vividly depicts the daily toil of the working man and woman, "the people who must sing or die." The smoke of spring fields, autumn leaves, steel mills, and battleship funnels is the emblem and extension of "the blood of a man," the life force which undergirds the industrial society and the larger human brotherhood: "Deep down are the cinders we came from—/You and I and our heads of smoke," he wrote in the title poem. Sandburg's American landscape broadens in *Smoke and Steel* from Chicago and the prairie to specific scenes in places such as Gary, Indiana; Omaha; Cleveland; Kalamazoo; Far Rockaway; the Blue Ridge; the Potomac; New York. In all of these places Sandburg found a common theme, the struggle of the common man, the quest of the "finders in the dark." "I hear America, I hear, *what* do I hear?," he wrote in "The Sins of Kalamazoo."

Sandburg's voyage to Sweden and his perspective of World War I are transcribed in the poems in two sections of *Smoke and Steel* titled "Passports" and "Playthings of the Wind." Harsh depictions of human cruelty (a lynching is graphically described in "Man, the Man-Hunter," for instance) are juxtaposed to the gentle, often joyous lyricism of poems about Paula Sandburg, family, home, the beauty of nature.

Smoke and Steel is a strong but uneven work, and it elicited contradictory critical views. In a review for the 15 January 1920 issue of the *New Republic* Louis Untermeyer hailed the book as "an epic of modern industrialism and a mighty paean

to modern beauty" and named Sandburg and Robert Frost as America's two major living poets. Other critics charged that Sandburg had no sense of the past or vision of the future and that he had begun to produce an undiscriminating quantity of work, often imitating himself in the process. In the 9 December 1920 issue of the London *Times* a reviewer mused that Sandburg's poems were true to a certain kind of life and that they were undoubtedly American but questioned whether Sandburg's work constituted "a high and right art."

The negative appraisals were overshadowed for Sandburg by the welcome acclaim of his friend Amy Lowell. "Reading these poems gives me more of a patriotic emotion than ever 'The Star-spangled Banner' has been able to do," she wrote in the *New York Times* (24 October 1920). "This is America and Mr. Sandburg loves her so much that suddenly we realize how much we love her, too." Earlier lectures about propagandistic poetry aside, Lowell forecast that posterity would rank Sandburg "high on the ladder of poetic achievement."

In 1921 Sandburg was forty-three years old, comfortably employed by Victor Lawson and Henry Justin Smith at the *Chicago Daily News*, and a poet whose three books had earned him a widening reputation and prestigious awards—including the Poetry Society of America Award, which he shared with Margaret Widdemer in 1919, and the Poetry Society of America Annual Book Award, which he shared with Stephen Vincent Benét in 1921. He lived with his wife and three small daughters in Elmhurst, Illinois, and traveled with increasing frequency on the college lecture circuit, reading his poetry and playing and singing American folk songs from his flourishing collection. His growing disillusionment with "the imbecility of a frightened world" was intensified by deep personal sorrow and anxiety at the discovery that his eldest child, Margaret, suffered from nocturnal epilepsy, an illness for which there was no effective treatment in 1921. Sandburg heightened his lecture activity to supplement his income so that Margaret could have every possible medical treatment for her mystifying illness, and he began to work in earnest on the *Rootabaga Stories* (1922), a charming, whimsical series of fables invented for his own children. A sequel, *Rootabaga Pigeons*, appeared in 1923.

He managed amid family stress to produce his fourth book of poetry, a slim volume entitled *Slabs of the Sunburnt West* (1922), dedicated to his youngest child, Helga. The book begins with a muted portrait of Chicago, "The Windy City," a catalog of the city's monotony and vitality, its weather and its people. "And So Today," an extended eulogy to an unknown soldier, brings a certain closure to the war poems of this period of the poet's life. There are poems to well-known subjects–including sculptor Constantin Brancusi, Charlie Chaplin, and Robert Frost. The title poem uses the vehicle of the journey of an overland passenger train to unite the past and present members of the great "procession" of "wonderful hungry people" who created the American nation. For the first time Sandburg made extended use of the catalog, the repetitive accrual of images in parallel forms and the quotation of American slang and platitudes.

These devices irritated some critics, who found Sandburg's work incoherent and his vocabulary dated. "Slang is last night's toadstool growth," Clement Wood wrote in the *Nation* (26 July 1922), warning that Sandburg wrote in "unfamiliar rhythms, and a vocabulary that tomorrow will speak only to the archaeologist." But other critics admired Sandburg's virility and originality, his mellower, more musical tone and his cogent style. Malcolm Cowley pointed out in the *Dial* (November 1922) that Sandburg's use of parallel constructions and repetition yielded verse which "is highly organized," producing effects "as complex and difficult sometimes as those of Swinburne's most intricate ballades. . . ." The *New York Times* reviewer warned that Sandburg "is already in danger of becoming the Professional Chanter of Virility" (4 July 1922), but on one point reviewers and Sandburg's large audience of readers agreed: he was a completely American poet, the Poet of the People.

Slabs of the Sunburnt West made frequent use of prose structures at a time when Sandburg was discovering an interesting fact of literary economics: prose paid better than poetry. His *Rootabaga Stories* were so successful that Alfred Harcourt proposed that Sandburg follow his longtime wish to write a juvenile biography of Abraham Lincoln. From the disillusioning realities of the world he had documented so long in poetry, journalism, and political speeches, Sandburg turned to the refuge of history and legend. He began to immerse himself in Lincoln research and in American folklore and folk music. For the next seventeen years, in the prime of his creative life, Sandburg focused on one central, overriding subject: Abraham Lincoln. He took "occasional detours" for po-

etry, producing two significant volumes, *Good Morning, America* in 1928 and *The People, Yes* in 1936. But the poet who had shown the American people the reality of their language and their lives in his innovative verse forms began the long work of presenting to them the higher reality of their mythology and legends in the tragic folk hero Lincoln and in *The American Songbag*, an anthology of American folk music that he edited in 1927.

The title poem of *Good Morning, America*, composed and delivered as the Phi Beta Kappa Poem at Harvard University in 1925, was Sandburg's strongest affirmation yet of "the little two-legged joker . . . Man." The collection begins with thirty-eight "Tentative (First Model) Definitions of Poetry" and moves–with a panoramic sweep reflecting Sandburg's departure from realism–into mythology, legend, history, and a universal humanism. Sandburg converts an informed view of history, the product of his mounting Lincoln research, into poetic subject matter. His extended catalog of proverbs and folk idioms foreshadows the content of *The People, Yes* as it dramatizes "the short miserable pilgrimage of mankind."

Sandburg's two-volume *Abraham Lincoln: The Prairie Years* brought him new celebrity and financial stability in 1926. *The American Songbag*, warmly received and reviewed in 1927, testified not only to Sandburg's versatility but to his comprehensive interest in documenting the American experience. If the Poet of the People needed further ratification of his place as a popular American literary figure, *Good Morning, America* received such an endorsement from the majority of critics. Sandburg was compared to Whitman, praised for his humor, his vision, the rhythms of his verse. Some critics, such as Perry Hutchison, chided that Sandburg demonstrated no real growth as a poet, that he had "sat too long at the feet of Walt Whitman" (*New York Times*, 21 October 1928). But the consensus was that "sunburned Carl Sandburg, in love with the earth," as Leon Whipple called him in *Survey* (1 November 1928), had found the subject and the style vigorous and free enough for "a Continental plateau and the Great Divide. . . ."

In the early 1930s Sandburg formed a life-long friendship with Archibald MacLeish, and the men carried on an introspective dialogue about the obligations of the poet to speak to the issues of his times. The Depression years provoked in Sandburg a profound desire to console "the people of the earth, the family of man," to lift the hopes of the people who, "In the darkness with a great bundle of grief," marched "in tune and step/with constellations of universal law." Sandburg relinquished his *Chicago Daily News* job in 1932 to devote his full time to writing biography and poetry; he began to take a "detour" from work on the last stages of *Abraham Lincoln: The War Years* to write a long, innovative poem based in part on the lessons he had learned from Lincoln and American history. *The People, Yes,* an epic prose-poem, is in many ways the culmination of Sandburg's work as a poet. He crafted it over an eight-year period, fusing the American vernacular with the details of history and contemporary events. Sandburg's immersion in the Lincoln era had given him an informed sense of history, and he saw striking parallels between Lincoln's time and the Depression years. Believing that economic inequity lay at the root of all social injustice, from labor conflict to racial and civil strife, he responded to the economic and social upheavals of the 1930s with *The People, Yes,* his testament to the seekers and the strugglers, the people who were the counterparts of his own immigrant parents. "Man is a long time coming," Sandburg concluded in the final, one hundred and seventh, stanza of the poem. "Man will yet win./Brother may yet line up with brother."

The critics looked for coherence and could not find it, sought structure and could not find that, and wondered anew if the Poet of the People could in fact write poetry at all. But there was generous praise for Sandburg's vision of the American people as heroic, for his lusty humor and vivid irony, for his success in rendering "the authentic accents of his brother." Sandburg's readers embraced the book and wrote to him in legions to thank him for it. He took all responses in stride. He had written the poem he wanted to write, and he called it the "best memorandum I could file for the present stress."

In 1940 Sandburg won the Pulitzer Prize for the four-volume *Abraham Lincoln: The War Years,* published in 1939. *The People, Yes* was his last major book of poetry. During the decade of the 1940s Sandburg lectured widely, wrote occasional poetry, involved himself actively in the war effort, and worked as a syndicated columnist. A collection of his newspaper columns and radio broadcasts was published as *Home Front Memo* (1943), along with the text and photographs from *Road to Victory,* a patriotic exhibit which he

and his brother-in-law, Edward Steichen, had created for the Museum of Modern Art in 1942.

Sandburg and MacLeish were critical of writers who remained detached from the national emergency of World War II, and Sandburg cautioned that "A writer's silence on living issues can in itself constitute a propaganda of conduct leading toward the deterioration or death of freedom."

Sandburg's commitment to speak to the issues of his times, his passion for American history, and his desire to try writing in every genre led him to sign a contract on 11 September 1943 to write an epic historical novel that Metro-Goldwyn-Mayer Studios could make into what the studio hoped would be a popular wartime film. Sandburg was an innovator, seldom afraid to risk new ventures; thus he set out in 1943, at age sixty-five, to write his first and only novel, *Remembrance Rock.* It was finally completed and published in 1948, but the film version was never made.

Sandburg had tried almost every genre by the time he won the Pulitzer Prize for poetry in 1951 for his *Complete Poems* (1950). In *Always the Young Strangers* (1953) he recorded the first twenty years of his life. Sandburg enjoyed the height of his celebrity in the 1950s, traveling widely as an increasingly visible public figure. He was a natural for the new medium of television, and his familiar face, with high cheekbones framed by the sweep of white hair, was photographed and recognized across the nation he celebrated throughout his life and work. In 1959 Sandburg and Edward Steichen traveled to the Soviet Union with *The Family of Man,* an exhibition of photographs and text which they had jointly arranged as a celebration of humanity. Sandburg made his second and final trip to Sweden at the end of that journey.

Sandburg wrote, traveled, and entertained audiences as long as he had the strength to do so. He went to Hollywood in 1960 to spend a year and a half as creative consultant to George Stevens and his film *The Greatest Story Ever Told.* The octogenarian Sandburg had by the 1960s become known as a legend in his time. "A legend in our time," he often exclaimed. "Jesus, it could be worse."

"Being a poet is a damn dangerous business," Sandburg observed at his eighty-fifth birthday dinner in 1963, on the event of the publication of his final book of poetry, *Honey and Salt.* The volume is notable for its variety, but its

Sandburg in 1948 (photograph by June Glenn, Jr.; courtesy of the Carl Sandburg Collection, University of Illinois Library at Urbana-Champaign)

quality is uneven. Some of the poems are sentimental caricatures of his early work, but many of them reveal powers which had stayed and grown. *Honey and Salt* is a summation of Sandburg's life and work weighted with reflections on the passage of time, the waning of physical and creative powers, the perdurability of the physical universe, and the transitory nature of human life. *Honey and Salt* contains whimsy and pain, sentimentality and strength, and Sandburg's enduring idealism, memory, and hope, as well as his rudimentary affirmation of the bonds of universal life and the family of man.

The Sandburgs left the midwestern heartland in 1945, moving to the mountains of North Carolina in search of more solitude and space for

the family and Paula Sandburg's thriving herd of champion dairy goats. They settled at Connemara, a 245-acre estate in Flat Rock, North Carolina. Carl Sandburg died there in the hush of the mountain summer on 22 July 1967 at age eighty-nine. His wife, Paula, survived him, along with daughters Margaret, Janet, and Helga, and Helga's children, John Carl and Karlen Paula, who as teenagers had legally taken their grandmother's maiden name, Steichen. At the simple funeral ceremony in a nearby chapel, Edward Steichen placed a pine bough on Sandburg's coffin, in memory of their years of fellowship.

Unlike American writers whose families had long been American citizens, Sandburg felt no compulsion to serve a literary apprenticeship abroad. While others found stimulation and sustenance in Paris, London, or Rome, Sandburg turned to Milwaukee and Chicago. Sandburg's immigrant father never learned to write the language his son used to explore, describe, interpret, and celebrate the American experience. August and Clara Sandburg were strangers to the American prairie and the robust complexity of the city Carl Sandburg sought to interpret for them and others like them. Witnessing the obstacles thrust before the modest hopes of simple working people such as his parents, he became the passionate champion for people who did not have the words or power to speak for themselves. During the turbulent events of nearly a century of American life, Sandburg sought to articulate and affirm the hopes of the average American citizen. "There are poets of streets and struggles, of dust and combat, of violence wanton or justified, of plain folk living close to a hard earth," Sandburg wrote in "Notes for a Preface" in his *Complete Poems*. He was convinced that "When men lose their poetic feeling for ordinary life, and cannot write poetry of ordinary things, their exalted poetry is likely to lose its strength of exaltation."

Sandburg found his subject and his themes in ordinary life. He viewed himself as "one more seeker" in the long procession of humanity. His celebration of the durable human spirit transcends time or place. This uniquely American poet found in the American experience symbols for the universal human experience. "The people take the earth/as a tomb of rest and a cradle of hope," he wrote in *The People, Yes*. "Who else speaks for the Family of Man?/They are in tune and step/with constellations of universal law."

Carl Sandburg spoke for the Family of Man in bold new forms and subjects. Twentieth-century critics have seriously underestimated his influence in legitimizing and popularizing the free-verse form in American literature. Sandburg was often his own best critic; he anticipated that some of his work would later be judged as dated and obsolete. If some of his poems seemed "to be not for this hour," he suggested, they could be "passed by as annals, chronicles or punctuation points of a vanished period." He was a conscientious public poet whose work, to be comprehended fully, must be read within the context of his times.

Yet as the spokesman for the great human family, Carl Sandburg, biographer, historian, troubadour, and poet, speaks to any period, any place.

Letters:

The Letters of Carl Sandburg, edited by Herbert Mitgang (New York: Harcourt, Brace & World, 1968).
Selected letters written by Sandburg from 1898 to 1963.

Carl Sandburg, Philip Green Wright, and the Asgard Press, 1900-1910, compiled by Joan St. C. Crane (Charlottesville: University of Virginia Press, 1975).
A series of letters written by Sandburg to his favorite college professor, the catalyst for his first poems; revealing portrait of the young Sandburg.

The Poet and the Dream Girl: The Love Letters of Lilian Steichen and Carl Sandburg, edited by Margaret Sandburg (Urbana: University of Illinois Press, 1987).
Love letters written by Sandburg and his future wife Lilian Steichen during their six-month long courtship in 1908, edited with helpful notes by their daughter.

Biographies:

Karl Detzer, *Carl Sandburg: A Study in Personality and Background* (New York: Harcourt, Brace, 1941).
An account of Sandburg's life up to World War II based on interviews with Sandburg as well as his books and papers.

Harry Golden, *Carl Sandburg* (Chicago: World, 1961).
An anecdotal account of certain periods and themes in Sandburg's life written by his friend and fellow journalist.

Joseph Haas and Gene Lovitz, *Carl Sandburg: A Pictorial Biography* (New York: Putnam's, 1967).
A short biography with emphasis on photographs of the photogenic Sandburg.

Paula Steichen, *My Connemara* (New York: Harcourt, Brace & World, 1969).
A memoir of life in the Sandburg home in the North Carolina mountains written by his only granddaughter.

North Callahan, *Carl Sandburg: Lincoln of Our Literature* (New York: New York University Press, 1970).
A short biographical study by an American

historian with emphasis on Sandburg's Lincoln biography.

Helga Sandburg, *A Great and Glorious Romance* (New York: Harcourt Brace Jovanovich, 1978).
Biography of Carl and Lilian Paula Steichen Sandburg up to 1920 by their youngest daughter.

Paula Steichen, "Hyacinths and Biscuits," in *Carl Sandburg Home Handbook 117* (Washington, D.C.: National Park Service, 1982).
Biographical study, with illustrations, written by Sandburg's granddaughter.

References:
Gay Wilson Allen, *Carl Sandburg, Pamphlets on American Writers,* No. 101 (Minneapolis: University of Minnesota Press, 1972).
Critical study of Sandburg's work, with some biographical data.

Norman Corwin, *The World of Carl Sandburg: A Stage Presentation* (New York: Harcourt, Brace, 1960).
The text of the Broadway production based on Sandburg's work, with biographical notes by Sandburg and Corwin.

Richard Crowder, *Carl Sandburg* (New York: Twayne, 1964).
Biographical, thematic and critical study of Sandburg's work.

Gregory D'Alessio, *Old Troubadour: Carl Sandburg with His Guitar Friends* (New York: Walker, 1987).
Memoir of Sandburg as folk musician and guitarist by an artist and classical guitarist who was Sandburg's friend and host during his extended visits to New York City; contains previously unpublished photographs and drawings of Sandburg.

Hazel Durnell, *The America of Carl Sandburg* (Seattle: University of Washington Press, 1965).
An exploration of the themes and landscapes in Sandburg's work.

Harry Hansen, *Midwest Portraits* (New York: Harcourt, Brace, 1923).
A series of essays on Midwestern figures, including a long essay on Sandburg by a literary critic who knew him personally and observed him at work and at home.

Amy Lowell, *Tendencies in Modern American Poetry* (New York: Macmillan, 1917), pp. 139-232.
A critical study of several American poets, with a chapter on Sandburg as a revolutionary poet; written by a poet who was also Sandburg's friend.

Harriet Monroe, *Poets and Their Art* (New York: Macmillan, 1926), pp. 29-38.
Critical study of American poets, including a chapter on Sandburg's early poetry.

Monroe, *A Poet's Life* (New York: Macmillan, 1938).
The autobiography of the founder of *Poetry* magazine, where Sandburg's poems were first published for a literary audience; only brief passages related to Sandburg.

Edward Steichen, ed., *Sandburg: Photographers View Carl Sandburg* (New York: Harcourt, Brace & World, 1966).
A collection of photographs of Sandburg selected and introduced by his brother-in-law the noted photographer.

Louis Untermeyer, *American Poetry Since 1900* (New York: Holt, 1923).
A critical survey of American poets and poetry, with a chapter on Sandburg.

Untermeyer, *Modern American Poetry* (New York: Harcourt, Brace, 1936).
An anthology of American poetry edited by a poet and critic who encouraged Sandburg to publish *Chicago Poems*, his first book of poetry.

Mark Van Doren, *Carl Sandburg, With a Bibliography of Sandburg Materials in the Collections of the Library of Congress* (Washington, D.C.: Library of Congress, 1969).
An annotated bibliography of Sandburg materials at the Library of Congress up to 1960, with an introductory essay on Sandburg's poetry by his friend and fellow poet Mark Van Doren, who delivered a Sandburg lecture at the Library of Congress on 8 January 1968.

Papers:
The principal repository of Carl Sandburg's papers and books is the Carl Sandburg Collection of the University of Illinois Library at Urbana-Champaign, which also includes an extensive photographic and tape archive, particularly the Carl Sandburg Oral History Collection, compiled by Penelope Niven. In addition, more than 10,000 of Sandburg's books and many of his papers are housed at Connemara, the Carl Sandburg Home, a National Historic Site and National Park in Flat Rock, North Carolina. A smaller collection of memorabilia and some early editions of his work may be seen at the Carl Sandburg Birthplace in Galesburg, Illinois.

Harriet Beecher Stowe

This entry was updated by Madeleine B. Stern from her entry in DLB 12, American Realists and Naturalists.

Places	Litchfield, Conn. Andover, Mass.	Hartford, Conn. Brunswick, Maine	Cincinnati, Ohio
Influences and Relationships	Henry Ward Beecher Charles Dudley Warner	Annie A. Fields	Frederick Douglass
Literary Movements and Forms	Realism	Didactic Fiction	
Major Themes	Abolition Defense of Women Puritan Life	Moral Rectitude Domesticity Colonial New England	Spiritual Regeneration Sentiment
Cultural and Artistic Influences	Black Culture	Black History	Calvinism
Social and Economic Influences	Slavery Temperance	Civil War	Racism

See also the Stowe entries in DLB 1, The American Renaissance in New England *and* DLB 42, American Writers for Children Before 1900.

BIRTH: Litchfield, Connecticut, 14 June 1811, to Lyman and Roxanna Foote Beecher.

MARRIAGE: January 1836 to Calvin E. Stowe; children: Eliza Tyler, Harriet Beecher, Henry Ellis, Frederick William, Georgiana May, Samuel Charles (died in infancy), Charles Edward.

DEATH: Hartford, Connecticut, 1 July 1896.

*SELECTED BOOKS: *Primary Geography for Children on an Improved Plan,* by Stowe and Catharine Beecher (Cincinnati: Corey, Webster & Fairbank, 1833);

Prize Tale: A New England Sketch (Lowell, Mass.: Gilman, 1834);

The Mayflower; or, Sketches of Scenes and Characters among the Descendants of the Pilgrims (New York: Harper, 1843); enlarged as *The Mayflower and Miscellaneous Writings* (Boston: Phillips, Sampson, 1855);

Uncle Tom's Cabin; or, Life Among the Lowly, 2 volumes (Boston: Jewett/Cleveland: Jewett, Proctor & Worthington, 1852);

Uncle Sam's Emancipation; Earthly Care, a Heavenly Discipline; and Other Sketches (Philadelphia: Hazard, 1853);

Sunny Memories of Foreign Lands, 2 volumes (Boston: Phillips, Sampson/New York: Derby, 1854);

The Christian Slave. A Drama Founded on a Portion of Uncle Tom's Cabin (Boston: Phillips, Sampson, 1855);

Dred; A Tale of the Great Dismal Swamp, 2 volumes (Boston: Phillips, Sampson, 1856); republished as *Nina Gordon: A Tale of the Great Dismal Swamp,* 2 volumes (Boston: Ticknor & Fields, 1866);

Our Charley, and What to Do With Him (Boston: Phillips, Sampson, 1858);

The Minister's Wooing (New York: Derby & Jackson, 1859);

The Pearl of Orr's Island: A Story of the Coast of Maine (Boston: Ticknor & Fields, 1862);

Agnes of Sorrento (Boston: Ticknor & Fields, 1862);

*This list omits British editions for books first published in the United States.

A Reply to "The Affectionate and Christian Address of Many Thousands of Women of Great Britain and Ireland to Their Sisters, the Women of the United States of America" (London: Low, 1863);

House and Home Papers, as Christopher Crowfield (Boston: Ticknor & Fields, 1865);

Little Foxes, as Crowfield (Boston: Ticknor & Fields, 1866);

Religious Poems (Boston: Ticknor & Fields, 1867);

Stories About Our Dogs (Edinburgh: Nimmo, 1867);

The Daisy's First Winter, and Other Stories (Boston: Fields, Osgood, 1867); republished with differing contents as *Queer Little Folks* (London: Nelson, 1886);

Queer Little People (Boston: Ticknor & Fields, 1867);

The Chimney Corner, as Crowfield (Boston: Ticknor & Fields, 1868);

Men of Our Times; or, Leading Patriots of the Day (Hartford, Conn.: Hartford Publishing Company/New York: Denison, 1868); republished as *The Lives and Deeds of Our Self-Made Men* (Hartford, Conn.: Worthington, Dustin, 1872);

Oldtown Folks (Boston: Fields, Osgood, 1869);

The American Woman's Home, by Stowe and Catharine Beecher (New York & Boston: Ford, 1869); revised and enlarged as *The New Housekeeper's Manual* (New York: Ford, 1874);

Lady Byron Vindicated. A History of the Byron Controversy, from Its Beginning in 1816 to the Present Time (Boston: Fields, Osgood, 1870);

Little Pussy Willow (Boston: Fields, Osgood, 1870);

My Wife and I; or, Harry Henderson's History (New York: Ford, 1871);

Pink and White Tyranny. A Society Novel (Boston: Roberts, 1871);

Six of One by Half a Dozen of the Other. An Every Day Novel, by Stowe, Edward Everett Hale, Lucretia Peabody Hale, and others (Boston: Roberts Brothers, 1872);

Sam Lawson's Oldtown Fireside Stories (Boston: Osgood, 1872);

Palmetto-Leaves (Boston: Osgood, 1873);

Woman in Sacred History (New York: Fords, Howard & Hulbert, 1873); republished as *Bible Heroines* (New York: Fords, Howard & Hulbert, 1878);

Betty's Bright Idea. Also Deacon Pitkin's Farm, and The First Christmas of New England (New York: National Temperance Society & Publishing House, 1875);

We and Our Neighbors; or, The Records of an Unfashionable Street (New York: Ford, 1875);

Footsteps of the Master (New York: Ford, 1877);

Poganuc People: Their Loves and Lives (New York: Fords, Howard & Hulbert, 1878);

A Dog's Mission; or, The Story of the Old Avery House and Other Stories (New York: Fords, Howard & Hulbert, 1880).

Collections: The Writings of Harriet Beecher Stowe, 16 volumes (Boston & New York: Houghton Mifflin, 1896);

Harriet Beecher Stowe (New York: Library of America, 1982)—includes Uncle Tom's Cabin, The Minister's Wooing, and Oldtown Folks, with notes and chronology by Kathryn Kish Sklar.

OTHER: A Key to Uncle Tom's Cabin; Presenting the Original Facts and Documents upon which the Story is Founded, compiled by Stowe (Boston: Jewett/Cleveland: Jewett, Proctor & Worthington, 1853);

"Nelly's Heroics," in Nelly's Heroics, with Other Heroic Stories (Boston: Lothrop, 1883).

Harriet Beecher Stowe's *Uncle Tom's Cabin* (1852) became not only a phenomenal best-seller but a moral instrument. Combining domesticity and sentiment with violence and realism, this novel was the target of vehement controversy upon publication and is still the subject of intense critical examination. Imbedded in fact, it was imbued by its author with moral fervor. Its influence on American attitudes toward slavery has become legendary.

Harriet Beecher Stowe was a product of New England, particularly of New England Calvinism. She was born in Litchfield, Connecticut, one of the eight children of Lyman and Roxanna Foote Beecher. When Harriet was four, her mother died, and two years later her father married Harriet Porter. The Beechers were a family driven to proselytize and convert, to teach and to preach. Lyman Beecher was a Congregational minister, and Harriet Beecher's brother, Henry Ward Beecher, later became well known as the pastor of Brooklyn's Plymouth Church. Harriet Beecher was reared in an atmosphere of "moral oxygen" charged with "intellectual electricity." Both these qualities would be injected into *Uncle Tom's Cabin*. In the parsonage where she grew up, the guiding principles of life were self-abnegation and spiritual regeneration. Harriet Beecher attended Miss Sarah Pierce's school in Litchfield for five years, and at the age of thirteen she went on to the Hartford Female Seminary, run by her sister Catharine. She subsequently taught there until 1832, when the family moved to Cincinnati upon Lyman Beecher's appointment as president of the Lane Theological Seminary. She taught at the Western Female Institute, founded by Catharine Beecher, and in 1834 she won first prize in a contest conducted by the *Western Monthly Magazine*. Her sketch appeared in the April 1834 issue of the magazine and was published separately as *Prize Tale: A New England Sketch* (1834).

In 1836 Harriet Beecher married a widower, Calvin Stowe, professor of biblical literature at Lane. During the first seven years of their marriage she bore him five children. To alleviate her domestic drudgery and overwork she occasionally wrote stories so that she could afford domestic help, and in 1843 a collection of her New England stories, *The Mayflower*, was published by Harper. While she was still living in southern Ohio, Stowe witnessed the miseries of black freedmen who lived across the river from slavery. The subject of her famous novel began to take shape in her mind, and she was also aware that she must write to help her family financially. As she said in a letter to a friend, "When a new carpet or mattress was going to be needed or when . . . it began to be evident that my family accounts . . . 'wouldn't add up' then I used to say to my faithful friend, and factotum, Anna, . . . 'now, if you will keep the babies and attend to the things in the house for one day, I'll write a piece and then we shall be out of the scrape.' " By 1850, when Calvin Stowe was appointed professor at Bowdoin College, Brunswick, Maine, the Stowes had two more children to support.

Stowe's New England and Beecher heritage had made her a crusader; her domestic needs provided financial motivation; her life in southern Ohio had given her knowledge, direct or second-hand, of the nature of slavery. Back in New England, spurred by the passage of the 1850 Fugitive Slave Law, she wrote *Uncle Tom's Cabin*. The story, for which she was paid three hundred dollars, was written for the antislavery weekly, the *National Era*, which published it in forty installments (5 June 1851-1 April 1852). According to Charles Dudley Warner, "The installments were mostly written during the morning, on a little desk in a corner of the diningroom of the cottage in Brunswick, subject to all the interruptions of housekeeping, her children bursting into the room continually. . . . With a smile and a word and a motion of the hand she would wave them off, and keep on. . . . Usually at night the chapters were read to the family, who followed the story with intense feeling."

The story the family–and soon most of the world–followed with intense feeling began as polemical literature and became folklore. Designed to expose the evils of slavery–the evils to master as well as to slave–*Uncle Tom's Cabin* presented a series of characters who, as John William Ward has said, have become "part of the collective experience of the American people."

According to Stowe, her object was to demonstrate black people's "wrongs and sorrows, under a system so necessarily cruel and unjust as to defeat and do away the good effects of all that can be attempted for them, by their best friends, under it." How well she succeeded in drawing attention to their plight is overwhelmingly demonstrated by the sales and publishing history of her work. Following its appearance in the *National Era, Uncle Tom's Cabin* (turned down by Phillips, Sampson who would not risk offending Southern readers) was published in two volumes by John P.

Jewett of Boston in March 1852. During the first nine months the first edition of five thousand copies was quickly exhausted, and after a total of one hundred thousand sets of the two-volume edition had been sold, a cheap one-volume edition and an illustrated edition for the Christmas trade were published. Both the publisher's staff and his premises were enlarged to accommodate production of this single title, which was becoming a runaway bestseller. By March 1853, three hundred thousand copies had been sold. In January 1853 Charles Briggs commented in *Putnam's Magazine*, "Never since books were first printed has the success of *Uncle Tom* been equalled; the history of literature contains nothing parallel to it, nor approaching it: it is, in fact, the first real success in book-making. . . ." Maintaining sales of one thousand copies a week, the book sold half a million copies by 1857. With pirated editions in England and translations into many languages, the historian Thomas Macaulay could accurately report to Stowe in the fall of 1856, "There is no place where Uncle Tom . . . is not to be found." Dramatic versions and "Tomitudes" (Tom artifacts) all touted *Uncle Tom's Cabin*.

There were many ingredients in the success of *Uncle Tom's Cabin*. One of these was realism, derived from the author's firsthand observations and use of authentic source materials. While she was living in southern Ohio, "on the confines of a slave state," she had conversed with former slaves, and, according to Annie A. Fields, Stowe had observed "the cruel sale and separation of a married woman from her husband" while she was aboard an Ohio River steamboat. Fields adds that Stowe's "husband and brother had once been obliged to flee with a fugitive slave woman by night . . . and she herself had been called to write the letters for a former slave woman, servant in her own family, to a slave husband in Kentucky." To this earlier personal experience Stowe added what she had gleaned from her readings. For example, the source of the famous episode of Eliza crossing the ice has been traced to an article in *A Friend of Youth*, a children's antislavery magazine edited by Mrs. Margaret Bailey, which in February 1851 carried an account of how a woman and her child escaped from Kentucky by crossing the ice of the Ohio River. Finally, Stowe pursued her research by seeking living sources. On 9 July 1851 she wrote to the freedman and abolitionist-orator Frederick Douglass about her project, explaining that because part of the book would be set on a cotton plantation, "I am very desirous, therefore, to gain information from one who has been an actual laborer on one, and it occurred to me that in the circle of your acquaintance there might be one who would be able to communicate to me some such information as I desire. I have before me an able paper written by a Southern planter, in which the details and *modus operandi* are given from his point of sight. I am anxious to have something more from another standpoint. I wish to be able to make a picture that shall be graphic and true to nature in its details." Thus, through personal experience and research, Stowe created a realistic account of her great subject.

To realism she added another major ingredient: the moral fervor that came from her Beecher inheritance and that could lead her to include in her novel pronouncements such as, "Not by combining together, to protect injustice and cruelty, and making a common capital of sin, is this Union to be saved–but by repentance, justice and mercy." Also demonstrated in *Uncle Tom's Cabin* is the skill of the increasingly professional writer who could wrest from the exigencies of writing for serial publication the triumph of suspense and who could reshape a sentimental story into what a British reviewer called an "Iliad of the blacks."

Many of Stowe's contemporaries appreciated her efforts. George Sand, perceiving that the book was "essentially domestic and of the family," went so far as to find its author endowed with the "genius . . . of the saint." A lengthy anonymous review in the *Times* (London) commented astutely that "the clever authoress . . . strikes at the convictions of her readers by assailing their hearts." At home *Uncle Tom's Cabin* won the praise of Henry Wadsworth Longfellow and Ralph Waldo Emerson, who wrote in "Success" that the novel spoke "to the universal heart, and was read with equal interest to three audiences, namely, in the parlor, in the kitchen, and in the nursery of every house." Henry James later remembered that, as a young boy, he found the dramatic version of *Uncle Tom's Cabin* a thrilling "aesthetic adventure." As it aroused support, the novel also stirred vituperative opposition primarily from the South. In the *Southern Literary Messenger* (October 1852) George F. Holmes wrote that Stowe "has shockingly traduced the slaveholding society of the United States." After exposing what he called "the inconsistencies and false assertions" of her "slanderous work," he concluded: "Indeed she is only entitled to criticism at all, as

the mouthpiece of a large and dangerous faction which if we do not put down with the pen, we may be compelled one day . . . to repel with the bayonet."

In an attempt to silence her critics, Stowe made public her sources in *A Key to Uncle Tom's Cabin* (1853). This book contains documentary evidence for her statements: records of court cases, eye-witness reports, ephemeral handbills, all of which substantiated as realistic the graphic picture of slavery she had drawn.

Long after its author's death *Uncle Tom's Cabin* continued to be the object of critical examination. In 1896, the year of her death, Charles Dudley Warner provided the *Atlantic Monthly* with a detailed account of its history. Its artistry or the lack of it, the significance of its message, even its use of Negro dialect, have preoccupied critics, and the book has continued to be the subject of controversy. In a 1949 issue of the *Partisan Review*, James Baldwin assailed it as not only "a very bad novel" but a racist one. Three years later, Langston Hughes defended it as "a good story, exciting in incident, sharp in characterization, and threaded with humor," concluding that "the love and warmth and humanity that went into its writing keep it alive a century later from Bombay to Boston." There is no doubt that *Uncle Tom's Cabin* is a book unlikely to be forgotten.

Four years after the publication of *Uncle Tom's Cabin* Stowe resumed the antislavery theme in her novel *Dred; A Tale of the Great Dismal Swamp* (1856). She was induced to return to the subject by three grave and almost simultaneous events in May 1856: the violent assault upon Charles Sumner in the Senate by Representative Preston Brooks of South Carolina; Henry Ward Beecher's staging of a mock slave auction in Plymouth Church to dramatize the antislavery protest; and the massacre in Pottawatomie, Kansas, of five proslavery men by John Brown and his followers. Set in North Carolina, Stowe's second antislavery novel describes Dred as a "tall black man, of magnificent stature and proportions," who is imbued with a passion for vengeance. Dred is balanced by the old slave woman Milly who, although she has lost fourteen children by death or sale, still believes in Christian love. The mulatto Harry Gordon faces the dilemma of choosing between these two forces of vengeance and patience. Although *Dred* has been called flawed and structurally disorganized, it paints such memorable scenes as the episode of "The Camp-Meeting," which Alice C. Crozier has called "a

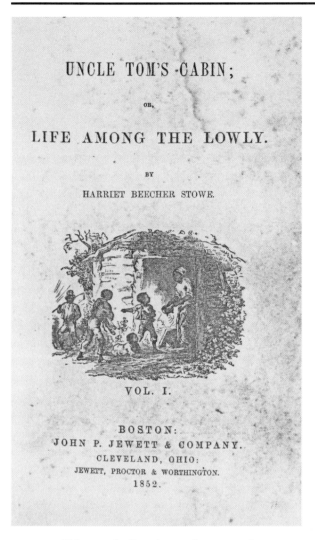

UNCLE TOM'S ·CABIN;

OR,

LIFE AMONG THE LOWLY.

BY

HARRIET BEECHER STOWE.

VOL. I.

BOSTON:
JOHN P. JEWETT & COMPANY.
CLEVELAND, OHIO:
JEWETT, PROCTOR & WORTHINGTON.
1852.

Title page for Stowe's most famous novel

piece of historical realism . . . a valuable document." Instead of compiling a separate key to her sources as she had done for *Uncle Tom's Cabin*, Stowe included appendices of citations to substantiate her assertions. Not unexpectedly the novel drew strong adverse criticism from the South, the *Southern Literary Messenger* concluding a review with the remark: "Were she a woman, we should blush for the sex–luckily she is only a Beecher."

As a Beecher she assumed the task of recording her father's recollections, and in the course of her labors she became fascinated with his reminiscence of New England and the theological wrangling that characterized it. In 1857 she lost her firstborn son, a student at Dartmouth who had not yet been converted. When, still urged on by economic need, she began another novel, she naturally turned to the two interwoven themes of

colonial New England and theological debate. Her series of New England novels begins with *The Minister's Wooing* (1859). Set in Newport, Rhode Island, the novel reanimates Puritan life and explores the beginnings of the slave trade as it focuses on Dr. Samuel Hopkins, a forthright colonial minister subject to "those interior crises in which a man is convulsed with the struggle of two natures, the godlike and the demoniac." As Stowe wrote: "In no other country were the soul and the spiritual life ever such intense realities, and everything contemplated so much . . . 'in reference to eternity.' " In *The Minister's Wooing*, as in the novels that followed it, Stowe recreated realistically colonial New England and the theological warfare that was so much a part of it. Lawrence Buell has aptly referred to the novel's "creative uses of orthodoxy."

The Pearl of Orr's Island (1862) is the second in the series of Stowe's New England novels. Set on the coast of Maine, it portrays "the primitive and Biblical people of that lonely shore," among them the mystical heroine Mara, the pearl of the title. In 1869 Stowe expanded her chronicle of colonial New England with *Oldtown Folks,* one of whose most interesting characters is the patriot Ellery Davenport, a man "at war with himself, at war with the traditions of his ancestry." Theological issues still dominate the book, but Bret Harte, reviewing the novel rather disparagingly for the *Overland Monthly,* credited her with a "quaint Puritan humor." The final New England novel was published in 1878. In *Poganuc People* Stowe produced "a fictional memoir of her childhood years in Litchfield" and glorified the "millennium . . . ever the star of hope in the eyes of the New England clergy; . . . They were children of the morning."

By the time *Poganuc People* was published, Stowe had written several other books that engaged public attention. Perhaps the most sensational was her *Lady Byron Vindicated* (1870). Now famous and well-traveled, Stowe had seen a "beautiful and terrible ministry" at work in the life of her late friend Anne, Lady Byron. They had first met in 1853, and the friendship had deepened during Stowe's 1856 journey abroad. The two women shared not only religious interests, but, it appears, confidences: Lady Byron had revealed to Stowe Lord Byron's incestuous relationship with his half sister. After Byron's mistress, Countess Teresa Guiccioli, criticized Lady Byron in *My Recollections of Lord Byron* (1869), Stowe was prompted to retaliate with an article in the *Atlan-*

tic Monthly. She later expanded this article into *Lady Byron Vindicated,* where she revealed the secret of Byron's incest, defended her late friend, and by defending one woman in particular, defended women in general. *Lady Byron Vindicated* aroused a storm of criticism. Justin McCarthy wrote in the *Independent:* "There is something positively painful about the sanctimonious imbecility of the manner in which Mrs. Stowe tries to regard her sickening task as a moral and religious duty." On the other hand, Elizabeth Cady Stanton reminded readers of the *Independent* that "the true relation of the sexes is the momentous question at this stage of our civilization, and Mrs. Stowe has galvanized the world to its consideration."

During the 1870s scandal came closer to home. The scandal involving her beloved brother Henry Ward Beecher and two of his parishioners, the *Independent*'s editor Theodore Tilton and Tilton's wife, Elizabeth, culminated in Tilton's suing Beecher, charging him with adultery with Elizabeth Tilton. The jury was unable to reach a verdict, but Stowe believed in her brother's innocence. Her literary productions during this difficult period consisted primarily of post-Civil war society novels. In *My Wife and I* (1871), *Pink and White Tyranny* (1871), and *We and Our Neighbors* (1875), Stowe attempted to delineate realistically the life of the times: its business and its morals, its alcoholism and its prostitution, the domestic role of its women. She could not resist the temptation to caricature Victoria Woodhull, the woman editor who had first exposed the Beecher scandal, and in *My Wife and I* she satirized her as Miss Audacia Dangereyes. William Dean Howells, reviewing *My Wife and I* in the *Atlantic Monthly,* remarked that "the reality of Mrs. Stowe's best work is not here, as it is absent from the other books in which she deals with fashion and wealth in a moralistic spirit."

While her reputation will rest forever upon her masterpiece, *Uncle Tom's Cabin,* many of Stowe's other works are worthy of reading and analysis. She developed into a truly professional writer, producing at least a book a year between 1862 and 1884 and providing for her family and educating her children. Neither her New England novels nor her novels of society are comparable in moral power with her antislavery novels, although in all her novels she attempted to recreate realistically the themes, backgrounds, and characters that engrossed her. The crusade which she helped document and advance has become history, but her novels continue to interest scholars. Her artistry and literary craftsmanship, her aesthetics and her theology, her ideology and her realism are all being examined. Harriet Beecher Stowe has not lost her audience.

Letters:

Life of Harriet Beecher Stowe Compiled from Her Letters and Journals, edited by Charles Edward Stowe (Boston: Houghton, Mifflin, 1889);

Life and Letters of Harriet Beecher Stowe, edited by Annie A. Fields (Boston: Houghton, Mifflin, 1897).

Biographies:

Charles Edward Stowe and L. B. Stowe, *Harriet Beecher Stowe, The Story of Her Life* (Boston: Houghton Mifflin, 1911);

Forest Wilson, *Crusader in Crinoline: The Life of Harriet Beecher Stowe* (Philadelphia: Lippincott, 1941).

References:

John R. Adams, *Harriet Beecher Stowe* (Boston: Twayne, 1963);
    Study of the author's life and career, with particular attention to her contributions to periodicals.

Elizabeth Ammons, ed., *Critical Essays on Harriet Beecher Stowe* (Boston: G. K. Hall, 1980);
    Highly useful compendium of reviews and critical analyses of Stowe's books with sections devoted to the antislavery books (*Uncle Tom's Cabin* and *Dred*), the Byron furor, New England matter, novels of manners, reminiscences.

Gillian Brown, "Getting in the Kitchen with Dinah: Domestic Politics in *Uncle Tom's Cabin,*" *American Quarterly,* 36 (1984): 503-523;
    Stowe's view of slavery as a threat to domestic life is examined.

Lawrence Buell, "Rival Romantic Interpretations of New England Puritanism: Hawthorne versus Stowe," *Texas Studies in Literature and Language,* 25 (1983): 77-99;
    Comparison of two novels, Stowe's *The Minister's Wooing* and Hawthorne's *The Scarlet Letter* in respect to their interpretations of Puritanism.

James M. Cox, "Harriet Beecher Stowe: From Sectionalism to Regionalism," *Nineteenth-Century Fiction*, 38 (1984): 444-466;
Examines *Uncle Tom's Cabin* as the expression of a "moral universe in a postsacred era."

Alice C. Crozier, *The Novels of Harriet Beecher Stowe* (New York: Oxford University Press, 1969);
Perceptive analysis of Stowe's novels, notably *Uncle Tom's Cabin* and *Dred,* classifying them as historical romance, and discussing their feminist implications as well as the role of mothers and family life they portray; with an interesting study of Stowe's exposure of Byron and vindication of Lady Byron.

Josephine Donovan, "Harriet Beecher Stowe's Feminism," *American Transcendental Quarterly,* 47-48 (1982): 141-157;
Studies Stowe's feminism as influenced adversely by Victoria Woodhull's exposure of the Beecher scandal.

Charles Foster, *The Rungless Ladder: Harriet Beecher Stowe and New England Puritanism* (Durham: Duke University Press, 1954);
Study of Stowe's Calvinist background as an influence upon her work, with detailed analyses of the novels.

Susan Geary, "Harriet Beecher Stowe, John P. Jewett, and Author-Publisher Relations in 1853," *Studies in the American Renaissance (1977):* 345-367;
Informative survey of the printing and publishing arrangements for *Uncle Tom's Cabin.*

Thomas F. Gossett, *Uncle Tom's Cabin and American Culture* (Dallas: Southern Methodist University Press, 1985);
Complete study of the author, her early life, the creation of her major novel and its reception.

Thomas P. Joswick, " 'The crown without the conflict,': Religious Values and Moral Reasoning in *Uncle Tom's Cabin,*" *Nineteenth-Century Fiction*, 39 (1984): 253-274;
Stresses Stowe's concept of "moral character" as a dominating societal force.

Gayle Kimball, *The Religious Ideas of Harriet Beecher Stowe: The Gospel of Womanhood* (New York & Toronto: Edwin Mellen Press, 1982);
Stowe's advocacy of women as agents of salvation is examined.

Stephen Railton, "Mothers, Husbands, and *Uncle Tom,*" *The Georgia Review*, 38 (1984): 129-144;
Traces the place of *Uncle Tom's Cabin* in literary history and analyzes its enormous popularity.

Moira Davison Reynolds, *Uncle Tom's Cabin and Mid-Nineteenth Century United States: Pen and Conscience* (Jefferson, N.C.: McFarland, 1985);
Uncle Tom's Cabin studied against the background of its times, specifically the contemporary state of slavery and women.

Madeleine B. Stern, "The Role of the Publisher in Mid-Nineteenth Century American Literature," *Publishing History*, 10 (1981): 5-26;
Examines the role played by the publisher in the literary history and reception of *Uncle Tom's Cabin.*

Edward Charles Wagenknecht, *Harriet Beecher Stowe: The Known and the Unknown* (New York: Oxford University Press, 1965);
Readable psychological biography of Stowe presenting a fresh portrait of the woman.

Papers:
Harriet Beecher Stowe's papers are in the Beecher-Stowe Collection at Schlesinger Library, Radcliffe College, Harvard University.

Edith Wharton

This entry was updated by Joseph Caldwell from the entry by James W. Tuttleton (New York University) in DLB 12, American Realists and Naturalists.

Places	Italy New England	France	New York City
Influences and Relationships	George Eliot Henry James William Carey Brownell Morton Fullerton	William Dean Howells Walter Berry Bernard Berenson	Paul Bourget Emile Zola Honoré de Balzac
Literary Movements and Forms	Short Story Satire	Realism Psychological Drama	Novel of Manners
Major Themes	Desire of the Individual vs. Authority of Social Convention Architecture and Gardening	The Aesthetic Poverty of America Entrapment	Female Psychology Free Will and Individual Responsibility
Cultural and Artistic Influences	Evolution Theories of Darwin, Huxley, and Spencer	Pragmatism	French Language and Culture
Social and Economic Influences	Abuses of the Industrial System	New York Social Aristocracy	World War I

See also the Wharton entries in DLB 4, American Writers in Paris, 1920-1939 *and* DLB 9, American Novelists, 1910-1945.

BIRTH: New York, New York, 24 January 1862, to George Frederic and Lucretia Rhinelander Jones.

MARRIAGE: 29 April 1885 to Edward Robbins Wharton (divorced).

DEATH: Pavillon Colombe, Saint Brice-sous-Forêt, France, 11 August 1937.

BOOKS: *Verses,* anonymous (Newport, R. I.: C. E. Hammett, Jr., 1878);

The Decoration of Houses, by Wharton and Ogden Codman, Jr. (New York: Scribners, 1897; London: Batsford, 1898);

The Greater Inclination (New York: Scribners, 1899; London: Lane/Bodley Head, 1899);

The Touchstone (New York: Scribners, 1900); republished as *A Gift from the Grave* (London: Murray, 1900);

Crucial Instances (New York: Scribners, 1901; London: Murray, 1901);

The Valley of Decision (2 volumes, New York: Scribners, 1902; 1 volume, London: Murray, 1902);

Sanctuary (New York: Scribners, 1903; London: Macmillan, 1903);

Italian Villas and Their Gardens (New York: Century, 1904; London: Lane/Bodley Head, 1904);

The Descent of Man and Other Stories (New York: Scribners, 1904; enlarged edition, London & New York: Macmillan, 1904);

Italian Backgrounds (New York: Scribners, 1905; London: Macmillan, 1905);

The House of Mirth (New York: Scribners, 1905; London & New York: Macmillan, 1905);

Madame de Treymes (New York: Scribners, 1907; London: Macmillan, 1907);

The Fruit of the Tree (New York: Scribners, 1907; London: Macmillan, 1907);

The Hermit and the Wild Woman and Other Stories (New York: Scribners, 1908; London: Macmillan, 1908);

A Motor-Flight Through France (New York: Scribners, 1908; London: Macmillan, 1908);

Artemis to Actaeon and Other Verse (New York: Scribners, 1909; London: Macmillan, 1909);

Tales of Men and Ghosts (New York: Scribners, 1910; London: Macmillan, 1910);

Ethan Frome (New York: Scribners, 1911; London: Macmillan, 1911);

The Reef (New York: Appleton, 1912; London: Macmillan, 1912);

The Custom of the Country (New York: Scribners, 1913; London: Macmillan, 1913);

Fighting France, from Dunkerque to Belfort (New York: Scribners, 1915; London: Macmillan, 1915);

Xingu and Other Stories (New York: Scribners, 1916; London: Macmillan, 1916);

Summer (New York: Appleton, 1917; London: Macmillan, 1917);

The Marne (New York: Appleton, 1918; London: Macmillan, 1918);

French Ways and Their Meaning (New York & London: Appleton, 1919; London: Macmillan, 1919);

The Age of Innocence (New York & London: Appleton, 1920);

In Morocco (New York: Scribners, 1920; London: Macmillan, 1920);

The Glimpses of the Moon (New York & London: Appleton, 1922; London: Macmillan, 1923);

A Son at the Front (New York: Scribners, 1923; London: Macmillan, 1923);

Old New York: False Dawn (The 'Forties), The Old Maid (The 'Fifties), The Spark (The 'Sixties), and New Year's Day (The 'Seventies) (New York & London: Appleton, 1924);

The Mother's Recompense (New York & London: Scribners, 1925);

The Writing of Fiction (New York & London: Scribners, 1925);

Here and Beyond (New York & London: Appleton, 1926);

Twelve Poems (London: Medici Society, 1926);

Twilight Sleep (New York & London: Appleton, 1927);

The Children (New York & London: Appleton, 1928); republished as *The Marriage Playground* (New York: Grosset & Dunlap, 1930);

Hudson River Bracketed (New York & London: Appleton, 1929);

Certain People (New York & London: Appleton, 1930);

The Gods Arrive (New York & London: Appleton, 1932);

Human Nature (New York & London: Appleton, 1933);

A Backward Glance (New York & London: Appleton-Century, 1934);

The World Over (New York & London: Appleton-Century, 1936);

Ghosts (New York & London: Appleton-Century, 1937);

The Buccaneers (New York & London: Appleton-Century, 1938).

OTHER: Hermann Sudermann, *The Joy of Living*, translated by Wharton (New York: Scribners, 1902);

The Book of the Homeless, compiled by Wharton (Paris, 1915; New York: Scribners, 1916);

Eternal Passion in English Poetry, edited by Wharton, Robert Norton, and Gaillard Lapsley, with a preface by Wharton (New York: Appleton-Century, 1939).

PERIODICAL PUBLICATIONS: "The Vice of Reading," *North American Review,* 177 (October 1903): 513-521;

"The Criticism of Fiction," *Times Literary Supplement,* 14 May 1914, p. 230;

"The Great American Novel," *Yale Review,* new series 16 (July 1927): 646-656;

"When New York Was Innocent," *Literary Digest,* 99 (15 December 1928): 27;

"Visibility in Fiction," *Yale Review,* new series 18 (March 1929): 480-488;

"Confessions of a Novelist," *Atlantic Monthly,* 151 (April 1933): 385;

"Permanent Values in Fiction" *Saturday Review of Literature,* 10 (7 April 1934): 603-604;

"Souvenirs du Bourget d'Outremer," *Review Hebdomadaire,* 45 (21 June 1936): 266-286.

Edith Wharton

While at the close of her career Edith Wharton was sometimes regarded as passé, a literary aristocrat whose fiction about people of high social standing had little to tell about the masses, particularly during the Jazz Age and the Depression, a countervailing view has begun to emerge in response to Edmund Wilson's call, after her death, for "justice" to Edith Wharton. In this counterview, Wharton is seen as a serious and deeply committed artist with a high respect for the professional demands of her craft, a woman praiseworthy for the generally high quality and range of her oeuvre, a novelist who wrote some of the most important fiction in the first quarter of the twentieth century, perhaps in American literary history. If this point of view has merit, her claim to attention arises from the clarity of her social vision, the particular angle of that vision (high society seen from the inside), and her subtle mastery of the techniques of fiction, which would be interesting to any reader concerned with the processes of writing. The novelist Gore Vidal remarked in "Of Writers and Class: In Praise of Edith Wharton" that "At best, there are only three or four American novelists who can be thought of as 'major' and Edith Wharton is one." He regards Wharton and Henry James as "the two great American masters of the novel." And he remarks that "now that the prejudice against the female writer is on the wane, they look to be exactly what they are: giants, equals, the tutelary and benign gods of our American literature." If that statement is not justice to Edith Wharton, it will be a long time in coming.

Born into the conservative, fashionable, and wealthy society of old New York in 1862, Edith Jones, the daughter of George Frederic and Lucretia Rhinelander Jones, was privately tutored, traveled extensively in Europe as a girl, and was married off on 29 April 1885 to Edward Wharton, a man considerably older than she and with few intellectual or artistic interests. During the early years of her marriage, she seems to have done little more than play the role of society matron and hostess in New York and Newport. Several years after her marriage, in 1894, she suffered a nervous breakdown, which resulted in convalescence in a sanatorium. There novel writing was prescribed therapy, and she thus commenced her professional writing career.

As a chronicler of the manners of New York society from the 1840s into the 1930s, an international novelist, and master of the short story, Wharton's principal focus, as indicated in her book *The Writing of Fiction* (1925), was the conflict between the desire of the individual and the authority of social convention. Blake Nevius has found the latent subject of her work to be two interlocking themes: "the spectacle of a large and generous nature . . . trapped by circumstances ironically of its own devising into consanguinity with a meaner nature"; and the related problem of trying to define "the nature and limits of individual responsibility, to determine what allowance of freedom or rebellion can be made for her trapped protagonist without at the same time threatening the structure of society." Since the publication of R. W. B. Lewis's *Edith Wharton: A Biography* (1975), based on her private papers, it has become vividly clear the extent to which these intensely felt issues arose from her personal situation.

Her first publication was a book of poems, *Verses* (1878), privately published in Newport while she was yet a girl. Together with *Artemis to Actaeon and Other Verse* (1909), and *Twelve Poems* (1926), Wharton's verse suggests a very conventional poetic sense, sometimes passionately eruptive, but never in connection with the great poetic revolution of the twentieth-century avantgarde. *Verses* was followed by *The Decoration of Houses* (1897), a work on interior decor written with Ogden Codman, Jr. (apparently to bury the taste of her mother's generation). And her first book publications of fiction were *The Greater Inclination* (1899), *The Touchstone* (1900), and *Crucial Instances* (1901).

At the publication of *The Greater Inclination*, Henry James remarked that he was able to detect, in these eight short stories, the echoes of George Eliot sounding through the book. But many early reviewers, among them John D. Barry in the *Boston Literary World*, remarked that, unfortunately, she had been most influenced by James himself—a claim that Wharton came more and more to resent, although she and James were to develop a close friendship. Harry Thurston Peck was perhaps more discriminating in his observation that *The Greater Inclination* had

caught the "English" manner of James's late style but had improved upon it. He concluded that "We have seen nothing this year that has impressed us so much as Mrs. Wharton's book." The stories in *The Greater Inclination* vary from a straight drawing-room scene written in dialogue, to a story–heavily freighted with psychological analysis–of a symbolic journey to death of a man and his wife. Several of the tales explore the power of social convention and the difficulty of transcending it; and a rather tough pragmatic attitude permeates Wharton's treatment of the theme. As one character remarks of conventions, "one may believe in them or not; but as long as they do rule the world it is only by taking advantage of their protection that one can find a *modus vivendi.*"

In *The Touchstone*, Wharton tried her hand at the *nouvelle*, a form she was to bring to perfection in *Ethan Frome* (1911). *The Touchstone* involves a man who secretly sells intimate love letters once written to him by a now-deceased novelist, Margaret Aubyn. After their publication, he confesses to his wife the sale of the letters, identifying himself as the heartless recipient who allowed her anguished love to be published to the world; this confession achieves an alleviation of his guilt and the rehabilitation of his marriage. No longer, in the Jamesian phrase, a "publishing scoundrel," Glennard becomes the deeply sensitive and moral man Margaret Aubyn had seen *in potentia* and loved.

While some of her early critics were to condemn the "flatness" of her characters in the short story and *nouvelle*, Wharton always felt that it was the business of the novel gradually to develop character and that the business of the short story was to reveal a significant situation. If therefore her personae in the stories seem less than fully "rounded," her practice was premeditated. As she was to observe in *The Writing of Fiction*, "No subject in itself, however fruitful, appears to be able to keep a novel alive; only the characters in it can. Of the short story the same cannot be said. Some of the greatest short stories owe their vitality entirely to the dramatic rendering of a situation. Undoubtedly the characters engaged must be a little more than puppets; but apparently, also, they may be a little less than individual human beings." None of her early critics would have objected to her description of the short story as "a shaft driven straight into the heart of human experience," but her view of characterization in short fiction doubtless accounts for the recurrent conviction that, for all her brilliance, Wharton's tales lack the human warmth of great art. Still, in praise of Wharton's psychological realism in *The Touchstone*, Aline Gorren remarked in the *Critic* that Wharton was to be praised for "the genius with which she will bring to the surface the underground movements of women's minds."

Crucial Instances was marked by a declining dependence on verbal irony and fin de siècle witticism and by a growth of her mastery of the short-story form. One of the predominant themes of this volume of tales is the futility of self-sacrifice (as in "The Angel at the Grave"); another was the aesthetic poverty of the American scene, particularly the New England small town, in contrast to Europe (as in "The Recovery"). These themes resonate throughout all Wharton's fiction, and the stories suggest, in their formal organization, what Wharton conceived short stories to be: "crucial instances" disengaged from "the welter of experience" that "illuminate our moral lives."

Wharton's annual excursions to Europe during her early married life account for the immediacy of the setting of her first novel, *The Valley of Decision* (1902), a long chronicle set in settecento Italy on the eve of the Napoleonic invasion. Out of a passion for Italy were also to come *Italian Villas and Their Gardens* (1904), a serious examination of Italian villa and garden architecture, illustrated by Maxfield Parrish's drawings, and *Italian Backgrounds* (1905), a series of nine travel sketches recording the impersonal impressions of the Whartons, the Paul Bourgets, and others of their entourage. The title sketch of *Italian Backgrounds* re-creates the color and variety of the settecento "world of appearances–of fine clothes, gay colours and graceful attitudes." *The Valley of Decision* was inspired by the same impulse to re-create that world in fiction, to vivify the colorful attitudes of the period. Like George Eliot's *Romola* (1863), however, the novel principally dramatizes the politics of a transitional age in which two political ideologies came into conflict with each other. An apt sense of the novel is suggested in Wharton's letter to William Crary Brownell, her Scribners editor. It was, she said, "an attempt to picture Italy at the time of the breaking-up of the small principalities at the end of the 18th century, when all the old forms and traditions of court life were still preserved, but the immense intellectual and moral movement of the new regime was at work beneath the surface of things. . . . I have tried to reflect the traditional influences and customs of the day, to-

gether with new ideas, in the mind of a cadet of one of the reigning houses, who is suddenly called to succeed to the dukedom of Pianura, and tries to apply the theories of the French encyclopedists to his small principality. Incidentally I have given sketches of Venetian life, and glimpses of Sir William Hamilton's circle at Naples, and the clerical milieu at Rome, where the suppression of the Society of Jesus, and the mysterious death of Ganganelli, had produced a violent reaction toward formalism and superstition. The close of the story pictures the falling to pieces of the whole business at the approach of Napoleon." Conservative in its social imagination, charged with contempt for radical Enlightenment political theorizing, *The Valley of Decision* thus took an indirect stand against the perfectibilitarian schemes for American social reform at the turn of the century, in the "progressive era." The general critical response was not favorable. Most reviewers felt it to be learned and labored and lacking in dramatic action, with characters put to the use of symbolizing various political positions. As an anonymous reviewer for the *Outlook* put it, "The story is not dramatic; it does not deal with the master passions in a masterly way; it is a carefully wrought study of a period and a temperament; an example of fine technique, a charmingly told story of deep and unusual interest."

Sanctuary (1903) deals once again with the theme of self-sacrifice. In this case, a woman marries a man guilty of fraud in order to prevent his unborn children from being "tainted" by their father's moral imperfection. In the end, Kate Orme saves their son Dick from replicating his father's financial dishonesty by having provided the sanctuary of love necessary to help him triumph over temptation where his father had not. In trying to render plausible Kate's motivation for marrying, Wharton writes of "mysterious primal influences," the "sacrificial instinct of her sex," and that "passion of spiritual motherhood that made her long to fling herself between the unborn child and its fate." But none of these phrases quite succeeds in making credible Kate's utterly fantastic motive in marrying Dick's father. As an anonymous reviewer in the *Independent* put it, *Sanctuary* is "the kind of book a woman writes when she conceives her characters all walking upon moral margins too narrow to be quite comfortable. And it does not demonstrate the growth of principles and manly stamina so much as it does a beautiful, tender sentimentality peculiar to women, whether they are writers, mothers or missionaries."

The Valley of Decision taught Wharton two principles about novel writing, she later observed. The first was that she ought to use the material she knew best; the second was that the value of any fictional subject would depend on how much significance she could see in it. Was the New York beau monde too shallow to yield deep significance? Some critics, notably Van Wyck Brooks and V. L. Parrington, have thought so. But Wharton saw her task–in re-creating this flat and futile commercial aristocracy in *The House of Mirth* (1905)–as that of extracting from New York society the human significance which would have universal meaning: as Wharton wrote in *A Backward Glance* (1934), "In what aspect could a society of irresponsible pleasure-seekers be said to have, on the 'old woe of the world,' any deeper bearing than the people composing such a society could guess? The answer was that a frivolous society can acquire dramatic significance only through what its frivolity destroys. Its tragic implication lies in its power of debasing people and ideals. The answer, in short, was my heroine, Lily Bart."

The story of Lily Bart is the story of a beautiful but fastidious girl of inadequate means who tries to maintain her social position in the wealthy but dissolute New York beau monde while, at twenty-nine, trying to find a suitably rich husband. As she loses her tenuous position with the idle rich, Lily falls in the social order and eventually drops out of it, only to die of an overdose of chloral in a cheap boardinghouse.

The product of the social forces that have shaped her, Lily is too poor to run with the fast crowd but too much enamored of its luxuries to give up wealth and glamour and make an independent life with Lawrence Selden, the relatively poor young man who loves her. Lily's social values, so reminiscent of those of Dreiser's Sister Carrie, and Lily's tragic fall, so suggestive of Hurstwood's gradual deterioration and suicide in a New York flophouse, suggest that Wharton's world view might have been that of scientific naturalism. On this issue critics have frequently disagreed. Blake Nevius, for example, did call Wharton a writer of naturalistic tragedy, but Robert Morss Lovett found in her a "spirit of comedy." Marilyn Jones Lyde has tried to prove that Wharton's view of life was that of ethical tragedy. E. K. Brown, however, argued that Wharton saw life as more ironic than tragic.

What Louis O. Coxe says of *The Age of Innocence* (1920) has seemed true of her other works: that one of the graces and delights of Wharton's fiction lies exactly "in the multifariousness of its thematic material, in its refusal to tie itself down to 'meaning,' the while that it glitters with a density, a hardness of surface that only a truly novelistic eye could have seen and an informing mind recreate." This celebration of Wharton's philosophical ambiguity returns to Percy Lubbock's claim that Wharton was not committed to any one philosophical view, to Frances Russell's complaint that Wharton was "full of standards, viewpoints."

Wharton was not a thoroughgoing determinist. A close investigation of *Ethan Frome, The House of Mirth* and *The Age of Innocence*–those works that most frequently provoke the question of her world view–shows that free will is ordinarily present. Lily Bart, for example, realizes that Selden has preserved a detached view of the society she aspires to, that he has "points of contact outside the great gilt cage in which they were all huddled for the mob to gape at": "How alluring the world outside the cage appeared to Lily, as she heard its door clang on her. In reality, as she knew, the door never clanged: it stood always open; but most of the captives were like flies in a bottle, and having once flown in, could never regain their freedom. It was Selden's distinction that he had never forgotten the way out." Lily defines her goal in life as "success," getting as much as one can out of life. For Selden, however, it is personal freedom–what he calls the republic of the spirit: freedom "from money, from ease and anxiety, from all the material accidents. To keep a kind of republic of the spirit–that's what I call success."

But the problem of free will, the ability to choose between alternatives, is more complex than this analysis has suggested–principally because of the influence of Wharton's reading in the sciences. Her knowledge of the forces of heredity and environment, gained from writers like Charles Darwin, Thomas Huxley, Herbert Spencer, and John Locke, complicates her portraits. While according Lily Bart a measure of freedom and responsibility for her behavior, Wharton could also write of her in such a way as to suggest that Lily is the poignant victim of hereditary and environmental forces which she cannot understand and over which she has little control: "Inherited tendencies had combined with early training to make her the highly specialized product she was: an organism as helpless out of its narrow range as the sea-anemone torn from the rock. She had been fashioned to adorn and delight; to what other end does nature round the rose-leaf and paint the humming-bird's breast? And was it her fault that the purely decorative mission is less easily and harmoniously fulfilled among social beings than in the world of nature? That it is apt to be hampered by material necessities or complicated by moral scruples?" But although the figurative language tends to suggest that Lily is a naturalistic victim, the irony in the rhetorical questions should not be lost on the reader.

In his Boston lectures on pragmatism in 1906, William James distinguished between a tender-minded and a tough-minded response to the question of free will and determinism. This distinction is relevant to Wharton's fiction. In her insistence that heredity and environment do strongly influence moral decisions, in her awareness that in a very special sense character is destiny, Wharton must be called a "tender-minded determinist" who realized, like Lawrence Selden, that Lily "was so evidently the victim of the civilization which had produced her, that the links of her bracelet seemed like manacles chaining her to her fate." She learns too late the alternative order of values based on freedom that Selden describes. She cannot balance, as he apparently can, the epicurean's delight in pleasure with the stoic's indifference to it. The novel thus weighs both Lily and contemporary New York society in the balance and finds them wanting. To complete the biblical phrase to which the title alludes: "The heart of the wise is in the house of mourning; but the heart of fools is in the house of mirth" (Ecclesiastes 7:3). The point of the novel is suggested by Wharton's remark in her review of Howard Sturgis's novel *Belchamber* (1905): "A handful of vulgar people, bent only on spending and enjoying, may seem a negligible factor in the social development of the race; but they become an engine of destruction through the illusions they kill and the generous ardor they turn to despair." Surely Lily Bart was in her mind when Wharton wrote those lines.

Written rapidly under pressure of a *Scribner's* magazine deadline, *The House of Mirth* reflects weaknesses of style and plotting and a strain of sentimentality that often mar Wharton's best fiction. But the book was a best-seller in 1905 and 1906. While most reviewers deplored the vanity and vulgarity of high society, William Payne Morton was typical in praising the novel as

"a work which has enlisted the matured powers of a writer whose performance is always distinguished, and whose coupling of psychological insight with the gift of expression is probably not surpassed by any other woman novelist of our time." The experience of writing the novel turned a drifting amateur into a professional writer, as Wharton herself confessed. It also revealed to her the possibilities inherent in the novel of manners set in New York. She celebrated her success by moving permanently to France in 1907, hoping to find in the exclusive Faubourg Saint-Germain quarter of Paris a literate and civilized high society lacking in New York.

Madame de Treymes (1907) dramatizes, after the manner of James's international tales (particularly *Madame de Mauves*, 1874), the conflict between the moral milieus of America and France. Set in Paris, which is celebrated for its physical beauty (Wharton always thought brownstone New York to be hideous), this *nouvelle* contrasts the individual goodness of the American with the moral and social complicities of a complex French social order. Henry James, who had just confessed in his preface to the New York edition of *The American* that he had not understood the French aristocracy in 1875, cautioned her about her subject matter: "All the same, with the rue de Varenne, &c, don't go in too much for the French or the 'Franco-American' subject–the real field of your extension is [England]–it has far more fusability with *our* native and primary material. . . ." But Wharton continued to feel more in command of the French scene than James had ever been. Even so, some reviewers wondered about *Madame de Treymes*'s sinister view of French familial solidarity, while Vernon Atwood claimed it to be "an absolutely flawless and satisfying piece of workmanship."

Wharton's third novel, *The Fruit of the Tree* (1907), sought to capitalize on the then-current vogue of muckraking and reform literature. This book abandoned the drawing-room milieu for the plight of the textile workers in a mill town in Massachusetts. Her aim, in telling the story of John Amherst, an assistant manager of a mill, was to expose and criticize the abuses of the industrial system, particularly the irresponsibility of managers who fail to look after the physical and spiritual welfare of their employees. That Wharton should have risked such a subject, about which she knew little, seems incredible. And, indeed, she got many of the details of factory life wrong. Then she shifted away from the reform topic midway through in order to explore the moral implications of euthanasia (Amherst's paralyzed wife is dispatched by an idealistic nurse who then marries him). The result is a structurally imperfect novel that concludes with the view that life is "not a matter of abstract principles, but a succession of pitiful compromises with fate, of concessions to old tradition, old beliefs, old charities and frailties." This observation, perhaps a latent theme of much of her fiction, suggests that the fruit of the tree is therefore a knowledge of the inextricable entanglements of good and evil.

A new invention, the motorcar, Wharton quickly discovered, had "restored the romance of travel." Her next book, *A Motor-Flight Through France* (1908), deals with a three-week tour taken by the Whartons and Henry James in the Whartons' new automobile. Perhaps the key to the work lies in what Wharton had to say about the effect of antiquities–like the Gothic cathedral at Rheims–on the American traveler who has, in effect, no roots in the past: "Yes–reverence is the most precious emotion that such a building inspires: reverence for the accumulated experiences of the past, readiness to puzzle out their meaning, unwillingness to disturb rashly results so powerfully willed, so laboriously arrived at– the desire, in short, to keep intact as many links as possible between yesterday and tomorrow, to lose, in the ardour of the new experiment, the least that may be of the long rich heritage of human experience." The operative terms for her point of view seem to be "enfranchisement of thought" combined with an "atavism of feeling." As an expression of medieval Catholicism, the cathedral represented both a bondage of superstition to be cast off in the modern age and yet a manifestation to be reverenced of the ancient attempt to struggle upward toward a clearer vision of the human condition. When the Germans shelled the cathedral at Rheims in World War I, James wrote to her: "Rheims is the most unspeakable & immeasurable horror & infamy–& what is appalling & heart-breaking is that it's *'forever & ever!'* . . . There *it was*–and now all the tears of rage of all the bereft millions & all the crowding curses of all the wondering ages will never bring a stone of it back!"

Meanwhile, between 1904 and 1909, Wharton had been steadily producing short stories, amid frequent motor trips through France and Italy. *The Hermit and the Wild Woman and Other Stories* (1908) is a collection of seven tales ranging from a saint's legend (the title story) through Jamesian tales of art and life ("The Verdict" and "The Pot Boiler") to a tale of politics ("The Best Man"). Of these seven stories, perhaps "The Last Asset," about a divorced couple's momentary conspiracy to get their daughter married off, is the best, despite the interest of the title story which, in its study of the abnegations of a morbidly spiritual hermit, may be a portrait of Henry James as the high priest of art.

Wharton's next volume–*Tales of Men and Ghosts* (1910)–was a diversion from the two big novels then partially completed in manuscript– *The Reef* (1912) and *The Custom of the Country* (1913). Only two of the ten tales are about "ghosts"–"The Eyes" and "Afterward." But several other stories deal with fantasies, delusions, and hysteria in such a way as to suggest the impact of her breakdown in the 1880s and of her husband's neurasthenia, which was growing worse. At their best, Wharton's ghost stories always have a doubleness of significance, a multiplicity of possible psychological interpretations that make the spectral tales plausible to the intellect.

In 1907 Wharton's knowledge of the French scene did not include a perfect command of a conversational idiom, even though she had spoken the language since childhood. At her request, Charles Du Bos found a tutor for her, but he turned out to be too amiable to correct her conversational errors. Instead, he asked her to prepare, for each of his visits, a written exercise, which he then corrected. In Wharton's exercise book is the germ of *Ethan Frome*: three chapters in French which introduce the three major characters and pose the complex relationship among them. The tragic ending of the story is nowhere in sight here: Wharton gave up her French lessons after a few weeks and the copybook, with its unfinished tale, was temporarily forgotten.

In the interim between the French version of the tale and the publication of *Ethan Frome* in English, there occurred perhaps the most passionate experience of Wharton's life–a brief but intense affair with Morton Fullerton, a ne'er-do-well American journalist then living in Paris. Her private diary suggests the intensity of her feelings: "Wir waren zusammen. Die süssesten Stunden meines Lebens." (We were together. The sweetest hours of my life.) And again: "Sometimes I am calm," she wrote, "exalted almost, so enclosed and satisfied in the thought of you, that I could say to you truly, as I did yesterday, 'I never wonder what you are doing when you are not with me.' At such moments I feel that all the mysticism in me–and the transcendentalism that in other women turns to religion–were poured into my feeling for you. . . . I am a little humbled, a little ashamed, to find how poor a thing I am, how the personality I had moulded into such strong firm lines has crumbled to a pinch of ashes in this flame! For the first time in my life *I can't read!* . . . I hold the book in my hand, and see your name all over the page."

At the same time Wharton was filled with guilt, for she believed in the marriage commitment, and she knew that no relationship could be satisfactory that was not a total sharing of all the experiences of life. Besides that, Fullerton was an unstable scapegrace whose amorous escapades, with both sexes, scandalized their circle of friends. The affair was brief and intense; but this happiest moment of her life could not last. The 1909 poem "Terminus," published in Lewis's biography of Wharton, suggests the inevitability of the end of the affair.

Ethan Frome, the *nouvelle* completed just after that intense liaison with Fullerton, deals less with character development than with the creation of an ironic situation–the entrapment of three crippled victims of love and hate shut up together under one roof in a snowbound New England farmhouse: Ethan, his wife, Zeena, and his beloved Mattie Silver, now crippled, like Frome, in the wake of their suicidal toboggan ride into an elm tree. Stunning in the spare economy of its realistic detail, yet richly symbolic in its network of recurrent images, this work is frequently advanced as one of Wharton's most "naturalistic" studies of human defeat and despair. Lionel Trilling, for example, once observed that whenever a character suffers in a piece of fiction, he does so at the behest of the author, who must justify his cruelty "by the seriousness of his moral intention"; and he concluded that Wharton "could not lay claim to any such justification." For Trilling, the mind can do nothing with the "perpetuity of suffering" which memorializes "a moment of passion." It is true that the setting of Starkfield is grim, snowbound, and stony. But neither heredity nor environment serves to explain the fate of the characters, nor are determinist considerations invoked to account for them. If Ethan remains with these querulous and droning women, it is less because he is morally inert than because he is exceptionally responsible for them, if not constrained by his guilt. Looked at in the light of Wharton's anguish over the Fullerton affair,

Ethan Frome is a stark projection, among other things, of Wharton's inability–much less her characters'–to escape the moral weight of self-punishment for illicit love. Contemporary reviewers seemed to grasp this point, in praising it as an analogue to Greek tragedy. As an anonymous reviewer for the *Nation* observed, "The wonder is that the spectacle of so much pain can be made to yield so much beauty."

Her next novel–*The Reef*–marked a significant departure from her characteristic mode as a novelist. It abandons the chronicle novel, like *The House of Mirth,* for a tightly constructed psychological drama focused on a central situation–again a love triangle–with a novelistic structure reminiscent of the manner of James's later works. Like *Ethan Frome, The Reef* deals with the power of sexual desire, the tortured frustrations of unrequited love, and the celebrations of suspicion and jealousy that afflict Anna Leath, a "sheltered American girl" who has grown up, much like Wharton, in a repressive New York environment. Once again, the theme of the "monstrousness of useless sacrifice" is invoked, by George Darrow, but Anna Leath cannot think of herself as Darrow's wife without remembering that Sophy Viner has had an affair with him, without imagining what they must have done together. So trapped is she by her genteel aversion to physical sexuality that she cannot accept this virile man because it would compromise her ideal of perfect love and thus would be a desecration of its sanctity. *The Reef* glitters with felicities of psychological insight and precision. Henry James called it a "beautiful book," marked by "supreme validity and distinction" and quite "the finest thing you have done." For most reviewers, however, it was a failure.

In the long run, however, the Jamesian novel developing all sides of a central situation was not to be Wharton's métier. In her next novel, *The Custom of the Country,* she returned to the long, rambling chronicle of manners, narrating the rise of a vulgar and aggressive girl to social prominence in the East and in Europe. Undine Spragg, the heroine, is a dazzlingly beautiful girl from the midwestern town of Apex City whose social ambition is so poisonous that it drives her to exploit everyone who crosses her path–her newly rich parents, whom she drags to New York and nearly bankrupts in her search for a rich husband; Ralph Marvell, the fashionable New Yorker whom she marries and drives to suicide; the Comte Raymond de Chelles, a French aristocrat of ancient family who seems more socially desirable as a husband than even Ralph; and finally Elmer Moffatt, an American billionaire railroad king with whom she eventually winds up. *The Custom of the Country* re-creates in a free-swinging satire the career of Undine Spragg, a type that Edmund Wilson once called the "international cocktail bitch," stripping off the skin of a decadent and lifeless New York social aristocracy, ridiculing the pretensions and provincialism of the American Midwest, and lambasting the American businessman as a crude materialist devoted only to mammon.

The year that *The Custom of the Country* was finished was in many ways a crucial one for Wharton. It marked, for one thing, the end of her marriage to Edward Wharton, whose mental derangement and embezzlement of funds in Wharton's trust made life with him unendurable. Her sense of liberation was reflected in what James called Wharton's "dazzling braveries of far excursionism" throughout the length and breadth of the Continent. Immediately after her April 1912 divorce she set out for Italy and then for Germany with her friends Walter Berry and Bernard Berenson, the art critic. In Germany she met Rainer Maria Rilke and other German artists, visited the great museums, saw *Faust*, and discovered the magic of Richard Strauss's operas. "They were," she later wrote, "vernal hours," echoing Sigmund, *"es war der Lenz!"* She began a new novel, an ambitious *Künstlerroman* (a novel of education in which the hero becomes an artist) to be called "Literature." But when World War I broke out in 1914, she abandoned her compulsive travels, returned to Paris, and threw herself into journalism and war charities, organizing, among other things, a workroom for unemployed seamstresses in her arrondissement and finding food and lodging for refugees pouring out of Belgium.

Out of this work developed her next two books—*Fighting France, From Dunkerque to Belfort* (1915) and *Le Livre des Sans-Foyer* (1915; *The Book of the Homeless*, 1916). The first recounts the experience of about six expeditions to the front line, where Wharton reported on trench warfare, the needs of the field hospitals, and the quiet heroism of the men and women who stood the rigors of frontline combat. Free of what she called "lyrical patriotism or post-card sentimentality," the book is nevertheless optimistic propaganda directed at the American public during the first fourteen months of the war. Her compilation,

Photograph inscribed to Morton Fullerton, circa 1907-1910 (courtesy of the Harry Ransom Humanities Research Center, University of Texas at Austin)

The Book of the Homeless, intended to assist the Children of Flanders Rescue Committee, contained poetry and music she solicited from such eminent artists as Rupert Brooke, Eleanora Duse, Sarah Bernhardt, Paul Claudel, Jean Cocteau, Thomas Hardy, William Dean Howells, George Santayana, William Butler Yeats, Igor Stravinsky, Joseph Conrad, Henry James, John Singer Sargent, and others. Like Wharton, Teddy Roosevelt—who wrote the introduction to the anthology—was concerned about America's continuing neutrality. "The part that America has played in this great tragedy is not an exalted part," he wrote, "and there is all the more reason why Americans should hold up the hands of those of their number who, like Mrs. Wharton, are endeavoring to some extent to remedy the national shortcomings." Meanwhile, in New York, Philadelphia, Boston, and Washington, "Edith Wharton" committees sprang up to collect funds for the perpetuation of her work.

Despite her inability to finish the manuscript of "Literature," Wharton did find time, amid her war work, to put together *Xingu and Other Stories* for publication in 1916. Most of the tales deal with typical Whartonian themes; some had been written well before the war commenced. "Xingu" is a broad satire on ladies' clubs which pretend to the mastery of "subjects" got up from week to week. "Kerfol" and "The Triumph of Night" are both ghost stories which hover between the occult and the psychologically aberrant. "The Choice" and "The Long Run" return to the theme of the moral ambiguities of love outside marriage in New York society. Surely Morton Fullerton must still have been in her mind when she protested to Charles Du Bos "the poverty, the miserable poverty, of any love that lies outside of marriage, of any love that is not a living together, a sharing of all!" "Autre Temps . . ." and "Bunner Sisters" are the most brilliant tales in the collection; "Bunner Sisters" is comparable to *Ethan Frome* in the intensity of its vision of poverty and despair. Written at the fin de siècle, "Bunner Sisters" is a work of such powerful urban realism that Stephan Crane or Dreiser could not have done better.

In June of 1916, while the war raged on, she took a brief vacation at Fontainebleau, where she wrote *Summer* (1917). This New England tragedy, a companion piece to the wintry *Ethan Frome*, was a work as remote as possible from the combat scenes around her. *Summer* records the story of a poor young New England girl, Charity Royall, who is seduced by a handsome city architect who has come to her town to study its old houses. Predictably, their summer romance results in her pregnancy, abandonment, but rescue by Mr. Royall, the foster father who takes her in again and marries her. While its portrait of the inbred and degenerate mountain people of the Berkshires angered local residents and led the *Boston Evening Transcript* reviewer to call the book unconvincing, Wharton continued to insist throughout her life that she knew, from the inside, the impoverished rural lives of the Fromes and the Royalls. And she made a continuing claim for the realism of her New England tales, contrasting them to the idealizations of the New England local colorists. The *Bookman* reviewer concurred in praising the authenticity of Wharton's setting and characterization, which showed "all the virtue of her style and none of its weakness."

With the entry of the United States into the war in 1917, Wharton's hopes for the survival of France soared. Her new enthusiasm was reflected in *The Marne* (1918), a badly written, embarrassingly sentimental *nouvelle* about an underage American boy whose love for France is so impassioned that he joins the U.S. Army Ambulance Service as a driver, only to be killed at the Marne. Unfortunately, the book exudes an "Over There" enthusiasm suggesting that it is indeed sweet and dignified to die for one's adopted country.

A Son at the Front, not published until 1923 but written at this time, is also a reflection of Wharton's war experience, specifically "that strange war-world of the rear, with its unnatural sharpness of outline and over-heightening of colour." In this novel, the artist-father John Campton reacts to the war personally and selfishly, as an inconvenience to his career, though he hopes that it may be the means by which his drafted son will gain a finer sense of values. When it becomes clear that the Allies will not win a quick victory, the defense of France becomes an obsession to him: "If France went, western civilization went with her; and then all they had believed in and been guided by would perish." The son is killed, and the grieving father is much chastened by the experience. But the point is clear: the defense of France is the salvation of Western civilization. Wharton's continual call for American intervention in the war was like that of Henry James, who renounced his American citizenship in 1915 as a gesture of protest at America's seeming indifference to this assault on civilization.

The ways in which France stood for civilization is suggested in Wharton's *French Ways and Their Meaning* (1919), a work published toward the end of the war and intended for Americans, especially soldiers, in France. In this work Wharton sought to explain her adopted country to those unfamiliar with its essential spirit, which she felt was typified by those "French" qualities of reverence, taste, continuity, and intellectual honesty. By "reverence" she meant the deeply rooted respect in France for old customs, traditions, rituals, and taboos—"les bienseances," the "always-have-beens," what she once called "the successive superpositions of experience that time brings." And by "continuity," she meant "the most homogeneous and uninterrupted culture" in the world. "France," she remarked, "has a lesson to teach and a warning to give [Americans]. It was our English forbears who taught us to flout tradition and break away from their own great inheritance; France may teach us that, side by side with the qualities of enterprise and innovation that English blood has put in us, we should cultivate the sense of continuity, that 'sense of the past' which enriches the present and binds us up with the world's great stabilising traditions of art and poetry and knowledge."

In *A Backward Glance* (1934) Wharton was to observe that "the really vital change" between 1870 and 1934 was that "in my youth, the Americans of the original States, who in moments of crisis still shaped the national point of view, were the heirs of an old tradition of European culture which the country has now totally rejected. This rejection . . . has opened a gulf between those days and these." In *The Age of Innocence*, a novel set in the old New York of her youth, Wharton sought to suggest some of those areas in which traditional society in old New York maintained the "old tradition of European culture" no longer characteristic of the postwar world. "To 'follow up' the traces of vanished old New York," Wharton felt, "one had to come to Europe;" there one found that the New York of the 1870s was very much like that of the English cathedral town or the French "ville de province" of the same era. In effect, she remarked on another occasion, "c'est seulement en ayant vu d'autres pays, étudié leurs moeurs, lu leurs livres, fréquenté leurs habitants, que l'on peut situer son propre pays dans l'histoire de la civilisation" ("it is only by having seen other countries, studied their customs, read their books, associated with the people, that one can place one's own country in the history of civilization").

Looking back, Wharton regarded old New York as having preserved an order of civilized values too precious to be forgotten in the age of jazz babies, flappers, and bathtub gin. Writing *The Age of Innocence* was therefore an act of piety for her, an attempt to atone for her youthful satire on the graceful, ordered civility of her parents' world. On one level the novel is a faithful record of the manners and mores of that New York City haut monde between 1870 and 1900: the opera evenings at the old Academy of Music, playgoing at Lester Wallack's theater, the formal dinners, the round of visits and leaving visiting cards, the betrothal visits, Grace Church weddings, the summers in Newport and winters in Washington Square, and the effect on her New Yorkers of "Arabian Night marvels" like the invention of electricity and the telephone.

The Age of Innocence interests today's readers, though, less for these archaeological exhumations than for the spiritual portrait of the age. What Wharton meant by innocence was partly sexual propriety and financial rectitude, but partly an aversion to the darker experiences of life, a fear of innovation, and a submissiveness to the power of social convention that characterized her parents' class. Wharton tests the value of this innocence in the character of Newland Archer, a young dilettante who grows bored with the stuffy, ordered world, falls in love with a Europeanized American, the Countess Ellen Olenska, contemplates running away to Europe with her but is maneuvered back into conformity within the dictates of his society when his rebellion threatens to destroy his marriage. Yet far from being the story of "a pathetic instance of vain frustration, of wasted forces," *The Age of Innocence* demonstrates that beneath the surface dullness were things so fine and sensitive and delicate that Ellen Olenska's spontaneity and social iconoclasm seem almost crass by comparison. In fact, the epilogue of the novel, set in 1900, affirms the balanced virtues of both the older ways of Archer's generation and the newer openness of the turn-of-the-century period, in the widower Archer's declining to renew his interest in Ellen (out of respect to the memory of his marriage) and in the marriage of Archer's son, Dallas, to a girl of marginal social position.

While *The Age of Innocence* did not match the 100,000-plus sales record of *The House of Mirth*, it did achieve best-seller status. Some reviewers complained that Wharton's art was wasted on a negligible high society and trivial people. V. L. Parrington claimed that there was "more hope for our literature in the honest crudities of the younger naturalists," and Katherine Mansfield begged for "a little wildness, a dark place or two in the soul." But readers generally agreed with the *Times Literary Supplement* reviewer, who described the novel as "a thorough mastery of the whole situation," and with William Lyon Phelps, who called her a writer who "brings glory on the name of America, and this is her best book." Indeed, it won for her the Pulitzer Prize in 1920.

The publication of *The Age of Innocence*—which Yvor Winters once called "the finest single flower of the Jamesian art; one which James fertilized but would have been unable to bring to maturity"—closed out the major phase of Wharton's career as a writer. Her best books were behind her, her war work was over, and many of her friends–Henry James, Howard Sturgis, Teddy Roosevelt, as well as young soldier-friends such as Ronald Simmons and her cousin Newbold Rhineland–were gone. It no longer seemed possible to stay at 53, rue de Varenne. Even Paris seemed too much. So Wharton gave up her Faubourg apartment and bought a large estate outside Paris at Saint Brice-sous-Forêt. Henceforth, in the summer, Pavillon Colombe was to be her home; and in the winter she journeyed to her other estate, Sainte-Claire Le Chateau, at Hyéres, on the Riviera. Writing in the postwar world seemed highly problematical to her. Yet stories kept clamoring to be told, and young writers such as F. Scott Fitzgerald and Sinclair Lewis wrote admiringly to her. Perhaps something could yet be done to record the moral history of the postwar world, she decided.

Looking about her at this world, Wharton was disgusted at the spectacle of the wealthy, denationalized, deracinated cosmopolites rushing about Europe from London to Paris, to St. Moritz and the Riviera. *The Glimpses of the Moon* (1922) deals with the four cornerstones of their existence–money, luxury, fashion, and pleasure. Her young couple, Susy Branch and Nick Lansing, resemble Lily Bart and Lawrence Selden of *The House of Mirth* in that they are in love and want to marry, but, also like Lily and Lawrence, they do not have enough money to maintain themselves in the rich crowd. Despite their desire to remain part of this group, they decide to marry, while each scouts for a wealthier spouse: "Why shouldn't they marry; belong to each other openly and honourably, if for ever so short a time, and with the definite understanding that whenever either of them got the chance to do better he or she should be immediately released? The law of their country facilitated such exchanges, and society was beginning to view them as indulgently as the law." In the end, their experiment a failure, Nick and Susy return to each other, poor but happy. Written for the *Pictorial Review*, a slick periodical aimed at American housewives, *The Glimpses of the Moon* marked a steep decline in Mrs. Wharton's powers. While some reviewers gave the obligatory nod to Wharton's stylistic powers, Ruth Hale memorably defined the critical view that would seal the book's fate: "Edith Wharton has no business to be writing such trash."

Nor was *A Son at the Front*, largely composed during the war, any improvement. At

sixty, living in her villa outside Paris, gardening and reading, Wharton wanted most to escape from the present. In 1923 she returned to the United States to receive an honorary doctorate from Yale University, but in many ways the trip was a failure. Most of her old friends were long dead or unrecognizable, and New York itself was measurably different from the prewar city she had left almost two decades before. Her parents' world, old New York, was gone without a trace.

In an effort to re-create that vanished world of her parents, Wharton produced in 1924 four *nouvelles* dealing with four decades of that vanished society's social history: *Old New York*, the collective title, is composed of *False Dawn (The 'Forties)*, *The Old Maid (The 'Fifties)*, *The Spark (The 'Sixties)*, and *New Year's Day (The 'Seventies)*. As glimpses of the social history of the time and place, *Old New York* is not compelling; but as a group of sharply realized moral dramas, the four parts do succeed as "crucial instances" of the complex struggle of four individuals in relation to the oppressive social order of a conventional society in the process of change.

The Mother's Recompense (1925) expands the theme of "Autre Temps . . ." in order to suggest certain transformations of moral and social values over two decades in contemporary New York. Kate Clephane, having abandoned her husband and child for a lover in Europe, returns to New York City eighteen years later to attend her daughter's wedding, only to discover that Anne's fiancé is a young man with whom Kate has had an affair in Europe. Unable openly to oppose the marriage without revealing her own dissipation (except to a New York gentleman who is still willing to marry her), Kate acquiesces in the marriage to protect her daughter and returns to Europe alone. Hers is a drama of renunciation, her only recompense being that "whenever she began to drift toward new uncertainties and fresh concessions," she could remind herself that "once at least she had stood fast, shutting away in a little space of peace and light the best thing that had ever happened to her."

By 1925 Edith Wharton had become the grande dame of American letters, had received an honorary doctorate from Yale, and was consistently identified as one of "the twelve greatest women in America." Few reviewers gave her really bad reviews, although there were veiled complaints at her "aristocratic status," her treatment of the beau monde rather then the toiling masses, her old-fashioned sensibility, the increasing slickness of her stories. Perhaps the *Independent* reviewer caught the general mood in his remarks about *The Mother's Recompense:* "Competent, skillful work, adequately chiseled and polished like a painting by a competent, but rather tired, artist."

Wharton had always felt that few English and American novelists had been really interested in the deeper processes of art. Perhaps with the exception of Henry James in mind, she had *The Writing of Fiction* published in 1925. A compilation of essays that had appeared in *Scribner's* magazine, the work deals prescriptively with the craft of fiction, as she had meditated and practiced it. Emphasizing in Jamesian terms such issues as selection, psychology, and the moral sense, Wharton devoted chapters to "Telling a Short Story," Constructing a Novel," and "Character and Situation." A concluding essay dealt with Marcel Proust. As a vade mecum for the aspiring writer, the volume has its uses, although the prescriptiveness suggests how conventional were her attitudes in the age of surrealism, dadaism, and stream-of-consciousness fiction. For she is a realist preeminently in the tradition of the early James, Howells, Honoré de Balzac, and Emile Zola.

Perhaps some episodes from her novels *Hudson River Bracketed* (1929) and *The Gods Arrive* (1932) will lay bare the theory implicit in her realistic art. In the former novel George Frenside, a literary critic and adviser, tells the aspiring novelist Vance Weston that he ought to get out and mix more often in society: "Manners are your true material, after all." This advice embodies Wharton's belief, as she put in *The Gods Arrive*, that "the surface of life was rich enough to feed the creator's imagination." This corresponds with the view she expressed in *The Writing of Fiction*–for the novelist "the proper study of mankind is man's conscious and purposive behaviour rather than its dim unfathomable sources." The point of interest in human behavior, for her, was "the conflicts . . . produced between the social order and individual appetites." The dramatization of such conflicts frequently produces the novel of manners, of which she was an expert practitioner. Her aim was like that of Vance Weston–not "to denounce or to show up, as most of the 'society' novelists did, but to take apart the works of the machine, and find out what all those people behind the splendid house fronts signified in the general scheme of things." Such an intention, well executed, delivers the novel of manners from the

charge of superficiality in its treatment of society. In fact, Wharton's realism makes great demands on the insight of the writer, for the surface must be probed and dissected by one on whom nothing is lost. Like James, she remarked that "As to experience, intellectual and moral, the creative imagination can make a little go a long way, provided it remains long enough in the mind and is sufficiently brooded on." But her conception of experience was not impressionistic and inward, as was James's. For Wharton, the novelist's subject was the individual in full engagement with the social world, its manners and mores, its rites and traditions, its liberties and constraints. And she did not hesitate to criticize Howells for not probing deeply enough or the later James for severing his characters from "that thick nourishing human air in which we all live and move," for stripping them of "all the *human fringes* we necessarily trail after us through life."

Between 1925 and her death in 1937, Wharton produced five more volumes of short stories, the final flowering of her art with the short tale: *Here and Beyond* (1926), *Certain People* (1930), *Human Nature* (1933), *The World Over* (1936), and *Ghosts* (1937). During this period she also wrote a volume of poems, her memoir, and five novels, one published posthumously.

Here and Beyond is composed of a half-dozen tales which deal about equally with this world and the next. Those which explore the supernatural–"Miss Mary Pask," "The Young Gentleman," and "Bewitched"–create, as always, an overpowering mood of occult strangeness, even while Wharton's steady rationalism usually provides us with a means of understanding the inexplicable. *Certain People* also offers six tales, of which the best is doubtless "After Holbein," a parable, in its way, of the fatal consequences of the life of social self-indulgence in New York City during the Gilded Age. *Human Nature*, dedicated to Bernard Berenson, whom she visited almost every year at his Villa I Tatti in Florence, contains only five tales, all but one of them ("A Glimpse") concerned with illness, disease, and death. Over seventy when the book was published, Wharton had been steadily deteriorating in health, and almost all of her contemporaries had died. Yet her theme was the inevitable fact that human nature had not changed as fast as Jazz Age social usages. Of the generally trivial group of tales in *The World Over*, one, "Roman Fever," is as good as anything she ever wrote. Again, the focus is on age, the function of memory, and death. The tale makes expert use of suspense; the controlled revelation of events which happened in the distant past has no equal in Wharton's oeuvre. It is at the same time a complex study of the sameness of, and the vital differences between, the generations, and a revelation of latent hatred which rises to a sudden and unexpected climax. In this tale, two widows in Rome, trying to keep up with their two fast-living, husband-hunting daughters, sit at a restaurant table overlooking the Palatine, the Forum, and the Colosseum. Constituted only of their conversation about the girls and their own girlhoods, and worked out against that vast Roman memento mori, the tale suggests that the real Roman fever is not the malaria that afflicted their grandmothers' generation, but that power of passionate love sufficient, once experienced, to nourish Mrs. Ansley through years of quiet obedience to the social forms of her New York City world. Leon Edel once observed that many of Wharton's stories suffered from "too close an adherence to the formula popular at the end of the nineteenth century, that of the sudden twist, the *coup de theatre*." Yet "Roman Fever" could not have succeeded as effectively with any other ending than the ironic bombshell that Mrs. Ansley quietly drops at the end, that Alida Slade's husband had fathered Grace Ansley's daughter.

In *Ghosts*, Wharton collected eleven tales already published in magazines and book form, dedicating the book to Walter de la Mare. This collection contains a preface on the nature of supernatural fiction which, together with her comments in *The Writing of Fiction*, constitutes the rationale of her spectral tales. In the preface to *Ghosts* she remarks that while the rational mind may not believe in ghosts, "it is in the warm darkness of the pre-natal fluid far below our conscious reason that the faculty dwells with which we apprehend the ghosts we may not be endowed with the gift of seeing." Only two requirements were necessary, she felt, for the supernatural tale: silence and continuity. But with jazz, the wireless, "the conflicting attractions of the gangster, the introvert and the habitual drunkard," the ghost and the ghostly story, she predicted, may succumb "to the impossibility of finding standing-room in a roaring and discontinuous universe."

"It is useless, at least for the story-teller," Wharton had observed in 1927, "to deplore what the new order of things has wiped out, vain to shudder at what it is creating; there it is, whether for better or worse, and the American novelist can best use his opportunity by plunging both hands into the motley welter." None of the five novels published in the last decade of her life– *Twilight Sleep* (1927), *The Children* (1928), *Hudson River Bracketed*, *The Gods Arrive*, and *The Buccaneers* (1938, posthumously submitted to Appleton-Century by her literary executor, Gaillard Lapsley)–matches the greatness of *The House of Mirth*, *Ethan Frome*, or *The Age of Innocence*; but high claims have been made for *Hudson River Bracketed* and *The Buccaneers*.

The first of these five–*Twilight Sleep*–bids fair to be one of Wharton's weakest novels. A satire on modern manners and morals, this novel ridicules the hurried, frenetic quality of modern social life, the ceaseless pursuit of pleasure and the fear of pain (focusing on the new anesthetic used in childbirth that is indicated by the title), the secular substitutions for religious value in society, and the shallowness of love in the age of Freud, jazz, and "quickie" divorces.

If *Twilight Sleep* reveals how the irresponsible adults victimize the young, *The Children* makes the point even more explicitly. As she grew older, the villains of Wharton's fiction became the middle generation of valueless hedonists–not irreverent youth, to whom society must now look for salvation. The final novels dramatize the fate in the modern world of young people who have rejected adults' inanities and who have discovered a value embedded in the cultural past unknown to their elders. Judith Wheater, a fifteen-year-old who tries desperately to keep her brothers and sisters together, despite the marryings and divorces and abandonments of parents and stepparents, is typical of all of the protagonists of the last five novels. They somehow develop the "memorial manner," which acknowledges and reverences the usable past, and a vivid moral sense (derived therefrom), by which their elders' conduct is weighed in the balance and found wanting. While many reviewers found the novel barely credible, Gorham Munson was perhaps typical in remarking that, although *The Children* "is not by the inspired Edith Wharton who wrote that finest of New England tragedies, *Ethan Frome*, it is a characteristically competent Wharton product, and the sun of Henry James, once refracted, still brings out the polish of pages that regret the decline in manners and record the new vulgarities."

The year *Hudson River Bracketed* appeared, thirty-one critics were asked to rank seventy-two contemporary American writers on the basis of literary merit. That Wharton still held her own was indicated by sixteen of them placing her in group one and ten in group two, generally judging her work as "superior." *Hudson River Bracketed* confirmed her general reputation by expertly tracing the apprenticeship of a young American novelist of manners, Vance Weston, while offering some lively comment on American life, the international literary scene, stream-of-consciousness fiction, dadaism and surrealism, and the artist's imagination. In brief, the novel deals with the necessity of Weston's discovering in Willows–an old house designed in the Hudson River Bracketed style–a symbol of continuity, history, and tradition–just what is needed to nourish the artist's imagination, according to Wharton.

In *The Gods Arrive,* written as a sequel, Wharton has Weston go to Europe in further pursuit of American cultural roots, and, at the same time, he descends deeper into himself to discover the source of his creative energies. The novel weaves together two interrelated themes: the age-old perplexing problem of love between men and women, both within and without the married estate; and the discovery of Europe and its old established traditions by a young writer inflamed with the recently discovered concept of continuity. Both books were received as competent and workmanlike, if old-fashioned in their literary attitudes, Isabel Paterson remarking how Wharton "satirizes the modernists in her own leisurely way, conceding not the fraction of an inch in either theory or practice to their literary claims."

One of the most interesting aspects of *Hudson River Bracketed* and *The Gods Arrive,* as well as of *The Buccaneers,* her last, uncompleted novel, is that they express an increasingly complex attitude toward the American Middle West, which she had consistently satirized in her earlier work. *The Buccaneers,* set in New York in the 1870s, deals with the efforts of the St. George family, indefatigable plutocrats from the Midwest, to launch their daughters into New York society. In Vance Weston and the St. George girls, who eventually discover the importance of the cultural roots and the traditions of an established society, Wharton celebrates the energy, passion, and power of the new Americans, especially as they try to assimilate cultural tradition. It is clear that, in Wharton's affection for the invading American beauties, who marry into the English aristocracy, in her satire upon the snobbishness of old New York, and upon the inanities of life among the British aristocracy, Wharton was sharply revising her views about the Midwestern nouveaux riches to

show how they might, after all, have a tonic effect on society and reinvigorate the meaning of the past and the value of tradition.

Vance Weston's successive experiments with several kinds of novels in *Hudson River Bracketed* and *The Gods Arrive* have the effect of highlighting what, to Wharton, were the limitations of novelistic genres. Even the naturalistic novel, for Wharton, had failed. The great French writers, she remarked, "invented the once-famous *tranche de vie,* the exact photographic reproduction of a situation or an episode, with all its sounds, smells, aspects realistically rendered, but with its deeper relevance and its suggestions of a larger whole either unconsciously missed or purposely left out." If they succeeded, she held, they did so only in spite of their theories. As early as 1914 she had left the hope that "some new theory of form, as adequate to its purpose as those preceding it, will be evolved from the present welter of experiment." But by the 1930s she did not find modernist theories of fiction to have produced a great narrative art. And in *The Gods Arrive,* she expressed her dismay at the literati in Paris who denounce tradition and argue that "fiction, as the art of narrative and the portrayal of social groups, had reached its climax, and could produce no more . . . –that unless the arts were renewed they were doomed, and that in fiction the only hope of renewal was in the exploration of the subliminal." For her, the realistic novel of manners, centering on the characters' conscious and purposive motives in the conflict between the social order and the individual's appetites, the novel of manners offering the social surface but probing for its deeper significance, would more than challenge the capacities of any artist.

In the process of dramatizing the vulgarity of the modern world and in defending the novel of manners against the emerging modernists, whom she largely misunderstood, Wharton lost, rather conspicuously, the sharp irony of her youthful style; and in its place readers increasingly encountered both the bitter distortions of satire and a mellow nostalgia for a vanished world that few could remember across the wreckage of the Great Depression and the war years. She was never at home in the postwar world. But although her novels became increasingly deprived of that rich and direct social experience that is the substance of the American novel of manners, she nevertheless tried to deal responsibly and realistically with her times up until her death in 1937. From this high seriousness and from her deep interest in the craft of fiction came a handful of superior novels–*The House of Mirth, Ethan Frome, The Custom of the Country,* and *The Age of Innocence*–and a score of excellent short stories– among them "Autre Temps . . . ," "Roman Fever," and "The Other Two." They will always be read with close attention and remembered with pleasure.

Bibliography:

James W. Tuttleton, "Edith Wharton: An Essay in Bibliography," *Resources for American Literary Study,* 3 (Fall 1973): 163-202.
> In addition to listings for editions, manuscripts, letters, and biography, includes a section of briefly annotated listings of reviews and essays concerning Wharton.

Biographies:

Louis Auchincloss, *Edith Wharton: A Woman in Her Time* (New York: Viking, 1971).
> Detailed and copiously illustrated popular biography.

R. W. B. Lewis, *Edith Wharton: A Biography* (New York, Evanston, San Francisco & London: Harper & Row, 1975).
> Definitive biography with critical commentary and background on major writings; makes use of diaries, letters, and other papers previously unavailable to scholars.

References:

Louis Auchincloss, *Edith Wharton* (Minneapolis: University of Minnesota Press, 1961).
> Brief critical introduction to major themes of Wharton's most important fiction as well as some discussion of her minor works; includes general biography and a bibliography.

Millicent Bell, *Edith Wharton and Henry James: The Story of Their Friendship* (New York: Braziller, 1965).
> Uses correspondence of both writers to detail their lengthy and complicated friendship.

Irving Howe, ed., *Edith Wharton: A Collection of Critical Essays* (Englewood Cliffs, N. J.: Prentice-Hall, 1962).
> Collects important critical essays on Wharton's writing and contains Howe's "The Achievement of Edith Wharton," an overview of her importance as a writer.

Margaret McDowell, *Edith Wharton* (Boston: Twayne, 1976).
> Brief critical introduction to Wharton's work.

Blake Nevius, *Edith Wharton: A Study of Her Fiction* (Berkeley: University of California Press, 1953).
> Exhaustive study of the major themes in Wharton's fiction.

James W. Tuttleton, *The Novel of Manners in America* (Chapel Hill: University of North Carolina Press, 1972), pp. 122-140.
> Includes a brief discussion of Wharton's novels of manners.

Cynthia Griffin Wolff, *A Feast of Words: The Triumph of Edith Wharton* (New York: Oxford University Press, 1977).
> Discusses Wharton's background and development as a writer and offers a psychological evaluation of her fictional works.

Contributors

Howard Baetzhold ....*Butler University*
J. M. Brook ....*Columbia, South Carolina*
Joseph Caldwell ....*Columbia, South Carolina*
Dennis Camp ....*Sangamon State University*
James B. Colvert ....*University of Georgia*
Eugene Current-Garcia ....*Auburn University*
Sara deSaussure Davis ....*University of Alabama*
Robert L. Gale ....*University of Pittsburgh*
Addison Gayle, Jr. ..... *Bernard M. Baruch College of the City University of New York*
Armida Gilbert ....*University of South Carolina*
Robert Gilbert ....*Columbia, South Carolina*
M. E. Grenander ....*State University of New York at Albany*
Hamlin Hill ....*Texas A&M University*
Nancy Carol Joyner ....*Western Carolina University*
Earle Labor ....*Centenary College of Louisiana*
Doris Lucas Laryea ....*North Carolina State University*
Ruth K. MacDonald ....*New Mexico State University*
Joseph R. McElrath, Jr. ....*Florida State University*
Ruth Miller ....*State University of New York at Stony Brook*
Penelope Niven ....*Hendersonville, North Carolina*
Donald Pizer ....*Tulane University*
Herbert K. Russell ....*John A. Logan College*
Michael D. Senecal ....*Columbia, South Carolina*
Daniel Shealy ....*Clemson University*
Madeleine B. Stern ....*New York, New York*
James W. Tuttleton ....*New York University*
Ben Merchant Vorpahl ....*University of Georgia*
James Woodress .... *University of California, Davis*

Cumulative Index

1640-1865: *Colonization to the American Renaissance*
1865-1917: *Realism, Naturalism, and Local Color*
1941-1968: *The New Consciousness*

Cumulative Index

Dictionary of Literary Biography